Philosophy of Religion

A Guide and Anthology

Brian Davies

OXFORD
UNIVERSITY PRESS

OXFORD

UNIVERSITY PRESS

Great Clarendon Street, Oxford OX2 6DP

Oxford University Press is a department of the University of Oxford.
It furthers the University's objective of excellence in research, scholarship,
and education by publishing worldwide in

Oxford New York

Auckland Bangkok Buenos Aires
Cape Town Chennai Dar es Salaam Delhi Hong Kong Istanbul
Karachi Kuala Lumpur Madrid Melbourne Mexico City Mumbai
Nairobi Paris São Paulo Singapore Taipei Tokyo Toronto

Oxford is a registered trade mark of Oxford University Press
in the UK and in certain other countries

Published in the United States
by Oxford University Press Inc., New York

British Library Cataloguing in Publication Data

Data available

Library of Congress Cataloging in Publication Data

Data available

ISBN 13: 978–0–19–875194–6
ISBN 10: 0–19–875194–X

10 9 8 7 6

Typeset in Adobe Minion
by RefineCatch Limited, Bungay, Suffolk
Printed in Great Britain by
Ashford Colour Press, Gosport, Hampshire

Philosophy of Religion

In memory of my mother, Lillian Davies (1916–98) and of H. P. Owen (1926–96)

Preface

How should we define 'philosophy of religion'? The task is not an easy one. We could say that it is 'philosophy as applied to religious belief'. But we would then need to recognize that definitions of 'philosophy' and 'religion' vary. 'What is philosophy?' and 'What is religion?' are questions to which different people give surprisingly different answers.

Yet philosophy of religion is now a thriving branch of philosophy. Many people currently describe themselves as students or teachers of the subject. And the literature devoted to it swells daily. Even if it is hard to say what philosophy of religion is exactly, there is no denying that it is currently very big business—every bit as big as, for example, philosophy of mind, philosophy of logic, or philosophy of language (phrases which also defy swift definition).

A good way to understand what philosophy of religion amounts to is to examine what would commonly be taken to be standard examples of it. And this is what this book aims to help you do. Most of it consists of extracts from the writings of various philosophers. So it is first and foremost an anthology. But it is more than that. For it also contains a lot of material setting its extracts in context and guiding readers through them. Taken as a whole, the volume amounts to a self-contained introduction to philosophy of religion, one which can be used both by readers working on their own and by students working under guidance.

In order to provide a helpful balance, I have selected extracts from authors of very different persuasions and philosophical traditions. In the source details at the start of each chapter, * indicates those extracts that have been edited by me, with the approval of the author. Since philosophers have reflected on religion for centuries, and since some of the most interesting and influential philosophy of religion comes from authors writing before the twentieth century, many of the extracts are from what one might call 'classical' rather than 'contemporary' sources. In so far as this volume allows readers to explore the 'classical' as well as the 'contemporary', it should help them to get a sense of what philosophy of religion has been and of how it has come to be the way it is today.

I should add that I have tried, throughout my own text, to avoid gender-specific reference to God. In some instances, however, I have used 'he'/'his' simply to avoid awkwardness in wording.

Brian Davies

Acknowledgements

I AM grateful to Fordham University for awarding me a Faculty Fellowship, which has helped me to prepare this book for publication. I am also grateful to several friends who read early drafts of some or all of my various introductions and bibliographies and made helpful comments on them. These include Victor Austin, Corey Beales, James Claffey, John Greco, Stephen Grimm, and Sara Penella. I owe thanks to Matthew Kent and Alan Rhoda for assistance in compiling the anthology sections, and to Angela Griffin of Oxford University Press for her graciousness and efficiency as an in-house editor. I am especially grateful to Sarah Dancy, whose careful and intelligent copy-editing of the text worked wonders.

Contents

Part III **Arguments for God's existence**

Cosmological arguments

Design arguments

Ontological arguments

God and human experience

Part IV **What is God?**

Omnipotent

Knowing

Part VI **Morality and religion**

Part VII **People and life after death**

Notes on contributors

William P. Alston is Professor Emeritus of Philosophy at Syracuse University. He has also been on the faculties of the University of Michigan, Rutgers University, and the University of Illinois. His recent books include *Divine Nature and Human Language* (1989), *Epistemic Justification* (1989), *Perceiving God, A Realist Perception of Truth* (1991), and *Illocutionary Acts and Sentence Meaning* (2000).

G. E. M. Anscombe Born in 1919, Elizabeth Anscombe studied philosophy at Oxford and then worked with Ludwig Wittgenstein at Cambridge. She is one of Wittgenstein's literary executors and has edited and translated many of his writings. She has taught both in Oxford and Cambridge. She has also lectured in many different countries. In 1959 she published *An Introduction to Wittgenstein's Tractatus*. In 1957 she published *Intention*, a very influential study of human agency. She is the author of many philosophical articles most of which can be found in her *Collected Philosophical Papers* (3 vols., 1981). She is married to P. T. Geach (see below).

Anselm of Canterbury was one of the most brilliant and influential of medieval philosophers. Much indebted to biblical thinking and by the thought of patristic authors such as St Augustine of Hippo, but also a seriously original thinker in his own right, he was especially expert at applying logical rigour to matters of theological significance. He is best known for his works *Monologion* and *Proslogion*. Other important works by Anselm include *On Truth* (*De Veritate*), *On Free Will* (*De Libertate Arbitrii*), *Why God Became Man* (*Cur Deus Homo*), and *The Compatibility of God's Foreknowledge, Predestination, and Grace with Human Freedom* (*De Concordia*).

Thomas Aquinas was an Italian Dominican friar and probably the greatest of the medieval Christian philosopher-theologians. He taught in France and Italy. His many writings deal with a huge range of religious, ethical, and logical questions. He also wrote commentaries on a number of philosophical texts (e.g. many of Aristotle's works). He is probably best known for his *Summa Theologiae* and *Summa Contra Gentiles*, but many of his less well known writings, and many of his shorter works, contain impressive and sophisticated material which those who wish to understand him would do well to consult. Aquinas has been treated as an important thinker by Roman Catholics since the time of his death, and he influenced some of sixteenth century Protestant theologians of the Reformation period (chiefly the Calvinist ones). In the last twenty years or so he has been much written about and reflected on by contemporary secular philosophers working in the analytical tradition. Aquinas's thinking is deeply affected by the Bible. It also reflects ideas to be found in the writings of Plato, Aristotle, and various Neoplatonists. And it anticipates ideas to be found in the modern philosophers Gottlob Frege and Ludwig Wittgenstein. For an introduction to Aquinas's philosophy, see Norman Kretzmann and Eleonore Stump (ed.), *The Cambridge Companion to Aquinas* (1993).

Augustine of Hippo was one of the most important and influential Christian thinkers of all time. Born in North Africa in 354, he was educated in Carthage. He became Bishop of Hippo in 391. In his most famous work, *Confessions*, he provides a memorable account of his conversion to Christianity. He wrote voluminously, and his writings did a great deal to affect the character of medieval philosophical and theological thinking. They also helped to determine the thought of many post-medieval writers, including some of the most famous Reformation figures. Augustine's philosophical thinking may be loosely described as Neoplatonic. But it would be foolish to try to classify him too quickly in terms of the history of ideas. An energetic, passionate, brilliant, original, and arguably inconsistent author, Augustine needs to be approached slowly and with careful attention to the details in his writings. His major works include: *Confessions*, *The City of God* (*De Civitate Dei*), *On Christian Doctrine* (*De Doctrina Christiana*), and *On the Trinity* (*De Trinitate*). For an account of Augustine and his influence, see Allan D. Fitzgerald (General Editor), *Augustine Through the Ages: An Encyclopedia* (1999).

A. J. Ayer was a British twentieth century philosopher. He taught mostly at Oxford, where he was a Fellow of Wolfson College and Wykeham Professor of Logic. He is, perhaps, most famous for his book *Language, Truth and Logic* (1936) which provided English speaking readers with a classic statement and defence of Logical Positivism. His other books include: *Foundations of Empirical Knowledge* (1940), *The Problem of Knowledge* (1954), *The Central Questions of Philosophy* (1973), and *Philosophy in the Twentieth Century* (1980). Ayer's autobiographical *Part of my Life* was published in 1978. For a general study of Ayer, see John Foster, *Ayer* (1985).

Boethius Ancius Manlius Severinus Boethius (usually just referred to as Boethius) was born into one of the great Roman senatorial families. He rose to high public office under Theodoric, the Ostragoth ruler of Italy (493–526), but was later accused of treason and magic, and was imprisoned (in Pavia), tortured, and executed. He helped to make some significant ancient Greek thought (notably Aristotle's logical writings) available to Latin authors. His best known work, the *Consolation of Philosophy* was written in prison shortly before his execution. He also wrote several treatises aiming to apply philosophy, especially logical skills, to the treatment of Christian doctrine. He was a highly significant influence on medieval philosophy and theology.

Johannes Caterus was born in Antwerp in 1590. Caterus (also known as Johan (or Jan) de Kater) was a Catholic priest and contemporary of René Descartes. Little is known of his life. He is best remembered as the author of the first set of replies to Descartes's *Meditations*. He was a student at Louvain. He was priest in charge of St Lawrens at Alkmaar from 1632–56. He was invited to comment on the *Meditations* by two priest friends of Descartes (Bannius and Bloemart). Correspondence by him survives in the archives of the Oud-Katholieke Kerk kept in the Rijksarchief in de Provincie Utrecht (Utrecht). Apart from his views as shown in the reply to Descartes, what we now know of Caterus mostly derives from the account of him given by Adrien Baillet in *La Vie de Monsieur Des-Cartes* (Paris, 1691).

W. K. Clifford was a nineteenth century British mathematician and philosopher. He taught at Cambridge and London Universities. He published little during his lifetime (though some of his writings appeared posthumously) and is now best known for the material by him reproduced in the present volume. Originally a Roman Catholic, he ended up an agnostic. For works by Clifford, see: Karl Pearson (ed.), *The Common Sense of the Exact Sciences* (1885), reissued with a preface by Bertrand Russell and a new introduction by James R. Newman (1955); F. Pollock (ed.), *Lectures and Essays* (2 vols., 1879).

Brian Davies is Professor of Philosophy, Fordham University, New York. His published works include *Thinking about God* (1985), *Language, Meaning and God* (Ed.) (1987), *The Thought of Thomas Aquinas* (1992), *An Introduction to the Philosophy of Religion* (2nd revised edition, 1993), and *Philosophy of Religion: A Guide to the Subject* (Ed.) (1998). He is General Editor of the series *Outstanding Christian Thinkers* (Geoffrey Chapman, London) and *Great Medieval Thinkers* (Oxford University Press).

Stephen T. Davis is professor of Philosophy at Claremont McKenna College in California. Professor Davis is the author or editor of eleven books and many articles in the philosophy of religion and Christian thought.

René Descartes, often called 'the father of modern philosophy', was born in La Haye, France, in 1596. He died in 1650. He is especially well known for his philosophy of human knowledge and his philosophy of mind, not to mention his arguments for the existence of God and his views about natural science. His influence on the history of philosophy has been enormous. His major works include: *Discourse on the Method of Rightly Conducting One's Reason and Seeking the Truth in the Sciences* (1637 and commonly referred to as the 'Discourse on Method'), and *Meditations on First Philosophy* (1641). For an introduction to Descartes see John Cottingham (ed.), *The Cambridge Companion to Descartes* (1992).

Peter Donovan completed a doctorate at Oxford in 1972 and was associate professor in Religious Studies at Massey University in New Zealand until January 2000. He is now an honorary research fellow, freelance writer, and gardener, living near Nelson. He has published books on religious language and experience, and on religion in New Zealand.

Paul Edwards is an American Philosopher who is mixed one part analytic philosopher to one part philosophe. Although Edwards is best known as the editor-in-chief of the *Encylopedia of Philosophy* (8 vols., 1967), a massive Enlightenment work with a notable analytic sensibility, his own widely discussed work focuses on such traditional philosophical issues as God, free will, immortality, induction, and the nature of value-judgements. Articles and books by him include: 'Bertrand Russell's Doubts about Induction' (1949), *The Logic of Mora Discourse* (1955), 'Hard and Soft Determinism' (1958), 'The Cosmological Argument' (1959), 'Atheism' (1967), *Buber and Buberism* (1970), *Heideger on Death* (1979), 'The Case against Reincarnation (1986–7, in four parts), *Voltaire* (1989), and *Immortality* (1992).

Antony Flew is Emeritus Professor of Philosophy in the University of Reading, England. His main relevant publications are *God: A Critical Enquiry* (formerly *God and Philosophy*, 1966), *God, Freedom and Immortality* (formerly *The Presumption of Atheism*, 1976), *The Logic of Immortality* (shortly to be reprinted under another title), and *Atheistic Humanism* (1993).

Pierre Gassendi was born in 1592. He died in 1655. He was a Catholic priest. As well as responding to Descartes's *Meditations* he was also an influential author in the field of philosophy of knowledge and philosophy of science. For a study of Gassendi, see Barry Brundell, *Pierre Gassendi: From Aristotelianism to a New Natural Philosophy* (1987).

Gaunilo of Marmoutiers was a contemporary of Anselm of Canterbury and the author of a famous reply to Anselm's *Proslogion*. Apart from his views as expressed in the reply to Anselm, we know nothing of him other than the fact that he was a Benedictine monk of the Abbey of Marmoutiers in France.

P. T. Geach Born in 1916, Peter Geach has taught philosophy at the Universities of Birmingham and Leeds. He has also taught at the University of Warsaw. A Fellow of the British Academy, he is very well known for his contributions to the study of logic, philosophy of religion, and philosophy of mind. His publications include: *Mental Acts* (1956), *Reference and Generality* (1962 and 1968), *God and the Soul* (1969), *Logic Matters*, (with G. E. M. Anscombe) *Three Philosophers* (1973), *Providence and Evil* (1977), and *The Virtues* (1977). He is married to G. E. M. Anscombe (see above). For discussion of Geach's philosophy, and for comments by him on the discussion, see Harry A. Lewis (ed.), *Peter Geach: Philosophical Encounters* (Dordrecht, 1991).

Robert Hambourger is an Associate Professor of Philosophy at North Carolina State University. He has taught at Northwestern University, the University of Wisconsin, New York University, Stanford University, and University of California, Los Angeles. When he wrote 'The Argument from Design' he had only recently come to believe in God but is now an active Catholic.

Paul Helm was formerly Reader in Philosophy at the University of Liverpool, U.K. He is currently Professor of the History and Philosophy of Religion at King's College, London. He has written extensively in the field of philosophy of religion. His books include *The Varieties of Belief* (1973), *Divine Revelation* (1983), *Eternal God* (1988), *The Providence of God* (1993) and *Faith with Reason* (2000).

David Hume was a Scottish eighteenth century philosopher (and also historian) especially known for his defence of an empiricist theory of knowledge (stressing the importance of sensory experience as a source of human knowledge). He is often taken to have been one of the greatest of eighteenth century philosophers, and his thinking has been extremely influential right down to present times. His main philosophical interests were in the areas of theory of knowledge, philosophy of the human person, ethics, and philosophy of religion. His most important works include *A Treatise of Human Nature* (1739/1740), *Essays: Moral and Political* (1741/1742), *An Enquiry concerning Human Understanding* (1748), *An Enquiry concerning the Principles of Morals* (1751), *The Natural History of Religion* (1757), and *Dialogues concerning Natural Religion* (1778). For an introductory volume on Hume's philosophy, see David Fate Norton (ed.), *The Cambridge Companion to Hume* (1993).

Immanuel Kant was a German eighteenth century philosopher born in Königsberg, where he taught for many years. Today he is widely regarded as one of the greatest of western philosophers. Influenced by the thought of authors such as Leibniz and Hume, he came to defend a position synthesizing some of the key elements in their thinking. In turn, Kant himself came to influence generations of philosophers. His main works include: *Critique of Pure Reason* (first edition, 1781), *Prolegomena to any Future Metaphysic* (1783), *Groundwork to the Metaphysic of Morals* (1785), *Metaphysical Foundations of Natural Science* (1786), *Critique of Practical Reason* (1788), *Critique of Judgement* (1790), *Religion within the Limits of Reason Alone* (1793), and *Metaphysics of Morals* (1797). For an introduction to Kant, see Paul Guyer (ed.), *The Cambridge Companion to Kant* (Cambridge, 1992).

Norman Kretzmann was a twentieth century American philosopher with special expertise both in contemporary analytical thinking and in medieval philosophy. He taught at a number of American universities, including Cornell University in New York, where he was Susan Linn Sage Professor of Philosophy. He died in 1998.

Kretzmann published scholarly editions of various medieval philosophical texts. He also published many learned articles and essays, and several edited collections. He was the principal editor of *The Cambridge History of Later Medieval Philosophy* (Cambridge, 1982). His other published books include *The Metaphysics of Theism* (1997) and *The Metaphysics of Creation* (1999).

Gottfried Wilhelm Leibniz was a late seventeenth and early eighteenth century German philosopher. Leibniz is now reckoned to be one of the greatest of the so-called 'rationalist' philosophers (along with Descartes and Spinoza). Born in Leipzig, and educated in Leipzig and Jena, he never held a university post (though he was offered one in 1667). Instead, he worked in the service of the Baron of Boineburg and, later, of the Dukes of Hanover. He had personal contacts with many of the greatest thinkers of his age (e.g. Antoine Arnauld, Robert Boyle, Samuel Clarke, Christian Huygens, Nicholas Malebranche, and Benedict de Spinoza). He wrote impressively on logic, mathematics, politics, jurisprudence, and philosophy of science. He also wrote voluminously about topics of interest to philosophers of religion. His philosophical system is very much a theistic one. His major works include *Discourse on Metaphysics* (1686), *New Essays in Human Understanding* (completed in 1704 but published posthumously), *Theodicy* (1710), and *Monadology* (1714). For a general introduction to Leibniz, see Nicholas Jolley (ed.), *The Cambridge Companion to Leibniz* (Cambridge, 1995).

J. L. Mackie Born in Australia in 1917, Mackie first taught in Australia and New Zealand. He then moved to England. At the time of his death in 1981 he was teaching philosophy at Oxford University, where he was a fellow of University College. His philosophical interests ranged over philosophy of religion, ethics, causality, and the history of philosophy (especially British empiricist philosophy). He published numerous influential articles. His books include: *Truth, Probability, and Paradox* (1973), *The Cement of the Universe* (1974), *Ethics: Inventing Right and Wrong* (1977), *Problems from Locke* (1976), *Hume's Moral Theory* (1980), and *The Miracle of Theism* (1982).

Norman Malcolm was one of the most distinguished of Wittgenstein's pupils and the main conveyor of his ideas to the USA, where Malcolm taught for many years at Cornell University. His writings were primarily in epistemology and philosophy of mind. They are distinguished not only by force of argument, but also by lucidity and simplicity of expression. His publications include *Memory and Mind* (1977) and (with D. M. Armstrong) *Consciousness and Causality* (1984). *Nothing is Hidden* (1986) is a valuable study of Wittgenstein's later phlosophical criticisms of his own earlier work.

C. B. Martin was formerly Professor of Philosophy at the University of Sydney, New

South Wales, Australia. His publications include *Religious Belief* (1959), (with D. M. Armstrong) *Locke and Berkeley: A Collection of Critical Essays* (1968), and (with D. M. Armstrong and U. T. Place) *Dispositions: A Debate* (1996).

Herbert McCabe is a Dominican friar currently teaching at Blackfriars Hall, Oxford. He was Editor of *New Blackfriars* from 1964 to 1965 and from 1970 to 1979. He has written extensively in the field of philosophy of religion. He has also written on ethics and sacramental theology. His publications include: *The New Creation* (1964), *Law, Love and Language* (1968), *The Teaching of the Catholic Church* (1985), and *God Matters* (1987).

Thomas V. Morris holds a Ph.D. in both Philosophy and Religious Studies from Yale University, and for fifteen years served as a Professor of Philosophy at the University of Notre Dame. He is now Chairman of the Morris Institute for Human Values in Wilmington, North Carolina, and works as a public philosopher. His latest book is *Philosophy for Dummies* (1999).

Kai Nielsen is an Emeritus Professor of the University of Calgary and a member of the Royal Society of Canada. His most recent books include *Naturalism without Foundations* (1996) and (with Hendrik Hart and Ronald Kuipers) *Walking the Tightrope of Faith* (1999).

H. P. Owen was a British twentieth century philosopher and theologian. Born in 1926, he died in 1996. He taught at the University of Wales and then at King's College, London, where he was Reader in Philosophy of Religion and, subsequently, Professor of Christian Doctrine. His writings include *Revelation and Existence* (1957), *The Moral Argument for Christian Theism* (1965), *The Christian Knowledge of God* (1969), *Concepts of Deity* (1971), and *Christian Theism: A Study in its Basic Principles* (1984). As well as defending the view that good philosophical thinking about morals provides grounds for belief in the existence of God, Owen (chiefly in *The Christian Knowledge of God*) also provided an impressive defence of the claim that people can have knowledge of God's existence (he called it an 'intuitive knowledge') which is solidly grounded in various aspects of human experience.

William Paley was an eighteenth century English theologian and moral philosopher. Born in Northamptonshire, he studied mathematics at Cambridge University. He subsequently became an Anglican priest and taught at Cambridge for nine years. Afterwards, he held a variety of ecclesiastical posts, including that of Archdeacon of Carlisle. He wrote three works, all of which were influential and much studied in eighteenth century Britain. These were: *The Principles of Moral and Political Philosophy* (1785), *A View of the Evidences of Christianity* (1794), and *Natural Theology* (1802).

D. Z. Phillips is Danforth Professor of Philosophy of Religion at Claremont Graduate University, California and Rush Rhees Research Professor at the University of Wales, Swansea. His works in philosophy of religion include: *The Concept of Prayer* (1965); *Faith and Philosophical Enquiry* (1971); *Death and Immortality* (1970); *Religion Without Explanation* (1976); *Belief Change and Forms of Life* (1986); *R.S. Thomas: Poet of the Hidden God* (1986); *From Fantasy to Faith* (1991); *Wittgenstein and Religion* (1994); *Philosophy's Cool Place* (1999); and *Recovering Religious Concepts* (2000).

Nelson Pike is Emeritus Professor of Philosophy, University of California, Irvine. He is the author of several books including *God and Timelessness* (1970) and *Mystic Union* (1992). He has been a contributor to numerous philosophical journals such as *Philosophical Review, Journal of Philosophy, Mind, American Philosophical Quarterly* and *International Journal for Philosophy of Religion.*

Alvin Plantinga is a 1954 Calvin College graduate who taught philosophy at his alma mater from 1963 to 1982 and then accepted an appointment as the John A. O'Brien Professor of Philosophy at the University of Notre Dame. He has given more than 200 guest lectures at conferences and on campuses in North America, Europe, and Australia. Known for the way in which he applies results of his work in other areas of analytic philosophy to traditional issues in philosophy of religion, he has published *God and Other* Minds (1967), *The Nature of Necessity* (1974), *Warranted Christian Belief* (1999), *The Analytic Theist: An Alvin Plantinga Reader* (1998), *Essays in Ontology* (2000) as well as many articles.

Plato was a hugely influential ancient Greek philosopher. He was born in Athens and lived there for most of his life. He was much influenced by Socrates, who features prominently in many of his writings (mostly composed in the form of dialogues). Plato's philosophical inquiries range chiefly around questions in the field of ethics, politics, theory of knowledge, philosophy of the human person, and logic. If only because of his extraordinary impact on intellectual history, all serious students of philosophy will need to study at least some of Plato's major works. For a general introduction to him, see Richard Kraut (ed.), *The Cambridge Companion to Plato* (1992).

Bertrand Russell was a very important twentieth century British philosopher. He taught at Cambridge University. His most important and original work lies in the areas of logic and mathematics (he thought that mathematics could be reduced to logic), but he also wrote on a variety of other subjects including theory of knowledge, the nature of the human person, the reasonableness of religious belief, and political theory. His major writings include: *A Critical Exposition of the Philosophy of Leibniz* (1900), *The Principles of Mathematics* (1903; 2nd Edition, 1937), (with A. N. Whitehead) *Principia Mathematica* (1925–7), *The*

Problems of Philosophy (1912), *The Philosophy of Logical Atomism* (1918), *The Analysis of Mind* (1927), *A History of Western Philosophy* (1945), and *Human Knowledge: Its Scope and Limits* (1948).

James Sadowsky is a Jesuit and Professor Emeritus at Fordham University in New York where he taught philosophy from 1960 to 1994. The following of his articles bear on the philosophy of religion: 'Did Darwin Destroy the Design Argument?' (*International Philosophical Quarterly*, 1980), 'Does Theism Need Middle Knowledge?' (co-authored with David Gordon, *Religious Studies*, 1990), 'Why Create Hitler?' (*New Blackfriars*, 1989), and 'Transubstantiation and Scholastic Philosophy' (*Proceedings of the American Philosophical Association*, 1965).

John Duns Scotus was a late thirteenth century philosopher and theologian sometimes referred to as the Subtle Doctor (*Doctor Subtilis*). Scotus was a native of Scotland. He became a Franciscan friar and subsequently taught in Oxford, Paris, and Cologne. He is often read as a vigorous critic of the thought of Thomas Aquinas. His influence on succeeding thinkers was considerable. His writings include lectures on the *Sentences* of Peter Lombard (the *Opus Oxoniense* and the *Reportata Parisiensia*), some commentaries on works of Aristotle, and a volume entitled *A Treatise on God as First Principle* (*De Primo Principio*).

Eleonore Stump is the Robert J. Henle, S.J., Professor of Philosophy at Saint Louis University. She has written extensively on various topics in medieval philosophy as well as in philosophy of religion and metaphysics. Her books include *Boethius's De topicis differentiis* (1978), *Boethius's In Ciceronis Topica* (1988), and *Dialectic and Its Place in the Development of Medieval Logic* (1989). Her recent articles include 'Ockham on Sensory Cognition', in the *Cambridge Companion to Ockham*, 'Aquinas on Justice', and 'Saadya Gaon and the Problem of Evil'.

Richard Swinburne has been Nolloth Professor of the Philosophy of the Christian Religion at Oxford University since 1985. He is the author of many books both on the philosophy of religion and on other philosophical areas. These include *The Existence of God* (2nd Edition, 1991), *The Evolution of the Soul* (1986), *Is There A God?* (1996), and *Providence and the Problem of Evil* (1998).

Illtyd Trethowan was a Benedictine monk, philosopher of religion, and theologian. He was born in 1907 and died in 1993. He lived and worked at Downside Abbey in Somerset. Trethowan was one of the most prolific and tough-minded twentieth century Catholics writing in English on philosophy and theology in the post-war years. Between 1948 and the time of his death he produced around 110 articles, numerous book reviews, a book written jointly with Dom Mark Pontifex (*The Meaning of Existence*, published in 1953), an edition of the writings of the fourteenth century English mystical author Walter Hilton (1975), and several translations of important French authors—most notably, Maurice Blondel, Louis Lavelle, Eugene Masure, Etienne Gilson, and Louis Bouyer. He also published seven books: *Christ in the Liturgy* (1952), *An Essay in Christian Philosophy* (1954), *The Basis of Belief* (1961), *Absolute Value* (1970), *The Absolute and the Atonement* (1971), *Mysticism and Theology* (1975), and *Process Theology and Christian Tradition* (1985). From 1946 to 1952, and from 1960 to 1964, he was Editor of *The Downside Review*.

Nicholas Wolterstorff received his BA degree from Calvin College in 1953, and his Ph.D. in philosophy from Harvard University in 1956. After spending a year in Europe on a fellowship from Harvard, the Sheldon Travelling Fellowship, he taught for two years in the philosophy department at Yale University. He then returned to his alma mater, Calvin College, where he taught philosophy for 30 years. In 1989 he left for his current position at Yale, as Noah Porter Professor of Philosophical Theology in the Divinity School, and as adjunct professor in the philosophy department and the religious studies department. He has taught, for one- or two-semester stints, at Haverford College, Notre Dame University, Princeton University, the University of Texas, the University of Michigan, and Temple University; and for five years he was a professor (half-time) at the Free University of Amsterdam. He has been President of the American Philosophical Association (Central Division), and of the Society of Christian Philosophers. After concentrating on metaphysics at the beginning of his career (*On Universals* (1970)), he spent a good many years working primarily on aesthetics and philosophy of art (*Works and Worlds of Art* (1980), and *Art in Action* (1980)). In more recent years, he has been concentrating on epistemology (*John Locke and the Ethics of Belief* (1996), and, forthcoming, *Thomas Reid and the Story of Epistemology*), philosophy of religion (*Divine Discourse* (1995)), and political philosophy (*Until Justice and Peace Embrace* (1983), and *Religion in the Public Square* (1997)), while maintaining his interest in aesthetics. In the fall of 1993 he gave the Wilde lectures at Oxford University (published as *Divine Discourse*). In the spring of 1995 he gave the Gifford lectures at St Andrews University (to be published under the title of *World, Mind, and Entitlement to Believe*). In the spring of 1998 he gave the Stone lectures at Princeton Seminary, on political philosophy and theology.

General introduction

What is this book about?

PHILOSOPHERS are people who try to think clearly. They typically seek to argue on the basis of reason. Confronted by an argument, they are fond of asking if its premises entail its conclusion. They also have a habit of trying to evaluate premises. 'Does it make sense to say this?' 'Is it unreasonable to believe that?' These are just the sort of questions which one can expect a philosopher to raise.[1]

But questions have a habit of leading to further ones. What is sense? What is the difference between the reasonable and the unreasonable? These, too, are questions which philosophers ask. And by doing so they remind us that there is no easy way to explain what philosophy is. The word 'philosophy' comes from the Greek words for 'love' and 'wisdom'. So we can think of philosophers as 'lovers of wisdom'. But what some think to be wisdom, others regard as folly (as St Paul famously said). And if we think we know what wisdom amounts to, we have already taken sides on a number of philosophical issues.[2]

Most contemporary philosophers would be none too keen to attempt a definition of 'philosophy'. But there are more ways than one of seeking to indicate what something is. Mary (from the United Kingdom) may find it hard to give Fred (from the USA) a definition of 'British humour'. Yet she can give him an understanding of it by getting him to view a lot of British comedy shows. And Mary (the philosopher) can give Fred (the non-philosopher) an understanding of what philosophy is by getting him to read through the writings of people commonly deemed to be philosophers. When asked what philosophy is, a famous philosopher once pointed to his bookshelves and said 'It's what that lot is all about'. He was trying to explain by example. And he was no fool in doing so.

What of 'philosophy of religion' ? As with 'philosophy' there are no easy definitions to be had. Nobody would deny that philosophers of religion are people who try to philosophize about religion. But what should we mean by 'religion'? In Henry Fielding's novel *Tom Jones*, Mr Thwakum declares: 'When I mention religion, I mean the Christian religion; and not only the Christian religion, but the Protestant religion; and not only the Protestant religion, but the Church of England.'[3] Yet there is surely more to be included under the rubric of religion than Mr Thwakum allows.

---

1. For a solid and reliable introduction to philosophical reasoning in general, one aimed at those approaching philosophy for the first time, see Peter Geach, *Reason and Argument* (Oxford, 1976).
2. In the current edition of the *Oxford English Dictionary*, we read that in 'the original and widest sense' philosophy is 'the love, study, or pursuit of wisdom, or of knowledge of things and their causes, whether theoretical or practical'. In this connection the Dictionary notes the influence of Cicero's *De Officiis*, II. ii. 5. It goes on to tell us that the 'most usual' sense of the word now is 'that department of knowledge or study which deals with ultimate reality, or with the most general causes and principles of things'. Most philosophers would say that even these definitions raise philosophical problems. What, for instance, is 'ultimate reality' supposed to mean?
3. Book III, ch. 3.

There is, alas, no simple way to explain what philosophy of religion is. Like philosophy in general, it defies quick definition.[4] But its nature can also be grasped by example. For you can think of it as what you find when you read what philosophers have been saying when reflecting on anything which might sensibly be thought of as a religious topic. The notion that there is a branch of philosophy to be called 'philosophy of religion' first clearly emerged in the writings of G. W. F. Hegel (1770–1831). But philosophy of religion has been around for as long as there have been philosophers. Almost all the great Western philosophers have things to say on matters which are recognizably religious. In this sense, almost all of them are philosophers of religion.

The contents of this book

In this book you will find many philosophers reflecting on religious matters. Aimed chiefly at students and general readers, it is intended to introduce you to philosophy of religion by means of anthology and commentary. It presupposes no previous training in philosophy and is intended to serve as a self-contained point of entry to its subject-matter. In this sense, you can think of it as a 'teach-yourself' manual.

On what basis have the topics and readings in what follows been chosen? An anthology can contain a lot of snippets touching on a lot of issues. Or it can provide substantial readings on a selection of some major ones. I have chosen to offer an anthology of the second kind. And, in doing so, I have focused on those questions which have most pre-occupied Western philosophers when thinking about religion, questions which have effectively made philosophy of religion the subject it is today. One of these is the relation between philosophy and religion—the subject of Part I. Another is that of the existence and nature of God (Parts II, III, and IV). The so-called 'problem of evil' has puzzled thinkers for centuries, so this topic is addressed in Part V. In Parts VI and VII you will find philosophers reflecting on ethics and religion, and on the question everyone asks at some time—'Is there life after death?'. In Part VII you will find a variety of answers to this question.

And a variety of answers to questions is what you will find all through the book. For I have aimed to anthologize texts from authors taking significantly different positions. I have also aimed to anthologize ones which will help you to see how philosophy of religion has been practised over time (on the sound philosophical principle that recent is not necessarily better). The texts to be found below follow no party line and no special historical bias. They come from authors of varying times and persuasions. Reading them should help you to gain a serious sense of philosophy of religion as a subject you can study while learning from all sorts of people. It should also help you to arrive at conclusions of your own. Philosophers of religion are people who seek to think for themselves. Thinking about their thinking should help you to become all that philosophers of religion seek to be.

To start with, however, you might be helped by a brief overview of philosophy of

---

4. For a helpful discussion of the difficulties involved in defining 'philosophy of religion', see the Introduction to M. J. Charlesworth, *Philosophy of Religion: The Historic Approaches* (London, 1972).

religion's history. The following one is very brief. But it will give you a sense of how the subject has developed over time and who has contributed to it.

A very short history of philosophy of religion

One could say that philosophy of religion is a worldwide phenomenon which has been around ever since there were human beings. Understood in this way, its story is part of the history of many countries and peoples, and it is long. But philosophy of religion, considered as a distinct branch of philosophy, is an essentially Western phenomenon, and its story is not vastly different from that of the history of Western philosophy in general. This is often said to have started with Plato (c.428–c.348 BC) and to have continued to what can be found in recently published journals and books devoted to philosophy. And much the same could be said of the history of philosophy of religion. For that can be thought of as something which starts with Plato and ends on the shelves of your local university library.

From Plato to Ockham There was significant reflection on religious matters prior to that of Plato. Xenophanes (c.570–c.475 BC) taught about one God who causes all. And Diogenes of Apollonia (5th century BC) spoke of an intelligence regulating the ways in which nature behaves. But it is in Plato's works that ancient Greek thinking rises to the level of a sustained philosophical treatment of matters recognizably religious. In his *Phaedo*, we find him debating the issue of life after death (see Part VII below).[5] And in other works we find him concerned with the notion of divinity and the role of the divine in the world of our experience. Is reality confined only to what we can discover with our senses? Is the world an effect of an intelligent cause or principle? Does it somehow depend on what is distinct from space and time? Can philosophical inquiry lead us to some kind of final happiness in relation to what lies beyond what we normally encounter? Plato has things to say on all these questions, and his answers had a big influence on later thinkers, especially ones within the Christian tradition. They also present a distinctive view of what people are, one which many would think of as religiously significant. For Plato teaches that people are not simply bodies. He holds that they have access to an immaterial realm, and are essentially immaterial. Scholars are currently divided when it comes to what exactly he believes about the existence and nature of God. But all of them would agree that he marks the start of sustained philosophical thinking on the subject.[6]

---

5. Philosophers have written in different literary forms. Plato liked to philosophize by writing conversations between different individuals (dialogues), a taste he shared with some later philosophers such as Augustine, Anselm, and Hume. In the Middle Ages, much (though by no means all) philosophy was written in a rather dry (though usually clear) question-and-answer format. Philosophers from the seventeenth century onwards have generally preferred to write straightforward expositions of their philosophical positions, though some have ventured into a more literary mode of expression, like the poem and the novel.

6. Key texts of Plato to study in this connection are *The Republic* and *The Laws*.

They would also agree that the next major exponent of such thinking is Aristotle (384–322 BC). As with Plato, scholars are divided when it comes to interpreting his teaching. He speaks much of the 'divine', but what exactly does he mean when doing so? In his *Metaphysics* he argues that there has to be a first, divine, immutable, and immaterial source of all change. But does he here take himself to be defending what we might call a 'religious' conclusion, as opposed to a 'physical' or 'scientific' one? Is Aristotle's divine cause of change anything like what God is taken to be by, for example, Jews and Christians? Commentators have differed in their answers to these questions. But there is no doubting Aristotle's commitment to a view of things which, by some standards, is 'religious' rather than 'secular'. He sees nature, for example, as a realm shaped by order and purpose. Unlike Plato, he does not think of people as essentially immaterial. But he argues that they have a non-material 'soul'.

Since he does not concentrate on religious themes, it can be argued that Aristotle is not a religious philosopher. But Plotinus (c.205–70) certainly is. So is Augustine of Hippo (354–430). For Plotinus (commonly referred to as the founder of Neoplatonism), philosophy can help us to rise to 'the One', which Plotinus takes to be the ultimate and immaterial source of the existence and value of everything.[7] According to Augustine (whose thinking was partly indebted to Plotinus), philosophy can lead us to see that there is a creator God who is good, timeless, immutable, and ubiquitous. Augustine also thinks that philosophy can help us to see the truth of certain beliefs which Christianity presupposes rather than lists in its creeds (beliefs also presupposed by religions such as Judaism and Islam): the belief that people have freedom of choice, for instance, or the belief that people are more than just physical objects. Augustine does not think that uniquely Christian beliefs (such as the doctrine of the Trinity or the doctrine of the Incarnation) can be proved by means of philosophy. But he holds that philosophy can help us to make some sense of them. He also argues that it can reasonably make room for the notion of faith. For him, reason and faith complement each other. For him, philosophy is a help, not a hindrance, to religion.[8]

This view of philosophy is fairly consistently upheld by many medieval philosophers. Once thought of as something of a dark period for philosophy, the Middle Ages are now generally acknowledged to have given rise to a vast amount of sophisticated work in the area of logic and ethics. They also gave rise to some impressive discussions of questions which are central to philosophy of religion.

Hence, for example, the Arabic philosopher Avicenna (980–1037) argues for a position which became something of a favourite with later (mostly Christian) religious thinkers. He distinguishes between what a thing is (its 'essence') and the fact that it exists at all (its 'existence'). And he uses this distinction to develop a philosophical argument for the

---

7. Our knowledge of Plotinus's teaching comes from a collection of his writings edited by Porphyry (c.232–c.305) and known as the *Enneads*. For a study of Plotinus, see Lloyd P. Gerson, *Plotinus* (London and New York, 1994).

8. Major texts by Augustine include: *City of God* (*De Civitate Dei*), *Christian Doctrine* (*De Doctrina Christiana*), *Confessions* (*Confessiones*), *Grace and Free Will* (*De Gratia et Libero Arbitrio*), and *The Trinity* (*De Trinitate*). For studies of Augustine, see Mary T. Clark, *Augustine* (London, 1994), John J. O'Meara, *Understanding Augustine* (Dublin, 1997), and John M. Rist, *Augustine* (Cambridge, 1994).

existence of God as something whose existence follows from its essence (a necessary existent).[9]

Then again, Anselm of Canterbury (1033–1109) defends the notion of 'faith seeking understanding' (*fides quaerens intellectum*) to offer a variety of arguments for God's existence—including the so-called 'Ontological Argument' (see Part III below). And in the twelfth century, the Jewish philosopher Maimonides (1135–1204) relentlessly struggled with what we might call 'theistic epistemology' (what can be known, as opposed to merely believed, of God). In his *Guide for the Perplexed*, he argues that our knowledge of God is essentially negative: we know best what God is *not*.[10]

The notion of knowing God by negation is also treated with considerable intellectual dexterity by the man who is normally thought of as the greatest medieval philosopher: the Dominican friar Thomas Aquinas (1224/6–74).[11] Though famous for developing the view that certain words used in talking about God and creatures are to be understood 'analogously' (see Part II below), Aquinas also argues that there is a serious sense in which people cannot know what God is. But he also provides sustained philosophical elaboration and defence of the belief that there exists a God who is simple, omnipotent, omniscient, and eternal (see Parts III and IV below). Taken as a whole, his writings cover all the major topics commonly thought of as belonging to philosophy of religion.

The history of medieval philosophy of religion does not end with Aquinas. One might, for example, mention one of his immediate contemporaries—Giovanni di Fidanza, commonly known as St Bonaventure (1221–74), the first great Franciscan philosopher.[12] One might also mention two other famous Franciscans: Duns Scotus (c.1266–1308) and William of Ockham (c.1285–1349).

For Scotus, who taught in Oxford and Paris, and who was thought of by the poet Gerald Manley Hopkins (1844–89) as the greatest of philosophers, a matter of central philosophical importance is Being. In thinking along these lines he is deferring to Aristotle, who argues that philosophers should study 'Being as being' (what it is for anything to be, as opposed to what it is for things to be the particulars that they are). Unlike Aristotle, however, Scotus reflects on this topic as a Christian. In doing so, he offers arguments for the existence of God (considered as Creator and as infinite being) which are distinctively different from those proposed by most of his Christian predecessors. They are, for example, different from arguments for the existence of God offered by Aquinas. Also in contrast to Aquinas, Scotus denies that philosophers can give adequate reason for thinking of God as omnipotent, just, or merciful. He believed that God was such, but he did not think that the matter could be settled by philosophical reasoning. And (again unlike Aquinas) he maintains that talk of God's being (including any talk of God) must (when compared with talk about what is not God) be construed as 'univocal'. He holds, for example, that when we say (a) that Fred exists or that Fred is good and (b) that God exists and that God is good, we mean 'exists' and 'is good' in exactly the same way. In doing so,

9. See L. E. Goodman, *Avicenna* (London and New York, 1992).
10. For a study of Maimonides, see Oliver Leaman, *Moses Maimonides* (London and New York, 1990).
11. The Dominicans are an order of friars founded by St Dominic Guzman (c.1170–1221).
12. The Franciscans are an order of friars founded by St Francis of Assisi (1181/2–1226).

he anticipates a lot of subsequent reflection on the topic of talk about God. In his reflections on the notions of possibility and necessity, he also anticipates those contemporary philosophers (practitioners of what is called 'modal logic') who make much of the notion of 'possible worlds' (see Parts III and IV below). For he conceives of God as choosing to create while selecting between many different universes which he could also have created (possible worlds).[13]

But can philosophy show that there is a God who creates? William of Ockham, in distinction from Scotus, said 'No'. Indeed, when it comes to the question of philosophy's ability to give us knowledge of God, Ockham is almost entirely sceptical. He believes in the existence of God, but he takes it to be something we can properly arrive at only by means of faith (considered as something sharply different from what can be attained by means of philosophical reflection). And on his account it is to faith alone that we must look for an answer to the question 'Do people live after death?'. For these reasons, he stands at something of a turning point in the history of philosophy of religion. With one foot firmly placed in an age of lively religious belief, there is a sense in which Ockham anticipates a later time when philosophers found themselves challenging such belief in the name of philosophy. He also anticipates a time when philosophers were to find themselves challenging the assumption that human beings can arrive at a knowledge of the world and of their place in it. For he argues that there is a sense in which God can directly cause us to be convinced that something that is not there *is* there—an idea which resembles one which features in the writings of René Descartes (1596–1650), who is often referred to as the 'father of modern philosophy'.[14]

From Descartes to Eliot In his *Discourse on Method* and his *Meditations on First Philosophy*, Descartes seeks to find a proposition which cannot be doubted. And in doing so, he entertains the possibility of an agent able to make us consistently to believe what is false. But Descartes is no friend of the view that we know nothing, and some of his most famous philosophical writings argue for the truth of various religious beliefs, notably the belief that God exists, and the belief that people are able to survive death. According to Descartes, the idea of God (a) must be caused by God and (b) implies God's necessary existence (see Part III below). Descartes also famously develops an understanding of human beings (sometimes referred to as 'substance dualism') according to which we are essentially non-material things who are, therefore, not necessarily extinguished when our bodies perish (see Part VII below). In some of his writings, he defends an account of God's nature which is much in line with that taught by some of the key medieval philosophers. He holds, for example, that God is both omnipotent and wholly simple.[15]

13. For more on Scotus, see Alan B. Wolter, *The Philosophical Theology of John Duns Scotus* (Ithaca, New York, and London, 1990) and Richard Cross, *Duns Scotus* (New York and Oxford, 1999).
14. For more on Ockham, see Marilyn McCord Adams, *William Ockham* (2 vols, Notre Dame, Indiana, 1987).
15. Good, general studies of Descartes include John Cottingham, *Descartes* (Oxford, 1986), Anthony Kenny, *Descartes: A Study of His Philosophy* (New York, 1968), Bernard Williams, *Descartes: The Project of Pure Enquiry* (Harmondsworth, 1978), and Margaret Dauler Wilson, *Descartes* (London, Henley, and Boston, 1978).

The notion of God stands at the heart of Descartes's philosophical system. It is crucial, too, in the one developed by G. W. Leibniz (1646–1716). Appealing to various versions of what he calls 'the principle of sufficient reason', and making much of a distinction between 'truths of reason' and 'truths of fact', Leibniz argues not only that there is a God but that the existence of God is a matter of strict necessity (see Part III below). Also appealing to 'sufficient reason', he seeks to explain why God creates and what God is like. Among other things, he proposes (a) that God is wholly good and (of necessity) is the producer of the 'best possible world', (b) that changes in the world are mostly effected by God alone, and (c) that God is distinct from, and the maker of, time (contrary to the thinking of Isaac Newton (1642–1727) and Samuel Clarke (1675–1729)).

The prominence given by Leibniz to the notion of 'possible worlds' has had an influence which extends to the present time and to the philosophy of religion as practised by contemporary authors such as Alvin Plantinga (see Part III below).[16] Some of Leibniz's major philosophical teachings about God also resemble those of Benedict de Spinoza (1632–77). But while Leibniz conceives of God as radically distinct from the universe, Spinoza, in his *Tractatus Theologico-Politicus* (*Theological-Political Treatise*), appears to think of God as identical with the laws of nature (a view which seems to be reaffirmed in his *Ethics*, published in 1677). And, unlike Leibniz, Spinoza has much to say on the question 'How should we read the Bible?'. In the light of the history of biblical scholarship during the last hundred years or so, some of his answers to this question seem strikingly contemporary.[17]

In histories and dictionaries of philosophy, Descartes, Leibniz, and Spinoza are often referred to as 'rationalists', for philosophers love to label each other (mostly to no useful effect). Another label beloved of philosophers is 'empiricist', and it is commonly used to characterize the thought of the next two figures who must be mentioned in a very brief history of philosophy of religion: John Locke (1632–1704) and David Hume (1711–76).[18]

From the viewpoint of philosophy of religion, Locke is chiefly important as a major seventeenth-century defender of natural theology (which we may, for the moment, think of as the attempt to ground beliefs about God on purely rational reflection).[19] He is also important as someone concerned to define the boundaries between religious faith and philosophical reason, and as concerned to defend Christianity as he understood it. Writing in the light of the account of the basis and range of human knowledge developed in his *An Essay Concerning Human Understanding* (1690), Locke maintains (in the *Essay*, but also in *The Reasonableness of Christianity*, published in 1695) that the existence of God can be demonstrated, that biblical moral teaching squares with what reason can discover, and that there are matters of faith which, though 'above reason', are yet rationally believable. Having developed a theory of what persons are, he also defends

16. For more on Leibniz, see Benson Mates, *The Philosophy of Leibniz* (New York and Oxford, 1986) and Nicholas Rescher, *Leibniz: An Introduction to his Philosophy* (Oxford, 1979).
17. For information on the history of biblical studies, see John Barton (ed.), *The Cambridge Companion to Biblical Interpretation* (Cambridge, 1998). For studies of Spinoza, see Alan Donagan, *Spinoza* (Brighton, 1988) and Stuart Hampshire, *Spinoza* (Harmondsworth, 1951).
18. Broadly speaking, empiricists are people who take all or most of our knowledge to be based on sensory experience or experienced sense-data (what seem to us to be sensory experiences).
19. For more on the notion of natural theology, see Part III below.

a much discussed view of human beings, one which carries forward Descartes's attempts to show that people need not expire with their bodies.[20]

Like those of Locke, Hume's writings on religion proceed on the basis of his understanding of human knowledge, which he presents in *A Treatise of Human Nature* (1739/ 1740) and his *Enquiry Concerning Human Understanding* (1748). But while Locke finds reason pointing towards the truth of various religious beliefs, Hume takes a different view. Hence, and especially in his *Dialogues Concerning Natural Religion* (posthumously published in 1779), we find him rejecting a variety of arguments for God's existence, while also arguing that philosophy is incapable of showing that God's nature is as most theists take it to be. 'If we take in our hand any volume; of divinity or school metaphysics', says Hume, 'let us ask, *Does it contain any abstract reasoning concerning quantity or number? No. Does it contain any experimental reasoning concerning matter of fact and existence?* No. Commit it then to the flames: for it can contain nothing but sophistry and illusion.'[21] In a famous section of the *Enquiry* Hume offers one of the best-known critiques of belief in the occurrence of miracles (see Part III, below). In *The Natural History of Religion* (1757), he argues that religion can have bad moral consequences and that it leads to superstition and fanaticism.[22]

Yet someone who is often described as having been led to his most mature reflections with a debt to Hume, follows a different line. For though Immanuel Kant (1724–1804), one of the most influential philosophers of modern times, says that Hume woke him up from certain 'dogmatic slumbers', he also writes positively and in defense of religious beliefs. In his *Critique of Pure Reason* (1781/1787) he famously maintains that it is impossible to demonstrate the existence of God by arguments like those of Descartes and Leibniz (see Part III below). Yet in his *Critique of Practical Reason* (1788) and in *Religion Within the Bounds of Pure Reason* (1793), he just as famously argues that moral considerations somehow imply both the existence of God and life after death for human beings (see Part VI below). Kant seems to have had little time for specifically Christian doctrine, for organized religion, or for religious practices such as prayer. But he stands a long way from Hume both in what he says about the existence of God and in what he says about the worth or significance of religion in general.[23] The same can be said of George Wilhelm Friedrich Hegel (1770–1831). He has seemed to some to be anything but a champion of religion. But his voluminous writings (notably his *Phenomenology of Spirit* (1807), his *Science of Logic* (1812–16), and his *Encyclopedia of the Philosophical Sciences* (1817, 1827, and 1830)) contain attempts to show that philosophy can view religion as vital to a right understanding of philosophy and human thinking, as something which reaches its proper and final expression in philosophy.[24]

20. Helpful introductions to Locke include John J. Jenkins, *Understanding Locke* (Edinburgh, 1983), E. J. Lowe, *Locke on Human Understanding* (London and New York, 1995), and R. S. Woolhouse, *Locke* (Brighton, 1983).

21. *An Enquiry Concerning Human Understanding*, ed. L. A. Selby-Bigge (3rd edn, Oxford, 1975), p. 165.

22. For a fine study of Hume on religion, see J. C. A. Gaskin, *Hume's Philosophy of Religion* (2nd edn, Basingstoke, 1988). Hume's writings on religion are conveniently collected in Antony Flew (ed.), *David Hume: Writings on Religion* (La Salle, Illinois, 1992).

23. See Bernard M. G. Reardon, *Kant as Philosophical Theologian* (Basingstoke, 1988).

24. For surveys of Hegel's thinking see Peter Singer, *Hegel* (Oxford, 1983) and Charles Taylor, *Hegel* (Cambridge, 1979).

Are Kant and Hegel truly religious thinkers? According to one of their most famous critics they are hardly religious at all. For in the judgement of Søren Kierkegaard (1813–55), true religious belief is different from what you might assent to by means of philosophical reflection (especially like that of Hegel). Like Kant, Kierkegaard argues that reason is limited when it comes to religious matters. Unlike Kant, however, he holds that it is totally limited. It can lead us only to the 'Unknown', beyond the range of knowledge, and it must give way to faith, which Kierkegaard described as a species of 'subjectivity', and which he conceived of as a passionate commitment and a way of life rather than as a speculative assent to a list of propositions. In developing this idea, Kierkegaard lays much stress on the importance of human freedom. He holds that religious faith is something we choose, not something to which our minds conform of necessity.

Kierkegaard's stress on freedom has led him to be labelled as an 'existentialist', a title he shares with later philosophers, most notably Jean-Paul Sartre (1905–80). Yet Sartre finds no truth in religion. And in the hundred or so years following Hegel's death, philosophers of note writing on religion are mostly critical of it. Hence, for example, Friedrich Nietzsche (1844–1900) famously declares 'God is dead'. He also spends much time insisting that Christian thinking springs from despicable human tendencies, like the desire to control people. Influenced by Nietzsche, Karl Marx (1818–83) argues that religion is 'the opium of the masses', a system of erroneous beliefs which befuddles people into accepting unacceptable ways of living together. Influenced, in turn, by Marx, Ludwig Feuerbach (1804–72) holds that belief in God is nothing but a 'projection' of the best human characteristics and aspirations. In *The Essence of Christianity* (1841) he maintains that those who believe in God take what we most value in ourselves and mistakenly think of it as something belonging to a being or beings distinct from the world of our experience. Feuerbach was translated into English by the Victorian novelist George Eliot (1819–80), and his thinking informs all of her most popular novels (such as *Adam Bede*, and *Middlemarch*). In the novels of George Eliot, you will find an impressive attempt to show how a philosophical critique of religion can seem credible when presented as literature.[25]

Philosophy of religion in the twentieth century Many important twentieth-century philosophers have regarded religious belief as of little interest. Some, like Bertrand Russell (1872–1970) dismiss it as wholly incredible or even as positively dangerous. Others pass over it in silence, as, for example, does Gottlob Frege (1848–1925), the founder of modern logic. In the 1920s, 1930s, 1940s, and 1950s, an influential group of philosophers, commonly referred to as 'Logical Positivists', argued that religious belief is meaningless or nonsensical (see Part II below), thereby depriving philosophy of religion of any intelligible subject-matter.[26]

Yet the period from 1900 to around 1960 also saw philosophers from many countries turning to religion as something of serious philosophical significance. Examples include the Austrian Ludwig Wittgenstein (1889–1951), the American John Dewey (1859–1952),

25. See Brian Davies, 'George Eliot and Christianity', *The Downside Review* (January 1982).
26. Examples of Logical Positivists include Otto Neurath (1882–1945), Friedrich Waismann (1896–1959), Rudolf Carnap (1891–1970), and (at one time, at least) A. J. Ayer (1910–89).

the German Hannah Arendt (1906–75), the English authors F. R. Tennant (1866–1957), I. T. Ramsey (1915–72), and Austin Farrer (1904–68), the Scottish A. E. Taylor (1869–1945), the Canadian Bernard Lonergan (1904–84), and the French thinkers Jacques Maritain (1882–1973) and Etienne Gilson (1884–1978). The same period also saw some major theologians employing philosophy to serious theological effect—people such as Rudolf Bultmann (1884–1976), Paul Tillich (1886–1965), and Karl Rahner (1904–84). And, since the middle of the 1960s or so, philosophy of religion has increasingly become a booming subject, even in quarters where it was deemed to be of little philosophical interest earlier in the century.

Why? Partly because large numbers of philosophers from the 1960s onward became disenchanted with Logical Positivism. The Positivists' dismissal of religious belief relied heavily on theories of meaning which came to be widely rejected.[27] Another factor to be reckoned with is the influence of Ludwig Wittgenstein, arguably the greatest of twentieth-century philosophers. His later writings, in particular the *Philosophical Investigations* and *On Certainty*, develop an approach to language, meaning, and knowledge which has led some of those influenced by it (notably Norman Malcolm, D. Z. Phillips, Rush Rhees, Gareth Moore, and Peter Winch) to develop a wholly new approach to philosophy of religion (see Part I below). A claim often stressed by these so-called 'Wittgensteinian' philosophers of religion is that religious belief does not need to be justified by means of philosophical argument. Writing not under Wittgenstein's influence but, rather, from independent reflection on the notions of 'reason' and 'evidence', and reacting to what is sometimes called 'classical foundationalism', other (largely American) twentieth-century philosophers have stimulated much discussion and research on religious knowledge and the relation between philosophy and religious belief. In this connection, the work of Alvin Plantinga and William Alston is especially to be noted.[28]

Plantinga and Alston are currently figures with a high profile in the American Society of Christian Philosophers, founded in 1978. The work of this Society and its members has been influential. Among other things, it has led to an increasingly growing interest in the philosophical discussion of specifically Christian teachings, such as the doctrines of the Trinity and the Incarnation. Since the 1980s, reflection on such doctrines has become very much part of what philosophers of religion have in mind when they refer to philosophy of religion. It was also very much part of philosophy of religion in its medieval form. So it is, perhaps, no accident that many of its current practitioners write with a special eye on medieval thinkers such as Anselm and Aquinas.

27. At the present time, verificationist attacks on religious belief are not taken very seriously by most philosophers. But they still have some defenders, notably Kai Nielsen and Michael Martin. See Nielsen's *Contemporary Critiques of Religion* (New York, 1971) and *An Introduction to the Philosophy of Religion* (New York, 1982). See Martin's *Atheism: A Philosophical Justification* (Philadelphia, 1990).
28. Some of Plantinga's major essays can be found in James F. Sennett (ed.), *The Analytic Theist: An Alvin Plantinga Reader* (Grand Rapids, Michigan, and Cambridge, 1998).

Advice on further reading

Many Western philosophers have had things to say on religious matters, and since almost all of their thinking is, in one way or another, relevant to those with an eye on philosophy of religion, you can be nothing but helped in your thinking on philosophy of religion by a study of Western philosophy in general.

To start with, you should consult some standard histories of philosophy. Especially to be recommended is F. C. Copleston, *A History of Philosophy* (9 vols, London, 1946–75) and the *Routledge History of Philosophy* (10 vols, London and New York, 1993–8). For recent one-volume guides, see Anthony Kenny, *A Brief History of Western Philosophy* (Oxford, 1998) and Anthony Kenny (ed.), *The Oxford Illustrated History of Western Philosophy* (Oxford, 1994). In the notes to the General Introduction above, I cite some useful, general studies of philosophers mentioned in it.

Dictionaries of philosophy are often very much worth consulting, since many of them contain entries by experts who pack a lot of information into a small space. A major reference work is Paul Edwards (ed.), *The Encyclopedia of Philosophy* (London, 1967). Others include Robert Audi (ed.), *The Cambridge Dictionary of Philosophy* (Cambridge, 1995) and T. Honderich (ed.), *The Oxford Companion to Philosophy* (Oxford, 1995). A useful, short reference work is Thomas Mautner (ed.), *Dictionary of Philosophy* (Harmondsworth, 1997). Cambridge University Press has for some years been publishing 'Companions' to major Western philosophers, all of which provide very good introductions to their subjects.

If you have no philosophical training, and if you want to pursue philosophy of religion armed with advice about philosophy in general, you should turn to some general introductions to philosophy. Ones to be recommended include:

Simon Blackburn, *Think* (Oxford, 1999).

A. C. Grayling (ed.), *Philosophy: A Guide Through the Subject* (Oxford, 1995).

A. C. Grayling (ed.), *Philosophy 2: Further Through the Subject* (Oxford, 1998).

A. Phillips Griffiths (ed.), *Key Themes in Philosophy* (Cambridge, 1989).

Adam Morton, *Philosophy in Practice* (Oxford, 1996).

Anthony O'Hear, *What Philosophy Is* (Harmondsworth, 1985).

Mel Thompson, *Teach Yourself Philosophy* (London, 1995).

Nigel Warburton, *Philosophy: The Basics* (3rd edn, London, 1999).

The best way to understand what philosophers are about is to read philosophers. If you do not feel able to spend your time ploughing through all of the writings of those commonly deemed to be the most significant philosophical thinkers, there are some good anthologies available. For example:

John Cottingham (ed.), *Western Philosophy: An Introduction* (Oxford, 1996).

Nigel Warburton (ed.), *Philosophy: Basic Readings* (London, 1999).

For basic information about who is who in philosophy, and for who is who in philosophy considered as more than a merely Western phenomenon, see Robert L. Arrington (ed.), *A Companion to the Philosophers* (Oxford, 1999) and Eliot Deutsch and Ron Bontekoe (eds), *A Companion to World Philosophy* (Oxford, 1997).

In *Philosophy of Religion: The Historic Approaches* (London, 1972), M. J. Charlesworth provides a most useful survey of philosophical thinking about religion, one which tries to sort out and to comment on the different ways in which philosophy of religion has been practised over the centuries. A comparable volume is J. Collins, *The Emergence of the Philosophy of Religion* (New Haven, Connecticut, 1967).

If you are looking for general introductions to philosophy of religion, the following can be recommended:

William Abraham, *An Introduction to the Philosophy of Religion* (Englewood Cliffs, New Jersey, 1985).

W. Norris Clarke SJ, *Explorations in Metaphysics: Being-God-Person* (Notre Dame, Indiana, and London, 1994).

Brian Davies, *An Introduction to the Philosophy of Religion* (2nd edn, Oxford, 1993).

Brian Davies (ed.), *Philosophy of Religion: A Guide to the Subject* (London, 1998).

J. C. A. Gaskin, *The Quest for Eternity* (Harmondsworth, 1984).

John Hick, *Philosophy of Religion* (4th edn, Englewood Cliffs, New Jersey, 1990).

H D. Lewis, *Philosophy of Religion* (London, 1965).

Anthony O'Hear, *Experience, Explanation and Faith* (London, 1984).

Michael Peterson, William Hasker, Bruce Reichenbach, and David Basinger, *Reason and Religious Belief: An Introduction to the Philosophy of Religion* (Oxford and New York, 1991).

Philip Quinn and Charles Taliaferro (eds), *A Companion to Philosophy of Religion* (Oxford, 1997).

William L. Rowe, *Philosophy of Religion* (Encino and Belmont, California, 1978).

Charles Taliaferro, *Contemporary Philosophy of Religion* (Oxford, 1998).

William J. Wainwright, *Philosophy of Religion* (2nd edn, Belmont, California, 1998).

Keith Yandell, *Philosophy of Religion: A Contemporary Introduction* (London and New York, 1999).

There are also several philosophy of religion anthologies currently available. Ones to be recommended are:

Baruch Brody (ed.), *Readings in the Philosophy of Religion* (2nd edn, Englewood Cliffs, New Jersey, 1992).

Steven M. Cahn and David Shatz (eds), *Contemporary Philosophy of Religion* (Oxford, 1982).

R. Douglas Geivett and Brendan Sweetman (eds), *Contemporary Perspectives on Religious Epistemology* (New York and Oxford, 1992).

Basil Mitchell (ed.), *The Philosophy of Religion* (Oxford, 1971).

William Peterson, William Hasker, Bruce Reichenbach, and David Basinger (eds), *Philosophy of Religion: Selected Readings* (New York and Oxford, 1996).

Louis P. Pojman (ed.), *Philosophy of Religion: An Anthology* (2nd edn, Belmont, California, 1993).

William L. Rowe and William J. Wainwright (eds), *Philosophy of Religion: Selected Readings* (3rd edn, New York and London, 1997).

Eleonore Stump and Michael J. Muray (eds), *Philosophy of Religion: The Big Questions* (Oxford, 1999).

As I note above, philosophers of religion have recently been devoting much energy to philosophy and Christian doctrine. If you want to see something of how their discussions have gone, you should consult the following works (all of which shall lead you to yet further reading):

William Charlton, *Philosophy and Christian Belief* (London, 1988).

R. J. Feenstra and C. Plantinga (ed.), *Trinity, Incarnation and Atonement* (Notre Dame, Indiana, 1989).

Thomas P. Flint (ed.), *Christian Philosophy* (Notre Dame, Indiana, 1990).

Hywel D. Lewis, *Jesus in the Faith of Christians* (London, 1981).

Hugo Meynell, *Is Christianity True?* (London, 1994).

Thomas V. Morris, *The Logic of God Incarnate* (Ithaca, New York, and London, 1986).

Thomas V. Morris (ed.), *Philosophy and the Christian Faith* (Notre Dame, Indiana, 1988).

Alan G. Padgett (ed.), *Reason and the Christian Religion* (Oxford, 1994).

E. Stump and T. Flint (eds), *Hermes and Athena: Biblical Exegesis and Philosophical Theology* (Notre Dame, Indiana, 1993).

Richard Sturch, *The Word and the Christ: An Essay in Analytic Christology* (Oxford, 1991).

Richard Swinburne, *Faith and Reason* (Oxford, 1981).

Richard Swinburne, *Responsibility and Atonement* (Oxford, 1989).

Richard Swinburne, *Revelation* (Oxford, 1992).

Richard Swinburne, *The Christian God* (Oxford, 1994).

Gijsbert van den Brink, Luco J. van den Brom, and Marcel Sarot (eds), *Christian Faith and Philosophical Theology* (Kampen, Netherlands, 1992).

Feminist thinking has recently begun to have an impact in contemporary literature on philosophy of religion. No extracts from feminist writers appear below, but if you want to learn something about feminist philosophy of religion you can consult:

Sue Anderson, *A Feminist Philosophy of Religion* (Oxford, 1998).

Alison M. Jaggar and Iris Marion Young (eds), *A Companion to Feminist Philosophy* (Oxford, 1998).

Grace M. Jantzen, *Becoming Divine: Towards a Feminist Philosophy of Religion* (Manchester, 1998).

Several contemporary journals either specialize in philosophy of religion or contain much that is relevant to the subject. These include:

Faith and Philosophy
International Journal for Philosophy of Religion
International Philosophical Quarterly
New Blackfriars
Religious Studies
Sophia
The Thomist

The Internet is now an excellent place to get information and help on philosophy (in general) and on philosophy of religion (in particular). Good sites from which to start browsing are:

The Blackwell Philosophy Resource Centre at *http:// www.blackwellpublishers.co.uk/philos /*
The Internet Encyclopedia of Philosophy at *http:// www.utm.edu/research/iep /*
The American Philosophical Association at *http:// www.udel.edu/apa /*

For further information on the Internet and philosophy, see Andrew T. Stull, *Philosophy on the Internet 1998–1999: A Prentice Hall Guide* (Upper Saddle River, New Jersey, 1999).

Part I

Philosophy and religious belief

Introduction

Philosophers and religious belief

PHILOSOPHERS have spent much time reflecting on specific religious beliefs (such as the belief that God exists, or the belief that miracles occur). And in later parts of this book we will be turning to some fruits of their reflection. But to start with we begin on a more abstract note. For philosophers have also wondered about the role of philosophy in general when it comes to religion. Should it be viewed as a friend of religious belief? Or as a foe? Should it seek to defend religious beliefs? Or should it seek to challenge them? Can philosophers welcome the notion of religious faith? Or should they treat it with suspicion? Can one philosophize about religion without taking sides on its truth or falsity? Or must one always pass judgement? These are the most prominent questions in this part of the book.

As you will realize from the General Introduction, some of them are implicitly answered by ancient philosophers. But the question of philosophy's role vis-à-vis religion was first explicitly discussed by medieval thinkers, especially those in the Christian tradition. It was, for example, tackled head-on by Anselm.

Anselm was a Benedictine monk. And his writings display a serene confidence in the value and truth of Christianity. Yet he is also convinced that the main items of Christian faith can be explored and defended by reason, and that they ought to be. Religious believers, so Anselm thinks, should not take human reasoning as the ultimate authority which determines what they should believe. But he also thinks that religious believers can seek to understand what they believe—a project he personally embarks on in his *Monologion*, *Proslogion*, and *Cur Deus Homo* (*Why God Became Man*). In the first of these works he argues not only that God exists, but that God is somehow three in one (the Christian doctrine of the Trinity). In the *Proslogion* he purports to prove that God is perfect. In the *Cur Deus Homo* he suggests that there are reasons which show that it was necessary that God should become incarnate.

Aquinas on reason and religion

But was Anselm over-optimistic in his view of what reason can show? With this question we come to Chapter 1, from Thomas Aquinas's *Summa Contra Gentiles*.[1] For, though Aquinas makes no mention of Anselm in it, we can read him as seeking to sympathize with Anselm while also politely disagreeing. Aquinas shares Anselm's respect for thinking

---

1. For medieval authors, who produced many of them, a 'summa' ('summary') was an extended treatise dealing with a variety of philosophical and/or theological questions. Completed by 1265, the *Summa Contra Gentiles* can be thought of as Aquinas's most extended attempt to show how philosophy can contribute to an understanding of the divine (though other readings of it have been defended). The title *Summa Contra Gentiles* is not Aquinas's. We do not know what title, if any, he gave to the work.

about religion with an eye on reason. But he also takes reason to be somewhat more limited than Anselm seems to do.

Why so? Since Aquinas writes clearly, you should not find it hard to work out his basic answer to this question. But to understand it properly you should also bear in mind some aspects of his thinking which lie behind it.

The first is his general approach to the topic of human knowledge. In his view, our knowledge is a consequence of the fact that we are physically acquainted with material objects. Since Aquinas takes God to be non-material, he therefore concludes that all human knowledge of God must be indirect and based on arguments starting from our knowledge of material things, arguments which he develops in texts such as Book 1 of his *Summa Contra Gentiles* and Part I of his *Summa Theologiae*.

The second is what we may call 'Aquinas's theistic agnosticism'. In many of his writings he insists that we cannot know what God is (*quid est*). By this he means that, since God is not an object of sensory experience, we are unable to have the sort of knowledge of God which we seek to have as we develop a scientific understanding of things in the world. Scientists typically try to analyse the natures of things and to frame explanations accordingly. According to Aquinas, however, God (being immaterial) is not an object of scientific inquiry. Or, as Aquinas often puts it, we cannot know God's 'essence'. As Herbert McCabe writes, in Aquinas's view, 'when we speak of God, although we know how to use our words, there is an important sense in which we do not know what they mean . . . We know how to talk about God, not because of any understanding of God, but because of what we know about his creatures.'[2]

The third is Aquinas's understanding of the terms 'belief' and 'knowledge' (and his corresponding understanding of the terms 'faith' and 'reason'). According to him, belief and knowledge are radically different. Working on the principle that, for example, 'Fred knows that John is dead' entails 'John is dead', while 'Fred believes that John is dead' does not, Aquinas thinks that we may have false beliefs which are obviously different from knowledge. He also thinks that when we know (rather than merely believe) that such and such is the case, we see not only that it is the case, but why. For Aquinas, knowledge comes with understanding. For this reason, he holds that though we may have many true religious beliefs, we are limited when it comes to religious *knowledge*. And he consequently thinks that we have to depend on divine revelation for religious truths which exceed what we can know. Or, as Aquinas frequently puts it, we cannot depend only on reason (considered as our ability to gain knowledge). We also need faith (considered as believing, on the basis of God's authority, truths which we cannot know to be true). By reason, Aquinas thinks, we can know that God exists and that various propositions of the form 'God is . . .' are true (see Parts II, III, and IV below). But we cannot, he argues, know that such teachings as that of the doctrine of the Trinity or the doctrine of the Incarnation are true. He holds that we can point to things which give us grounds for accepting them. And he holds that we can defend them in the light of arguments brought against them. But we cannot

2. Herbert McCabe, Appendix 3 to volume 3 of the Blackfriars edition of the *Summa Theologiae*.

know them to be true.[3] They are matters of faith. And, so Aquinas also argues, for those unable to arrive at the religious knowledge which is, in principle, open to people, even this must be viewed as a matter of faith. A doctor may know what a human kidney is, but those unable or unwilling to engage in medical studies may simply have to believe the doctor's account. By the same token, so Aquinas argues, many people may need to take on faith religious truths which can, in principle, be known.[4]

Evidence and religious belief

Aquinas clearly assumes that it is not necessarily improper or unreasonable to believe what one cannot know. But is he right to do so? The author of Chapter 2 would seem to think not. For in this extract we find W. K. Clifford (1845–79) famously asserting: 'It is wrong always, everywhere, and for any one, to believe anything upon insufficient evidence.' Clifford does not tell us what exactly he means by 'evidence'. Nor does he tell us when evidence is 'sufficient' for belief. He condemns those who accept statements which are 'unproved and unquestioned'. But he does not say what he means by 'proof', or when questioning leads to proper belief. So he and Aquinas might, in the end, be able to shake hands and be philosophical friends, especially when we remember how Aquinas claims that even those who believe on faith need not be believing without reason. But Clifford certainly strikes a note which you do not find in Aquinas. For he seems to be insisting that everyone is morally obliged to go through a fairly extensive course of research before accepting any belief. He also seems to be insisting that one is somehow to blame if one believes that such and such is the case without being able to cite grounds which show that it is the case (or that it is more likely than not to be the case). And Aquinas is evidently of a different mind.

In that case, however, who is right? Many Western philosophers, especially since the seventeenth century, seem to side with something like Clifford's line of thinking. For many of them insist that we are only rationally entitled to believe when we can back up our beliefs with 'reasons', 'grounds', or 'evidence'. Hence, for example, Locke holds that one should only believe what reason shows to be believable (presumably implying that one should not believe that something is the case without reason to suppose that it is so). According to Locke, though God can reveal what lies 'beyond reason', it is reason which must determine what God has revealed, since 'Reason must be our last judge and guide in everything'.[5] 'Whatever God has revealed', says Locke, 'is certainly true; no doubt can be made of it. This is the proper object of faith. But whether it be a divine revelation or no, reason must judge, which can never permit the mind to reject a greater evidence to

3. Why not? Aquinas's answer to this question is: (1) Our knowledge of (as opposed to our faith in) God is confined to what we can infer of God on the basis of the world as we experience it; (2) Knowing that God is Trinity or that God became incarnate would involve having a knowledge of God which is equal to the knowledge which God has of himself, a knowledge which we currently lack. See Brian Davies, *The Thought of Thomas Aquinas* (Oxford, 1992), ch. 10.
4. Aquinas's position here is ratified by the first Vatican Council. See chapter 4 ('On Faith and Reason') of its *Dogmatic Constitution on the Catholic Faith.*
5. John Locke, *An Essay Concerning Human Understanding*, Book IV, ch. XIX.

embrace what is less evident, nor allow it to entertain probability in opposition to know-ledge and certainty.'[6]

But what should we mean by 'reason'? You can see what Locke means by reading his *Essay Concerning Human Understanding*. To find someone strongly echoing both him and Clifford, you can turn to Chapter 3, in which Antony Flew argues that the onus of proof lies on believers when it comes to belief in God.

What does Flew mean by 'the onus of proof'? Some philosophers have said that we have a proof that such and such is the case only if we can show that it can be strictly deduced from indubitably true premises. But this notion of proof is not what Flew has primarily in mind. For him, the onus of proof lies on believers in the sense that it is up to them to provide 'sufficient reason'. Flew's basic idea seems to be that we can distinguish between conclusions which are well supported and ones which are not. And, on this basis, he argues that the belief that God exists needs to be well supported. In courts of law it is assumed that the prosecution must establish its case against the defendant. In a similar way, so Flew argues, those who believe in God need to establish their case before the court of the human race. Like legal prosecutors, they propose that we should think thus and so about a certain matter. So, also like legal prosecutors, they need to convince us of the truth of the verdict they support.

Does religious belief need evidence?

Flew's line of thinking is shared by many contemporary philosophers of religion. Hence, for example, Anthony Kenny writes: 'To me it seems that if belief in the existence of God cannot be rationally justified, there can be no good reasons for adopting any of the traditional monotheistic religions.'[7] And both friends and foes of religious belief have written as though agreeing with what Kenny says. Notable examples include Richard Swinburne and J. L. Mackie. In several well-known books, Swinburne takes pains to show that belief in God can overcome what Flew seems to mean by 'the presumption of athe-ism'. According to Swinburne, rational reflection can show that God's existence is more probable than not.[8] According to Mackie, arguments for God's existence should certainly be looked at if we are to arrive at a sensible conclusion regarding God's existence. Unlike Swinburne, however, Mackie finds that the balance of probability does not favour those who believe in God.[9]

Yet is it so obvious that it is intrinsically wrong to believe what one cannot defend by argument or by appeal to 'evidence' or 'grounds'? According to Alvin Plantinga, the answer is 'No', and in Chapter 4 he defends this conclusion with direct reference to Clifford and Flew. He does so by concentrating on belief in God and by defending what he calls the 'Reformed objection to natural theology'.

In the General Introduction I said that 'natural theology' can be loosely defined as 'the

6. Ibid. Book IV, ch. XVII.
7. Anthony Kenny, *The Five Ways* (London, 1969), p. 4.
8. See Richard Swinburne, *The Existence of God* (Oxford, 1979; revised edn, 1991) and Richard Swinburne, *Is There A God?* (Oxford and New York, 1996).
9. J. L. Mackie, *The Miracle of Theism* (Oxford, 1982).

attempt to ground beliefs about God on purely rational reflection'. We might also think of it as the attempt to show that belief in God's existence can be defended by reason or argument which ought to be acceptable to anyone, not simply those who already believe in God's existence. And, with such understandings in mind, we should note straight away that Plantinga is no foe of natural theology (see Part III below, where he defends a version of the so-called 'Ontological Argument'). But do those who believe in God need natural theology? Clifford and Flew can be taken as saying (a) that they do, and (b) that they should abandon their belief if they cannot produce some compelling natural theology. Plantinga, however, argues otherwise. He maintains that belief in God can be thought of as 'properly basic'.[10]

What does Plantinga mean by this suggestion? His main idea can be presented fairly simply. For think about something as ordinary as your conviction that you are now reading a book. Is it a reasonable conviction? You will probably say that it is. But is it something you have arrived at and can justify by technical philosophical argument? You will probably say that it is a conviction you just have. And why should you not say this? Why should you not have convictions or beliefs from which you start rather than to which you argue? That is the question which Plantinga presses with respect to belief that God exists. And his answer is that people need not be thought of as unreasonable if their belief that God exists is something they start with rather than something they have concluded to on the basis of argument or some other kind of intellectual exercise. This is what he means when he says that 'God exists' can be taken as a 'properly basic' belief. According to Plantinga, 'it is entirely right, rational, reasonable, and proper to believe in God without any evidence or argument at all'. If we are tempted to argue otherwise, he adds, it will be because we subscribe to 'classical foundationalism', a theory of rationality which Plantinga finds wholly unconvincing since it implausibly requires us to accept that someone (call him John) is only entitled to believe without evidence that such and such is the case (call this P) if P is self-evident to John, or evident to John's senses, or certain or incorrigible for John in some way. Plantinga argues that this theory is incoherent since it does not meet its own criteria for reasonable belief: it is not self-evident, or evident to the senses, or certain or incorrigible; nor can it be argued to from any such premises.

Plantinga's views on the 'proper basicality' of belief that God exists have provoked much discussion among twentieth-century philosophers of religion. But are they correct? The author of Chapter 5 argues that they are not. In 'Evidence Against Anti-Evidentialism', Norman Kretzmann suggests that Plantinga only manages to defend his basic claim (a) by misrepresenting the relationship between classical foundationalism and 'evidentialism' (construed as the thesis that 'it is irrational to believe anything on insufficient evidence'), and (b) by employing the word 'evidence' in a way which would not be used by those (such as Aquinas) who think it proper and necessary to explore the question of evidence for God's existence. For Plantinga, evidentialism depends on classical foundationalism. For Kretzmann, things are the other way around. For Plantinga, evidentialism is bound up with a certain way of reasoning or arriving at beliefs. For

10. For a brief account of Reformed thinking on natural theology, see Nicholas Wolterstorff, 'The Reformed Tradition', in Philip Quinn and Charles Taliaferro (eds), *A Companion to Philosophy of Religion* (Oxford, 1997).

Kretzmann, it is not. According to Kretzmann, therefore, Plantinga has done nothing to show why we should believe that 'it is entirely right, rational, reasonable, and proper to believe in God without any evidence or argument at all'.

Light from Wittgenstein?

Yet should we reject evidentialism for some reason other than those offered by Plantinga? And are there other grounds than his for resisting it with respect to religious belief? If we think of evidentialism as holding that Fred is making some grave intellectual error by believing *P* while not being able to produce evidence or grounds of *P*'s truth, we might be suspicious of it in view of what the contemporary philosopher Elizabeth Anscombe calls 'believing the person'. She notes that 'the greater part of our knowledge of reality rests upon the belief that we repose in things we have been taught and told'. In developing this idea she writes:

Nor is what testimony gives us entirely a detachable part, like the thick fringe of fat on a chunk of steak. It is more like the flecks and streaks of fat that are often distributed through good meat; though there are lumps of pure fat as well. Examples could be multiplied indefinitely. You have received letters; how did you ever learn what a letter was and how it came to you? You will take up a book and look in a certain place and see 'New York, Dodd Mead and Company, 1910.' So do you know from personal observation that that book was published by that company, and then, and in New York? Well, hardly. But you do know it *purports* to have been so. How? Well, you know that is where the publisher's name is always put, and the name of the place where his office belongs. How do you know that? You were taught it ... You may think you know that New York is in North America. What is New York, what is North America? You may say you have been to these places. But how much does that fact contribute to your knowledge? Nothing, in comparison with testimony. How did you know you were there? Even if you inhabit New York and you have simply learned its name as the name of the place you inhabit, there is the question: How extensive a region is this place you are calling 'New York'? And what has New York got to do with this bit of a map? Here is a complicated network of received information.[11]

According to Anscombe, my claiming to know that such and such is the case is not to be dismissed as 'unreasonable' just because I cannot produce 'evidence', 'grounds', or 'reasons' for its truth. Unlike Plantinga, however, Anscombe makes no reference to 'properly basic' beliefs. She concentrates, instead, on what we already believe and how our beliefs fit together to give us what we call 'knowledge'. And in doing so she is echoing some teaching of Wittgenstein, teaching applied to religious belief in Chapters 6 and 7, from D. Z. Phillips and Norman Malcolm.

   In his last notes *On Certainty*, Wittgenstein writes:

The child learns by believing the adult. Doubt comes after belief. I learned an enormous amount and accepted it on human authority, and then I found some things confirmed or disconfirmed by my own experience. In general I take as true what is found in text-books, of geography for example. Why? I say: All these facts have been confirmed a hundred times over. But how do I know that? What is my evidence for it? I have a world picture. Is it true or false? Above all it is the substratum of all my

11. G. E. M. Anscombe, 'What Is It to Believe Someone?', in C. F. Delaney (ed.), *Rationality and Religious Belief* (Notre Dame, Indiana, and London, 1979), pp. 143 f.

enquiring and asserting . . . Doesn't testing come to an end? . . . The difficulty is to realize the groundlessness of our believing . . . Think of chemical investigations. Lavoisier makes experiments with substances in his laboratory and now he concludes that this and that takes place when there is burning. He does not say that it might happen otherwise another time. He has got hold of a definite world-picture—not of course one that he invented: he learned it as a child. I say world-picture and not hypothesis, because it is the matter-of-course foundation for his research and as such also goes unmentioned.[12]

On Wittgenstein's account, demands for evidence and grounds only make sense in the light of ways of thinking which do not themselves rest on evidence or grounds. And, so Phillips and Malcolm argue, religious beliefs, such as belief in God, (a) need not be (and should not be) thought of as beliefs resting on evidence or grounds, and (b) are none the worse for that. But not for reasons such as Plantinga gives. According to Malcolm and Phillips, the demand for evidence with respect to religious belief is mistaken since it misconstrues the nature of religious belief and fails to grasp that religious belief is something like the 'world-picture' ascribed to Lavoisier by Wittgenstein.

Malcolm, as you will see, lays great stress on passages from Wittgenstein such as the one quoted above. He also suggests that we will not understand religious belief by focusing on sentences such as 'God exists' and by taking them to express propositions which people accept on the basis of evidence or grounds. For Malcolm, 'I believe in God' does not mean 'I believe on the basis of evidence that "God exists" is true'. It is something believers say as they view the world and themselves in a certain way. It is 'language embedded in action' and is best viewed as resting on a complicated network of human reactions which cannot be thought of as either justified or unjustified.

But is that so? According to Phillips, it is. Wittgenstein distinguishes between 'surface grammar' and 'depth grammar'.[13] Roughly speaking, this is a distinction between what utterances or sentences might *seem* to mean by virtue of their appearance, and what they *really* mean. Consider the sentence 'I have a pain in my foot'. From a grammatical point of view, this resembles 'I have a key in my pocket'. But we would be wrong if we took pain to be some sort of physical object with a precise physical location (we can look at the key in your pocket, but we cannot look at the pain in your foot). Here, then, we can distinguish between what the first sentence seems to mean and what it really means. And, so Phillips argues, what religious believers say really means something different from what is said by those whose way of talking might rightly be thought of as standing in need of evidence, grounds, or justification—like people who tell us that there are keys in their pockets.

Hence, for example, in Chapter 6, Phillips distinguishes between belief in God and acceptance of 'matters of fact'. A fact, he says, 'might not have been'. But 'it makes no sense to say that God might not exist'. Elsewhere in his writings he argues that belief in God is not a hypothesis based on grounds, that it is not an empirical hypothesis, that it is

12. Ludwig Wittgenstein, *On Certainty* (trans. D. Paul and G. E. M. Anscombe, Oxford, 1974), §§160–7.
13. Cf. Ludwig Wittgenstein, *Philosophical Investigations* (trans. G. E. M. Anscombe, Oxford, 1958), §664. For an account of Wittgenstein on 'grammar', see Hans-Johann Glock *A Wittgenstein Dictionary* (Oxford, 1996), pp. 150 ff.

not open to falsification, and that it is not held tentatively.[14] He also holds that 'God exists' is not an indicative statement:

To ask whether God exists is not to ask a theoretical question. If it is to mean anything at all, it is to wonder about praising and praying; it is to wonder whether there is anything in all that. This is why philosophy cannot answer the question 'Does God exist?' with either an affirmative or a negative reply . . . 'There is a God', though it appears to be in the indicative mood, is an expression of faith.[15]

In short, Phillips's view is that much philosophical discussion of religious belief has misconstrued its nature.[16] And, with this idea in mind, he insists that philosophy's role vis-à-vis religion is one of conceptual clarification. Instead of asking whether, for example, there is evidence for 'God exists', it should be asking what it means to believe in God. And, so Phillips adds, answers to such a question lie within religious belief. As he puts it in Chapter 6: 'The role of philosophy in this context is not to justify, but to understand.' Or, as he says in his book *Religion Without Explanation*:

Instead of stipulating what *must* constitute intelligible uses of language, one should look and see how language is in fact used. If one does, one comes across the use of language found in magical and religious rite and rituals. Such language is not based on opinions or hypotheses, but is expressive . . . Faced by it, the philosopher's task is not to attempt to verify or falsify what he sees, for that makes no sense in this context. His task is a descriptive one; he gives an account of the use of language involved. He can only say that these language games are played.[17]

This seems to have been the view to which Wittgenstein came before he died. And, indeed, authors such as Malcolm and Phillips owe much to texts like Wittgenstein's *Lectures on Religious Belief*, from which Phillips often quotes.[18] At one time, however, Wittgenstein was teaching that religious assertions are strictly 'nonsensical'. Why? We will see in Part II. There, we will also find other authors worrying about what it means to believe in God.

14. Cf. D. Z. Phillips, *The Concept of Prayer* (London, 1965), pp. 67 f. and p. 81. Also cf. D. Z. Phillips, *Faith and Philosophical Enquiry* (London, 1970), pp. 87–92 and 101–5.

15. *Religion Without Explanation* (Oxford, 1976) p. 181. Cf. also pp. 149, 171, and 174. Also cf. D. Z. Phillips, *Faith After Foundationalism* (London and New York, 1988), pp. 21 and 324.

16. Critics of Phillips frequently argue that his own account of religious belief misrepresents it. They have especially argued that belief in God, as Phillips construes it, is not at all what most of those who believe in God take it to be.

17. *Religion Without Explanation*, p. 41. You will note that Malcolm's paper also uses the phrase 'language-game'. It derives from Wittgenstein. For Wittgenstein on 'language-games', see *Wittgenstein Dictionary*, pp. 193 ff. Note that even some of Wittgenstein's fans occasionally express unease about applying the term 'language-game' as Phillips and Malcolm do. Hence, for example, Anthony Kenny has written: 'Unfortunately, Wittgenstein's influence on the philosophy of religion has been disastrous . . . The concept of language-game is an obscure and ambiguous one in Wittgenstein's own writings; in the hands of some of his admirers it has become a stone-wall defence against any demand for a justification of belief in God' ('In Defence of God', *Times Literary Supplement*, 7 February 1975, p. 145).

18. Cf. Ludwig Wittgenstein, *Lectures and Conversations on Aesthetics, Psychology and Religious Belief* (ed. Cyril Barrett, Oxford, 1966).

Chapter 1

Faith and reason in harmony

Thomas Aquinas

On the way in which divine truth is to be made known

Tʜᴇʀᴇ is a twofold mode of truth in what we profess about God. Some truths about God exceed all the ability of the human reason. Such is the truth that God is triune. But there are some truths which the natural reason also is able to reach. Such are that God exists, that He is one, and the like. In fact, such truths about God have been proved demonstratively by the philosophers, guided by the light of the natural reason.

That there are certain truths about God that totally surpass man's ability appears with the greatest evidence. Since, indeed, the principle of all knowledge that the reason perceives about some thing is the understanding of the very substance of that being it is necessary that the way in which we understand the substance of a thing determines the way in which we know what belongs to it. Hence, if the human intellect comprehends the substance of some thing, for example, that of a stone or of a triangle, no intelligible characteristic belonging to that thing surpasses the grasp of the human reason. But this does not happen to us in the case of God. For the human intellect is not able to reach a comprehension of the divine substance through its natural power. For, according to its manner of knowing in the present life, the intellect depends on the sense for the origin of knowledge; and so those things that do not fall under the senses cannot be grasped by the human intellect except in so far as the knowledge of them is gathered from sensible things. Now, sensible things cannot lead the human intellect to the point of seeing in them the nature of the divine substance; for sensible things are effects that fall short of the power of their cause. Yet, beginning with sensible things, our intellect is led to the point of knowing about God that He exists, and other such characteristics that must be attributed to the First Principle. There are, consequently, some intelligible truths about God that are open to the human reason; but there are others that absolutely surpass its power.

Thomas Aquinas edited extracts from 'Summa Contra Gentiles' Book 1, from Thomas Aquinas *Summa Contra Gentiles*, translated by Anton Pegis (University of Notre Dame Press, 1975).

That the truth about God to which the natural reason reaches is fittingly proposed to men for belief

Since, therefore, there exists a twofold truth concerning the divine being, one to which the inquiry of the reason can reach, the other which surpasses the whole ability of the human reason, it is fitting that both of these truths be proposed to man divinely for belief. This point must first be shown concerning the truth that is open to the inquiry of the reason; otherwise, it might perhaps seem to someone that, since such a truth can be known by the reason, it was uselessly given to men through a supernatural inspiration as an object of belief.

Yet, if this truth were left solely as a matter of inquiry for the human reason, three awkward consequences would follow.

The first is that few men would possess the knowledge of God. For there are three reasons why most men are cut off from the fruit of diligent inquiry which is the discovery of truth. Some do not have the physical disposition for such work. As a result, there are many who are naturally not fitted to pursue knowledge; and so, however much they tried, they would be unable to reach the highest level of human knowledge which consists in knowing God. Others are cut off from pursuing this truth by the necessities imposed upon them by their daily lives. For some men must devote themselves to taking care of temporal matters. Such men would not be able to give so much time to the leisure of contemplative inquiry as to reach the highest peak at which human investigation can arrive, namely, the knowledge of God. Finally, there are some who are cut off by indolence. In order to know the things that the reason can investigate concerning God, a knowledge of many things must already be possessed. For almost all of philosophy is directed towards the knowledge of God, and that is why metaphysics, which deals with divine things, is the last part of philosophy to be learned. This means that we are able to arrive at the inquiry concerning the aforementioned truth only on the basis of a great deal of labor spent in study. Now, those who wish to undergo such a labor for the mere love of knowledge are few, even though God has inserted into the minds of men a natural appetite for knowledge.

The second awkward effect is that those who would come to discover the above-mentioned truth would barely reach it after a great deal of time. The reasons are several. There is the profundity of this truth, which the human intellect is made capable of grasping by natural inquiry only after a long training. Then, there are many things that must be presupposed, as we have said. There is also the fact that, in youth, when the soul is swayed by the various movements of the passions, it is not in a suitable state for the knowledge of such lofty truth. On the contrary, 'one becomes wise and knowing in repose,' as it is said in the *Physics*. The result is this. If the only way open to us for the knowledge of God were solely that of the reason, the human race would remain in the blackest shadows of ignorance. For then the knowledge of God, which especially renders men perfect and good, would come to be possessed only by a few, and these few would require a great deal of time in order to reach it.

The third awkward effect is this. The investigation of the human reason for the most part has falsity present within it, and this is due partly to the weakness of our intellect in judgment, and partly to the admixture of images. The result is that many, remaining ignorant of the power of demonstration, would hold in doubt those things that have been most truly demonstrated. This would be particularly the case since they see that, among those who are reputed to be wise men, each one teaches his own brand of doctrine. Furthermore, with the many truths that are demonstrated, there sometimes is mingled something that is false, which is not demonstrated but rather asserted on the basis of some probable or sophistical argument, which yet has the credit of being a demonstration. That is why it was necessary that the unshakeable certitude and pure truth concerning divine things should be presented to men by way of faith.

Beneficially, therefore, did the divine Mercy provide that it should instruct us to hold by faith even those truths that the human reason is able to investigate In this way, all men would easily be able to have a share in the knowledge of God, and this without uncertainty and error.

That the truths the human reason is not able to investigate are fittingly proposed to men for belief

Now, perhaps some will think that men should not be asked to believe what the reason is not adequate to investigate, since the divine Wisdom provides in the case of each thing according to the mode of its nature. We must therefore prove that it is necessary for man to receive from God as objects of belief even those truths that are above the human reason.

No one tends with desire and zeal towards something that is not already known to him. But, as we shall examine later on in this work, men are ordained by the divine Providence towards a higher good than human fragility can experience in the present life. That is why it was necessary for the human mind to be called to something higher than the human reason here and now can reach, so that it would thus learn to desire something and with zeal tend towards something that surpasses the whole state of the present life. This belongs especially to the Christian religion, which in a unique way promises spiritual and eternal goods. And so there are many things proposed to men in it that transcend human sense.

It is also necessary that such truth be proposed to men for belief so that they may have a truer knowledge of God. For then only do we know God truly when we believe Him to be above everything that it is possible for man to think about Him; for the divine substance surpasses the natural knowledge of which man is capable. Hence, by the fact that some things about God are proposed to man that surpass his reason, there is strengthened in man the view that God is something above what he can think.

Another benefit that comes from the revelation to men of truths that exceed the reason is the curbing of presumption, which is the mother of error. For there are some who have such a presumptuous opinion of their own ability that they deem themselves able to measure the nature of everything; I mean to say that, in their estimation, everything is true that seems to them so, and everything is false that does not. So that the human mind, therefore, might be freed from this presumption and come to a humble inquiry after truth, it was necessary that some things should be proposed to man by God that would completely surpass his intellect.

A still further benefit may also be seen in what Aristotle says in the *Ethics*. There was a certain Simonides who exhorted people to put aside the knowledge of divine things and to apply their talents to human occupations. He said that 'he who is a man should know human things, and he who is mortal, things that are mortal.' Against Simonides Aristotle says that 'man should draw himself towards what is immortal and divine as much as he can.' And so he says in the *De animalibus* that, although what we know of the higher substances is very little, yet that little is loved and desired more than all the knowledge that we have about less noble substances. He also says in the *De caelo et mundo* that when questions about the heavenly bodies can be given even a modest and merely plausible solution, he who hears this experiences intense joy. From all these considerations it is clear that even the most imperfect knowledge about the most noble realities brings the greatest perfection to the soul. Therefore, although the human reason cannot grasp fully the truths that are above it, yet, if it somehow holds these truths at least by faith, it acquires great perfection for itself.

That to give assent to the truths of faith is not foolishness even though they are above reason

Those who place their faith in this truth, however, 'for which the human reason offers no experimental evidence,' do not believe foolishly, as though 'following artificial fables' (2 Peter 1: 16). For these 'secrets of divine Wisdom' (Job 11: 6) the divine Wisdom itself, which knows all things to the full, has deigned to reveal to men. It reveals its own presence, as well as the truth of its teaching and inspiration, by fitting arguments; and in order to confirm those truths that exceed natural knowledge, it gives visible manifestation to works that surpass the ability of all nature. Thus, there are the wonderful cures of illnesses, there is the raising of the dead, and the wonderful immutation in the heavenly bodies; and what is more wonderful, there is the inspiration given to human minds, so that simple and untutored persons, filled with the gift of the Holy Spirit, come to possess instantaneously the highest wisdom and the readiest eloquence. When these arguments were examined, through the efficacy of the abovementioned proof, and not the violent assault of arms or the promise of pleasures, and (what is most wonderful of all) in the midst of the tyranny of the persecutors, an innumerable throng of people, both simple and most learned, flocked to the Christian faith. In this faith there are truths preached that surpass every human intellect; the pleasures of the flesh are curbed; it is taught that the things of the world should be spurned. Now, for the minds of mortal men to assent to these things is the greatest of miracles, just as it is a manifest work of divine inspiration that, spurning visible things, men should seek only what is invisible. Now, that this has happened neither without preparation nor by chance, but as a result of the disposition of God, is clear from the fact that through many pronouncements of the ancient prophets God had foretold that He would do this. The books of these prophets are held in veneration among us Christians, since they give witness to our faith.

This wonderful conversion of the world to the Christian faith is the clearest witness of the signs given in the past; so that it is not necessary that they should be further repeated, since they appear most clearly in their effect. For it would be truly more wonderful than all signs if the world had been led by simple and humble men to believe such lofty truths, to accomplish such difficult actions, and to have such high hopes. Yet it is also a fact that, even in our own time, God does not cease to work miracles through His saints for the confirmation of the faith.

That the truth of reason is not opposed to the truth of the Christian faith

Now, although the truth of the Christian faith which we have discussed surpasses the capacity of the reason, nevertheless that truth that the human reason is naturally endowed to know cannot be opposed to the truth of the Christian faith. For that with which the human reason is naturally endowed is clearly most true; so much so, that it is impossible for us to think of such truths as false. Nor is it permissible to believe as false that which we hold by faith, since this is confirmed in a way that is so clearly divine. Since, therefore, only the false is opposed to the true, as is clearly evident from an examination of their definitions, it is impossible that the truth of faith should be opposed to those principles that the human reason knows naturally.

Furthermore, that which is introduced into the soul of the student by the teacher is contained in the knowledge of the teacher—unless his teaching is fictitious, which it is improper to say of God. Now, the knowledge of the principles that are known to us naturally has been implanted in us by God; for God is the Author of our nature. These principles, therefore, are also contained by the divine Wisdom. Hence, whatever is opposed to them is opposed to the divine Wisdom, and, therefore, cannot come from God. That which we hold by faith as divinely revealed, therefore cannot be contrary to our natural knowledge.

Again. In the presence of contrary arguments our intellect is chained, so that it cannot proceed to the knowledge of the truth. If, therefore, contrary knowledges were implanted in us by God, our intellect would be hindered from knowing truth by this very fact. Now, such an effect cannot come from God.

And again. What is natural cannot change as long as nature does not. Now, it is impossible that contrary opinions should exist in the same knowing subject at the same time. No opinion or belief, therefore, is implanted in man by God which is contrary to man's natural knowledge.

From this we evidently gather the following conclusion: whatever arguments are brought forward against the doctrines of faith are conclusions incorrectly derived from the first and self-evident principles imbedded in nature. Such conclusions do not have the force of demonstration; they are arguments that are either probable or sophistical. And so, there exists the possibility to answer them.

Chapter 2
The ethics of belief

W. K. Clifford

A SHIPOWNER was about to send to sea an emigrant ship. He knew that she was old, and not over-well built at the first; that she had seen many seas and climes, and often had needed repairs. Doubts had been suggested to him that possibly she was not seaworthy. These doubts preyed upon his mind, and made him unhappy; he thought that perhaps he ought to have her thoroughly overhauled and refitted, even though this should put him to great expense. Before the ship sailed, however, he succeeded in overcoming these melancholy reflections. He said to himself that she had gone safely through so many voyages and weathered so many storms that it was idle to suppose she would not come safely home from this trip also. He would put his trust in Providence, which could hardly fail to protect all these unhappy families that were leaving their fatherland to seek for better times elsewhere. He would dismiss from his mind all ungenerous suspicions about the honesty of builders and contractors. In such ways he acquired a sincere and comfortable conviction that his vessel was thoroughly safe and seaworthy; he watched her departure with a light heart, and benevolent wishes for the success of the exiles in their strange new home that was to be; and he got his insurance money when she went down in mid-ocean and told no tales.

What shall we say of him? Surely this, that he was verily guilty of the death of those men. It is admitted that he did sincerely believe in the soundness of his ship; but the sincerity of his conviction can in no wise help him, because *he had no right to believe on such evidence as was before him.* He had acquired his belief not by honestly earning it in patient investigation, but by stifling his doubts. And although in the end he may have felt so sure about it that he could not think otherwise, yet inasmuch as he had knowingly and willingly worked himself into that frame of mind, he must be held responsible for it.

Let us alter the case a little, and suppose that the ship was not unsound after all; that she made her voyage safely, and many others after it. Will that diminish the guilt of her owner? Not one jot. When an action is once done, it is right or wrong for ever; no accidental failure of its good or evil fruits can possibly alter that. The man would not have been innocent, he would only have been not found out. The question of right or wrong has to do with the origin of his belief, not the matter of

W. K. Clifford edited extracts from 'The Ethics of Belief' from W. K. Clifford *Lectures and Essays*, 2nd edition, edited by Leslie Stephen and Frederick Pollock (Macmillan, 1886).

it; not what it was, but how he got it; not whether it turned out to be true or false, but whether he had a right to believe on such evidence as was before him.

There was once an island in which some of the inhabitants professed a religion teaching neither the doctrine of original sin nor that of eternal punishment. A suspicion got abroad that the professors of this religion had made use of unfair means to get their doctrines taught to children. They were accused of wresting the laws of their country in such a way as to remove children from the care of their natural and legal guardians; and even of stealing them away and keeping them concealed from their friends and relations. A certain number of men formed themselves into a society for the purpose of agitating the public about this matter. They published grave accusations against individual citizens of the highest position and character, and did all in their power to injure these citizens in the exercise of their professions. So great was the noise they made, that a Commission was appointed to investigate the facts; but after the Commission had carefully inquired into all the evidence that could be got, it appeared that the accused were innocent. Not only had they been accused on insufficient evidence, but the evidence of their innocence was such as the agitators might easily have obtained, if they had attempted a fair inquiry. After these disclosures the inhabitants of that country looked upon the members of the agitating society, not only as persons whose judgment was to be distrusted, but also as no longer to be counted honourable men. For although they had sincerely and conscientiously believed in the charges they had made, yet *they had no right to believe on such evidence as was before them*. Their sincere convictions, instead of being honestly earned by patient inquiring, were stolen by listening to the voice of prejudice and passion.

Let us vary this case also, and suppose, other things remaining as before, that a still more accurate investigation proved the accused to have been really guilty. Would this make any difference in the guilt of the accusers? Clearly not; the question is not whether their belief was true or false, but whether they entertained it on wrong grounds. They would no doubt say, 'Now you see that we were right after all; next time perhaps you will believe us.' And they might be believed, but they would not thereby become honourable men. They would not be innocent, they would only be not found out. Every one of them, if he chose to examine himself *in foro conscientiæ*, would know that he had acquired and nourished a belief, when he had no right to believe on such evidence as was before him; and therein he would know that he had done a wrong thing.

It may be said, however, that in both of these supposed cases it is not the belief which is judged to be wrong, but the action following upon it. The shipowner might say, 'I am perfectly certain that my ship is sound, but still I feel it my duty to have her examined, before trusting the lives of so many people to her.' And it might be said to the agitator, 'However convinced you were of the justice of your cause and the truth of your convictions, you ought not to have made a public attack upon any man's character until you had examined the evidence on both sides with the utmost patience and care.'

In the first place, let us admit that, so far as it goes, this view of the case is right and necessary; right, because even when a man's belief is so fixed that he cannot think otherwise, he still has a choice in regard to the action suggested by it, and so cannot escape the duty of investigating on the ground of the strength of his convictions; and necessary, because those who are not yet capable of controlling their feelings and thoughts must have a plain rule dealing with overt acts.

But this being premised as necessary, it becomes clear that it is not sufficient, and that our previous judgment is required to supplement it. For it is not possible so to sever the belief from the action it suggests as to condemn the one without condemning the other. No man holding a strong belief on one side of a question, or even wishing to hold a belief on one side, can investigate it with such fairness and completeness as if he were really in doubt and unbiassed; so that the existence of a belief not founded on fair inquiry unfits a man for the performance of this necessary duty.

Nor is that truly a belief at all which has not some influence upon the actions of him who holds it. He who truly believes that which prompts him to an action has looked upon the action to lust after it, he has committed it already in his heart. If a belief is not realized immediately in open deeds, it is stored up for the guidance of the future. It goes to make a part of that aggregate of beliefs which is the link between sensation and action at every moment of all our lives, and which is so organized and compacted together that no part of it can be isolated from the rest, but every new addition modifies the structure of the whole. No real belief, however trifling and fragmentary it may seem, is ever truly insignificant; it prepares us to receive more of its like, confirms those which resembled it before, and weakens others; and so gradually it lays a stealthy train in our inmost thoughts, which may some day explode into overt action, and leave its stamp upon our character for ever.

And no one man's belief is in any case a private matter which concerns himself alone. Our lives are guided by that general conception of the course of things which has been created by society for social purposes. Our words, our phrases, our forms and processes and modes of thought, are common property, fashioned and perfected from age to age; an heirloom which every succeeding generation inherits as a precious deposit and a sacred trust to be handed on to the next one, not unchanged but enlarged and purified, with some clear marks of its proper handiwork. Into this, for good or ill, is woven every belief of every man who has speech of his fellows. An awful privilege, and an awful responsibility, that we should help to create the world in which posterity will live.

In the two supposed cases which have been considered, it has been judged wrong to believe on insufficient evidence, or to nourish belief by suppressing doubts and avoiding investigation. The reason of this judgment is not far to seek: it is that in both these cases the belief held by one man was of great importance to other men. But forasmuch as no belief held by one man, however seemingly trivial the belief, and however obscure the believer, is ever actually insignificant or without its effect on the fate of mankind, we have no choice but to extend our judgment to all cases of belief whatever. Belief, that sacred faculty which prompts the decisions of our will, and knits into harmonious working all the compacted energies of our being, is ours not for ourselves, but for humanity. It is rightly used on truths which have been established by long experience and waiting toil, and which have stood in the fierce light of free and fearless questioning. Then it helps to bind men together, and to strengthen and direct their common action. It is desecrated when given to unproved and unquestioned statements, for the solace and private pleasure of the believer; to add a tinsel splendour to the plain straight road of our life and display a bright mirage beyond it; or even to drown the common sorrows of our kind by a self-deception which allows them not only to cast down, but also to degrade us. Whoso would deserve well of his fellows in this matter will guard the purity of his belief with a very fanaticism of jealous care, lest at any time it should rest on an unworthy object, and catch a stain which can never be wiped away.

It is true that this duty is a hard one, and the doubt which comes out of it is often a very bitter thing. It leaves us bare and powerless where we thought that we were safe and strong. To know all about anything is to know how to deal with it under all circumstances. We feel much happier and more secure when we think we know precisely what to do, no matter what happens, than when we have lost our way and do not know where to turn. And if we have supposed ourselves to know all about anything, and to be capable of doing what is fit in regard to it, we naturally do not like to find that we are really ignorant and powerless, that we have to begin again at the beginning, and try to learn what the thing is and how it is to be dealt with—if indeed anything can be learnt about it. It is the sense of power attached to a sense of knowledge that makes men desirous of believing, and afraid of doubting.

The sense of power is the highest and best of pleasures when the belief on which it is founded is a true belief, and has been fairly earned by investigation. For then we may justly feel that it is common property, and holds good for others as well as for ourselves. Then we may be glad, not that *I* have learned secrets by which I am safer and stronger, but that *we men* have got mastery over more of the world; and we shall be strong, not for ourselves, but in the name of Man and in his strength. But if the belief has been accepted on insufficient evidence, the pleasure is a stolen one. Not only does it deceive ourselves by giving us a sense of power which we do not really possess, but it is sinful, because it is stolen in defiance of our duty to mankind. That duty is to guard ourselves from such beliefs as from a pestilence, which may shortly master our own body and then spread to the rest of the town. What would be thought of one who, for the sake of a sweet fruit, should deliberately run the risk of bringing a plague upon his family and his neighbours?

And, as in other such cases, it is not the risk only which has to be considered; for a bad action is always bad at the time when it is done, no matter what happens afterwards. Every time we let ourselves believe for unworthy reasons, we weaken our powers of self-control, of doubting, of judicially and fairly weighing evidence. We all suffer severely enough from the maintenance and support of false beliefs and the fatally wrong actions which they lead to, and the evil born when one such belief is entertained is great and wide. But a greater and wider evil arises when the credulous character is maintained and supported, when a habit of believing for unworthy reasons is fostered and made permanent.

To sum up: it is wrong always, everywhere, and for anyone, to believe anything upon insufficient evidence.

Chapter 3

The presumption of atheism

Antony Flew

1. What it is, and why it matters

THE presumption of atheism, which I want to discuss is not a form of presumptuousness. Indeed it might be regarded as an expression of the very opposite, a modest teachability. What I want to examine of God should properly begin from the presumption of atheism, that the onus of proof must lie upon the theist.

The word 'atheism', however, has in this contention to be construed unusually. Whereas nowadays the usual meaning of 'atheist' in English is 'someone who asserts that there is no such being as God', I want the word to be understood not positively but negatively. I want the originally Greek prefix 'a' to be read in the same way in 'atheist' as it customarily is read in such other Greco-English words as 'amoral', 'atypical', and 'asymmetrical'. In this interpretation an atheist becomes: not someone who positively asserts the non-existence of God; but someone who is simply not a theist. Let us, for future ready reference, introduce the labels 'positive atheist' for the former and 'negative atheist' for the latter. What the protagonist of my presumption of atheism wants to show is that the debate about the existence of God ought to be conducted in a particular way, and that the issue should be seen in a certain perspective. His thesis about the onus of proof involves that it is up to the theist: first, to introduce and to defend his proposed concept of God; and, second, to provide sufficient reason for believing that this concept of his does in fact have an application.

It is the first of these two stages which needs perhaps to be emphasised even more strongly than the second. Where the question of existence concerns, for instance, a Loch Ness Monster or an Abominable Snowman, this stage may perhaps reasonably be deemed to be more or less complete before the argument begins. But in the controversy about the existence of God this is certainly not so: not only for the quite familiar reason that the word 'God' is used—or misused—in many different ways; but also, and much more interestingly, because it cannot be taken for granted that even the would-be mainstream theist is operating with a legitimate concept which theoretically could have an application to an actual being.

This last suggestion is not really as new-fangled and factitious as it is sometimes

Antony Flew edited extracts from 'The Presumption of Atheism' from *The Presumption of Atheism and Other Essays on God, Freedom and Immortality* (Elek Books, Pemberton Publishing Co, 1976), reprinted by permission of the author.

thought to be. But its pedigree has been made a little hard to trace. For the fact is that, traditionally, issues which should be seen as concerning the legitimacy or otherwise of a proposed or supposed concept have by philosophical theologians been discussed, either as surely disposable difficulties in reconciling one particular feature of the Divine nature with another, or else as aspects of an equally surely soluble general problem of saying something about the infinite Creator in language intelligible to His finite creatures. These traditional and still almost universally accepted forms of presentation are fundamentally prejudicial. For they assume that there is a Divine Being, with an actual nature the features of which we can investigate. They assume that there is an Infinite Creator, whose existence—whatever difficulties we finite creatures may have in asserting anything else about Him—we may take for granted.

The general reason why this presumption of atheism matters is that its acceptance must put the whole question of the existence of God into an entirely fresh perspective. Most immediately relevant here is that in this fresh perspective problems which really are conceptual are seen as conceptual problems; and problems which have tended to be regarded as advanced and, so to speak, optional extras now discover themselves as both elementary and indispensable. The theist who wants to build a systematic and thorough apologetic finds that he is required to begin absolutely from the beginning. This absolute beginning is to ensure that the word 'God' is provided with a meaning such that it is theoretically possible for an actual being to be so described.

Although I shall later be arguing that the presumption of atheism is neutral as between all parties to the main dispute, in as much as to accept it as determining a procedural framework is not to make any substantive assumptions, I must give fair warning now that I do nevertheless believe that in its fresh perspective the whole enterprise of theism appears even more difficult and precarious than it did before. In part this is a corollary of what I have just been suggesting; that certain difficulties and objections, which may previously have seemed peripheral or even factitious, are made to stand out as fundamental and unavoidable. But it is also in part, as we shall be seeing soon, a consequence of the emphasis which it places on the imperative need to produce some sort of sufficient reason to justify theist belief.

2. The presumption of atheism and the presumption of innocence

One thing which helps to conceal this need is a confusion about the possible varieties of proof, and this confusion is one which can be resolved with the help of the first of a series of comparisons between my proposed presumption of atheism and the legal presumption of innocence.

(i) It is frequently said nowadays, even by professing Roman Catholics, that everyone knows that it is impossible to prove the existence of God. The first objection to this putative truism is, as my reference to Roman Catholics should have suggested, that it is not true. For it is an essential dogma of Roman Catholicism, defined as such by the First Vatican Council, that 'the one and true God our creator and lord can be known for certain through the creation by the natural light of human reason'.[1] So even if this dogma is, as I myself believe, false, it is certainly not known to be false by those many Roman Catholics who remain, despite all the disturbances consequent upon the Second Vatican Council, committed to the complete traditional faith.

To this a sophisticated objector might reply that the definition of the First Vatican Council speaks of knowing for certain rather than of proving or demonstrating; adding perhaps, if he was very sophisticated indeed, that the word 'demonstrari' in an earlier draft was eventually replaced by the expression 'certo cognosci'. But, allowing that this is correct, it is certainly not enough to vindicate the conventional wisdom. For the word 'proof' is not ordinarily restricted in its application to demonstratively valid arguments, that is, in which the conclusion cannot be denied without thereby contradicting the premises. So it is too flattering to suggest that most of those who make this facile claim, that everyone knows that it is impossible to prove the existence of God, are intending only the strictly limited assertion that one special sort of proof, demonstrative proof, is impossible.

The truth, and the danger, is that wherever there is any awareness of such a limited and specialised interpretation, there will be a quick and illegitimate move to the much wider general conclusion that it is impossible and, furthermore, unnecessary to provide any sufficient reason for believing. It is, therefore, worth underlining that when the presumption of atheism is explained as insisting that the onus of proof must be on the theist, the word 'proof' is being used in the ordinary wide sense in which it can embrace any and every variety of sufficient reason. It is, of course, in this and only this sense that the word is interpreted when the presumption of innocence is explained as laying the onus of proof on the prosecution.

(ii) A second element of positive analogy between these two presumptions is that both are defeasible; and that they are, consequently, not to be identified with assumptions. The presumption of innocence indicates where the court should start and how it must proceed. Yet the prosecution is still able, more often than not, to bring forward what is in the end accepted as sufficient reason to warrant the verdict 'Guilty'; which appropriate sufficient reason is properly characterised as a proof of guilt. The defeasible presumption of innocence is thus in this majority of cases in fact defeated. Were the indefeasible innocence of all accused persons an assumption of any legal system, then there could not be within that system any provision for any verdict other than 'Not Guilty'. To the extent that it is, for instance, an assumption of the English Common Law that every citizen is cognisant of all that the law requires of him, that law cannot admit the fact that this assumption is, as in fact it is, false.

The presumption of atheism is similarly defeasible. It lays it down that thorough

---

1. H. Denzinger, *Enchiridion Symbolorum* (29th rev. edn, Freiburg im Breisgau, 1953, §1806).

and systematic inquiry must start from a position of negative atheism, and that the burden of proof lies on the theist proposition. Yet this is not at all the same thing as demanding that the debate should proceed on either a positive or a negative atheist assumption, which must preclude a theist conclusion. Counsel for theism no more betrays his client by accepting the framework determined by this presumption than counsel for the prosecution betrays the state by conceding the legal presumption of innocence. The latter is perhaps in his heart unshakably convinced of the guilt of the defendant. Yet he must, and with complete consistency and perfect sincerity may, insist that the proceedings of the court should respect the presumption of innocence. The former is even more likely to be persuaded of the soundness of his brief. Yet he too can with a good conscience allow that a thorough and complete apologetic must start from, meet, and go on to defeat, the presumption of atheism.

(iii) However—and here we come to a third element in the positive analogy—to say that such presumptions are in themselves procedural and not substantive is not to say that the higher-order questions of whether to follow this presumption or that are trifling and merely formal rather than material and substantial. These higher-order questions are not questions which can be dismissed cynically as 'issues of principle as opposed to issues of substance'. It can matter a lot which presumption is adopted. Notoriously there is a world of difference between legal systems which follow the presumption of innocence, and those which do not.

(iv) Next, as a fourth element in the positive analogy, it is a paradoxical consequence of the fact that these presumptions are procedural and not substantive that particular defeats do not constitute any sort of reason, much less a sufficient reason, for a general surrender. The fact that George Joseph Smith was in his trial proved guilty of many murders defeats the original presumption of his innocence. But this particular defeat has no tendency at all to show that even in this particular case the court should not have proceeded on this presumption. Still less does it tend to establish that the legal system as a whole was at fault in incorporating this presumption as a general principle. It is the same with the presumption of atheism. Suppose that someone is able to prove the existence of God. This achievement must, similarly, defeat our presumption. But it does not thereby show that the original contention about the onus of proof was mistaken.

3. The case for the presumption of atheism

What does show the presumption of atheism to be the right one is what we have now to investigate.

(i) An obvious first move is to appeal to the old legal axiom: 'Ei incumbit probatio qui dicit, non qui negat.' Literally and unsympathetically translated this becomes: 'The onus of proof lies on the man who affirms, not on the man who denies.' To this the objection is almost equally obvious. Given just a very little verbal ingenuity, the content of any motion can be rendered alternatively in either a negative or a positive form: either, 'That this house affirms the existence of God'; or,

'That this house takes its stand for positive atheism'. So interpreted, therefore, our axiom provides no determinate guidance.

Suppose, however, that we take the hint already offered in the previous paragraph. A less literal but more sympathetic translation would be: 'The onus of proof lies on the proposition, not on the opposition.' The point of the change is to bring out that this maxim was offered in a legal context, and that our courts are institutions of debate. An axiom providing no determinate guidance outside that framework may nevertheless be fundamental for the effective conduct of orderly and decisive debate. Here the outcome is supposed to be decided on the merits of what is said within the debate itself, and of that alone. So no opposition can set about demolishing the proposition case until and unless that proposition has first provided them with a case for demolition: 'You've got to get something on your plate before you can start messing it around'.[2]

Of course our maxim even when thus sympathetically interpreted still offers no direction on which contending parties ought to be made to undertake which roles. Granting that courts are to operate as debating institutions, and granting that this maxim is fundamental to debate, we have to appeal to some further premise principle before we become licensed to infer that the prosecution must propose and the defence oppose. This further principle is, once again, the familiar presumption of innocence. Were we, while retaining the conception of a court as an institution for reaching decisions by way of formalised debate, to embrace the opposite presumption, the presumption of guilt, we should need to adopt the opposite arrangements. In these the defence would first propose that the accused is after all innocent, and the prosecution would then respond by struggling to disintegrate the case proposed.

(ii) The first move examined cannot, therefore, be by itself sufficient. To have considered it does nevertheless help to show that to accept such a presumption is to adopt a policy. And policies have to be assessed by reference to the aims of those for whom they are suggested. If for you it is more important that no guilty person should ever be acquitted than that no innocent person should ever be convicted, then for you a presumption of guilt must be the rational policy. For you, with your preference structure, a presumption of innocence becomes simply irrational. To adopt this policy would be to adopt means calculated to frustrate your own chosen ends; which is, surely, paradigmatically irrational.

What then are the aims by reference to which an atheist presumption might be justified? One key word in the answer, if not the key word, must be 'knowledge'. The context for which such a policy is proposed is that of inquiry about the existence of God; and the object of the exercise is, presumably, to discover whether it is possible to establish that the word 'God' does in fact have application. Now to establish must here be either to show that you know or to come to know. But knowledge is crucially different from mere true belief. All knowledge involves true

2. J. L. Austin, *Sense and Sensibilia* (Oxford, 1962, p. 142).

belief; not all true belief constitutes knowledge. To have a true belief is simply and solely to believe that something is so, and to be in fact right. But someone may believe that this or that is so, and his belief may in fact be true, without its thereby and necessarily constituting knowledge. If a true belief is to achieve this more elevated status, then the believer has to be properly warranted so to believe. He must, that is, be in a position to know. It is, therefore, not only incongruous but also scandalous in matters of life and death, and even of eternal life and death, to maintain that you know either on no grounds at all, or on grounds of a kind which on other and comparatively minor issues you yourself would insist to be inadequate.

It is by reference to this inescapable demand for grounds that the presumption of atheism is justified. If it is to be established that there is a God, then we have to have good grounds for believing that this is indeed so. Until and unless some such grounds are produced we have literally no reason at all for believing; and in that situation the only reasonable posture must be that of either the negative atheist or the agnostic. So the onus of proof has to rest on the proposition. It must be up to them: first, to give whatever sense they choose to the word 'God', meeting any objection that so defined it would relate only to an incoherent pseudo-concept; and, second, to bring forward sufficient reasons to warrant their claim that, in their present sense of the word 'God', there is a God. The same applies, with appropriate alterations, if what is to be made out is, not that theism is known to be true, but only—more modestly—that it can be seen to be at least more or less probable.

Chapter 4

Religious belief as 'properly basic'

Alvin Plantinga

BELIEF in God is the heart and center of the Christian religion—as it is of Judaism and Islam. Of course Christians may disagree, at least in emphasis, as to how to think of God; for example, some may emphasize his hatred of sin; others, his love of his creatures. Furthermore, one may find, even among professedly Christian theologians, supersophisticates who proclaim the liberation of Christianity from belief in God, seeking to replace it by trust in 'Being itself' or the 'Ground of Being' or some such thing. It remains true, however, that belief in God is the foundation of Christianity.

In this essay I want to discuss a connected constellation of questions: Does the believer-in-God accept the existence of God by *faith*? Is belief in God contrary to reason, unreasonable, irrational? Must one have *evidence* to be rational or reasonable in believing in God? Suppose belief in God is *not* rational; does that matter? And what about proofs of God's existence? Many Reformed or Calvinist thinkers and theologians have taken a jaundiced view of natural theology, thought of as the attempt to give proofs or arguments for the existence of God; are they right? What underlies this hostility to an undertaking that, on the surface, at least, looks perfectly harmless and possibly useful? These are some of the questions I propose to discuss. They fall under the general rubric *faith and reason*, if a general rubric is required. I believe Reformed or Calvinist thinkers have had important things to say on these topics and that their fundamental insights here are correct. What they say, however, has been for the most part unclear, ill-focused, and unduly inexplicit. I shall try to remedy these ills; I shall try to state and clearly develop their insight; and I shall try to connect these insights with more general epistemological considerations.

Like the Missouri River, what I have to say is best seen as the confluence of three streams—streams of clear and limpid thought, I hasten to add, rather than turbid, muddy water. These three streams of thought are first, reflection on the evidentialist objection to theistic belief, according to which belief in God is unreasonable or irrational because there is insufficient evidence for it; second, reflection on the Thomistic conception of faith and reason; and third, reflection on the Reformed

Alvin Plantinga edited extracts from 'Reason and Belief in God' from *Faith and Rationality* edited by Alvin Plantinga and Nicholas Wolterstorff (University of Notre Dame Press, 1983), reprinted by permission of the publisher and author. Some passages of the original text, written mainly for the benefit of the specialist, have been omitted with the permission of the author.

rejection to natural theology. In Part I I shall explore the evidentialist objection, trying to see more clearly just what it involves and what it presupposes. Part II will begin with a brief look at Thomas Aquinas' views on faith and knowledge; I shall argue that the evidentialist objection and the Thomistic conception of faith and knowledge can be traced back to a common root in *classical foundationalism*—a pervasive and widely accepted picture or total way of looking at faith, knowledge, belief, rationality, and allied topics. I shall try to characterize this picture in a revealing way and then go on to argue that classical foundationalism is both false and self-referentially incoherent; it should therefore be summarily rejected. In Part III I shall explore the Reformed rejection of natural theology; I will argue that it is best understood as an implicit rejection of classical foundationalism in favor of the view that belief in God is properly basic. What the Reformers meant to hold is that it is entirely right, rational, reasonable, and proper to believe in God without any evidence or argument at all; in this respect belief in God resembles belief in the past, in the existence of other persons, and in the existence of material objects. I shall try to state and clearly articulate this claim and in Part IV to defend it against objections.

Part I: The evidentialist objection to belief in God

My first topic, then, is the evidentialist objection to theistic belief. Many philosophers—W. K. Clifford,[1] Brand Blanshard,[2] Bertrand Russell,[3] Michael Scriven,[4] and Antony Flew,[5] to name a few—have argued that belief in God is irrational or unreasonable or not rationally acceptable or intellectually irresponsible or somehow noetically below par because, as they say, there is *insufficient evidence* for it. Bertrand Russell was once asked what he would say if, after dying, he were brought into the presence of God and asked why he had not been a believer. Russell's reply: 'I'd say "Not enough evidence God! Not enough evidence!"'[6] We may have our doubts as to just how that sort of response would be received; but Russell, like many others, held that theistic belief is unreasonable because there is insufficient evidence for it.

1. W. K. Clifford, 'The Ethics of Belief' in *Lectures and Essays* (London: Macmillan, 1879), pp. 345 f.
2. Brand Blanshard, *Reason and Belief* (London: Allen & Unwin, 1974), pp. 400 f.
3. Bertrand Russell, 'Why I am not a Christian' in *Why I Am Not a Christian* (New York: Simon & Schuster, 1957), p. 3 ff.
4. Michael Scriven, *Primary Philosophy* (New York: McGraw-Hill, 1966), p. 87 ff.
5. Antony Flew, *The Presumption of Atheism* (London: Pemberton, 1976), pp. 22 ff.
6. Wesley Salmon, 'Religion and Science: A New Look at Hume's Dialogues,' *Philosophical Studies* 33 (1978): 176.

A. How shall we construe 'theistic belief'?

But how shall we construe 'theistic belief' here? I have been speaking of 'belief in God'; but this is not entirely accurate. For the subject under discussion is not really the rational acceptability of belief *in* God, but the rationality of belief that God exists—that there *is* such a person as God. And belief in God is not at all the same thing as belief that there is such a person as God. To believe that God exists is simply to accept as true a certain proposition: perhaps the proposition that there is a personal being who has created the world, who has no beginning, and who is perfect in wisdom, justice, knowledge, and power. According to the book of James, the devils do that, and they tremble. The devils do not believe *in* God, however; for belief in God is quite another matter. One who repeats the words of the Apostles' Creed 'I believe in God the Father Almighty, . . .' and means what he says is not simply announcing the fact that he accepts a certain proposition as true; much more is involved than that. Belief in God means *trusting* God, accepting God, accepting his purposes, committing one's life to him and living in his presence. To the believer the entire world speaks of God. Great mountains, surging ocean, verdant forests, blue sky and bright sunshine, friends and family, love in its many forms and various manifestations—the believer sees these things and many more as gifts from God. The universe thus takes on a personal cast for him; the fundamental truth about reality is truth about a *person*. So believing in God is indeed more than accepting the proposition that God exists. But if it is more than that, it is also at least that. One cannot sensibly believe in God and thank him for the mountains without believing that there *is* such a person to be thanked and that he is in some way responsible for the mountains. Nor can one trust in God and commit oneself to him without believing that he exists; as the author of Hebrews says, 'He who would come to God must believe that he is and that he is a rewarder of those who seek him.' (Heb. 11: 6)

So belief in God must be distinguished from the belief that God exists. Having made this distinction, however, I shall ignore it for the most part, using 'belief in God' as a synonym for 'belief that there is such a person as God.' The question I want to address, therefore, is the question whether belief in God—belief in the existence of God—is rationally acceptable. But what is it to believe or assert that God exists? Just which belief is it into the rational acceptability of which I propose to inquire? Which God do I mean to speak of? The answer, in brief, is: the God of Abraham, Isaac, and Jacob; the God of Jewish and Christian revelation: the God of the Bible.

To believe that God exists, therefore, is first of all to hold a *belief* of a certain sort—an existential belief. To assert that God exists is to make an *assertion* of a certain sort—an existential assertion. It is to answer at the most basic level the ontological question 'What is there?' This may seem excessively obvious. I would not so much as mention it, were it not for the fact that some philosophers and theologians seem to disagree. Oddly enough, they seem to use the phrase 'belief in

God' and even 'belief that God exists' in such a way that to believe in God is not to hold any such existential beliefs at all. Much of what Rudolph Bultmann says, for example, seems to suggest that to believe in God is not at all to believe that there exists a being of a certain sort. Instead, it is to adopt a certain attitude or policy, or to make a kind of resolve: the resolve, perhaps, to accept and embrace one's finitude, giving up the futile attempt to build hedges and walls against guilt, failure, and death. And according to the philosopher Richard Braithwaite, a religious assertion is 'the assertion of an intention to carry out a certain behavioral policy, subsumable under a sufficiently general principle to be a moral one, together with the implicit statement, but not necessarily the assertion, of certain stories.'[7] But then it looks as if according to Braithwaite when the Christian asserts 'I believe in God the Father Almighty' he is not, contrary to appearances, asserting that he believes that there exists a *being* of a certain kind; instead he is asserting that he intends to carry out a certain behavioral policy. As *I* use the phrase 'belief in God,' however, that phrase denotes a *belief* not a resolve or the adoption of a policy. And the assertion that God exists is an *existential* assertion, not the assertion of an intention to carry out a certain policy, behavioral or otherwise. To believe or assert that God exists is to believe or assert that there exists a being of a certain very special sort.

What sort? Some contemporary theologians, under the baneful influence of Kant, apparently hold that the name 'God,' as used by Christians and others, denotes an *idea*, or a *concept*, or a *mental construct* of some kind. The American theologian Gordon Kaufman, for example, claims that the word 'God' 'raises special problems of meaning because it is a noun which by definition refers to a reality transcendent of and thus not locatable within experience.'[8] In a striking echo of one of Kant's famous distinctions, Kaufman distinguishes what he calls the 'real referent' of the term 'God' from what he calls 'the available referent':

The real referent for 'God' is never accessible to us or in any way open to our observation or experience. It must remain always an unknown X, a mere limiting idea with no content.[9]

For all practical purposes, it is the *available referent*—a particular imaginative construct— that bears significantly on human life and thought. It is the 'available God' whom we have in mind when we worship or pray; . . . it is the available God in terms of which we speak and think whenever we use the word 'God.' In this sense 'God' denotes for all practical purposes what is essentially a mental or imaginative construct.[10]

Professor John Hick makes a similar suggestion; in his inaugural address at the Claremont School of Theology he suggested that when Christians speak to God, they are speaking of a certain *image*, or *mental construction*, or *imaginative creation* of some sort.

7. Richard Braithwaite, *An Empiricist's View of the Nature of Religious Belief* (Cambridge: Cambridge University Press, 1955), p. 32.
8. Gordon Kaufman, *God the Problem* (Cambridge: Harvard University Press, 1972), p. 8.
9. Ibid., p. 85.
10. Ibid., p. 86.

Now these are puzzling suggestions. If it is Kaufman's 'available referent' 'in terms of which we speak whenever we use the word "God",' and if the available referent is a mental or imaginative construct, then presumably when we say 'there is a God' or 'God exists' we are affirming the existence of a certain kind of mental or imaginative construct. But surely we are not. And when Christians say that God has created the world, for example, are they really claiming that an image or imaginative construct, whatever precisely that may be, has created the world? That seems at best preposterous. In any event, the belief I mean to identify and discuss is not the belief that there exists some sort of imaginative construct or mental construction or anything of the sort. It is instead the belief, first, that there exists a *person* of a certain sort—a being who acts, holds beliefs, and has aims and purposes. This person, secondly, is immaterial, exists *a se*, is perfect in goodness, knowledge, and power, and is such that the world depends on him for its existence.

B. Objections to theistic belief

Now many objections have been put forward to belief in God. First, there is the claim that as a matter of fact there is no such thing as belief in God, because the sentence 'God exists' is, strictly speaking, nonsense.[11] This is the positivists' contention that such sentences as 'God exists' are unverifiable and hence 'cognitively meaningless' (to use their charming phrase), in which case they altogether fail to express propositions. On this view those who claim to believe in God are in the pitiable position of claiming to believe a proposition that as a matter of fact does not so much as exist. This objection, fortunately, has retreated into the obscurity it so richly deserves, and I shall say no more about it.[12]

Second, there is the claim that belief in God is *internally inconsistent* in that it is impossible, in the broadly logical sense, that there be any such person as theists say God is. For example, theists say that God is a person who has no body but nonetheless acts in the world; some philosophers have retorted that the idea of a bodiless person is impossible, and the idea of a bodiless person *acting* is *obviously* impossible. Some versions of some of these objections are of great interest, but I do not propose to discuss them here. Let me just record my opinion that none of them is at all compelling; so far as I can see, the concept of God is perfectly coherent. Third, some critics have urged that the existence of God is incompatible with other beliefs that are plainly true and typically accepted by theists. The most widely urged objection to theistic belief, the deductive argument from evil, falls into this category. According to this objection the existence of an omnipotent, omniscient, and wholly good God is *logically incompatible* with the presence of evil in the world—a

---

11. A. J. Ayer, *Language, Truth and Logic*, 2nd edn (London: Gollantz, Ltd., 1946), pp. 114–20.
12. For further discussion of positivism and its dreaded verifiability criterion of meaning, see Alvin Plantinga, *God and Other Minds* (Ithaca, New York: Cornell University Press, 1968), pp. 156–68.

presence conceded and indeed insisted upon by theists.[13] For their part, theists have argued that there is no inconsistency here;[14] and I think the present consensus, even among those who urge some form of the argument from evil, is that the deductive form of the argument from evil is unsuccessful.

More recently, philosophers have claimed that the existence of God, while perhaps not inconsistent with the existence of the amount and kinds of evil we actually find, is at any rate *unlikely* or *improbable* with respect to it; that is, the probability of God's existence with respect to evil is less than that of its denial with respect to evil. Hence the existence of God is improbable with respect to what we know. But if theistic belief *is* improbable with respect to what we know, then, so goes the claim, it is irrational or intellectually improper to accept it. Although this objection—the probabilistic argument from evil—is not of central concern here, it bears an interesting relation to one of my main topics—the question whether belief in God is properly basic. So suppose we briefly examine it. The objector claims that

(1) God is the omnipotent, omniscient, wholly good creator of the world

is improbable or unlikely with respect to the amounts and varieties of evil we find in the world. Perhaps *some* of the evil is necessary to achieve certain good states of affairs, but there is so *much* evil, much of which seems, on the face of things, utterly gratuitous. The objector claims, therefore, that (1) is improbable or unlikely, given

(2) There are 10^{13} turps of evil

where the turp is the basic unit of evil—equal, as you may have guessed, to $1/10^{13}$ (the evil in the actual world).

Suppose we stipulate for purposes of argument that (1) is in fact improbable on (2). Let us agree that it is unlikely, given the existence of 10^{13} turps of evil, that the world has been created by a God who is perfect in power, knowledge, and goodness. What is supposed to follow from that? How is this to be construed as an objection to theistic belief? How does the argument go from there? It does not follow, of course, that theism is false. Nor does it follow that one who accepts both (1) and (2) (and, let us add, recognizes that (1) is improbable with respect to (2)) has an irrational system of beliefs or is in any way guilty of noetic impropriety. For it *could* be, obviously enough, that (1) is improbable with respect to (2) but probable with respect to something else we know. I might know, for example, both that

(3) Feike is a Frisian, and 9 out of 10 Frisians cannot swim,

13. This claim has been made by Epicurus, perhaps by David Hume, by some of the French Encyclopedists, by F. H. Bradley, J. McTaggart, and many others. For an influential contemporary statement of the claim, see J. Mackie, 'Evil and Omnipotence,' *Mind* 64 (1955): 200 ff.
14. C. S. Lewis, *The Problem of Pain* (New York: Macmillan, 1943); and see Plantinga, *God and Other Minds*, pp. 115–55; idem, *The Nature of Necessity* (Oxford: Clarendon Press, 1974), chapter 9. A more accessible form of the argument can be found in Alvin Plantinga, *God, Freedom and Evil* (1974; reprint edn, Grand Rapids, Michigan: Eerdmans, 1978), pp. 1–50.

and

(4) Feike is a Frisian lifeguard, and 99 out of 100 Frisian lifeguards can swim;

it is plausible to hold that

(5) Feike can swim

is probable with respect to (4) but improbable with respect to (3). If, furthermore, (3) and (4) are all we know about Feike's swimming ability, then the view that he can swim is epistemically more acceptable for us than the view that he cannot— even though we know something with respect to which the former is improbable.

Indeed, we might very well *know* both (3) and (5); we might very well know a pair of propositions A and B such that A is improbable on B. So even if it were a fact that (2) is evidence against (1) or that (1) is improbable on (2), that fact would not be of much consequence. But then how can this objection be developed? How can the objector proceed?

Presumably what he means to hold is that (1) is improbable, not just on (2) but on some appropriate body of *total evidence*—perhaps all the evidence the theist has, or perhaps the body of evidence he is rationally obliged to have. The objector must be supposing that there is a relevant body of total evidence here, a body of evidence that includes (2); and his claim is that (1) is improbable with respect to this relevant body of total evidence.

Suppose we step back a moment and reconsider the overall structure of the probabilistic argument. The objector's claim is that the theist is irrational in accepting belief in God because it is improbable with respect to (2), the proposition that there are 10^{13} turps of evil—a proposition whose truth the theist acknowledges. As we have seen, however, even if the existence of God is improbable with respect to (2), that fact is utterly insufficient for demonstrating irrationality in the theist's structure of beliefs; there may be many propositions A and B such that even though A is improbable on B, we can nonetheless accept both in perfect propriety. What the objector must be supposing, then, is something like this. For any theist T you pick, there is a set of propositions T_s that constitute his *total evidence*; and now for any proposition A the theist accepts, he is rational in accepting A only if A is not improbable with respect to T_s. And the objector's claim is that the existence of God *is* improbable with respect to T_s for any (or nearly any) theist.

Suppose we say that T_s is the theist's *evidential set*. This is the set of propositions to which, as we might put it, his beliefs are responsible. A belief is rationally acceptable for him only if it is not improbable with respect to T_s. Now so far we have not been told what sorts of propositions are to be found in T_s. Perhaps these are the propositions the theist *knows* to be true, or perhaps the largest subset of his beliefs that he can rationally accept without evidence from other propositions, or perhaps the set of propositions he knows *immediately*—knows, but does not know on the basis of other propositions. However exactly we characterize this set T_s, the presently pressing question is this: Why cannot belief in God be itself a member of

T_s? Perhaps for the theist—for some theists, at any rate—belief in God is a member of T_s in which case it obviously will not be improbable with respect to T_s. Perhaps the theist is entirely within his epistemic rights in *starting from* belief in God, taking that proposition to be one of the ones probability with respect to which determines the rational propriety of *other* beliefs he holds. If so, the fact, if it is a fact, that theistic belief is improbable with respect to the existence of evil does not even begin to show that the theist is irrational in accepting it. The high-road reply to the probabilistic argument from evil, therefore, leads directly to one of the questions I am fundamentally concerned with: What sorts of beliefs, if any, is it rational or reasonable to *start from*? Which beliefs are such that one may properly accept them without evidence, that is, without the evidential support of other beliefs? One who offers the probabilistic argument from evil simply *assumes* that belief in God does not have that status; but perhaps he is mistaken.

C. The evidentialist objection stated

Now suppose we turn explicit attention to the evidentialist objection. Many philosophers have endorsed the idea that the strength of one's belief ought always to be proportional to the strength of the evidence for that belief. Thus, according to John Locke a mark of the rational person is 'the not entertaining any proposition with greater assurance than the proofs it is built upon will warrant.' According to David Hume 'A wise man ... proportions his belief to the evidence.' In the nineteenth century we have W. K. Clifford, that 'delicious *enfant terrible*' as William James calls him, insisting that it is wicked, immoral, monstrous, and maybe even impolite to accept a belief for which you do not have sufficient evidence:

Whoso would deserve well of his fellows in this matter will guard the purity of his belief with a very fanaticism of jealous care, lest at any time it should rest on an unworthy object, and catch a stain which can never be wiped away.[15]

He adds that if a

belief has been accepted on insufficient evidence, the pleasure is a stolen one. Not only does it deceive ourselves by giving us a sense of power which we do not really possess, but it is sinful, because it is stolen in defiance of our duty to mankind. That duty is to guard ourselves from such beliefs as from a pestilence, which may shortly master our body and spread to the rest of the town. (p. 184)

And *finally*: 'To sum up: it is wrong always, everywhere, and for anyone to believe anything upon insufficient evidence' (p. 186). (It is not hard to detect, in these quotations, the 'tone of robustious pathos' with which James credits him.) Clifford, of course, held that one who accepts belief in God *does* accept that belief on

15. Clifford, 'The Ethics of Belief,' p. 183.

insufficient evidence and has therefore defied his duty to mankind. More recently, Bertrand Russell has endorsed the same idea: 'Give to any hypothesis which is worth your while to consider,' he says, 'just that degree of credence which the evidence warrants'; and in his view the evidence warrants no credence in the existence of God.

1. A. Flew: the presumption of atheism Still more recently Antony Flew has commended what he calls Clifford's 'luminous and compulsive essay' (perhaps 'compulsive' here is to be understood as 'compelling'); and Flew goes on to claim that there is, in his words, a 'presumption of atheism.' What is a presumption of atheism, and why should we think there is one? Flew puts it as follows:

What I want to examine is the contention that the debate about the existence of God should properly begin from the presumption of atheism, that the onus of proof must lie upon the theist.

The word 'atheism,' however, has in this contention to be construed unusually. Whereas nowadays the usual meaning of 'atheist' in English is 'someone who asserts there is no such being as God,' I want the word to be understood not positively but negatively. I want the original Greek preface 'a' to be read in the same way in 'atheist' as it is customarily read in such other Greco-English words as 'amoral,' 'atypical,' and 'asymmetrical.' In this interpretation an atheist becomes: not someone who positively asserts the non-existence of God; but someone who is simply not a theist.

. . .

What the protagonist of my presumption of atheism wants to show is that the debate about the existence of God ought to be conducted in a particular way, and that the issue should be seen in a certain perspective. His thesis about the onus of proof involves that it is up to the theist: first to introduce and to defend his proposed concept of God; and second, to provide sufficient reason for believing that this concept of his does in fact have an application.[16]

How shall we understand this? What does it mean, for example, to say that the debate 'should properly begin from the presumption of atheism?' What sorts of things do debates begin from, and what is it for one to begin from such a thing? Perhaps Flew means something like this: to speak of where a debate should begin is to speak of the sorts of premises to which the affirmative and negative sides can properly appeal in arguing their cases. Suppose you and I are debating the question whether, say, the United States has a right to seize Mideast oil fields if the OPEC countries refuse to sell us oil at what we think is a fair price. I take the affirmative and produce for my conclusion an argument one of whose premises is the proposition that the United States has indeed a right to seize these oil fields under those conditions. Doubtless that maneuver would earn me few points. Similarly, a debate about the existence of God cannot sensibly start from the assumption that God does indeed exist. That is to say, the affirmative cannot properly appeal, in its

16. Flew, *The Presumption of Atheism*, pp. 13–15.

arguments, to such premises as that there is such a person as God; if she could, she would have much too easy a time of it. So in this sense of 'start' Flew is quite right: the debate cannot start from the assumption that God exists.

Of course, it is also true that the debate cannot start from the assumption that God does *not* exist; using 'atheism' in its ordinary sense, there is equally a presumption of aatheism. So it looks as if there is in Flew's sense a presumption of atheism, alright, but in that same sense an equal presumption of aatheism. If this is what Flew means, then what he says is entirely correct, if something of a truism.

In other passages, however, Flew seems to understand the presumption of atheism in quite a different fashion:

It is by reference to this inescapable demand for grounds that the presumption of atheism is justified. If it is to be established that there is a God, then we have to have good grounds for believing that this is indeed so. Until or unless some such grounds are produced we have literally no reason at all for believing; and in that situation the only reasonable posture must be that of either the negative atheist or the agnostic. (p. 22)

Here we have a claim much more contentious than the mere suggestion that a debate about the existence of God ought not to start from the assumption that indeed there is such a person as God; here Flew is claiming that it is irrational or unreasonable to accept theistic belief in the absence of arguments or evidence for the existence of God. That is, Flew claims that if we know of no propositions that serve as evidence for God's existence, then we cannot rationally believe in God. And of course Flew, along with Russell, Clifford, and many others, holds that in fact there are not sufficient grounds or evidence for belief in God. Flew, therefore, seems to endorse the following two principles:

(6) It is irrational or unreasonable to accept theistic belief in the absence of sufficient evidence or reasons

and

(7) We have no evidence or at any rate not sufficient evidence for the proposition that God exists.

2. M. Scriven: atheism is obligatory in the absence of evidence   According to Michael Scriven, if the arguments for God's existence fail, then the only rational posture is not merely not believing in God; it is atheism, the belief that there is no God. Speaking of the theistic proofs, he says, 'It will now be shown that if they fail, there is no alternative to atheism.'[17] He goes on to say: 'we need not have a proof that God does not exist in order to justify atheism. Atheism is obligatory in the absence of any evidence for God's existence . . . The proper alternative, where there is no evidence, is not mere suspension of belief, e.g., about Santa Claus; it is *disbelief'*. (p. 103) But Scriven's claim seems totally arbitrary. He holds that if the

17. Scriven, *Primary Philosophy*, pp. 102–3.

arguments *for* God's existence fail and the arguments *against* God's existence *also* fail, then atheism is rationally obligatory. If you have no evidence *for* the existence of God, then you are rationally obliged to believe there is no God—whether or not you have any evidence *against* the existence of God. The first thing to note, then, is that Scriven is not treating

(8) God exists

and

(9) God does not exist

in the same way. He claims that if there is no evidence for (8), then the only rational course is to believe its denial, namely (9). But of course he does not propose the same treatment for (9); he does not suggest that if there is no evidence for (9), then we are rationally obliged to believe *its* denial, namely (8). (If he *did* propose that (9) should be treated like (8), then he would be committed to supposing that if we had no evidence either way, the rational thing to do would be to believe the denial of (8) namely (9), and *also* the denial of (9), namely (8).) Why then does he propose this lack of parity between (8) and (9)? What is the justification for treating these propositions so differently? Could not the theist just as sensibly say, 'If the arguments for *atheism* fail and there is no evidence for (9), then theism is rationally obligatory'? Scriven's claim, initially at any rate, looks like a piece of merely arbitrary intellectual imperialism.

Scriven's extravagant claim, then, does not look at all promising. Let us therefore return to the more moderate evidentialist position encapsulated by

(6) It is irrational or unreasonable to accept theistic belief in the absence of sufficient evidence or reasons

and

(7) There is no evidence or at any rate not sufficient evidence for the proposition that God exists.

3. The evidentialist objection and intellectual obligation Now (7) is a strong claim. What about the various arguments that have been proposed for the existence of God—the traditional cosmological and teleological arguments for example? What about the versions of the *moral* argument as developed, for example, by A. E. Taylor and more recently by Robert Adams? What about the broadly inductive or probabilistic arguments developed by F. R. Tennant, C. S. Lewis, E. L. Mascall, Basil Mitchell, Richard Swinburne, and others? What about the ontological argument in its contemporary versions?[18] Do none of these provide evidence? Notice: the question is not whether these arguments, taken singly or in

---

18. See, for example, Plantinga, *The Nature of Necessity*, chapter 10.

combinations, constitute *proofs* of God's existence; no doubt they do not. The question is only whether someone might be rationally justified in believing in the existence of God on the basis of the alleged evidence offered by them; and that is a radically different question.

At present, however, I am interested in the objector's other premise—the claim that it is irrational or unreasonable to accept theistic belief in the absence of evidence or reasons. Why suppose *that* is true? Why should we think a theist must have evidence, or reason to think there *is* evidence, if he is not to be irrational? Why not suppose, instead, that he is entirely within his epistemic rights in believing in God's existence even if he has no argument or evidence at all? This is what I want to investigate. Suppose we begin by asking what the objector means by describing a belief as *irrational*. What is the force of his claim that theistic belief is irrational, and how is it to be understood? The first thing to see is that this objection is rooted in a *normative* view. It lays down conditions that must be met by anyone whose system of beliefs is *rational*, and here 'rational' is to be taken as a normative or evaluative term. According to the objector there is a right way and a wrong way with respect to belief. People have responsibilities, duties, and obligations with respect to their believings just as with respect to their actions, or if we think believings are a kind of action, their *other* actions. Professor Brand Blanshard puts this clearly:

everywhere and always belief has an ethical aspect. There is such a thing as a general ethics of the intellect. The main principle of that ethic I hold to be the same inside and outside religion. This principle is simple and sweeping: Equate your assent to the evidence.[19]

and according to Michael Scriven:

Now even belief in something for which there is no evidence, i.e., a belief which goes beyond the evidence, although a lesser sin than belief in something which is contrary to well-established laws, is plainly irrational in that it simply amounts to attaching belief where it is not justified. So the proper alternative, when there is no evidence, is not mere suspension of belief, e.g., about Santa Claus; it is disbelief. It most certainly is not faith.[20]

Perhaps this sort of obligation is really just a special case of a more general moral obligation; perhaps, on the other hand, it is unique and *sui generis*. In any event, says the objector, there are such obligations: to conform to them is to be rational and to go against them is to be irrational.

Now here what the objector says seems plausible; there do seem to be duties and obligations with respect to belief, or at any rate in the general *neighborhood* of belief. One's own welfare and that of others sometimes depends on what one believes. If we are descending the Grand Teton and I am setting the anchor for the 120-foot rappel into the Upper Saddle, I have an obligation to form such beliefs as *this anchor point is solid* only after careful scrutiny and testing. One commissioned

19. Blanshard, *Reason and Belief*, p. 401.
20. Scriven, *Primary Philosophy*, p. 103.

to gather intelligence—the spies Joshua sent into Canaan, for example—has an obligation to get it right. I have an obligation with respect to the belief that Justin Martyr was a Greek apologist—an obligation arising from the fact that I teach medieval philosophy, must make a declaration on this issue, and am obliged not to mislead my students here. The precise nature of these obligations may be hard to specify: What exactly *is* my obligation here? Am I obliged to believe that Justin Martyr was a Greek apologist if and only if Justin Martyr *was* a Greek apologist? Or to form a belief on this topic only after the appropriate amount of checking and investigating? Or maybe just to tell the students the truth about it, whatever I myself believe in the privacy of my own study? Or to tell them what is generally thought by those who should know? In the rappel case, do I have a duty to believe that the anchor point is solid if and only if it is? Or only only if it is? Or just to check carefully before forming the belief? Or perhaps there is no obligation to *believe* at all, but instead an obligation to *act on* a certain belief only after appropriate investigation. In any event, it seems plausible to hold that there are obligations and norms with respect to belief, and I do not intend to contest this assumption.

Now perhaps the evidentialist objector thinks there are intellectual obligations of the following sorts. With respect to certain kinds of propositions perhaps I have a duty not to believe them unless I have evidence for them. Perhaps I have a duty not to accept the denial of an apparently self-evident proposition unless I can see that it conflicts with other propositions that seem self-evident. Perhaps I have a duty to accept such a proposition as *I see a tree* under certain conditions that are hard to spell out in detail but include at least my entertaining that proposition and my having a certain characteristic sort of visual experience along with no reason to think my perceptual apparatus is malfunctioning.

Of course these obligations would be *prima facie* obligations; in special sorts of circumstances they could be overridden by other obligations. I have an obligation not to take bread from the grocery store without permission and another to tell the truth. Both sorts of obligation can be overridden, in specific circumstances, by other obligations—in the first case, perhaps, an obligation to feed my starving children and in the second (when the Nazis are pounding on the door) an obligation to protect a human life. So we must distinguish *prima facie* duties or obligations from *all-things-considered* or *on-balance (ultima facie?)* obligations. I have a *prima facie* obligation to tell the truth; in a given situation, however, that obligation may be overridden by others, so that my duty, all things considered, is to tell a lie. This is the grain of truth contained in situation ethics and the ill-named 'new morality.'

And *prima facie* intellectual obligations, like obligations of other sorts, can conflict. Perhaps I have a *prima facie* obligation to believe what seems to me self-evident, and what seems to me to follow self-evidently from what seems to me self-evident. But what if, as in the Russell paradoxes, something that seems self-evidently false apparently follows, self-evidently, from what seems self-evidently true? Here *prima facie* intellectual obligations conflict, and no matter what I do, I will violate a *prima facie* obligation. Another example: in reporting the Grand Teton rappel I neglected to mention the violent electrical storm coming in from the southwest; to escape it we must get off in a hurry, so that I have a *prima facie* obligation to inspect the anchor point carefully, but another to set up the rappel rapidly, which means I cannot spend a lot of time inspecting the anchor point.

Thus lightly armed, suppose we return to the evidentialist objector. Does he mean to hold that the theist without evidence is violating some intellectual obligation? If so, which one? Does he claim, for example, that the theist is violating his all-things-considered intellectual obligation in thus believing? Perhaps he thinks anyone who believes in God without evidence is violating his all-things-considered intellectual duty. This, however, seems unduly harsh. What about the 14-year-old theist brought up to believe in God in a community where everyone believes? This 14-year-old theist, we may suppose, does not believe in God on the basis of evidence. He has never heard of the cosmological, teleological, or ontological arguments; in fact no one has ever presented him with any evidence at all. And although he has often been told about God, he does not take that testimony as evidence; he does not reason thus: everyone around here says God loves us and cares for us; most of what everyone around here says is true; so probably *that is* true. Instead, he simply believes what he is taught. Is he violating an all-things-considered intellectual duty? Surely not. And what about the mature theist— Thomas Aquinas, let us say—who thinks he *does* have adequate evidence? Let us suppose he is wrong; let us suppose all of his arguments are failures. Nevertheless he has reflected long, hard, and conscientiously on the matter and thinks he *does* have adequate evidence. Shall we suppose he is violating an all-things-considered intellectual duty here? I should think not. So construed, the objector's contention is totally implausible.

Perhaps, then, the objector is to be understood as claiming that there is a *prima facie* intellectual duty not to believe in God without evidence. This duty can be overridden by circumstances, of course, but there is a *prima facie* obligation to believe propositions of this sort only on the basis of evidence. The theist without evidence, he adds, is flouting this obligation and is therefore not living up to his intellectual obligations. But here too there are problems. The suggestion is that I now have the *prima facie* duty to comply with the following command: either have evidence or do not believe. But this may be a command I cannot obey. I may not know of any way to acquire evidence for this proposition; and of course if the objector is right, there is no adequate evidence for it. But it is also not within my power to refrain from believing this proposition. My beliefs are not for the most part directly within my control. If you order me now, for example, to cease believing that the earth is very old, there is no way I can comply with your order. But in the same way it is not now within my power to cease believing in God now. So this alleged *prima facie* duty is one such that it is not within my power to comply with it.

But how can I have a duty, *prima facie* or otherwise, to do what it is not within my power to do?

4. Can I have intellectual obligations if my beliefs are not within my control? This is a difficult and vexing question. The suggestion here is that I cannot now have a *prima facie* obligation to comply with a command which it is not now within my power to obey. Since what I believe is not normally within my power, I cannot have an obligation to believe a certain proposition or to refrain from believing it; but then, *contra* the objector, I do not have an obligation to refrain from believing in God if I have no evidence. This response to the objector is, I think, inadequate. In the first place the response is unbecoming from the theist, since many of those who believe in God follow St Paul (for example, Romans 1) in holding that under certain circumstances failure to believe in God is culpable. And there are cases where most of us—theist and nontheist alike—do in fact believe that a person is culpable or condemnable for holding a given belief, as well as cases where we hold a person responsible for *not* accepting certain beliefs. Consider the following. Suppose someone comes to believe that Jews are inferior, in some important way, to Gentiles. Suppose he goes on to conclude that Jews should not be permitted to share public facilities such as restaurants and hotels with the rest of us. Further reflection leads him to the view that they should not be provided with the protection of law and that the rest of us have a right to expropriate their property if that is convenient. Finally, he concludes that they ought to be eliminated in order to preserve the purity of the alleged Aryan race. After soul-searching inquiry he apparently believes in all honesty that it is his duty to do what he can to see that this view is put into practice. A convincing sort, he gets the rest of us to see things his way: we join him in his pogroms, and his policy succeeds.

Now many of us will agree that such a person is culpable and guilty. But wherein does his guilt consist? Not, presumably, in doing what he believes he ought to do, in trying to carry out his duty as he sees it. Suppose, to vary the example, he tries to encourage and institute these abhorrent policies at considerable cost to himself: he loses his job; his friends turn their backs on him; he is finally arrested and thrown into prison. Nonetheless he valiantly persists. Does he not deserve moral *credit* for doing what he sees as his duty? His guilt, surely, does not consist solely in his taking the *actions* he takes; at least part of the guilt lies in accepting those abhorrent views. If he *had not* acted on his beliefs—out of fear of the consequences, perhaps—would he not have been guilty nonetheless? He would not have caused as much trouble, but would he not have been guilty? I should think so. We do in fact sometimes think that a person is guilty—has violated norms or obligations—by virtue of the beliefs he holds.

The theist, accordingly, should not reply to the evidentialist objector by claiming that since our beliefs are not within our control, we cannot have a *prima facie* duty to refrain from believing certain propositions. But there is a second reason why this response to the evidentialist is inadequate. I have been using the terms 'accept' and 'believe' interchangeably, but in fact there is an important distinction they can nicely be used to mark. This distinction is extremely hard to make clear but nonetheless, I think, important. Perhaps we can make an initial stab at it as follows. Consider a Christian beset by doubts. He has a hard time believing certain crucial Christian claims—perhaps the teaching that God was in Christ, reconciling the world to himself. Upon calling that belief to mind, he finds it cold, lifeless, without warmth or attractiveness. Nonetheless he is committed to this belief; it is his position; if you ask him what he thinks about it, he will unhesitatingly endorse it. He has, so to speak, thrown in his lot with it. Let us say that he *accepts* this proposition, even though when he is assailed by doubt, he may fail to *believe* it—at any rate explicitly—to any appreciable degree. His commitment to this proposition may be much stronger than his explicit and occurrent belief in it; so these two—that is, acceptance and belief—must be distinguished.

Take another example. A person may accept the proposition that alleged moral distinctions are unreal, and our tendency to make them is a confused and superstitious remnant of the infancy of our race—while nonetheless sometimes finding himself compelled to believe, for example, that gross injustice is wicked. Such a person adopts as his position the proposition that moral distinctions are unreal, and he accepts that proposition; but (at certain times and in certain conditions) he cannot help believing, *malgré lui*, that such distinctions are not unreal. In the same way, someone with solipsistic inclination—acquired, perhaps, by an incautious reading of Hume—could *accept* the proposition that, say, there really is no external world—no houses, horses, trucks, or trees—but find himself, under certain conditions, regularly believing that there are such things.

Now I am quite aware that I have not been able to make this distinction between acceptance and belief wholly clear. I think there is such a distinction in the neighborhood, however, and I believe it is important. It is furthermore one the objector may be able to make use of; for while it is plausible to hold that what I believe is not within my direct control, it is also plausible to suppose that what I *accept* is or can be at least in part a matter of deliberate decision, a matter of voluntarily taking up a certain position. But then the objector can perhaps restate his objection in terms of *acceptance*. Perhaps (because of an unfortunate upbringing, let us say) I cannot refrain from believing in God. Nevertheless it is within my power, says the evidentialist objector, to refuse to *accept* that proposition. And now his claim that there are duties with respect to our beliefs may be reconstrued as the claim that we have *prima facie* duties with respect to our acceptances, one of these duties being not to accept such a proposition as *there is such a person as God* in the absence of evidence.

Finally, while we may perhaps agree that what I believe is not *directly* within my control, some of my beliefs are indirectly within my control, at least in part. First, what I accept has a long-term influence upon what I believe. If I refuse to accept belief in God, and if I try to ignore or suppress my tendency to believe, then perhaps eventually I will no longer believe. And as Pascal pointed out, there are other ways to influence one's beliefs. Presumably, then, the evidentialist objector could hold that it is my *prima facie* duty not to accept belief in God without evidence, and to do what I can to bring it about that I no longer believe. Although it is not within my power now to cease believing now, there may be a series of actions, such that I can now take the first and, after taking the first, will be able to take the second, and so on; and after taking the whole series of actions I will no longer believe in God. Perhaps the objector thinks it is my *prima facie* duty to undertake whatever sort of regimen will at some time in the future result in my not believing without evidence. Perhaps I should attend a Universalist-Unitarian church, for example, and consort with members of the Rationalist Society of America. Perhaps I should read a lot of Voltaire and Bertrand Russell and Thomas Paine, eschewing St Augustine and C. S. Lewis and, of course, the Bible. Even if I cannot now stop believing without evidence, perhaps there are other actions I can take, such that if I were to take them, then at some time in the future I will not be in this deplorable condition.

So far, then, we have been construing the evidentialist objector as holding that the theist without sufficient evidence—evidence in the sense of other propositions that prove or make probable or support the existence of God—is violating a *prima facie* intellectual obligation of some sort. As we have seen, the fact that belief is not within direct control may give him pause; he is not, however, without plausible replies. But the fact is there is a quite different way of construing the evidentialist objection; the objector need not hold that the theist without evidence is violating or has violated some duty, *prima facie*, *ultima facie*, or otherwise. Consider someone who believes that Venus is smaller than Mercury, not because he has evidence, but because he read it in a comic book and always believes everything he reads—or consider someone who holds this belief on the basis of an outrageously bad argument. Perhaps there is no obligation he has failed to meet; nevertheless his intellectual condition is defective in some way; or perhaps alternatively there is a commonly achieved excellence he fails to display. Perhaps he is like someone who is easily gulled, or has a serious astigmatism, or is unduly clumsy. And perhaps the evidentialist objection is to be understood, not as the claim that the theist without evidence has failed to meet some obligation, but that he suffers from a certain sort of intellectual deficiency. If this is the objector's view, then his proper attitude toward the theist would be one of sympathy rather than censure.

But of course the crucial question here is this: Why does the objector think these things? Why does he think there *is* a *prima facie* obligation to try not to believe in God without evidence? Or why does he think that to do so is to be in a deplorable condition? Why is it not permissible and quite satisfactory to believe in God without any evidence—proof or argument—at all? Presumably the objector does not mean to suggest that *no* propositions can be believed or accepted without evidence, for if you have evidence for *every* proposition you believe, then (granted certain plausible assumptions about the formal properties of the evidence relation) you will believe infinitely many propositions; and no one has time, these busy days, for that. So presumably *some* propositions can properly be believed and accepted without evidence. Well, why not belief in God? Why is it not entirely acceptable, desirable, right, proper, and rational to accept belief in God without any argument or evidence whatever?

Part II: Aquinas and foundationalism

In this section I shall give what I take to be the evidentialist objector's answer to these questions; I shall argue that his answer is not in the least compelling and that the prospects for his project are not bright. But it is not only evidentialist objectors that have thought theists need evidence if their belief is to be rational; many Christians have thought so too. In particular, many Christian thinkers in the tradition of natural theology have thought so. Thomas Aquinas, of course, is the natural theologian *par excellence*. Thomist thought is also, as it seems to me, the natural starting point for philosophical reflection on these topics, Protestant as well as Catholic. No doubt there are mountains between Rome and Geneva; nevertheless Protestants should in these matters be what Ralph McInerny calls 'peeping Thomists'—at any rate they should *begin* as peeping Thomists. We must therefore look at some of Aquinas' views on these matters.

A. Aquinas and evidentialism

1. Aquinas on knowledge According to Aquinas it is possible for us to have scientific knowledge—*scientia*—of the existence and immateriality, unity, simplicity, and perfection of God. As Aquinas sees it, *scientia* is knowledge that is inferred from what is *seen* to be true:

Any science is possessed by virtue of principles known immediately and therefore seen. Whatever, then, is an object of science is in some sense seen.[21]

Aristotle suggests that the principles of a science must be *self-evident*; and Aquinas sometimes seems to follow him in holding that *scientia*, properly speaking, consists in a body of propositions deduced syllogistically from self-evident first principles— or perhaps *scientia* consists not just in those syllogistic conclusions but in the syllogisms themselves as well. Logic and mathematics seem to be the best examples of science so thought of. Consider, for example, propositional logic: here one can start from self-evident axioms and proceed to deduce theorems by argument forms—*modus ponens*, for example—that are themselves self-evidently valid in an

---

21. Aquinas, *Summa Theologiae* (hereafter 'ST'), IIa, IIae, 1, 5.

obvious sense.[22] Other good examples of science, so thought of, would be first order logic and arithmetic.[23] And here it would be the *theorems*, not the axioms, of these systems that would constitute science. *Scientia* is *mediate* knowledge, so that one does not have *scientia* of what is self-evident. Strictly speaking, then, only those arithmetical truths that are not self-evident would constitute science. The proposition $3 + 1 = 4$ is unlikely to appear as an axiom in a formulation of arithmetic; since it is self-evident, however, it does not constitute *scientia*, even if it appears as a theorem in some axiomatization of arithmetic.

Of course the 'first principles' of a science—the axioms as opposed to the theorems, so to say—are also *known*. They are known *immediately* rather than mediately, and are known by 'understanding.'

Now a truth can come into the mind in two ways, namely, as known in itself, and as known through another. What is known in itself is like a principle, and is perceived immediately by the mind. And so the habit which perfects the intellect in considering such a truth is called 'understanding'; it is a firm and easy quality of mind which sees into principles. A truth, however, which is known through another is understood by the intellect, not immediately, but through an inquiry of reason of which it is the terminus.[24]

Like many of Aquinas' distinctions, this one comes from Aristotle:

Now of the thinking states by which we grasp truth, some are unfailingly true; others admit of error—opinion, for example, and calculation, whereas scientific knowledge and intuition are always true; further, no other kind of thought except intuition is more accurate than scientific knowledge, whereas primary premises are more knowable than demonstrations, and all scientific knowledge is discursive. From these considerations it follows that there will be no scientific knowledge of the primary premises, and since, except intuition, nothing can be truer than scientific knowledge, it will be intuition that apprehends the primary premises. (*Posterior Analytics*, II, 19)

Following Aristotle, then, Aquinas distinguishes what is self-evident, or known through itself (*per se nota*), from what is known through another (*per aliud nota*);

---

22. In fact, these argument forms are self-evidently valid in two senses: (a) it is self-evident that for any instance of the form in question, if the premises are true, then so is the conclusion, and (b) the corresponding conditional of the argument form is itself self-evident.

23. Although the quantification rule presents a bit of a problem in some formulations, in that it does not have the sheer see-through-ability demanded by self-evidence. The fact, incidentally, that propositional and first order logic are not *uniquely* axiomatizable is no obstacle to seeing them as sciences in this Aristotelian sense; nor does the incompleteness of arithmetic show that arithmetic is not a science in this sense.

24. Verum autem est dupliciter considerabile: uno modo, sicut per se notum; alio modo, sicut per aliud notum. Quod autem est per se notum se habet ut principium, et percipitur statim ab intellectu. Et ideo habitus perficiens intellectum ad hujusmodi veri considerationem vocatur *intellectus*, qui est habitus principiorum.

   Verum autem quod est per aliud notum, non statim percipitur ab intellectu, sed per inquisitionem rationis, et se habet in ratione termini. (Aquinas, *Summa Theologiae*, Ia, q. 84, a.2; my italics)

the former are 'principles' and are apprehended by understanding, while the latter constitute science. Aquinas' central point here is that self-evident propositions are known *immediately*. Consider a proposition like

(1) $2 + 1 = 3$

and contrast it with one like

(2) $281 \times 29 = 8{,}149$.

We know the first but not the second *immediately*: we know it, and we do not know it by way of inference from other propositions or on the basis of our knowledge of other propositions. Instead, we can simply see that it is true. Elsewhere Aquinas says that a proposition that is self-evident to us (*per se notam quod nos*) is such that we cannot grasp or apprehend it without believing, indeed, knowing it. (2), on the other hand, does not have this status for us; few of us can simply see that it is true. Instead we must resort to calculation; we go through a chain of inferences, the ultimate premises of which are self-evident.

Of course self-evident propositions are *known*, even though they do not consti-tute *scientia* in the strict sense. Indeed, their epistemic status, according to Aquinas, is higher than that of propositions known by demonstration. More exactly, *our* epistemic condition, in grasping a truth of this sort, is superior to the condition we are in with respect to a proposition of which we have knowledge by demonstration. The emerging picture of scientific knowledge, then, is the one to be found in Aristotle's *Posterior Analytics*: we know what is self-evident and what follows from what is self-evident by self-evident argument forms. Knowledge consists of *scientia* and *intellectus*, or understanding. By understanding we grasp first principles, self-evident truths; from these we infer or deduce further truths. What we know consists in what we find self-evident together with what we can infer from it by logical means. And if we take this picture seriously, it looks as if knowledge is restricted to what is necessarily true in the broadly logical sense.[25] Presumably a proposition is *per se nota* only if it is necessarily true, and any proposition that follows from necessary truths by self-evident argument forms will itself be necessarily true. As Aristotle puts it, 'Since the object of pure scientific knowledge cannot be other than it is, the truth obtained by demonstrative knowledge [Aquinas' *scientia*] will be necessary' (*Posterior Analytics*, I, 3).

As a picture of Aquinas' view of science, however, this is at best incomplete; for Aquinas obviously believes we have knowledge, scientific knowledge, of much that is not logically necessary. He thinks there is such a thing as natural science (*scientia naturalis*), whose subject matter is changeable material objects:

On the other hand there is the fact that demonstrative knowledge (*scientia*) is found in the intellect. Had the intellect no knowledge of material things, it could not have demonstrative

25. See Plantinga, *The Nature of Necessity*, chapter 1.

knowledge (*scientia*) of them. Thus there would be no natural science (*scientia naturalis*) dealing with changeable material beings. (ST, Ia, 84, 1)

Aquinas means to say, furthermore, not merely that in natural science we know some necessary truths about contingent and changeable objects (as we do in knowing, for example, that whatever is moved is moved by another); he means that among the truths we know are such contingent propositions as that there is a tree outside the window and that its branches are moving in the wind. There are two sorts of propositions whose truth we simply *see*. First, there are those that are self-evident, or *per se nota*; these are the object of *intellectus* or understanding, and we see their truth in the way in which we see that $2 + 1 = 3$. Second, there are propositions 'evident to the senses,' as he puts it: 'That some things move is evident to the senses' (ST, Ia, 2, 3), as is the proposition that the sun moves.[26] His examples of propositions evident to the senses are for the most part propositions whose truth we determine by *sight*. Although of course Aquinas did not think of vision as the only sense yielding knowledge, he did give it pride of place; because it is immaterial, he says, it is 'more of a knower' than the other senses. It is not easy to see just what Aquinas means by 'evident to the senses,' but perhaps the following is fairly close: a proposition is evident to the senses if we human beings have the power to determine its truth by looking at, listening to, tasting, touching, or smelling some physical object. Thus

(3) There is a tree outside my window,
(4) The cat on the mat is fuscous,

and

(5) This wall is yellow

are propositions evident to the senses.

In the first place, then, there are those propositions we simply see to be true; in the second place there are those propositions we see to follow from those in the first group. These propositions can be deduced from those in the first group by arguments we see to be valid.[27] So the basic picture of knowledge is this: we know what we see to be true together with what we can infer from what we see to be true by arguments we can see to be valid.

2. Aquinas on knowledge of God Now Aquinas believes that human beings (even in our earthly condition here below) can have knowledge, *scientific* knowledge, of God's existence, as well as knowledge that he has such attributes as simplicity, eternity, immateriality, immutability and the like. In *Summa Theologiae* Aquinas sets out his famous 'Five Ways,' or five proofs of God's existence: in *Summa Contra Gentiles* he sets out the proof from motion in much greater detail; and in each case he follows these alleged demonstrations with alleged demonstra-

---

26. Aquinas, *Summa Contra Gentiles* (hereafter 'SCG'), I, 13, 3.
27. That is, by arguments whose corresponding conditionals are self-evident to us.

tions that God possesses the attributes just mentioned. So natural knowledge of God is possible. But the vast majority of those who believe in God, he thinks, do not have knowledge of God's existence but must instead take it on faith. Only a few of us have the time, inclination, and ability to follow the theistic proofs; the rest of us take this truth on faith. And even though God's existence is demonstrable—even though we are capable of *knowing* it—nevertheless it is appropriately proposed to human beings as an object of faith. The reason, in brief, is that our welfare demands that we believe the proposition in question, but *knowledge* of it is exceedingly hard to come by:

For the rational truth about God would have appeared to only a few, and even so after a long time and mixed with many errors; whereas on knowing this depends our whole welfare, which is in God. (ST, Ia, I, 1)

From all this it is clear that, if it were necessary to use a strict demonstration as the only way to reach a knowledge of the things we must know about God, very few could ever construct such a demonstration and even these could do it only after a long time. From this it is evident that the provision of the way of faith, which gives all easy access to salvation at any time, is beneficial to man.[28]

So most of those who believe in God do so on faith. Fundamentally, for Aquinas, to accept a proposition on faith is to accept it on God's authority; faith is a matter of 'believing God' (ST, IIa, IIae, ii, 2): 'for that which is above reason we believe only because God has revealed it' (SCG, I, 9). Now what about those who believe in God on faith even though they do not know that God exists? How can that be a rational procedure? So far as I know, Aquinas does not explicitly address this question. He does discuss a closely related question, however: the question whether those who believe (take on faith) what is 'above reason' are irrational or foolish, or in his terms, 'believe with undue levity':

[1] Those who place their faith in this truth, however, 'for which the human reason offers no experimental evidence,' do not believe foolishly, as though 'following artificial fables' (2 Peter 1: 16). For these 'secrets of divine Wisdom' (Job 11: 6) the divine Wisdom itself, which knows all things to the full, has deigned to reveal to men. It reveals its own presence, as well as the truth of its teaching and inspiration, by fitting arguments; and in order to confirm those truths that exceed natural knowledge, it gives visible manifestation to works that surpass the ability of all nature. Thus, there are the wonderful cures of illnesses, there is the raising of the dead, and the wonderful immutation in the heavenly bodies; and what is more wonderful, there is the inspiration given to human minds, so that simple and untutored persons, filled with the gift of the Holy Spirit, come to possess instantaneously the highest wisdom and the readiest eloquence. When these arguments were examined, through the efficacy of the above-mentioned proof, and not the violent assault of arms or the promise of pleasures, and (what is most wonderful of all) in the midst of the tyranny of the persecutors, an innumerable throng of people, both simple and most learned, flocked to the Christian faith. In this faith there are truths preached that surpass every human intellect; the pleasures

28. Aquinas, *De Veritate*, question 14, article 10.

of the flesh are curbed; it is taught that the things of the world should be spurned. Now, for the minds of mortal men to assent to these things is the greatest of miracles, just as it is a manifest work of divine inspiration that, spurning visible things, men should seek only what is invisible. Now, that this has happened neither without preparation nor by chance, but as a result of the disposition of God, is clear from the fact that through many pronouncements of the ancient prophets God had foretold that He would do this. The books of these prophets are held in veneration among us Christians, since they give witness to our faith. (SCG, I, 6)

Here the point, I think, is the following. It is of course totally proper and entirely sensible to take a belief on God's say-so, to accept it on his authority. Clearly I am not foolish or irrational in believing something on the authority of my favorite mathematician, even if I cannot work it out for myself. I may thus come to believe, for example, that the four-color problem has been solved. But then a fortiori I would not be foolish or irrational in accepting a belief on the basis of *God's* authority. If I know that God proposes *p* to me for belief, then, clearly enough, it is eminently sensible to believe *p*. The question is not whether it is foolish to believe something on God's authority, but whether it is foolish to believe that God has in fact proposed a given item for my belief. Obviously, if he *has*, then I should believe it; but what is my reason or motive for supposing that in fact it is *God* who has proposed for our belief, for example, the teaching of the Trinity?

This is the question Aquinas addresses in the above passage; he means to argue that it is not foolish or irrational to take it that God has proposed for our belief just those items Christians suppose that he has—the articles of faith. What he means to say, I think, is that to believe in the mysteries of the faith is not to be foolish or to believe with undue levity, because we have *evidence for* the conclusion that God has proposed them for our belief. This evidence consists in the fulfillment of prophecy and in the signs and wonders accompanying the proclamation of these mysteries. Aquinas refers here to 'works that surpass the ability of all nature,' such as 'wonderful cures of illness,' 'the raising of the dead,' and the like. The greatest miracle of all, he says, is the marvelous rapidity with which the Christian faith has spread, despite the best efforts of tyrants and despite the fact that 'In this faith there are truths preached that surpass every human intellect; the pleasures of the flesh are curbed; it is taught that the things of the world should be spurned.'

I think he means to suggest, furthermore, that if we did *not* have this evidence, or some other evidence, we would be foolish or irrational in accepting the mysteries of the faith. It is just because we have evidence for these things that we are not irrational in accepting them. Here by way of contrast he cites the followers of Mohammed, who, he says, do not have evidence: 'It is thus clear that those who place any faith in his words believe foolishly' (SCG, I, 6).

What is important to see here is the following. Aquinas clearly believes that there are some propositions we are rationally justified in accepting, even though we do not have evidence for them, or reason to them from other propositions, or accept them on the basis of other propositions. Let us say that a proposition is *basic* for me if I believe it and do not believe it on the basis of other propositions. This relationship is familiar but hard to characterize in a revealing and nontrivial fashion. I believe that the word 'umbrageous' is spelled u-m-b-r-a-g-e-o-u-s: this belief is based on another belief of mine, the belief that that is how the dictionary says it is spelled. I believe that $72 \times 71 = 5112$. This belief is based upon several other beliefs I hold: that $1 \times 72 = 72$; $7 \times 2 = 14$; $7 \times 7 = 49$; $49 + 1 = 50$; and others. Some of my beliefs, however, I accept but do not accept on the basis of any other beliefs. Call these beliefs *basic*. I believe that $2 + 1 = 3$, for example, and do not believe it on the basis of other propositions. I also believe that I am seated at my desk, and that there is a mild pain in my right knee. These too are basic for me; I do not believe them on the basis of others. Now the propositions we are rationally justified in accepting as basic, thinks Aquinas, are the ones we see to be true: those that are self-evident or evident to the senses. As for the rest of the propositions we believe, we are rational in accepting them only if they stand in a certain relationship to those that are properly basic. Among the nonbasic propositions we rationally accept, some we see to follow from those that *are* basic; these are the propositions we know. Others are not known to us, do not follow from basic propositions, but are nonetheless rationally acceptable because they are *probable* or likely with respect to them. I believe Aquinas means to hold, more generally, that a proposition is rationally acceptable for us only if it is at least probable with respect to beliefs that are properly basic for us—that is, with respect to beliefs that are self-evident or evident to the senses. And hence on his view, as on the evidentialist objector's, belief in God is rational for us only if we have evidence for it.

B. Foundationalism

Aquinas and the evidentialist objector concur, then, in holding that belief in God is rationally acceptable only if there is evidence for it—only if, that is, it is probable with respect to some body of propositions that constitutes the evidence. And here we can get a better understanding of Aquinas and the evidentialist objector if we see them as accepting some version of *classical foundationalism*. This is a *picture* or total way of looking at faith, knowledge, justified belief, rationality, and allied topics. This picture has been enormously popular in Western thought; and despite a substantial opposing groundswell, I think it remains the dominant way of thinking about these topics. According to the foundationalist some propositions are properly basic and some are not; those that are not are rationally accepted only on the basis of *evidence*, where the evidence must trace back, ultimately, to what *is* properly basic. The existence of God, furthermore, is not among the propositions that are properly basic; hence a person is rational in accepting theistic belief only if he has evidence for it. The vast majority of those in the western world who have thought about our topic have accepted some form of classical foundationalism. The evidentialist objection to belief in God, furthermore, is obviously rooted in this way of looking at things. So suppose we try to achieve a deeper understanding of it.

Earlier I said the first thing to see about the evidentialist objection is that it is a *normative* contention or claim. The same thing must be said about foundational-ism: this thesis is a normative thesis, a thesis about how a system of beliefs *ought* to be structured, a thesis about the properties of a correct, or acceptable, or rightly structured system of beliefs. According to the foundationalist there are norms, or duties, or obligations with respect to belief just as there are with respect to actions. To conform to these duties and obligations is to be rational; to fail to measure up to them is to be irrational. To be rational, then, is to exercise one's epistemic powers *properly*—to exercise them in such a way as to go contrary to none of the norms for such exercise.

I think we can understand foundationalism more fully if we introduce the idea of a *noetic structure*. A person's noetic structure is the set of propositions he believes, together with certain epistemic relations that hold among him and these proposi-tions. As we have seen, some of my beliefs may be based upon others; it may be that there are a pair of propositions A and B such that I believe B, and believe A *on the basis of B*. An account of a person's noetic structure, then, would specify which of his beliefs are basic and which nonbasic. Of course it is abstractly possible that *none* of his beliefs is basic; perhaps he holds just three beliefs, A, B, and C, and believes each of them on the basis of the other two. We might think this improper or irrational, but that is not to say it could not be done. And it is also possible that *all* of his beliefs are basic; perhaps he believes a lot of propositions but does not believe any of them on the basis of any others. In the typical case, however, a noetic structure will include both basic and nonbasic beliefs. It may be useful to give some examples of beliefs that are often basic for a person. Suppose I seem to see a tree; I have that characteristic sort of experience that goes with perceiving a tree. I may then believe the proposition that I see a tree. It is *possible* that I believe that pro-position *on the basis of* the proposition that I seem to see a tree; in the typical case, however, I will not believe the former on the basis of the latter because in the typical case I will not believe the latter at all. I will not be paying any attention to my experience but will be concentrating on the tree. Of course I *can* turn my attention to my experience, notice how things look to me, and acquire the belief that I seem to see something that looks like *that*; and if you challenge my claim that I see a tree, perhaps I *will* thus turn my attention to my experience. But in the typical case I will not believe that I see a tree on the basis of a proposition about my experience; for I believe A on the basis of B only if I believe B, and in the typical case where I perceive a tree I do not believe (or entertain) any propositions about my experience. Typic-ally I take such a proposition as basic. Similarly, I believe I had breakfast this morning; this too is basic for me. I do not believe this proposition on the basis of some proposition about my experience—for example, that I seem to remember having had breakfast. In the typical case I will not have even considered *that* question—the question whether I *seem* to remember having had breakfast; instead I simply believe that I had breakfast; I take it as basic.

Second, an account of a noetic structure will include what we might call an index of *degree* of belief. I hold some of my beliefs much more firmly than others. I believe both that $2 + 1 = 3$ and that London, England, is north of Saskatoon, Saskatchewan; but I believe the former more resolutely than the latter. Some beliefs I hold with maximum firmness; others I do in fact accept, but in a much more tentative way.

Third, a somewhat vaguer notion: an account of S's noetic structure would include something like an index of *depth of ingression*. Some of my beliefs are, we might say, on the periphery of my noetic structure. I accept them, and may even accept them firmly, but I could give them up without much change elsewhere in my noetic structure. I believe there are some large boulders on the top of the Grand Teton. If I come to give up this belief (say by climbing it and not finding any), that change need not have extensive reverberations throughout the rest of my noetic structure; it could be accommodated with minimal alteration elsewhere. So its depth of ingression into my noetic structure is not great. On the other hand, if I were to come to believe that there simply is no such thing as the Grand Teton, or no mountains at all, or no such thing as the state of Wyoming, that would have much greater reverberations. And suppose I were to come to think there had not been much of a past (that the world was created just five minutes ago, complete with all its apparent memories and traces of the past) or that there were not any other persons: these changes would have even greater reverberations; these beliefs of mine have great depth of ingression into my noetic structure.

Now foundationalism is best construed, I think, as a thesis about *rational* noetic structures. A noetic structure is rational if it could be the noetic structure of a person who was completely rational. To be completely rational, as I am here using the term, is not to believe only what is true, or to believe all the logical consequences of what one believes, or to believe all necessary truths with equal firmness, or to be uninfluenced by emotion in forming belief; it is, instead, to do the right thing with respect to one's believings. It is to violate no epistemic duties. From this point of view, a rational person is one whose believings meet the appropriate standards; to criticize a person as irrational is to criticize her for failing to fulfill these duties or responsibilities, for failing to conform to the relevant norms or standards. To draw the ethical analogy, the irrational is the impermissible; the rational is the permissible.

A rational noetic structure, then, is one that could be the noetic structure of a wholly rational person; and foundationalism, as I say, is a thesis about such noetic structures. We may think of the foundationalist as beginning with the observation that some of our beliefs are based upon others. According to the foundationalist a rational noetic structure will *have a foundation*—a set of beliefs not accepted on the basis of others; in a rational noetic structure some beliefs will be basic. Nonbasic beliefs, of course, will be accepted on the basis of other beliefs, which may be accepted on the basis of still other beliefs, and so on until the foundations are reached. In a rational noetic structure, therefore, every nonbasic belief is ultimately accepted on the basis of basic beliefs.

According to the foundationalist, therefore, every rational noetic structure has a foundation, and all nonbasic beliefs are ultimately accepted on the basis of beliefs in the foundations. But a belief cannot properly be accepted on the basis of just *any* other belief; in a rational noetic structure, A will be accepted on the basis of B only if B *supports* A or is a member of a set of beliefs that together support A. It is not clear just what this relation—call it the 'supports' relation—is; and different foundationalists propose different candidates. Presumably, however, it lies in the neighborhood of *evidence*; if A supports B, then A is evidence for B, or makes B evident; or perhaps B is likely or probable with respect to B. This relation admits of degrees. My belief that Feike can swim is supported by my knowledge that nine out of ten Frisians can swim and Feike is a Frisian; it is supported more strongly by my knowledge that the evening paper contains a picture of Feike triumphantly finishing first in the fifteen-hundred meter freestyle in the 1980 summer Olympics. And the foundationalist holds, sensibly enough, that in a rational noetic structure the strength of a nonbasic belief will depend upon the degree of support from foundational beliefs.

By way of summary, then, let us say that according to foundationalism: (1) in a rational noetic structure the believed-on-the-basis-of relation is asymmetric and irreflexive, (2) a rational noetic structure has a foundation, and (3) in a rational noetic structure nonbasic belief is proportional in strength to support from the foundations.

C. Conditions on proper basicality

Next we note a further and fundamental feature of classic varieties of foundationalism: they all lay down certain conditions of proper basicality. From the foundationalist point of view not just any kind of belief can be found in the foundations of a rational noetic structure; a belief to be properly basic (that is, basic in a rational noetic structure) must meet certain conditions. It must be capable of functioning foundationally, capable of bearing its share of the weight of the whole noetic structure. Thus Thomas Aquinas, as we have seen, holds that a proposition is properly basic for a person only if it is self-evident to him or 'evident to the senses.'

Suppose we take a brief look at self-evidence. Under what conditions does a proposition have it? What kinds of propositions are self-evident? Examples would include very simple arithmetical truths such as

(6) $2 + 1 = 3$;

simple truths of logic such as

(7) No man is both married and unmarried;

perhaps the generalizations of simple truths of logic, such as

(8) For any proposition p the conjunction of p with its denial is false;

and certain propositions expressing identity and diversity; for example,

(9)   Redness is distinct from greenness,

(10) The property of being prime is distinct from the property of being composite,

and

(11) The proposition *all men are mortal* is distinct from the proposition *all mortals are men.*

There are others; Aquinas gives as examples:

(12) The whole is greater than the part,

where, presumably, he means by 'part' what we mean by 'proper part,' and, more dubiously,

(13) Man is an animal.

Still other candidates—candidates which may be less than entirely uncontroversial—come from many other areas; for example,

(14) If p is necessarily true and p entails q, then q is necessarily true,

(15) If e^1 occurs before e^2 and e^2 occurs before e^3, then e^1 occurs before e^3,

and

(16) It is wrong to cause unnecessary (and unwanted) pain just for the fun of it.

What is it that characterizes these propositions? According to the tradition the outstanding characteristic of a self-evident proposition is that one simply sees it to be true upon grasping or understanding it. Understanding a self-evident proposition is sufficient for apprehending its truth. Of course this notion must be relativized to *persons*; what is self-evident to you might not be to me. Very simple arithmetical truths will be self-evident to nearly all of us, but a truth like $17 + 18 = 35$ may be self-evident only to some. And of course a proposition is self-evident to a person only if he does in fact grasp it, so a proposition will not be self-evident to those who do not apprehend the concepts it involves. As Aquinas says, some propositions are self-evident only to the learned; his example is the truth that immaterial substances do not occupy space. Among those propositions whose concepts not everyone grasps, some are such that anyone who *did* grasp them would see their truth; for example,

(17) A model of a first-order theory T assigns truth to the axioms of T.

Others—$17 + 13 = 30$, for example—may be such that some but not all of those who apprehend them also see that they are true.

But how shall we understand this 'seeing that they are true'? Those who speak of self-evidence explicitly turn to this visual metaphor and expressly explain self-evidence by reference to vision. There are two important aspects to the metaphor and two corresponding components to the idea of self-evidence. First, there is the *epistemic* component: a proposition *p* is self-evident to a person *S* only if *S* has *immediate* knowledge of *p*—that is, knows *p*, and does not know *p* on the basis of his knowledge of other propositions. Consider a simple arithmetic truth such as $2 + 1 = 3$ and compare it with one like $24 \times 24 = 576$. I know each of these propositions, and I know the second but not the first on the basis of computation, which is a kind of inference. So I have immediate knowledge of the first but not the second.

But there is also a phenomenological component. Consider again our two propositions; the first but not the second has about it a kind of luminous aura or glow when you bring it to mind or consider it. Locke speaks, in this connection, of an 'evident luster'; a self-evident proposition, he says, displays a kind of 'clarity and brightness to the attentive mind.' Descartes speaks instead of 'clarity and distinctness'; each, I think, is referring to the same phenomenological feature. And this feature is connected with another: upon understanding a proposition of this sort one feels a strong inclination to accept it; this luminous obviousness seems to compel or at least impel assent. Aquinas and Locke, indeed, held that a person, or at any rate a normal, well-formed human being, finds it impossible to withhold assent when considering a self-evident proposition. The phenomenological component of the idea of self-evidence, then, seems to have a double aspect: there is the luminous aura that $2 + 1 = 3$ displays, and there is also an experienced tendency to accept or believe it. Perhaps, indeed, the luminous aura *just is* the experienced impulsion toward acceptance; perhaps these are the very same thing. In that case the phenomenological component would not have the double aspect I suggested it did have; in either case, however, we must recognize this phenomenological aspect of self-evidence.

Aquinas therefore holds that self-evident propositions are properly basic. I think he means to add that propositions 'evident to the senses' are also properly basic. By this latter term I think he means to refer to *perceptual* propositions—propositions whose truth or falsehood we can determine by looking or employing some other sense. He has in mind, I think, such propositions as

(18) There is a tree before me,
(19) I am wearing shoes,

and

(20) That tree's leaves are yellow.

So Aquinas holds that a proposition is properly basic if and only if it is either self-evident or evident to the senses. Other foundationalists have insisted that propositions basic in a rational noetic structure must be *certain* in some important sense. Thus it is plausible to see Descartes as holding that the foundations of a rational noetic structure include, not such propositions as (18)–(20), but more cautious claims—claims about one's own mental life; for example,

(21) It seems to me that I see a tree,

(22) I seem to see something green,

or, as Professor Chisholm puts it,

(23) I am appeared greenly to.

Propositions of this latter sort seem to enjoy a kind of immunity from error not enjoyed by those of the former. I could be mistaken in thinking I see a pink rat; perhaps I am hallucinating or the victim of an illusion. But it is at the least very much harder to see that I could be mistaken in believing that I *seem* to see a pink rat, in believing that I am appeared pinkly (or pink ratly) to. Suppose we say that a proposition with respect to which I enjoy this sort of immunity from error is incorrigible for me; then perhaps Descartes means to hold that a proposition is properly basic for S only if it is either self-evident or incorrigible for S.

By way of explicit definition:

(24) *p* is incorrigible for S if and only if (a) it is not possible that S believe *p* and *p* be false, and (b) it is not possible that S believe ~*p* and *p* be true.

Here we have a further characteristic of foundationalism: the claim that not just any proposition is properly basic. Ancient and medieval foundationalists tended to hold that a proposition is properly basic for a person only if it is either self-evident or evident to the senses: modern foundationalists—Descartes, Locke, Leibniz, and the like—tended to hold that a proposition is properly basic for S only if either self-evident or incorrigible for S. Of course this is a historical generalization and is thus perilous; but perhaps it is worth the risk. And now let us say that a *classical foundationalist* is any one who is either an ancient and medieval or a modern foundationalist.

D. The collapse of foundationalism

Now suppose we return to the main question: Why should not belief in God be among the foundations of my noetic structure? The answer, on the part of the classical foundationalist, was that even if this belief is *true* it does not have the characteristics a proposition must have to deserve a place in the foundations. There is no room in the foundations for a proposition that can be rationally accepted only on the basis of other propositions. The only properly basic propositions are those that are self-evident or incorrigible or evident to the senses. Since the proposition that God exists is none of the above, it is not properly basic for anyone; that is, no well-formed, rational noetic structure contains this proposition in its foundations. But now we must take a closer look at this fundamental principle of classical foundationalism:

(25) A proposition *p* is properly basic for a person S if and only if *p* is either self-evident to S or incorrigible for S or evident to the senses for S.

(25) contains two claims: first, a proposition is properly basic *if* it is self-evident,

incorrigible, or evident to the senses, and, second, a proposition is properly basic *only if* it meets this condition. The first seems true enough; suppose we concede it. But what is to be said for the second? Is there any reason to accept it? Why does the foundationalist accept it? Why does he think the theist ought to?

We should note first that if this thesis, and the correlative foundationalist thesis that a proposition is rationally acceptable only if it follows from or is probable with respect to what is properly basic—if these claims are true, then enormous quantities of what we all in fact believe are irrational. One crucial lesson to be learned from the development of modern philosophy—Descartes through Hume, roughly—is just this: relative to propositions that are self-evident and incorrigible, most of the beliefs that form the stock in trade of ordinary everyday life are not probable—at any rate there is no reason to think they are probable. Consider all those propositions that entail, say, that there are enduring physical objects, or that there are persons distinct from myself, or that the world has existed for more than five minutes: none of these propositions, I think, is more probable than not with respect to what is self-evident or incorrigible for me; at any rate no one has given good reason to think any of them is. And now suppose we add to the foundations propositions that are evident to the senses, thereby moving from modern to ancient and medieval foundationalism. Then propositions entailing the existence of material objects will of course be probable with respect to the foundations, because included therein. But the same cannot be said either for propositions about the past or for propositions entailing the existence of persons distinct from myself; as before, these will not be probable with respect to what is properly basic.

And does not this show that the thesis in question is false? The contention is that

(26) *A* is properly basic for me only if *A* is self-evident or incorrigible or evident to the senses for me.

But many propositions that do not meet these conditions *are* properly basic for me. I believe, for example, that I had lunch this noon. I do not believe this proposition on the basis of other propositions; I take it as basic; it is in the foundations of my noetic structure. Furthermore, I am entirely rational in so taking it, even though this proposition is neither self-evident nor evident to the senses nor incorrigible for me. Of course this may not convince the foundationalist; he may think that in fact I do *not* take that proposition as basic, or perhaps he will bite the bullet and maintain that if I really *do* take it as basic, then the fact is I *am*, so far forth, irrational.

Perhaps the following will be more convincing. According to the classical foundationalist (call him *F*) a person *S* is rational in accepting (26) only if either (26) is properly basic (self-evident or incorrigible or evident to the senses) for him, or he believes (26) on the basis of propositions that are properly basic for him and support (26). Now presumably if *F* knows of some support for (26) from propositions that are self-evident or evident to the senses or incorrigible, he will be able to provide a good argument—deductive, inductive, probabilistic or whatever—whose premises are self-evident or evident to the senses or incorrigible and whose conclusion is (26). So far as I know, no foundationalist has provided such an argument. It therefore appears that the foundationalist does not know of any support for (26) from propositions that are (on his account) properly basic. So if he is to be rational in accepting (26), he must (on his own account) accept it as basic. But according to (26) itself, (26) is properly basic for F only if (26) is self-evident or incorrigible or evident to the senses for him. Clearly (26) meets none of these conditions. Hence it is not properly basic for F. But then F is self-referentially inconsistent in accepting (26); he accepts (26) as basic, despite the fact that (26) does not meet the condition for proper basicality that (26) itself lays down.

Furthermore, (26) is either false or such that in accepting it the foundationalist is violating his epistemic responsibilities. For F does not know of any argument or evidence for (26) Hence if it is true, he will be violating his epistemic responsibilities in accepting it. So (26) is either false or such that F cannot rationally accept it. Still further, if the theist were to accept (26) at the foundationalist's urging but without argument, he would be adding to his noetic structure a proposition that is either false or such that in accepting it he violates his noetic responsibilities. But if there is such a thing as the ethics of belief, surely it will proscribe believing a proposition one knows to be either false or such that one ought not to believe it. Accordingly, I ought not to accept (26) in the absence of argument from premises that meet the condition it lays down. The same goes for the foundationalist: if he cannot find such an argument for (26), he ought to give it up. Furthermore, he ought not to urge and I ought not to accept any objection to theistic belief that crucially depends upon a proposition that is true only if I ought not believe it.

Nearly everyone accepts as basic some propositions entailing the existence of other persons and some propositions about the past; not nearly everyone accepts the existence of God as basic. Struck by this fact, we might propose:

(27) p is properly basic for S if and only if p is self-evident or incorrigible or evident to the senses for S, or is accepted as basic by nearly everyone.

There are problems with (27). It is meant to legitimize my taking as basic such deliverances of memory as that I had lunch this noon; but not nearly everyone takes that proposition as basic. Most of you, I daresay, have not so much as given it a thought; you are much too busy thinking about your own lunch to think about mine. So (27) will not do the job as it stands. That is of no real consequence, however; for even if we had an appropriate statement of (27), it would suffer from the same sort of malady as does (26). Not nearly everyone takes (27) as basic; I do not, for example. Nor is it self-evident, incorrigible, or evident to the senses. So unless we can find an argument for it from propositions that meet the conditions it lays down, we shall, if we believe it, be believing a proposition that is probably either false or such that we ought not believe it. Therefore we ought not believe it, at least until someone produces such an argument for it.

Now we could continue to canvass other revisions of (26), and in Part III I shall look into the proper procedure for discovering and justifying such criteria for proper basicality. It is evident, however, that classical foundationalism is bankrupt, and insofar as the evidentialist objection is rooted in classical foundationalism, it is poorly rooted indeed.

Of course the evidentialist objection *need* not presuppose classical foundationalism; someone who accepted quite a different version of foundationalism could no doubt urge this objection. But in order to evaluate it, we should have to see what criterion of proper basicality was being invoked. In the absence of such specification the objection remains at best a promissory note. So far as the present discussion goes, then, the next move is up to the evidentialist objector. He must specify a criterion for proper basicality that is free from self-referential difficulties, rules out belief in God as properly basic, and is such that there is some reason to think it is true.

Part III: The reformed objection to natural theology

Suppose we think of natural theology as the attempt to prove or demonstrate the existence of God. This enterprise has a long and impressive history—a history stretching back to the dawn of Christendom and boasting among its adherents many of the truly great thinkers of the Western world. One thinks, for example, of Anselm, Aquinas, Scotus, and Ockham, of Descartes, Spinoza, and Leibniz. Recently—since the time of Kant, perhaps—the tradition of natural theology has not been as overwhelming as it once was; yet it continues to have able defenders both within and without officially Catholic philosophy.

Many Christians, however, have been less than totally impressed. In particular Reformed or Calvinist theologians have for the most part taken a dim view of this enterprise. A few Reformed thinkers—B. B. Warfield, for example—endorse the theistic proofs, but for the most part the Reformed attitude has ranged from tepid endorsement, through indifference, to suspicion, hostility, and outright accusations of blasphemy. And this stance is initially puzzling. It looks a little like the attitude some Christians adopt toward faith healing: it can't be done, but even if it could it shouldn't be. What exactly, or even approximately, do these sons and daughters of the Reformation have against proving the existence of God? What *could* they have against it? What could be less objectionable to any but the most obdurate atheist?

A. The objection initially stated

By way of answering this question, I want to consider three representative Reformed thinkers. Let us begin with the nineteenth-century Dutch theologian Herman Bavinck:

A distinct natural theology, obtained apart from any revelation, merely through observation and study of the universe in which man lives, does not exist. . . .

Scripture urges us to behold heaven and earth, birds and ants, flowers and lilies, in order that we may see and recognize God in them. 'Lift up your eyes on high, and see who hath created these.' Is. 40: 26. Scripture does not reason in the abstract. It does not make God the conclusion of a syllogism, leaving it to us whether we think the argument holds or not. But it speaks with authority. Both theologically and religiously it proceeds from God as the starting point.

We receive the impression that belief in the existence of God is based entirely upon these proofs. But indeed that would be 'a wretched faith, which, before it invokes God, must first prove his existence.' The contrary, however, is the truth. There is not a single object the existence of which we hesitate to accept until definite proofs are furnished. Of the existence of self, of the world round about us, of logical and moral laws, etc., we are so deeply convinced because of the indelible impressions which all these things make upon our consciousness that we need no arguments or demonstration. Spontaneously, altogether involuntarily: without any constraint or coercion, we accept that existence. Now the same is true in regard to the existence of God. The so-called proofs are by no means the final grounds of our most certain conviction that God exists. This certainty is established only by faith; that is, by the spontaneous testimony which forces itself upon us from every side.[29]

According to Bavinck, then, belief in the existence of God is not based upon proofs or arguments. By 'argument' here I think he means arguments in the style of natural theology—the sort given by Aquinas and Scotus and later by Descartes, Leibniz, Clarke, and others. And what he means to say, I think, is that Christians do not *need* such arguments. Do not need them for what?

Here I think Bavinck means to hold two things. First, arguments or proofs are not, in general, the source of the believer's confidence in God. Typically the believer does not believe in God on the basis of arguments; nor does he believe such truths as that God has created the world on the basis of arguments. Second, argument is not needed for *rational justification*; the believer is entirely within his epistemic right in believing, for example, that God has created the world, even if he has no argument at all for that conclusion. The believer does not need natural theology in order to achieve rationality or epistemic propriety in believing; his belief in God can be perfectly rational even if he knows of no cogent argument, deductive or inductive, for the existence of God—indeed, even if there is no such argument.

Bavinck has three further points. First he means to add, I think, that we cannot come to knowledge of God on the basis of argument; the arguments of natural theology just do not work. (And he follows this passage with a more or less traditional attempt to refute the theistic proofs, including an endorsement of some of Kant's fashionable confusions about the ontological argument.) Second, Scripture 'proceeds from God as the starting point,' and so should the believer. There is

29. Herman Bavinck, *The Doctrine of God*, tr. William Hendricksen (Grand Rapids: Eerdmans, 1951), pp. 78–9. *The Doctrine of God* is the translation of the second volume of Bavinck's *Gereformeede Dogmatiek*, published 1895–9.

nothing by way of proofs or arguments for God's existence in the Bible; that is simply presupposed. The same should be true of the Christian believer then; he should *start* from belief in God rather than from the premises of some argument whose conclusion is that God exists. What is it that makes those premises a better starting point anyway? And third, Bavinck points out that belief in God relevantly resembles belief in the existence of the self and of the external world—and, we might add, belief in other minds and the past. In none of these areas do we typically *have* proof or arguments, or *need* proofs or arguments.

Suppose we turn next to John Calvin, who is as good a Calvinist as any. According to Calvin God has implanted in us all an innate tendency, or nisus, or disposition to believe in him:

'There is within the human mind, and indeed by natural instinct, an awareness of divinity.' This we take to be beyond controversy. To prevent anyone from taking refuge in the pretense of ignorance, God himself has implanted in all men a certain understanding of his divine majesty. Ever renewing its memory, he repeatedly sheds fresh drops. Since, therefore, men one and all perceive that there is a God and that he is their Maker, they are condemned by their own testimony because they have failed to honor him and to consecrate their lives to his will. If ignorance of God is to be looked for anywhere, surely one is most likely to find an example of it among the more backward folk and those more remote from civilization. Yet there is, as the eminent pagan says, no nation so barbarous, no people so savage, that they have not a deep-seated conviction that there is a God. So deeply does the common conception occupy the minds of all, so tenaciously does it inhere in the hearts of all! Therefore, since from the beginning of the world there has been no region, no city, in short, no household, that could do without religion, there lies in this a tacit confession of a sense of deity inscribed in the hearts of all.

Indeed, the perversity of the impious, who though they struggle furiously are unable to extricate themselves from the fear of God, is abundant testimony that this conviction, namely, that *there is some God*, is naturally inborn in all, and is fixed deep within, as it were in the very marrow. . . . From this we conclude *that it is not a doctrine that must first be learned in school* but one of which each of us is master from his mother's womb and which nature itself permits no one to forget.[30]

Calvin's claim, then, is that God has created us in such a way that we have a strong tendency or inclination toward belief in him. This tendency has been in part overlaid or suppressed by sin. Were it not for the existence of sin in the world, human beings would believe in God to the same degree and with the same natural spontaneity that we believe in the existence of other persons, an external world, or the past. This is the natural human condition; it is because of our presently unnatural sinful condition that many of us find belief in God difficult or absurd. The fact is, Calvin thinks, one who does not believe in God is in an epistemically substandard position—rather like a man who does not believe that his wife exists, or thinks she is like a cleverly constructed robot and has no thoughts, feelings, or consciousness.

---

30. John Calvin, *Institutes of the Christian Religion*, tr. Ford Lewis Battles (Philadelphia: Westminster Press, 1960), book 1, chapter 3, pp. 43–4.

Although this disposition to believe in God is partially suppressed, it is nonetheless universally present. And it is triggered or actuated by a widely realized condition:

Lest anyone, then, be excluded from access to happiness, he not only sowed in men's minds that seed of religion of which we have spoken, but revealed himself and daily discloses himself in the whole workmanship of the universe. As a consequence, men cannot open their eyes without being compelled to see him. (p. 1)

Like Kant, Calvin is especially impressed in this connection, by the marvelous compages of the starry heavens above:

Even the common folk and the most untutored, who have been taught only by the aid of the eyes, cannot be unaware of the excellence of divine art, for it reveals itself in this innumerable and yet distinct and well-ordered variety of the heavenly host. (p. 50)

And Calvin's claim is that one who accedes to this tendency and in these circumstances accepts the belief that God has created the world—perhaps upon beholding the starry heavens, or the splendid majesty of the mountains, or the intricate, articulate beauty of a tiny flower—is entirely within his epistemic rights in so doing. It is not that such a person is justified or rational in so believing by virtue of having an implicit argument—some version of the teleological argument, say. No; he does not need any argument for justification or rationality. His belief need not be based on any other propositions at all; under these conditions he is perfectly rational in accepting belief in God in the utter absence of any argument, deductive or inductive. Indeed, a person in these conditions, says Calvin, *knows* that God exists.

Elsewhere Calvin speaks of 'arguments from reason' or rational arguments:

The prophets and apostles do not boast either of their keenness or of anything that obtains credit for them as they speak; nor do they dwell upon rational proofs. Rather, they bring forward God's holy name, that by it the whole world may be brought into obedience to him. Now we ought to see how apparent it is not only by plausible opinion but by clear truth that they do not call upon God's name heedlessly or falsely. If we desire to provide in the best way for our consciences—that they may not be perpetually beset by the instability of doubt or vacillation, and that they may not also boggle at the smallest quibbles—we ought to seek our conviction in a higher place than human reasons, judgments, or conjectures, that is, in the secret testimony of the Spirit. (book 1, chapter 7, p. 78)

Here the subject for discussion is not belief in the existence of God, but belief that God is the author of the Scriptures; I think it is clear, however, that Calvin would say the same thing about belief in God's existence. The Christian does not *need* natural theology, either as the source of his confidence or to justify his belief. Furthermore, the Christian *ought* not to believe on the basis of argument; if he does, his faith is likely to be 'unstable and wavering,' the 'subject of perpetual doubt.' If my belief in God is based on argument, then if I am to be properly rational, epistemically responsible, I shall have to keep checking the philosophical journals to see whether, say, Antony Flew has finally come up with a good objection to my favorite argument. This could be bothersome and time-consuming; and what do I do if someone does find a flaw in my argument? Stop going to church? From Calvin's point of view believing in the existence of God on the basis of rational argument is like believing in the existence of your spouse on the basis of the analogical argument for other minds—whimsical at best and unlikely to delight the person concerned.

B. The Barthian dilemma

The twentieth-century theologian Karl Barth is particularly scathing in his disapproval of natural theology. *That* he disapproves is overwhelmingly clear. His *reasons* for thus disapproving, however, are much less clear; his utterances on this topic, as on others, are fascinating but Delphic in everything but length. Sometimes, indeed, he is outrageous, as when he suggests that the mere act of believing or accepting the Christian message is a manifestation of human pride, self-will, contumacy, and sin. Elsewhere, however, he is both more moderate and thoroughly intriguing:

Now suppose the partner in the conversation [that is, natural theology] discovers that faith is trying to use the well-known artifice of dialectic in relation to him. We are not taking him seriously because we withhold from him what we really want to say and represent. It is only in appearance that we devote ourselves to him, and therefore what we say to him is only an apparent and unreal statement. What will happen then? Well, not without justice—although misconstruing the friendly intention which perhaps motivates us—he will see himself despised and deceived. He will shut himself up and harden himself against the faith which does not speak out frankly, which deserts its own standpoint for the standpoint of unbelief. What use to unbelief is a faith which obviously knows different? And how shocking for unbelief is faith which only pretends to take up with unbelief a common position. . . . This dilemma betrays the inner contradiction in every form of a 'Christian' natural theology. It must really represent and affirm the standpoint of faith. Its true objective to which it really wants to lead unbelief is the knowability of the real God through Himself in his revelation. But as a 'natural' theology, its initial aim is to disguise this and therefore to pretend to share in the life-endeavour of natural man. It therefore thinks that it should appear to engage in the dialectic of unbelief in the expectation that here at least a preliminary decision in regard to faith can and must be reached. Therefore, as a natural theology it speaks and acts improperly. . . . We cannot experiment with unbelief, even if we think we know and possess all sorts of interesting and very promising possibilities and recipes for it. We must treat unbelief seriously. Only one thing can be treated more seriously than unbelief; and that is faith itself—or rather, the real God in whom faith believes. But faith itself—or rather, the real God in whom faith believes—must be taken so seriously that there is no place at all for even an apparent transposition to the standpoint of unbelief, for the pedagogic and playful self-lowering into the sphere of its possibilities.[31]

31. Karl Barth, *Church Dogmatics*, tr. G. T. Thompson and Harold Knight (Edinburgh: T & T Clark, 1956), volume 1, part 1, pp. 93–5.

We must try to penetrate a bit deeper into these objections to natural theology, and suppose we start with Barth. Precisely what is the objection to which he is pointing? That somehow it is improper or un-Christian or dishonest or impious to try to prove God's existence; but *how* exactly? Barth speaks here of a *dilemma* that confronts the natural theologian. Dilemmas have horns; what are the horns of this one? The following, I think. In presenting a piece of natural theology, either the believer must adopt what Barth calls 'the standpoint of unbelief' or he must pretend to his unbelieving interlocutor to do so. If he does the former, he deserts his Christian standpoint; but if he does the latter, he is dishonest, in bad faith, professing to believe what in fact he does not believe. But what *is* the standpoint of unbelief and what is it to adopt it? And how could one fall into this standpoint just by working at natural theology, just by making a serious attempt to prove the existence of God?

Perhaps Barth is thinking along the following lines. In *arguing* about the existence of God, in attempting to prove it, one implicitly adopts a certain stance. In adopting this stance one presupposes that it is not yet known whether there is a God; that remains to be seen; that is what is up for discussion. In adopting this stance, furthermore, the natural theologian implicitly concedes that what one ought to believe here depends on the result of the inquiry; if there are good arguments *for* the existence of God, then we—that is, we believers and unbelievers who together are engaged in this inquiry—ought to accept God's existence; if there are good arguments *against* the existence of God, we ought to accept its denial; and if the arguments on both sides are equally strong (and equally weak) then perhaps the right thing to do is to remain agnostic.

In adopting this stance one concedes that the rightness or propriety of belief and unbelief depends upon the outcome of a certain inquiry. Belief in God is right and proper only if there is on balance better reason to believe than not to believe—only if, that is, the arguments for the existence of God are stronger than those against it. But of course an inquiry has a starting point, and arguments have premises. In supposing the issue thus dependent upon the outcome of argument, one supposes the appropriate premises are available. What about these premises? In adopting this stance the natural theologian implicitly commits himself to the view that there is a certain set of propositions from which the premises of theistic and antitheistic arguments are to be drawn—a set of propositions such that belief in God is rational or proper only if it stands in the right relation to that set. He concurs with his unbelieving interlocutor that there is a set of propositions both can appeal to, a set of propositions accepted by all or nearly all rational persons; and the propriety or rightness of belief in God depends on its relation to these propositions.

What are these propositions and where do they come from? We shall have to enter that question more deeply later; for the moment let us call them 'the deliverances of reason.' Then to *prove* or *demonstrate* that God exists is to exhibit a deductive argument whose conclusion is that God exists, whose premises are drawn from the deliverances of reason, and each of whose steps is by way of an argument whose corresponding conditional is among the deliverances of reason. Aquinas' first three ways would be attempts to demonstrate the existence of God in just this sense. A demonstration that God does not exist, of course, would be structurally isomorphic; it would meet the second and third condition just mentioned but have as conclusion the proposition that there is no such person as God. An alleged example would be the deductive argument from evil—the claim that the existence of evil is among the deliverances of reason and is inconsistent with the existence of God.

Of course it might be that the existence of God does not thus follow from the deliverances of reason but is nonetheless *probable* or *likely* with respect to them. One could then give a probabilistic or inductive argument for the existence of God, thus showing that theistic belief is rational, or epistemically proper, in that it is more likely than not with respect to the deliverances of reason. Perhaps Aquinas' Fifth Way and Paley's argument from design can be seen as falling into this category, and perhaps the probabilistic argument from evil—the claim that it is unlikely that God exists, given all the evil there is—can then be seen as a structurally similar argument for the conclusion that unbelief is the proper attitude.

According to Barth, then, the natural theologian implicitly concedes that the propriety of belief in God is to be tested by its relationship to the deliverances of reason. Belief is right, or rational, or rationally acceptable only if it stands in the proper relationship to the deliverances of reason—only if, for example, it is more likely than not or at any rate not unlikely with respect to them.

Now to adopt the standpoint of unbelief is not, as Barth sees it, to reject belief in God. One who enthusiastically accepts and believes in the existence of God can nonetheless be in the standpoint of unbelief. To be in that standpoint it is sufficient to hold that belief in God is rationally permissible for a person *only if he or she has a good argument for it.* To be in the standpoint of unbelief is to hold that belief in God is rationally acceptable *only if it is more likely than not with respect to the deliverances of reason.* One who holds this belief, says Barth, is in the standpoint of unbelief; his ultimate commitment is to the deliverances of reason rather than to God. Such a person 'makes reason a judge over Christ,' or at any rate over the Christian faith. And to do so, says Barth, is utterly improper for a Christian.

The horns of the Barthian dilemma, then, are bad faith or dishonesty on the one hand and the standpoint of unbelief on the other. Either the natural theologian accepts the standpoint of unbelief or he does not. In the latter case he misleads and deceives his unbelieving interlocutor and thus falls into bad faith. In the former case he makes his ultimate commitment to the deliverances of reason, a posture that is for a Christian totally inappropriate, a manifestation of sinful human pride.

And this attempt to prove the existence of God certainly cannot end in any other way than with the affirmation that even apart from God's grace, already preceding God's grace, already anticipating it, he is ready for God, so that God is knowable to him otherwise than from and through himself. Not only does it end with this. In principle, it begins with it. For in what does it consist but in the arrogation, preservation and affirmation of the self-sufficiency of man and therefore his likeness with God? (p. 135)

C. Rejecting classical foundationalism

Now I think the natural theologian has a sound response to Barth's dilemma: she can execute the maneuver known to dialectician and matador alike as 'escaping between the horns.' As a natural theologian she offers or endorses theistic arguments, but why suppose that her own belief in God must be based upon such argument? And if it is not, why suppose she must pretend that it is? Perhaps her aim is to point out to the unbeliever that belief in God follows from other things he already believes, so that he can continue in unbelief (and continue to accept these other beliefs) only on pain of inconsistency. We may hope this knowledge will lead him to give up his unbelief, but in any event she can tell him quite frankly that her belief in God is not based on its relation to the deliverances of reason. Indeed, she can follow Calvin in claiming that belief in God *ought* not to be based on arguments from the deliverances of reason or anywhere else. So even if 'the standpoint of unbelief' is as reprehensible as Barth says it is, his dilemma seems to evaporate.

What is most interesting here is not Barth's claim that the natural theologian faces this dilemma; here he is probably wrong, or at any rate not clearly right. More interesting is his view that belief in God need not be based on argument. Barth joins Calvin and Bavinck in holding that the believer in God is entirely within his rights in believing as he does even if he does not know of any good theistic argument (deductive or inductive), even if he does not believe there is any such argument, and even if in fact no such argument exists. Like Calvin, Kuyper, and Bavinck, Barth holds that belief in God is *properly basic*—that is, such that it is rational to accept it without accepting it on the basis of any other propositions or beliefs at all. In fact, they think the Christian ought not to accept belief in God on the basis of argument; to do so is to run the risk of a faith that is unstable and wavering, subject to all the wayward whim and fancy of the latest academic fashion. What the Reformers held was that a believer is entirely rational, entirely within his epistemic rights, in *starting with* belief in God, in accepting it as basic, and in taking it as premise for argument to other conclusions.

In rejecting natural theology, therefore, these Reformed thinkers mean to say first of all that the propriety or rightness of belief in God in no way depends upon the success or availability of the sort of theistic arguments that form the natural theologian's stock in trade. I think this is their central claim here, and their central insight. As these Reformed thinkers see things, one who takes belief in God as basic is not thereby violating any epistemic duties or revealing a defect in his noetic structure; quite the reverse. The correct or proper way to believe in God, they thought, was not on the basis of arguments from natural theology or anywhere else; the correct way is to take belief in God as basic.

I spoke earlier of classical foundationalism, a view that incorporates the following three theses:

(1) In every rational noetic structure there is a set of beliefs taken as basic—that is, not accepted on the basis of any other beliefs,

(2) In a rational noetic structure nonbasic belief is proportional to support from the foundations,

and

(3) In a rational noetic structure basic beliefs will be self-evident or incorrigible or evident to the senses.

Now I think these three Reformed thinkers should be understood as rejecting classical foundationalism. They may have been inclined to accept (1); they show no objection to (2); but they were utterly at odds with the idea that the foundations of a rational noetic structure can at most include propositions that are self-evident or evident to the senses or incorrigible. In particular, they were prepared to insist that a rational noetic structure can include belief in God as basic. As Bavinck put it, 'Scripture . . . does not make God the conclusion of a syllogism, leaving it to us whether we think the argument holds or not. But it speaks with authority. Both theologically and religiously it proceeds from God as the starting point' (above, p. 75). And of course Bavinck means to say that we must emulate Scripture here.

In the passages I quoted earlier, Calvin claims the believer does not need argument—does not need it, among other things, for epistemic respectability. We may understand him as holding, I think, that a rational noetic structure may very well contain belief in God among its foundations. Indeed, he means to go further, and in two separate directions. In the first place he thinks a Christian *ought* not to believe in God on the basis of other propositions; a proper and well-formed Christian noetic structure will *in fact* have belief in God among its foundations. And in the second place Calvin claims that one who takes belief in God as basic can *know* that God exists. Calvin holds that one can *rationally accept* belief in God as basic; he also claims that one can *know* that God exists even if he has no argument, even if he does not believe on the basis of other propositions. A foundationalist is likely to hold that some properly basic beliefs are such that anyone who accepts them *knows* them. More exactly, he is likely to hold that among the beliefs properly basic for a person S, some are such that if S accepts them, S knows them. He could go on to say that *other* properly basic beliefs cannot be known if taken as basic, but only rationally believed; and he might think of the existence of God as a case in point. Calvin will have none of this; as he sees it, one needs no arguments to know that God exists.

Part IV: *Is* belief in God properly basic?

According to the Reformed thinkers discussed in the last section the answer is 'Yes indeed.' I enthusiastically concur in this contention, and in this section I shall try to clarify and develop this view and defend against some objections. I shall argue first that one who holds that belief in God is properly basic is not thereby committed to the view that just about *anything* is; I shall argue secondly that even if belief in God is accepted as basic, it is not *groundless*; I shall argue thirdly that one who accepts belief in God as basic may nonetheless be open to arguments *against* that belief; and finally I shall argue that the view I am defending is not plausibly thought of as a species of *fideism*.

A. The Great Pumpkin objection

It is tempting to raise the following sort of question. If belief in God is properly basic, why cannot *just any* belief be properly basic? Could we not say the same for any bizarre aberration we can think of? What about voodoo or astrology? What about the belief that the Great Pumpkin returns every Halloween? Could I properly take *that* as basic? Suppose I believe that if I flap my arms with sufficient vigor, I can take off and fly about the room; could I defend myself against the charge of irrationality by claiming this belief is basic? If we say that belief in God is properly basic, will we not be committed to holding that just anything, or nearly anything, can properly be taken as basic, thus throwing wide the gates to irrationalism and superstition?

Certainly not. According to the Reformed epistemologist certain beliefs are properly basic in certain circumstances; those same beliefs may *not* be properly basic in other circumstances. Consider the belief that I see a tree: this belief is properly basic in circumstances that are hard to describe in detail, but include my being appeared to in a certain characteristic way; that same belief is not properly basic in circumstances including, say, my knowledge that I am sitting in the living room listening to music with my eyes closed. What the Reformed epistemologist holds is that there are widely realized circumstances in which belief in God is properly basic; but why should that be thought to commit him to the idea that just about *any* belief is properly basic in any circumstances, or even to the vastly weaker claim that for any belief there are circumstances in which it is properly basic? Is it just that he rejects the criteria for proper basicality purveyed by classical foundationalism? But why should *that* be thought to commit him to such tolerance of irrationality? Consider an analogy. In the palmy days of positivism the positivists went about confidently wielding their verifiability criterion and declaring meaningless much that was clearly meaningful. Now suppose someone rejected a formulation of that criterion—the one to be found in the second edition of A. J. Ayer's *Language, Truth and Logic*, for example. Would that mean she was committed to holding that

(1) T' was brillig; and the slithy toves did gyre and gymble in the wabe,

contrary to appearances, makes good sense? Of course not. But then the same goes for the Reformed epistemologist: the fact that he rejects the criterion of proper basicality purveyed by classical foundationalism does not mean that he is committed to supposing just anything is properly basic.

But what then is the problem? Is it that the Reformed epistemologist not only rejects those criteria for proper basicality but seems in no hurry to produce what he takes to be a better substitute? If he has no such criterion, how can he fairly reject belief in the Great Pumpkin as properly basic?

This objection betrays an important misconception. How *do* we rightly arrive at or develop criteria for meaningfulness, or justified belief, or proper basicality? Where do they come from? Must one have such a criterion before one can sensibly make any judgments—positive or negative—about proper basicality? Surely not. Suppose I do not know of a satisfactory substitute for the criteria proposed by classical foundationalism; I am nevertheless entirely within my epistemic rights in holding that certain propositions in certain conditions are not properly basic.

Some propositions seem self-evident when in fact they are not; that is the lesson of some of the Russell paradoxes. Nevertheless it would be irrational to take as basic the denial of a proposition that seems self-evident to you. Similarly, suppose it seems to you that you see a tree; you would then be irrational in taking as basic the proposition that you do not see a tree or that there are no trees. In the same way, even if I do not know of some illuminating criterion of meaning, I can quite properly declare (1) (above) meaningless.

And this raises an important question—one Roderick Chisholm has taught us to ask.[32] What is the status of criteria for knowledge, or proper basicality, or justified belief? Typically these are universal statements. The modern foundationalist's criterion for proper basicality, for example, is doubly universal:

(2) For any proposition *A* and person *S*, *A* is properly basic for *S* if and only if *A* is incorrigible for *S* or self-evident to *S*.

But how could one know a thing like that? What are its credentials? Clearly enough, (2) is not self-evident or just obviously true. But if it is not, how does one arrive at it? What sorts of arguments would be appropriate? Of course a foundationalist might find (2) so appealing he simply takes it to be true, neither offering argument for it nor accepting it on the basis of other things he believes. If he does so, however, his noetic structure will be self-referentially incoherent. (2) itself is neither self-evident nor incorrigible; hence if he accepts (2) as basic, the modern foundationalist violates in accepting it the condition of proper basicality he himself lays down. On the other hand, perhaps the foundationalist will try to produce some argument for it from premises that are self-evident or incorrigible: it is exceedingly hard to see,

---

32. Roderick Chisholm, *The Problem of the Criterion* (Milwaukee: Marquette University Press, 1973), pp. 14 ff.

however, what such an argument might be like. And until he has produced such arguments, what shall the rest of us do—we who do not find (2) at all obvious or compelling? How could he use (2) to show us that belief in God, for example, is not properly basic? Why should we believe (2) or pay it any attention?

The fact is, I think, that neither (2) nor any other revealing necessary and sufficient condition for proper basicality follows from clearly self-evident premises by clearly acceptable arguments. And hence the proper way to arrive at such a criterion is, broadly speaking, *inductive*. We must assemble examples of beliefs and conditions such that the former are obviously properly basic in the latter, and examples of beliefs and conditions such that the former are obviously *not* properly basic in the latter. We must then frame hypotheses as to the necessary and sufficient conditions of proper basicality and test these hypotheses by reference to those examples. Under the right conditions, for example, it is clearly rational to believe that you see a human person before you: a being who has thoughts and feelings, who knows and believes things, who makes decisions and acts. It is clear, furthermore, that you are under no obligation to reason this belief from others you hold; under those conditions that belief is properly basic for you. But then (2) must be mistaken; the belief in question, under those circumstances, is properly basic, though neither self-evident nor incorrigible for you. Similarly, you may seem to remember that you had breakfast this morning, and perhaps you know of no reason to suppose your memory is playing you tricks. If so, you are entirely justified in taking that belief as basic. Of course it is not properly basic on the criteria offered by classical foundationalists, but that fact counts not against you but against those criteria.

Accordingly, criteria for proper basicality must be reached from below rather than above; they should not be presented *ex cathedra* but argued to and tested by a relevant set of examples. But there is no reason to assume, in advance, that everyone will agree on the examples. The Christian will of course suppose that belief in God is entirely proper and rational; if he does not accept this belief on the basis of other propositions, he will conclude that it is basic for him and quite properly so. Followers of Bertrand Russell and Madelyn Murray O'Hare may disagree; but how is that relevant? Must my criteria, or those of the Christian community, conform to their examples? Surely not. The Christian community is responsible to *its* set of examples, not to theirs.

So, the Reformed epistemologist can properly hold that belief in the Great Pumpkin is not properly basic, even though he holds that belief in God is properly basic and even if he has no full-fledged criterion of proper basicality. Of course he is committed to supposing that there is a relevant *difference* between belief in God and belief in the Great Pumpkin if he holds that the former but not the latter is properly basic. But this should prove no great embarrassment; there are plenty of candidates. These candidates are to be found in the neighborhood of the conditions that justify and ground belief in God—conditions I shall discuss in the next section. Thus, for example, the Reformed epistemologist may concur with Calvin in holding that God has implanted in us a natural tendency to see his hand in the world around us; the same cannot be said for the Great Pumpkin, there being no Great Pumpkin and no natural tendency to accept beliefs about the Great Pumpkin.[33]

B. The *ground* of belief in God

My claim is that belief in God is properly basic; it does not follow, however, that it is *groundless*. Let me explain. Suppose we consider perceptual beliefs, memory beliefs, and beliefs ascribing mental states to other persons, such beliefs as:

(3) I see a tree,
(4) I had breakfast this morning,

and

(5) That person is in pain.

Although beliefs of this sort are typically taken as basic, it would be a mistake to describe them as *groundless*. Upon having experience of a certain sort, I believe that I am perceiving a tree. In the typical case I do not hold this belief on the basis of other beliefs; it is nonetheless not groundless. My having that characteristic sort of experience—to use Professor Chisholm's language, my being appeared treely to— plays a crucial role in the formation of that belief. It also plays a crucial role in its *justification*. Let us say that a belief is *justified* for a person at a time if (a) he is violating no epistemic duties and is within his epistemic rights in accepting it then and (b) his noetic structure is not defective by virtue of his then accepting it.[34] Then my being appeared to in this characteristic way (together with other circumstances) is what confers on me the right to hold the belief in question; this is what justifies me in accepting it. We could say, if we wish, that this experience is what justifies me in holding it; this is the *ground* of my justification, and, by extension, the ground of the belief itself.

If I see someone displaying typical pain behavior, I take it that he or she is in pain. Again, I do not take the displayed behavior as *evidence* for that belief; I do not infer that belief from others I hold; I do not accept it on the basis of other beliefs. Still, my perceiving the pain behavior plays a unique role in the formation and justification of that belief; as in the previous case it forms the ground of my justification for the belief in question. The same holds for memory beliefs. I seem to remember having breakfast this morning; that is, I have an inclination to believe the proposition that I had breakfast, along with a certain past-tinged experience that is familiar to all but hard to describe. Perhaps we should say that I am appeared to pastly; but perhaps that insufficiently distinguishes the experience in question from

---

33. For further comment on the Great Pumpkin objection see Alvin Plantinga, 'On Reformed Episte- mology,' *Reformed Journal*, April 1982.
34. I do not mean to suggest, of course, that if a person believes a true proposition and is justified (in this sense) in believing it, then it follows that he *knows* it; that is a different (and stronger) sense of the term.

that accompanying beliefs about the past not grounded in my own memory. The phenomenology of memory is a rich and unexplored realm; here I have no time to explore it. In this case as in the others, however, there is a justifying circumstance present, a condition that forms the ground of my justification for accepting the memory belief in question.

In each of these cases a belief is taken as basic, and in each case *properly* taken as basic. In each case there is some circumstance or condition that confers justification; there is a circumstance that serves as the ground of justification. So in each case there will be some true proposition of the sort

(6) In condition *C*, *S* is justified in taking *p* as basic.

Of course *C* will vary with *p*. For a perceptual judgment such as

(7) I see a rose-colored wall before me

C will include my being appeared to in a certain fashion. No doubt *C* will include more. If I am appeared to in the familiar fashion but know that I am wearing rose-colored glasses, or that I am suffering from a disease that causes me to be thus appeared to, no matter what the color of the nearby objects, then I am not justified in taking (7) as basic. Similarly for memory. Suppose I know that my memory is unreliable; it often plays me tricks. In particular, when I seem to remember having breakfast, then, more often than not, I have not had breakfast. Under these conditions I am not justified in taking it as basic that I had breakfast, even though I seem to remember that I did.

So being appropriately appeared to, in the perceptual case, is not sufficient for justification; some further condition—a condition hard to state in detail—is clearly necessary. The central point here, however, is that a belief is properly basic only in certain conditions; these conditions are, we might say, the ground of its justification and, by extension, the ground of the belief itself. In this sense basic beliefs are not, or are not necessarily, *groundless* beliefs.

Now similar things may be said about belief in God. When the Reformers claim that this belief is properly basic, they do not mean to say, of course, that there are no justifying circumstances for it, or that it is in that sense groundless or gratuitous. Quite the contrary. Calvin holds that God 'reveals and daily discloses himself in the whole workmanship of the universe,' and the divine art 'reveals itself in the innumerable and yet distinct and well ordered variety of the heavenly host.' God has so created us that we have a tendency or disposition to see his hand in the world about us. More precisely, there is in us a disposition to believe propositions of the sort *this flower was created by God* or *this vast and intricate universe was created by God* when we contemplate the flower or behold the starry heavens or think about the vast reaches of the universe.

Calvin recognizes, at least implicitly, that other sorts of conditions may trigger this disposition. Upon reading the Bible, one may be impressed with a deep sense that God is speaking to him. Upon having done what I know is cheap, or wrong, or wicked, I may feel guilty in God's sight and form the belief *God disapproves of what I have done*. Upon confession and repentance I may feel forgiven, forming the belief *God forgives me for what I have done*. A person in grave danger may turn to God, asking for his protection and help; and of course he or she then has the belief that God is indeed able to hear and help if he sees fit. When life is sweet and satisfying, a spontaneous sense of gratitude may well up within the soul; someone in this condition may thank and praise the Lord for his goodness, and will of course have the accompanying belief that indeed the Lord is to be thanked and praised.

There are therefore many conditions and circumstances that call forth belief in God: guilt, gratitude, danger, a sense of God's presence, a sense that he speaks, perception of various parts of the universe. A complete job would explore the phenomenology of all these conditions and of more besides. This is a large and important topic, but here I can only point to the existence of these conditions.

Of course none of the beliefs I mentioned a moment ago is the simple belief that God exists. What we have instead are such beliefs as:

(8) God is speaking to me,
(9) God has created all this,
(10) God disapproves of what I have done,
(11) God forgives me,

and

(12) God is to be thanked and praised.

These propositions are properly basic in the right circumstances. But it is quite consistent with this to suppose that the proposition *there is such a person as God* is neither properly basic nor taken as basic by those who believe in God. Perhaps what they take as basic are such propositions as (8)–(12), believing in the existence of God on the basis of propositions such as those. From this point of view it is not wholly accurate to say that it is belief in God that is properly basic; more exactly, what are properly basic are such propositions as (8)–(12), each of which self-evidently entails that God exists. It is not the relatively high-level and general proposition *God exists* that is properly basic, but instead propositions detailing some of his attributes or actions.

Suppose we return to the analogy between belief in God and belief in the existence of perceptual objects, other persons, and the past. Here too it is relatively specific and concrete propositions rather than their more general and abstract colleagues that are properly basic. Perhaps such items as:

(13) There are trees,
(14) There are other persons,

and

(15) The world has existed for more than five minutes

are not in fact properly basic; it is instead such propositions as:

(16) I see a tree,
(17) That person is pleased,

and

(18) I had breakfast more than an hour ago

that deserve that accolade. Of course propositions of the latter sort immediately and self-evidently entail propositions of the former sort, and perhaps there is thus no harm in speaking of the former as properly basic, even though so to speak is to speak a bit loosely.

The same must be said about belief in God. We may say, speaking loosely, that belief in God is properly basic; strictly speaking, however, it is probably not that proposition but such propositions as (8)–(12) that enjoy that status. But the main point, here, is this: belief in God, or (8)–(12), are properly basic; to say so, however, is not to deny that there are justifying conditions for these beliefs, or conditions that confer justification on one who accepts them as basic. They are therefore not groundless or gratuitous.

C. Is argument irrelevant to basic belief in God?

Suppose someone accepts belief in God as basic. Does it not follow that he will hold this belief in such a way that no argument could move him or cause him to give it up? Will he not hold it come what may, in the teeth of any evidence or argument with which he could be presented? Does he not thereby adopt a posture in which argument and other rational methods of settling disagreement are implicitly declared irrelevant? Surely not. Suppose someone accepts

(19) There is such a person as God

as basic. It does not for a moment follow that he will regard argument irrelevant to this belief of his; nor is he committed in advance to rejecting every argument against it. It could be, for example, that he accepts (19) as basic but also accepts as basic some propositions from which, by arguments whose corresponding conditionals he accepts as basic, it follows that (19) is false. What happens if he is apprised of this fact, perhaps by being presented with an argument from those propositions to the denial of (19)? Presumably some change is called for. If he accepts these propositions more strongly than (19), presumably he will give the latter up.

Similarly, suppose someone believes there is no God but also believes some propositions from which belief in God follows by argument forms he accepts. Presented with an argument from these propositions to the proposition that God exists, such a person may give up his atheism and accept belief in God. On the other hand, his atheistic belief may be stronger than his belief in some of the propositions in question, or his belief in their conjunction. It is possible, indeed, that he *knows* these propositions, but believes some of them less firmly than he believes that there is no God; in that case, if you present him with a valid argument from these propositions to the proposition that God exists, you may cause him to give up a proposition he knows to be true. It is thus possible to reduce the extent of some-one's knowledge by giving him a sound argument from premises he knows to be true.

So a person can accept belief in God as basic without accepting it dogmatically—that is, in such a way that he will ignore any contrary evidence or argument. And now a second question: Suppose the fact is belief in God *is* properly basic. Does it follow that one who accepts it dogmatically is within his epistemic rights? Does it follow that someone who is within his rights in accepting it as basic *remains* justi-fied in this belief, no matter what counterargument or counterevidence arises?

Again, surely not. The justification-conferring conditions mentioned above must be seen as conferring *prima facie* rather than *ultima facie*, or all-things-considered, justification. This justification can be overridden. My being appeared to treely gives me a *prima facie* right to take as basic the proposition *I see a tree*. But of course this right can be overridden; I might know, for example, that I suffer from the dreaded dendrological disorder, whose victims are appeared to treely only when there are no trees present. If I do know that, then I am not within my rights in taking as basic the proposition *I see a tree* when I am appeared to treely. The same goes for the conditions that confer justification on belief in God. Like the 14-year-old theist (above, p. 55), perhaps I have been brought up to believe in God and am initially within my rights in so doing. But conditions can arise in which perhaps I am no longer justified in this belief. Perhaps you propose to me an argument for conclu-sion that it is impossible that there be such a person as God. If this argument is convincing for me—if it starts from premises that seem self-evident to me and proceeds by argument forms that seem self-evidently valid—then perhaps I am no longer justified in accepting theistic belief. Following John Pollock, we may say that a condition that overrides my *prima facie* justification for *p* is *defeating condition* or *defeater* for *p* (for me). Defeaters, of course, are themselves *prima facie* defeaters, for the defeater can be defeated. Perhaps I spot a fallacy in the initially convincing argument; perhaps I discover a convincing argument for the denial of one of its premises; perhaps I learn on reliable authority that someone else has done one of those things. Then the defeater is defeated, and I am once again within my rights in accepting *p*. Of course a similar remark must be made about defeater-defeaters: they are subject to defeat by defeater-defeater-defeaters and so on.

Many believers in God have been brought up to believe, but then encountered potential defeaters. They have read books by skeptics, been apprised of the atheo-logical argument from evil, heard it said that theistic belief is just a matter of wish fulfillment or only a means whereby one socioeconomic class keeps another in bondage. These circumstances constitute potential defeaters for justification in theistic belief. If the believer is to remain justified, something further is called for—something that *prima facie* defeats the defeaters. Various forms of theistic apologetics serve this function (among others). Thus the *free-will defense* is a defeater for the atheological argument from evil, which is a potential defeater for theistic belief. Suppose I am within my epistemic rights in accepting belief in God as basic; and suppose I am presented with a plausible argument—by Democritus, let us say—for the conclusion that the existence of God is logically incompatible with the existence of evil. (Let us add that I am strongly convinced that there *is* evil.) This is a potential defeater for my being rational in accepting theistic belief. What is required, if I am to continue to believe rationally, is a defeater for that defeater. Perhaps I discover a flaw in Democritus' argument, or perhaps I have it on reliable authority that Augustine, say, has discovered a flaw in the argument; then I am once more justified in my original belief.

D. Fideism

I take up one final question. In *Reflections on Christian Philosophy* Ralph McInerny suggests that what I have been calling Reformed epistemology is *fideism*. Is he right? Is the Reformed epistemologist perforce a fideist? That depends: it depends, obviously enough, on how we propose to use the term 'fideism.' According to my dictionary fideism is 'exclusive or basic reliance upon faith alone, accompanied by a consequent disparagement of reason and utilized especially in the pursuit of philosophical or religious truth.' A fideist therefore urges reliance on faith rather than reason, in matters philosophical and religious; and he may go on to disparage and denigrate reason. We may thus distinguish at least two grades of fideism: moderate fideism, according to which we must rely upon faith rather than reason in religious matters, and extreme fideism, which disparages and denigrates reason.

Now let us ask first whether the Reformed epistemologist is obliged to be an extreme fideist. Of course there is more than one way of disparaging reason. One way to do it is to claim that to take a proposition on faith is higher and better than accepting it on the basis of reason. Another way to disparage reason is to follow Kant in holding that reason left to itself inevitably falls into paradox and antimony on ultimate matters. According to Kant pure reason offers us conclusive argument for supposing that the universe had no beginning, but also, unfortunately, conclusive arguments for the denial of that proposition. I do not think any of the alleged arguments are anywhere nearly conclusive, but if Kant were right, then presumably reason would not deserve to be paid attention to, at least on this topic. According to the most common brand of extreme fideism, however, reason and faith *conflict* or *clash* on matters of religious importance; and when they do, faith is to be preferred and reason suppressed. Thus according to Kierkegaard faith teaches 'the absurdity that the eternal is the historical.' He means to say, I think, that this proposition is among the deliverances of faith but absurd from the point of view of reason; and it should be accepted despite this absurdity. The turn-of-the-century Russian theologian Shestov carried extreme fideism even further; he held that one can attain religious truth only by rejecting the proposition that $2 + 2 = 4$ and accepting instead $2 + 2 = 5$.

Now it is clear, I suppose, that the Reformed epistemologist need not be an extreme fideist. His views on the proper basicality of belief in God surely do not commit him to thinking that faith and reason conflict. So suppose we ask instead whether the Reformed epistemologist is committed to *moderate* fideism. And again that depends; it depends upon how we propose to use the terms 'reason' and 'faith.' One possibility would be to follow Abraham Kuyper, who proposes to use these terms in such a way that one takes on faith whatever one accepts but does not accept on the basis of argument or inference or demonstration:

There is thus no objection to the use of the term 'faith' for that function of the soul by which it attains certainty immediately or directly, without the aid of discursive demonstration. This places faith over against demonstration, but *not* over against knowing.[35]

On this use of these terms, anything taken as basic is taken on faith; anything believed on the basis of other beliefs is taken on reason. I take $2 + 1 = 3$ as basic; accordingly, I take it on faith. When I am appropriately appeared to, I take as basic such propositions as *I see a tree before me* or *there is a house over there*; on the present construal I take these things on faith. I remember that I had lunch this noon, but do not accept this belief on the basis of other propositions; this too, then, I take on faith. On the other hand, what I take on the basis of reason is what I believe on the basis of argument or inference from other propositions. Thus I take $2 + 1 = 3$ on faith, but $21 \times 45 = 945$ by reason; for I accept the latter on the basis of calculation, which is a form of argument. Further, suppose I accept supralapsarianism or premillenialism or the doctrine of the virgin birth on the grounds that God proposes these doctrines for our belief and God proposes only truths; then on Kuyper's use of these terms I accept these doctrines not by faith but by reason. Indeed, if with Kierkegaard and Shestov I hold that the eternal is the historical and that $2 + 2 = 5$ because I believe God proposes *these* things for my belief, then on the present construal I take them not on faith but on the basis of reason.

And here we can see, I think, that Kuyper's use of these terms is not the relevant one for the discussion of fideism. For consider Shestov. Shestov is an extreme fideist because he thinks faith and reason conflict; and when they do, he says, it is reason that must be suppressed. To paraphrase the poem, 'When faith and reason clash, let reason go to smash!' But he is not holding that faith teaches something—$2 + 2 = 5$, for example—that conflicts with a belief—$2 + 2 = 4$—that one arrives at by reasoning from other propositions. On the contrary, the poignancy of the clash is just that what faith teaches conflicts with an *immediate* teaching of reason—a proposition that is apparently self-evident. On the Kuyperian use of these terms Shestov would

35. Abraham Kuyper, *Encyclopedia of Sacred Theology*, tr. J. DeVries (New York: Charles Scribner's Sons, 1898), pp. 128–9.

be surprised to learn that he is not a fideist after all. For what he takes faith to conflict with here is not something one accepts by reason—that is, on the basis of other propositions. Indeed on the Kuyperian account Shestov not only does not qualify as a fideist; he probably qualifies as an antifideist. Shestov probably did not recommend taking $2 + 2 = 5$ as basic; he probably held that God proposes this proposition for our belief and that we should therefore accept it. On the other hand he also believed, no doubt, that $2 + 2 = 4$ is apparently self-evident So given the Kuyperian use, Shestov would be holding that faith and reason conflict here, but it is $2 + 2 = 4$ that is the deliverance of faith and $2 + 2 = 5$ the deliverance of reason! Since he recommends accepting $2 + 2 = 5$, the deliverance of reason, he thus turns out to be a rationalist or antifideist at least on this point.

And this shows that Kuyper's use of these terms is not the relevant use. What we take on faith is not simply what we take as basic, and what we accept by reason is not simply what we take on the basis of other propositions. The deliverances of reason include propositions taken as basic and the deliverances of faith include propositions accepted on the basis of others.

The Reformed epistemologist, therefore, is a fideist only if he holds that some central truths of Christianity are not among the deliverances of reason and must instead be taken on faith. But just what are the deliverances of reason? What do they include? First, clearly enough, self-evident propositions and propositions that follow from them by self-evidently valid arguments are among the deliverances of reason. But we cannot stop there. Consider someone who holds that according to correct scientific reasoning from accurate observation the earth is at least a couple of billion years old; nonetheless, he adds, the fact is it is no more than some 6,000 years old, since that is what faith teaches. Such a person is a fideist, even though the proposition *the earth is more than 6,000 years old* is neither self-evident nor a consequence of what is self-evident. So the deliverances of reason include more than the self-evident and its consequences. They also include basic perceptual truths (propositions 'evident to the senses'), incorrigible propositions, certain memory propositions, certain propositions about other minds, and certain moral or ethical propositions.

But what about the belief that there is such a person as God and that we are responsible to him? Is that among the deliverances of reason or an item of faith? For Calvin it is clearly the former. 'There is within the human mind, and indeed by natural instinct, an awareness of divinity. . . . God himself has implanted in all men a certain understanding of his divine majesty . . . men one and all perceive that there is a God and that he is their Maker' (*Institutes* I, 3, 1). According to Calvin, everyone, whether in the faith or not, has a tendency or nisus, in certain situations, to apprehend God's existence and to grasp something of his nature and actions. This natural knowledge can be and is suppressed by sin, but the fact remains that a capacity to apprehend God's existence is as much part of our natural noetic equipment as is the capacity to apprehend perceptual truths, truths about the past, and truths about other minds. Belief in the existence of God is in the same boat as belief in other minds, the past, and perceptual objects; in each case God has so constructed us that in the right circumstances we form the belief in question. But then the belief that there is such a person as God is as much among the deliverances of reason as those other beliefs.

From this vantage point we can see, therefore, that the Reformed epistemologist is not a fideist at all with respect to belief in God. He does not hold that there is any conflict between faith and reason here, and he does not even hold that we cannot attain this fundamental truth by reason; he holds, instead, that it is among the deliverances of reason.

Of course the nontheist may disagree; he may deny that the existence of God is part of the deliverances of reason. A former professor of mine for whom I had and have enormous respect once said that theists and nontheists have different conceptions of reason. At the time I did not know what he meant, but now I think I do. On the Reformed view I have been urging, the deliverances of reason include the existence of God just as much as perceptual truths, self-evident truths, memory truths, and the like. It is not that theist and nontheist agree as to what reason delivers, the theist then going on to accept the existence of God by faith; there is, instead, disagreement in the first place as to what are the deliverances of reason. But then the Reformed epistemologist is no more a fideist with respect to belief in God than is, for example, Thomas Aquinas. Like the latter, he will no doubt hold that there are other truths of Christianity that are not to be found among the deliverances of reason—such truths, for example, as that God was in Christ, reconciling the world to himself. But he is not a fideist by virtue of his views on our knowledge of God.

By way of summary: I have argued that the evidentialist objection to theistic belief is rooted in classical foundationalism; the same can be said for the Thomistic conception of faith and reason. Classical foundationalism is attractive and seductive; in the final analysis, however, it turns out to be both false and self-referentially incoherent. Furthermore, the Reformed objection to natural theology, unformed and inchoate as it is, may best be seen as a rejection of classical foundationalism. As the Reformed thinker sees things, being self-evident, or incorrigible, or evident to the senses is not a necessary condition of proper basicality. He goes on to add that belief in God is properly basic. He is not thereby committed to the idea that just any or nearly any belief is properly basic, even if he lacks a criterion for proper basicality. Nor is he committed to the view that argument is irrelevant to belief in God if such belief is properly basic. Furthermore, belief in God, like other properly basic beliefs, is not groundless or arbitrary; it is grounded in justification-conferring conditions. Finally, the Reformed view that belief in God is properly basic is not felicitously thought of as a version of fideism.

Chapter 5

Evidence and religious belief

Norman Kretzmann

Plantinga's project

ALVIN Plantinga has avowedly been trying to establish the rationality of believing without evidence that God exists.[1] Others are also engaged in this project, which they sometimes call 'Reformed epistemology'. The following quotation from Plantinga can serve as a statement of the thesis of Reformed epistemology: 'it is entirely right, rational, reasonable, and proper to believe in God without any evidence or argument at all' (RBG, p. 43).

The wording of that statement is clearly designed to raise eyebrows as well as questions. A natural first question, closely associated with the raised eyebrows, is this: Why would a philosopher take up a thesis that appears to be contrary to a plain canon of rationality? In particular, why would Plantinga, who has himself contributed notably to uncovering evidence for theism, take up this thesis? His own answer is that the thesis of Reformed epistemology expresses '[w]hat the Reformers [especially Calvin and Calvinists] meant to hold', but that '[w]hat they say . . . has been for the most part unclear, ill-focused, and unduly inexplicit', and that he is going to 'try to remedy these ills', because the Reformers' 'fundamental insights here are correct' (RBG, pp. 42–3). The natural second question, of course, is why he thinks they are correct.

As I will try to show, the position Plantinga actually develops is nothing like so controversial or so opposed to evidentialism as the thesis of Reformed epistemology makes it seem. But because he conceives of his position in the terms in which he expresses the thesis, he naturally takes evidentialism to be the main obstacle in the way of his project.

As befits a canon of rationality, evidentialism is truistic: *It is irrational to believe anything on insufficient evidence.* Then how can Plantinga or anyone else take up *anti*-evidentialism? Only, I think, by giving the evidentialist canon an unnatural interpretation, as I'll try to show.

In the process of focusing on evidentialism as the obstacle to his rational theism without evidence, Plantinga presents it first in the form of 'the evidentialist objection to theistic belief [in general], according to which belief in God is unreasonable

Norman Kretzmann edited extract from 'Evidence Against Anti-Evidentialism' from *Our Knowledge of God* edited by K. J. Clark (Kluwer Academic Press, 1992), reprinted by permission of the publisher.

1. See Plantinga, 'Reason and Belief in God' (hereafter RBG), in this vol., Chapter 4, 'Religious belief as "properly basic" ', from which page numbers are taken.

or irrational because there is insufficient evidence for it' (RBG, pp. 42, 43), later in a limiting-case version more clearly relevant to his particular project: 'it is irrational and unreasonable to accept theistic belief in the absence of arguments or evidence for the existence of God' (RBG, p. 51). So the success, even the feasibility, of Plantinga's project as he conceives of it requires anti-evidentialism in the form of a refutation of the evidentialist objection.

My project

In my examination of theistic anti-evidentialism I will focus exclusively on Plantinga's work, which has been at least as influential as any work of this sort. Some of my criticisms apply only to his version of anti-evidentialism, but others apply generally. I will try to show how and why his position misinterprets evidentialism, that his direct examination of the evidentialist objection turns up nothing that weakens it in any way, that his claim to have found the root of evidentialism in classical foundationalism is unfounded, that his effort at refuting evidentialism by way of refuting classical foundationalism is therefore misdirected, and that his attempt to establish theism (the belief that God exists) as typically or often a properly basic belief does not succeed. Finally and most importantly, I will try to show that the position Plantinga actually develops needn't be construed as and really isn't opposed to evidentialism. What Plantinga's anti-evidentialism actually opposes is an artificial position much narrower than the natural, evident evidentialism that has been for thousands of years taken for granted by all who prize rationality, theists and atheists alike. In expounding and examining his position, however, I will begin by following his own account of it.

Theistic evidentialists and evidentialist objectors

Plantinga acknowledges that '[m]any philosophers have endorsed' evidentialism (RBG, p. 63). Just about all philosophers, along with other rational beings, have regularly applied it, usually unselfconsciously; those who have gone so far as to endorse it may be thought of as explicit evidentialists. Among these are theistic evidentialists as well as evidentialist objectors to theism. Thomas Aquinas is Plantinga's paradigmatic theistic evidentialist (RBG, pp. 59–65). I think that that's a correct and important characterization of Aquinas, and that in this respect he represents a long, invaluable tradition within Christian theology and philosophy, a tradition apparently denigrated if not repudiated by anti-evidentialism. But my main concern now is with the other sort of explicit evidentialists Plantinga opposes— those whose evidentialism leads them to object to at least some forms of theistic belief—just because it is, naturally, their evidentialism that Plantinga focuses on.

Obviously, no one could be a theistic evidentialist without maintaining that some evidence for theism is generally available, and the evidentialist objectors Plantinga considers appear to share that view. Their objection to theism is simply that the available evidence is not *sufficient*, quantitatively or qualitatively—whether for theistic belief at all, or for theistic belief held as strongly as theists are expected to hold it.

It's not surprising that the evidentialist objection should be raised by people who acknowledge the availability of some evidence for theism. Their objection would clearly miss its target of ordinary theistic belief without such an acknowledgement. Scripture itself alludes to natural evidence, and versions of the cosmological, teleological, and ontological arguments (to mention only the big three) have been employed by theistic evidentialists for a long, long time. If the evidentialist objectors Plantinga cites had actually encountered theism maintained along with an avowed ignoring or avoiding of all the available evidence for it, their stated position suggests that they would have left it alone to collapse of its own weight. Evidentialism is naturally suited to license the house founded upon a rock, condemn the house built upon the sand, and disregard castles in the air.

Most evidentialists would indeed recognize some beliefs as rational without *ulterior* evidence—evidence beyond any evidence that may be provided either in the very circumstances in which the belief is formed or in the very proposition that is the object of the belief—e.g., evidence beyond the evidence you have for your belief that you are now having such-and-such experiences, or that everything is what it is. Because such beliefs need no ulterior evidence, they do not suffer from *insufficient* evidence. But because the belief that God exists is not of a type standardly recognized as rationally believable without ulterior evidence, theism without ulterior evidence is generally characterized as theism with insufficient evidence. Still, evidentialism as an objection against theism is, historically and naturally, an objection against the sufficiency of the evidence expressly relied on in *evidentialist* theism, Aquinas's sort, not against the absence of any evidence at all in theism of the sort Plantinga seems to approve of.

Alluding to the evidentialist objection as often as he does, Plantinga naturally makes use of summary statements of it. He tends to begin by summarizing it as directed against believing *with insufficient evidence* that God exists. But he soon moves to representing the objection as directed against believing *without any evidence at all* that God exists, and he understandably favors this no-evidence version of the objection, more appositely opposed to his declared position.

The evidentialist argument

Plantinga's anti-evidentialism might reasonably be expected to take shape in his most sustained direct examination of the reasoning behind the evidentialist objection, in which he presents what he describes as its two principles (RBG, p. 51) or premises (RBG, p. 53). Here they are:

(6) It is irrational or unreasonable to accept theistic belief in the absence of sufficient evidence or reasons.

(7) There is no evidence or at any rate not sufficient evidence for the proposition that God exists.[2]

The conclusion, left implicit, is of course the objection itself:

It is irrational to believe that God exists.

Plantinga's rejection of the objection requires him to attack either the validity of this argument or the truth of (6) or (7). But he does not advance to the attack at once and the attack, when it comes, is surprisingly tentative and altogether inconclusive. It is directed first against (7), the second premiss. 'Now (7) is a strong claim. What about the various arguments that have been proposed for the existence of God . . . ?' 'Do none of these provide evidence?' he asks. He admits that they don't 'singly or in combinations, constitute *proofs* of God's existence. . . . The question is only whether someone might be justified in believing in the existence of God on the basis of the alleged evidence offered by them; and that is a radically different question' (RBG, pp. 52–3). And that is all he has to say about (7).

What does it come to? As far as I can see, it comes to no more than a suggestion that (7) is *perhaps* an exaggeration. It isn't clear from these passages that he is ready even to delete '*no* evidence' from (7); but, as we've seen, the general availability of some evidence for theism really is undeniable. If we suppose that he is ready to make that deletion, then he would replace (7) with (7') 'There is *not sufficient* evidence for the proposition that God exists', which, given the wording of (6), is still adequate for the conclusion, if the argument is valid.

Is (7') true? Judging on the basis of his discussion of it, Plantinga's response appears to be 'That's a good question'. As might have been expected, given the thesis of Reformed epistemology, and especially in the aftermath of his ambivalent handling of (7), Plantinga expresses more interest 'in the objector's *other* premise—the claim that it is irrational or unreasonable to accept theistic belief in the absence of evidence or reasons'. (RBG, p. 53; emphasis added). Absence of *sufficient* evidence or reasons is what (6) actually talks about. With 'sufficient', (6) is perfectly linked with (7'), 'There is not sufficient evidence for the proposition that God exists'. Without 'sufficient', (6) is less well suited to the argument (though perhaps even more plausible), but perfectly adapted to Plantinga's transition from the direct consideration of the evidentialist argument to Reformed epistemology proper: 'Why suppose *that* is true? Why should we think a theist must have evidence, or reason to think there is evidence, if he is not to be irrational? Why not suppose, instead, that he is entirely within his epistemic rights in believing in God's existence even if he has no argument or evidence at all?' (RBG, p. 53). And with that transition his direct attack on the argument comes to an end, having apparently consisted in no more than raising leading questions about each of the two premises.

Of course this direct attack is not all Plantinga offers against the evidentialist argument. The sentence immediately following the passage I just quoted completes

2. See RBG, p. 52.

the transition with the announcement 'This is what I want to investigate'. The remaining pages of RBG contain that investigation, and it is helpful for present purposes to recognize that the referent of 'This' can be construed as (6), the first premiss. Theistic evidentialists would take this evidentialist argument to be valid but unsound in virtue of the falsity of (7) alone. Plantinga's treatment of the argument in RBG strongly suggests that he takes it to be valid but unsound in virtue of the falsity of (6) alone. (6) just is evidentialism applied specifically to theism. Plantinga's project as he presents it cannot succeed unless (6) is shown to be false, and his direct examination of the evidentialist objection makes no discernible progress toward that goal. And so the success of his stated project depends entirely on the indirect refutation of evidentialism he goes on to attempt.

Plantinga's attempt to tie evidentialism to foundationalism

Plantinga's indirect anti-evidentialism has two main components: tying the evidentialist objection to classical foundationalism, and showing that classical foundationalism is untenable. I don't think either of those two components is successful, but I won't have anything to say here about his attempted refutation of classical foundationalism (often hereafter just 'foundationalism'). If I'm right about his not succeeding in showing that the evidentialist objection stands or falls with foundationalism, then he can't defend his position by refuting foundationalism; and so I will examine his attempt to tie evidentialism to foundationalism.

Near the beginning of RBG he says 'I shall argue that the evidentialist objection and the Thomistic conception of faith and knowledge can be traced back to a common root in *classical foundationalism*' (RBG, p. 43). Later, after a survey of what he takes to be Aquinas's application to systematic theology of the principles and practices of Aristotelian demonstrative science, he begins a section labeled 'Foundationalism' by saying 'Aquinas and the evidentialist objector concur, then, in holding that belief in God is rationally acceptable only if there is evidence for it—only if, that is, it is probable with respect to some body of propositions that constitutes the evidence. And here we can get a better understanding of Aquinas and the evidentialist objector if we see them as accepting some version of *classical foundationalism*' (RBG, p. 65). As far as I can tell, that is all he does by way of arguing that evidentialism is rooted in or even merely tied to foundationalism.

For present purposes I will simply assent to everything he says in RBG about the interrelations of Aquinas's theology, Aristotelian science, and classical foundationalism. But none of it has any tendency to show that evidentialism in general or the evidentialist objection is rooted in foundationalism. Aquinas's philosophical theology is an elaborately developed, sophisticated system of knowledge modeled more or less closely on Aristotelian demonstrative science. Evidentialism is logically, psychologically, and, no doubt, historically prior to any such system; it is a truistic, pre-theoretic, typically implicit canon of rationality itself. It's easy enough to imagine the Aristotelian conception of demonstrative science developing in an effort to make precise and systematic the universal intuition expressed in 'it is irrational to believe anything on insufficient evidence'. It's unthinkable that that intuition could have grown out of foundationalism or, for that matter, coherentism or any other epistemological system. Plantinga really offers no argument to show that 'the evidentialist objection . . . can be traced back to a . . . root in classical foundationalism', and he seems to be hanging the picture upside down when he says that 'we can get a better understanding of . . . the evidentialist objector if we see [him]   as accepting some version of *classical foundationalism*'. On the contrary, we can get a better understanding of the classical foundationalist if we see him as attempting to elaborate and codify the intuition expressible as evidentialism. Foundationalism is rooted in evidentialism.

Classical foundationalism's technical details, which Plantinga relies on in his attempted refutation of it, do not extend down to its evidentialist roots. So whatever Plantinga might think he could do to evidentialism as a result of tying it to foundationalism can have no effect on the evidentialist objection itself.

The notion of evidence narrowed in two respects

Although Plantinga has inverted the root-to-shoot relationship between evidentialism and foundationalism, they are, as I've just been saying, naturally associated. In virtue of that association, some of what is true of foundationalism is true of evidentialism as well, and many an evidentialist might find foundationalism congenial if not indispensable. In particular, there is no good reason for the evidentialist to object to Plantinga's clarifying his crucial phrase 'without evidence' in the context of his examination of foundationalism.

We already have some reasons to think there is something problematic about the very meaning of Plantinga's 'without evidence'. In view of the apparent status of evidentialism as a canon of rationality, the undeniable general availability of some evidence for theism, and, in particular, his own apparent rejection of the 'no evidence' element in (7), can his claim that theism without evidence is rational really mean just what it seems to mean? In fact, as might have been expected, it means something a good deal narrower than it seems to mean.

Plantinga does not expressly introduce his narrow notion of evidence at any one point in RBG. It remains mostly implicit and can be discerned best in connection with his consideration of foundationalism. The clearest indications begin at the very end of his examination of the evidentialist argument, in his efforts to clarify the evidentialist objection and thereby to weaken it. 'But of course the crucial question here is this: Why does the objector think these things? . . . Why is it not permissible and quite satisfactory to believe in God without any evidence—proof or argument—at all? Presumably the objector does not mean to suggest that *no* propositions can be believed or accepted without evidence, for if you have evidence for *every* proposition you believe, then (granted certain plausible assumptions about the formal properties of the evidence relation) you will believe infinitely many propositions; and no one has time, these busy days, for that. So presumably *some* propositions can properly be believed and accepted without evidence. Well, why not belief in God? Why is it not entirely acceptable, desirable, right, proper, and rational to accept belief in God without any argument or evidence whatever?' (RBG, pp. 58–9).

The tactical purpose of this passage is to weaken the opposition by showing that even the evidentialist objector must acknowledge the rationality of believing *some* propositions without evidence. But the passage rests on assumptions that narrow the notion of evidence in ways that characterize all of Plantinga's anti-evidentialism. Two such assumptions, easy to discern and important in the remainder of this discussion, are these: *all* evidence is (what I have been calling) *ulterior* evidence, grounds other than the nature of the believed proposition or the circumstances of the formation of the belief, and *all* evidence is *propositional*. Although these assumptions present a familiar philosophical conception of evidence, they strike me as simply failing to capture all of evidentialism's conception of evidence. And in the absence of these assumptions the objector might very well mean to suggest that '*no* propositions can be [rationally] believed or accepted without evidence'.

It is of course true and important that rationality as ordinarily construed requires one to recognize some beliefs as capable of standing on their own, as needing no evidence beyond the evidence supplied in the nature of their propositional objects (beliefs whose objects are self-evident propositions) or the circumstances of their formation (incorrigible beliefs). And, as I've pointed out, evidentialism embraces that requirement. Such beliefs can't be characterized as having *insufficient* evidence, but the sufficient evidence they have is neither *ulterior* evidence nor purely *propositional*.

The evidentialist can fully assent to Plantinga's claim that 'Aquinas and the evidentialist objector concur . . . in holding that belief in God is rationally acceptable only if there is evidence for it' without fully accepting his exposition of the claim: 'only if, that is, it is probable with respect to some body of propositions that constitutes the evidence' (RBG, p. 65). However well such a notion of evidence may serve Aquinas's systematic philosophical theology, it is far too narrowly sophisticated to suit evidentialism in general, which is not now and never was expressible as 'It is irrational to believe anything on insufficient evidence, by which is meant anything that is not probable with respect to some body of propositions that constitutes the evidence'. All that the evidentialist canon demands for beliefs that do not carry their evidence with them is sufficient support or backing of *some* sort, and 'evidence' has long been and is still the ordinary English word for that ordinary notion. Someone's evidence for a rational belief might, of course, sometimes be purely propositional and as fully cooked as Plantinga's exposition here suggests it must always be, but it might equally well be raw experience itself.

When Plantinga expresses the evidentialist criterion in (6) as 'sufficient evidence *or reasons*', he comes as near as makes no difference to the degree of breadth required in a criterion as fundamental as evidentialism is, even if 'evidence' in that phrase is given the narrow interpretation he develops for it. But the broadening effect of 'or reasons' is only momentary and no doubt inadvertent; almost every-where else he relies exclusively on his artificially narrow notion of evidence when characterizing evidentialism or his own position. Without that artifice he would not be an anti-evidentialist; without that artifice he would have no means at all of defending the rationality of theism without any evidence at all.

In the context of foundationalism beliefs maintained without ulterior propo-sitional evidence are interpretable as *basic* beliefs, where S's belief that *p* is basic for S if and only if S believes that *p* but not on the basis of any other belief(s) of S. And in that context the question of the *rationality* of believing without ulterior propositional evidence becomes the question whether a given basic belief is *prop-erly* basic, whether the nature of the believed proposition itself or the circumstances of the formation of the belief provide sufficient evidence for it. When evidentialism is specifically applied to theism in the context of foundationalism, its precision is enhanced—as Plantinga shows in a passage that suits evidentialism well as long as we bear in mind his narrow notion of evidence. 'According to the foundationalist some propositions are properly basic and some are not; those that are not are rationally accepted only on the basis of *evidence*, where the evidence must trace back, ultimately, to what *is* properly basic. The existence of God, furthermore, is not among the propositions that are properly basic; hence a person is rational in accept-ing theistic belief only if he has evidence for it' (RBG, p. 65). Of course a classical foundationalist prepared to show that the proposition that God exists is self-evident, incorrigible, or evident to the senses could on that basis alone assert that he was a rational theist without (ulterior propositional) evidence, and there have been theists prepared at least to claim one or another of those properly basic statuses for 'God exists', but Plantinga is not among them. Therefore, *his* claim that theism without (ulterior propositional) evidence is rational depends in part on his length-ening the short list of classes of properly basic beliefs to include, somehow, the belief that God exists.

The notion of belief narrowed in two respects

In maintaining that the belief that God exists can be and often is properly basic Plantinga appears to be maintaining

(AP) S can be rational in believing that God exists, even if that belief of S is based on no other belief(s) of S.

But, as we will see, the position he actually develops is

(AP') S can be rational in believing that God exists, even if S's *acquisition* of that belief is based on no other *occurrent* belief(s) of S.

(AP) is controversial. (AP'), on the other hand, by narrowing the notion of belief from believing generally to *acquiring* belief, and from belief generally to *occurrent* belief, leaves controversy behind. It might fairly be read as claiming no more than that in forming one's religious beliefs one need not first engage in conscious apologetics or philosophical theology of any sort, which is just what the great theistic evidentialists have always claimed, although of course they went on to insist that faith thus formed seeks understanding if it isn't deficient. But (AP′), congenial to theistic evidentialism, neither supports Plantinga's claim of proper basicality for theism nor commits him to anti-evidentialism, as I will try to show.

That Plantinga's notion of belief is artificially narrow is already apparent before he introduces foundationalism, on the basis of his first detailed example of theism 'without evidence', undertaken in aid of showing that the deontological version of the evidentialist objection is 'unduly harsh'. 'What about the 14-year-old theist brought up to believe in God in a community where everyone believes? This 14-year-old theist, we may suppose, does not believe in God on the basis of evidence. He has never heard of the cosmological, teleological, or ontological arguments; in fact no one has ever presented him with any evidence at all. And although he has often been told about God, he does not take that testimony as evidence; he does not reason thus: everyone around here says God loves us and cares for us; most of what everyone around here says is true; so probably *that is* true. Instead, he simply believes what he is taught. Is he violating an all-things-considered intellectual duty? Surely not' (RBG, p. 55).

The theism of this 14-year-old, call him Ted, exemplifies what it is, in Plantinga's view, to believe in God *without any evidence at all.* As long as Ted has had any beliefs of any kind, we may suppose, he has believed that God exists; theism is not a belief he came to. As a child of three or four Ted may literally have had no evidence at all for his belief that God exists. But for several years now he has been reading the Bible, which was presented to him as the word of God. He has been receiving religious instruction from his parents and other figures of authority. He has thought about religious issues at least a little, in the manner of 14-year-old theists. As a consequence of all these developments, his faith has surely deepened and is no longer utterly infantile; to some degree and in some respects he has achieved understanding where once he had only faith.

What would an evidentialist say about Ted's theism? I would say that Ted is rational to believe as he does, that the evidence he has, considered relative to Ted's age and circumstances, is sufficient for his theism. Considered objectively, however, the sort of evidence Ted has is obviously insufficient for theism on the part of an educated, sophisticated adult. In any case, no evidentialist worth attending to would say that Ted's theism was without any evidence at all. Why does Plantinga say it?

His description of Ted and Ted's circumstances rules out the possibility that Ted takes 'God exists' to be self-evident, incorrigible, or evident to the senses. Since all the support Ted is said to have for his belief is propositional and might fairly be described even as a 'body of propositions', Plantinga's reason for denying that Ted has evidence can't be that the grounds for his belief are sub-propositional, merely experiential. His reason for denying that Ted has or ever had evidence for his belief that God exists seems to be that the propositions that would strike an evidentialist as Ted's evidence for theism were never used by Ted as a basis for *acquiring* his belief. Ted 'does not believe in God *on the basis* of evidence'; 'he does not take that testimony as evidence' just because he doesn't employ it in an argument that leads him to accept what he's been told. Plantinga, it seems, considers something to be evidence for *S*'s belief that *p* only if it is *ulterior* evidence, *propositional* evidence, and evidence *relied on by S in coming to believe that p*. *S*'s theism without evidence, therefore, may be theism with lots of experiential support and even lots of sophisti-cated supporting argumentation recognized as such and approved by *S*, as long as *S* didn't come to theism as a consequence of seeing the force of the arguments. That position isn't even anti-evidentialist in a way many if any evidentialists would recognize as such, and it's theism without evidence only in a sense that could hardly raise an eyebrow, except perhaps at the misleading designation for it.

Plantinga's attending exclusively to the *generative* interpretation of 'believe on the basis of' results in his neglecting the far more common and more important interpretation of that phrase as concerned only with the *support* of belief. But, of course, it is only the support and not the generation of belief that is at issue between Plantinga and the evidentialist.

This particular aspect of his narrow notions of evidence and belief seems to be at least enhanced by his attention to foundationalism. When presenting Aristotelian demonstrative science as the model for ancient and medieval foundationalism he says, 'Logic and mathematics seem to be the best examples of science so thought of. Consider, for example, propositional logic: here one can *start from* self-evident axioms and *proceed* to deduce theorems . . .' (RBG, p. 59; emphasis added). This account seems intended to present demonstrative science as a heuristic device. But, as Jonathan Barnes has observed, 'Aristotle does not pretend to be offering guid-ance to the scientist—or, for that matter, to the historian or the philosopher—on how best to pursue his researches or how most efficiently to uncover new truths. Rather, it [Book A of the *Posterior Analytics*] is concerned with the organization and presentation of the results of research: its aim is to say how we may collect into an intelligible whole the scientist's various discoveries—how we may so arrange the facts that their interrelations, and in particular their explanations, may best be revealed and grasped. In short, the primary purpose of [Aristotelian] demonstra-tion is to expound and render intelligible what is already discovered, not to discover what is still unknown'.[3]

Precisely the same sort of thing must be said about Aquinas (the perceptive Aristotelian) and his natural theology. It should go without saying that none of the Five Ways is one along which Thomas himself came to theism or expected any of his readers to do so (since he was writing for students of theology). The Five Ways,

---

3. Jonathan Barnes, *Aristotle's Posterior Analytics* (Clarendon Press, Oxford, 1975), pp. x–xi.

like all the other arguments and evidence in the *Summa Theologiae* devoted to rational faith's enterprise of seeking understanding, are meant 'to expound and render intelligible what is already discovered, not to discover what is still unknown' or even to record the route by which such theological discoveries were made.

And evidence of just that sort is what I contend Ted surely has and ought to have. Because of his tender years and his sheltered upbringing, what he would offer when asked why he believed in God would no doubt fall short of the highest standards of theistic evidentialism, but in offering it he would be doing his best to support what he already believed by expounding it and rendering it intelligible, which is just what Augustine, Anselm, and Aquinas were doing, too.

What the evidentialist counts as belonging to Ted's evidence for theism is what Ted would offer if asked why he believes in God. He has beliefs supportive of that belief. He must have such beliefs, given the life he's led and the education he's had. We can suppose that he believes, for instance, that God answered his prayers for his mother's recovery from a dangerous illness, and that Jesus rose from the dead. Those supportive beliefs are, to be sure, not steps by which he came to theism. And it would be implausible to suppose that such beliefs are even very often among his occurrent beliefs, or that he has ever actually offered them in support of his theism. But he knows that he is expected to 'be ready always to give an answer to every man that asketh you a reason of the hope that is in you' (1 Peter 3: 15), and it is his deeply ingrained dispositional beliefs of just those sorts that he would offer without a moment's hesitation when the question brought them into his consciousness. If Ted, improbably, had absolutely nothing to say when asked for a reason, his family, teachers, and friends would be shocked and disappointed, and Ted would be ashamed. Conscientious believers as well as objectors live by the evidentialist canon. There *is* deficiency in a faith that can give no reason, even if not everyone who holds such a faith is epistemically deficient.

Circumstances, grounds, warrant, justification, etc.

Plantinga's project of expounding and defending theism without evidence involves one final obstacle to the evidentialist's denial that Plantinga has presented us with anything that matches that description. This obstacle doesn't arise clearly in the case of Ted's theism, the support for which is all propositional. It consists in Plantinga's account of the credentials he admits a belief must have if it is to qualify as properly basic in his extended sense, according to which 'I see a tree' and 'God exists' can rightly be and typically are properly basic.

We are in a position to expect certain things of this account: the credentials required by such a properly basic belief that p will lie outside the nature of p itself, they will not include anything propositional that plays a part in S's acquiring of his belief that p, and they will be called anything but *evidence* for S's belief that p. These expectations are amply fulfilled, as a few passages will quickly show. 'Consider the belief that I see a tree: this belief is properly basic in *circumstances* that are hard to describe in detail, but include my being appeared to in a certain characteristic way' (RBG, p. 83). 'Upon having experience of a certain sort, I believe that I am perceiving a tree. In the typical case I do not hold this belief on the basis of other beliefs; it is nonetheless *not groundless*. My having that characteristic sort of experience . . . plays a crucial role in the formation of that belief. It also plays a crucial role in its *justification*' (RBG, p. 86). It is worth noting that in this second passage the justifying sub-propositional experience is also assigned 'a crucial role' in *S*'s *acquisition* of his belief that *p*.

It is clear that Plantinga not only acknowledges but insists that so-called properly basic beliefs of the sort represented by 'I see a tree' and 'God exists' must present credentials. But he also insists that these credentials must be non-propositional, which, given his narrow notion of evidence, is enough to prevent their counting as evidence for these beliefs. The first and most obvious thing to say about such 'circumstances', 'warrant', 'grounds', or 'justification' is that they all are and ought to be included in what the evidentialist normally assesses when assessing the rationality of a belief that has such backing. Evidence by any other name is still subject to the evidentialist canon. Plantinga seems close to acknowledging this when he says regarding the 'circumstances' required for the proper basicality of his belief that he sees a tree that 'that same belief is not properly basic in circumstances including, say, my knowledge that I am sitting in the living room listening to music with my eyes closed' (RBG, p. 83). The evidentialist's verdict on Plantinga's believing in such circumstances that he sees a tree is not that it is not properly basic—a possibility too remote in such circumstances to be seriously considered—but that it is irrational absolutely in virtue of having not merely no evidence to warrant it, but also overwhelming evidence to the contrary.

In order to show that Plantinga's theism 'without evidence' is *not* without evidence, I've just been pointing out that the 'warrant' and 'justification' he locates in sub-propositional experiential circumstances are now and always have been among the things whose adequacy concerns the evidentialist, among the things the evidentialist would count as evidence; and that therefore Plantinga hasn't shown that propositions such as 'I see a tree' and 'God exists' are rationally believable without evidence. And if all his sub-propositional warrant and justification for such beliefs is part of what evidentialism has always been concerned with in assessing the rationality of beliefs, then the real difference between the theistic evidentialist and Plantinga as he presents himself in these articles seems to lie in their different treatments of sub-propositional evidence. Plantinga's refusal to countenance it as evidence leads to a neglect of its inchoate, unorganized state, below the level of consciousness. The theistic evidentialist, on the other hand, is interested in employing 'Chisholm-like' questions in order to raise sub-propositional evidence to the propositional level, where it can be properly organized and assessed. Plantinga's project yields not so much theism without evidence as see-no-evidence theism.

Someone might think these observations miss the mark. After all, there's plausibility in Plantinga's repeated claim that a necessary condition for anything's counting as evidence for S's belief that he sees a tree is that S at least *believes* whatever is supposed to count in that way, and surely anything S believes is *propositional*. It would, of course, enhance the plausibility of the claim that anything that can count as S's evidence for S's belief that p must be among S's other beliefs *if* those other beliefs included S's dispositional beliefs. And while the object of belief must be propositional, for some of S's dispositional beliefs, and especially for those at issue here, the object need be only potentially propositional. Sub-propositional experiential circumstances C that require no more than the simple stimulus of the question 'Do you believe that you are now in C?' in order to be raised to the propositional level and made the object of an occurrent experiential belief are eminently recognizable as potentially propositional, as objects of dispositional beliefs, and thus as justifying conditions to which the believer has ready access.

If a relatively sophisticated S believes that she sees a tree and believes it in circumstances Plantinga accepts as warranting S's belief as properly basic, then all the evidentialist has to do in order to convert S's properly basic belief into what Plantinga would recognize as a properly *based* belief is to ask her 'Do you believe that you are now having the visual experience ordinarily associated with seeing a tree, and do you believe that that experience is your basis for your belief that you see a tree?'. And if the status of proper basicality Plantinga has won for 'I see a tree' and 'God exists' is evanescent to that amazing degree, it isn't worth working for or having.

This concentration on propositional evidence can easily go too far, however. It must often happen that an unsophisticated S believes that he sees a tree, believes it in circumstances Plantinga accepts as warranting S's belief as properly basic, and simply wouldn't understand the question 'Do you believe that you are now having the visual experience ordinarily associated with seeing a tree, and do you believe that that experience is your basis for your belief that you see a tree?'. It would stretch the notion of belief too far to claim that S may be believing, even dispositionally, a proposition S wouldn't understand if it were put to him. All the same, in such a case S's belief is (typically) based on S's visual experience *itself*. That experience, the *cause* of the belief, is still evidence of a sort the evidentialist canon is concerned with. And at least in many cases S could eventually be brought to focus his attention on the experience itself and to understand the evidentialist's questions.

More generally and much more importantly, even a sophisticated S's incorrigible belief that she is now having such-and-such a visual experience will (typically) have as its evidence only that experience itself, the very circumstances in which she forms the belief. Ultimately, sub-propositional evidence is indispensable. While evidentialism certainly recognizes evidence at this lowest level, it can't pretend to *assess* it, and so is likely to acknowledge incorrigible beliefs as properly basic.

As regards belief generally and as regards theism in particular, the 'evidentialist challenge' has *not* been 'challenged and overcome'. The evidentialist challenge hasn't even been challenged.

Chapter 6
Grammar and religious belief
D. Z. Phillips

WHAT kind of philosophical and theological account does the concept of divine reality call for? To answer this question one must determine the grammar of the concept to be investigated. All too often in the case of the reality of God this requirement has been overlooked or taken for granted. Because the question of divine reality can be construed as 'Is God real or not?' it has often been assumed that the dispute between the believer and the unbeliever is over *a matter of fact*. The philosophical investigation of the reality of God then becomes the philosophical investigation appropriate to an assertion of a matter of fact. That this is a misrepresentation of the religious concept is made obvious by a brief comparison of talk about facts with talk about God.

When do we say, 'It is a fact that . . . ' or ask, 'Is it a fact that . . . ?'? Often, we do so where there is some uncertainty. For example, if the police hear that a wanted criminal has died in some remote part of the world, their reaction might be, 'Check the facts'. Again, we often say that something is a fact in order to rule out other possibilities. A student asks, 'Is the professor coming in today?' and receives the reply, 'No, as a matter of fact he never comes in on Monday.' A fact might not have been: it is conceivable that the wanted criminal had not died, just as it is conceivable that it had been the custom of the professor to come in on Mondays. On the other hand, the religious believer is not prepared to say that God might not exist. It is not that as a *matter of fact* God will always exist, but that it *makes no sense* to say that God might not exist.

We decide the truth or falsity of many matters of fact by taking account of the truth or falsity of other matters of fact. What is to count in deciding whether something is a fact or not is agreed upon in most cases. Refusal to admit that something is a fact in certain situations might be cause for alarm, as in the case of someone who sees chairs in a room which in fact is empty. Is this akin to the dispute between the believer and the unbeliever; one sees God, but the other does not? The believer is not like someone who sees objects when they are not there, since his reaction to the absence of factual evidence is not at all like that of the man suffering from hallucinations. In the case of the chairs there is no dispute over *the kind of evidence* needed to settle the issue. When the positivist claims that there is no God because God cannot be located, the believer does not object on the grounds that the investigation has not been thorough enough, but on the grounds that the

D. Z. Phillips 'Philosophy, Theology and the Reality of God' from *The Philosophical Quarterly* 13 (1963), copyright © The Editors of The Philosophical Quarterly 1963, reprinted by permission of Blackwell Publishers and the author.

investigation fails to understand the grammar of what is being investigated—namely, the reality of God.

It makes as little sense to say, 'God's existence is not a fact' as it does to say, 'God's existence is a fact.' In saying that something either is or is not a fact, I am not describing the 'something' in question. To say that x is a fact is to say something about the grammar of x; it is to indicate what it would and would not be sensible to say or do in connection with it. To say that the concept of divine reality does not share this grammar is to reject the possibility of talking about God in the way in which one talks about matters of fact. I suggest that more can be gained if one compares the question, 'What kind of reality is divine reality?' not with the question, 'Is this physical object real or not?' but with the different question, 'What kind of reality is the reality of physical objects?'. To ask whether physical objects are real is not like asking whether this appearance is real or not where often one can find out. I can find out whether unicorns are real or not, but how can I find out whether the physical world is real or not? This latter question is not about the possibility of carrying out an investigation. It is a question of whether it is possible to speak of truth and falsity in the physical world; a question prior to that of determining the truth or falsity of any particular matter of fact. Similarly, the question of the reality of God is a question of the possibility of sense and nonsense, truth and falsity, in religion. When God's existence is construed as a matter of fact, it is taken for granted that the concept of God is at home within the conceptual framework of the reality of the physical world. It is as if we said, 'We know where the assertion of God's existence belongs, we understand what kind of assertion it is; all we need do is determine its truth or falsity.' But to ask a question about the reality of God is to ask a question about *a kind of reality*, not about the reality of *this* or *that*, in much the same way as asking a question about the reality of physical objects is not to ask about the reality of this or that physical object.

What then is the appropriate philosophical investigation of the reality of God? Suppose one asks, 'His reality as opposed to what?'. The possibility of the unreality of God does not occur *within* any religion, but it might well arise in disputes *between* religions. A believer of one religion might say that the believers of other religions were not worshipping the same God. The question how he would decide the identity of God is connected in many ways with what it means to talk of divine reality.

In a dispute over whether two people are discussing the same person there are ways of removing the doubt, but the identity of a god is not like the identity of a human being. To say that one worships the same God as someone else is not to point to the same object or to be confronted with it. How did Paul, for example, know that the God he worshipped was also the God of Abraham? What enabled him to say this was not anything like the method of agreement one has in the case of two astronomers who check whether they are talking of the same star. What enabled Paul to say that he worshipped the God of Abraham was the fact that although many changes had taken place in the concept of God, there was nevertheless a common religious tradition in which both he and Abraham stood. To say that a god is not the same as one's own God involves saying that those who believe in him are in a radically different religious tradition from one's own. The criteria of what can sensibly be said of God are to be found *within* the religious tradition. This conclusion has an important bearing on the question of what account of religion philosophy and theology can give. It follows from my argument that the criteria of meaningfulness cannot be found *outside* religion, since they are given by religious discourse itself. Theology can claim justifiably to show what is meaningful in religion only when it has an internal relation to religious discourse. Philosophy can make the same claim only if it is prepared to examine religious concepts in the contexts from which they derive their meaning.

Some theologians have claimed that theology gives a justification of religion. E. L. Mascall, for instance, says: 'The primary task of rational theology is to ask what grounds can be found for asserting the existence of God.'[1]

Mascall implies that theology is external to religion and seeks a rational justification of religious truth. This view differs sharply from what I claim to be the internal role of theology in religion. This role can be explained as follows.

One cannot have religion without religious discourse. This is taught to children through stories by which they become acquainted with the attributes of God. As a result of this teaching the child forms an idea of God. We have far less idea than we sometimes suppose of what the nature of the child's idea is, but for our purposes its content is irrelevant. What is relevant to note is that the child does not listen to the stories, observe religious practices, reflect on all this, and then form an idea of God out of the experience. The idea of God is being formed in the actual story-telling and religious services. To ask which came first, the story-telling or the idea of God, is to ask a senseless question. Once one has an idea of God, what one has is a primitive theology. This is in many ways far removed from the theology of the professional theologian, but what makes it far removed is a difference in complexity or maturity, not a difference in kind or function. In each case theology decides what it makes sense to say to God and about God. In short, theology is the grammar of religious discourse.

There is a limited analogy between the relation of theology to religious discourse and the relation of logic to language. One cannot have a language without a logic, although one can have a language without explicitly formulated logical principles. On the other hand, logical principles can have no meaning apart from the language in which they are found. This is not refuted by the fact that the meaning of a formal system can be explained in terms of the rules of that system. The question remains whether the possibility of any such system is dependent on the existence of language. The argument appears circular and contradictory if one thinks of either logic or language as being prior to the other. But as in the case of the child's stories

---

1. *Existence and Analogy* (London: Longmans, 1949), p. 1.

and the concept of God, to ask which came first is to ask a senseless question. As soon as one has language one has logic which determines what can and what cannot be said in that language without being prior to it. As soon as one has religious discourse one has a theology which determines what it will be sensible to say and what it will be nonsensical to say within that religious discourse without being prior to it.

The limited nature of the analogy is evident when we want to talk of alternative theologies. To understand the need for a new theology, the need for a revised grammar of religious discourse, it is more helpful to consider an analogy with the development of scientific laws. In the course of scientific experimentation, in order to account for new phenomena, scientific laws have to be modified or changed. One would not say that the old laws are wrong, or that the new ones are nearer the truth, but simply that they differ in their range of application. There is an analogy here with the way in which old ideas of God are supplanted and new ones take their place. This will not seem arbitrary if one remembers that the need for a new theology, for a different idea of God, does not occur *in vacuo*. The development of scientific laws can only be understood by reference to the tradition of scientific enquiry, and the changes in the idea of God can only be understood in terms of a developing religion. This is not to say that the role of the concept of God is akin to the role of a scientific model, for the analogy with developing scientific laws, like the analogy with logic and language, is a limited one. I use it simply to re-emphasise the internal relation of theology to religion.

Theology cannot impose criteria of meaningfulness on religion from without. Neither can philosophy. Mascall, on the other hand, maintains that like theology, philosophy has a special role to play, namely to seek rational grounds for asserting the existence of God. This view misrepresents the relation of philosophy to religion. The role of philosophy in this context is not to justify, but to understand. Mascall says of the Christian: 'He knows what he means by God because the Bible and the Church have told him. He can then institute a purely rational enquiry into the grounds for asserting that God exists.'[2]

Why not remain with an understanding of what the Bible and the Church teach? What extra is this rational enquiry supposed to achieve? This question might be answered by indicating the problems connected with the existence of a plurality of religions. If one accepts the internal relation of theology to religion and the religious tradition as the means of identifying God, what is one to say of the conflicting claims of different religions? In much the same spirit in which I have been talking about the relation of theology to religion, Peter Winch says:

criteria of logic are not a direct gift of God, but arise out of, and are only intelligible in the context of, ways of living or modes of social life. It follows that one cannot apply criteria of

2. Ibid., p. 17.

logic to modes of social life as such. For instance, science is one such mode and religion is another; and each has criteria of intelligibility peculiar to itself. So within science or religion actions can be logical or illogical . . . in religion it would be illogical to suppose that one could pit one's strength against God's . . . But we cannot sensibly say that either the practice of science itself or that of religion is either illogical or logical; both are non-logical.[3]

But can this thesis hold in face of a plurality of religions? The problem is brought out if one considers the way in which the analogy between theology, logic and scientific laws which we have considered breaks down. In the development of scientific laws there is eventual agreement that such development is desirable. The same could be said, roughly speaking, of the development of the idea of God in the Old Testament. But this need not be true of modern developments in theology: opposing theologians will stick to their respective positions and declare the others to be wrong. This brings up the question of authority or reference to an authoritative system. Both logic and science are *public* in so far as it can be decided whether a statement is logical or illogical, or whether a given practice is scientific or not. Illogical and non-scientific statements are refutable. But because of the nature of theology one may only say that a religious statement is refuted by *a* theology. There is no analogy here with either logic or science. This is due to what might be called *the personal element* in theology. In the formulation of logical and scientific principles there is no personal element involved. This is not true of theology.

As I have already said, the systematic theology is a sophistication of that theology which is necessarily present in so far as religious language is present. The theological system is often constructed to answer certain questions and problems which may arise. But the foundation of a theological system is based on the non-formalised theology which is within the religious way of life carried on by the person who is constructing the theological system. In so far as this is true, theology is personal, since it is based on one's own experience of God. Where the connection between theology and experience is missing, there is a danger of theology becoming an academic game.

It is extremely difficult to steer a course between the personal and the public in this whole question. Theology must be personal in so far as it is concerned with one's own idea of God, and in this context religion must always be personal. On the other hand, in so far as religious language must be learnt, religion is public. One cannot have *any* idea of God. Once one has embraced a theology, one has established 'what can be said' in that particular religion, but what can be said does not depend on the fact that an *individual* is saying it.

Some philosophers have held that in face of theological differences *within* religions and the more pronounced theological differences *between* religions, philosophy itself must decide what are the meaningful religious assertions. This view is expressed in no uncertain terms by Peter Munz in his book, *Problems of Religious*

3. *The Idea of a Social Science* (London: Routledge, 1958), pp. 90–1.

Knowledge. In face of the plurality of religious traditions Munz thinks it foolish to identify the truth with any *one* of them. On the other hand, he also objects to saying that religious truth is the *sum* of religious traditions. One of Munz's aims is ' . . . to enquire whether it is not possible to find a criterion of religious truth which would enable us to avoid the identification of religious truth with any one provincial or with the alleged cosmopolitan tradition.'[4]

Munz thinks that such a criterion can be found in philosophy: ' . . . the philosophy of religion imposes its own criterion of what is good theological reasoning and what is bad theological reasoning. And in doing this, it ceases to be purely descriptive of religious knowledge and begins to be normative.'[5]

Munz's disagreement with Winch is obvious. He thinks that the norm of truth and falsity is not to be found within religion, but *outside* it. One reason why he thinks that philosophical criteria of theological reasoning are needed is the absence of real discussion between adherents of different religions. He describes the contact that does occur as follows: 'These arguments are therefore no more than affirmations of positions. They are monologues. A real argument must be a dialogue, an exchange of opinions and a weighing of evidence. Only a *real* argument can be more than an exercise in self-assertion. But to argue *really*, one must be clear as to the things one is arguing about.'[6]

Munz says more than he realises in the last sentence of the above quotation. In order for adherents of different religions to talk to each other, they must have something to talk about! But this is a religious matter, not a philosophical one. Philosophical speculation may help to distinguish religion from superstition, but where *religions* are concerned, whether they have enough in common to promote discussion depends on the content of their beliefs. No general answer is possible. In some cases, for instance between Christians and Jews, a wealth of discussion is possible. Between others—Christians and Buddhists, say—discussion is more difficult. When one considers tribal religions, one wonders whether one is talking about the same thing at all; whether here religion has a different meaning. The possibility of discussion then depends, not as Munz suggests on the intervention of philosophy from without, but on the theologies of the religions in question. If there were a union of religions this would be because of changes within the religions united. One might object to my analysis on the grounds that it stresses religious meaning at the expense of religious truth. The analysis does not indicate which religion is the true one. But why should anyone suppose that philosophy can answer that question?

One final objection. An opponent of religion might claim that far from leaving the question of religious truth unanswered, I have guaranteed that any possible answer

4. *Problems of Religious Knowledge* (London: SCM Press, 1959), p. 9.
5. Ibid., p. 28.
6. Ibid., p. 11.

is favourable to religion by insisting that the criteria of intelligibility in religious matters are to be found within religion. The objection confuses my epistemological thesis with an absurd religious doctrine. To say that the criteria of truth and falsity in religion are to be found within a religious tradition is to say nothing of the truth or falsity of the religion in question. On the contrary, my thesis is as necessary in explaining unbelief as it is in explaining belief. It is because many have seen religion for what it is that they have thought it important to rebel against it. The rebel sees what religion is and rejects it. What can this 'seeing' be? Obviously, he does not see the point of religion as the believer does, since for the believer seeing the point of religion is believing. Nevertheless, the rebel has knelt in the church even if he has not prayed. He has taken the sacrament of Communion even if he has not communed. He knows the story from the inside, but it is not a story that captivates him. Nevertheless, he can see what religion is supposed to do and what it is supposed to be. At times we stand afar off saying, 'I wish I could be like that.' We are not like that, but we know what it must be like. The rebel stands on the threshold of religion seeing what it must be like, but saying, 'I do not want to be like that. I rebel against it all.' It is in this context, as Camus has said, that 'every blasphemy is, ultimately, a participation in holiness'.

Chapter 7

The groundlessness of religious belief

Norman Malcolm

I

IN his final notebooks Wittgenstein wrote that it is difficult 'to realize the ground-lessness of our believing.'[1] He was thinking of how much mere acceptance, on the basis of no evidence, forms our lives. This is obvious in the case of small children. They are told the names of things. They accept what they are told. They do not ask for grounds. A child does not demand a proof that the person who feeds him is called 'Mama.' Or are we to suppose that the child reasons to himself as follows: 'The others present seem to know this person who is feeding me, and since they call her "Mama" that probably is her name'? It is obvious on reflection that a child cannot consider evidence or even doubt anything until he has already learned much. As Wittgenstein puts it: 'The child learns by believing the adult. Doubt comes *after* belief' (*OC*, 160).

What is more difficult to perceive is that the lives of educated, sophisticated adults are also formed by groundless beliefs. I do not mean eccentric beliefs that are out on the fringes of their lives, but fundamental beliefs. Take the belief that familiar material things (watches, shoes, chairs) do not cease to exist without some physical explanation. They don't 'vanish in thin air.' It is interesting that we do use that very expression: 'I *know* I put the keys right here on this table. They must have vanished in thin air!' But this exclamation is hyperbole; we are not speaking in literal seriousness. I do not know of any adult who would consider, in all gravity, that the keys might have inexplicably ceased to exist.

Our attitude in this matter is striking. We would not be willing to consider it as even improbable that a missing lawn chair had 'just ceased to exist.' We would not

Norman Malcolm extract from 'The Groundlessness of Belief' from *Reason and Religion* edited by Stuart C. Brown (Cornell University Press, 1977), copyright © Royal Institute of Philosophy 1977, reprinted by permission of the publisher.

1. Ludwig Wittgenstein, *On Certainty*, ed. G. E. M. Anscombe and G. H. von Wright; English translation by D. Paul and G. E. M. Anscombe (Oxford, 1969), paragraph 166. Henceforth I include references to this work in the text, employing the abbreviation '*OC*' followed by paragraph number. References to Wittgenstein's *The Blue and Brown Books* (Oxford, 1958) are indicated in the text by '*BB*' followed by page number. References to his *Philosophical Investigations,* ed. G. E. M. Anscombe and R. Rhees; English translation by Anscombe (Oxford, 1967) are indicated by '*PI*' followed by paragraph number. In *OC* and *PI*, I have mainly used the translations of Paul and Anscombe but with some departures.

entertain such a suggestion. If anyone proposed it we would be sure he was joking. It is no exaggeration to say that this attitude is part of the foundations of our thinking. I do not want to say that this attitude is *un*reasonable; but rather that it is something that we do not *try* to support with grounds. It could be said to belong to 'the framework' of our thinking about material things.

Wittgenstein asks: 'Does anyone ever test whether this table remains in existence when no one is paying attention to it?' (*OC*, 163). The answer is: Of course not. Is this because we would not call it 'a table' if that were to happen? But we do call it 'a table' and none of us makes the test. Doesn't this show that we do not regard that occurrence as a possibility? People who did so regard it would seem ludicrous to us. One could imagine that they made ingenious experiments to decide the question; but this research would make us smile. Is this because experiments were conducted by our ancestors that settled the matter once and for all? I don't believe it. The principle that material things do not cease to exist without physical cause is an unreflective part of the framework within which physical investigations are made and physical explanations arrived at.

Wittgenstein suggests that the same is true of what might be called 'the principle of the continuity of nature':

Think of chemical investigations. Lavoisier makes experiments with substances in his laboratory and now concludes that this and that takes place when there is burning. He does not say that it might happen otherwise another time. He has got hold of a world picture—not of course one that he invented: he learned it as a child. I say world-picture and not hypothesis, because it is the matter-of-course (*selbstverständliche*) foundation for his research and as such also goes unmentioned. (*OC*, 167)

But now, what part is played by the presupposition that a substance A always reacts to a substance B in the same way, given the same circumstances? Or is that part of the definition of a substance? (*OC*, 168)

Framework principles such as the continuity of nature or the assumption that material things do not cease to exist without physical cause belong to what Wittgenstein calls a 'system.' He makes the following observation, which seems to me to be true: 'All testing, all confirmation and disconfirmation of a hypothesis takes place already within a system. And this system is not a more or less arbitrary and doubtful point of departure for all our arguments: no, it belongs to the nature of what we call an argument. The system is not so much the point of departure, as the element in which arguments have their life' (*OC*, 105).

A 'system' provides the boundaries within which we ask questions, carry out investigations, and make judgments. Hypotheses are put forth, and challenged, *within* a system. Verification, justification, the search for evidence, occur *within* a system. The framework propositions of the system are not put to the test, not backed up by evidence. This is what Wittgenstein means when he says: 'Of course there is justification; but justification comes to an end' (*OC*, 192); and when he asks: 'Doesn't testing come to an end?' (*OC*, 164); and when he remarks that 'whenever we test anything we are already presupposing something that is not tested' (*OC,* 163).

That this is so is not to be attributed to human weakness. It is a conceptual requirement that our inquiries and proofs stay within boundaries. Think, for example, of the activity of calculating a number. Some steps in a calculation we will check for correctness, but others we won't: for example, that $4 + 4 = 8$. More accurately, some beginners might check it, but grown-ups won't. Similarly, some grown-ups would want to determine by calculation whether $25 \times 25 = 625$, whereas others would regard that as laughable. Thus the boundaries of the system within which *you* calculate may not be exactly the same as *mine.* But we do calculate; and, as Wittgenstein remarks, 'In certain circumstances . . . we regard a calculation as sufficiently checked. What gives us a right to do so? . . . Somewhere we must be finished with justification, and then there remains the proposition that *this* is how we calculate' (*OC,* 212). If someone did not accept any boundaries for calculating this would mean that he had not learned *that* language-game: 'If someone supposed that *all* our calculations were uncertain and that we could rely on none of them (justifying himself by saying that mistakes are always possible) perhaps we would say he was crazy. But can we say he is in error? Does he not just react differently? We rely on calculations, he doesn't; we are sure, he isn't' (*OC,* 217). We are taught, or we absorb, the systems within which we raise doubts, make inquiries, draw conclusions. We grow into a framework. We don't question it. We accept it trustingly. But this acceptance is not a consequence of reflection. We do not decide to accept framework propositions. We do not decide that we live on the earth, any more than we decide to learn our native tongue. We do come to adhere to a framework proposition, in the sense that it forms the way we think. The framework propositions that we accept, grow into, are not idiosyncrasies but common ways of speaking and thinking that are pressed on us by our human community. For our acceptances to have been withheld would have meant that we had not learned how to count, to measure, to use names, to play games, or even *to talk.* Wittgenstein remarks that 'a language-game is only possible if one trusts something.' Not *can,* but *does* trust something (*OC,* 509). I think he means by this trust or acceptance what he calls belief 'in the sense of religious belief' (*OC,* 459). What does he mean by belief 'in the sense of religious belief'? He explicitly distinguishes it from *conjecture* (*Vermutung:* ibid.). I think this means that there is nothing tentative about it; it is not adopted as a hypothesis that might later be withdrawn in the light of new evidence. This also makes explicit an important feature of Wittgenstein's understanding of belief, in the sense of 'religious belief,' namely, that it does not rise or fall on the basis of evidence or grounds: it is 'groundless.'

II

In our Western academic philosophy, religious belief is commonly regarded as unreasonable and is viewed with condescension or even contempt. It is said that religion is a refuge for those who, because of weakness of intellect or character, are unable to confront the stern realities of the world. The objective, mature, *strong* attitude is to hold beliefs solely on the basis of *evidence*.

It appears to me that philosophical thinking is greatly influenced by this veneration of evidence. We have an aversion to statements, reports, declarations, beliefs, that are not based on grounds. There are many illustrations of this philosophical bent.

For example, in regard to a person's report that he has an image of the Eiffel Tower we have an inclination to think that the image must *resemble* the Eiffel Tower. How else could the person declare so confidently what his image is *of? How could he know?*

Another example: A memory-report or memory-belief must be based, we think, on some mental *datum* that is equipped with various features to match the corresponding features of the memory-belief. This datum will include an image that provides the *content* of the belief, and a peculiar feeling that makes one refer the image to a *past* happening, and another feeling that makes one believe that the image is an *accurate* portrayal of the past happening, and still another feeling that informs one that it was *oneself* who witnessed the past happening. The presence of these various features makes memory-beliefs thoroughly reasonable.

A final illustration: Consider the fact that after a comparatively few examples and bits of instruction a person can go on to carry out a task, apply a word correctly in the future, continue a numerical series from an initial segment, distinguish grammatical from ungrammatical constructions, solve arithmetical problems, and so on. These correct performances will be dealing with new and different examples, situations, combinations. The performance output will be far more varied than the instruction input. How is this possible? What carries the person from the meager instruction to his rich performance? The explanation has to be that an effect of his training was that he abstracted the Idea, perceived the Common Nature, 'internalized' the Rule, grasped the Structure. What else could bridge the gap between the poverty of instruction and the wealth of performance? Thus we postulate an intervening mental act or state which removes the inequality and restores the balance.

My illustrations belong to what could be called the *pathology* of philosophy. Wittgenstein speaks of a 'general disease of thinking' which attempts to explain occurrences of discernment, recognition, or understanding, by postulating mental states or processes from which those occurrences flow 'as from a reservoir' (*BB*, p. 143). These mental intermediaries are assumed to contribute to the causation of the various cognitive performances. More significantly for my present purpose, they are supposed to *justify* them; they provide our *grounds* for saying or doing this rather than that; they *explain how we know*. The Image, or Cognitive State, or Feeling, or Idea, or Sample, or Rule, or Structure, *tells* us. It is like a road map or a signpost. It guides our course.

What is 'pathological' about these explanatory constructions and pseudoscientific inferences? Two things at least. First, the movement of thought that demands these intermediaries is circular and empty, unless it provides criteria for determining their presence and nature *other than* the occurrence of the phenomena they are postulated to explain—and, of course, no such criteria are forthcoming. Second, there is the great criticism by Wittgenstein of this movement of philosophical thought: namely, his point that no matter what kind of state, process, paradigm, sample, structure, or rule, is conceived as giving us the necessary guidance, it could be taken, or understood, as indicating a *different* direction from the one in which we actually did go. The assumed intermediary Idea, Structure, or Rule, does not and cannot reveal that because of it we went in the only direction it was reasonable to go. Thus the internalized intermediary we are tempted to invoke to bridge the gap between training and performance, as being that which shows us what we must do or say if we are to be rational, cannot do the job it was invented to do. It cannot fill the epistemological gap. It cannot provide the bridge of justification. It cannot put to rest the How-do-we-know? question. Why not? Because it cannot tell us how *it itself* is to be taken, understood, applied. Wittgenstein puts the point briefly and powerfully: 'Don't always think that you read off your words from facts; that you portray these in words according to rules. For even so you would have to apply the rule in the particular case without guidance' (*PI*, 292). Without guidance! Like Wittgenstein's signpost arrow that cannot tell us whether to go in the direction of the arrow tip or in the opposite direction, so too the Images, Ideas, Cognitive Structures, or Rules, that we philosophers imagine as devices for guidance, cannot interpret themselves to us. The signpost does not tell the traveler how to read it. A second signpost might tell him how to read the first one; we can imagine such a case. But this can't go on. If the traveler is to continue his journey he will have to do something on his own, without guidance.

The parable of the traveler speaks for *all* of the language-games we learn and practice; even those in which there is the most disciplined instruction and the most rigorous standards of conformity. Suppose that a pupil has been given thorough training in some procedure, whether it is drawing patterns, building fences, or proving theorems. But then he has to carry on by himself in new situations. How does he know what to do? Wittgenstein presents the following dialogue: ' "However you instruct him in the continuation of a pattern—how can he *know* how he is to continue by himself"—Well, how do *I* know?—If that means "Have I grounds?", the answer is: the grounds will soon give out. And then I shall act, without grounds' (*PI*, 211). Grounds come to an end. Answers to How-do-we-know? questions come to an end. Evidence comes to an end. We must speak, act, live, without evidence. This is so, not just on the fringes of life and language, but at the center of our most regularized activities. We do learn rules and learn to follow them. But our training was in the past! We had to leave it behind and proceed on our own.

It is an immensely important fact of nature that as people carry on an activity in which they have received a common training, they do largely *agree* with one another, accepting the same examples and analogies, taking the same steps. We agree in what to say, in how to apply language. We agree in our responses to particular cases.

As Wittgenstein says: 'That is not agreement in opinions but in form of life' (*PI*, 241). We cannot explain this agreement by saying that we are just doing what the rules tell us—for our agreement in applying rules, formulae, and signposts is what gives them their *meaning*.

One of the primary pathologies of philosophy is the feeling that we must *justify* our language-games. We want to establish them as well-grounded. But we should consider here Wittgenstein's remark that a language-game 'is not based on grounds. It is there—like our life' (*OC*, 559).

Within a language-game there is justification and lack of justification, evidence and proof, mistakes and groundless opinions, good and bad reasoning, correct measurements and incorrect ones. One cannot properly apply these terms to a language-game itself. It may, however, be said to be 'groundless,' not in the sense of a groundless opinion, but in the sense that we accept it, we live it. We can say, 'This is what we do. This is how we are.'

In this sense religion is groundless; and so is chemistry. Within each of these two systems of thought and action there is controversy and argument. Within each there are advances and recessions of insight into the secrets of nature or the spiritual condition of humankind and the demands of the Creator, Savior, Judge, Source. Within the framework of each system there is criticism, explanation, justification. But we should not expect that there might be some sort of rational justification of the framework itself.

A chemist will sometimes employ induction. Does he have evidence for a Law of Induction? Wittgenstein observes that it would strike him as nonsense to say, 'I know that the Law of Induction is true.' ('Imagine such a statement made in a law court.') It would be more correct to say, 'I believe in the Law of Induction' (*OC*, 500). This way of putting it is better because it shows that the attitude toward induction is belief in the sense of 'religious' belief—that is to say, an acceptance which is not conjecture or surmise and for which there is no reason—it is a groundless acceptance.

It is intellectually troubling for us to conceive that a whole system of thought might be groundless, might have no rational justification. We realize easily enough, however, that grounds soon give out—that we cannot go on giving reasons for our reasons. There arises from this realization the conception of a reason that is *self-justifying*—something whose credentials as a reason cannot be questioned.

This metaphysical conception makes its presence felt at many points—for example, as an explanation of how a person can tell what his mental image is *of*. We feel that the following remarks, imagined by Wittgenstein, are exactly right: ' "The image must be more similar to its object than any picture. For however similar I make the picture to what it is supposed to represent, it can always be the picture of something else. But it is essential to the image that it is the image of *this* and of nothing else" ' (*PI*, 389). A pen and ink drawing represents the Eiffel Tower; but it could represent a mine shaft or a new type of automobile jack. Nothing prevents this drawing from being taken as a representation of something other than the Eiffel Tower. But my mental image of the Eiffel Tower is *necessarily* an image of the Eiffel Tower. Therefore it must be a 'remarkable' kind of picture. As Wittgenstein observes: 'Thus one might come to regard the image as a super-picture' (ibid.). Yet we have no intelligible conception of how a super-picture would differ from an ordinary picture. It would seem that it has to be a *super-likeness*—but what does this mean?

There is a familiar linguistic practice in which one person *tells* another what his image is of (or what he intends to do, or what he was about to say) and no question is raised of how the first one *knows* that what he says is true. This question is imposed from outside, artificially, by the philosophical craving for justification. We can see here the significance of these remarks: 'It isn't a question of explaining a language-game by means of our experiences, but of noting a language-game' (*PI*, 655). 'Look on the language-game as the *primary* thing' (*PI*, 656). Within a system of thinking and acting there occurs, *up to a point*, investigation and criticism of the reasons and justifications that are employed in that system. This inquiry into whether a reason is good or adequate cannot, as said, go on endlessly. We stop it. We bring it to an end. We come upon something that *satisfies* us. It is as if we made a decision or issued an edict: '*This* is an adequate reason!' (or explanation, or justification). Thereby we fix a boundary of our language-game.

There is nothing wrong with this. How else could we have disciplines, systems, games? But our fear of groundlessness makes us conceive that we are under some logical compulsion to terminate at *those particular* stopping points. We imagine that we have confronted the self-evident reason, the self-justifying explanation, the picture or symbol whose meaning cannot be questioned. This obscures from us the *human* aspect of our concepts—the fact that what we call 'a reason,' 'evidence,' 'explanation,' 'justification,' is what appeals to and satisfies *us*.

III

The desire to provide a rational foundation for a form of life is especially prominent in the philosophy of religion, where there is an intense preoccupation with purported proofs of the existence of God. In American universities there must be hundreds of courses in which these proofs are the main topic. We can be sure that nearly always the critical verdict is that the proofs are invalid and consequently that, up to the present time at least, religious belief has received no rational justification.

Well, of course not! The obsessive concern with the proofs reveals the assumption that in order for religious belief to be intellectually respectable it *ought* to have a rational justification. *That* is the misunderstanding. It is like the idea that we are not justified in relying on memory until memory has been proved reliable.

Roger Trigg makes the following remark: 'To say that someone acts in a certain way because of his belief in God does seem to be more than a redescription of his action ... It is to give a *reason* for it. The belief is distinct from the commitment which may follow it, and is the justification for it.'² It is evident from other remarks that by 'belief in God' Trigg means 'belief in the existence of God' or 'belief that God exists'. Presumably by the acts and *commitments* of a religious person Trigg refers to such things as prayer, worship, confession, thanksgiving, partaking of sacraments, and participation in the life of a religious group.

For myself I have great difficulty with the notion of belief in *the existence* of God, whereas the idea of belief *in* God is to me intelligible. If a man did not ever pray for help or forgiveness, or have any inclination toward it; nor ever felt that it is 'a good and joyful thing' to thank God for the blessings of this life; nor was ever concerned about his failure to comply with divine commandments—then, it seems clear to me, he could not be said to believe in God. Belief in God is not an all or none thing; it can be more or less; it can wax and wane. But belief in God in any degree does require, as I understand the words, some religious action, some commitment, or if not, at least a bad conscience.

According to Trigg, if I take him correctly, a man who was entirely devoid of any inclination toward religious action or conscience, might believe in *the existence* of God. What would be the marks of this? Would it be that the man knows some theology, can recite the Creeds, is well-read in Scripture? Or is his belief in the existence of God something different from this? If so, what? What would be the difference between a man who knows some articles of faith, heresies, scriptural writings, and in addition believes in the existence of God, and one who knows these things but does not believe in the existence of God? I assume that both of them are indifferent to the acts and commitments of religious life.

I do not comprehend this notion of belief in *the existence* of God which is thought to be distinct from belief *in* God. It seems to me to be an artificial construction of philosophy, another illustration of the craving for justification.

Religion is a form of life; it is language embedded in action—what Wittgenstein calls a 'language-game.' Science is another. Neither stands in need of justification, the one no more than the other.

Present-day academic philosophers are far more prone to challenge the credentials of religion than of science, probably for a number of reasons. One may be the illusion that science can justify its own framework. Another is the fact that science is a vastly greater force in our culture. Still another may be the fact that by and large religion is to university people an alien form of life. They do not participate in it and do not understand what it is all about.

2. *Reason and Commitment* (Cambridge, 1973), p. 75.

Questions for discussion

1. Can we offer some clear tests which an argument or a reason must pass if it is rightly to be considered as a good one?
2. Is Aquinas right to hold that items of specifically Christian teaching (such as the doctrines of the Trinity and the Incarnation) are not open to rational demonstration?
3. Should we share Aquinas's sharp distinction between faith and knowledge?
4. Flew invokes the presumption of atheism. But why should one not say that the onus of proof lies on the atheist?
5. Can we know that what we take to be evidence really *is* evidence?
6. How might one determine whether or not a belief is 'properly basic'?
7. Is religious belief seriously different from other kinds of belief?
8. Do we have a 'normal understanding' of notions such as 'meaning' and 'understanding'? If so, does it tie them closely to empirical confirmation and refutation?
9. Is it possible to draw a sharp distinction between philosophy and theology?
10. What should be the role of philosophy when it comes to religious belief?

Advice on further reading

Many of the issues discussed by authors of the preceding extracts have been recently written about in books dealing with the topic of religion and philosophy in general. Ones especially worth consulting include:

Robert Audi and William Wainwright (eds), *Rationality, Religious Belief and Moral Commitment* (Ithaca, New York, 1986).

Stuart Brown (ed.), *Reason and Religion* (Ithaca, New York, and London, 1977).

Jack A. Bonsor, *Athens and Jerusalem: The Role of Philosophy in Theology* (New York, 1993).

Vincent Brümmer, *Theology and Philosophical Inquiry* (London and Basingstoke, 1981).

Anthony Kenny, *What is Faith?* (Oxford and New York, 1992).

J. Pelikan, *Christianity and Classical Culture* (New Haven, Connecticut, 1993).

Terence Penelhum, *Reason and Religious Faith* (Oxford, 1995).

Alvin Plantinga and Nicholas Wolterstorff (eds), *Faith and Rationality* (Notre Dame, Indiana, and London, 1983).

John E. Smith, *Reason and God: Encounters of Philosophy with Religion* (New Haven, Connecticut and London 1961).

Richard Swinburne, *Faith and Reason* (Oxford, 1981).

Timothy Tessin and Mario von der Ruhr (eds), *Philosophy and the Grammar of Religious Belief* (New York, 1995).

Roger Trigg, *Rationality and Religion* (Oxford, 1998).

For a splendid survey and discussion of the history of thinking on the relation between faith and reason, see Avery Dulles, S J, *The Assurance of Things Hoped For* (New York and Oxford, 1994). For a brief survey of medieval approaches to the topic, see John F. Wippel, *Mediaeval Reactions to the Encounter between Faith and Reason* (Milwaukee,Wisconsin, 1995). As I have noted, Anselm is an important figure in discussions of the relationship between reason and religious belief. See Brian Davies and G. R. Evans (eds), *Anselm of Canterbury: The Major Works* (Oxford, 1998). For a sensitive, historical account of Anselm, see R. W. Southern, *Saint Anselm: A Portrait in a Landscape* (Cambridge, 1991). For philosophical approaches to Anselm on faith and reason, see:

David B. Burrell, 'Anselm: Formulating the Quest for Understanding', in David B. Burell, *Exercises in Religious Understanding* (Notre Dame, Indiana, and London, 1974).

G. R. Evans, *Anselm and Talking about God* (Oxford, 1978).

Jasper Hopkins, *A Companion to the Study of St. Anselm* (Minneapolis, Minnesota, 1972).

The extract from Aquinas which appears as Chapter 1 is best read with a knowledge of Aquinas's overall thinking. For a general survey of that, see Brian Davies, *The Thought of Thomas Aquinas* (Oxford, 1992). For more historically oriented surveys, see Jean-Pierre Torrell, *Saint Thomas Aquinas: Volume 1, The Person and His Work* (Washington, DC, 1996) and James A. Weisheipl, *Friar Thomas D'Aquino* (Oxford, 1974; republished with Corrigenda and Addenda, Washington, DC, 1983). Aquinas's discussion of reason and religious belief in the *Summa Contra Gentiles* has been recently and expertly explored by Norman Kretzmann in *The Metaphysics of Theism: Aquinas's Natural Theology in Summa Contra Gentiles I* (Oxford, 1997) and *The Metaphysics of Creation: Aquinas's Natural Theology in Summa*

Contra Gentiles II (Oxford, 1999). For other useful studies of Aquinas on philosophy and religious belief, see:

Leo J. Elders, *The Philosophical Theology of St Thomas Aquinas* (Leiden, 1990).

Etienne Gilson, *The Christian Philosophy of St Thomas Aquinas* (London, 1957).

John Jenkins, *Knowledge and Faith in Thomas Aquinas* (Cambridge, 1997).

C. F. J. Martin, *Thomas Aquinas: God and Explanations* (Edinburgh, 1997).

In reading the extract from Aquinas in Chapter 1, you might be helped by some attempts to explain what Aquinas thought of human knowledge in general. See Scott MacDonald, 'Theory of Knowledge', in Norman Kretzmann and Eleonore Stump (eds), *The Cambridge Companion to Aquinas* (Cambridge, 1993) and Eleonore Stump, 'Aquinas on the Foundations of Knowledge', *Canadian Journal of Philosophy*, supplementary volume 17 (1992).

Authors such as Clifford and Flew argue in ways reminiscent of John Locke, who is well worth reading with an eye on the topic of philosophy and religion. He deals with faith and reason in Part IV of the *Essay Concerning Human Understanding* and in *The Reasonableness of Christianity*. For editions of these texts, see Peter H. Nidditch (ed.), *An Essay Concerning Human Understanding* (Oxford, 1975) and I. T. Ramsey (ed.), *The Reasonableness of Christianity* (Stanford, California, 1958). For discussions of Locke on faith and reason, see Paul Helm, 'Locke on Faith and Knowledge', *The Philosophical Quarterly* 90 (1973), Alan P. F. Sell, *John Locke and the Eighteenth-Century Divines* (Cardiff, 1997), and Nicholas Wolterstorff, *John Locke and the Ethics of Belief* (Cambridge, 1996).

If you wish to read more by Plantinga on the themes touched on in Chapter 4, see:

Alvin Plantinga, 'Is Belief in God Rational?', in C. F. Delaney (ed.), *Rationality and Religious Belief* (Notre Dame, Indiana, 1979).

Alvin Plantinga, 'The Reformed Objection to Natural Theology', *Christian Scholar's Review* 11 (1982).

Alvin Plantinga, 'The Reformed Objection Revisited', *Christian Scholar's Review* 12 (1983).

Alvin Plantinga, 'Advice to Christian Philosophers', *Faith and Philosophy* 1 (1984).

Alvin Plantinga, *Warrant and Proper Function* (Oxford, 1993).

Alvin Plantinga, *Warranted Christian Belief* (New York, 2000).

Nicholas Wolterstorff is another notable author arguing along lines similar to those of Plantinga. See his 'The Migration of the Theistic Arguments: From Natural Theology to Evidentialist Apologetics', in Audi and Wainwright, *Rationality, Religious Belief*, and 'Can Belief in God be Rational if it has no Foundations?' in Plantinga and Wolterstorff, *Faith and Rationality*. For some discussions of Plantinga on belief in God and proper basicality, see:

Philip Quinn, 'In Search of the Foundations of Theism', *Faith and Philosophy* 2 (1985).

D. Z. Phillips, *Faith After Foundationalism* (London and New York, 1988).

Gary Gutting, 'Plantinga and the Rationality of Religious Belief ', in Tessin and von der Ruhr (eds), *Philosophy and the Grammar of Religious Belief*.

Linda Zagzebski (ed.), *Rational Faith: Catholic Responses to Reformed Epistemology* (Notre Dame, Indiana, 1983).

Plantinga has replied to Quinn in 'The Foundations of Theism: A Reply', *Faith and Philosophy* 3 (1986).

Among the many available general studies of Wittgenstein's thinking, three can be especially recommended as reliable, concise, and clearly written. These are:

Robert J. Fogelin, *Wittgenstein* (2nd edn, London, 1987).

A. C. Grayling, *Wittgenstein* (Oxford, 1988).

Anthony Kenny, *Wittgenstein* (Harmondsworth, 1973).

For a superb account of Wittgenstein's thinking on religious matters, see Cyril Barrett, *Wittgenstein on Ethics and Religious Belief* (Oxford, 1991). Also see Brian R. Clack *An Introduction to Wittgenstein's Philosophy of Religion* (Edinburgh, 1999), which, as well as containing some fine expositions of Wittgenstein, also includes very helpful introductions to and discussions of authors such as Malcolm and Phillips.

The extract from Phillips in Chapter 6 is but the tip of an iceberg. To get a serious sense of his thinking, you should consult the following works by him:

The Concept of Prayer (London, 1965).

Faith and Philosophical Enquiry (London, 1970).

Death and Immortality (London, 1970).

Religion Without Explanation (Oxford, 1976).

Belief, Change and Forms of Life (Atlantic Highlands, New Jersey, 1986).

Faith after Foundationalism (London and New York, 1988).

Wittgenstein and Religion (London, 1993).

Recovering Religious Concepts (Basingstoke and New York, 2000).

If you are interested in exploring what might be said about religion with an eye on Wittgenstein's philosophy, there are several authors worth reading apart from Malcolm and Phillips. In *Religion, Truth and Language-Games* (London, 1977), Patrick Sherry provides a sober and insightful discussion of the importance of Wittgenstein to philosophy of religion, which takes a stance somewhat different from that of Phillips. In *Does God's Existence Need Proof?* (Oxford, 1993), Richard Meser offers an extremely judicious and balanced discussion of the question contained in his book's title, a discussion which deals with Plantinga, Phillips, and a number of other authors. For a critical evaluation of Wittgensteinan trends in philosophy of religion, see Roger Trigg, *Reason and Commitment* (Cambridge, 1973).

Part II

The problem of God-Talk

Introduction

'God-Talk' and concepts of God

BERTRAND Russell had views on the morality of war. And for these he spent time in prison. A gaoler once asked him what his religion was. Russell said: 'Agnostic'. The gaoler replied: 'Well, there may be many religions, but we all worship the same God'.

But do we? Or, rather, do all who use the word 'God' mean the same thing by it? Can we assume that there is just one concept of God? Or should we think of there being many notions of the divine?

As a glance through a book such as H. P. Owen's *Concepts of Deity* ought quickly to convince you, the answer is that people have thought of God in radically different ways.[1] It is, perhaps, natural to assume that Judaism, Islam, and Christianity share a common concept of God. For their followers profess agreement on some major issues, such as that God is the Creator of all things, or that God is all-knowing (omniscient), all-powerful (almighty or omnipotent), and perfectly good. But verbal agreement between people does not guarantee that they have a common mind. And it does not do so when it comes to the God-Talk shared by Jews, Muslims, and Christians.[2] It does not even do so when it comes to what is said by members of just one of these traditions. Christians, for instance, often subscribe to similar or identical talk of God while understanding it in different ways.[3] For some of them, to call God 'Creator' implies that everything that happens is somehow God's doing. For others, it implies no such thing. For some of them, God's omniscience and omnipotence are to be chiefly understood on the model of human knowledge and power. For others, they cannot be. For some of them, God's goodness is to be thought of as moral goodness (as exhibited by people). For others it should not be thought of in this way at all.

We shall be directly turning to such disagreements later in this book (chiefly in Parts IV and V). For now, though, we need to note that the very possibility of talking of God significantly has been a major topic of discussion among philosophers of religion.

What is the problem supposed to be? Hume alludes to it through the character of Philo in his *Dialogues Concerning Natural Religion* (1779):

But when we look beyond human affairs . . . when we carry our speculations into the two eternities, before and after the present state of things; into the creation and formation of the universe; the existence and properties of spirits; the powers and operations of one universal Spirit existing without

---

1. H. P. Owen, *Concepts of Deity* (London, 1971).
2. I borrow the helpful phrase 'God-Talk' from John Macquarrie. See his *God-Talk: An Examination of the Language and Logic of Theology* (New York, 1967).
3. Authors such as D. Z. Phillips often refer to 'religious belief', 'religious believers', and to what 'belief in God' amounts to. But one might wonder to what extent such language betrays a failure to appreciate the diversity in what 'religious believers' think about what they say. Cf. my 'The Doctrine of God', in Michael Walsh (ed.), *Commentary on the Catechism of the Catholic Church* (London, 1994).

beginning and without end; omnipotent, omniscient, immutable, infinite, and incomprehensible: We must be far removed from the smallest tendency to scepticism not to be apprehensive, that we have here got quite beyond the reach of our faculties.[4]

Hume is suggesting that God-Talk is talk of what we *cannot understand*. And in doing so he is echoing many earlier thinkers, including some religious ones.

Understanding God-Talk

There are some words which seem only to be used when talking of God (or which are used when talking of what is not God only in the light of their use in God-Talk). Examples include 'omnipotent' and 'omniscient'. But God-Talk chiefly consists of nouns, adjectives, and verbs which are most frequently used in discourse concerning what few people think of as divine. Noun examples include terms such as 'agent', 'person', 'father', and 'lord'. Adjective examples include 'good', 'just', 'merciful', 'active', 'living', 'powerful', and 'loving'. Verb examples include words such as 'act', 'cause', and 'know'. Nouns, adjectives, and verbs such as these seem to have their primary sense in talk of what we might refer to as 'things in the world'.

Yet God is not supposed to be a thing in the world. God is also said to be what nothing in the world seems to be, such as infinite and wholly immaterial (and, on some accounts, timeless and immutable). So how can God-Talk tell us what God is? If we take its words in their usual sense, are we not clearly failing to talk of God? And if we use them to talk about God, are we not seeking to employ them to say something of which they are incapable? For many people, these are questions to be taken very seriously.

Augustine and his heirs

They are, for instance, taken with great seriousness by Augustine of Hippo, some of whose reflections on them can be found in Chapter 8. Influenced by what we may loosely call a 'Platonic way of thinking', Augustine holds that the senses give us no serious knowledge. In his view, true knowledge derives from God, who 'illuminates' our minds as the sun throws light on the ground.[5] Yet (like Hume and many others) he also thinks that God-Talk raises serious problems for human understanding. For to his way of thinking, much influenced by his reading of the Bible, God is not the sort of thing we can get our minds around. Among other things, Augustine's reading of the Bible leads him to think that God is 'simple'—as not to be thought of as a distinct individual with distinct attributes.[6] We may say that God is good and that God is wise. But, so Augustine concludes,

4. David Hume, *Dialogues Concerning Natural Religion* (ed. Norman Kemp Smith, Indianapolis, 1977), pp. 134 f.
5. For Augustine and his theory of divine illumination, see his *De Magistro*. For secondary reading, see ch. IV of Volume II of Copleston's *A History of Philosophy*, Mary T. Clark, *Augustine* (London, 1994), ch. 2, and John M. Rist, *Augustine* (Cambridge, 1994), ch. 3. Also see M. F. Burnyeat, 'Wittgenstein and Augustine *De Magistro*', in Gareth B. Matthews (ed.), *The Augustinian Tradition* (Berkeley, Los Angeles, and London, 1999).
6. For more on this notion of divine simplicity, see Part IV below.

God's goodness and wisdom cannot be thought of as distinguishable, as, for example, can Fred's strength and intelligence. His strength and intelligence are different attributes (so that he can get weak without becoming stupid). They are also different from Fred herself (in the sense that he can still be there even though he has become weak and stupid). According to Augustine, however, all that we ascribe to God *is* God, which leads him to conclude that God basically defies the logic of our language. We commonly talk by singling out individuals and by ascribing properties which we take to be distinguishable from each other and from the subjects to which we ascribe them. And, in Aristotle's *Categories*, Augustine (while a student in Carthage) took himself to have found a philosophical documentation of our common way of talking. But he also found it inadequate as a way of dealing with God-Talk, as he firmly says in Chapter 8 below.[7]

Chapter 8 comes from Augustine's *Confessions*. And if you go on to read the whole of that work you will find Augustine striving hard to explain how we can talk sensibly and truthfully when trying to speak about God. But Augustine never suggests that the task is an easy one. Christian though he was, it would be quite wrong to think of him as someone who thinks God-Talk to be unproblematic. And the same can be said of many of his Christian successors.

Take, for example, the author commonly referred to as 'Pseudo-Dionysius' or 'Dionysius the Areopagite'. His writings were enormously influential on Christian thinking (especially Eastern Christian thinking) from around the ninth to the fourteenth century. And they are still read and respected today (in some quarters, anyway).[8] Yet Dionysius effectively ends up feeling himself obliged to conclude that the language we use to talk of things in the world must inevitably fail to capture what God is. In the end, so he thinks, we are forced into silence. Dionysius agrees that we can ascribe attributes to God which we normally ascribe to what is not divine. But, so he adds, as soon as we say that God is X, Y, or Z, we must instantly deny that God is so. Why? Because no names or concepts strictly reach the divine reality. According to Dionysius, God transcends the limits signified by the words we normally use. He is always more than whatever we can say about him. God 'is beyond assertion', but also 'beyond denial'. He is beyond assertion since he is 'the perfect and unique cause of all things'. He is beyond denial by virtue of his 'preeminently simple and absolute nature, free of every limitation, beyond every limitation'.[9]

---

7. For a text of the *Categories* with notes and commentary, see *Aristotle's Categories and De Interpretatione* (translated with notes by J. L. Ackrill, Oxford, 1963).

8. Dionysius the Areopagite wrote four major works which circulated from around the sixth century: *The Divine Names, The Mystical Theology, The Celestial Hierarchy*, and *The Ecclesiastical Hierarchy*. But we do not actually know who he was. In the New Testament we are told that when St Paul preached at Athens 'some men joined him and believed, among them Dionysius the Areopagite', and he was long thought to be this person. But we now know that his writings must have been completed well after the New Testament period (hence the 'Pseudo' in 'Pseudo-Dionysius'). His writings were commented on by medieval thinkers such as John Scotus Eriugena (*c.*810–*c.*877), Albert the Great (d. 1280) and Thomas Aquinas. A great deal of what is often called 'Western mysticism' is deeply indebted to him. He was an influence, for instance, on the author of the famous text known as *The Cloud of Unknowing*.

9. *The Mystical Theology*, ch. 5. I quote from *Pseudo-Dionysius: The Complete Works*, translated by Colm Luibheid (New York and Mahwah, New Jersey, 1987).

Is God-Talk empty?

Yet struck though they were by the problems presented by God-Talk, writers such as Augustine and Dionysius saw them as ones to be struggled with from the position of belief in God. They did not take them to argue against such belief. But others have disagreed. As I noted in Part I, Wittgenstein, at one time, took the view that religious assertions are strictly nonsensical. And, with varying degrees of emphasis, others have endorsed this conclusion.

Wittgenstein's philosophy is often said to fall into two phases. The second is represented by texts such as the *Philosophical Investigations*, *On Certainty*, and the *Lectures on Religious Belief*. The first is represented by a work called *Tractatus Logico-Philosophicus*, in which Wittgenstein's chief question is 'How does language connect with the world?'.[10] His basic answer here is that it does so since it consists of 'propositions' which 'picture' (or depict) 'facts', or 'states of affairs', composed of 'objects'. From this answer, Wittgenstein concludes that meaningful language is essentially empirical (that it reports what is in principle open to sensory investigation)—or, as he observes, 'The totality of true propositions is the whole of natural science.'[11] Wittgenstein also concludes that, when language tries to go beyond picturing the world, it is nonsensical since it is seeking to talk about that of which we cannot talk significantly, something we can only 'pass over in silence'.[12]

What follows if the basic theses of the *Tractatus* are correct? In the *Tractatus* itself Wittgenstein thinks that the language of religion must be meaningless if taken as trying to refer to what lies beyond the world. And, though he does not employ this conclusion so as to denigrate religious belief, the Logical Positivists (which I mentioned in the General Introduction) sought to do just that. For, claiming to be influenced by Wittgenstein, they developed a theory of meaning known as the 'Verification Principle', in the light of which they argued that religious belief is unreservedly unintelligible or straightforwardly lacking in sense.[13]

Different Logical Positivists (sometimes called 'Verificationists') formulated the Verification Principle differently. In particular, they came to distinguish between what has

---

10. For useful beginner's companions to the *Tractatus*, see G. E. M. Anscombe, *An Introduction to Wittgenstein's Tractatus* (London, 1959) and H. O. Mounce, *Wittgenstein's Tractatus: An Introduction* (Oxford, 1981).
11. Ludwig Wittgenstein, *Tractatus Logico-Philosophicus* (trans. D. F. Pears and B. F. McGuiness, London, 1961), 4. 11.
12. *Tractatus* 7. Evidently, then, Wittgenstein had firmly rejected some major theses of the *Tractatus* by the time he was saying the sort of thing we find in his *Lectures on Religious Belief*. It is not the Wittgenstein of the *Tractatus* which is influencing what you find in Chapters 6 and 7.
13. One should not suppose that Wittgenstein would have endorsed the teaching of Logical Positivists regarding religious belief. For the *Tractatus* is not hostile to religion in the way that they were. Cf. Paul Engelmann, *Letters from Ludwig Wittgenstein with a Memoir* (Oxford, 1967), p. 97: 'A whole generation of disciples was able to take Wittgenstein for a positivist because he has something of enormous importance in common with the positivists: he draws the line between what we can speak about and what we must be silent about just as they do. The difference is only that they have nothing to be silent about. Positivism holds—and this is its essence—that what we can speak about is all that matters in life. *Whereas Wittgenstein passionately believes that all that really matters in human life is precisely what, in his view, we must be silent about.*'

been called its 'weak' and 'strong' versions. Basically, however, all versions relied on the conviction that meaningful statements fall into two groups: (1) mathematical statements (e.g. '2 + 2 = 4'), tautologies (e.g. 'All cats are cats'), and logically necessary statements (e.g. 'Not both p and not-p'), and (2) statements which can be confirmed through the use of human senses, especially using methods commonly employed in physics, chemistry, and biology. In the early days of Logical Positivism it was the strong version of the Verification Principle that was in vogue. Friedrich Waismann stated it thus: 'Anyone uttering a sentence must know under what conditions he calls it true and under what conditions he calls it false. If he is unable to state these conditions, he does not know what he has said. A statement which cannot be conclusively verified cannot be verified at all. It is simply devoid of any meaning.'[14] But it was the weak version of the Verification Principle that became the most popular. It held that (forgetting about mathematical statements, tautologies, and truths of logic) a statement is factual and meaningful only if sense experience can go at least some way to confirming it.

It is this version of the Verification Principle which lies behind what A. J. Ayer has to say in Chapter 9. But is it cogent? Many of its defenders came to feel unhappy with it, including Ayer. In response to an argument originating from Alonzo Church, he acknowledged that the Verification Principle cannot be formulated in any satisfactory way.[15] For a recent, critical treatment of the Principle as applied to religious belief, you can turn to Chapter 10, from Richard Swinburne, in which he rejects both its strong and (as invoked by Ayer) weak versions. But you should note that forms of verificationism are still defended by some philosophers. According, for instance, to Michael Dummett (writing with no special reference to religion): 'An understanding of a statement consists in a capacity to recognize whatever is counted as verifying it.'[16] According to Kai Nielsen (writing directly on religious belief), any utterances purportedly referring to and/or describing God (as traditionally conceived, rather than as conceived by those who take God to be a physical object) are neither true nor false and are, therefore, factually meaningless.[17] Why? Because they are not confirmable by sense experience. Nielsen is aware of standard criticisms of verificationist approaches to the topic of meaning. But he takes them to be answerable. He argues, for example, that our normal understanding of

14. Friedrich Waismann, 'Logische Analyse des Wahrscheinlichkeitsbegriffs', *Erkenntnis* 1 (1930–1). At one time, Wittgenstein seems to have endorsed a strong version of the Verification Principle. For he is reported as saying: 'If I can never verify the sense of a proposition completely, then I cannot have meant anything by the proposition either. Then the proposition signifies nothing whatsoever.' Cf. Brian McGuiness (ed.), *Ludwig Wittgenstein and the Vienna Circle: Conversations Recorded by Friedrich Waismann* (New York, 1979).
15. For Church's discussion, see his review of *Language, Truth and Logic* (2nd edn) in *Journal of Symbolic Logic* (1949), pp. 52 f. For Ayer's admission, see *The Central Questions of Philosophy* (London, 1973).
16. Michael Dummett, 'What is a Theory of Meaning?' in G. Evans and J. McDowell (eds), *Truth and Meaning* (Oxford, 1976). Dummett is a Roman Catholic, so it should not be supposed that he takes the sentence I have quoted as grounds for challenging religious belief.
17. For works by Nielsen, see the General Introduction above, fn. 27. For a brief and approving account of Nielsen's position, see Michael Martin, 'The Verificationist Challenge', in Philip Quinn and Charles Taliaferro (eds), *A Companion to Philosophy of Religion* (Oxford, 1997), pp. 204 ff.

notions such as 'meaning' and 'understanding' ties them closely to empirical confirmation and refutation.[18]

And others have thought along similar lines. A good example is Antony Flew, who in
Chapter 11 suggests that there is a 'peculiar danger' and an 'endemic evil' present in
'theological utterance'. Why? Because, says Flew, God-Talk looks suspiciously like an
exercise in linguistic cheating. On the one hand, it consists of assertions (e.g. 'God loves
us') expressed by means of words which rightly give rise to certain expectations in those
who hear them. Presented with such assertions, we naturally look for things to be such
and such a way and not otherwise. But, so Flew observes, God-Talk seems to be taken by
its advocates as compatible with any and every eventuality. What it gives with one hand
it effectively takes back with another. It cancels itself out. Or, in Flew's words, it dies a
'death by a thousand qualifications'.[19]

Does it though? Flew's discussion of the matter is clear, concise, and provocative. I have
included it since, more than many comparable texts, it nicely represents an approach to
problems involved in talking of God which many people share.[20] But it seems to proceed
as though we could reasonably come to a proper philosophical evaluation of God-Talk
without considering why people who believe in God might want to speak as they do
concerning him. It also seems to proceed as though words used in talking of God can only
be deemed to have the sense which they bear when used to talk about what is not divine
(that, for example, talk of God's love should be bound by expectations we have when we
talk of human love). And one might wonder whether or not Flew is right in proceeding
on these assumptions.

As we have seen, authors such as D. Z. Phillips suggest that we should not pass judgements on the significance of what religious believers say without first looking carefully at
religious belief in practice. I assume that he would say that our extract from Flew simply
fails to appreciate what talk of God amounts to. Think, for example, of his insistence that
'There is a God', though it appears to be in the indicative mood, is an expression of faith.
So when reflecting on Flew, you might consider what Phillips has to say. But you might
also want to consider yet another way of arguing that God-Talk is not as objectionable as
Flew takes it to be, one which seeks to ground it in reasons for speaking of God in certain

18. Cf. Moritz Schlick, who held that the Verification Principle is 'nothing but a simple statement of the
    way in which meaning is actually assigned to propositions in everyday life and in science'. Accord-
    ing to Schlick: 'There never has been any other way, and it would be a grave error to suppose that we
    have discovered a new conception of meaning which is contrary to common opinion and which we
    want to introduce into philosophy' ('Meaning and Verification', reprinted in Herbert Feigl and
    Wilfrid Sellars (eds), *Readings in Philosophical Analysis* (New York, 1949)).
19. As Flew says, the 'parable' he uses to introduce his case is developed from a story told in an essay by
    the Cambridge philosopher John Wisdom (1904–93). In this, two people return to their old garden
    to find it containing some healthy plants but also a lot of weeds. One of them is convinced that a
    gardener has been at work. The other is not. But Wisdom does not develop his story to suggest that
    God-Talk is somehow to be rejected. Instead, he develops it to suggest that, though belief in God
    might not be something the truth of which can be established by ordinary empirical investigation,
    it can still be thought of as based on serious reasoning. Wisdom's essay is well worth reading as a
    complement to that of Flew.
20. It also takes a line on what is usually called 'the problem of evil'. So it is relevant to the topic of Part
    V of this book. Many would take it to present the problem of evil in its starkest form.

ways, one which also challenges the notion that words which we use in non-theological contexts come with rules for their usage which prevent us from wielding them significantly when talking of God. I am here referring to the suggestion that words used in God-Talk and in talk of what is not divine can be thought of as being 'analogous'. Sometimes called 'The Theory of Analogy', this move in philosophy of religion is chiefly associated with Thomas Aquinas—which brings us to Chapter 12, from the first part of the *Summa Theologiae*.[21]

Aquinas and analogy

According to the recently published *Catechism of the Catholic Church*, God is incomprehensible and ineffable.[22] This teaching is a traditional one among writers in the Christian tradition (as well as among Jewish and Islamic authors). But many people now deny (either directly or by implication) that God is strictly incomprehensible and ineffable. They would agree that God is in some sense a mystery. But, so they would add, we can have a pretty good understanding of what God is, and we can capture him quite effectively in language.[23]

Why so? The usual answer given is that God belongs to the same class as we do. I am a person. You are a person. And, so it is frequently said, God is a person. Hence, for example, Richard Swinburne maintains that theism (the belief that there is a God) is the belief that there is 'something like a "person" without a body (i.e. a spirit) who is eternal, free, able to do anything, knows everything, is perfectly good, is the proper object of human worship and obedience, the creator and sustainer of the universe'.[24] According to Swinburne, God is a conscious agent existing through time. He perceives. He learns. He

21. In reading Chapter 12 (and in reading Chapters 40, 43, 46, and 50), you should bear in mind that the *Summa Theologiae* is divided into sections called 'Questions'. These consist of a series of 'Articles' which raise detailed problems bearing on the topic of the 'Question' to which they belong. Each 'article' typically consists of 'Objections' and 'Replies' together with what is usually referred to as the *corpus* (body) of the 'article'. In the 'Objections' Aquinas typically raises some of the strongest arguments he knows *against* the position he wants to defend. In the *corpus* he presents his own arguments for this position. In the 'Replies' he tries to explain why the objections he has cited *do not* count against it.

22. The *Catechism* was originally published in Rome in 1994. The section on God comprises paragraphs 198–231.

23. This is a rather recent view, though its exponents sometimes cite the medieval author Duns Scotus in defence of it. For someone doing just this, see Richard Swinburne, *The Coherence of Theism* (revised edn, Oxford, 1993), ch. 4. In Scotus, see *Reportata Parisiensia*, I, d.3, q.l, n.7.

24. Swinburne, *The Coherence of Theism*, p. 1. The word 'theism' seems to have originated in English in the seventeenth century as a way of referring (often abusively) to the beliefs of religious thinkers who rejected the Christian doctrine of the Trinity while also insisting that they believed in God. In the twentieth century (as in Swinburne's usage) it has come to be used as a term to describe the beliefs of anyone who subscribes to what seems common to Judaism, Islam, and Christianity. As I have noted, however, Jews, Christians, and Muslims have significantly differed in their beliefs about what they call 'God'. And, even within their own religious traditions, they have disagreed among themselves with respect to what is and what is not true of God. So 'theism' (and its corresponding adjective 'theistic') is a term to be approached with some caution, though I frequently use it in what follows.

changes. He even has beliefs. And Swinburne is by no means alone in speaking of God in this way. John Lucas, for instance, explains that: 'The ultimate reality is a person . . . To be a person is to be conscious and to be an agent . . . We cannot understand the actions and feelings attributed to God in the Bible unless we can, at least to a limited extent, have some idea of God reaching a decision and caring about what happens.'[25] According to Alvin Plantinga: 'God is the premier person, the first and chief exemplar of personhood . . . We men and women are image bearers of God, and the properties most important for an understanding of our personhood are properties we share with him.'[26] Swinburne, Lucas, and Plantinga accept that God is in various respects different from human persons. But, like many other writers who could be cited, they are also convinced that God is much like people and that people are much like God.

Such, however, is not the view of Aquinas. According to him, God is deeply mysterious. 'The divine substance', he says, 'surpasses every form that our intellect reaches. Thus we are unable to apprehend it by knowing what it is.'[27] God, he maintains, 'is greater than all we can say, greater than all we can know; and not merely does he transcend our language and our knowledge, but he is beyond the comprehension of every mind whatsoever, even of angelic minds, and beyond the being of every substance.'[28]

In that case, however, what about God-Talk? Does it serve to express anything of God's nature? Can it do nothing to tell us what God is? Aquinas's teaching on analogy is designed to show that, mysterious though God is, we can reasonably take ourselves to speak truly when talking of God. And its basic idea is that words applied to God and to creatures can be thought of having a sense which is somewhere in between the 'univocal' and the 'equivocal'.

How are we to understand the words 'univocal' and 'equivocal'? We shall best do so by example.

First let us consider the sentences 'Tommy has a cat called "Moo," ' and 'Jim has a cat called "Thor." ' In the *Oxford English Dictionary*, we find 'cat' defined as 'A well-known carnivorous quadruped (*Felis domesticus*) which has long been domesticated, being kept to destroy mice, and as a house pet.' So let us assume that Moo and Thor are both cats in the sense given by the *Oxford English Dictionary*. Aquinas would say that in 'Moo is a cat' and 'Thor is a cat' the word 'cat' is being used *univocally*. It means precisely the same thing in each sentence.

But now consider the word 'bat'. As the *Oxford English Dictionary* also tells us, this can mean: 'An animal . . . consisting of mouse-like quadrupeds . . . having the fingers extended to support a thin membrane which stretches from the side of the neck by the toes of both pairs of feet to the tail . . . which they fly with a peculiar quivering motion." But a bat can also be 'a stick or stout piece of wood'. So what if Mary has a bat with wings, while Fred has a bat made of wood? Then, so Aquinas would say, in 'Mary has a

25. J. R. Lucas, *The Future* (Oxford, 1989), pp. 212 ff.
26. 'Advice to Christian Philosophers', *Faith and Philosophy* 1 (1984), p. 265. Throughout this essay Plantinga repeatedly uses the words 'that there is such a person as God' to identify the issue at stake between those who believe in God and those who do not. Cf. pp. 261, 262, 264. For more on 'God is a person', see Part IV below.
27. *Summa Contra Gentiles*, I, 14.
28. *Commentary on Dionysius's 'Divine Names'*, I, iii, 77.

bat' and 'Fred has a bat' the word 'bat' means something completely different, and its usage is equivocal. It means something completely different in each sentence.

   Might we say that terms applied both to God and to what is not divine ('creatures', as Aquinas would say) can be thought of as doing so univocally or equivocally? Take, for example, 'good' in 'God is good' and 'Mary is good'. Shall we say that 'good' here is to be understood as meaning exactly the same thing? Or shall we say that it means something entirely different? Aquinas replies 'No' to both questions. We cannot, he thinks, take 'good' to be used univocally of God and creatures, since, like Augustine, he holds that God is 'simple'. All words describing creatures, he thinks, do so by signifying (referring to) what lacks the divine simplicity. They fail to signify (or to give us an understanding of) what God is. Or, as Aquinas puts it: 'Words expressing creaturely perfections express them as distinct from one another: *wise*, for example, used of a human being expresses a perfection distinct from his nature, his powers, his existence, and so on; but when we use it of God, we don't want to express anything distinct from his substance, power, and existence.' And yet, so Aquinas adds, we cannot take words such as 'good' to be used equivocally of God and creatures. Why not? Because they would fail to signify properly when applied to God, and we could never begin to reason about God by using them. Or, as Aquinas puts it, if terms applied to God and creatures are purely equivocal in meaning, 'nothing could be known or proved about God from creatures, but all such argument would commit the logical fallacy of equivocation'.[29]

   Yet might we not use a word on different occasions without employing it univocally or purely equivocally? In fact, we do so frequently. We say, for example, 'I love my wife', 'I love my country', and 'I love a rare steak', without meaning exactly the same thing by 'love', yet without meaning something entirely different either. We say 'John's a good father' and 'John's a good chemist', without meaning exactly the same thing by 'good', yet without meaning something entirely different either. If we say that in instances such as these we are employing one and the same word 'analogously', we shall pretty well see what Aquinas means in his teaching on analogy. For his basic point is that one and the same word can be significantly applied both to God and to creatures without meaning exactly the same and without meaning something entirely different.[30]

29. An argument illustrating what Aquinas calls the 'fallacy of equivocation' would be: (1) bats have lungs; (2) cricket players use bats; (3) therefore cricket players use things with lungs.

30. In the *Philosophical Investigations*, Wittgenstein develops a notion of 'family resemblance' which might be compared to Aquinas's notion of analogy. Defending the idea that a word can significantly be used in different but related senses without it being true that the word is being used figuratively, Wittgenstein writes (§66): 'Consider for example the proceedings that we call "games". I mean board-games, card-games, ball-games, Olympic games, and so on. What is common to them all?—Don't say: "There *must* be something common, or they would not be called 'games' "—but *look and see* whether there is anything common to them all.—For if you look at them you will not see something that is common to *all*, but similarities, relationships, and a whole series of them at that. To repeat: don't think, but look!—Look for example at board-games, with their multifarious relationships. Now pass to card-games; here you find many correspondences with the first group, but many common features drop out, and others appear. When we pass next to ball-games, much that is common is retained, but much is lost.—Are they all "amusing"? Compare chess with noughts and crosses. Or is there always winning and losing, or competition between players? Think of patience . . . And we can go through the many, many other groups of games in the same way; can see how similarities crop up and disappear.'

But why does Aquinas think that there are words which can be used analogously of God and creatures? One might agree that there is such a thing as analogous use of words without supposing that words can be applied both to God and to creatures with some sameness of meaning. One might, for instance, hold that we can only talk sense when using words analogously if we are talking of things which belong to the world of space and time. Or one might hold that we can speak of God by *only* saying what God is *not* as for example Maimonides is commonly taken to teach.[31] Yet as you will see below, Aquinas denies that talk about God can only be thought of as saying what God is not. On his account there are positive reasons for thinking that at least some things said of God are *literally* true.

Why so? He alludes to his reasons in the extract below. But to understand the allusions you need to note how, as a philosopher, he approaches the topic of God's existence in general. We saw in Part I why he wants to say that we cannot know what God is. We also saw that he takes human knowledge of God to be indirect and based on arguments starting from our knowledge of material things. But what sort of arguments?

Aquinas is particularly intrigued by the fact that there is any world at all, by the fact that there is something rather than *nothing*. He explicitly denies that philosophy can show that the world ever began to be, so he does not hold that God exists, since something must have got the world going at some time in the past (though he believes that God did this).[32] But he frequently teaches that everything we can conceive of or understand is continually dependent on God for its sheer existence (*esse*). The ancient philosophers, says Aquinas, asked causal questions about things in the world, but some 'climbed higher to the prospect of being as being' and 'observed the cause of things inasmuch as they are beings, not merely as things of such a kind or quality'.[33] If something exists, Aquinas argues, its existence either follows from its nature or is brought about by something other than itself. Aquinas then maintains that there cannot be an endless series of things bringing about the existence of others while themselves being brought about by something else. There has to be something which exists by nature. Following the biblical tradition, Aquinas calls this 'God'. In doing so, he was the first Christian author seriously, and in detail, to focus on the notion of existence as of primary importance for reflecting on God, whom he speaks of as 'Being Itself' (*ipsum esse subsistens*).

31. This is how Aquinas reports the teaching of Maimonides. And with some reason. According to Maimonides: 'God exists of necessity and . . . He is non-composite . . . and we can only apprehend that He is, not what He is. It is therefore meaningless that He should have any positive attribute, since the fact that He is is not something outside of what He is, so that the attribute might indicate one of these too . . . It is the negative attributes which we must employ to guide our mind to that which we ought to believe concerning God' (*Maimonides: The Guide of the Perplexed*, ed. Julius Guttmann, trans. Chaim Rabin, Indianapolis, 1995, Book I, ch. lviii, p. 80). But Maimonides certainly thought that some God-Talk is literally true and can be understood as such. And a case can be made for viewing Aquinas's treatment of God-Talk as, effectively, very similar to that of Maimonides. See Alexander Broadie, 'Maimonides and Aquinas on the Names of God', *Religious Studies* 23 (1987).

32. Cf. his text *De Aeternitate Mundi* (*On the Eternity of the World*). For an English translation of this, see C. Vollert, L. Kendzierski, and P. Byrne (eds), *St Thomas Aquinas, Siger of Brabant, St Bonaventure 'On the Eternity of the World'* (Milwaukee, Wisconsin, 1964).

33. *Summa Theologiae*, Ia. 44. 2.

And it is this notion of God as 'Being Itself' which lies at the centre of what Aquinas says about God-Talk.

For, so he reasons, everything which comes from God must somehow reflect what God is. Why? Because, so Aquinas thinks, effects always resemble their causes. He does not, of course, mean that effects always *look* like their causes (though he thinks that they sometimes do, since, for example, children often look like their parents). Rather, his thesis is that causes (in the sense of agents in the world which bring about changes in the world) explain their effects and do so precisely because of what they are. For him, we have an explanation of some development in the world when we reach the point of saying, 'Oh, I see. Of course that explains it.' And we have this, he thinks, when we see how a cause is expressing its nature in its effect.

Suppose that Fred is staggering around. We ask, 'How come?' Then we learn that he has drunk a lot of whisky, and we say, 'Oh, I see. Of course that explains it.' But what do we 'see'? One might be tempted to say something like 'We see that it is not surprising that Fred should be staggering, since people who drink whisky often do that.' One might say that what 'seeing' means here is that we note that what is now occurring has happened a large number of times before. But if one occurrence is puzzling (if, for example, Fred's staggering is puzzling), why should a thousand such occurrences be less puzzling? That drinking whisky is followed (or regularly followed) by staggering does not *explain* what has happened. It simply reports what we have become used to experiencing. It does not help us to see why the drinking is connected with the staggering.[34]

Nobody did see the connection until quite recent times. To see it you need a chemical account of alcohol and an account of its effect on the brain. Only when you have developed this kind of understanding can you be said to *see* why drunken people stagger. And what you would at last see is why it has to be the case that they do so. You would see what Aquinas means in talking of effects resembling their causes. If you pour exactly the right amount of sulphuric acid on a quantity of zinc, the zinc will always fizz, and disappear, and give off an inflammable gas, and the sulphuric acid will lose its corrosive power. But why? Because:

$$Zn + H_2SO_4 \rightarrow ZnSO_4 + H_2$$

Here you see (in a literal sense) that what is on the right side of the $\rightarrow$ resembles what is on the left side. So you can now say, 'Yes, I see, of course.' Effects really do reflect what their causes are. What Aquinas calls the likeness of an effect to its cause is precisely what we are seeking as we look for scientific explanations.

So when Aquinas says that causes are like their effects, he means that seeing why the effects spring from their causes is seeing how the nature of the cause explains the effect and renders its effect necessary, and therefore unsurprising. He means that though, when drunk, I cannot be described as looking like alcohol, I am, when drunk, certainly showing forth what alcohol is. And in this sense, so he thinks, I resemble it.

And, so he also thinks, the world made by God resembles God. So we can speak of God by means of words which we use when talking of God's creatures. But Aquinas also holds that we need to be careful as we do so. He is happy, for instance, to endorse talk which

34. Cf. Aristotle, *Metaphysics*, I, 1.

speaks of God as being like a creature. For this is how God is often spoken of in the Bible, which encourages us to think of God as, for example, a mother, an eagle, a father, a king, and a case of dry rot. But, so Aquinas believes, talk like this cannot be taken literally, and we need to be aware of the fact. He also believes that even such assertions as 'God is good' and 'God is wise' need to be approached on the assumption that goodness in God and wisdom in God is not something we can get our minds around by thinking of the goodness or wisdom of anything with which we are personally acquainted.

Reasons and belief in God

Yet Aquinas does think that we have reasons to say such things as that God is good or that God is wise. And he holds that our understanding of God-Talk depends much on these reasons. In the *Summa Theologiae* (and elsewhere) Aquinas only mentions analogy after he has explained why God must be spoken of in certain specific ways. Ia. 13 (from which Chapter 12 is taken) follows a set of questions in which Aquinas argues for the truth of a number of positive assertions concerning God. And most of it looks as though it can be read as a general account of what Aquinas has been doing since Ia. 1. To understand texts such as Ia. 13, then, we need to consider what has led up to them.

And, so one might argue, we need to do something similar when presented by any examples of God-Talk and with an eye on the question of whether or not they make sense. For why should we suppose that the question of God-Talk's sense or nonsense can be settled in some general way—by appeal, for example, to some criterion of meaning such as that endorsed by Logical Positivists? Should we not look at specific examples of God-Talk and consider why people use them? Can we settle questions of meaning without considering the reasons people have for speaking as they do? Can we, for instance, pronounce on the meaningfulness of the claim that God is eternal without considering why people have wanted to defend it? Can we settle the issue of the meaningfulness of sentences such as 'God is omnipotent' or 'God is good' without examining reasons which people offer for asserting them with conviction? Can we, as some philosophers would put it, reasonably decide on the matter *a priori*?[35]

In Part IV we will be turning to some specific reasons which have been given for saying particular things about God. Before doing that, however, we move on to reasons which have been given for believing that God exists in the first place.

35. You can look up definitions of *a priori* (and its corresponding expression *a posteriori*) in some of the standard dictionaries of philosophy. Generally, it is said that those matters we can decide on *a priori* are those which we do not settle on with an eye to empirical investigation, while matters settled on *a posteriori* are decided on the basis of empirical investigation.

Chapter 8
How believers find God-Talk puzzling

Augustine of Hippo

How shall I call upon my God, my God and Lord? Surely when I call on him, I am calling on him to come into me. But what place is there in me where my God can enter into me? 'God made heaven and earth' (Gen. I: I). Where may he come to me? Lord my God, is there any room in me which can contain you? Can heaven and earth, which you have made and in which you have made me, contain you? Without you, whatever exists would not exist. Then can what exists contain you? I also have being. So why do I request you to come to me when, unless you were within me, I would have no being at all? I am not now possessed by Hades; yet even there are you (Ps. 138: 8): for 'even if I were to go down to Hades, you would be present'. Accordingly, my God, I would have no being, I would not have any existence, unless you were in me. Or rather, I would have no being if I were not in you 'of whom are all things, through whom are all things, in whom are all things' (Rom. 11: 36). Even so, Lord, even so. How can I call on you to come if I am already in you? Or where can you come from so as to be in me? Can I move outside heaven and earth so that my God may come to me from there? For God has said 'I fill heaven and earth' (Jer. 23: 24).

Who then are you, my God? What, I ask, but God who is Lord? For 'who is the Lord but the Lord', or 'who is God but our God?' (Ps. 17: 32). Most high, utterly good, utterly powerful, most omnipotent, most merciful and most just, deeply hidden yet most intimately present, perfection of both beauty and strength, stable and incomprehensible, immutable and yet changing all things, never new, never old, making everything new and 'leading' the proud 'to be old without their knowledge' (Job 9: 5, Old Latin version); always active, always in repose, gathering to yourself but not in need, supporting and filling and protecting, creating and nurturing and bringing to maturity, searching even though to you nothing is lacking: you love without burning, you are jealous in a way that is free of anxiety, you 'repent' (Gen. 6: 6) without the pain of regret, you are wrathful and remain tranquil. You will a change without any change in your design. You recover what you find, yet have never lost. Never in any need, you rejoice in your gains (Luke 15: 7); you are never

Augustine of Hippo extracts from *Confessions* translated with an introduction and notes by Henry Chadwick (OUP, 1991), Translation, Introduction and Notes copyright © Henry Chadwick 1991, reprinted by permission of Oxford University Press.

avaricious, yet you require interest (Matt. 25: 27). We pay you more than you require so as to make you our debtor, yet who has anything which does not belong to you? (I Cor. 4: 7). You pay off debts, though owing nothing to anyone; you cancel debts and incur no loss. But in these words what have I said, my God, my life, my holy sweetness? What has anyone achieved in words when he speaks about you? Yet woe to those who are silent about you because, though loquacious with verbosity, they have nothing to say.

What good did it do me that at about the age of twenty there came into my hands a work of Aristotle which they call the *Ten Categories*? My teacher in rhetoric at Carthage, and others too who were reputed to be learned men, used to speak of this work with their cheeks puffed out with conceit, and at the very name I gasped with suspense as if about to read something great and divine. Yet I read it without any expositor and understood it. I had discussions with people who said they had understood the *Categories* only with much difficulty after the most erudite teachers had not only given oral explanations but had drawn numerous diagrams in the dust. They could tell me nothing they had learnt from these teachers which I did not already know from reading the book on my own without having anyone to explain it. The book seemed to me an extremely clear statement about substances, such as man, and what are in them, such as a man's shape, what is his quality of stature, how many feet, and his relatedness, for example whose brother he is, or where he is placed, or when he was born, or whether he is standing or sitting, or is wearing shoes or armour, or whether he is active or passive, and the innumerable things which are classified by these nine genera of which I have given some instances, or by the genus of substance itself.

What help was this to me when the book was also an obstacle? Thinking that absolutely everything that exists is comprehended under the ten categories, I tried to conceive you also, my God, wonderfully simple and immutable, as if you too were a subject of which magnitude and beauty are attributes. I thought them to be in you as if in a subject, as in the case of a physical body, whereas you yourself are your own magnitude and your own beauty. By contrast a body is not great and beautiful by being body; if it were less great or less beautiful, it would nevertheless still be body. My conception of you was a lie, not truth, the figments of my misery, not the permanent solidity of your supreme bliss. You had commanded and it so came about in me, that the soil would bring forth thorns and brambles for me, and that with toil I should gain my bread (Gen. 3: 18).

Chapter 9
God-Talk is evidently nonsense
A. J. Ayer

IT is now generally admitted, at any rate by philosophers, that the existence of a being having the attributes which define the god of any non-animistic religion cannot be demonstratively proved. What is not so generally recognised is that there can be no way of proving that the existence of a god, such as the God of Christianity, is even probable. Yet this also is easily shown. For if the existence of such a god were probable, then the proposition that he existed would be an empirical hypothesis. And in that case it would be possible to deduce from it, and other empirical hypotheses, certain experiential propositions which were not deducible from those other hypotheses alone. But in fact this is not possible. It is sometimes claimed, indeed, that the existence of a certain sort of regularity in nature constitutes sufficient evidence for the existence of a god. But if the sentence 'God exists' entails no more than that certain types of phenomena occur in certain sequences, then to assert the existence of a god will be simply equivalent to asserting that there is the requisite regularity in nature; and no religious man would admit that this was all he intended to assert in asserting the existence of a god. He would say that in talking about God, he was talking about a transcendent being who might be known through certain empirical manifestations, but certainly could not be defined in terms of those manifestations. But in that case the term 'god' is a metaphysical term. And if 'god' is a metaphysical term, then it cannot be even probable that a god exists. For to say that 'God exists' is to make a metaphysical utterance which cannot be either true or false. And by the same criterion, no sentence which purports to describe the nature of a transcendent god can possess any literal significance.

It is important not to confuse this view of religious assertions with the view that is adopted by atheists, or agnostics. For it is characteristic of an agnostic to hold that the existence of a god is a possibility in which there is no good reason either to believe or disbelieve; and it is characteristic of an atheist to hold that it is at least probable that no god exists. And our view that all utterances about the nature of God are nonsensical, so far from being identical with, or even lending any support to, either of these familiar contentions, is actually incompatible with them. For if the assertion that there is a god is nonsensical, then the atheist's assertion that there is no god is equally nonsensical, since it is only a significant proposition that can be significantly contradicted. As for the agnostic, although he refrains from saying either that there is or that there is not a god, he does not deny that the question

A. J. Ayer extract from *Language, Truth and Logic* (Dover Publications Inc., 1946), reprinted by permission of the publisher.

whether a transcendent god exists is a genuine question. He does not deny that the two sentences 'There is a transcendent god' and 'There is no transcendent god' express propositions one of which is actually true and the other false. All he says is that we have no means of telling which of them is true, and therefore ought not to commit ourselves to either. But we have seen that the sentences in question do not express propositions at all. And this means that agnosticism also is ruled out.

It is to be remarked that in cases where deities are identified with natural objects, assertions concerning them may be allowed to be significant. If, for example, a man tells me that the occurrence of thunder is alone both necessary and sufficient to establish the truth of the proposition that Jehovah is angry, I may conclude that, in his usage of words, the sentence 'Jehovah is angry' is equivalent to 'It is thundering.' But in sophisticated religions, though they may be to some extent based on men's awe of natural process which they cannot sufficiently understand, the 'person' who is supposed to control the empirical world is not himself located in it; he is held to be superior to the empirical world, and so outside it; and he is endowed with super-empirical attributes. But the notion of a person whose essential attributes are non-empirical is not an intelligible notion at all. We may have a word which is used as if it named this 'person,' but, unless the sentences in which it occurs express propositions which are empirically verifiable, it cannot be said to symbolize anything. And this is the case with regard to the word 'god,' in the usage in which it is intended to refer to a transcendent object. The mere existence of the noun is enough to foster the illusion that there is a real, or at any rate a possible entity corresponding to it. It is only when we enquire what God's attributes are that we discover that 'God,' in this usage, is not a genuine name.

It is not within the scope of this enquiry to enter more deeply into the causes of religious feeling, or to discuss the probability of the continuance of religious belief. We are concerned only to answer those questions which arise out of our discussion of the possibility of religious knowledge. The point which we wish to establish is that there cannot be any transcendent truths of religion. For the sentences which the theist uses to express such 'truths' are not literally significant.

An interesting feature of this conclusion is that it accords with what many theists are accustomed to say themselves. For we are often told that the nature of God is a mystery which transcends the human understanding. But to say that something transcends the human understanding is to say that it is unintelligible. And what is unintelligible cannot significantly be described. Again, we are told that God is not an object of reason but an object of faith. This may be nothing more than an admission that the existence of God must be taken on trust, since it cannot be proved. But it may also be an assertion that God is the object of a purely mystical intuition, and cannot therefore be defined in terms which are intelligible to the reason. And I think there are many theists who would assert this. But if one allows that it is impossible to define God in intelligible terms, then one is allowing that it is impossible for a sentence both to be significant and to be about God. If a mystic admits that the object of his vision is something which cannot be described, then he must also admit that he is bound to talk nonsense when he describes it.

For his part, the mystic may protest that his intuition does reveal truths to him, even though he cannot explain to others what these truths are; and that we who do not possess this faculty of intuition can have no ground for denying that it is a cognitive faculty. But the mystic, so far from producing propositions which are empirically verified, is unable to produce any intelligible propositions at all. And therefore we say that his intuition has not revealed to him any facts. It is no use his saying that he has apprehended facts but is unable to express them. For we know that if he really had acquired any information, he would be able to express it. He would be able to indicate in some way or other how the genuineness of his discovery might be empirically determined. The fact that he cannot reveal what he 'knows,' or even himself devise an empirical test to validate his 'knowledge,' shows that his state of mystical intuition is not a genuinely cognitive state. So that in describing his vision the mystic does not give us any information about the external world; he merely gives us indirect information about the condition of his own mind.

These considerations dispose of the argument from religious experience, which many philosophers still regard as a valid argument in favour of the existence of a god. They say that it is logically possible for men to be immediately acquainted with God, as they are immediately acquainted with a sense-content, and that there is no reason why one should be prepared to believe a man when he says that he is seeing a yellow patch, and refuse to believe him when he says that he is seeing God. The answer to this is that if the man who asserts that he is seeing God is merely asserting that he is experiencing a peculiar kind of sense-content, then we do not for a moment deny that his assertion may be true. But, ordinarily, the man who says that he is seeing God is saying not merely that he is experiencing a religious emotion, but also that there exists a transcendent being who is the object of this emotion; just as the man who says that he sees a yellow patch is ordinarily saying not merely that his visual sense-field contains a yellow sense-content, but also that there exists a yellow object to which the sense-content belongs. And it is not irrational to be prepared to believe a man when he asserts the existence of a yellow object, and to refuse to believe him when he asserts the existence of a transcendent god. For whereas the sentence 'There exists here a yellow-coloured material thing' expresses a genuine synthetic proposition which could be empirically verified, the sentence 'There exists a transcendent god' has, as we have seen, no literal significance.

We conclude, therefore, that the argument from religious experience is altogether fallacious. The fact that people have religious experiences is interesting from the psychological point of view, but it does not in any way imply that there is such a thing as religious knowledge, any more than our having moral experiences implies that there is such a thing as moral knowledge. The theist, like the moralist, may believe that his experiences are cognitive experiences, but, unless he can formulate his 'knowledge' in propositions that are empirically verifiable, we may be sure that he is deceiving himself. It follows that those philosophers who fill their books with assertions that they intuitively 'know' this or that moral or religious 'truth' are merely providing material for the psychoanalyst. For no act of intuition can be said to reveal a truth about any matter of fact unless it issues in verifiable propositions. And all such propositions are to be incorporated in the system of empirical propositions which constitutes science.

Chapter 10

God-Talk is not evidently nonsense

Richard Swinburne

Iɴ its earliest form, the doctrine first put forward by the logical positivists of the late 1920s claimed that to be factual a statement had to be verifiable 'in principle' by an observation-statement or, more loosely, by observation. By 'verifiable' was meant 'conclusively verifiable'. An observation-statement is one which reports something observed, or, in a wide sense, experienced. By a statement being verifiable 'in principle' by observation was meant that the statement was such that it made sense to suppose an observation might verify it if that observation could be made, even if it was not in practice possible to make the observation. 'This table is brown' is a factual statement, on this form of verficationist doctrine, because it is possible 'in principle' for someone to make an observation which would conclusively establish that the table is brown. It makes sense to suppose that someone could make an observation which would consist in seeing that the table is brown—even if in fact the table is not brown, it *makes sense* to suppose that a man could make such an observation. That the star Sirius has five planets is not something which anyone could conclusively verify at present. But one day telescopes or space travel might be so developed that the observation that Sirius has five planets, it makes sense to suppose, could be made.

The above form of verificationism may be called the strong verificationist theory. It is generally agreed to be false. The argument most influential in persuading logical positivists to abandon it was the argument that it would show all universal statements to have no factual meaning; and since clearly some such statements have factual meaning, the theory must be false. A universal statement is a statement of the form 'all A's are B' where 'the class of A's is an open class, that is A's are such that however many A's you have observed, it always makes sense to suppose that there is another one. The class of ravens is open. The class of the twelve Apostles is not. Examples of universal statements are 'all ravens are (at all times) black', 'all material bodies near the surface of the earth are (at all times) subject to an acceleration towards the earth of $c.32$ ft/sec.^{2}'. Such statements cannot be conclusively verified. However many ravens you have observed to be black, there may always be another one and that one may be white.

So the logical positivists abandoned strong verificationism and tried the strong falsificationist principle that to be factual a statement had to be falsifiable in principle by an observation-statement. A statement is falsifiable 'in principle' if it makes

R. G. Swinburne extract from *The Coherence of Theism* (Revised edition, OUP, 1997), copyright © Oxford University Press 1997, reprinted by permission of the publisher and the author.

sense to suppose that it be (conclusively) falsified. A universal statement 'all *A*'s are *B*' is falsified by finding an *A* that is not *B*, and if an *A* which is not *B* is the sort of thing which can be observed, then 'all *A*'s are *B*' can be falsified by an observation-statement. 'All ravens are black' would be falsified by observing a white raven. However, although at any rate many universal statements prove to be factually meaningful on this criterion, existential statements asserting the existence of a member of an open class do not. An existential statement is a statement asserting the existence at some time or other of an object of a certain kind, such as 'there is, was, or will be a man with two heads' or 'there is, was, or will be a centaur (somewhere)'. No observation can falsify such statements. However many observations you make and fail to find a two-headed man, there may be one somewhere where you have not looked, or one may be born tomorrow. Yet clearly such existential statements are factual.

One might suggest that to be factual a statement has to be *either* conclusively falsifiable *or* conclusively verifiable 'in principle' by an observation-statement. But counter-examples, of what are clearly factual statements, to this principle are also not hard to find. Consider what are known as mixed universal-and-existential statements, such as 'all badgers are mortal', that is 'all badgers die at some time or other'. You cannot conclusively falsify such a statement. For however old a badger you find, he may die one day. Nor can you conclusively verify such a statement, for however many badgers you find which eventually die, there may be yet another one which you have not yet found which will live for ever. Faced with these difficulties logical positivists retreated to what I shall call the weak verification-or-falsification criterion, or, for short, the weak verificationist principle. This is that a statement *q* is factual if and only if either it is itself an observation-statement or there are observation-statements which, if true, would confirm or disconfirm *q*. By 'confirm' I mean 'raise the probability of', that is 'count as evidence in favour of'; by 'disconfirm' I mean 'lower the probability of' or 'count as evidence against'. Thus although you cannot conclusively verify 'all ravens are black', you can make observations which would count as evidence in favour of this statement. Observing many ravens in different parts of the world and finding them all to be black would count as good evidence favouring 'all ravens are black'. And even though you cannot conclusively verify or conclusively falsify 'all badgers are mortal', you can have good evidence in favour of it—e.g. that all of many reliable reports available to you about the lives of many badgers show that all have died within at any rate fifty years.

The weak verificationist principle expresses the very weak form which verificationism reached in A. J. Ayer's influential *Language, Truth and Logic*, first published in 1936. Much subsequent philosophical controversy has been devoted to attempting to state criteria for when one statement confirms another. But whether or not any simple general account can be given of this matter, that has no tendency to cast doubt on the applicability of the weak verificationist principle itself. So long as we can recognize intuitively when one statement confirms another (as of course we often can) we can apply the principle. In *Language, Truth and Logic* Ayer seems at times to be introducing the principle as a definition of a 'factual' or 'synthetic' statement. If so, the only objection which can be made to his procedure is that it is misleading. There may well in that case be non-analytic propositions which are not 'synthetic', and as propositions are generally supposed to be either synthetic or analytic, a definition which allowed an intermediate category is out of accord with normal philosophical usage, and might mislead someone who was not paying close attention to Ayer's peculiar usage. However, at other times Ayer seems to assume that if a statement is 'meaningful' (i.e. coherent) and non-analytic it must be synthetic. On that understanding of 'synthetic' the weak verficationist principle is an interesting further claim about 'synthetic' or 'factual' propositions. Most philosophers have understood the principle in this way, and many have taken for granted that it is true. I shall also understand it in this way and shall investigate whether or not it is true.

Let us begin, however, by noting a preliminary point. Even if the principle were true, it would not be of great value in sorting out factual statements from others. Like other forms of verificationism, it relies on the notion of an observation-statement. An observation-statement is a statement which reports an observation which could 'in principle' be made. But what does 'in principle' mean? An observation could be made 'in principle' if it makes sense to suppose that it could be made, if it is coherent or logically possible to suppose that it be made. So what has happened is that being uncertain about whether a statement is a factual statement, that is a statement which is logically possible while its negation is also logically possible, the advocate of the weak verificationist principle suggests that a statement is factual if and only if either it describes a logically possible state of affairs which is observable or it would be confirmed or disconfirmed by some statement which described a logically possible state of affairs which is observable. Hence the principle will be useful only if men are agreed better about which statements report observable logically possible states of affairs than about which statements report logically possible states of affairs in general. Are they? I doubt it. Consider all the things that some men have claimed to be observable: 'the end of the world', 'my own death', 'the devil', 'heaven', 'the fourth dimension', 'Poseidon', 'men turned into stones', etc. etc. Some men have held these things to be observable 'in principle' and others have denied it. Is there any simple way to settle the issue? One way which has been suggested is to suppose that the observable must be describable by some simple sensory vocabulary; to suppose that we can *really* observe objects which are square or round, red or blue, move, utter noises, etc.; but that we cannot observe quarrelsome men, a lump of gold, or the planet Venus; and that when we claim to have observed the latter, we ought rather to claim to have inferred these things from things of the former kind which we can truly be said to have observed. But this kind of move constitutes a highly arbitrary restriction on the normal use of 'observe'. Philosophers now recognize that there is no simple and obvious limit on the observable—we can observe bacteria (under a microscope), the moons of Jupiter (in a telescope), John Major (on the television). So if men claim to have observed the objects and events cited earlier how can we show them wrong? One or two of the purported observations *might* be eliminable in virtue of some logical property of the word 'observe', such as that it is not logically possible to observe the future. From this it would follow, for example, that an inhabitant of the world cannot observe its end. For many p, however, the proof, if it can be given, that p is not something which it is logically possible to observe, will, I suspect, consist of a proof (by means other than the weak verficationist principle) that p is not logically possible *simpliciter*. So although men may be agreed *by and large* about which statements are observation-statements, I see no reason to suppose that the degree of consensus is vastly greater here than over which statements are factual. And if that is so, the weak verificationist principle is not going to be of great help in clearing up the latter.

Even if men were to agree for any given statement about whether or not it is an observation-statement, there is a second difficulty which arises with any attempt to show that the statement expressed by some sentence is *not* a factual statement. To show this you have to show that it is not confirmable or disconfirmable by *any* observation-statement. Yet we hardly have before us a catalogue of types of observation-statement which we can run over quickly to see whether they have any confirmation relations to some given statement. So we may easily make a mistake in concluding that a statement p is not confirmable or disconfirmable by any observation-statement through not having thought of a certain observation-statement q, which does in fact confirm (or disconfirm) p.

For these reasons, but primarily the first, I conclude that the weak verificationist principle may not be of much use in separating 'factual statements' from others. Nevertheless the principle may be true. Is it? I know of only two arguments in its favour. The first is the argument from examples; that if we consider any statement which we judge to be factual, we will find that it is confirmable or disconfirmable through observation (or experience in wide sense). The trouble is, however, that there are plenty of examples of statements which *some* people judge to be factual which are not apparently confirmable or disconfirmable through observation. For example:

p_1.   There is a being like men in his behaviour, physiology, and history who nevertheless has no thoughts, feelings, or sensations.

or p_2.   Some of the toys which to all appearances stay in the toy cupboard while people are asleep and no one is watching, actually get up and dance in the middle of the night and then go back to the cupboard, leaving no traces of their activity.

Now such statements are apparently unconfirmable—to all appearances there is no possible evidence of observation which would count for or against them. If it is known that something looks like a man, has the body of a man, reacts like a man, talks like a man, and has been born and has grown up like a man, there is no further observational test which could be done to show whether or not he really feels anything when you stick a pin into him and he screams. So the claim that (some-where in the universe) there exists a being of the kind described in P_1 cannot be confirmed or disconfirmed. Some philosophers think that such statements are nevertheless factual, and others deny this. If the former are right, the weak verifica-tionist principle is false; and if the latter are right, that perhaps counts in its favour. But you cannot show that the weak verificationist principle is true by appealing to examples, because people disagree about whether the statements cited as examples are factual. Only if you can prove by some *other* acceptable principle that the disputed statements are not factual can you use them as evidence for the verifica-tionist principle.

The other argument in favour of the weak verficationist principle is the follow-ing. It is claimed that a man could not understand a factual claim unless he knew what it would be like to observe it to hold or knew which observations would count for or against it; from which it follows that a statement could not *be* factually meaningful unless there could be observational evidence which would count for or against it. But then the premiss of this argument seems clearly false. A man can understand the statement 'once upon a time, before there were men or any other rational creatures, the earth was covered by sea', without his having any idea of what geological evidence would count for or against this proposition, or any idea of how to establish what geological evidence would count for or against the proposition. Surely we understand a factual claim if we understand the words which occur in the sentence which expresses it, and if they are com-bined in a grammatical pattern of which we understand the significance. It may be that in order to understand the words we have observed cases where they would be correctly applied or where terms definitionally related to them would be cor-rectly applied—or at least to have observed events which are evidence for or against the occurrence of such cases. And it may be that in order to understand the signifi-cance of the pattern in which the terms are combined (e.g. a subject–predicate sentence) we have to have observed cases where such a sentence-pattern would be correctly used. But none of this shows that in order to understand a particular statement we have to know what it would be like to observe *it* to hold or know which observations would be evidence for or against *it*.

I conclude that arguments in favour of the weak verificationist principle do not work. We have no reason for supposing this principle to be true. If we did have such reason, and if we were able to apply the principle without begging crucial questions, we would have a test which we could apply to credal sentences to see if they expressed factual statements. We could ask whether credal sentences made observation-statements or made statements which were confirmable or discon-firmable by observation-statements. Yet our conclusion is that, despite the verifica-tionist's arguments, there may well be factual statements which no evidence of observation can count for or against. Hence, even if it could be shown that credal sentences did not make observation-statements or statements which evidence of observation could count for or against (and I do not wish to suggest that this could be shown), that would not show—without further argument—that they did not make factual statements. Verificationism does not provide principles which are of use for settling the character of theological sentences.

Chapter 11

'Death by a thousand qualifications'

Antony Flew

L ET us begin with a parable. It is a parable developed from a tale told by John Wisdom in his haunting and revelatory article 'Gods'.[1] Once upon a time two explorers came upon a clearing in the jungle. In the clearing were growing many flowers and many weeds. One explorer says, 'Some gardener must tend this plot'. The other disagrees, 'There is no gardener'. So they pitch their tents and set a watch. No gardener is ever seen. 'But perhaps he is an invisible gardener.' So they set up a barbed-wire fence. They electrify it. They patrol with bloodhounds. (For they remember how H. G. Wells's *The Invisible Man* could be both smelt and touched though he could not be seen.) But no shrieks ever suggest that some intruder has received a shock. No movements of the wire ever betray an invisible climber. The bloodhounds never give cry. Yet still the Believer is not convinced. 'But there is a gardener, invisible, intangible, insensible to electric shocks, a gardener who has no scent and makes no sound, a gardener who comes secretly to look after the garden which he loves.' At last the Sceptic despairs, 'But what remains of your original assertion? Just how does what you call an invisible, intangible, eternally elusive gardener differ from an imaginary gardener or even from no gardener at all?'

In this parable we can see how what starts as an assertion, that something exists or that there is some analogy between certain complexes of phenomena, may be reduced step by step to an altogether different status, to an expression perhaps of a 'picture preference'.[2] The Sceptic says there is no gardener. The Believer says there is a gardener (but invisible, etc.). One man talks about sexual behaviour. Another man prefers to talk of Aphrodite (but knows that there is not really a superhuman person additional to, and somehow responsible for, all sexual phenomena). The process of qualification may be checked at any point before the original assertion is completely withdrawn and something of that first assertion will remain (Tautology). Mr. Wells's invisible man could not, admittedly, be seen, but in all other respects he was a man like the rest of us. But though the process of qualification may be, and of course usually is, checked in time, it is not always judiciously so

Antony Flew extract from 'Theology and Falsification' from *New Essays in Philosophical Theology* edited by Antony Flew and Alasdair MacIntyre (SCM Press, 1955, Macmillan, NY, 1964), copyright © Antony Flew and Alasdair MacIntyre 1955, reprinted by permission of the publishers SCM Press and Simon and Schuster, Inc. and the author.

1. *P.A.S.*, 1944–5, reprinted as ch. X of *Logic and Language*, vol I (Blackwell, 1951), and in his *Philosophy and Psychoanalysis* (Blackwell, 1953).
2. Cf. J. Wisdom, 'Other Minds', *Mind*, 1940; reprinted in his *Other Minds* (Blackwell, 1952).

halted. Someone may dissipate his assertion completely without noticing that he has done so. A fine brash hypothesis may thus be killed by inches, the death by a thousand qualifications.

And in this, it seems to me, lies the peculiar danger, the endemic evil, of theological utterance. Take such utterances as 'God has a plan', 'God created the world', 'God loves us as a father loves his children'. They look at first sight very much like assertions, vast cosmological assertions. Of course, this is no sure sign that they either are, or are intended to be, assertions. But let us confine ourselves to the cases where those who utter such sentences intend them to express assertions. (Merely remarking parenthetically that those who intend or interpret such utterances as crypto-commands, expressions of wishes, disguised ejaculations, concealed ethics, or as anything else but assertions, are unlikely to succeed in making them either properly orthodox or practically effective).

Now to assert that such and such is the case is necessarily equivalent to denying that such and such is not the case. Suppose then that we are in doubt as to what someone who gives vent to an utterance is asserting, or suppose that, more radically, we are sceptical as to whether he is really asserting anything at all, one way of trying to understand (or perhaps it will be to expose) his utterance is to attempt to find what he would regard as counting against, or as being incompatible with, its truth. For if the utterance is indeed an assertion, it will necessarily be equivalent to a denial of the negation of that assertion. And anything which would count against the assertion, or which would induce the speaker to withdraw it and to admit that it had been mistaken, must be part of (or the whole of) the meaning of the negation of that assertion. And to know the meaning of the negation of an assertion, is as near as makes no matter, to know the meaning of that assertion. And if there is nothing which a putative assertion denies then there is nothing which it asserts either: and so it is not really an assertion. When the Sceptic in the parable asked the Believer, 'Just how does what you call an invisible, intangible, eternally elusive gardener differ from an imaginary gardener or even from no gardener at all?' he was suggesting that the Believer's earlier statement had been so eroded by qualification that it was no longer an assertion at all.

Now it often seems to people who are not religious as if there was no conceivable event or series of events the occurrence of which would be admitted by sophisticated religious people to be a sufficient reason for conceding 'There wasn't a God after all' or 'God does not really love us then'. Someone tells us that God loves us as a father loves his children. We are reassured. But then we see a child dying of inoperable cancer of the throat. His earthly father is driven frantic in his efforts to help, but his Heavenly Father reveals no obvious sign of concern. Some qualification is made—God's love is 'not a merely human love' or it is 'an inscrutable love', perhaps—and we realize that such sufferings are quite compatible with the truth of the assertion that 'God loves us as a father (but, of course, . . .)'. We are reassured again. But then perhaps we ask: what is this assurance of God's (appropriately qualified) love worth, what is this apparent guarantee really a guarantee against?

Just what would have to happen not merely (morally and wrongly) to tempt but also (logically and rightly) to entitle us to say 'God does not love us' or even 'God does not exist'? I therefore put to the succeeding symposiasts the simple central questions, 'What would have to occur or to have occurred to constitute for you a disproof of the love of, or of the existence of, God?'

Chapter 12

One way of understanding God-Talk

Thomas Aquinas

The words we use for God

Can we use words for God?

It seems we have no words for God.

For (1) pseudo-Dionysius[1] says: *of him there is neither name nor opinion.* And Proverbs 30 (4) asks: *What is his name or his son's name? Do you know?*

Moreover, (2) nouns are either abstract or concrete. Neither are appropriate to God: concrete nouns because he is simple, abstract nouns because they don't express complete subsistent things. So no nouns apply to God.

Moreover, (3) nouns express sorts of things, verbs and participles are tensed, pronouns are either demonstrative or relative. None of this is appropriate to God, who is without qualities or incidental properties, exists out of time, can't be ostensively demonstrated to our senses, nor referred to by any pronoun referring back to a noun or participle or demonstrative pronoun. So no sort of word can apply to him.

BUT AGAINST THAT: We read in Exodus 15 (3): *The Lord is a great warrior: Almighty is his name.*

IN REPLY: Aristotle[2] says *words express thoughts and thoughts represent things*; so clearly words refer mediately to things by way of our mental conceptions: we talk about things in the way we know them. Now we have already seen that in this life we cannot see God's substance but know him only from creatures: as their non-creaturely and transcendent cause. So this is where our words for God come from: from creatures. Such words, however, will not express the substance of God as he is in himself, in the way words like *human being* express the substance of what human beings are in themselves, expressing what defines human beings and declaring what

Thomas Aquinas extracts from *Summa Theologiae* from *Thomas Aquinas Selected Philosophical Writings*, selected and translated with an introduction and notes by Timothy McDermott (Oxford World's Classics, 1993) copyright © Timothy McDermott 1993, reprinted by permission of Oxford University Press.

1. *Divine Names*, 1 (5).
2. *Int.* 1 (1.16ᵃ 3).

makes them human beings; for the meaning of a word is the definition of some thing.

HENCE: To 1: God is said to have no name or be beyond naming because his substance lies outside what we understand of him or can express in words.

To 2: Because our knowledge and our words for God come from creatures, the words we use for him express him in ways more appropriate to the kind of creatures we know naturally, and these, as we have said, are material creatures. In such creatures subsistent wholes are composed (of formed material), the form not being a subsistent whole itself but determining what subsists. So all our words for expressing subsistent wholes are concrete terms, appropriate to composite things; whereas to express the non-composite forms we use words that don't express them as subsistent but as determining what subsists: as *whiteness*, for example, names what makes things white. Now God is both non-composite *and* subsistent, so we use abstract terms to express his lack of composition and concrete terms to express his subsistence and wholeness. But neither way of talking fully measures up to his way of existing, for in this life we do not know him as he is in himself.

To 3: To express something as a sort of thing is to express it as a subject subsisting under a determinate nature or form. So just as we have said concrete nouns are used to express God's subsistent wholeness, so too are words that express him as a sort of thing. In the same way, tensed verbs and participles are used to express God's eternity (which includes all time); for just as we can only grasp and express non-composite subsistent things in the way we do composite things, so we can understand and express in words the simpleness of eternity only in terms of things in time: the reason being our mind's kinship with composite temporal things. We use demonstrative pronouns of God in the way we use them of certain other things, pointing them out not to our senses but to our minds, for the way in which we point out things depends on the way we know them. And so because there are ways in which nouns and participles and demonstrative pronouns apply to God, there are ways in which relative nouns and pronouns can express him.

Do any of the words we use for God express what he essentially is?

It seems that no word used of God can express what he essentially is: For (1) John Damascene[3] says: *Of necessity each word said of God expresses not what he essentially is but what he is not, or some relationship he has, or something following from his nature or activity.*

Moreover, (2) pseudo-Dionysius[4] says: *You will find that the utterances of all God's holy teachers articulate the names of God, in praise and revelation, in accordance with*

---

3. *De Fide Orthodoxa*, 1.9.
4. *Divine Names*, 1 (4).

blessed outpourings of his divinity. And what he means is that the words the holy teachers use in praise of God differ according to what issues from God. But words expressing what issue from something don't express anything of its substance. So the words we use of God don't express what he essentially is.

Moreover, (3) we talk of things in the way we understand them. But we don't understand God's substance in this life, so no words we use can express God's substance.

BUT AGAINST THAT: Augustine[5] says: *The being strong of God is his being, and the being wise, and whatever other phrase we use to express the very substance of that simple being.* So all such names express God's substance.

IN REPLY: Clearly negative names for God and names relating him to creatures don't in any way express his substance; rather they express an absence of something in him, or a relationship he has to other things (or better, that other things have). Opinions have differed, however, about non-relative affirmative terms like *good* and *wise*.

Some have said that all such names, though ascribed affirmatively to God, are actually designed to exclude something from God rather than to ascribe something positive to him. So, according to them, when we say *God is alive* we mean that God is not like inanimate things, and other propositions are to be understood in the same way. And this was Moses Maimonides' view. Others say that such names are used to express God's relationship to creatures, so that when we say *God is good* we mean that God causes goodness in things, and so on for other propositions.

Both views seem unacceptable, for three reasons. In the first place, neither view explains why some words are used of God rather than others. God causes bodies just as he causes goodness, so if all that we are expressing by saying *God is good* is that God causes goodness, why don't we say *God is a body* because he causes bodies? Or we could say *God is a body* in order to exclude his being merely unformed potentiality like ultimate matter. In the second place, all words used of God would apply to him only secondarily, in the way the word *healthy* applies secondarily to medicine, where it means only that medicine causes bodies to be healthy, that being the primary meaning of the word. In the third place, it isn't what people talking of God want to say. When we talk of the *living* God, we want to say something else than that he causes life in us or differs from non-living bodies.

So we must rather say that such words do express God's substance and say something of what God essentially is, but represent him inadequately. And we explain this as follows. We can only talk of God as we know him, and since we know him through creatures, we only know him as creatures represent him. But we have said above that all creaturely perfections pre-exist in God in one simple all-embracing perfection. So creatures having any perfection represent and resemble him, but not as things of one type or kind represent each other, but as effects

---

5. *De Trinitate*, 6 (4).

partially resemble a cause of a higher kind though falling short of reproducing its form: the way earthly bodily forms, for example, reproduce the power of the sun. We explained all this earlier when talking of God's perfection. So the sort of words we are considering express God's substance, but do it imperfectly just as creatures represent him imperfectly.

So when we say *God is good* we mean neither *God causes goodness* nor *God is not bad*, but *What in creatures we call goodness pre-exists in a higher way in God*. Thus God is not good because he causes goodness; rather because he is good, goodness spreads through things. As Augustine[6] says, *because* he *is good*, we *exist*.

HENCE: To 1: The reason John Damascene says such words don't express what God is is that none of them perfectly express what he is; but each expresses him imperfectly in the imperfect way creatures represent him.

To 2: *Why* a word gets used to mean something differs sometimes from *what* it is used to mean: the Latin word *lapis* derives from *laedens pedem*—hurting the feet, but it doesn't mean any and every kind of thing that hurts our feet, but the particular kind of body we call a rock. And so we answer that *why* certain words get used of God depends on the outpourings of his divinity: for just as creatures represent him, however imperfectly, according to differing outpourings of perfection, so our minds know and name God in accordance with each outpouring. Nevertheless, these words don't mean those outpourings: *God is alive* doesn't mean life pours out from him, but expresses the fact that life pre-exists in him as the source of all things, though in a way surpassing anything we can understand or express.

To 3: We can't know God's substance in this life for what it is in itself, but we can know it as represented by creaturely perfections, and that is how our words for him express it.

Do some of the words we use for God apply to him literally, or are they all metaphorical?

It seems that no words apply literally to God: For (1), as we have said, all words used of God come from creatures. But to apply names of creatures to God—calling him a rock or a lion, for example—is to use metaphor. So the words we use of God apply to him metaphorically.

Moreover, (2) no word applies literally to something of which it is more truly denied than asserted. But all words like *good* and *wise*, pseudo-Dionysius[7] says, are more truly denied of God than asserted. So none of these names apply to him literally.

Moreover, (3) words for bodies can only apply to an incorporeal God metaphorically. But all the words we are considering carry with them features

6. *De Doctrina Christiana* (1.32).
7. *Celestial Hierarchy*, 2 (3).

characteristic of bodies: tense, for example, or concreteness, or other bodily conditions. So all these words apply to God metaphorically.

BUT AGAINST THAT: Ambrose[8] says *There are certain words which reveal clearly what is proper to divinity, and some which express the evident truth of divine majesty; but others are used of him by simile and metaphor.* So not all words are used metaphorically of God; some apply literally.

IN REPLY: As we have said, we know God from the perfections that are poured out from him into creatures, and exist in him in a way surpassing the way they exist in creatures. Now our minds apprehend those perfections in the way they exist in creatures, and give them names suiting the way we apprehend them. So in using such words of God we must consider on the one hand the perfections they express—goodness, life, and the like—and on the other their manner of expressing them. In regard to what they express, these words apply literally to God, and indeed more properly to him than to creatures, and so primarily to him. But as regards their manner of expressing it, they don't apply literally to God; for their manner of expression is appropriate only to creatures.

HENCE: To 1: Some words so express the perfections issuing from God into created things that the imperfect way in which the creature shares God's perfection is included in what the word means, as materiality is included in the meaning of *rock*. Such words can apply to God only metaphorically. But other words express the perfections without including in what the word means any particular way of sharing those perfections: words like *existent* and *good* and *living*, for example. And such words apply to God literally.

To 2: The reason pseudo-Dionysius says we should deny such words of God is that what they express doesn't belong to him in the way they express it but in a surpassing way. Thus in the same place he says that God *exists beyond all substance and life*.

To 3: Words applying literally to God carry with them features characteristic of bodies not in what they express but in the way they express it; whereas words that apply metaphorically to him carry some bodily feature as part of what they mean.

Are these words used for God synonymous?

It seems that the words we use about God are all synonymous: For (1) synonyms are words meaning exactly the same thing. Now the words we use about God mean exactly the same thing: for his goodness is his substance, and his wisdom is his substance, and so on. So these words are completely synonymous.

Moreover, if it's said that the words refer to one reality but express different notions,

8. *De Fide*, 2 (prologue).

then against that: (2) notions not corresponding to reality are empty. So if reality is one and the notions many, it seems the notions are empty.

Moreover, (3) what is really and notionally one is more one than what is really one but notionally complex. Now God is supremely one. So it seems he isn't really one and notionally complex. So the words used of him don't express different notions, and so are synonymous.

BUT AGAINST THAT: All joining of synonyms results in tautological triviality, as when one says a *clothing garment*. So if every word used of God was synonymous it wouldn't be acceptable to talk of *the good God* and so on. Yet scripture says: *Most powerful, great, and mighty one, Lord of hosts is your name!*

IN REPLY: The words we use of God are not synonymous. It wouldn't be difficult to see this if such words were designed to exclude something from God or signify some causal relationship he has to creatures: for they would then differ in meaning according to the different things denied or the different effects referred to. But what we have said about these words expressing, however imperfectly, God's substance, will also make clear, if we recall it, that they express different notions.

For the meaning of a word is our mental conception of the thing meant. Now, because the mind knows God from creatures, the conceptions it forms in order to understand God correspond to the perfections that issue from God into creatures. In creatures these shared perfections are many and various, but in God they pre-exist in a simple unity. So just as the various perfections of creatures correspond to one simple source, which they represent in many and various ways by their different perfections, so too to our many and various mental conceptions there corresponds something altogether one and simple, understood imperfectly by way of these conceptions. And so the words we use of God, though all expressing one thing, do so by way of many and various conceptions, and so are not synonymous.

HENCE: To 1: The answer to this is now clear. Synonyms signify the same thing under the same notion. Words that express the same thing with different notions don't have one meaning in the primary and simple sense of that expression, since words mean things only by way of our mental conceptions of them, as we said earlier.

To 2: The many notions expressed by these words are not useless or empty, for there corresponds to them all one simple reality that they all represent in various imperfect ways.

To 3: The very fact that God contains in one simple unity what other things share in many different ways shows the perfection of God's unity. And it is this that makes him really one and notionally complex, since our minds apprehend him in the many different ways creatures represent him.

Are words used of God and creatures univocally or equivocally?

It seems that words used of God and creatures are used univocally (i.e. in exactly the same sense) of both: For (1) the equivocal presupposes the univocal, as many-ness presupposes unity (the equivocal use of the word *dog*, for example, to signify things that bark and a type of fish must presuppose its univocal use to signify all things that bark); otherwise we would go on for ever. Now there are univocal agents that share with their effects a single name and definition (human beings, for instance, reproducing human beings), and equivocal agents (the sun, for example, causing heat, though it itself is hot only in an equivocal sense). Seemingly then the first of agents, to which all agency is traced back, will be a univocal agent; and so the words used of God and creatures must be univocal.

Moreover, (2) there is no likeness between things equivocally the same. Since, however, creatures are like God in some respect—*Let us make the human to our own image and likeness*, God says in Genesis 1 (26)—it seems that something is said univocally of God and creatures.

Moreover, (3) Aristotle[9] says that a measure must be generically one with what it measures. Now God is the first measure of everything, and therefore generically one with creatures; so something can be said univocally of God and creatures.

BUT AGAINST THAT: (1) When the same word is used but with different meanings it is used equivocally. But no word means the same used of God as it does used of creatures: in creatures, for example, wisdom is a property, but not in God, and such a change in genus alters the meaning, since a thing's genus is part of its definition. The same applies to all other words, so whatever word we use of God and creatures is used equivocally.

Moreover, (2) God is much further from creatures than any creatures are from one another. But some creatures are so far from one another that nothing can be said univocally of them: things not in the same genus, for example. Much less, then, can anything be said univocally of God and creatures, but everything must be said equivocally.

IN REPLY: Nothing can be said univocally of God and creatures. For effects that don't measure up to the power of their cause resemble it inadequately, not repro-ducing its nature, so that what exists in simple unity in the cause exists in many various forms in the effects: the uniform energy of the sun, for example, produces manifold and varied forms of effect on earth. And in the same way, as we have said, all the many and various perfections existing in creatures pre-exist in God in simple unity.

9. *Metaph*, 10 (1.1053[a]24).

In this way then words expressing creaturely perfections express them as distinct from one another: *wise*, for example, used of a human being expresses a perfection distinct from his nature, his powers, his existence, and so on; but when we use it of God we don't want to express anything distinct from his substance, powers, and existence. So the word *wise* used of human beings somehow contains and delimits what is meant; when used of God, however, it doesn't, but leaves what it means uncontained and going beyond what the word can express. Clearly then the word *wise* isn't used in the same sense of God and man, and the same is true of all the other words. No word, then, is said of God and creatures univocally.

But neither are they said purely equivocally, as some people have held. For that would mean nothing could be known or proved about God from creatures, but all such argument would commit the logical fallacy of equivocation. And that contradicts both the philosophers who have demonstrated many truths about God, and St Paul, who said in Romans 1 (20) that *the hidden things of God can be clearly understood from the things that he has made.*

Our answer then is that these words apply to God and creatures by analogy or proportion. There are two ways in which this happens with words. It happens when two or more things are 'proportioned' to another one: the word *healthy*, for example, is applied both to medicines and to urine because both are related or 'proportioned' to the health of some organism, the one as its cause and the other as its symptom. It also happens when one thing is 'proportioned' directly to another: the word *healthy* applies to the medicine and to the organism itself, since the medicine is cause of health in the organism. And it is in this way that words are used analogically of God and creatures, not purely equivocally and not purely univocally; for our only words for God come from creatures, as we have said, and so whatever we say of God and creatures is said in virtue of the relationship creatures bear to God as to the source and cause in which all their creaturely perfections pre-exist in a more excellent way.

And this way of sharing a word lies somewhere between pure equivocation and straightforward univocalness. For analogical use doesn't presuppose one and the same sense as univocalness does, nor totally different senses as equivocation does, but a word said in senses that differ by expressing different proportions to one and the same thing, as *healthy* said of urine means it is a symptom of the organism's health, and said of medicine means it is a cause of the same health.

HENCE: To 1: In our use of words the equivocal presupposes the univocal, but in activity univocal agents necessarily presuppose a non-univocal agency. Non-univocal causes are general causes of entire species, in the way the sun has been the cause of the whole human race. But univocal causes can't be general causes of entire species—if that were so they would cause themselves as members of the species—but they are particular causes of this or that individual becoming a member of the species. So the general causes of entire species can't be univocal causes. Now the particular causes of individuals presuppose a general cause of the species. Such general causes, though not univocal, are not wholly equivocal either, since they are expressing themselves in their effects; but we can call them analogical causes, paralleling the way our use of univocal terms presupposes the one first non-univocal but analogical term, namely, *being*.

To 2: The likeness of creatures to God is imperfect, since they don't even represent him generically, as we have said.

To 3: God is not a measure proportionate to what is measured, and so God and creatures don't have to be generically one.

As to the arguments against: They prove that such words are not used univocally of God and creatures, but not that they are used equivocally.

If we say they are used analogically, do they apply primarily to God or to creatures?

It seems our words apply primarily to creatures, not God: For (1) we talk about things as we know them: *words express thoughts*, as Aristotle[10] says. But we know creatures before we know God. So the words we use apply first to creatures and then to God.

Moreover, (2) pseudo-Dionysius[11] says that *we name God from creatures*. But names like *lion* and *rock* transferred to God from creatures apply first to the creatures and then to God. So all names used of God and creatures apply first to creatures and then to God.

Moreover, (3) words used in common of God and creatures apply to God as cause of creatures, says pseudo-Dionysius.[12] Now words said of something as cause of something else apply to it secondarily: *healthy* is first said of organisms, and only secondarily of the medicines that cause the organisms' health. So such words apply first to creatures, and then to God.

BUT AGAINST THAT: We read in Ephesians 3 (14–15): *I bow my knee to the Father of our Lord Jesus Christ, from whom all fatherhood in heaven and earth is named*; and why should other words used of God and creatures be any different? Such words then apply first to God, and then to creatures.

IN REPLY: Whenever words are used analogically of several things, it is because they are all related to some one thing; so that one thing must help define the others. And because, as Aristotle[13] says, the meanings of words are definitions, the word must

10. *Int.* 1.1.16ᵃ3.
11. *Divine Names,* 1 (6).
12. *Mystical Theology,* 1.2.
13. *Metaph,* 4 (7.1012ᵃ23).

apply first to what helps define the others and only after that to the others in the order of their approximation to the first thing: thus *healthy* as it applies to organisms helps define *healthy* as used of medicines (called healthy because they cause health in organisms) and of urine (called healthy because it is symptomatic of health in organisms). In the same way then all words used metaphorically of God apply first to creatures and then to God, since said of God they only express some likeness to creatures. Just as talking of a *smiling* meadow expresses a proportion: that flowers adorn a meadow like a smile on a man's face, so talking of God as a *lion* expresses this proportion: that God is powerful in his doings like lions in theirs. And so clearly we can't define what such words mean when used of God unless we refer to what they mean used of creatures.

And this would also be the case with words used of God non-metaphorically, if all they expressed was God's causality, as some have supposed. For then saying *God is good* would mean simply *God causes the goodness of creatures*, and then the goodness of creatures would be helping to define what was meant by the word *good* said of God. So good would apply first to creatures and then to God. But, as we have seen, such names don't simply express God's causality but his substance, for calling God *good* or *wise* doesn't only mean that he causes wisdom or goodness, but that these perfections pre-exist in him in a more excellent way. So taking this into account we say rather that as expressing these perfections such words apply first to God and then to creatures (since the perfections flow into creatures from God); but as applied by us we apply them first to creatures, which we know first. And that is why the way in which they express the perfections is appropriate to creatures, as we already mentioned.

HENCE: To 1: The objection here is talking of our application of the words.

To 2: The case is different with words used metaphorically of God, as we have said.

To 3: This objection would hold if such words expressed only God's causality and not his substance, as *healthy* said of medicine . . .

Can we make affirmative statements about God?

It seems we can't make affirmative statements about God: For (1) pseudo-Dionysius[14] says *denials are true of God but affirmations disconnected*.

Moreover, (2) Boethius[15] says *A simple form can't be a subject*. But as we have shown, God above all is simple form; so he can't be a subject. But whatever affirmative propositions are about is accounted its subject. So affirmative propositions can't be made about God.

Moreover, (3) all understanding of things in a way other than they are is

14. *Celestial Hierarchy,* 2 (3).
15. *De Trinitate,* 2.

false. Now God, as we have proved, is altogether free of compositeness. So since affirmative statements understand things as composite (connecting a subject with a predicate), it seems they can't truly be made about God.

BUT AGAINST THAT: Faith can't profess falsehood, yet it makes certain affirmations, as, for example, that God is three persons in one nature, and that he is almighty. So affirmative propositions can be made about God.

IN REPLY: We can make true affirmations about God.

To make this clear note that in every true affirmative statement subject and predicate signify under different aspects what is in some way identical: and this whether the predicate expresses some incidental property of the subject or what it substantially is. For clearly (if we say *The man is a white man,*) *man* and *white man* refer to one subject under different aspects, the notion of man and the notion of white man being different. And similarly if I say *humans are animals* it is precisely whatever is human that is truly animal—one and the same subject is called an animal because of its sense-nature and human because of its reasoning nature. So here too predicate and subject refer to one subject under different aspects. And this happens in a way even in propositions of identity, for there the mind treats the subject-term as though it referred to some subject the form of which is expressed in the predicate-term, in accordance with the saying: *predicates must be interpreted as forms and subjects as matter.*

To the different aspects then there corresponds the plurality of subject and predicate, and the mind expresses the underlying identity by connecting the two in one proposition. Now God, altogether one and simple in himself, is nevertheless known to us by way of many different conceptions, since we can't see him as he is in himself. But all of these different conceptions we have of him correspond, as we know, to one and the same simple thing. So we represent this conceptual plurality by the plurality of subject and predicate, and God's unity by the mental connecting of subject and predicate.

HENCE: To 1: Pseudo-Dionysius says affirmations about God are disconnected (or unfitting, as another translation has it) because no word used of God expresses him in an appropriate way, as we have said.

To 2: Our minds can't comprehend the way subsistent simple forms exist in themselves, but understands them as though they were composite things, subjects existing under a form. And so simple forms are understood as subjects, and then something is attributed to them.

To 3: This proposition: *All understanding of things in a way other than they are is false,* is ambiguous, because the words *in a way other than* can describe the *understanding* in relation to the thing understood or in relation to the mind understanding. In relation to the thing understood the proposition says that *any understanding of things which understands them to exist in a way other than they do is false;* which is true but irrelevant, since our mind when it composes propositions about God doesn't assert that he is composite but that he is simple. But if the proposition is interpreted in relation to the mind understanding then it is false. For our way of understanding things is clearly different from the way things exist: our mind understands material things below its own level immaterially, not in the sense of thinking *them* immaterial, but in the sense that thinking them is an immaterial act; and in a similar way it understands simple things above its own level in the way natural to it, compositely, but not in the sense of thinking *them* composite. So our minds aren't false because their statements about God are composite.

Questions for discussion

1. How should we understand the word 'God'?
2. Is there reason to suppose that God is incomprehensible or in some way beyond human understanding?
3. Is there some way of determining whether a sentence has or lacks meaning?
4. Is God-Talk more puzzling than other kinds of talk?
5. Is there any reason for saying that language is intrinsically inadequate for talking of God?
6. Does belief in God suffer from a death by a thousand qualifications?
7. Can one defend an account of God-Talk which takes it to be basically negative in character?
8. Can God be thought of as reflected in creatures?
9. Is the notion of analogy of any help when it comes to making sense of God-Talk?
10. Can one evaluate God-Talk without looking at why people use it?

Advice on further reading

Discussions of the meaningfulness of God-Talk in general can be found in all the introductions to philosophy of religion cited above. For book-length discussions see:

William P. Alston, *Divine Nature and Human Language* (Ithaca and London, 1989).

Frederick Ferré, *Language, Logic and God* (London and Glasgow, 1970).

R. S. Heimbeck, *Theology and Meaning* (London, 1969).

John McQuarrie, *God-Talk* (London, 1967).

Kai Nielsen, *Scepticism* (London, 1973).

Kai Nielsen, *An Introduction to the Philosophy of Religion* (London, 1982).

I. T. Ramsey, *Religious Language* (New York, 1963).

Patrick Sherry, *Religion, Truth and Language-Games* (London, 1977).

Janet Martin Soskice, *Metaphor and Religious Language* (Oxford, 1985).

David Tracy *The Analogical Imagination* (London, 1981).

Contemporary philosophers using the word 'God' frequently take themselves to be speaking of God as depicted in the Old and New Testaments. So, when addressing the issue of God-Talk it is worth looking at how the word 'God' was understood by biblical authors. For some guidance in this venture see the entries on 'God OT' and 'God NT' in David Noel Freedman (ed.), *The Anchor Bible Dictionary*, vol. 2 (New York, London, Toronto, Sydney, Auckland, 1992). Also see the entry on 'God' in vol. 2 of Colin Brown (ed.), *The New International Dictionary of New Testament Theology* (Grand Rapids, Michigan, 1976). In order to learn about biblical teaching on the nature of God, you might also turn to some standard accounts of Old and New Testament theology. Examples include:

Walter Brueggemann, *Theology of the Old Testament* (Minneapolis, Minnesota, 1997).

G. B. Caird, *New Testament Theology* (Oxford, 1994).

Hans Conzelmann, *An Outline of the Theology of the New Testament* (2nd edn, New York and Evanston, 1968).

Walter Eichrodt, *Theology of the Old Testament* (2 vols, Philadelphia and London, 1961).

Alan Richardson, *An Introduction to the Theology of the New Testament* (London, 1958).

For introductions to Islamic thinking on God, see:

John L. Esposito, *Islam: The Straight Path* (New York and Oxford, 1991).

Alfred Guillaume, *Islam* (Harmondsworth, 1956).

Malise Ruthven, *Islam* (Oxford and New York, 1997).

W. Montgomery Watt, *Islamic Philosophy and Theology* (Edinburgh, 1962).

For an account of Christian teaching about God in the period following that of the New Testament, see:

J. N. D. Kelly, *Early Christian Creeds* (3rd edn, Harlow and New York, 1972).

J. N. D. Kelly, *Early Christian Doctrines* (5th edn, London, 1977).

G. L. Prestige, *God in Patristic Thought* (2nd edn, London, 1952).

The problem of God's unknowability (leading to an emphasis on what is commonly called 'negative theology') is very much a feature in the thought of patristic and medieval authors. For an excellent survey, see Deirdre Carabine, *The Unknown God* (Louvain, 1995). For studies of Eastern Christian thinking on God-Talk, see Vladimir Lossky, *The Mystical Theology of the Eastern Church* (Cambridge and London, 1957), and *The Vision of God* (2nd edn, Leighton Buzzard, 1973). For a recent discussion of negative theology coming from an especially famous contemporary philosopher, see Hilary Putnam, 'On Negative Theology', *Faith and Philosophy* 14 (1997).

The best English version of the *Confessions* is *St Augustine Confessions*, translated with an introduction and notes by Henry Chadwick (Oxford, 1991). A helpful companion to this is Henry Chadwick, *Augustine* (Oxford, 1986). For a detailed commentary on the *Confessions*, see James J. O'Donnell, *Augustine Confessions* (3 vols, Oxford, 1992). For more student-oriented treatments, see Gillian Clark, *Augustine The Confessions* (Cambridge, 1993) and Robert J. O'Connell, SJ, *St Augustine's Confessions* (2nd edn, New York, 1989).

For more on Dionysius, see Paul Rorem, *Pseudo-Dionysius: A Commentary on the Texts and an Introduction to Their Influence* (New York and Oxford, 1993). Also see 'Albert and the Dionysian Tradition' in Simon Tugwell (ed.), *Albert and Thomas: Selected Writings* (New York and Mahwah, New Jersey, 1988), pp. 39 ff. Andrew Louth's *Denys the Areopagite* (London, 1989) provides an overview of Dionysius's thinking aimed at general readers, as does chapter VIII of Louth's *The Origins of the Christian Mystical Tradition* (Oxford, 1981), which also contains an overview of Augustine's *Confessions*.

For an introductory discussion of verificationism and religious belief, see Frederick Ferré, *Language, Logic and God* (London and Glasgow, 1970). For a more technical discussion, see R. S. Heimbeck, *Theology and Meaning* (London, 1969). For a reader on verificationism and religious belief, see Malcolm L. Diamond and Thomas V. Litzenburg Jr. (eds), *The Logic of God: Theology and Verification* (Indianapolis, Indiana, 1975). For an introduction to Logical Positivism, see Oswald Hanfling, *Logical Positivism* (Oxford, 1981) and Oswald Hanfling (ed.), *Essential Readings in Logical Positivism* (Oxford, 1981). For subtle criticism of certain verificationist assumptions, see W. V. Quine, 'Two Dogmas of Empiricism', in W. V. Quine, *From a Logical Point of View* (Cambridge, Massachusetts, and London, 1953). See also C. T. Hughes, 'Martin on the Meaninglessness of Religious Language', *International Journal for Philosophy of Religion* 34 (1993).

The extract from Flew (Chapter 11) is discussed by R. M. Hare, Basil Mitchell, and I. M. Crombie in Antony Flew and Alasdair MacIntyre (eds), *New Essays in Philosophical Theology* (London, 1955). Other discussions of it can be found in most of the introductions to philosophy of religion listed in the Advice on Reading section for the General Introduction. Flew develops what he says in his extract in *God and Philosophy* (London, 1966) and in chapter 3 of *The Presumption of Atheism and Other Essays* (London, 1976).

For a general account of Aquinas on God-Talk, see chapters 3 and 4 of my *The Thought of Thomas Aquinas*. Also see my 'Aquinas on What God is Not', *Revue Internationale de Philosophie* 52 (1998). For a study of Aquinas on God-Talk which relates it to the teaching of Maimonides and Avicenna, see David B. Burrell, *Knowing the Unknowable God* (Notre Dame, Indiana, 1986). In *Aquinas God and Action* (London and Henley, 1979), Burrell also offers a focused treatment of Aquinas on God-Talk, one which sets it in the context of Aquinas's overall thinking. For a book-length study of Aquinas on God-Talk, see Ralph McInerny, *Aquinas and Analogy* (Washington, DC, 1996).

In the Middle Ages, Aquinas's treatment of analogy was famously rejected by Duns Scotus. For an introduction to Scotus on God-Talk, see Richard Cross, *Duns Scotus* (New York and Oxford, 1999), chapter 3.

For a detailed and sophisticated study of analogy in language as a whole, the definitive work is James F. Ross, *Portraying Analogy* (Cambridge, 1981). Here Ross argues that analogy is all-pervasive in our discourse. The book contains a section on God-Talk. For a discussion by Ross of religious discourse and analogy, one explicitly aimed at students, see chapter 4 of Brian Davies (ed.), *Philosophy of Religion: A Guide to the Subject* (London, 1998).

Part III

Arguments for God's existence

Introduction

The notion of natural theology

I N *The City of God* (*De Civitate Dei*), St Augustine tells of an ancient attempt to divide theology into three parts: 'civic' (*civile*), 'mythical' (*mythikon*), and 'natural' (*phusikon*). Focusing on 'natural theology', he describes it as 'that in which philosophers have left many books (in which) they discuss what gods there are, where they are, of what kind they are, of what quality, for how long they have existed, whether they have always existed, whether they are made of fire, as Heraclitus believes, or of numbers, as Pythagoras thinks, or of atoms, as Epicurus says'.[1]

In terms of this account, natural theology is a philosophical enterprise which advances conclusions about divinity based on purely rational reflection. And, considered as such, it can be found in the writings of many ancient Greek thinkers and in the writings of many medieval authors. It can be found in a lot of eighteenth-century European thinking, much of which distinguished between 'natural' and 'revealed' religion. It can also be found in the writings of many contemporary philosophers of religion.

As I have said above, one might define 'natural theology' as the attempt to show that beliefs about God (especially the belief that God exists) can be defended on the basis of reason or argument which ought to be acceptable to anyone, not simply to those who already believe in God's existence. Or, along with James Barr, one might think of it as what is endorsed by those who hold that 'just by being human beings, men and women have a certain degree of knowledge of God and awareness of him, or at least a capacity for such an awareness, and this knowledge or awareness exists anterior to the special revelation of God made through Jesus Christ, through the Church, through the Bible'.[2] Either way, advocates of natural theology can be thought of as people who hold that there are grounds for beliefs about God which it makes sense to embrace without already starting with such beliefs.

Arguments for God's existence

In *Perceiving God: The Epistemology of Religious Experience*, William Alston offers the following definition of 'natural theology':

Natural theology is the enterprise of providing support for religious beliefs by starting from premises that neither are nor presuppose any religious beliefs. We begin from the mere existence of the world, or the teleological order of the world, or the concept of God, and we try to show that when we think through the implications of our starting point we are led to recognize the existence of a being that

---

1. *Augustine: The City of God against the Pagans* (edited and translated by R. W. Dyson, Cambridge, 1998), Book VI, ch. 5. For information on Varro, see E. J. Kenny (ed.), *The Cambridge History of Classical Literature II: Latin Literature* (Cambridge, 1982), pp. 286 ff.
2. James Barr, *Biblical Faith and Natural Theology* (Oxford, 1993), p. 1.

possesses attributes sufficient to identify Him as God. Once we get that foothold we may seek to show that a being could not have the initial attributes without also possessing certain others; in this manner we try to go as far as we can in building up a picture of God without relying on any supposed experience of God or communication from God, or on any religious authority. The credentials of this enterprise have often been challenged in the modern era. Hume and Kant are prominent among the challengers. Its death has repeatedly been reported, but like the phoenix it keeps rising from its ashes in ever new guises.[3]

Some advocates of natural theology (I take Aquinas to be an obvious example) might feel somewhat unhappy with the idea that it can give us a 'picture of God' considered as *having* 'attributes'.[4] But Alston's definition is a helpful one for our purposes since it nicely homes in on three of the main kinds of argument which have been defended or considered by those with an interest in natural theology—three kinds of argument considered in this part.

Note Alston's words: 'We begin from the mere existence of the world, or the teleological order of the world, or the concept of God.' Here he is broadly referring to what I am calling 'Cosmological Arguments', 'Design Arguments', and 'Ontological Arguments'. Together with appeal to what is sometimes called 'religious experience' or 'experience of God', such arguments constitute what most contemporary philosophers have in mind when they use the expression 'natural theology'.[5]

What do they amount to, and how should they be evaluated? The chapters in Part III offer some answers. Part III is divided into different sections, and my introductions to them are chiefly designed to help you to understand them and to place them in an historical context. The 'Advice on further reading' appended to each section should help you profitably to reflect on them further.

3. William Alston, *Perceiving God: The Epistemology of Religious Experience* (Ithaca, New York, and London, 1991), p. 289.
4. See my comments on Aquinas and analogy in the Introduction to Part II. Also see Chapters 50 and 52.
5. I should note that in *Perceiving God* Alston does not consider himself to be providing an argument from religious experience. He concentrates on the suggestion that experience can itself be the grounds for beliefs about God.

Advice on further reading

Arguments for God's existence are discussed in all of the introductions to philosophy of religion cited so far. Among other books dealing with a variety of arguments for God's existence, the following can be recommended as of historical and/or philosophical help when it comes to thinking about them in general:

Bernadino M. Bonansea, *God and Atheism* (Washington, DC, 1979).

Mark Comer, *Does God Exist?* (Bristol, 1991).

Stephen T. Davis, *God, Reason and Theistic Proofs* (Grand Rapids, Michigan, 1997).

Antony Flew, *God and Philosophy* (London, 1966).

Richard M. Gale, *On the Nature and Existence of God* (Cambridge, 1991).

John Hick, *Arguments for the Existence of God* (London, 1971).

Hans Küng, *Does God Exist?* (London, 1980).

H. D. Lewis, *Our Experience of God* (London, 1959).

J. L. Mackie, *The Miracle of Theism* (Oxford, 1982).

Hugo Meynell, *God and the World* (London, 1971).

Alvin Plantinga, *God and Other Minds* (Ithaca, New York, and London, 1967).

Alvin Plantinga, *God, Freedom and Evil* (London, 1975).

Robert Prevost, *Probability and Theistic Explanation* (Oxford, 1990).

James F. Ross, *Philosophical Theology* (2nd edn, Indianapolis, Indiana, 1980).

J. J. C. Smart and J. J. Haldane, *Atheism and Theism* (Oxford, 1996).

Richard Swinburne, *The Existence of God* (Oxford, 1979; revised edn, 1991).

Richard Swinburne, *Is There a God?* (Oxford, 1996).

Peter Vardy, *The Puzzle of God* (London, 1990).

James Barr's *Biblical Faith and Natural Theology* (Oxford, 1993) is the currently most erudite and distinguished available discussion of natural theology with an eye on biblical texts. For introductions to Karl Barth and natural theology, see:

John Bowden, *Karl Barth* (London, 1971).

David Ford (ed.), *The Modern Theologians* (2nd edn, Oxford, 1997).

Alasdair Heron, *A Century of Protestant Theology* (Guildford and London, 1980).

S. W. Sykes (ed.), *Karl Barth—Studies of his Theological Method* (Oxford, 1979).

John Webster, *Barth* (London, 2000).

According to the first Vatican Council: 'God, the source and end of all things, can be known with certainty from the consideration of created things, by the natural power of human reason' (cf. Norman P. Tanner (ed.), *Decrees of the Ecumenical Councils*, vol. 2, London, 1990, p. 806). And Roman Catholics in general have commonly been well disposed to the idea of natural theology. For some introduction to their thinking on the matter, see the *Catechism of the Catholic Church* (Vatican City, 1994), Part I, section 1, ch. 1, and the papal encyclical by John Paul II, *Fides et Ratio* (Vatican City, 1998). In *The Metaphysics of Theism: Aquinas's Natural Theology in Summa contra gentiles I* (Oxford, 1997), Norman Kretzmann considers what we might mean by 'natural theology' and argues that Aquinas is an unusually impressive representative of it.

For an introduction to ancient natural theology, see Sarah Broadie, 'Rational Theology', in A. A. Long (ed.), *The Cambridge Companion to Early Greek Philosophy* (Cambridge, 1999). Also see L. P. Gerson, *God and Greek Philosophy: Studies in the History of Natural Theology* (London and New York, 1990). For a contemporary philosophical discussion of natural theology in general, see Alvin Plantinga, 'The Prospects for Natural Theology', in James Tomberlin (ed.), *Philosophical Perspectives* (5th edn, Atascadero, California, 1991).

Cosmological arguments

Introduction

Where does it all come from?

When people who believe in God are asked why they do so, they often say 'Well, something must have started it all' or 'The world cannot have come from nothing'. The idea here is that the sheer existence of the universe demands a cause, reason, or explanation, and that God can be thought of as just what is needed—that God must exist to account for there being a *cosmos*. And this is the idea which links all that I am calling 'cosmological arguments'. In many works of philosophy you will find authors referring to 'the cosmological argument' as if there were just one particular argument for God which alone deserves the name 'cosmological'. In fact, however, the history of philosophy has thrown up a variety of arguments for God's existence, all of which can fairly be referred to as 'cosmological'.[1]

One could argue that they go back a long way. Plato, for instance, reasons to the existence of a divine craftsman and to the existence of something which accounts for change in the world.[2] And Aristotle maintains that we need to seek for the causes of things, including such phenomena as earthly and celestial motion.[3] But their teachings on these matters are often hard to interpret. One might also reasonably suggest that they are not so much concerned with the existence of the world as with features that it exhibits, and that they are not attempting to defend belief in God's existence, as most classical defenders of cosmological arguments can be thought of as trying to do.

When we turn, however, to Arabic authors writing from around the ninth to the twelfth centuries we find arguments clearly designed to defend the notion that the world has a cause of its being, a cause which can certainly be thought of as divine. In particular, we find arguments maintaining that the universe must have been brought into existence by God a finite time ago. We also find arguments holding that everything other than God is 'contingent' and can only exist because given existence (or made to exist) by God, whose existence is absolutely 'necessary'.

1. The phrase 'the cosmological argument' was introduced into philosophy by Kant. See Immanuel Kant, *Critique of Pure Reason*, A591/B619.
2. See Plato's Dialogues *Timaeus* and *Laws*.
3. See, for example, *Physics*, Book VII.

Islamic cosmological arguments

The arguments of the first kind are causal and temporal. And they rest heavily on the belief that the universe had a beginning. The arguments of the second kind are also causal. But they are compatible with supposing that the universe never had a beginning or that it is, as some would say, 'eternal'. The arguments of the first kind are commonly associated with authors known as *mutakallimūn*, writing within the so-called kalām tradition of Islamic thinking—authors such as Al-Kindī (c.801–c.83) and al-Ghāzālī (1058–1111). The arguments of the second kind are commonly associated with authors belonging to the Islamic *falsafa* tradition—authors such as Avicenna.

The basic thrust of kalām cosmological arguments can be presented thus:

1.   Whatever has a beginning of existence must have a cause.
2.   The universe began to exist.
3.   The universe must have been caused to exist.

But what kind of cause? Defenders of kalām cosmological arguments think that only something such as free, intelligent choice can account for the coming to pass of what, like the beginning of the universe, cannot be explained in terms of unfree, non-intelligent, physical processes. The occurrence of such processes depends on the universe being there in the first place. According to defenders of kalām cosmological arguments, therefore, the cause of the beginning of the universe cannot be an unfree, non-intelligent, physical process. It must be a personal being. Or, as a prominent contemporary defender of this line of thinking puts it:

> Since everything that begins to exist has a cause of its existence, and since the universe began to exist, we conclude, therefore, the universe has a cause of its existence . . . Transcending the entire universe there exists a cause which brought the universe into being . . . But even more: we may plausibly argue that the cause of the universe is a personal being . . . If the universe began to exist, and if the universe is caused, then the cause of the universe must be a personal being who freely chooses to create the world.[4]

What of cosmological arguments other than those of the kalām type? As represented by thinking to be found in writings by people such as Avicenna, their basic thrust can be presented thus:

1.   Everything must either have a reason or cause of its existence, or not.
2.   If something does not, then there is at least one thing which exists of necessity.
3.   If something does not exist of necessity, its existence derives from a reason or cause (it is a contingent being).
4.   There cannot be an infinite series of reasons or causes for the existence of contingent beings.
5.   So contingent beings ultimately derive from what exists of necessity.

---

4. William Lane Craig, *The Kalām Cosmological Argument* (London, 1979), pp. 149 ff.

Or, as Avicenna put it:

Whatever has being must either have a reason for its being or have no reason for it. If it has a reason, then it is contingent, equally before it comes into being (if we make this mental hypothesis) and when it is in a state of being—for in the case of a thing whose being is contingent the mere fact of its entering upon being does not remove from it the contingent nature of its being. If on the other hand it has no reason for its being in any way whatsoever, then it is necessary in its being. This rule having been confirmed, I shall now seek to prove that there is in being a being which has no reason for its being.

A being which has no reason for its being . . . is either contingent or necessary. If it is necessary, then the point we sought to prove is established. If on the other hand it is contingent, that which is contingent cannot enter upon being except for some reason which sways the scales in favour of its being and against its not-being. If the reason is also contingent, then there is a chain of contingents linked one to the other, and there is no being at all; for this being which is the subject of our hypothesis cannot enter into being so long as it is not preceded by an infinite succession of beings, which is absurd. Therefore, contingent beings end in a Necessary Being.[5]

Note that this argument is indifferent as to whether or not 'contingent' things have a temporal origin. It is, we may say, an argument which turns on the sheer existence of things—as are all the examples of cosmological arguments presented in the chapters below. For all of them, in their different ways, are arguing not that the beginning of the universe had a cause, but that there must be a cause of why something exists rather than nothing.

Anselm, Aquinas, and Scotus

Outside Islamic circles, cosmological arguments were defended by significant medieval Jewish thinkers—Maimonides, for example.[6] They were also given rigorous attention by Christian authors anxious to explore what philosophy can say about God as the source of the world.[7] Anselm is a good example of such an author, and in Chapter 13 he offers one of the most concise cosmological arguments ever. It comes from his *Monologion*, which he calls a 'meditation' on 'the essence of the divine' observing the conditions: 'nothing whatsoever to be argued on the basis of the authority of Scripture, but the constraints of reason concisely to prove, and the clarity of truth clearly to show, in the plain style, with everyday arguments, and down-to-earth dialectic, the conclusions of distinct investigations'.[8]

What Anselm says in Chapter 13 needs no explanatory comment, since it is abundantly clear what he is saying and why.[9] But the extracts from Aquinas and Scotus are different from Anselm's in this respect. So at this stage it might help if I make the following points:

First, in reading the extract from Aquinas, you should bear in mind that, in article 1, he

---

5. Avicenna *al-Risālat al'Arshīya*, quoted from Arthur J. Arberry, *Avicenna on Theology* (London, 1951), p. 25.
6. See *The Guide of the Perplexed*, Book II, ch. 1.
7. In the light, of course, of the Christian doctrine of creation according to which the world is made and sustained in its existence by God. See the volumes by Kelly cited at the end of Part II.
8. Brian Davies and G. R. Evans (eds), *Anselm of Canterbury: The Major Works* (Oxford, 1998), p. 5.
9. Note that Anselm does not use the word 'God' in developing his argument. That word only appears late in the *Monologion*. But Anselm clearly thought of his argument as pointing to the truth of what he said when professing belief in God.

is relying on the notion of causality which I sought to explain in Part II when introducing his teaching that effects somehow resemble their causes. In Chapter 14 Aquinas's idea is that existing things must be caused to exist by something the nature of which is reflected by their sheer existence (as opposed to particular features they might possess). He thinks that such a thing can best be described as 'sheer existence subsisting of his very nature' since what it accounts for is *not* that things are like this or like that, but *that* they exist at all.

Second, in article 2 of Chapter 14 we encounter the terms 'matter' and 'form', which Aquinas derives from Aristotle. Matter, for Aquinas, is opposed to form. Form is that by which something actually *is* (e.g. a cow), while matter is that by which what it is might *not be* (that by which a cow can become a corpse). According to Aquinas, it is because we have a material world that the food a cow's mother eats, while actually food, is potentially a cow (could cease to be food and be turned into an embryo cow in the womb, with the same matter). It is because we have a material world that a cow can cease to be a cow and be turned into beef—with the same matter—which, in turn, might become something else.

Third, Scotus presents his cosmological argument right at the beginning of Chapter 15. The argument starts from the fact that something is produced and concludes that there has to be an unproduced producer. And it is very briefly stated. But Scotus feels that an objection to it needs to be dealt with at length, and it is his treatment of this which comprises the bulk of the chapter. Here Scotus is concerned with what is often called 'the infinite regress argument' (one frequently invoked by critics of cosmological arguments). For suppose that A is produced by B and that B is produced by C. Why does there *have* to be something unproduced which ultimately accounts for A? Why may there not be a chain of producers going on to infinity and with nothing unproduced producing them? Scotus's reply leads him to distinguish between things 'ordered essentially' and things 'ordered accidentally', and you might find his argument hard to follow. Basically, however, he is only saying that if one instance of production raises the question of a cause, the same is true of an infinite number. On his account, some things can be causally related (or 'ordered') in a series that does *not* imply the need for a first member *of that series*. But he also thinks of things as causally related (or 'ordered') in a way which implies the need for something which is not just one more member of the series to which they belong. And in denying that the series of produced producers can be infinite he is thinking of just such a series. Effectively, he is saying: 'Yes, B might produce A, and C might produce B, and D might produce C, and so on to infinity. But how come *any* members of the series B, C, D and so on? Whatever accounts for this cannot be something produced.'[10]

---

10. Aquinas argues in a similar way. Cf. *Summa Theologiae*, Ia. 46. 2 and 7: 'It is not impossible to proceed to infinity accidentally as regards efficient causes; for instance, if all the causes thus infinitely multiplied should have the order of only one cause, while their multiplication is accidental: e.g. as an artificer acts by means of many hammers accidentally, because one after the other is broken. It is accidental, therefore, that one particular hammer should act after the action of another, and it is likewise accidental to this particular man as generator to be generated by another man; for he generates as a man, and not as the son of another man. For all men generating hold one grade in the order of efficient causes—viz., the grade of a particular generator. Hence it is not impossible for a man to be generated by man to infinity; but such a thing would be impossible if the generation of this man depended upon this man, and on an elementary body, and on the sun, and so on to infinity'.

More modern cosmological arguments

Medieval philosophers of various religious persuasions differ in their approach to cosmological arguments. But they also share a common conviction when it comes to the idea that the existence of what we encounter (including ourselves) cannot be thought of as a 'brute fact' lacking what we might call an 'extra-mundane' cause. And many of their philosophical successors agree with them in this respect. Hence, for example, Locke defends a cosmological argument for God's existence in *An Essay Concerning Human Understanding*. Here he writes:

I think it is beyond Question, that *Man has a clear perception of his own Being*; he knows certainly, that he exists, and that he is something ... In the next place, Man knows by an intuitive Certainty, that bare *nothing can no more produce any real Being, than it can be equal to two right angles* ... If therefore we know that there is some real Being, and that Non-entity cannot produce any real Being, it is an evident demonstration, that from Eternity there has been something; Since what was not from Eternity, had a Beginning; and what had a Beginning, must be produced by something else.[11]

Is that argument sound? Commenting on it in his *New Essays on Human Understanding*, Leibniz thinks not. He says:

I find an ambiguity there. If it means that *there has never been a time when nothing existed*, then I agree with it, and it really does follow with entirely mathematical rigour from the preceding propositions. For if there had ever been nothing, there would always have been nothing, since a being cannot be produced by nothing; and in that case we ourselves would not have existed, which conflicts with the first truth of experience. But you go straight on in a way which shows that when you say that something has existed from all eternity you mean an eternal thing. But from what you have asserted so far it does not follow that if there has always been something then one certain thing has always been, i.e. that there is an eternal being.[12]

Here Leibniz is suggesting that we cannot validly argue that since something has always existed it follows that some one thing (e.g. God) has always existed. Yet Leibniz himself defends a cosmological argument, as you can see from Chapter 16. Unlike those of Anselm, Aquinas, and Scotus, however, his argument is not an explicitly causal one arguing that there must be something which produces or brings about the existence of the world. Instead, it invokes the notion of 'sufficient reason'. For Leibniz, God must exist since there has to be a 'sufficient reason of existence' which lies in 'necessity itself'.

What does Leibniz mean by 'sufficient reason'? He often takes causes to be reasons. He would have said, for example, that you have given a reason for Fred's death by noting that he was shot by Mike. But he also understands 'reason' in a broader sense—as what explains. And, for Leibniz, there are different kinds of explanation.

There is, for example, explanation in terms of intention ('Fred died because Mike

---

11. John Locke, *An Essay Concerning Human Understanding* (edited with an introduction by Peter H. Nidditch, Oxford, 1975), Book IV, ch. X, pp. 619 f.
12. G. W. Leibniz, *New Essays on Human Understanding* (trans. and ed. Peter Remnant and Jonathan Bennett, Cambridge, 1981), 436.

wanted him out of the way'). There is also explanation in terms of what cannot consistently be denied. If, for example, we ask why all triangles are three-sided, the obvious answer is: because it follows from the notion of a triangle that anything triangular is three-sided. And it is this last kind of explanation (or reason) for which Leibniz is always seeking when thinking about the existence of God. In looking for a 'sufficient reason for existence', Leibniz is basically thinking that everything in the end is the way it is because it *has* to be—in the way that it *has* to be that all triangles are three-sided. So he thinks of God as something the existence of which one could only deny by contradicting oneself—as one would contradict oneself by asserting that no triangles have three sides.

The conclusion that God is a being whose existence can only be denied by means of contradiction came to be taken by many philosophers after Leibniz (and much under his influence) as what cosmological arguments are essentially concerned to establish. Kant, for example, is clearly thinking along these lines in what he says about what he calls 'the' cosmological argument in *The Critique of Pure Reason*, for he dismisses it on the ground that there can be nothing the denial of the existence of which implies a contradiction.[13] As we have seen, however, there are cosmological arguments which do not turn on views about logical possibility and logical necessity. In Chapter 17 you will find a contemporary one, which you can read as a complement to Chapter 14 since it is written by a supporter of Aquinas seeking to express his (often hard to understand) writings on the question 'Why believe in God?'.

Evaluating cosmological arguments

How should we think of cosmological arguments? Are they cogent? Do any of them give us good reason to believe in the existence of God? Do they contain fallacies? Do they rest on premises we have no reason to believe? Do they fail because their conclusions do not follow from their premises? Critics of cosmological arguments have attacked them on various grounds, some of which can be highlighted by the following questions:

1. Why should we suppose that beginnings of existence need to be caused?
2. Why should we accept that the universe had a beginning?
3. Why should we not say that the universe (whether it had a beginning or not) is a brute fact requiring no explanation or cause?
4. Even if we agree that various things in the world need to be accounted for causally, why should we suppose that the same is true of the world as a whole?
5. Why is it absurd to suppose that there cannot be an infinite regress of causes?
6. Even if particular causal chains have a first member, why suppose that there is some first member which accounts for there being anything in need of a cause?
7. How do we know that everything must have a 'sufficient reason'?

In the end, you can only answer these questions by trying to think about them for yourself; and Chapters 18 and 19, by Paul Edwards and J. L. Mackie, should help you to do

---

13. *Critique of Pure Reason* A592/620–A602/630.

this. Between them, Edwards and Mackie present the strongest contemporary case against cosmological arguments. So they should help to give you a good idea of how one might develop a substantial critique of them. They presume no background knowledge, so they need no explanatory comments.[14] Since Hume provides an especially famous rejection of the principle that beginnings of existence must be caused, I have included what Hume has to say in Chapter 20, followed in Chapter 21 by a response to Hume from the contemporary philosopher Elizabeth Anscombe. Hume writes with great clarity, as does Anscombe. So, like those of Edwards and Mackie, these chapters are also self-explanatory. The same is true of Chapter 22 in which James Sadowsky offers a particularly succinct discussion of what I have called 'the infinite regress argument'—often thought decisively to show that cosmological arguments are inherently defective.

14. Note, however, that Mackie alludes to Kant on ontological arguments, for which see 'Ontological arguments' below.

Chapter 13

A concise cosmological argument from the eleventh century

Anselm of Canterbury

> That there exists a nature, through which everything that exists exists, which exists through itself, and which is, of all things that exist, supreme

FURTHERMORE, not only is it the case that all good things are good, and all great things great, through one and the same thing, but also it would seem to be the case that whatever is, is through one thing. For everything that exists, exists either through something or through nothing. But nothing exists through nothing. For it is impossible even to conceive of something existing through nothing. Whatever exists, then, exists only through something.

Now since this is the case, there is either one or more than one thing through which all existing things exist. If there are more than one, then they are either themselves reducible to some one thing through which they exist, or each of them exists individually through itself, or they all exist mutually through one another. Suppose then, first, that they exist through some one thing, then all the existing things do exist through one, and not more than one, thing—that one thing through which the more than one exist. Suppose, then, secondly, that each of them exists individually through itself. In order for each to exist through itself, there must of course be some single power-to-exist-through-oneself (or some single nature-of-existing-through-oneself) that each possesses. And then, doubtless, they would exist through this one thing—that through which they possess the capacity to exist through oneself. It is therefore closer to the truth to say that all existing things exist through this one thing, than to say that they exist through things which, without it, are incapable of existing. The third possibility, that they should exist mutually through one another, defies reason. For the notion that something could exist through that to which it gives existence, is just irrational. For not even do things spoken of by means of mutually related terms exist mutually through one another. Master and servant are spoken of with reference to each other. Yet the human beings themselves who are thus spoken of do not exist through each other at all, nor do the relations themselves by which they are spoken of exist through each other at all. (The relations exist through the subjects.) Truth therefore rules out altogether

Anselm of Canterbury extract from 'Monologion 3' translated by Simon Harrison from *Anselm of Canterbury The Major Works* edited with an introduction and notes by Brian Davies and G. R. Evans (Oxford World's Classics, 1998), copyright © Simon Harrison 1998; editorial matter copyright © Brian Davies and G. R. Evans 1998, reprinted by permission of Oxford University Press.

the possibility that there is more than one thing through which everything exists. Therefore there is necessarily some one thing through which all existing things exist.

Therefore, since all things exist through this one thing, beyond a shadow of a doubt this one thing exists through itself. Therefore all the other things exist through something other than themselves, while this alone exists through itself. But what exists through something other than itself, is less than that through which all other things exist, and which alone exists through itself. Therefore, that which exists through itself, exists most of all. There exists, therefore, some one thing, which alone of all things most exists and exists supremely. But that which exists most of all, that through which whatever is good is good, whatever is great is great, and indeed through which whatever exists exists—this is necessarily supremely good, supremely great, and is of all the things that exist, the supreme. Therefore there is some thing which, whether it is called an essence, a substance, or a nature, is the best and the greatest, and of all the things that are, the supreme.

Chapter 14

A thirteenth-century cosmological argument

Thomas Aquinas

The first cause of things

Must everything that is have been caused by God?

THE FIRST POINT: 1. This does not appear necessary. There is nothing against our meeting with a thing lacking a non-essential, for instance a human being who is not white. Now the relationship of effect to cause does not seem of the very nature of beings, for some are conceivable without it. And hence can exist without it. What then is there to stop some beings existing which are not created by God?

2. Moreover, a thing requires an efficient cause in order to be an existing fact. Hence that which cannot but exist does not require one. Now no necessary thing is able not to be, for what has to be cannot fail to be. Since there are many such in reality, all beings are not from God.

3. Further, whatever has a cause can be demonstrated through that cause. Yet Aristotle brings out how mathematical demonstrations are not conducted through an efficient cause. Not all entities, therefore, come from God as an efficient cause.

ON THE OTHER HAND in *Romans* we read, *For from him and through him and unto him are all things.*

REPLY: We are bound to conclude that everything that is at all real is from God. For when we encounter a subject which shares in a reality then this reality must needs be caused there by a thing which possesses it of its nature, as when, for example, iron is made red-hot by fire. Now ... God is sheer existence subsisting of his very nature. And such being, as we have also noted, cannot but be unique, rather as whiteness would be were it subsistent, for its repetition depends on there being many receiving subjects. We are left with the conclusion that all things other than God are not their own existence but share in existence.

It follows strictly that all things which are diversified by their diverse sharing in

Thomas Aquinas extracts from Volume 8 of the Blackfriars edition of *The Summa Theologiae* edited by Thomas Gilby (Eyre and Spottiswoode and McGraw Hill, 1967).

existence, so that some are fuller beings than others, are caused by one first being which simply *is* in the fullest sense of the word.

On these grounds Plato held that before the many you must place the one; and Aristotle that the supremely real and true is the cause of everything that is real and true, his illustration being fire, which is *hottest and the cause of heat in everything else.*

HENCE: 1. While a relationship to a cause does not enter into the definition of a being that is caused, nevertheless it follows from what is bound up in a being by participation, for from the fact that a thing is such it follows that it is caused by another. Such a being cannot exist without being caused, no more than a human being can without a sense of the comic. Yet since to be caused is not essential to the meaning of being as such we can meet with a being that is uncaused.

2. This was the objection, as noticed in the *Physics*, which prompted the conclusion that what is necessary has no cause. Yet the demonstrative sciences bring out how fallacious it is, for necessary premises there offer grounds for necessary conclusions. Accordingly Aristotle remarks in the *Metaphysics* that there are some objects which have a cause for their necessity. The reason why an efficient cause is required is not just because the effect is such that it may or may not exist, but because it would not exist did its cause not exist. This conditional judgment is true whether the antecedent clause or the consequent clause express what is possible or impossible.

3. Mathematical objects are taken as abstract concepts of reason, all the same they are not abstract where they exist in reality. Now having an efficient cause is due to having real existence. And so, although the things mathematics are about do have an efficient cause, it is not under that aspect that a mathematician studies them. That is why mathematical demonstration does not work through the medium of efficient causality.

Is primary matter caused by God?

THE SECOND POINT: 1. No, it would seem. For a thing that is made is composed of that in which it is made and of some other principle, as the *Physics* point out. Primary matter, however, does not have any subject. Therefore it cannot have been made by God.

2. Besides, to act on and to be acted on are divided as not overlapping. Now as the first active principle is God so the first passive principle is matter. They are two opposite principles, neither of which comes from the other.

3. Also, every agent produces its like, and, since it is because it is actual that it is productive, it follows that what it produces is also actual in some manner. But primary matter precisely as such is purely potential. It is against its very meaning to be something produced.

ON THE OTHER HAND St Augustine cries, *Two hast thou made, O Lord, one close to thyself,* namely angelic nature, *the other close to nothing,* namely prime matter.

REPLY: The ancient philosophers entered into the truth step by step and as it were haltingly. Somewhat raw to begin with, they reckoned that the only realities were sensible bodies. Those of them who maintained these were subject to change thought of this only in terms of outward modification, for instance according to rarefaction and condensation, or to mingling or separating out. They supposed that bodily substance was unproduced, and the changes of condition which happened to it they ascribed to such causes as love and strife, mind, and so forth.

They advanced further when they grasped the distinction between substantial form and matter—which they held was unproduced—and gathered that it was according to their essential forms that bodily things were changed from one thing into another. Such transformations they attributed to more universal causes, for instance Aristotle's 'inclined circle', or Plato's Ideas.

Yet notice that form pins matter down to a determinate kind of thing, rather as a supplementary property shapes a substance of a species to a determinate mode of being, as a human being is limited by being white. On both sides, therefore, they were still looking at being under a particular aspect, namely as this sort of being or as existing in such and such a manner. That is why they remained at the particular efficient causes for things.

Later others climbed higher to the prospect of being as being, and observed the cause of things inasmuch as they are beings, not merely as things of such a kind or quality. To be the cause of things in that they are beings is to be the cause of all that belongs to their existence in any way whatsoever, not merely as regards what they are like by the properties which shape them or what kind they are by their substantial forms. So we have to lay down that even primary matter is caused by the all-embracing cause of beings.

HENCE: 1. Aristotle is there speaking of a particular coming into existence, that is by transformation, whether with respect to substance or properties. We, however, are now speaking of things in their issuing from the universal source of being. Not even matter is left out of this, though it is not produced in the first way referred to.

2. To be the effect of action, that is what passion is. Hence it is reasonable that the primary passive principle should be the effect of the first active principle, for whatever is incomplete depends causally on what is complete. And, as Aristotle says, this must be the utterly complete.

3. The argument shows that matter is not produced without form, not that it is not produced. For although everything that is caused in actuality is, it is not nevertheless pure actuality. Hence even what is potential in it has to be caused if all that belongs to it as an existent is caused.

Chapter 15

A fourteenth-century cosmological argument

John Duns Scotus

Sᴏᴍᴇ being is an effect because it is produced. Now either nothing produces it, or it produces itself, or it is produced by another. It is not produced by nothing, for nothing is the cause of nothing. Neither does it produce itself, for according to book 1, chapter nine of Augustine's *De trinitate*, 'nothing begets itself.' Therefore it is produced by another. If by another, then this other is produced by nothing, by itself, or by another—and so the process would continue indefinitely. Consequently, one must stop with something that is not produced but that produces by its own power and not in virtue of any other; and this I call the first.

I raise an objection to this reasoning:

It is not incongruous that productions of the same sort should continue indefinitely, according to the philosophers. Thus this son is from that father, and the latter from another father, and so on ad infinitum. Fire, too, can come from fire indefinitely.

(*Solution to the objection*) I refute the objection thus: in things essentially ordered, I declare, there is no progression to infinity, nor do any philosophers admit such, though they do concede this where accidentally ordered things are concerned, as is clear from Avicenna's *Metaphysics*, book 8, chapter 5.

To demonstrate this, however, I introduce one prefatory remark, namely, to speak of per se and per accidens causes is not the same as speaking of essentially ordered and accidentally ordered causes. For in the first case, there is a one-to-one comparison, namely, of a cause to its effect. And we have a per se cause when something causes by virtue of its proper nature, not by something incidental to it. Thus a subject is the per se cause of its proper attribute; and there are many other instances, such as when something white expands (the diaphanous medium) or a builder builds. But the converse is true of a per accidens cause, such as Polycletus building.

In the second case, however, there is a comparison of two causes with each other insofar as some third thing is caused by them. And then it turns out that per se or essentially ordered causes differ from those accidentally ordered in three ways. And this triple difference provides a threefold demonstration for proving that something is a first efficient cause in an unqualified sense.

John Duns Scott extract from 'Reportatio IA' from *Duns Scotus, Metaphysician* by William A. Frank and Allan B. Wolter (Purdue University Press, 1995).

The first difference is that with causes that are essentially ordered, the second cause, insofar as it causes, depends upon the first, whereas in accidentally ordered causes the second does not depend upon the first in this way, though it may be dependent on the first for its existence or in some other respect. For though a son depends upon his father for his existence, he does not depend upon him in causing, since when his father is dead he can act as effectively as if his father were alive.

There is a second difference, since the causality of per se and essentially ordered causes is of different sorts and is ordered (to the effect) in different ways. For the superior cause is more perfect inasmuch as the second cause causes by virtue of the former. But this is not so with accidentally ordered causes, for a son can procreate, just as a father can; and he does not depend in this except upon a cause of the same sort—not upon a more perfect cause.

There is a third difference, because all the per se and essentially ordered causes are needed simultaneously to cause the effect; were this not so, some per se and essential causality would be lacking the effect. But such simultaneity is not required where accidentally ordered causes are concerned, for they exercise their causality successively, one after the other.

From the first difference I argue thus: In essentially ordered causes, where our adversary postulates an infinity, each second cause, insofar as it is causing, depends upon a first. If there were an infinity of causes, therefore, it would be such that each one of them—not just each posterior cause—depended upon its immediately prior cause. Rather, the whole collection of what is caused depends upon some other prior cause that is not a part of that collection, for then something would be a cause of itself. Since the whole collection of dependents depends, it does so not upon something that is part of that collection, because everything there is dependent. Consequently it depends upon something that is not part of that totality. And this I call the first efficient. Hence, even if there is an infinity of causes, they still depend upon something that is not a part of that infinity.

From the second difference I argue thus: If all essentially ordered causes are of a different order, because they are of different orders, the higher will always be more perfect. Therefore a cause that is infinitely superior will be infinitely more perfect. Hence if there is an infinity of such, there will be infinite causes that are simply perfect. But no cause that is simply perfect causes by virtue of another; therefore if there is an infinity of causes, then they are not essentially ordered. For if you grant that they cause by virtue of another, none would be simply supreme or perfect.

From the third argument I argue thus: If an infinity of essentially ordered causes would concur in the production of some effect, and—by virtue of this third difference—all such must act at once, it would follow that an actual infinity is simultaneously causing this effect—something that no philosopher admits.

(*Two persuasive reasons*) Two other persuasive arguments are adduced to prove this (primacy of efficiency), the first of which is this. If in essentially ordered causes, the process went on to infinity, each would be caused, and hence by some cause. If this were not a first cause, then all would be equally intermediate causes, for there would be no first with reference to which one could be said to be more proximate or remote than another. And hence the argument given by the Philosopher in book 2 of the *Metaphysics* would hold good. This is virtually the same as the argument derived from the first difference.

The second reason is this. To be an efficient cause does not imply imperfection. But what includes no imperfection can be assumed to exist without imperfection in some being. But if no cause exists that is not itself dependent upon something prior, then no cause exists without imperfection. Since this negates our initial assumption, it follows from that assumption that effectibility could exist in some nature that is simply first. Therefore, effectibility that is first in an unqualified sense is possible, and if it can exist and yet cannot be from another, then it exists of itself.

You may object that these reasons are valid only if one assumes an essential order among the causes, something you deny and avow instead that everything produced is adequately accounted for by some particular total cause of the same sort, like a son produced by a father, and so on ad infinitum.

I say against this: Either this product is produced by a cause of some other order, and then it follows that an essential order does exist, or else the product is caused by something of the same sort. As such it would be a possible to be produced by the cause that produces it, and that cause, too, would be only a possible to be produced by some other cause, which in turn was only a possible to be produced by something else, and so on ad infinitum. For where all are of the same sort, their natures would have the same sort of existence, so that if one were only something able to be produced, then all would be such successively. But no succession can continue indefinitely except by virtue of something permanent that is coextensive with the succession as a whole. For no change in form (i.e., from possibility to actuality) is perpetuated save by virtue of something uniform that is not a part of the succession itself, since no part can persist throughout the entire succession and still be only just a part of it. Therefore, there is something that is essentially prior to the whole succession, since the latter depends upon it. Hence everything that depends upon an accidentally ordered cause also depends upon a per se and essentially ordered cause as well. Indeed, if this essential order is denied, the accidental order will also be denied, because the accidentals have no order except in relation to something fixed and permanent. Neither would a multitude, then, have any order proceeding to infinity. And in this way the first objection is refuted, namely, that there will be no infinite process of accidentally ordered causes unless there be a stage where the essential order ends.

Chapter 16

A seventeenth-century cosmological argument

Gottfried Wilhelm Leibniz

B ESIDES the world or aggregate of finite things we find a certain Unity which is dominant, not only in the sense in which the soul is dominant in me, or rather in which the self or *I* is dominant in my body, but also in a much more exalted manner. For the dominant Unity of the universe not only rules the world, but also constructs or makes it; and it is higher than the world and, if I may so put it, extramundane; it is thus the ultimate reason of things. For neither in any one single thing, nor in the whole aggregate and series of things, can there be found the sufficient reason of existence. Let us suppose the book of the elements of geometry to have been eternal, one copy always having been written down from an earlier one; it is evident that, even though a reason can be given for the present book out of a past one, nevertheless out of any number of books taken in order going backwards we shall never come upon a full reason; since we might always wonder why there should have been such books from all time—why there were books at all, and why they were written in this manner. What is true of the books is true also of the different states of the world; for what follows is in some way copied from what precedes (although according to certain laws of change). And so, however far you go back to earlier states, you will never find in those states a full reason why there should be any world rather than none, and why it should be such as it is.

Therefore, even if you suppose the world eternal, as you will still be supposing nothing but a succession of states and will not in any of them find a sufficient reason, nor however many states you assume will you advance one step towards giving a reason, it is evident that the reason must be sought elsewhere. For in things which are eternal, though there may be no cause, nevertheless a reason must he discerned; which reason in things that are permanent is necessity itself or essence, but in the series of changeable things (if this is supposed *a priori* to be eternal) it will be, as will be presently understood, the prevailing of inclinations, in a sphere where reasons do not necessitate (by an absolute or metaphysical necessity, in which the contrary implies a contradiction), but incline. From this it is evident that even by supposing the world to be eternal we cannot escape the ultimate, extra-mundane reason of things, or God.

Gottfried Leibniz edited extract from 'On the Ultimate Origination of Things' from *Leibniz Philosophical Writings* edited by G. H. R. Parkinson (Dent and Sons, 1973), reprinted by permission of Everyman Publishers Plc.

The reasons of the world then lie in something extramundane, different from the chain of states, or series of things, whose aggregate constitutes the world. And so we must pass from physical or hypothetical necessity, which determines the sub-sequent things of the world by the earlier, to something which is of absolute or metaphysical necessity, for which no reason can be given. For the present world is necessary physically or hypothetically, but not absolutely or metaphysically. In other words, granted that it is once such and such, it follows that such and such things will come into being. Since then the ultimate root must be in something which is of metaphysical necessity, and since there is no reason of any existent thing except in an existent thing, it follows that there must exist some one Being of metaphysical necessity, that is, to whose essence existence belongs; and so there must exist something different from the plurality of beings, that is the world, which, as we have allowed and have shown, is not of metaphysical necessity.

Chapter 17

A modern cosmological argument

Herbert McCabe

Iɴ my view to assert that God exists is to claim the right and need to carry on an activity, to be engaged in research, and I think this throws light on what we are doing if we try to prove the existence of God. To prove the existence of God is to prove that some questions still need asking, that the world poses these questions for us.

To prove the existence of God, then, would be rather like proving the validity of science—I don't mean science as a body of established facts set out in textbooks or journals, but science as an intellectual activity, the activity of research currently going on; and not just routine research which consists in looking for the answers to clearly formulated questions by means of clearly established techniques, but the research which is the growing point of science, the venture into the unknown.

It is perfectly possible to deny the validity of this. It is perfectly possible to say we now *have* science (we didn't have it in the eighth century, let us say, but we have it now). It is just there; from now on it is all really just a matter of tidying up a few details. Now of course all the really great advances in science have come by questioning just that, by questioning, let us say, whether the Newtonian world is really the last word, by digging down and asking questions of what everybody has come to take for granted. But you could imagine quite easily a society which discouraged such radical questioning. In this century we have seen totalitarian societies which have been extremely keen on improving their technology and answering detailed questions within the accepted framework of science, but extremely hostile to the kind of radical thinking I am envisaging; the kind of society where Wernher von Braun is honoured and Einstein is exiled. I also think that the same effect can be produced in more subtle ways in societies that don't look totalitarian. And of course it was notoriously produced in the Church confronted by Galileo. The asking of radical questions is discouraged by any society that believes in itself, believes it has found the answers, believes that only its authorised questions are legitimate.

Faced with such hostility or such incomprehension, you can, of course, say: well, wait and see: you will find that in spite of everything, science will make startling and quite unexpected changes, that our whole world view will shift in ways we cannot now predict or imagine. But that is just to assert your *belief*. And this I think is parallel to asserting your belief in God. I think a belief in God—in the sense of a

Herbert McCabe 'Creation' from *New Blackfriars*, vol. 61 (1980), reprinted by permission of the author.

belief in the validity of the kind of radical question to which God would be the answer—is a part of human flourishing and that one who closes himself off from it is to that extent deficient. For this reason I welcome such belief in God, but what I am asking myself now is not whether I believe, but what grounds I have for such belief. And here again I think the analogy with proving the validity of fundamental thinking in science is helpful. How, after all, do we show that there is still a long and probably unexpected road to travel in science? By pointing to anomalies in the present scientific world picture. If your world picture includes, for example, the idea of ether as the medium in which light waves occur, then there is an anomaly if it turns out to be impossible to determine the velocity of a light source with respect to the ether; and so on. Now in a parallel way, it seems to me, proofs for the existence of God point to anomalies in a world picture which excludes the God question. It is, it seems to me, quite anomalous to hold that while it is legitimate and valid to ask 'How come?' about any particular thing or event in the world, it is illegitimate and invalid to ask it about the whole world. To say that we aren't allowed to ask it merely because we can't answer it seems to me to be begging the question. The question is: is there an unanswered question about the existence of the world? Can we be puzzled by the existence of the world instead of nothing? I can be and am; and this is to be puzzled about God.

The question 'How come?' can have a whole lot of different meanings and be asked at several levels, and the deeper the question you ask about an individual thing the more it is a question about a world to which that thing belongs; there is finally a deepest question about a thing which is also a question about everything. Let me explain that enigmatic remark.

Supposing you ask 'How come Fido?' You may be asking whether his father is Rover or whether it was that promiscuous mongrel down the lane. In such a case the answer is satisfactorily given by naming Fido's parents. At this level no more need be said; the question is fully answered *at this level*. But now suppose you ask: 'But how come Fido's a dog?' The answer could be: 'His parents were dogs, and dogs just are born of other dogs'. Here you have moved to what I call a deeper level of questioning and begun to talk about what dogs are. You are saying: for Fido to *be* is for him to be a *dog*, and Fido's parents are the sort of things whose activities result in things being dogs. Now your original question 'How come Fido?' has deepened into a question about the dog species. It remains a question about this individual dog Fido, but it is also a question about dogs—not about dogs in the abstract, but about the actual dog species in the world. Your question 'How come Fido?' at this new level is a question 'How come dogs anyway?'

And of course there is an answer to that too in terms of things like genetics and natural selection and what not. Here we have a new and deeper level of the question 'How come Fido?'—still a question about this particular puppy, but one that is answered in terms of its membership of a still wider community; no longer now simply the community of dogs, but the whole biological community within which dogs come to be and have their place. Then of course we can ask a question about

Fido at a deeper level still. When we ask how come the biological community, we no doubt answer in terms of biochemistry. (I am not of course pretending that we actually have the answers to all these questions, as though we fully understood how it came about, and had to come about, that there are now dogs around the place, but we expect eventually to answer these questions.)

And now we can go on from the level of biochemistry to that of physics and all the time we are asking more penetrating questions concerning Fido and each time we go further in our questioning we are seeing Fido in a wider and wider context.

We can put this another way by saying that each time we ask the question we are asking about Fido over against some other possibility. Our first question simply meant: How come Fido is this dog rather than another; he's Rover's son rather than the mongrel's son. At the next level we were asking: How come he's a dog rather than, say, a giraffe. At the next level: How come he's a living being rather than an inanimate, and so on.

Now I want to stress that all the time we are asking about this individual Fido. It is just that we are seeing further problematics within him. Fido's parents brought it about that he is this dog not another, but in that act they also brought it about that he is *this dog* (not a giraffe), that he is *this living dog*, that he is this *biochemically complex, living dog*, that he is this *molecularly structured, biochemically complex, living dog*, and so on. We are probing further into what it is for Fido to come to be and always by noting what he is not, but might have been. Every 'How come' question is how come this *instead of* what is not. And every time, of course, we answer by reference to some thing or state of affairs, some existing reality, in virtue of which Fido is this rather than what he is not.

Now our ultimate radical question is not how come Fido exists as this dog instead of that, or how come Fido exists as a dog instead of a giraffe, or exists as living instead of inanimate, but how come Fido exists *instead of nothing*, and just as to ask how come he exists as dog is to put him in the context of dogs, so to ask how come he exists instead of nothing is to put him in the context of *everything*, the universe or world. And this is the question I call the God-question, because whatever the answer is, whatever the thing or state of affairs, whatever the existing reality that answers it we call 'God'.

Now of course it is always possible to stop the questioning at any point; a man may refuse to ask why there are dogs. He may say there just *are* dogs and perhaps it is impious to enquire how come—there were people who actually said that to Darwin. Similarly it is possible to refuse to ask this ultimate question, to say as Russell once did: the universe is just there. This seems to me just as arbitrary as to say: dogs are just there. The difference is that we now know by hindsight that Darwin's critics were irrational because we have familiarised ourselves with an *answer* to the question, how come there are dogs? We have not familiarised ourselves with the answer to the question, how come the world instead of nothing? but that does not make it any less arbitrary to refuse to ask it. To ask it is to enter on an exploration which Russell was simply refusing to do, as it seems to me. It is of course perfectly right to point out the mysteriousness of a question about *every-thing*, to point to the fact that we have no way of answering it, but that is by no means the same as saying it is an unaskable question. As Wittgenstein said 'Not *how* the world is, but *that* it is, is the mystery'.

There is indeed a difficulty about having a concept of 'everything', for we ordinarily conceive of something with, so to say, a boundary around it: this is a sheep and not a giraffe. But *everything* is bounded by *nothing*, which is just to say that it is not bounded by anything. To put what is the same point another way: we can have no concept of *nothing*, absolutely speaking. We can use the word relatively; we can say, 'There is nothing in the cupboard' meaning there are no largish objects—we are understood not to be saying there is no dust or no air. 'There is nothing between Kerry and New York' means there is no land. It does not mean there is absolutely nothing, no sea or fishes. The notions of everything and of absolutely nothing, are not available to us in the sense that the notions of sheep or scarlet or savagery are available to us. And this means that we are asking our ultimate radical question with tools that will not do the job properly, with words whose meaning has to be stretched beyond what we can comprehend. It would be very strange if it were not so. As Wittgenstein says, what we have here is the mystery. If the question of God were a neat and simple question to be answered in terms of familiar concepts, then whatever we are talking about, it is not God. A God who is in this sense comprehensible would not be worth worshipping, or even of talking about (except for the purpose of destroying him).

It is clear that we reach out to, but do not reach, an answer to our ultimate question, how come anything instead of nothing? But we are able to exclude some answers. If God is whatever answers our question, how come everything? then evidently he is not to be included amongst everything. God cannot be a thing, an existent among others. It is not possible that God and the universe should add up to make two. Again, if we are to speak of God as causing the existence of everything, it is clear that we must not mean that he makes the universe out of anything. Whatever creation means it is not a process of making.

Again it is clear that God cannot *interfere* in the universe, not because he has not the power but because, so to speak, he has too much; to interfere you have to be an alternative to, or alongside, what you are interfering with. If God is the cause of everything, there is nothing that he is alongside. Obviously God makes no difference to the universe; I mean by this that we do not appeal specifically to God to explain why the universe is this way rather than that, for this we need only appeal to explanations within the universe. For this reason there can, it seems to me, be no feature of the universe which indicates it is God-made. What God accounts for is that the universe is there instead of nothing. I have said that whatever God is, he is not a member of everything, not an inhabitant of the universe, not a thing or a kind of thing. And I should add, I suppose, that it cannot be possible to ask of him, how come God instead of nothing? It must not be possible for him to be nothing. Not just in the sense that God must be imperishable, but that it must make no sense to consider that God might not be. Of course it is still possible to *say*, without manifest contradiction, 'God might not be', but that is because when we speak of God by using the word 'God', we do not understand what we mean, we have no concept of God; what governs our use of the word 'God' is not an understanding of what God is but the validity of a question about the world. That is why we are not protected by any *logical* laws from saying 'God might not exist' even though it makes no sense. What goes for our rules for the use of 'God' does not go for the God we try to name with the word. (And a corollary of this, incidentally, is why a famous argument for the existence of God called the ontological argument does not work.)

What I have been saying may seem to make God both remote and irrelevant. He is not part of the universe and he makes no difference to it. It is therefore necessary to stress that God must be in everything that happens and everything that exists in the universe. If Fido's parents make Fido to exist instead of nothing it is because in their action God is acting, just as if a pen writes it is because in its action a writer is acting. It is because it is God that wields every agent in the universe that agents bring things into existence, make things new. Every action in the world is an action of God; not because it is not an action of a creature but because it is by God's action that the creature is *itself* and has its *own* activity.

For the moment may I just say that it seems to me that what we often call atheism is not a denial of the God of which I speak. Very frequently the man who sees himself as an atheist is not denying the existence of some answer to the mystery of how come there is anything instead of nothing, he is denying what he thinks or has been told is a *religious* answer to this question. He thinks or has been told that religious people, and especially Christians, claim to have discovered what the answer is, that there is some grand architect of the universe who designed it, just like Basil Spence only bigger and less visible, that there is a Top Person in the universe who issues arbitrary decrees for the rest of the persons and enforces them because he is the most powerful being around. Now if denying this claim makes you an atheist, then I and Thomas Aquinas and a whole Christian tradition are atheistic too.

But a genuine atheist is one who simply does not see that there is any problem or mystery here, one who is content to ask questions within the world, but cannot see that the world itself raises a question. This is the man I compare to those who are content to ask questions within the established framework of science, but cannot see that there are genuine though ill-formulated questions on the frontiers. I have made a comparison with scientific research, but just the same parallel could be made with any kind of creative activity. The poet is trying to write a poem but he does not know what he is trying to say until he has said it and recognised it. Until he has done this it is extremely difficult to show that he is writing a poem or that he could write a poem. I can show, by pointing to the existence of bricks and cement and so on and the availability of a work-force, that there could be more *houses* made. I cannot show that there will *ever* be another poem.

I called this paper 'God and Creation' in order to indicate what I and the main-stream Christian tradition understand by creation as a path towards God. We come across God, so to speak, or rather we search and do *not* come across him, when the universe raises for us a radical question concerning its existence at all. And creation is the name we give to God's answering this question.

I hope it will be evident that creation is here being used in a quite different sense from the way it is used by people who seek to discover the origin of the universe (was it a big bang or a lot of little pops or whatever). Whatever processes took place in remote periods of time is of course in itself a fascinating topic but it is irrelevant to the question of creation in the sense that makes us speak of God. When we have concluded that God created the world, there still remains the scientific question to ask about what kind of world it is and was and how, if ever, it began. It is probably unnecessary to say that the proposition that the universe is made by God and that everything that is, is begun and sustained in existence by God, does not entail that the universe has only existed for a finite time. There may be reasons for thinking that the universe is finite in time and space but the fact that its existence depends on God is not one of them.

Coming to know that the universe is dependent on God does not in fact tell us anything about the character of the universe. How could it? Since everything we know about God (that he exists and what he is not) is derived from what we know of the universe, how could we come back from God with some additional informa-tion about the world? If we think we can it is only because we have smuggled something extra into our concept of God—for example, when we make God in our own image and ask ourselves quite illegitimate questions like 'What would I have done if I were God?' It should be evident that this is a temptation to be avoided.

Chapter 18
Objections to cosmological arguments
Paul Edwards

I

T HE cosmological proof has taken a number of forms, the most important of which are known as the causal argument and the argument from contingency, respectively. In some writers, in Samuel Clarke for example, they are combined, but it is best to keep them apart as far as possible. The causal argument is the second of the 'five ways' of Aquinas and proceeds roughly as follows: we find that the things around us come into being as the result of the activity of other things. These causes are themselves the result of the activity of other things. But such a causal series cannot 'go back to infinity.' Hence there must be a first member, a member which is not itself caused by any preceding member—an uncaused or 'first' cause.

It has frequently been pointed out that even if this argument were sound it would not establish the existence of God. It would not show that the first cause is all-powerful or all-good or that it is in any sense personal. Somebody believing in the eternity of atoms, or of matter generally, could quite consistently accept the conclusion. Defenders of the causal argument usually concede this and insist that the argument is not in itself meant to prove the existence of God. Supplementary arguments are required to show that the first cause must have the attributes assigned to the Deity. They claim, however, that the argument, if valid, would at least be an important step towards a complete proof of the existence of God.

Does the argument succeed in proving so much as a first cause? This will depend mainly on the soundness of the premise that an infinite series of causes is impossible. Aquinas supports this premise by maintaining that the opposite belief involves a plain absurdity. To suppose that there is an infinite series of causes logically implies that nothing exists now; but we know that plenty of things do exist now; and hence any theory which implies that nothing exists now must be wrong. Let us take some causal series and refer to its members by the letters of the alphabet:

$$A \rightarrow B \ldots W \rightarrow X \rightarrow Y \rightarrow Z$$

Z stands here for something presently existing, e.g. Margaret Truman. Y represents the cause or part of the cause of Z, say Harry Truman. X designates the cause or

Paul Edwards 'The Cosmological Argument' from *The Rationalist Annual* 1959, reprinted by permission of The Rationalist Press and the author.

part of the cause of Y, say Harry Truman's father, etc. Now, Aquinas reasons, whenever we take away the cause, we also take away the effect: if Harry Truman had never lived, Margaret Truman would never have been born. If Harry Truman's father had never lived, Harry Truman and Margaret Truman would never have been born. If A had never existed, none of the subsequent members of the series would have come into existence. But it is precisely A that the believers in the infinite series is 'taking away.' For in maintaining that the series is infinite he is denying that it has a first member; he is denying that there is such a thing as a first cause; he is, in other words, denying the existence of A. Since without A, Z could not have existed, his position implies that Z does not exist now; and that is plainly false.

This argument fails to do justice to the supporter of the infinite series of causes. Aquinas has failed to distinguish between the two statements:

(1) A did not exist, and
(2) A is not uncaused.

To say that the series is infinite implies (2), but it does not imply (1). The following parallel may be helpful here: Suppose Captain Spaulding had said, 'I am the greatest explorer who ever lived,' and somebody replied, 'No, you are not.' This answer would be denying that the Captain possessed the exalted attribute he had claimed for himself, but it would not be denying his existence. It would not be 'taking him away.' Similarly, the believer in the infinite series is not 'taking A away.' He is taking away the privileged status of A; he is taking away its 'first causeness.' He does not deny the *existence* of A or of any particular member of the series. He denies that A or anything else *is the first member* of the series. Since he is not taking A away, he is not taking B away, and thus he is also not taking X, Y, or Z away. His view, then, does not commit him to the absurdity that nothing exists now, or more specifically, that Margaret Truman does not exist now. It may be noted in this connection that a believer in the infinite series is not necessarily denying the existence of supernatural beings. He is merely committed to denying that such a being, if it exists, is uncaused. He is committed to holding that whatever other impressive attributes a supernatural being might possess, the attribute of being a first cause is not among them.

The causal argument is open to several other objections. Thus, even if otherwise valid, the argument would not prove a *single* first cause. For there does not seem to be any good ground for supposing that all the various causal series in the universe ultimately merge. Hence, even if it is granted that no series of causes can be infinite, the possibility of a plurality of first members has not been ruled out. Nor does the argument establish the *present* existence of the first cause. It does not prove this, since experience clearly shows that an effect may exist long after its cause has been destroyed.

II

Many defenders of the causal argument would contend that at least some of these criticisms rest on a misunderstanding. They would probably go further and contend that the argument was not quite fairly stated in the first place—or at any rate that if it was fair to some of its adherents it was not fair to others. They would in this connection distinguish between two types of causes—what they call 'causes *in fieri*' and what they call 'causes *in esse*.' A cause *in fieri* is a factor which brought or helped to bring an effect into existence. A cause *in esse* is a factor which 'sustains' or helps to sustain the effect 'in being.' The parents of a human being would be an example of a cause *in fieri*. If somebody puts a book in my hand and I keep holding it up, his putting it there would be the cause *in fieri*, and my holding it would be the cause *in esse* of the book's position. To quote Father Joyce:

If a smith forges a horse-shoe, he is only a cause *in fieri* of the shape given to the iron. That shape persists after his action has ceased. So, too, a builder is a cause *in fieri* of the house which he builds. In both these cases the substances employed act as causes *in esse* as regards the continued existence of the effect produced. Iron, in virtue of its natural rigidity, retains in being the shape which it has once received; and, similarly, the materials employed in building retain in being the order and arrangement which constitute them into a house.[1]

Using this distinction, a defender of the argument now reasons in the following way. To say that there is an infinite series of causes *in fieri* does not lead to any absurd conclusions. But Aquinas is concerned only with causes *in esse* and an infinite series of *such* causes is impossible. In the words of the American Thomist, R. P. Phillips:

Each member of the series of causes possess being solely by virtue of the actual present operation of a superior cause. .... Life is dependent, *inter alia*, on a certain atmospheric pressure, this again on the continual operation of physical forces, whose being and operation depends on the position of the earth in the solar system, which itself must endure relatively unchanged, a state of being which can only be continuously produced by a definite—if unknown—constitution of the material universe. This constitution, however, cannot be its own cause. That a thing should cause itself is impossible: for in order that it may cause it is necessary for it to exist, which it cannot do, on the hypothesis, until it has been caused. So it must *be* in order to cause itself. Thus, not being uncaused nor yet its own cause, it must be caused by another, which produces and preserves it. It is plain, then, that as no member of this series possesses being except in virtue of the actual present operation of a superior cause, if there be no first cause actually operating none of the dependent causes could operate either. We are thus irresistibly led to posit a first efficient cause which, while itself uncaused, shall impart causality to a whole series. ....

The series of causes which we are considering is not one which stretches back into the past; so that we are not demanding a beginning of the world at some definite moment

---

1. *The Principles of Natural Theology* (London and New York, 1924), p. 58.

reckoning back from the present, but an actual cause now operating, to account for the present being of things.[2]

Professor Phillips offers the following parallel to bring out his point:

In a goods train each truck is moved and moves by the action of the one immediately in front of it. If then we suppose the train to be infinite, i.e. that there is no end to it, and so no engine which starts the motion, it is plain that no truck will move. To lengthen it out to infinity will not give it what no member of it possesses of itself, viz. the power of drawing the truck behind it. If then we see any truck in motion we know there must be an end to the series of trucks which gives causality to the whole.[3]

Father Joyce introduces an illustration from Aquinas to explain how the present existence of things may be compatible with an infinite series of causes *in fieri* but not with an infinite series of causes *in esse*.

When a carpenter is at work, the series of efficient causes on which his work depends is necessarily limited. The final effect, e.g. the fastening of a nail, is caused by a hammer: the hammer is moved by the arm: and the motion of his arm is determined by the motor-impulses communicated from the nerve centres of the brain. Unless the subordinate causes were limited in number, and were connected with a starting-point of motion, the hammer must remain inert; and the nail will never be driven in. If the series be supposed infinite, no work will ever take place. But if there is question of causes on which the work is not essentially dependent, we cannot draw the same conclusion. We may suppose the carpenter to have broken an infinite number of hammers, and as often to have replaced the broken tool by a fresh one. There is nothing in such a supposition which excludes the driving home of the nail.[4]

The supporter of the infinite series of causes, Joyce also remarks, is 'asking us to believe that although each link in a suspended chain is prevented from falling simply because it is attached to the one above it, yet if only the chain be long enough, it will, taken as a whole, need no support, but will hang loose in the air suspended from nothing.'[5]

This formulation of the causal argument unquestionably circumvents one of the objections mentioned previously. If Y is the cause *in esse* of an effect, Z, then it must exist as long as Z exists. If the argument were valid in this form it would therefore prove the present and not merely the past existence of a first cause. In this form the argument is, however, less convincing in another respect. To maintain that all 'natural' or 'phenomenal' objects—things like tables and mountains and human beings—require a cause *in fieri* is not implausible, though even here Mill and others have argued that, strictly speaking, only *changes* require a causal explanation. It is far from plausible, on the other hand, to claim that all natural objects require a cause *in esse*. It may be granted that the air around us is a cause *in esse* of human life

2. *Modern Thomistic Philosophy*, vol. II (London, 1935), pp. 284–5.
3. Ibid., p. 278.
4. Joyce, *Principles of Natural Theology*, pp. 67–8.
5. Ibid., p. 82.

and further that certain gravitational forces are among the causes *in esse* of the air being where it is. But when we come to gravitational forces or, at any rate, to material particles like atoms or electrons it is difficult to see what cause *in esse* they require. To those not already convinced of the need for a supernatural First Cause, some of the remarks by Professor Phillips in this connection appear merely dogmatic and question-begging. Most people would grant that such particles as atoms did not cause themselves, since, as Professor Phillips observes, they would in that event have had to exist before they began existing. It is not at all evident, however, that these particles cannot be uncaused. Professor Phillips and all other supporters of the causal argument immediately proceed to claim that there is something else which needs no cause *in esse*. They themselves admit thus, that there is nothing self-evident about the proposition that everything must have a cause *in esse*. Their entire procedure here lends substance to Schopenhauer's gibe that supporters of the cosmological argument treat the law of universal causation like 'a hired cab which we dismiss when we have reached our destination.'[6]

But waiving this and all similar objections, the restatement of the argument in terms of causes *in esse* in no way avoids the main difficulty which was previously mentioned. A believer in the infinite series would insist that his position was just as much misrepresented now as before. He is no more removing the member of the series which is supposed to be the first cause *in esse* than he was removing the member which had been declared to be the first cause *in fieri*. He is again merely denying a privileged status to it. He is not denying the reality of the cause *in esse* labelled A. He is not even necessarily denying that it possesses supernatural attributes. He is again merely taking away its 'first causeness.'

The advocates of the causal argument in either form seem to confuse an infinite series with one which is long but finite. If a book, Z, is to remain in its position, say 100 miles up in the air, there must be another object, say another book, Y, underneath it to serve as its support. If Y is to remain where it is, it will need another support, X, beneath it. Suppose that this series of supports, one below the other, continues for a long time, but eventually, say after 100,000 members, comes to a first book which is not resting on any other book or indeed on any other support. In that event the whole collection would come crashing down. What we seem to need is a first member of the series, a first support (such as the earth) which does not need another member as *its* support, which in other words is 'self-supporting.'

This is evidently the sort of picture that supporters of the First Cause argument have before their minds when they rule out the possibility of an infinite series. But such a picture is not a fair representation of the theory of the infinite series. A *finite* series of books would indeed come crashing down, since the first or lowest member would not have a predecessor on which it could be supported. If the series, however, were infinite this would not be the case. In that event every member *would* have a predecessor to support itself on and there would be no crash. That is to say: a crash

6. *The Fourfold Root of the Principle of Sufficient Reason.*

can be avoided either by a finite series with a first self-supporting member or by an infinite series. Similarly, the present existence of motion is equally compatible with the theory of a first unmoved mover and with the theory of an infinite series of moving objects; and the present existence of causal activity is compatible with the theory of a first cause *in esse* as much as with the theory of an infinite series of such causes.

The illustrations given by Joyce and Phillips are hardly to the point. It is true that a carpenter would not, *in a finite time-span*, succeed in driving in a nail if he had to carry out an infinite number of movements. For that matter, he would not accomplish this goal in a finite time if he broke an infinite number of hammers. However, to make the illustrations relevant we must suppose that he has infinite time at his disposal. In that case he would succeed in driving in the nail even if he required an infinite number of movements for this purpose. As for the goods train, it may be granted that the trucks do not move unless the train has an engine. But this illustration is totally irrelevant as it stands. A relevant illustration would be that of engines, each moved by the one in front of it. Such a train would move if it were infinite. For every member of this series there would be one in front capable of drawing it along. The advocate of the infinite series of whose members are not really causally connected with one another. In the series he believes in, every member is genuinely the cause of the one that follows it.

III

No staunch defender of the cosmological argument would give up at this stage. Even if there were an infinite series of causes *in fieri* or *in esse*, he would contend, this still would not do away with the need for an ultimate, a first cause. As Father Copleston put it in his debate with Bertrand Russell:

Every object has a phenomenal cause, if you insist on the infinity of the series. But the series of phenomenal causes is an insufficient explanation of the series. Therefore, the series has not a phenomenal cause, but a transcendent cause.[7]

An infinite series of contingent beings will be, to my way of thinking, as unable to cause itself as one contingent being.[8]

The demand to find the cause of the series as a whole rests on the erroneous assumption that the series is something over and above the members of which it is composed. It is tempting to suppose this, at least by implication, because the word *series* is a noun like *dog* or *man*. Like the expression 'this dog' or 'this man,' the phrase 'this series' is easily taken to designate an individual object. But reflection shows this to be an error. If we have explained the individual members there is nothing additional left to be explained. Suppose I see a group of five

7. Bertrand Russell, *Why I Am Not a Christian* (London, Allen and Unwin, 1957), pp. 152–3.
8. Ibid., p. 151.

Eskimos standing on the corner of Sixth Avenue and 50th Street and I wish to explain why the group came to New York. Investigation reveals the following stories:

Eskimo No. 1 did not enjoy the extreme cold in the polar region and decided to move to a warmer climate.

No. 2 is the husband of Eskimo No. 1. He loves her dearly and did not wish to live without her.

No. 3 is the son of Eskimos 1 and 2. He is too small and too weak to oppose his parents.

No. 4 saw an advertisement in the *New York Times* for an Eskimo to appear on television.

No. 5 is a private detective engaged by the Pinkerton Agency to keep an eye on Eskimo No. 4.

Let us assume that we have now explained in the case of each of the five Eskimos why he or she is in New York. Somebody then asks: 'All right, but what about the group as a whole; why is *it* in New York?' This would plainly be an absurd question. There is no group over and above the five members, and if we have explained why each of the five members is in New York we have ipso facto explained why the group is there. It is just as absurd to ask for the cause of the series as a whole, as distinct from asking for the causes of individual members.

IV

It is most unlikely that a determined defender of the cosmological line of reasoning would surrender even here. He would probably admit that the series is not a thing over and above its members and that it does not make sense to ask for the cause of the series if the cause of each member has already been found. He would insist, however, that when he asked for the explanation of the entire series, he was not asking for its *cause*. He was really saying that a series, finite or infinite, is not 'intelligible' or 'explained' if it consists of nothing but 'contingent' members. To quote Father Copleston once more:

What we call the world is intrinsically unintelligible apart from the existence of God. The infinity of the series of events, if such an infinity could be proved, would not be in the slightest degree relevant to the situation. If you add up chocolates, you get chocolates, after all, and not sheep. If you add up chocolates to infinity, you presumably get an infinite number of chocolates. So, if you add up contingent beings to infinity, you still get contingent beings, not a necessary being.[9]

This last quotation is really a summary of the 'contingency argument,' the other main form of the cosmological proof and the third of the five ways of Aquinas. It may be stated more fully in these words: All around us we perceive contingent

9. Ibid.

beings. This includes all physical objects and also all human minds. In calling them 'contingent' we mean that they might not have existed. We mean that the universe can be *conceived* without this or that physical object, without this or that human being, however certain their actual existence may be. These contingent beings we can trace back to other contingent beings—for example, a human being to his parents. However, since these other beings are also contingent, they do not provide a real or full explanation. The contingent beings we originally wanted explained have not yet become intelligible, since the beings to which they have been traced are no more necessary than they were. It is just as true of our parents, for example, as it is of ourselves, that they might not have existed. We can then properly explain the contingent beings around us only by tracing them ultimately to some necessary being, to something which exists necessarily, which has 'the reason for its existence within itself.' The existence of contingent beings, in other words, implies the existence of a necessary being.

This form of the cosmological argument is even more beset with difficulties than the causal variety. In the first place, there is the objection, stated with great force by Kant, that it really commits the same error as the ontological argument, in tacitly regarding existence as an attribute or characteristic. To say that there is a necessary being is to say that it would be a self-contradiction to deny its existence. This would mean that at least one existential statement is a necessary truth; and this in turn presupposes that in at least one case existence is contained in a concept. But only a characteristic can be contained in a concept and it has seemed plain to most philosophers since Kant that existence is not a characteristic, that it can hence never be contained in a concept, and that hence no existential statement can ever be a necessary truth. To talk about anything 'existing necessarily' is, in their view, about as sensible as to talk about round squares, and they have concluded that the contingency-argument is quite absurd.

It would lead too far to discuss here the reasons for denying that existence is a characteristic. I will assume that this difficulty can somehow be surmounted and that the expression 'necessary being,' as it is intended by the champions of the contingency argument, might conceivably apply to something. There remain other objections which are of great weight. I shall try to state these by first quoting again from the debate between Bertrand Russell and Father Copleston:

RUSSELL: . . . It all turns on this question of sufficient reason, and I must say you haven't defined 'sufficient reason' in a way that I can understand—what do you mean by sufficient reason? You don't mean cause?

COPLESTON: Not necessarily. Cause is a kind of sufficient reason. Only contingent being can have a cause. God is his own sufficient reason; and he is not cause of himself. By sufficient reason in the full sense I mean an explanation adequate for the existence of some particular being.

RUSSELL: But when is an explanation adequate? Suppose I am about to make a flame with a match. You may say that the adequate explanation of that is that I rub it on the box.

COPLESTON: Well for practical purposes—but theoretically, that is only a partial explanation.

An adequate explanation must ultimately be a total explanation, to which nothing further can be added.

RUSSELL: Then I can only say that you're looking for something which can't be got, and which one ought not to expect to get.

COPLESTON: To say that one has found it is one thing; to say that one should not look for it seems to me rather dogmatic.

RUSSELL: Well, I don't know. I mean, the explanation of one thing is another thing which makes the other thing dependent on yet another, and you have to grasp this sorry scheme of things entire to do what you want, and that we can't do.[10]

Russell's main point here may be expanded in the following way. The contingency argument rests on a misconception of what an explanation is and does, and similarly on what it is that makes phenomena 'intelligible.' Or else it involves an obscure and arbitrary redefinition of 'explanation,' 'intelligible,' and related terms. Normally, we are satisfied that we have explained a phenomenon if we have found its cause or if we have exhibited some other uniform or near-uniform connection between it and something else. Confining ourselves to the former case, which is probably the most common, we might say that a phenomenon, Z, has been explained if it has been traced back to a group of factors, a, b, c, d, etc., which are its cause. These factors are the full and real explanation of Z, quite regardless of whether they are pleasing or displeasing, admirable or contemptible, necessary or contingent. The explanation would not be adequate only if the factors listed are not really the cause of Z. If they are the cause of Z, the explanation would be adequate, even though each of the factors is merely a 'contingent' being.

Let us suppose that we have been asked to explain why General Eisenhower won the elections of 1952. 'He was an extremely popular general,' we might answer, 'while Stevenson was relatively little known; moreover there was a great deal of resentment over the scandals in the Truman Administration.' If somebody complained that this was only a partial explanation we might mention additional antecedents, such as the widespread belief that the Democrats had allowed communist agents to infiltrate the State Department, [the fact] that Eisenhower was a man with a winning smile, and [the fact] that unlike Stevenson he had shown the good sense to say one thing on race relations in the North and quite another in the South. Theoretically, we might go further and list the motives of all American voters during the weeks or months preceding the election. If we could do this we would have explained Eisenhower's victory. We would have made it intelligible. We would 'understand' why he won and why Stevenson lost. Perhaps there is a sense in which we might make Eisenhower's victory even more intelligible if we went further back and discussed such matters as the origin of American views on Communism or of racial attitudes in the North and South. However, to explain the outcome of the election in any ordinary sense, loose or strict, it would not be necessary to go back to prehistoric days or to the amoeba or to a first cause, if such a first cause exists.

10. Ibid., p. 150.

Nor would our explanation be considered in any way defective because each of the factors mentioned was a 'contingent' and not a necessary being. The only thing that matters is whether the factors were really the cause of Eisenhower's election. If they were, then it has been explained although they are contingent beings. If they were not the cause of Eisenhower's victory, we would have failed to explain it even if each of the factors were a necessary being.

If it is granted that, in order to explain a phenomenon or to make it intelligible, we need not bring in a necessary being, then the contingency argument breaks down. For a series, as was already pointed out, is not something over and above its members; and every contingent member of it could in that case be explained by reference to other contingent beings. But I should wish to go further than this, and it is evident from Russell's remarks that he would do so also. Even if it were granted, both that the phrase 'necessary being' is meaningful and that all explanations are defective unless the phenomena to be explained are traced back to a necessary being, the conclusion would still not have been established. The conclusion follows from this premise together with the additional premise that *there are* explanations of phenomena in the special sense just mentioned. It is this further premise which Russell (and many other philosophers) would question. They do not merely question, as Copleston implies, whether human beings can ever obtain explanations in this sense, but whether they *exist*. To assume without further ado that phenomena have explanations, or an explanation in this sense, is to beg the very point at issue. The use of the same word, *explanation*, in two crucially different ways lends the additional premise a plausibility it does not really possess. It may indeed be highly plausible to assert that phenomena have explanations, whether we have found them or not, in the ordinary sense in which this usually means that they have causes. It is then tempting to suppose, because of the use of the same word, that they also have explanations in a sense in which this implies dependence on a necessary being. But this is a gross non sequitur.

V

It is necessary to add a few words about the proper way of formulating the position of those who reject the main premise of the cosmological argument, in either of the forms we have considered. It is sometimes maintained in this connection that in order to reach a 'self-existing' entity it is not necessary to go beyond the universe: the universe itself (or 'Nature') is 'self-existing.' And this in turn is sometimes expanded into the statement that while all individual things 'within' the universe are caused, the universe itself is uncaused. Statements of this kind are found in Büchner, Bradlaugh, Haeckel, and other freethinkers of the nineteenth and early twentieth century. Sometimes the assertion that the universe is 'self-existing' is elaborated to mean that *it* is the 'necessary being.' Some eighteenth-century unbelievers, apparently accepting the view that there is a necessary being, asked why Nature or the material universe could not fill the bill as well as or better than God.

'Why,' asks one of the characters in Hume's *Dialogues*, 'may not the material universe be the necessarily existent Being? . . . We dare not affirm that we know all the qualities of matter; and for aught we can determine, it may contain some qualities, which, were they known, would make its non-existence appear as great a contradiction as that twice two is five.'[11] Similar remarks can be found in Holbach and in several of the Encyclopedists.

The former of these formulations immediately invites the question why the universe, alone of all 'things,' is exempted from the universal sway of causation. 'The strong point of the cosmological argument,' writes Dr Ewing, 'is that after all it does remain incredible that the physical universe should just have happened. . . . It calls out for some further explanation of some kind.'[12] The latter formulation is exposed to the criticism that there is nothing any more 'necessary' about the existence of the universe or Nature as a whole than about any particular thing within the universe.

I hope some of the earlier discussions in this article have made it clear that in rejecting the cosmological argument one is not committed to either of these propositions. If I reject the view that there is a supernatural first cause, I am not thereby committed to the proposition that there is a *natural* first cause, and even less to the proposition that a mysterious thing called the universe qualifies for this title. I may hold that there is no universe over and above individual things of various sorts; and, accepting the causal principle, I may proceed to assert that all these things are caused by other things, and these other things by yet other things, and so on, ad infinitum. In this way no arbitrary exception is made to the principle of causation. Similarly, if I reject the assertion that God is a 'necessary being,' I am not committed to the view that the universe is such an entity. I may hold that it does not make sense to speak of anything as a 'necessary being' and that even if there were such a thing as the universe it could not be properly considered a necessary being.

However, in saying that nothing is uncaused or that there is no necessary being, one is not committed to the view that everything, or for that matter anything, is merely a 'brute fact.' Dr Ewing laments that 'the usual modern philosophical views opposed to theism do not try to give any rational explanation of the world at all, but just take it as a brute fact not to be explained.' They thus fail to rationalize the universe. Theism, he concedes, cannot completely rationalize things either since it does not show 'how God can be his own cause or how it is that he does not need a cause.'[13] Now, if one means by 'brute fact' something for which there *exists* no explanation (as distinct from something for which no explanation is in our possession), then the theists have at least one brute fact on their hands, namely God. Those who adopt Büchner's foundation also have one brute fact on their hands, namely the universe. Only the position I have been supporting dispenses with brute facts altogether. I don't know if this is any special virtue, but the defenders of the cosmological argument seem to think so.

11. Hume, *Dialogues*, Part IX.
12. A. C. Ewing, *Fundamental Questions of Philosophy* (New York, 1951), p. 225.
13. Ibid.

Chapter 19

More objections to cosmological arguments

J. L. Mackie

THE cosmological argument is *par excellence* the philosophers' argument for theism. It has been presented in many forms, but in one version or another it has been used by Greek, Arabic, Jewish, and Christian philosophers and theologians, including Plato, Aristotle, al Farabi, al Ghāzālī, ibn Rushd (Averroes), Maimonides, Aquinas, Spinoza, and Leibniz.[1] What is common to the many versions of this argument is that they start from the very fact that there is a world or from such general features of it as change or motion or causation—not, like the argument from consciousness or the argument for design, from specific details of what the world includes or how it is ordered—and argue to God as the uncaused cause of the world or of those general features, or as its creator, or as the reason for its existence. I cannot examine all the variants of this argument that have been advanced, but I shall discuss three intendedly demonstrative approaches and an inductive, probabilistic, approach. And although arguments to a first cause or a creator are more immediately attractive, and appeared earlier in history, than those which argue from the contingency of the world to a necessary being, the latter are in some respects simpler and perhaps more fundamental, so I shall begin with one of these.

(a) Contingency and sufficient reason

Leibniz gives what is essentially the same proof in slightly different forms in different works; we can sum up his line of thought as follows.[2] He assumes the *principle of sufficient reason*, that nothing occurs without a sufficient reason why it is so and not otherwise. There must, then, be a sufficient reason for the world as a whole, a reason why something exists rather than nothing. Each thing in the world is contingent, being causally determined by other things: it would not occur if other things were otherwise. The world as a whole, being a collection of such things, is therefore itself contingent. The series of things and events, with their causes, with causes of

1. W. L. Craig, *The Cosmological Argument from Plato to Leibniz* (Macmillan, London, 1980). Quotations from al Farabi and al Ghazali are taken from this work.
2. The clearest account is in 'On the Ultimate Origination of Things', printed, e.g., in G. W. Leibniz, *Philosophical Writings* (Dent, London, 1934), pp. 32–41. (See Chapter 16 of this volume.)

those causes, and so on, may stretch back infinitely in time; but, if so, then however far back we go, or if we consider the series as a whole, what we have is still contingent and therefore requires a sufficient reason outside this series. That is, there must be a sufficient reason *for* the world which is *other than* the world. This will have to be a necessary being, which contains its own sufficient reason for existence. Briefly, things must have a sufficient reason for their existence, and this must be found ultimately in a necessary being. There must be something free from the disease of contingency, a disease which affects everything in the world and the world as a whole, even if it is infinite in past time.

This argument, however, is open to criticisms of two sorts, summed up in the questions 'How do we know that everything must have a sufficient reason?' and 'How can there be a necessary being, one that contains its own sufficient reason?' These challenges are related: if the second question cannot be answered satisfactorily, it will follow that things as a whole cannot have a sufficient reason, not merely that we do not know that they must have one.

Kant's criticism of the Leibnizian argument turns upon this second objection; he claims that the cosmological proof depends upon the already criticized ontological proof.[3] The latter starts from the concept of an absolutely necessary being, an *ens realissimum*, something whose essence includes existence, and tries to derive from that concept itself alone the fact that there is such a being. The cosmological proof 'retains the connection of absolute necessity with the highest reality, but instead of reasoning . . . from the highest reality to necessity of existence, it reasons from the previously given unconditioned necessity of some being to the unlimited reality of that being'. However, Kant's claim that the cosmological proof 'rests' or 'depends' on the ontological one, that 'the so-called cosmological proof really owes any cogency which it may have to the ontological proof from mere concepts' is at least misleading. The truth is rather this. The cosmological argument purports to show, from the contingency of the world, in conjunction with the principle of sufficient reason, that there must be something else which is not contingent, which exists necessarily, which is or contains its own sufficient reason. When we ask how there could be such a thing, we are offered the notion of an *ens realissimum* whose essence includes existence. This is the notion which served as the starting-point of (in particular) Descartes's ontological proof. But the notion is being used quite differently in the two cases. Does this connection imply that successful criticism of the ontological proof undermines the cosmological one also? That depends on the nature of the successful criticism. If its outcome is that the very concept of something's essence including existence is illegitimate—which would perhaps have been shown by Kant's thesis that existence is not a predicate, or by the quantifier analysis of existence in general, if either of these had been correct and uncontroversial—then at least the final step in the cosmological proof is blocked, and Leibniz must either find some different explanation of how something might

3. *Critique of Pure Reason*, Transcendental Dialectic, Book II, Chapter III, Section 5.

exist necessarily and contain its own sufficient reason, or else give up even the first step in his proof, abandoning the search for a sufficient reason of the world as a whole. But if the outcome of the successful criticism of the ontological proof were merely that we cannot validly start from a mere concept and thence derive actual existence—if we allowed that there was nothing illegitimate about the concept of a being whose essence includes existence, and insisted only that whatever a concept contains, it is always a further question whether there is something that instantiates it—then the cosmological proof would be unaffected by this criticism.

But perhaps we can still make something like Kant's point. Since it is always a further question whether a concept is instantiated or not, no matter how much it contains, the existence even of a being whose essence included existence would not be self-explanatory: there might have failed to be any such thing. This 'might' expresses at least a conceptual possibility; if it is alleged that this being none the less exists by a metaphysical necessity, we are still waiting for an explanation of this kind of necessity. The existence of this being is not logically necessary; it does not exist in all logically possible worlds; in what way, then, does it necessarily exist in this world and satisfy the demand for a sufficient reason?

It might be replied that we understand what it is for something to exist contingently, in that it would not have existed if something else had been otherwise: to exist necessarily is to exist but not contingently in this sense. But then the premiss that the natural world as a whole is contingent is not available: though we have some ground for thinking that each part, or each finite temporal stretch, of the world is contingent in this sense upon something else, we have initially no ground for thinking that the world as a whole would not have existed if something else had been otherwise; inference from the contingency of every part to the contingency *in this sense* of the whole is invalid. Alternatively, we might say that something exists contingently if and only if it might not have existed, and by contrast that something exists necessarily if and only if it exists, but it is not the case that it might not have existed. In this sense we could infer the contingency of the whole from the contingency of every part. But once it is conceded, for reasons just given, that it is not logically impossible that the alleged necessary being might not have existed, we have no understanding of how it could be true of this being that it is not the case that it might not have existed. We have as yet no ground for believing that it is even possible that something should exist necessarily in the sense required.

This criticism is reinforced by the other objection, 'How do we know that everything must have a sufficient reason?'. I see no plausibility in the claim that the principle of sufficient reason is known *a priori* to be true. Leibniz thought that reliance on this principle is implicit in our reasoning both about physics and about human behaviour: for example, Archimedes argued that if, in a symmetrical balance, equal weights are placed on either side, neither will go down, because there is no reason why one side should go down rather than the other; and equally a rational being cannot act without a motive.[4] But what is being used by Archimedes is just the rule that like causes produce like effects. This, and in general the search for, and expectation of, causes and regularities and reasons, do indeed guide inquiry in many fields. But the principles used are not known *a priori*, and Samuel Clarke pointed out a difficulty in applying them even to human behaviour: someone who has a good reason for doing either A or B, but no reason for doing one of these rather than the other, will surely choose one arbitrarily rather than do neither.[5] Even if, as is possible, we have some innate tendency to look for and expect such symmetries and continuities and regularities, this does not give us an *a priori* guarantee that such can always be found. In so far as our reliance on such principles is epistemically justified, it is so *a posteriori*, by the degree of success we have had in interpreting the world with their help. And in any case these principles of causation, symmetry, and so on refer to how the world works; we are extrapolating far beyond their so far fruitful use when we postulate a principle of sufficient reason and apply it to the world as a whole. Even if, within the world, everything seemed to have a sufficient reason, that is, a cause in accordance with some regularity, with like causes producing like effects, this would give us little ground for expecting the world as a whole, or its basic causal laws themselves, to have a sufficient reason of some different sort.

The principle of sufficient reason expresses a demand that things should be intelligible *through and through*. The simple reply to the argument which relies on it is that there is nothing that justifies this demand, and nothing that supports the belief that it is satisfiable even in principle. As we have seen in considering the other main objection to Leibniz's argument, it is difficult to see how there even could be anything that would satisfy it. If we reject this demand, we are not thereby committed to saying that things are utterly unintelligible. The sort of intelligibility that is achieved by successful causal inquiry and scientific explanation is not undermined by its inability to make things intelligible through and through. Any particular explanation starts with premises which state 'brute facts', and although the brutally factual starting-points of one explanation may themselves be further explained by another, the latter in turn will have to start with something that it does not explain, *and so on however far we go*. But there is no need to see this as unsatisfactory.

A sufficient reason is also sometimes thought of as a final cause or purpose. Indeed, if we think of each event in the history of the world as having (in principle) been explained by its antecedent causes, but still want a further explanation of the whole sequence of events, we must turn to some other sort of explanation. The two candidates that then come to mind are two kinds of purposive or teleological explanation. Things are as they are, Plato suggested, because it is *better* that they

4. *The Leibniz–Clarke Correspondence*, edited by H. G. Alexander (Manchester University Press, 1956 and 1976), Leibniz's Second Paper.
5. *The Leibniz–Clarke Correspondence*, Clarke's Third and Fifth Replies.

should be so.[6] This can be construed either as implying that (objective) value is in itself creative or as meaning that some intelligent being sees what would be better, chooses it, and brings it about. But why must we look for a sufficient reason of either of these sorts? The principle of sufficient reason, thus understood, expresses a demand for some kind of absolute purposiveness. But if we reject this demand, we are not thereby saying that 'man and the universe are ultimately meaningless'.[7] People will still have the purposes that they have, some of which they can fulfil, even if the question 'What is the purpose of the world as a whole?' has no positive answer.

The principle of sufficient reason, then, is more far-reaching than the principle that every occurrence has a preceding sufficient cause: the latter, but not the former, would be satisfied by a series of things or events running back infinitely in time, each determined by earlier ones, but with no further explanation of the series as a whole. Such a series would give us only what Leibniz called 'physical' or 'hypothetical' necessity, whereas the demand for a sufficient reason for the whole body of contingent things and events and laws calls for something with 'absolute' or 'metaphysical' necessity. But even the weaker, deterministic, principle is not an *a priori* truth, and indeed it may not be a truth at all; much less can this be claimed for the principle of sufficient reason. Perhaps it just expresses an arbitrary demand; it may be intellectually satisfying to believe that there is, objectively, an explanation for everything together, even if we can only guess at what the explanation might be. But we have no right to assume that the universe will comply with our intellectual preferences. Alternatively, the supposed principle may be an unwarranted extension of the determinist one, which, in so far as it is supported, is supported only empirically, by our success in actually finding causes, and can at most be accepted provisionally, not as an *a priori* truth. The form of the cosmological argument which relies on the principle of sufficient reason therefore fails completely as a demonstrative proof.

(b) The regress of causes

There is a popular line of thought, which we may call the first cause argument, and which runs as follows: things must be caused, and their causes will be other things that must have causes, and so on; but this series of causes cannot go back indefinitely; it must terminate in a first cause, and this first cause will be God. This argument envisages a regress of causes in time, but says (as Leibniz, for one, did not) that this regress must stop somewhere. Though it has some initial plausibility, it also has obvious difficulties. Why must the regress terminate at all? Why, if it terminates, must it lead to a single termination, to one first cause, rather than to a number—perhaps an indefinitely large number—of distinct uncaused causes? And

6. Plato, *Phaedo*, 97–9.
7. Craig, op. cit., p. 287.

even if there is just one first cause, why should we identify this with God? I shall come back to this argument and to possible replies to these objections; but first I want to look at a more elaborate philosophical argument that has some, though not much, resemblance to it.

Of Aquinas's 'five ways', the first three are recognizably variants of the cosmological proof, and all three involve some kind of terminated regress of causes.[8] But all of them are quite different from our first cause argument. The first way argues to a first mover, using the illustration of something's being moved by a stick only when the stick is moved by a hand; here the various movings are simultaneous, we do not have a regress of causes in time. Similarly the 'efficient causes' in the second way are contemporary agents. Both these arguments, as Kenny has shown, depend too much on antiquated physical theory to be of much interest now. The third way is much more significant. This argument is in two stages, and can be freely translated, with some condensation, as follows:

First stage: If everything were able-not-to-be, then at some time there would have been nothing (because what is able-not-to-be, at some time is not); and then (since what does not exist cannot begin to be except through something which is) even now there would be nothing. It is plainly not true that there is nothing now; so it cannot be true that everything is able-not-to-be. That is, there must be at least one thing which is necessary.
Second stage: Everything that is necessary either has a cause of its necessity outside itself, or it does not. But it is not possible to go to infinity in a series of necessary things each of which has a cause of its necessity outside itself; this is like what has been proved about efficient causes. Therefore we must assume something which is necessary through itself, which does not have a cause of its necessity outside itself, but which is the cause of the necessity of the other things; and this men all call God.

This argument is quite different from our first cause argument and also from Leibniz's argument from contingency. Although it uses the contrast between things which are able-not-to-be (and therefore contingent) and those which are necessary, it is not satisfied with the conclusion that there is something necessary; it allows that there may be many necessary things, and reaches God only at the end of the second stage, as what has its necessity 'through itself' (*per se*). Clearly 'necessary' does not mean the same for Aquinas as for Leibniz. What it does mean will become clearer as we examine the reasoning.

In the first stage, the premiss 'what is able-not-to-be, at some time is not' seems dubious: why should not something which is *able* not to be nevertheless just happen to exist always? But perhaps Aquinas means by 'things that are able-not-to-be' (*possibilia non esse*) something like 'impermanent things', so that this premiss is analytic. Even so, the statement that if everything were such, at some time there would have been nothing, does not follow: some impermanent things might have

lasted through all past time, and be going to display their impermanence by perishing only at some time in the future. But we may be able to understand Aquinas's
thought by seeing what is said more explicitly by Maimonides, by whom Aquinas
appears to have been influenced here.[9] His corresponding proof seems to assume
that past time has been finite—and reasonably so, for if past time has been finite
there would seem to be an easier argument for a divine creator, such as we shall
consider below. The suggestion is that it would not have been possible for
impermanent things to have lasted throughout an infinite time, and hence they
would have perished already.

However, another objection is that there might be a series of things, each of
which was impermanent and perished after a finite period, but whose periods of
existence overlapped so that there never was a time when there was nothing. It
would be a clear logical fallacy (of which some commentators have accused Aquinas) to infer 'at some time everything is not' from 'each thing at some time is not'.
But we might defend Aquinas in either of two ways. First, if each thing were
impermanent, it would be the most improbable good luck if the overlapping
sequence kept up through infinite time. Secondly, even if this improbable luck
holds, we might regard the series of overlapping things as itself a thing which had
already lasted through infinite time, and so could not be impermanent. Indeed, if
there were such a series which never failed, this might well indicate that there was some
permanent stock of material of which the perishable things were composed and into
which they disintegrated, thereby contributing to the composition of other things.

A third objection concerns the premiss that 'what does not exist cannot begin to
be except through something that is'. This is, of course, a form of the principle that
nothing can come from nothing; the idea then is that if our series of impermanent
things had broken off, it could never have started again after a gap. But is this an *a
priori* truth? As Hume pointed out, we can certainly conceive an uncaused
beginning-to-be of an object; if what we can thus conceive is nevertheless in some
way impossible, this still requires to be shown.[10] Still, this principle has some
plausibility, in that it is constantly confirmed in our experience (and also used,
reasonably, in interpreting our experience).

Altogether, then, the first stage of Aquinas's argument falls short of watertight
demonstration, but it gives some lower degree of support to the conclusion that
there is at least one thing that is necessary in the sense, which has now become clear,
that it is permanent, that *for some reason* it is not able-not-to-be.

The second stage takes this conclusion as its starting-point. One permanent
thing, it allows, may be caused to be permanent, sustained always in existence, by
another. But, it holds, there cannot be an infinite regress of such things. Why not?
Aquinas refers us to his earlier proof about efficient causes, in the second way. This
runs:

9. Craig, op. cit., Chapter 4.
10. *Treatise*, Book I, Part iii, Section 3; contrast Kenny, op. cit., p. 67.

It is not possible to go to infinity in a series of efficient causes. For in all ordered efficient causes the first item is the cause of the intermediate one and the intermediate is the cause of the last (whether there is only one intermediate or more than one); now if the cause is removed, so is the effect. Therefore if there has not been a first item among efficient causes there will not be a last or an intermediate. But if one goes to infinity in a series of efficient causes, there will not be a first efficient cause, and so there will not be a last effect or intermediate efficient causes . . .

Unfortunately this argument is unsound. Although in a *finite* ordered series of causes the intermediate (or the earliest intermediate) is caused by the first item, this would not be so if there were an infinite series. In an infinite series, every item is caused by an earlier item. The way in which the first item is 'removed' if we go from a finite to an infinite series does not entail the removal of the later items. In fact, Aquinas (both here and in the first way) has simply begged the question against an infinite regress of causes. But is this a sheer mistake, or is there some coherent thought behind it? Some examples (some of which would not themselves have been available to Aquinas, though analogues of them would have been) may suggest that there is. If we were told that there was a watch without a mainspring, we would hardly be reassured by the further information that it had, however, an infinite train of gear-wheels. Nor would we expect a railway train consisting of an infinite number of carriages, the last pulled along by the second last, the second last by the third last, and so on, to get along without an engine. Again, we see a chain, consisting of a series of links, hanging from a hook; we should be surprised to learn that there was a similar but infinite chain, with no hook, but links supported by links above them for ever. The point is that in these examples, and in the series of efficient causes or of necessary things, it is assumed that there is a relation *of dependence*—or, equivalently, one in the reverse direction of *support*—and, if the series were infinite, there would in the end be nothing for the effects to depend on, nothing to support them. And the same would be true if the regress were not infinite but circular.

There is here an implicit appeal to the following general principle: Where items are ordered by a relation of dependence, the regress must end somewhere; it cannot be either infinite or circular. Perhaps this principle was intended by al Farabi in the dictum that is translated 'But a series of contingent beings which would produce one another cannot proceed to infinity or move in a circle' (p. 83). As our examples show, this principle is at least highly plausible; the problem will be to decide when we have such a relation of dependence.

In the second stage of Aquinas's argument, therefore, the key notion is that any necessary—that is, permanent—thing either depends for its permanence on something else or is *per se necessarium* in a sense which can apply only to God. The actual text of the third way does not reveal Aquinas's thinking about this. But comparison of it with other passages in his writings and with Maimonides's proof suggests that the implicit assumption is that anything whose essence does not involve existence must, even if it is permanent, depend for its existence on something else.[11] This assumption would give the dependence which would call for an end to the regress and also ensure that nothing could end it but a being whose essence involved existence—which would explain the assertion that what is *per se necessarium* is what men all call God.

But the final objection to the argument is that we have no reason for accepting this implicit assumption. Why, for example, might there not be a permanent stock of matter whose essence did not involve existence but which did not derive its existence from anything else?

It is obvious that, as I said earlier, Aquinas's third way is very different from Leibniz's cosmological proof. Yet there has been a tendency to assimilate the former to the latter.[12] This is understandable, in that Aquinas would need something like the principle of sufficient reason to support what I have called the implicit assumption against our final objection: for example, there being a permanent stock of matter would be just a brute fact that had no sufficient reason, whereas something whose essence involved existence would seem to have, in itself, *per se*, a sufficient reason for its permanence. But in view of our criticisms of Leibniz's argument, no borrowing from it can rescue that of Aquinas.

But what about the popular first cause argument? Can we not now answer our earlier queries? Why must the regress of causes in time terminate? Because things, states of affairs, and occurrences *depend* on their antecedent causes. Why must the regress lead to one first cause rather than to many uncaused causes, and why must that one cause be God? Because anything other than God would need something else causally to depend upon. Moreover, the assumption needed for this argument is more plausible than that needed for Leibniz's proof, or for Aquinas's. The notion that everything must have a sufficient reason is a metaphysician's demand, as is the notion that anything permanent must depend for its permanence on something else unless its essence involves existence. But the notion that an effect *depends* on a temporally earlier cause is part of our ordinary understanding of causation: we all have some grasp of this asymmetry between cause and effect, however hard it may be to give an exact analysis of it.[13]

Nevertheless, this argument is not demonstratively cogent. Though we understand that where something has a temporally antecedent cause, it depends somehow upon it, it does not follow that everything (other than God) *needs* something else to depend on in this way. Also, what we can call al Farabi's principle, that where items are ordered by a relation of dependence, the regress must terminate somewhere, and cannot be either infinite or circular, though plausible, may not be really sound. But the greatest weakness of this otherwise attractive argument is that some reason is required for making God the one exception to the supposed need for something else to depend on: why should God, rather than anything else, be taken

11. Craig, op. cit., pp. 142–3, 146–8.
12. Craig, op. cit., p. 283.
13. Cf. Chapter 7 of *The Cement of the Universe*.

as the only satisfactory termination of the regress? If we do not simply accept this as a sheer mystery (which would be to abandon rational theology and take refuge in faith), we shall have to defend it in something like the ways that the metaphysicians have suggested. But then this popular argument takes on board the burdens that have sunk its more elaborate philosophical counterparts.

(c) Finite past time and creation

There is, as Craig explains, a distinctive kind of cosmological argument which, unlike those of Aquinas, Leibniz, and many others, assumes or argues that the past history of the world is finite.[14] This, which Craig calls, by its Arabic name, the *kalām* type of argument, was favoured by Islamic thinkers who were suspicious of the subtleties of the philosophers and relied more on revelation than on reason. Nevertheless, they did propound this as a rational proof of God's existence, and some of them used mathematical paradoxes that are descended from Zeno's, or that anticipate Cantor's, to show that there cannot be an actual infinite—in particular, an infinite past time. For example, if time past were infinite, an infinite stretch would have actually to have been traversed in order to reach the present, and this is thought to be impossible. Then there is an ingenious argument suggested by al Ghāzālī: the planet Jupiter revolves in its orbit once every twelve years, Saturn once every thirty years; so Jupiter must have completed more than twice as many revolutions as Saturn; yet if past time were infinite they would each have completed the same (infinite) number; which is a contradiction. (pp. 101–2) The first of these (which Kant also uses in the thesis of his First Antinomy) just expresses a prejudice against an actual infinity. It assumes that, even if past time were infinite, there would still have been a starting-point of time, but one infinitely remote, so that an actual infinity would have had to be traversed to reach the present from there. But to take the hypothesis of infinity seriously would be to suppose that there was no starting-point, not even an infinitely remote one, and that from any specific point in past time there is only a finite stretch that needs to be traversed to reach the present. Al Ghāzālī's argument uses an instance of one of Cantor's paradoxes, that in an infinite class a part can indeed be equal to the whole: for example, there are just as many even numbers (2, 4, 6, etc.) as there are whole numbers (1, 2, 3, etc.), since these classes can be matched one–one with each other. But is this not a contradiction? Is not the class of even numbers both equal to that of the integers (because of this one–one correlation) and smaller than it (because it is a proper part of it, the part that leaves out the odd numbers)? But what this brings out is that we ordinarily have and use a criterion for one group's being smaller than another—that it is, or can be correlated one–one with, a proper part of the other—and a criterion for two groups' being equal in number—that they can be correlated one–one with each other—which together ensure that *smaller than* and *equal to* exclude

14. Craig, op. cit., Chapter 3.

one another for all pairs of finite groups, but not for pairs of infinite groups. Once we understand the relation between the two criteria, we see that there is no real contradiction.

In short, it seems impossible to disprove, *a priori*, the possibility of an infinite past time. Nevertheless, many people have shared, and many still do share, these doubts about an actual infinite in the real world, even if they are willing to leave mathematicians free to play their Cantorian games—which, of course, not all mathematicians, or all philosophers of mathematics, want to play. Also the view that, whatever we say about *time*, the *universe* has a finite past history, has in recent years received strong empirical support from the cosmology that is a branch of astronomy. So let us consider what the prospects would be for a proof of the existence of a god if we were supplied, from whatever source, with the premiss that the world has only a finite past history, and therefore a beginning in time, whether or not this is also the beginning of time. Here the crucial assumption is stated by al Ghāzālī: '[We] know by rational necessity that nothing which originates in time originates by itself, and that, therefore, it needs a creator' (p. 102). But *do* we know this by rational necessity? Surely the assumption required here is just the same as that which is used differently in the first cause argument, that anything other than a god needs a cause or a creator to depend on. But there is *a priori* no good reason why a sheer origination of things, not determined by anything, should be unacceptable, whereas the existence of a god with the power to create something out of nothing is acceptable.

When we look hard at the latter notion we find problems within it. Does God's existence have a sheer origination in time? But then this would be as great a puzzle as the sheer origination of a material world. Or has God existed for ever through an infinite time? But this would raise again the problem of the actual infinite. To avoid both of these, we should have to postulate that God's own existence is not in time at all; but this would be a complete mystery.

Alternatively, someone might not share al Ghāzālī's worries about the actual infinite, and might rely on an empirical argument—such as the modern cosmological evidence for the 'big bang'—to show that the material world had a beginning in time. For him, therefore, God's existence through an infinite time would be unproblematic. But he is still using the crucial assumptions that God's existence and creative power would be self-explanatory whereas the unexplained origination of a material world would be unintelligible and therefore unacceptable. But the first of these leads us back to the criticism stated in section (a). The notion, embedded in the ontological argument, of a being whose existence is self-explanatory because it is not the case that it might not have existed, is *not* defensible; so we cannot borrow that notion to complete any form of the cosmological argument. The second assumption is equally questionable. We have no good ground for an *a priori* certainty that there could not have been a sheer unexplained beginning of things. But in so far as we find this improbable, it should cast doubt on the interpretation of the big bang as an absolute beginning of the material universe; rather, we should

224 J. L. MACKIE

infer that it must have had *some* physical antecedents, even if the big bang has to be taken as a discontinuity so radical that we cannot explain it, because we can find no laws which we can extrapolate backwards through this discontinuity.

In short, the notion of creation seems more acceptable than any other way out of the cosmological maze only because we do not look hard either at it or at the human experiences of making things on which it is modelled. It is vaguely explanatory, apparently satisfying; but these appearances fade away when we try to formulate the suggestion precisely.

(d) Swinburne's inductive cosmological argument

We might well have anticipated, from the beginning, the conclusion that our discussion in this chapter has thus laboriously reached. We have no general grounds for expecting to be able to demonstrate, by deductively valid arguments, using premises that are known with certainty, conclusions which go far beyond the empirical data on which they are based. And particularly since Hume and Kant philosophers have tended to be very sceptical about such a possibility. On the other hand we do have good general grounds for expecting to be able to confirm, provisionally but sometimes quite strongly, hypotheses that go far beyond the observational data that support them, and to confirm them in a sense that makes it reasonable for us to rely, for practical purposes, on their being either true or at any rate fairly close to the truth. The successful growth of the empirical sciences over the last 400 years justifies such a general expectation, no matter what problems there may still be in developing a satisfactory theory of the confirmation of hypotheses or of the justification of inductive reasoning. Though the theologians of the past wanted much more, many thinkers today would be content if theism were as well confirmed as one of the better-established scientific theories. So we might well consider whether there is a good inductive or hypothesis-confirming variant of the cosmological argument; and this is what Swinburne has tried to present.[15]

Swinburne prefixes to his whole discussion of the existence of a god an account of inductive reasoning in general. The statement that a hypothesis is 'confirmed' by certain evidence is ambiguous: it may mean that the evidence has raised the probability of the hypothesis as compared with what it was, or would have been, apart from that evidence; or it may mean that the evidence makes the hypothesis more likely than not to be true. Swinburne speaks of a 'good C-inductive argument', meaning one in which the premises or evidence confirm the conclusion or hypothesis in the former sense, and of a 'good P-inductive argument' where they confirm it in the latter sense. As he says, it is harder to tell when we have a good P-inductive argument than when we have a good C-inductive argument. But in either

---

15. In Chapter 7 of *The Existence of God* (Oxford University Press, 1979). References in the text are to pages in this work

case it is a question of an *argument*: we are concerned with relations of non-deductive support between certain evidence, in the light of some body of background knowledge or belief, and a hypothesis or conclusion. Any judgment that we reasonably make will be provisional, in that further evidence, or a change in the background knowledge or belief, may alter the degree of confirmation or the balance of probabilities, and one important kind of change in the background is the introduction of further, rival, possible explanatory hypotheses, or a change in the initial probability of such hypotheses.

There is an important principle which serves as a criterion for a good C-inductive argument. A hypothesis is confirmed by certain evidence if and only if (apart from or prior to that evidence's being observed) the addition of the hypothesis to the background knowledge or belief makes it more probable that that evidence would occur than it would be in relation to the background knowledge or belief alone. Symbolically, if 'h' stands for the hypothesis, 'e' for the evidence, 'k' for the background knowledge or belief, and '$P(x/y)$' for the probability of x in relation to y, then h is confirmed—in the sense of having its probability raised—by e if and only if $P(e/h\&k) > P(e/k)$. Or, equivalently, a hypothesis is in this sense confirmed by evidence if and only if that evidence would have been more likely to occur if the hypothesis had been true than if it had been false: h is confirmed by e if and only if $P(e/h\&k) > P(e/ \sim h\&k)$. In other words, the evidence raises the probability of the hypothesis if and only if the addition of the hypothesis raises the antecedent probability of the evidence. This holds provided that the initial probability of the hypothesis in relation to the background knowledge or belief is not zero.

This principle may be illustrated by a simple detective story example. The finding, in the dried mud of a path, of footmarks which closely match Fred's shoes in shape, size, and degree of wear, and the distances between which match the ordinary length of his stride, makes it more likely that Fred walked along that path when it was last wet than it would have been without this evidence. Why? Because the hypothesis that Fred walked there then raises the probability that there would now be just such footmarks as compared with what it would be without that hypothesis, or on the supposition that he did not walk there then. If our background information makes it quite likely that there would be such marks even if Fred had not walked there—for example, if Fred has a twin brother who frequently borrows Fred's shoes and who uses that path—the addition of the hypothesis that Fred walked there does not raise the antecedent probability of the footmarks so much (since it was fairly high without that hypothesis, or even in relation to the denial of that hypothesis), and finding the marks is no longer so good a confirmation that Fred was there. Again (even if Fred has no twin brother) if our background knowledge makes it impossible that Fred should have walked on the path when it was last wet—for example, if Fred died before the last heavy rain—then although the addition of the hypothesis would raise the antecedent probability of that evidence, the evidence cannot confirm the hypothesis: its zero initial probability cannot be raised.

This principle concerns C-inductive arguments, the conditions for the raising of the probability of a hypothesis by evidence. When we come to P-inductive arguments, to the question whether the evidence makes the hypothesis on balance more likely than not, the initial probability of the hypothesis is very significant. Even if the evidence *raises* the probability of the hypothesis in comparison with what it was otherwise, it may fail to make it more likely than not, because the initial probability of the hypothesis was low. Because the initial probability of a miracle's occurring is so low, it would need very good evidence indeed to make it more likely than not that one had occurred. Even evidence which the miracle's occurrence would explain and make probable, but which would have been very unlikely to come about without the miracle, may be insufficient to overcome the antecedent improbability of the miracle so as to make it now more likely than not that it occurred.

These can be taken as agreed principles of inductive reasoning; the problem is to apply them to the cosmological argument. Swinburne's first point is an adaptation of one of Leibniz's. Even if the universe has an infinite history in which each event is causally explained by the conjunction of laws and earlier events, that history as a whole is still unexplained. It might have been radically different—either with different laws or with the same laws but different specific situations all the way along—or there might have been nothing at all; no explanation has been given to show why neither of these possibilities was fulfilled. But, secondly, Swinburne suggests, the hypothesis that there is a god would to some extent explain the existence and the actual history of the universe. He is claiming that there is a kind of explanation, quite different from causal explanation, which is used when we explain something as the intentional action of a rational being; he calls this 'personal explanation'. On the assumption that there is a god such as traditional theism proclaims, it follows that he could make a physical universe if he chose, and that he might have had some reason to do so. Swinburne does not, indeed, say that the hypothesis (h) that there is such a god makes it very probable that (e) there should be such a universe as this:

However I do not claim that $P(e/h.k)$ is especially high. $P(e/h.k)$ measures how likely it is if there is a God that there will be a physical universe. The choice before God among worlds to create includes a world where there is just God; a world where there are one or more finite non-physical objects (e.g. non-embodied spirits); a world consisting of a simple physical universe (e.g. just one round steel ball); and a world which is a complex physical universe. There are good reasons why God should make a complex physical universe. For such a universe can be beautiful, and that is good; and also it can be a theatre for finite agents to develop and make of it what they will . . . But I cannot see that God has overriding reason to make such a universe . . . Nor can I see that he has overriding reason to make or not to make any alternative world. (pp. 130–1)

Swinburne is not saying, then, that this is obviously the best of all possible worlds; so $P(e/h\&k)$ is not high. On the other hand, he thinks that $P(e/k)$ is still lower: a complex physical universe is 'very unlikely to come about but for God's agency'. Consequently we do have that $P(e/h\&k) > P(e/k)$, and therefore that there is a good C-inductive argument from the existence of a complex physical universe to the existence of the god of traditional theism.

As we have seen, this will hold only if $P(h/k)$, the initial probability of the existence of such a god, is not zero. Let us grant this. Still, all that is being said is that the existence of a complex physical universe *raises* the likelihood of a god, makes it more probable than it would have been otherwise, that is, if there had been no such universe. But it is hard to see how this helps us. How can we even think about the antecedent probability that there should be a god, given that there was no such universe? Presumably we must think of an initial probability of there being a god, relative only to tautological information, and if we have rejected the ontological argument this will be pretty low. But there is very little analogy with Fred's case, where it was, perhaps, apart from the footmarks, not very likely that he had walked along that path, but the discovery of the footmarks makes it much more probable. The trouble is that if the evidence, e, is to be that there is a complex physical universe, then the background knowledge or belief k must exclude this, and so will be able to include only logical and mathematical truths. What likelihood could the God-hypothesis have had in relation to these?

We may be asking the wrong question, then, if we ask whether there is a good C-inductive argument from the sheer existence of a complex physical universe to the existence of a god. Swinburne's summary puts the issue differently:

There is quite a chance that if there is a God he will make something of the finitude and complexity of a universe. It is very unlikely that a universe would exist uncaused, but rather more likely that God would exist uncaused. The existence of the universe is strange and puzzling. It can be made comprehensible if we suppose that it is brought about by God. This supposition postulates a simpler beginning of explanation than does the supposition of an uncaused universe, and that is grounds for believing the former supposition to be true. (pp. 131–2)

We are now comparing the two rival hypotheses, one that there is no further cause or explanation of the complex physical universe, the other that there is a god who created it. That there is this universe is common ground, shared by the two hypotheses. Swinburne is arguing that in relation to our background knowledge—which can now include everything that we ordinarily know about ourselves and the world, though it must exclude any specifically religious beliefs—it is more likely that there should be an uncaused god who created the world than simply an uncaused universe—that is, a universe with internal causal relationships, but no further cause for its basic laws being as they are or for its being there at all. The analogy would be with the reasoning in which we postulate a common ancestor for a group of similar manuscripts, on the ground that their otherwise unexplained and therefore improbable resemblances can be explained as being due to their having been copied, directly or indirectly, from this ancestor; the surviving-manuscripts-plus-common-ancestor hypothesis is more acceptable than a surviving-manuscripts-with-no-common-ancestor hypothesis.

But now the fact that the uncaused universe would, by definition, have no further explanation does not justify the claim that it is 'strange and puzzling' or 'very unlikely'. The mere fact that it is a complex physical universe does not mean that it includes anything comparable to the resemblances between our manuscripts that would be surprising if not further explained. On the other side, the hypothesis of divine creation is very unlikely. Although *if* there were a god with the traditional attributes and powers, he would be able and perhaps willing to create such a universe as this, we have to weigh in our scales the likelihood or unlikelihood *that* there is a god with these attributes and powers. And the key power, involved in Swinburne's use of 'personal explanation', is that of fulfilling intentions *directly*, without any physical or causal mediation, without materials or instruments. There is nothing in our background knowledge that makes it comprehensible, let alone likely, that anything should have such a power. All our knowledge of intention-fulfilment is of *embodied* intentions being fulfilled *indirectly* by way of bodily changes and movements which are *causally* related to the intended result, and where the ability thus to fulfil intentions itself has a *causal history*, either of evolutionary development or of learning or of both. Only by ignoring such key features do we get an analogue of the supposed divine action. But even apart from this I see no plausibility in the statement that it is 'rather more likely that God would exist uncaused'. Swinburne's backing for this is that 'the supposition that there is a God is an extremely simple supposition; the postulation of a God of infinite power, knowledge, and freedom is the postulation of the simplest kind of person which there could be', whereas 'There is a complexity, particularity, and finitude about the universe which cries out for explanation' (p. 130). (It is somewhat ironic that whereas God seemed to Anselm and others to be self-explanatory because he is something than which nothing greater can be conceived, he now seems to Swinburne to be relatively self-explanatory because he is simple.) But, first, the 'simplicity' achieved by taking everything to infinity is bought at the cost of asserting a whole series of real actual infinites, about which, as I mentioned, many thinkers, like al Ghazali above, have had doubts. Secondly, the particularity has not been removed, but only shelved: we should have to postulate particularities in God, to explain his choice of the particular universe he decided to create. And the very notion of a non-embodied spirit, let alone an infinite one, is intrinsically improbable in relation to our background knowledge, in that our experience reveals nothing of the sort.

Some of the themes we encountered in dealing with the older forms of cosmological argument recur here. Like Leibniz, Swinburne is looking for explanation and intelligibility. He does not, like Leibniz, demand a complete explanation, a sufficient reason for everything, or intelligibility through and through; but he is trying to minimize the unexplained part of our total picture. But without introducing the concept of something that contains its own sufficient reason, or whose essence includes existence—unsatisfactory though, in the end, these notions are—he has nothing to support the claim that by adding a god to the world we *reduce* the unexplained element. Although his starting-point is like Leibniz's, his conclusion is more like that of the *kalām* argument, in taking creation by a person as the one satisfactory beginning of things. But when we look hard at it, such 'personal explanation' is not a satisfactory beginning at all, and certainly not one that is given any initial probability by the ordinary information that we have to take as our background knowledge.

The prospects for an inductive or probabilistic or hypothesis-confirming variant of the cosmological argument are, therefore, no better than those for a demonstrative one. However, our criticisms have been directed particularly against a *cosmological* argument in the sense explained at the beginning of this chapter, that is, one whose empirical datum is either the mere fact that there is a world at all or such very general facts about it as that there is change or motion or causation. These criticisms leave open the possibility that the hypothesis that there is a god may be confirmed by evidence of more detailed and specific kinds, for example by the existence of conscious beings, or the presence of what have been seen as 'marks of design'.

Chapter 20

Why is a cause always necessary?

David Hume

Why a cause is always necessary

To begin with the first question concerning the necessity of a cause: 'Tis a general maxim in philosophy, that *whatever begins to exist, must have a cause of existence*. This is commonly taken for granted in all reasonings, without any proof given or demanded. 'Tis suppos'd to be founded on intuition, and to be one of those maxims, which tho' they may be deny'd with the lips, 'tis impossible for men in their hearts really to doubt of. But if we examine this maxim by the idea of knowledge above-explain'd, we shall discover in it no mark of any such intuitive certainty; but on the contrary shall find, that 'tis of a nature quite foreign to that species of conviction.

All certainty arises from the comparison of ideas, and from the discovery of such relations as are unalterable, so long as the ideas continue the same. These relations are *resemblance, proportions in quantity and number, degrees of any quality, and contrariety*; none of which are imply'd in this proposition, *Whatever has a beginning has also a cause of existence*. That proposition therefore is not intuitively certain. At least any one, who wou'd assert it to be intuitively certain, must deny these to be the only infallible relations, and must find some other relation of that kind to be imply'd in it; which it will then be time enough to examine.

But here is an argument, which proves at once, that the foregoing proposition is neither intuitively nor demonstrably certain. We can never demonstrate the necessity of a cause to every new existence, or new modification of existence, without shewing at the same time the impossibility there is, that any thing can ever begin to exist without some productive principle; and where the latter proposition cannot be prov'd, we must despair of ever being able to prove the former. Now that the latter proposition is utterly incapable of a demonstrative proof, we may satisfy ourselves by considering, that as all distinct ideas are separable from each other, and as the ideas of cause and effect are evidently distinct, 'twill be easy for us to conceive any object to be non-existent this moment, and existent the next, without conjoining to it the distinct idea of a cause or productive principle. The separation, therefore, of the idea of a cause from that of a beginning of existence, is plainly possible for the imagination; and consequently the actual separation of these objects is so far

David Hume 'A Treatise of Human Nature' from *David Hume A Treatise of Human Nature* edited by L. A. Selby-Bigge, revised by P. H. Nidditch (OUP, 1978), copyright © Oxford University Press 1978, reprinted by permission of the publisher.

possible, that it implies no contradiction nor absurdity; and is therefore incapable of being refuted by any reasoning from mere ideas; without which 'tis impossible to demonstrate the necessity of a cause.

Accordingly we shall find upon examination, that every demonstration, which has been produc'd for the necessity of a cause, is fallacious and sophistical. All the points of time and place, say some philosophers, in which we can suppose any object to begin to exist, are in themselves equal; and unless there be some cause, which is peculiar to one time and to one place, and which by that means determines and fixes the existence, it must remain in eternal suspence; and the object can never begin to be, for want of something to fix its beginning. But I ask; Is there any more difficulty in supposing the time and place to be fix'd without a cause, than to suppose the existence to be determin'd in that manner? The first question that occurs on this subject is always, *whether* the object shall exist or not: The next, *when* and *where* it shall begin to exist. If the removal of a cause be intuitively absurd in the one case, it must be so in the other: And if that absurdity be not clear without a proof in the one case, it will equally require one in the other. The absurdity, then, of the one supposition can never be a proof of that of the other; since they are both upon the same footing, and must stand or fall by the same reasoning.

The second argument, which I find us'd on this head, labours under an equal difficulty. Every thing, 'tis said, must have a cause; for if any thing wanted a cause, *it* wou'd produce *itself*; that is, exist before it existed; which is impossible. But this reasoning is plainly unconclusive; because it supposes, that in our denial of a cause we still grant what we expressly deny, *viz.* that there must be a cause; which therefore is taken to be the object itself; and *that*, no doubt, is an evident contradiction. But to say that any thing is produc'd, or to express myself more properly, comes into existence, without a cause, is not to affirm, that 'tis itself its own cause; but on the contrary in excluding all external causes, excludes *a fortiori* the thing itself, which is created. An object, that exists absolutely without any cause, certainly is not its own cause; and when you assert, that the one follows from the other, you suppose the very point in question, and take it for granted, that 'tis utterly impossible any thing can ever begin to exist without a cause, but that upon the exclusion of one productive principle, we must still have recourse to another.

'Tis exactly the same case with the third argument, which has been employ'd to demonstrate the necessity of a cause. Whatever is produc'd without any cause, is produc'd by *nothing*; or in other words, has nothing for its cause. But nothing can never be a cause, no more than it can be something, or equal to two right angles. By the same intuition, that we perceive nothing not to be equal to two right angles, or not to be something, we perceive, that it can never be a cause; and consequently must perceive, that every object has a real cause of its existence.

I believe it will not be necessary to employ many words in shewing the weakness of this argument, after what I have said of the foregoing. They are all of them founded on the same fallacy, and are deriv'd from the same turn of thought. 'Tis sufficient only to observe, that when we exclude all causes we really do exclude them, and neither suppose nothing nor the object itself to be the causes of the existence; and consequently can draw no argument from the absurdity of these suppositions to prove the absurdity of that exclusion. If every thing must have a cause, it follows, that upon the exclusion of other causes we must accept of the object itself or of nothing as causes. But 'tis the very point in question, whether every thing must have a cause or not; and therefore, according to all just reasoning, it ought never to be taken for granted.

They are still more frivolous, who say, that every effect must have a cause, because 'tis imply'd in the very idea of effect. Every effect necessarily pre-supposes a cause; effect being a relative term, of which cause is the correlative. But this does not prove, that every being must be preceded by a cause; no more than it follows, because every husband must have a wife, that therefore every man must be marry'd. The true state of the question is, whether every object, which begins to exist, must owe its existence to a cause; and this I assert neither to be intuitively nor demonstratively certain, and hope to have prov'd it sufficiently by the foregoing arguments.

Since it is not from knowledge or any scientific reasoning, that we derive the opinion of the necessity of a cause to every new production, that opinion must necessarily arise from observation and experience. The next question, then, shou'd naturally be, *how experience gives rise to such a principle?* But as I find it will be more convenient to sink this question in the following, *Why we conclude, that such particular causes must necessarily have such particular effects, and why we form an inference from one to another?* we shall make that the subject of our future enquiry. 'Twill, perhaps, be found in the end, that the same answer will serve for both questions.

Chapter 21
'Whatever has a beginning of existence must have a cause'

G. E. M. Anscombe

HUME distinguishes two questions, the one: *Why a beginning of existence must necessarily always have a cause?* and the other, a double one: *why such particular causes must always have such particular effects*, and *what is the nature of the inference, from the one to the other?*

Not only are these distinct questions but a person may consistently hold that a beginning of existence must always have a cause, without holding that 'such particular causes must have such particular effects' (or that such particular effects must have such particular causes). It isn't clear whether Hume saw this.

His most famous thesis is that the ideas of cause and effect are always separable; that is, that one may, without contradiction or absurdity, suppose a given sort of cause to occur without its characteristic effect, and vice versa. This *seems* to be very generally true. There is a counter-example. If I ask how something comes to be in a certain place, I may learn that it arrived there from somewhere else; i.e. it travelled from point A to point B from time t to t' and so was at point B at t'. This is a causal explanation of its coming to be at point B at t' and it cannot 'without contradiction or absurdity' be supposed to happen without the thing's coming to be at point B— an event that might, however, have occurred otherwise, if for example it came into existence at that moment at that place. Thus, we can't accept Hume's principle as impregnable. But it is *prima facie* true in a vast number of cases.

Section III of Part II, Book 1 of the *Treatise* is devoted to proving that 'Whatever begins to exist must have a cause of existence' is not intuitively or demonstrably certain, i.e. is not what would nowadays be called a proposition whose truth is logically necessary.

What Hume calls 'intuitively certain' is a proposition whose truth is discoverable purely from examining the ideas contained in it, and what he calls 'demonstrably certain' is apparently a proposition which follows from something intuitively certain.

He first produces a 'proof', which we shall soon examine, that that first 'principle of causality' cannot possibly be intuitively or demonstrably certain; and he devotes the rest of the section to disposing of such arguments as he knows, purporting to demonstrate it. He considers four arguments, of which he is able to refute the last three quite easily; indeed they do not deserve attention. One says that something that came into existence without a cause must produce itself, which is impossible; another, that it is produced by *nothing*, which is incapable of producing anything. As Hume says, these arguments assume what they set out to prove, and so can hardly prove it. This is not 'just reasoning'. The point is obvious indeed. Not that the arguments are invalid; but they cannot prove the conclusion, if they cannot prove it except to someone who already accepts it. Another argument Hume reasonably calls still more frivolous: every effect must have a cause, since cause and effect are relative terms. As he says, this does not show that every beginning of existence must be an effect, any more than the truth that every husband must have a wife shows that every man must be married. His making this point will be of some importance for our understanding of his positive argument that this 'principle of causality' cannot possibly be intuitively or demonstrably certain. So much for the second, third and fourth arguments which he considers.

The first argument, however, is obscure and is dealt with rather sketchily. It is that 'all the points of time and space, in which we can suppose any object to begin to exist, are in themselves equal; and unless there be some cause, which is peculiar to one time and to one place, and which by that means determines and fixes the existence, it must remain in eternal suspense'. Hume replies 'Is there any more difficulty in supposing the time and place to be fix'd without a cause, than to suppose the existence to be determin'd in that manner? The first question that occurs on this subject is always, *whether* the object shall exist or not: the next, *when* and *where* it shall begin to exist. If the removal of a cause be intuitively absurd in the one case, it must be so in the other: And if that absurdity be not clear without a proof in the one case, it will equally require one in the other. The absurdity, then, of the one supposition can never be a proof of that of the other, since they are both upon the same footing, and must stand or fall by the same reasoning.'

Why does he say 'The first question is whether an object shall exist'? This seems to consider the matter from the point of view of a creator, which suggests that Hume is consciously in Leibniz country; for Leibniz argues for the identity of indiscernibles on the ground that God must have a reason for putting A here and now, and B there and then, which there could not be unless something distinguished A from B. Yet Hume doesn't consider this. The questions are not easy to reformulate and seem better left out.

What is Hume's argument? He is saying: You cannot argue to the absurdity of *p*, from the fact that it entails *q*, which is absurd, for if someone saw no difficulty in *p*, he'd see no difficulty in *q*. (Rather as if the argument were a shaggy dog story.) This is somewhat cavalier. The arguer is not saying 'There is no absurdity in *p*' but rather 'There is at any rate *this* absurdity in *p*, that it entails *q*, which is absurd'.

Hume is saying 'But why should I find *q* absurd, if I don't *already* find *p* absurd?'. And to this there may well be an answer in this case. It is not fair to say: you *cannot* argue like that, because you are initially supposing that *p* is *not* absurd. One is not initially supposing anything of the sort. Well, Hume says, by producing an argu-ment instead of simply saying p is absurd, you are conceding it is not intuitively absurd; now *if* it is not intuitively absurd, then neither is q. Well, even that is not clear; but anyway, perhaps q is not 'intuitively' absurd but there are further argu-ments to show that q is absurd.

And this is indeed the case. Without existing at a definite place and time, a particular finite and non-eternal thing won't exist at all. Hobbes' argument, as cited by Hume, seems to go on as follows: Antecedently to a thing's existence at a place and time nothing can connect it with that time and place more than with any other, unless something already existent makes that the time and place of the thing's existence. This argument indeed seems very uncertain. Hume could say: the thing is and can be connected with the time and place *only* by the brute fact of existing then and there: you can think of that without invoking something else that makes it exist at that time and place.

But the argument suggests another one. Namely: Space and time are relative; that is, antecedently to a thing's existence at a place and time, there can be no distinction of that place and time from any other unless something else distinguishes them. In this passage, Hume writes as if the place and time for a thing's existence could be specified independently of its existence. The argument that he is considering assumes that too; and also it is the truth. Since, then, space and time are relative, this specifiability requires a determinant other than the thing which is supposed to exist, or to have existed in the place and at the time.

That is the argument, and Hume does not deal with the questions suggested by the argument he cited from Hobbes, which give rise to this one; he has apparently not seen that the question arises what the requisite specification of place and time could mean without a prior existence. Or at least *some* other existence. For as far as concerns time, it may not be prior; it might be posterior. Thus we specify a time as n years ago. This is not to give a cause, but the requirement of other existences by which to specify time and place does disprove Hume's great principle 'That there is nothing in any object consider'd in itself, which can afford us a reason for drawing a conclusion beyond it'. Or if he should say: 'consider'd in itself' excludes 'consider'd as existing at a given time and place', then, if a thing that comes into existence must come into existence at a given time and place, 'consider'd in itself' it can't be considered as coming into existence at all. But as soon as you consider it as existing at a given time and place, the question arises as to how that time and place could be specified.

This is a very obscure topic, and we will leave it, with the observation that Hume has hardly done it justice. Let us now attend to our main business: the argument, already given by him, to show that a beginning of existence without a cause is not demonstrably absurd.

It is an argument from imagination.

as all distinct ideas are separable from each other, and as the ideas of cause and effect are evidently distinct, 'twill be easy for us to conceive any object to be non-existent this moment, and existent the next, without conjoining to it the distinct idea of a cause or productive principle. The separation, therefore, of the idea of a cause from that of a beginning of existence is plainly possible for the imagination, and consequently the actual separation of these objects is so far possible, that it implies no contradiction or absurdity.

His argument is rather prolix—more so than my quotation shows. Let us set it out proposition by proposition.

(1)   All distinct ideas are separable.
(2)   The ideas of cause and effect are distinct.
(3)   ∴ It will be easy to think of an object's coming into existence without thinking of a cause.

So far, so good: 'separable' presumably means 'such that one can think of one without *eo ipso* thinking of the other'.

We might query (2) on the grounds that cause and effect are correlative, like husband and wife. But from Hume's giving an example of an effect in (3), and especially in view of his calling 'frivolous' the argument that the ideas of cause and effect are correlative, we must take him to mean that the ideas of whatever objects are causes and effects are distinct from one another. The next step is the crucial one:

(4)   ∴ The separation of the idea of a cause from that of a beginning of existence is possible for the imagination.

What does this mean? There are two possibilities: that it is possible to imagine a beginning of existence without imagining a cause, and that it is possible to imagine a beginning of existence without a cause. The first certainly follows from (3) but is too close to it in sense for us seriously to suppose it is what Hume means. He must, then, mean the second, so we have

(4)   (a)   ∴ It is possible to imagine something's beginning to exist without a cause.

From this he draws the conclusion

(5)   ∴ The actual separation of these objects is so far possible, that it implies no contradiction or absurdity.

This makes one ask 'What objects?' The answer, as far as concerns one of them, is plain: it is 'a beginning of existence'.

For example, I imagine a star or a rabbit beginning to exist. To supply such a particular case is both reasonable and conformable to Hume's doctrine of abstract ideas; for neither in reality nor according to Hume can there be a bare image of a beginning of existence which is not the beginning of existence of anything in particular. But what is the other 'object'? The only answer we have is 'a cause'. Now we can go two ways. We can either forsake the doctrine of abstract ideas and say that that is to be a sufficient description of our image in the particular case, or we can, as we did with 'a beginning of existence', supply a specific cause, as, another rabbit, or the compacting of nebulous material. And here arises the difficulty. For the argument from imaginability to possibility has a good deal of force on the second interpretation: let me imagine any event—say the boiling of a kettle—and any particular cause of it—say the heat of a fire, and not only can I imagine the one's happening without the other, but the imaginability is of a sort to convince me of the possibility in the sense of 'implying no contradiction or absurdity'. 'I know what it would be like to find the kettle boiled without a fire', I may say, similarly I know what it would be like to find a rabbit coming into being *not* from a parent rabbit. So here the argument from imagination is sound. But this sound argument does not yield the desired conclusion. Let it hold for any particular cause I care to introduce. Let us even suppose that Hume is right in saying it holds universally. Then I can say

(6) For any beginning (or modification) of existence E and any particular cause C, I can imagine E's happening without C,

and infer from this

(7) For any beginning (or modification) of existence E, and any particular cause C, E can be supposed to happen without C: i.e. there is no contradiction or absurdity in the supposition.

But the proposition does not give me the possibility of imagining an effect without any cause at all. That is, it does not give me:

(8) I can imagine this: there is a beginning (or modification) of existence without any cause.

For quite generally from

For *any*, it is possible that not . . .

there does not follow:

It is possible that for *none* . . .

E.g., from:

For *any* colour, I can imagine that a rose is not that colour does not follow:

I can imagine that a rose has no colour.

Nor does, (6), the possible exclusion of any particular cause in the imagination, or what (we are granting) follows from it, (7), the possibility of a beginning of existence without any given cause, yield

(9) A beginning of existence can *happen* without any cause,

i.e. this supposition is without contradiction or absurdity.

So if we go this way we have (perhaps) a sound argument from imagination. 'This can be imagined, therefore this is possible', but the *this* is not the desired conclusion, but is only the conclusion that the effect can occur without any particular cause which you have imagined it without.

We must, then, try the other tack, in which we forget Hume's doctrine of abstract ideas, and accept that the second 'object' is just 'a cause' and no more. Then the argument is simply:

We can imagine something's coming into existence without a cause. ∴ It is possible (i.e. there is no contradiction in supposing) that something comes into existence without a cause.

If this is the right interpretation, one wonders why Hume did not give the argument straight in this form. The trouble about it is that it is very unconvincing. For if I say I can imagine a rabbit coming into being without a parent rabbit, well and good: I imagine a rabbit coming into being, and our observing that there is no parent rabbit about. But what am I to imagine if I imagine a rabbit coming into being without a cause? Well, I just imagine a rabbit coming into being. That this *is* the imagination of a rabbit coming into being without a cause is nothing but, as it were, the *title* of the picture. Indeed I can form an image and give my picture that title. But from my being able to do *that*, nothing whatever follows about what is possible to suppose 'without contradiction or absurdity' as holding in reality.

Hume's argument can be rendered more intelligible to us if we attribute to him the following principle:

If a circumstance need not be thought of in thinking of a thing, then that thing can be thought of as lacking that circumstance and hence can exist without it.

The attribution is probably correct; for we know that Hume thought that '*the mind cannot form any notion of quantity or quality without forming a precise notion of degrees of each*'. His argument for this is that, e.g., the 'precise degree of any quality' cannot be distinguished from the quality. Holding it obviously absurd to suppose a quality to exist, though in no particular degree, Hume thought there could be no such thing as an idea of it which was not an idea of any particular degree of it. Generalizing, we may put it:

If something cannot be without such and such, it cannot be thought of without thinking of such and such.

The principle we have attributed to Hume as inspiring the argument we have been examining is essentially this one contraposed, though an extra step has been put in.

With some caution and restriction, we may grant the Parmenidean principle that 'It is the same thing that can be thought and can be'. But Hume's extension of it is certainly wrong. It is even wrong in the particular case from which we formed the generalization. I can imagine or think of a sprig of leaves as existing without there being any definite number of leaves that I think of it as having. Naturally, this does not mean that I can think of it as existing without having a definite number of leaves.

Chapter 22

Can there be an endless regress of causes?

James A. Sadowsky

T HE operative principle in the Cosmological Argument is that if each cause of A were itself in need of a cause, then no cause of A could exist and hence A itself could not exist. Since A does exist and does need a cause, it follows that not all of A's causes are in need of a cause. In other words the need for causes must come to an end: there must be or have been a cause that was not itself in need of a cause.

Kai Nielsen and a number of other philosophers such as Paul Edwards and Ronald Hepburn reject this argument. They see no reason why an endless series of caused causes could not do the same job that is done by a series ending with an uncaused cause. But let us hear Nielsen himself:

Why could there not be an infinite series of caused causes? An infinite series is not a long or even a very, very long *finite* series. The person arguing for an infinite series is not arguing for something that came from nothing, nor need he be *denying* that *every* event has a cause. He is asserting that we need not assume that there is a *first* cause that started everything. Only if the series were finite would it be impossible for there to be something if there were no first cause or uncaused cause. But if the series were literally infinite, there would be no need for there to be a first cause to get the causal order started, for there would always be a causal order since an infinite series can have no first member . . .[1]

The contention seems to be that if each member is supported by another member, the series will somehow be able to exist on its own. And of course it would have to stand on its own because its very endlessness precludes the intervention of an outside cause.

But it is just as difficult for any supporting member to exist as the member it supports. This brings back the question of how any member can do any causing unless it first exists. B cannot cause A until B exists. C cannot cause B until C exists, and C cannot cause until D brings it into existence. What is true of D is equally true of E and F, without end. Since each condition for the existence of A requires the fulfillment of a prior condition, it follows that none of them can ever be fulfilled. In

James A. Sadowsky, S.J., 'The Cosmological Argument and the Endless Regress' from *International Philosophical Quarterly*, Vol. XX, No. 4 (1980), reprinted by permission of International Philosophical Quarterly and the author.

1. Kai Nielsen, *Reason and Practice* (New York: Harper and Row, 1971), p. 171. Cf. Edwards: 'The Cosmological Argument' in *Critiques of God*, edit. Paul Angeles (Buffalo: Prometheus Books, 1976), pp. 44–50 and Ronald Hepburn in 'Cosmological Argument,' *The Encyclopedia of Philosophy* (New York: Macmillan Company, 1967).

each case what is offered as part of the solution turns out instead to be part of the problem.

How can Nielsen account for the independence of the series? Since it is a closed system, the independence can come only from the members of the series. By supposition, however, each member is wholly lacking in independence. While in some cases collections have properties that its members, taken individually, do not have, the fact remains that they must be derived from their members. Each member must have something of its own that it can contribute. But in the case we are considering no member has anything of its own: whatever it has is received from another.

No such problem arises in the case of a series whose first member is an *uncaused* cause. Although all the other members are totally dependent, the series as a whole derives its independence from that one independent being. In the same way we can say that the Universe (in the sense of 'all that there is') is independent because one of the beings that make it up (God) is independent—even though all the other things totally depend on him.[2]

If we reject the principle of the Cosmological Argument, we have to agree that nothing (including causes) can exist without a cause. But if that makes sense, is not the following equally intelligible: 'No one may do anything (including asking for permission) without asking for permission.' Clearly there is no way in which this precept can be observed because there is no legitimate way of asking for permission. The problem in both cases is that *no* condition can ever be met without the fulfillment of a preceding condition. No permission may be asked for because each asking for permission requires a prior asking for permission. Likewise, no causation can take place because each act of causation requires a prior act of causation

Gilbert Ryle uses the same tactic to demolish what he calls *The Intellectualist Legend*. Roughly, the principle that he is attacking amounts to saying: 'Never do anything (including thinking) without first thinking about it.' Of this he says:

The crucial objection to the intellectualist legend is this. The consideration of propositions is itself an operation the execution of which can be more or less intelligent, less or more stupid. But if, for any operation to be intelligently executed, a prior theoretical operation had first to be performed and performed intelligently, it would be a logical impossibility for anyone to break into the circle.

And:

To put it quite generally, the absurd assumption made by the intellectualist legend is this, that a performance of any sort inherits all its title to intelligence from some anterior internal operation of planning what to do . . . By the original argument, therefore, our intellectual planning must inherit its title to shrewdness from yet another interior process of planning to plan, and this process in its turn could be either silly or shrewd. The regress is infinite, and

---

2. It is in this sense that I can agree with Hepburn when he says: 'John Laird's suspicion seems justified—that while the world is indeed the *theatre* of causes and effects, we are not entitled to claim that it itself is an effect of some super-cause.' Hepburn, *Christianity and Paradox* (London: Watts, 1958), p. 169.

this reduces to absurdity the theory that for an operation to be intelligent it must be steered by prior intellectual operation. What distinguished sensible from silly operations is not their parentage but their procedure. . . .[3]

Ryle's point is that if there is to be intellectual planning at all, there must have been at least one act that was not intellectually planned. If all intelligent action required to be intelligently planned, there could be no intelligent action: not everything can be intelligent because something else was intelligent. Does not the same logic force us to say that not everything exists because something else exists? Must we not say that something exists in and of itself?

It seems to me that Nielsen has, perhaps without knowing it, advanced an argument which, if sound, would license *any* infinite regress. Why not accept the intellectualist legend, for example? All we have to do is postulate an infinity of acts of planning. Pointing out that a theory involves an infinite regress has always been an important weapon in the philosophical armory. The loss of this weapon to the rest of philosophy is too high a price to pay for the rejection of the Cosmological Argument.[4]

3. Gilbert Ryle, *The Concept of Mind* (New York: Barnes & Noble, 1949), pp. 30–2.
4. The infinite regress argument will not, however, work for Humean causes. For Hume to say that every event is caused by another event is to say little more than that every event is preceded by another event. This statement does not involve an infinite regress because being preceded by an event is not a necessary condition for being an event. The second ring of the doorbell could just as well have been the first. Humean causes are not necessary conditions and consequently he is not saying that every thing *needs* a cause. Since he denies that there are any caused beings in our sense of 'cause', he is perhaps unwittingly conceding that there is at least one uncaused being (in our sense). This parallels his attempt to get rid of substances by putting qualities in their place, but all he succeeds in doing is transforming the qualities into so many substances. Similarly here he gets rid of effects (in our sense), leaving only uncaused beings.

Questions for discussion

1. Are there reasons for supposing that the universe began to exist?
2. Must anything that begins to exist be caused to do so? To what extent is this question crucial when it comes to the existence of God?
3. Is there any reason for saying that we should ask 'Why is there something rather than nothing?' Is the question of relevance when it comes to the topic of God's existence?
4. 'The Universe is just there.' Discuss.
5. Can there be an endless series of causes for the things that exist now?

Advice on further reading

For book-length treatments of one or more cosmological arguments, the following can all be recommended as serious studies:

David Braine, *The Reality of Time and the Existence of God* (Oxford, 1988).

Hugo Meynell, *The Intelligible Universe: A Cosmological Argument* (London, 1982).

Barry Miller, *From Existence to God* (London and New York, 1992).

Milton K. Munitz, *The Mystery of Existence* (New York, 1965).

Bruce R. Reichenbach, *The Cosmological Argument: A Reassessment* (Springfield, Illinois, 1972).

William Rowe, *The Cosmological Argument* (Princeton and London, 1975).

John J. Shepherd, *Experience, Inference and God* (London, 1975).

   The phrase 'cosmological argument' has been used in a somewhat bewildering variety of ways. In this book I am thinking of cosmological arguments in accordance with the suggested understanding of them offered by Antony Flew in 'What Are Cosmological Arguments?', to be found in his *The Presumption of Atheism* (London, 1976). This essay is most helpful when it comes to deciding on whether or not to call arguments for God 'cosmological'.

   Cosmological arguments depend much on notions such as 'cause', 'explanation', 'existence', and 'proof'. The literature on these notions is vast, but some helpful essays bearing on them with an eye on natural theology include:

Peter Geach, 'Causality and Creation', in Peter Geach, *God and the Soul* (London, 1969).

Dudley Knowles (ed.), *Explanation and its Limits* (Cambridge, 1990).

A. N. Prior, 'On Some Proofs of the Existence of God', in A. N. Prior, *Papers in Logic and Ethics* (London, 1976).

Ernest Sosa (ed.), *Causation and Conditionals* (Oxford, 1975).

Keith Ward, 'Explanation and Mystery in Religion', *Religious Studies* 9 (1973).

C. J. F. Williams, 'Being', in Philip L. Quinn and Charles Taliaferro, *A Companion to Philosophy of Religion* (Oxford, 1997).

   For a research bibliography on cosmological arguments, see Clement Dore, *Theism* (Dordrecht, 1984). For a good account of some major cosmological arguments, see William Lane Craig, *The Cosmological Argument from Plato to Leibniz* (London, 1980). For a scholarly survey of cosmological arguments in ancient thinking, see L. P. Gerson, *God and Greek Philosophy: Studies in the History of Natural Theology* (London and New York, 1990). For an expert guide through medieval Islamic and Jewish thinking on cosmological arguments, the book to read is Herbert A. Davidson, *Proofs for Eternity, Creation and the Existence of God in Medieval Islamic and Jewish Philosophy* (Oxford, 1987). For a contemporary exposition and defence of kalām cosmological arguments, see William Lane Craig, *The Kalām Cosmological Argument* (London, 1979). Craig replies to Mackie's discussion of him in William Lane Craig, 'Professor Mackie and the *Kalām* Cosmological Argument', *Religious Studies* 20 (1985).

   For criticism of kalām cosmological arguments, see:

Quentin Smith, 'A Big Bang Cosmological Argument for God's Nonexistence', *Faith and Philosophy* 9 (1992).

Graham Oppy, 'Professor William Craig's Criticisms of Critiques of *Kalām* Cosmological Arguments by Paul Davies, Stephen Hawking, and Adolf Grünbaum', *Faith and Philosophy* 12 (1995).

Graham Oppy, 'Kalām Cosmological Arguments: Reply to Professor Craig', *Sophia* 34 (1995).

For an erudite and lively discussion of historical and philosophical issues bearing on kalām cosmological arguments, see Richard Sorabji, *Time, Creation and the Continuum* (London, 1983). For an introduction to Avicenna, see L. E. Goodman, *Avicenna* (London and New York, 1992).

In Chapter 15 Aquinas presents ideas which also feature in his so-called 'Five Ways' (*Summa Theologiae*, Ia. 2. 3. These have been much invoked as examples of cosmological arguments. For a good and non-technical introduction to them, see G. E. M. Anscombe and P. T. Geach, *Three Philosophers* (Oxford, 1961), pp. 109–25. For sympathetic evaluations of them, see C. F. J. Martin, *Thomas Aquinas: God and Explanations* (Edinburgh, 1997) and Lubor Velecky, *Aquinas' Five Arguments in the* Summa Theologiae *Ia. 2. 3.* (Kampen, 1994). For a critical evaluation of them, see Anthony Kenny, *The Five Ways* (London, 1969). For explanation of terms in Aquinas such as 'matter' and 'form', see his text *On the Principles of Nature* (*De Principiis Naturae*), for a translation of which see Timothy McDermott (ed.), *Thomas Aquinas: Selected Philosophical Writings* (Oxford, 1993), pp. 67–80. For secondary reading on Aquinas's terminology, see F. C. Copleston, *Aquinas* (Harmondsworth, 1955), ch. 2. For Aquinas's cosmological arguments in the *Summa Contra Gentiles*, see Norman Kretzmann, *The Metaphysics of Theism* (Oxford, 1997). An especially helpful essay on Aquinas and cosmological arguments is Scott MacDonald, 'Aquinas's Parasitic Cosmological Argument', *Medieval Philosophy and Theology* 1 (1991).

For introductions to and discussions of Scotus on cosmological arguments, see:

Efrem Bettoni, *Duns Scotus: The Basic Principles of His Philosophy* (Washington, DC, 1961).

Richard Cross, *Duns Scotus* (New York and Oxford, 1999).

William A. Frank and Allan B. Wolter, *Duns Scotus, Metaphysician* (West Lafayette, Indiana, 1995).

Allan Wolter, *The Philosophical Theology of Duns Scotus* (Ithaca and London, 1990), especially ch. 11.

Helpful background reading to Leibniz on cosmological arguments can be found in Craig's *The Cosmological Argument from Plato to Leibniz*, ch. 8. See also:

Nicholas Jolley (ed.), *The Cambridge Companion to Leibniz* (Cambridge, 1995), chs 4, 5, and 10.

G. H. R. Parkinson, *Logic and Reality in Leibniz's Metaphysics* (Oxford, 1965), ch. IV.

Nicholas Rescher, *Leibniz: An Introduction to his Philosophy* (Oxford, 1979), chs II and XIV.

For a famous debate on cosmological arguments, see Frederick Copleston and Bertrand Russell, 'The Argument from Contingency', reprinted in John Hick (ed.), *The Existence of God* (New York and London, 1964). For a reply to Anscombe on causation and beginnings, see David Gordon, 'Anscombe on Coming into Existence and Causation', *Analysis* 44 (1984).

Design arguments

Introduction

Goals and order

Cosmological arguments can be thought of as sparked by a desire to account for the sheer existence of things. But with design arguments the focus changes from the fact *that* the world exists to the fact that it exhibits certain *features*. What features? The basic answer given by all forms of design argument is: features that suggest mind or intelligence. According to the Old Testament: 'The heavens are telling out the glory of God; and the firmament proclaims his handiwork.'[1] And defenders of design arguments are out to maintain that the world works in a way which suggests that it is governed, planned, or ordered, though not by any mind or intelligence within it. Their basic idea is that it is governed, planned, or ordered by what we might call an 'author of nature' or a 'cosmic manufacturer' or 'God'.

But why? One answer given has centred on the suggestion that the world contains things which act or behave in ways that seem goal-oriented rather than random. We often say that some processes occur by chance. But is it by chance that hearts function as they do? Is it by chance that the wombs of female animals foster the embryos contained in them? Many would say that hearts, wombs, and many other comparable things, work according to a purpose or function and that they can therefore be thought of as goal-directed. We can ask 'What are they *for*?'. Yet if that is true, how are we to account for their tending to their goals as they do? If we think of them as having a function or purpose, it cannot be one which we have built into them. The parts of a computer have functions or purposes because they have been designed by technologists. But no human technologist can be appealed to as responsible for the functions or purposes displayed by things in nature. So could it be that function or purpose in nature reflects the intentions of something like a 'cosmic technologist'? According to some kinds of design argument, that is exactly what we should suppose. As some philosophers would put it, we should think of nature in 'teleological' terms.[2] And we should then account for its 'teleology'

---

1. *Psalm* 19.
2. The adjective 'teleological', and the related noun 'teleology', come from the Greek *telos* (end) and *logos* (speech). 'Teleology' originally signified teaching about ends and goals in nature. It then came to refer to their actual presence. So people often use the word 'teleology' to refer to what they take to be indications of function or purpose in nature.

with reference to non-human intention. Hence it is that in much philosophical literature you will find design arguments described as 'teleological arguments'.

Some design arguments, however, tend to focus more on the notion of regularity than on the notion of function or purpose. For suppose we do not feel happy with the suggestion that things in nature have 'functions' or act with a 'purpose'. We might still find it hard to deny that the world as a whole behaves in an exceedingly regular way. Some have insisted that it is governed by 'laws of nature'. And even if we do not like that suggestion (more on which in Part IV), all of us assume that there are basic and regular ways in which things in nature work, ones which have allowed us to develop sciences such as biology, chemistry, and physics. So how are we to account for natural regularity like this? We might say that it calls for no explanation since it is unremarkable. But some people have found it both remarkable and in need of explanation. And they have subsequently appealed to it as a ground for supposing that there is non-human mind at work in the world. These, too, can be taken as defenders of design arguments.

The history of the arguments: early days

Design arguments, like cosmological ones, go back a long way. Plato, for instance, suggested that order in the material world is the work of a divine craftsman, or Demiurge, and that mind accounts for order and motion in the cosmos as a whole.[3] In Cicero's *De Natura Deorum* (*On the Nature of the Gods*), a figure called Lucilius asks: 'What could be more clear or obvious when we look up to the sky and contemplate the heavens, than that there is some divinity of superior intelligence?' The point he seems to be making is that the operation of the universe must be somehow controlled or caused by a mind much greater than any of ours.[4]

But should we use the word 'God' in this context? And should we say that the way the world goes is evidence for the existence of God as thought of in religions such as Judaism, Islam, and Christianity? For clear affirmative answers to these questions, we need to jump from philosophers such as Plato to medieval authors such as Aquinas, who offers a design argument in Chapter 23. Here he argues that nature is ruled by an 'intellect' which gives 'order to nature'.

What does he mean in saying this? His discussion makes much of the terms 'material cause', 'efficient cause', and 'final cause'. But what does he mean by them?

A cause (*causa*), for Aquinas, is what Aristotle called an *aition*.[5] The Greek word *aition* (often translated as 'cause') is connected with the verb 'to blame' or 'to hold accountable', and it signified that which somehow accounts for something. According to Aristotle, an *aition* is an explanation. It answers questions of the form 'How come?' or 'On account of what?' And, so Aristotle argues, there are four kinds of answer to questions of this form (answers referring to four kinds of causes).

---

3. Cf. the *Timaeus* and the *Laws*.
4. Cicero, *The Nature of the Gods* (trans. Horace C. P. McGregor, Harmondsworth, 1972), p. 24.
5. In Chapter 23 Aquinas is explicitly alluding to what Aristotle says about causes in Book 1 (A) of Aristotle's *Metaphysics*. Aristotle's treats more fully of causes in his *Physics*.

Suppose I drop a cup. You might expect it to shatter. But it does not. You ask 'Why didn't the cup shatter?' I explain: 'It's made of plastic.'

Suppose I drop an ornament and it shatters. You ask 'Why did it shatter?' I explain: 'It's made of glass.'

In each case here I offer an explanation which refers you to *what something is made of*, and, so Aristotle would have said, I here invoke a 'material cause'. The cup did not smash because it was made of plastic. The ornament smashed because it was made of glass.

But now suppose that we are looking at a cat cleaning its whiskers. You might wonder which cats are its parents. I might say: 'Tibbles and Ginger.' You might know nothing of cats and might therefore ask 'Why is this thing doing that?' I might reply: 'Because it's a cat.' And I might flesh out what I say by noting what cats are: things which characteristically behave as we see this cat behaving.

In the first case here, Aristotle would take me to be invoking an 'efficient cause' (or a pair of efficient causes). For in referring to Tibbles and Ginger I am explaining *what produced* something. In the second case, I would be offering an explanation which refers to *what a thing is by nature*, or, in Aristotle's language, I would be invoking a 'formal cause'.

And, so Aristotle would add, we would be looking for a 'final cause' if, for example, we wonder what the tablets in my medicine cabinet are *for*. My doctor might say: 'These are to lower your blood-pressure, and these are to regulate your heart-beat.' According to Aristotle, my doctor would here be offering an explanation in terms of *an end or goal*. And, says Aristotle, this would be to refer to a *final cause* or to *final causality*

For Aristotle, then, there are four kinds of cause (material, efficient, formal, and final). And in Chapter 23 Aquinas basically reiterates this teaching. In doing so, however, he emphasizes final causation as something found in nature, not just in the products of human inventors. Nature, so he suggests, contain many things which act in an orderly manner so that results come about in a way that cannot be captured by talking of matter, efficient cause, or chance. And he holds that this fact cannot be explained except in terms of intention lying beyond the world.

The history of the argument: later days

One way of reading Aquinas on final causation is to see him as arguing that we live in a *context* rather than a *chaos* and that this fact is reason for supposing that we live in a world that is *planned*. And as the intricate structures of nature came to be more and more discovered by scientists, design arguments became increasingly popular with religious apologists, often themselves distinguished scientists such as Isaac Newton (1642–1727) and Robert Boyle (1627–91). Newton saw his scientific theories as confirming that the world shows forth the wisdom and power of a 'non-mechanical' deity working on the mechanisms of nature by 'immaterial forces'.[6] Boyle argued in a similar way. In *The*

6. Cf. Isaac Newton, *The Mathematical Principles of Natural Philosophy* (1687; 2nd edn, 1713; 3rd edn, 1726).

Origin of Forms and Qualities (1666) he compares natural organisms with machines whose parts function with a definite purpose.[7] In *The Usefulness of Experimental Natural Philosophy* (1663), Boyle compares the world as a whole with clocks and watches—like the cathedral clock in Strasbourg, in which, says Boyle,

the several pieces making up that curious engine are so framed and adapted, and are put into such motion, that though the numerous wheels, and other parts of it, move several ways, and that without any thing either of knowledge or design; yet each performs its part in order to the various end, for which it was contrived, as regularly and uniformly as if it knew and were concerned to do its duty.[8]

The analogy between the universe and a time-piece was taken up by many defenders of design arguments after Boyle. But it is especially well known from its employment by William Paley (1743–1805). In his *Natural Theology; or Evidences of the Existence and Attributes of the Deity, Collected from the Appearances of Nature*, Paley notes that the parts of a watch are obviously put together to achieve a definite result. And, so he suggests, the universe resembles a watch and must therefore be accounted for in terms of intelligent and purposive agency.

You can read what he has to say in Chapter 24. This requires no explanatory comment since it contains no technical terminology. But is Paley right? Even before he published his *Natural Theology*, philosophers were challenging the value of design arguments. Notable examples include Hume and Kant.

Hume and Kant on design arguments

Hume's major treatment of the claim that nature exhibits divine design is to be found in his *Dialogues Concerning Natural Religion* (1779).[9] This text, from which Chapter 25 comes, has given rise to much speculation as to which of its characters (if any) represents the views of its author. Yet abstracting from such considerations, one can clearly identify in the *Dialogues* a number of objections to arguments suggesting that the way the world goes is evidence for the existence of God. We may summarize some of them by means of the following questions:

1. Design arguments depend on there being a strong resemblance between the universe and artefacts produced by people. But is there such a resemblance?
2. Why should we suppose that our experience of designing agents can furnish us with a model for understanding the operations of the entire universe? 'Is a part of nature a rule for another part very wide of the former?'
3. Since we can only infer the presence of design in the light of our experience of many instances of this, and since the world is not something examples of which we

---

7. For the text, see M. A. Stewart (ed.), *Selected Philosophical Papers of Robert Boyle* (Manchester, 1979).
8. Marie Boas Hall, *Robert Boyle on Natural Philosophy: An Essay with Selections from His Writings* (Bloomington, Indiana, 1965), p. 146.
9. But also see Hume's *An Inquiry Concerning Human Understanding*, Section XI.

have experience (there is only one world), why suppose that it should be taken to be something designed?

4. If we argue for the existence of God by comparing the world with artefacts produced by people, should we not conclude that God is finite and imperfect?
5. Human artefacts are often constructed by many people. So should we not conclude that there might be many gods?
6. If we argue for the existence of God by comparing the world with artefacts designed by people, should we not conclude that God is exactly like a human being? Why not become 'a perfect anthropomorphite'?
7. How can we be sure that the present orderly state of the universe is not a temporary one?

In Hume's treatment of design arguments the focus is definitely on a supposed analogy between human products and what we find in nature, one which Hume seems seriously to challenge. In Kant's treatment, the analogy is challenged once again, though much less severely. Kant allows that there is an analogy between artefacts and things which we find in nature. He is even prepared to grant that it is not unreasonable to argue from nature to 'a causality similar to that responsible for artificial products'. But he denies that this amounts to a proof of God's existence. For that, he says, we need other arguments— 'transcendental' ones, which he discusses in the *Critique of Pure Reason* before he gets to the topic of God as a designer. He sees them as intended to establish that there is something which can be known to exist of absolute necessity (for more on which, see 'Ontological arguments' section below). He also finds them to be fatally flawed. So his ultimate verdict on design arguments is unfavourable.

And onwards?

The negative approach to design arguments found in Hume and Kant has been much echoed since their time. You can find it, for example, in the writings of Charles Darwin (1809–82). Should we say that the existence and working of living things is evidence of divine design? Darwin suggests that we should not. According to him, living things have arisen because of conditions favouring the development of species which come about due to chance factors at a genetic level. Appealing to the notion of 'Natural Selection', Darwin argues that the living organisms we know about are those which have survived a struggle for existence owing to useful variations. We may take them to manifest design. But what accounts for the appearance of design is the disappearance of the unfit. There are no hostile witnesses to testify against design. They have all been killed off.

Other critics of design arguments have, among other things, challenged the suggestion that what we might take to be order in nature is something actually there as an objective reality. In the *Critique of Pure Reason*, Kant maintains that we are unable to experience 'things in themselves'. According to him, we are presented in experience with an undifferentiated manifold, and we order our experience of things in themselves as our understanding imposes such categories as unity and plurality, cause and effect. Influenced by this view, some thinkers have suggested that the argument from design fails because order is only a product of the human mind: it is 'people imposed' not 'God imposed'.

Yet design arguments continue to be defended by large numbers of philosophers. Two contemporary supporters of them are Richard Swinburne and Robert Hambourger, whose views can be found in Chapters 27 and 28. Focusing especially on Hume, Swinburne defends a design argument which turns on the notion of 'regularities of succession'. In his discussion, Hambourger concentrates on the notions of chance, cause, and explanation. Reading these philosophers with an eye on the other chapters in this section should give you plenty worth thinking about when it comes to evaluating design arguments as specimens of natural theology.

Chapter 23

Is the world ruled by providence?

Thomas Aquinas

Providence is concerned with the direction of things to an end. Therefore, whoever denies final causality should also deny providence. Now, those who deny final causality take two positions.

Some of the very ancient philosophers admitted only a material cause. Since they would not admit an efficient cause, they could not affirm the existence of an end, for an end is a cause only in so far as it moves the efficient cause. Other and later philosophers admitted an efficient cause, but said nothing about a final cause. According to both schools, everything was necessarily caused by previously existing causes, material or efficient.

This position, however, was criticized by other philosophers on the following grounds. Material and efficient causes, as such, cause only the existence of their effects. They are not sufficient to produce goodness in them so that they be aptly disposed in themselves, so that they could continue to exist, and toward others so that they could help them. Heat, for example, of its very nature and of itself can break down other things, but this breaking down is good and helpful only if it happens up to a certain point and in a certain way. Consequently, if we do not admit that there exist in nature causes other than heat and similar agents, we cannot give any reason why things happen in a good and orderly way.

Moreover, whatever does not have a determinate cause happens by accident. Consequently, if the position mentioned above were true, all the harmony and usefulness found in things would be the result of chance. This was actually what Empedocles held. He asserted that it was by accident that the parts of animals came together in this way through friendship—and this was his explanation of an animal and of a frequent occurrence! This explanation, of course, is absurd, for those things that happen by chance, happen only rarely; we know from experience, however, that harmony and usefulness are found in nature either at all times or at least for the most part. This cannot be the result of mere chance; it must be because an end is intended. What lacks intellect or knowledge, however, cannot tend directly toward an end. It can do this only if someone else's knowledge has established an end for it, and directs it to that end. Consequently, since natural things have no knowledge, there must be some previously existing intelligence directing them to an end, like an archer who gives a definite motion to an arrow so that it will wing its

Thomas Aquinas from *De Veritate* translated by Robert W. Mulligan (Henry Regnery Co, 1952).

way to a determined end. Now, the hit made by the arrow is said to be the work not of the arrow alone but also of the person who shot it. Similarly, philosophers call every work of nature the work of intelligence.

Consequently, the world is ruled by the providence of that intellect which gave this order to nature; and we may compare the providence by which God rules the world to the domestic foresight by which a man rules his family, or to the political foresight by which a ruler governs a city or a kingdom, and directs the acts of others to a definite end. There is no providence, however, in God with respect to Himself, since whatever is in Him is an end, not a means to it.

Chapter 24

An especially famous design argument

William Paley

State of the argument

IN crossing a heath, suppose I pitched my foot against a *stone*, and were asked how the stone came to be there, I might possibly answer, that, for anything I knew to the contrary, it had lain there for ever; nor would it, perhaps, be very easy to show the absurdity of this answer. But suppose I had found a *watch* upon the ground, and it should be inquired how the watch happened to be in that place, I should hardly think of the answer which I had before given—that, for anything I knew, the watch might have always been there. Yet why should not this answer serve for the watch as well as for the stone? Why is it not as admissible in the second case as in the first? For this reason, and for no other, viz., that, when we come to inspect the watch, we perceive (what we could not discover in the stone) that its several parts are framed and put together for a purpose, e.g. that they are so formed and adjusted as to produce motion, and that motion so regulated as to point out the hour of the day; that, if the different parts had been differently shaped from what they are, of a different size from what they are, or placed after any other manner, or in any other order than that in which they are placed, either no motion at all would have been carried on in the machine, or none which would have answered the use that is now served by it. To reckon up a few of the plainest of these parts, and of their offices, all tending to one result:—We see a cylindrical box containing a coiled elastic spring, which, by its endeavour to relax itself, turns round the box. We next observe a flexible chain (artificially wrought for the sake of flexure) communicating the action of the spring from the box to the fusee. We then find a series of wheels, the teeth of which catch in, and apply to, each other, conducting the motion from the fusee to the balance, and from the balance to the pointer, and, at the same time, by the size and shape of those wheels, so regulating that motion as to terminate in causing an index, by an equable and measured progression, to pass over a given space in a given time. We take notice that the wheels are made of brass, in order to keep them from rust; the springs of steel, no other metal being so elastic; that over the face of the watch there is placed a glass, a material employed in no other part of the work, but in the room of which, if there had been any other than a transparent

William Paley 'Natural Theology', chapters 1–3, from William Paley *Natural Theology* (C. Knight, 1836).

substance, the hour could not be seen without opening the case. This mechanism being observed, (it requires indeed an examination of the instrument, and perhaps some previous knowledge of the subject, to perceive and understand it; but being once, as we have said, observed and understood,) the inference, we think, is inevitable, that the watch must have had a maker: that there must have existed, at some time, and at some place or other, an artificer or artificers who formed it for the purpose which we find it actually to answer; who comprehended its construction, and designed its use.

I. Nor would it, I apprehend, weaken the conclusion, that we had never seen a watch made; that we had never known an artist capable of making one; that we were altogether incapable of executing such a piece of workmanship ourselves, or of understanding in what manner it was performed; all this being no more than what is true of some exquisite remains of ancient art, of some lost arts, and, to the generality of mankind, of the more curious productions of modern manufacture. Does one man in a million know how oval frames are turned? Ignorance of this kind exalts our opinion of the unseen and unknown artist's skill, if he be unseen and unknown, but raises no doubt in our minds of the existence and agency of such an artist, at some former time, and in some place or other. Nor can I perceive that it varies at all the inference, whether the question arise concerning a human agent, or concerning an agent of a different species, or an agent possessing, in some respect, a different nature.

II. Neither, secondly, would it invalidate our conclusion, that the watch sometimes went wrong, or that it seldom went exactly right. The purpose of the machinery, the design, and the designer, might be evident, and, in the case supposed, would be evident, in whatever way we accounted for the irregularity of the movement, or whether we could account for it or not. It is not necessary that a machine be perfect, in order to show with what design it was made: still less necessary, where the only question is, whether it were made with any design at all.

III. Nor, thirdly, would it bring any uncertainty into the argument, if there were a few parts of the watch, concerning which we could not discover, or had not yet discovered, in what manner they conduced to the general effect; or even some parts, concerning which we could not ascertain whether they conduced to that effect in any manner whatever. For, as to the first branch of the case, if by the loss, or disorder, or decay of the parts in question, the movement of the watch were found in fact to be stopped, or disturbed, or retarded, no doubt would remain in our minds as to the utility or intention of these parts, although we should be unable to investigate the manner according to which, or the connexion by which, the ultimate effect depended upon their action or assistance; and the more complex is the machine, the more likely is this obscurity to arise. Then, as to the second thing supposed, namely, that there were parts which might be spared without prejudice to the movement of the watch, and that he had proved this by experiment, these superfluous parts, even if we were completely assured that they were such, would not vacate the reasoning which we had instituted concerning other parts.

The indication of contrivance remained, with respect to them, nearly as it was before.

IV. Nor, fourthly, would any man in his senses think the existence of the watch, with its various machinery, accounted for, by being told that it was one out of possible combinations of material forms; that whatever he had found in the place where he found the watch, must have contained some internal configuration or other; and that this configuration might be the structure now exhibited, viz., of the works of a watch, as well as a different structure.

V. Nor, fifthly, would it yield his inquiry more satisfaction, to be answered, that there existed in things a principle of order, which had disposed the parts of the watch into their present form and situation. He never knew a watch made by the principle of order; nor can he even form to himself an idea of what is meant by a principle of order, distinct from the intelligence of the watchmaker.

VI. Sixthly, he would be surprised to hear that the mechanism of the watch was no proof of contrivance, only a motive to induce the mind to think so:

VII. And not less surprised to be informed, that the watch in his hand was nothing more than the result of the laws of *metallic* nature. It is a perversion of language to assign any law as the efficient, operative cause of anything. A law presupposes an agent; for it is only the mode according to which an agent proceeds: it implies a power; for it is the order according to which that power acts. Without this agent, without this power, which are both distinct from itself, the *law* does nothing, is nothing. The expression, 'the law of metallic nature,' may sound strange and harsh to a philosophic ear; but it seems quite as justifiable as some others which are more familiar to him, such as 'the law of vegetable nature,' 'the law of animal nature,' or, indeed, as 'the law of nature' in general, when assigned as the cause of phenomena, in exclusion of agency and power, or when it is substituted into the place of these.

VIII. Neither, lastly, would our observer be driven out of his conclusion, or from his confidence in its truth, by being told that he knew nothing at all about the matter. He knows enough for his argument: he knows the utility of the end: he knows the subserviency and adaptation of the means to the end. These points being known, his ignorance of other points, his doubts concerning other points, affect not the certainty of his reasoning. The consciousness of knowing little need not beget a distrust of that which he does know.

State of the argument continued

Suppose in the next place, that the person who found the watch should, after some time, discover that, in addition to all the properties which he had hitherto observed in it, it possessed the unexpected property of producing, in the course of its movement, another watch like itself (the thing is conceivable); that it contained within it a mechanism, a system of parts, a mould, for instance, or a complex adjustment of lathes, files, and other tools, evidently and separately calculated for this purpose; let us inquire what effect ought such a discovery to have upon his former conclusion.

I. The first effect would be to increase his admiration of the contrivance, and his conviction of the consummate skill of the contriver. Whether he regarded the object of the contrivance, the distinct apparatus, the intricate, yet in many parts intelligible mechanism by which it was carried on, he would perceive, in this new observation, nothing but an additional reason for doing what he had already done—for referring the construction of the watch to design, and to supreme art. If that construction *without* this property, or which is the same thing, before this property had been noticed, proved intention and art to have been employed about it, still more strong would the proof appear, when he came to the knowledge of this further property, the crown and perfection of all the rest.

II. He would reflect, that though the watch before him were, in *some sense*, the maker of the watch which was fabricated in the course of its movements, yet it was in a very different sense from that in which a carpenter, for instance, is the maker of a chair—the author of its contrivance, the cause of the relation of its parts to their use. With respect to these; the first watch was no cause at all to the second; in no such sense as this was it the author of the constitution and order, either of the parts which the new watch contained, or of the parts by the aid and instrumentality of which it was produced. We might possibly say, but with great latitude of expression, that a stream of water ground corn; but no latitude of expression would allow us to say, no stretch of conjecture could lead us to think, that the stream of water built the mill, though it were too ancient for us to know who the builder was. What the stream of water does in the affair is neither more nor less than this; by the application of an unintelligent impulse to a mechanism previously arranged, arranged independently of it, and arranged by intelligence, an effect is produced, viz., the corn is ground. But the effect results from the arrangement. The force of the stream cannot be said to be the cause or the author of the effect, still less of the arrangement. Understanding and plan in the formation of the mill were not the less necessary for any share which the water has in grinding the corn; yet is this share the same as that which the watch would have contributed to the production of the new watch, upon the supposition assumed in the last section. Therefore,

III. Though it be now no longer probable that the individual watch which our observer had found was made immediately by the hand of an artificer, yet doth not this alteration in anywise affect the inference, that an artificer had been originally employed and concerned in the production. The argument from design remains as it was. Marks of design and contrivance are no more accounted for now than they were before. In the same thing, we may ask for the cause of different properties. We may ask for the cause of the colour of a body, of its hardness, of its heat; and these causes may be all different. We are now asking for the cause of that subserviency to a use; that relation to an end, which we have remarked in the watch before us. No answer is given to this question, by telling us that a preceding watch produced it. There cannot be design without a designer; contrivance, without a contriver; order, without choice; arrangement, without anything capable of arranging; subserviency and relation to a purpose, without that which could intend a purpose; means suitable to an end, and executing their office in accomplishing that end, without the end ever having been contemplated, or the means accommodated to it. Arrangement, disposition of parts, subserviency of means to an end, relation of instruments to a use, imply the presence of intelligence and mind. No one, therefore, can rationally believe, that the insensible, inanimate watch, from which the watch before us issued, was the proper cause of the mechanism we so much admire in it;—could be truly said to have constructed the instrument, disposed its parts, assigned their office, determined their order, action, and mutual dependency, combined their several motions into one result, and that also a result connected with the utilities of other beings. All these properties, therefore, are as much unaccounted for as they were before.

IV. Nor is anything gained by running the difficulty farther back, *i.e.*, by supposing the watch before us to have been produced from another watch, that from a former, and so on indefinitely. Our going back ever so far, brings us no nearer to the least degree of satisfaction upon the subject. Contrivance is still unaccounted for. We still want a contriver. A designing mind is neither supplied by this supposition, nor dispensed with. If the difficulty were diminished the farther we went back, by going back indefinitely we might exhaust it. And this is the only case to which this sort of reasoning applies. Where there is a tendency, or, as we increase the number of terms, a continual approach towards a limit, *there*, by supposing the number of terms to be what is called infinite, we may conceive the limit to be attained; but where there is no such tendency or approach, nothing is effected by lengthening the series. There is no difference as to the point in question, (whatever there may be as to many points,) between one series and another; between a series which is finite, and a series which is infinite. A chain, composed of an infinite number of links, can no more support itself than a chain composed of a finite number of links. And of this we are assured; (though we never *can* have tried the experiment,) because, by increasing the number of links, from ten for instance to a hundred, from a hundred to a thousand, &c., we make not the smallest approach, we observe not the smallest tendency towards self-support. There is no difference in this respect (yet there may be a great difference in several respects,) between a chain of a greater or less length, between one chain and another, between one that is finite and one that is infinite. This very much resembles the case before us. The machine which we are inspecting demonstrates, by its construction, contrivance and design. Contrivance must have had a contriver; design, a designer; whether the machine immediately proceeded from another machine or not. That circumstance alters not the case. That other machine may, in like manner, have proceeded from a former machine: nor does that alter the case; the contrivance must have had a contriver. That former one from one preceding it: no alteration still; a contriver is still necessary. No tendency is perceived, no approach towards a diminution of this necessity. It is the same with any and every succession of these machines; a succession of ten, of a hundred, of a thousand; with one series, as with another; a series which is finite, as with a series which is infinite. In whatever other respects they may differ, in this they do not. In all, equally, contrivance and design are unaccounted for.

The question is not simply, How came the first watch into existence? which question, it may be pretended, is done away by supposing the series of watches thus produced from one another to have been infinite, and consequently to have had no such *first*, for which it was necessary to provide a cause. This, perhaps, would have been nearly the state of the question, if nothing had been before us but an unorganized, unmechanized substance, without mark or indication of contrivance. It might be difficult to show that such substance could not have existed from eternity, either in succession (if it were possible, which I think it is not, for unorganized bodies to spring from one another,) or by individual perpetuity. But that is not the question now. To suppose it to be so, is to suppose that it made no difference whether he had found a watch or a stone. As it is, the metaphysics of that question have no place: for, in the watch which we are examining, are seen contrivance, design; an end, a purpose; means for the end, adaptation to the purpose. And the question which irresistibly presses upon our thoughts, is, Whence this contrivance and design? The thing required is the intending mind, the adapted hand, the intelligence by which that hand was directed. This question, this demand, is not shaken off, by increasing a number or succession of substances, destitute of these properties; nor the more, by increasing the number to infinity. If it be said, that, upon the supposition of one watch being produced from another in the course of that other's movements, and by means of the mechanism within it, we have a cause for the watch in my hand, viz., the watch from which it proceeded,—I deny, that for the design, the contrivance, the suitableness of means to an end, the adaptation of instruments to a use, (all of which we discover in the watch,) we have any cause whatever. It is in vain, therefore, to assign a series of such causes, or to allege that a series may be carried back to infinity; for I do not admit that we have yet any cause at all for the phenomena, still less any series of causes either finite or infinite. Here is contrivance, but no contriver; proofs of design, but no designer.

V. Our observer would further also reflect, that the maker of the watch before him was, in truth and reality, the maker of every watch produced from it: there being no difference (except that the latter manifests a more exquisite skill,) between the making of another watch with his own hands, by the mediation of files, lathes, chisels, &c., and the disposing, fixing, and inserting of these instruments, or of others equivalent to them, in the body of the watch already made in such a manner, as to form a new watch in the course of the movements which he had given to the old one. It is only working by one set of tools instead of another.

The conclusion which the *first* examination of the watch, of its works, construction, and movement, suggested, was, that it must have had, for cause and author of that construction, an artificer who understood its mechanism, and designed its use. This conclusion is invincible. A *second* examination presents us with a new discovery. The watch is found, in the course of its movement, to produce another watch, similar to itself; and not only so, but we perceive in it a system, or organization, separately calculated for that purpose. What effect would this discovery have, or ought it to have, upon our former inference? What, as hath already been said, but to increase, beyond measure, our admiration of the skill which had been employed in the formation of such a machine? Or shall it, instead of this, all at once turn us round to an opposite conclusion, viz., that no art or skill whatever has been concerned in the business, although all other evidences of art and skill remain as they were, and this last and supreme piece of art be now added to the rest? Can this be maintained without absurdity? Yet this is atheism.

Application of the argument

This is atheism: for every indication of contrivace, every manifestation of design, which existed in the watch, exists in the works of nature; with the difference, on the side of nature, of being greater and more, and that in a degree which exceeds all computation. I mean that the contrivances of nature surpass the contrivances of art, in the complexity, subtilty, and curiosity of the mechanism; and still more, if possible, do they go beyond them in number and variety; yet in a multitude of cases, are not less evidently mechanical, not less evidently contrivances, not less evidently accommodated to their end, or suited to their office, than are the most perfect productions of human ingenuity.

Chapter 25

We cannot know that the world is designed by God

David Hume

N ot to lose any time in circumlocutions, said Cleanthes, addressing himself to Demea, much less in replying to the pious declamations of Philo; I shall briefly explain how I conceive this matter. Look round the world: Contemplate the whole and every part of it: You will find it to be nothing but one great machine, subdivided into an infinite number of lesser machines, which again admit of sub-divisions, to a degree beyond what human senses and faculties can trace and explain. All these various machines, and even their most minute parts, are adjusted to each other with an accuracy, which ravishes into admiration all men, who have ever contemplated them. The curious adapting of means to ends, throughout all nature, resembles exactly, though it much exceeds, the productions of human contrivance; of human design, thought, wisdom, and intelligence. Since therefore the effects resemble each other, we are led to infer, by all the rules of analogy, that the causes also resemble; and that the Author of nature is somewhat similar to the mind of man; though possessed of much larger faculties, proportioned to the grandeur of the work, which he has executed. By this argument *a posteriori*, and by this argument alone, do we prove at once existence of a Deity, and his similarity to human mind and intelligence.

I shall be so free, Cleanthes, said Demea, as to tell you, that from the beginning, I could not approve of your conclusion concerning the similarity of the Deity to men; still less can I approve of the mediums, by which you endeavour to establish it. What! No demonstration of the being of a God! No abstract arguments! No proofs *a priori*! Are these, which have hitherto been so much insisted on by philosophers, all fallacy, all sophism? Can we reach no farther in this subject than experience and probability? I will not say that this is betraying the cause of a Deity: But surely by this affected candour, you give advantage to atheists, which they never could obtain, by the mere dint of argument and reasoning.

What I chiefly scruple in this subject, said Philo, is not so much, that all religious arguments are by Cleanthes reduced to experience, as that they appear not to be even the most certain and irrefragable of that inferior kind. That a stone will fall, that fire will burn, that the earth has solidity, we have observed a thousand and a

David Hume extracts from 'Dialogues Concerning Natural Religion' *David Hume Dialogues Concerning Natural Religion and The Natural History of Religion* edited with an introduction by J. C. A. Gaskin (Oxford World's Classics, 1993), editorial matter copyright © J. C. A. Gaskin 1993, reprinted by permission of Oxford University Press.

thousand times; and when any new instance of this nature is presented, we draw without hesitation the accustomed inference. The exact similarity of cases gives us a perfect assurance of a similar event; and a stronger evidence is never desired nor sought after. But wherever you depart, in the least, from the similarity of the cases, you diminish proportionably the evidence; and may at last bring it to a very weak *analogy*, which is confessedly liable to error and uncertainty. After having experienced the circulation of the blood in human creatures, we make no doubt that it takes place in Titius and Mævius: But from its circulation in frogs and fishes, it is only a presumption, though a strong one, from analogy, that it takes place in men and other animals. The analogical reasoning is much weaker, when we infer the circulation of the sap in vegetables from our experience that the blood circulates in animals; and those, who hastily followed that imperfect analogy, are found, by more accurate experiments, to have been mistaken.

If we see a house, Cleanthes, we conclude, with the greatest certainty, that it had an architect or builder; because this is precisely that species of effect, which we have experienced to proceed from that species of cause. But surely you will not affirm, that the universe bears such a resemblance to a house, that we can with the same certainty infer a similar cause, or that the analogy is here entire and perfect. The dissimilitude is so striking, that the utmost you can here pretend to is a guess, a conjecture, a presumption concerning a similar cause; and how that pretension will be received in the world, I leave you to consider.

It would surely be very ill received, replied Cleanthes; and I should be deservedly blamed and detested, did I allow, that the proofs of a Deity amounted to no more than a guess or conjecture. But is the whole adjustment of means to ends in a house and in the universe so slight a resemblance? The œconomy of final causes? The order, proportion, and arrangement of every part? Steps of a stair are plainly contrived, that human legs may use them in mounting; and this inference is certain and infallible. Human legs are also contrived for walking and mounting; and this inference, I allow, is not altogether so certain, because of the dissimilarity which you remark; but does it, therefore, deserve the name only of presumption or conjecture?

Good God! cried Demea, interrupting him, where are we? Zealous defenders of religion allow, that the proofs of a Deity fall short of perfect evidence! And you, Philo, on whose assistance I depended, in proving the adorable mysteriousness of the divine nature, do you assent to all these extravagant opinions of Cleanthes? For what other name can I give them? Or why spare my censure, when such principles are advanced, supported by such an authority, before so young a man as Pamphilus?

You seem not to apprehend, replied Philo, that I argue with Cleanthes in his own way; and by showing him the dangerous consequences of his tenets, hope at last to reduce him to our opinion. But what sticks most with you, I observe, is the representation which Cleanthes has made of the argument *a posteriori*; and finding that that argument is likely to escape your hold and vanish into air, you think it so disguised, that you can scarcely believe it to be set in its true light. Now, however much I may dissent, in other respects, from the dangerous principles of Cleanthes, I must allow, that he has fairly represented that argument; and I shall endeavour so to state the matter to you, that you will entertain no farther scruples with regard to it.

Were a man to abstract from every thing which he knows or has seen, he would be altogether incapable, merely from his own ideas, to determine what kind of scene the universe must be, or to give the preference to one state or situation of things above another. For as nothing, which he clearly conceives, could be esteemed impossible or implying a contradiction, every chimera of his fancy would be upon an equal footing; nor could he assign any just reason, why he adheres to one idea or system, and rejects the others; which are equally possible.

Again; after he opens his eyes, and contemplates the world, as it really is, it would be impossible for him, at first, to assign the cause of any one event; much less, of the whole of things or of the universe. He might set his fancy a rambling; and she might bring him in an infinite variety of reports and representations. These would all be possible; but being all equally possible, he would never, of himself, give a satisfactory account for his preferring one of them to the rest. Experience alone can point out to him the true cause of any phenomenon.

Now according to this method of reasoning, Demea, it follows (and is, indeed, tacitly allowed by Cleanthes himself) that order, arrangement, or the adjustment of final causes is not, of itself, any proof of design; but only so far as it has been experienced to procceed from that principle. For aught we can know *a priori*, matter may contain the source or spring of order originally, within itself, as well as mind does; and there is no more difficulty in conceiving, that the several elements, from an internal unknown cause, may fall into the most exquisite arrangement, than to conceive that their ideas, in the great, universal mind, from a like internal, unknown cause, fall into that arrangement. The equal possibility of both these suppositions is allowed. But by experience we find (according to Cleanthes), that there is a difference between them. Throw several pieces of steel together, without shape or form; they will never arrange themselves so as to compose a watch: Stone, and mortar, and wood, without an architect, never erect a house. But the ideas in a human mind, we see, by an unknown, inexplicable œconomy, arrange themselves so as to form the plan of a watch or house. Experience, therefore, proves, that there is an original principle of order in mind, not in matter. From similar effects we infer similar causes. The adjustment of means to ends is alike in the universe, as in a machine of human contrivance. The causes, therefore, must be resembling.

I was from the beginning scandalised, I must own, with this resemblance, which is asserted, between the Deity and human creatures; and must conceive it to imply such a degradation of the supreme Being as no sound theist could endure. With your assistance, therefore, Demea, I shall endeavour to defend what you justly call the adorable mysteriousness of the divine nature, and shall refute this reasoning of Cleanthes; provided he allows, that I have made a fair representation of it.

When Cleanthes had assented, Philo, after a short pause, proceeded in the following manner.

That all inferences, Cleanthes, concerning fact, are founded on experience, and that all experimental reasonings are founded on the supposition, that similar causes prove similar effects, and similar effects similar causes; I shall not, at present, much dispute with you. But observe, I entreat you, with what extreme caution all just reasoners proceed in the transferring of experiments to similar cases. Unless the cases be exactly similar, they repose no perfect confidence in applying their past observation to any particular phenomenon. Every alteration of circumstances occasions a doubt concerning the event; and it requires new experiments to prove certainly, that the new circumstances are of no moment or importance. A change in bulk, situation, arrangement, age, disposition of the air, or surrounding bodies; any of these particulars may be attended with the most unexpected consequences: And unless the objects be quite familiar to us, it is the highest temerity to expect with assurance, after any of these changes, an event similar to that which before fell under our observation. The slow and deliberate steps of philosophers, here, if any where, are distinguished from the precipitate march of the vulgar, who, hurried on by the smallest similitude, are incapable of all discernment or consideration.

But can you think, Cleanthes, that your usual phlegm and philosophy have been preserved in so wide a step as you have taken, when you compared to the universe houses, ships, furniture, machines; and from their similarity in some circumstances inferred a similarity in their causes? Thought, design, intelligence, such as we dis-cover in men and other animals, is no more than one of the springs and principles of the universe, as well as heat or cold, attraction or repulsion, and a hundred others, which fall under daily observation. It is an active cause, by which some particular parts of nature, we find, produce alterations on other parts. But can a conclusion, with any propriety, be transferred from parts to the whole? Does not the great disproportion bar all comparison and inference? From observing the growth of a hair, can we learn any thing concerning the generation of a man? Would the manner of a leaf's blowing, even though perfectly known, afford us any instruction concerning the vegetation of a tree?

But allowing that we were to take the *operations* of one part of nature upon another for the foundation of our judgment concerning the *origin* of the whole (which never can be admitted); yet why select so minute, so weak, so bounded a principle as the reason and design of animals is found to be upon this planet? What peculiar privilege has this little agitation of the brain which we call thought, that we must thus make it the model of the whole universe? Our partiality in our own favour does indeed present it on all occasions: But sound philosophy ought care-fully to guard against so natural an illusion.

So far from admitting, continued Philo, that the operations of a part can afford us any just conclusion concerning the origin of the whole, I will not allow any one part to form a rule for another part, if the latter be very remote from the former. Is there any reasonable ground to conclude, that the inhabitants of other planets possess thought, intelligence, reason, or any thing similar to these faculties in men? When nature has so extremely diversified her manner of operation in this small globe; can we imagine, that she incessantly copies herself throughout so immense a universe? And if thought, as we may well suppose, be confined merely to this narrow corner, and has even there so limited a sphere of action; with what propriety can we assign it for the original cause of all things? The narrow views of a peasant, who makes his domestic œconomy the rule for the government of kingdoms, is in comparison a pardonable sophism.

But were we ever so much assured, that a thought and reason, resembling the human, were to be found throughout the whole universe, and were its activity elsewhere vastly greater and more commanding than it appears in this globe: Yet I cannot see, why the operations of a world, constituted, arranged, adjusted, can with any propriety be extended to a world, which is in its embryo-state, and is advancing towards that constitution and arrangement. By observation, we know somewhat of the œconomy, action, and nourishment of a finished animal; but we must transfer with great caution that observation to the growth of a fœtus in the womb, and still more, to the formation of an animalcule in the loins of its male parent. Nature, we find, even from our limited experience, possesses an infinite number of springs and principles, which incessantly discover themselves on every change of her position and situation. And what new and unknown principles would acturate her in so new and unknown a situation as that of the formation of a universe, we cannot, without the utmost temerity, pretend to determine.

A very small part of this great system, during a very short time, very imperfectly discovered to us: And do we thence pronounce decisively concerning the origin of the whole?

Admirable conclusion! Stone, wood, brick, iron, brass, have not, at this time, in this minute globe of earth, an order or arrangement without human art and contrivance: Therefore the universe could not originally attain its order and arrangement, without something similar to human art. But is a part of nature a rule for another part very wide of the former? Is it a rule for the whole? Is a very small part a rule for the universe? Is nature in one situation, a certain rule for nature in another situation, vastly different from the former?

And can you blame me, Cleanthes, if I here imitate the prudent reserve of Simonides, who, according to the noted story, being asked by Hiero, *What God was*? desired a day to think of it, and then two days more; and after that manner continually prolonged the term, without ever bringing in his definition or description? Could you even blame me, if I had answered at first, that *I did not know*, and was sensible that this subject lay vastly beyond the reach of my faculties? You might cry out sceptic and raillier as much as you pleased: But having found, in so many other subjects, much more familiar, the imperfections and even contradictions of human reason, I never should expect any success from its feeble conjectures, in a subject, so sublime, and so remote from the sphere of our observation. When two *species* of objects have always been observed to be conjoined together, I can *infer*, by custom, the existence of one wherever I *see* the existence of the other: And this I call an argument from experience. But how this arguument can have place, where the objects, as in the present case, are single, individual, without parallel, or specific resemblance, may be difficult to explain. And will any man tell me with a serious countenance, that an orderly universe must arise from some thought and art, like the human; because we have experience of it? To ascertain this reasoning, it were requisite, that we had experience of the origin of worlds; and it is not sufficient surely, that we have seen ships and cities arise from human art and contrivance. . . .

Now, Cleanthes, said Philo, with an air of alacrity and triumph, mark the consequences. *First,* By this method of reasoning, you renounce all claim to infinity in any of the attributes of the Deity. For as the cause ought only to be proportioned to the effect, and the effect, so far as it falls under our cognisance, is not infinite; what pretensions have we, upon your suppositions, to ascribe that attribute to the divine Being? You will still insist, that, by removing him so much from all similarity to human creatures, we give in to the most arbitrary hypothesis, and at the same time weaken all proofs of his existence.

Secondly, You have no reason, on your theory, for ascribing perfection to the Deity, even in his finite capacity; or for supposing him free from every error, mistake, or incoherence in his undertakings. There are many inexplicable difficulties in the works of nature, which, if we allow a perfect Author to be proved *a priori,* are easily solved, and become only seeming difficulties, from the narrow capacity of man, who cannot trace infinite relations. But according to your method of reasoning, these difficulties become all real; and perhaps will be insisted on, as new instances of likeness to human art and contrivance. At least, you must acknowledge, that it is impossible for us to tell, from our limited views, whether this system contains any great faults, or deserves any considerable praise, if compared to other possible, and even real systems. Could a peasant, if the Æneid were read to him, pronounce that poem to be absolutely faultless, or even assign to it its proper rank among the productions of human wit; he, who had never seen any other production?

But were this world ever so perfect a production, it must still remain uncertain, whether all the excellencies of the work can justly be ascribed to the workman. If we survey a ship, what an exalted idea must we form of the ingenuity of the carpenter, who framed so complicated, useful, and beautiful a machine? And what surprise must we entertain, when we find him a stupid mechanic, who imitated others, and copied an art, which, through a long succession of ages, after multiplied trials, mistakes, corrections, deliberations, and controversies, had been gradually improving? Many worlds might have been botched and bungled, throughout an eternity, ere this system was struck out: Much labour lost: Many fruitless trials made: And a slow, but continued improvement carried on during infinite ages in the art of world-making. In such subjects, who can determine, where the truth; nay, who can conjecture where the probability, lies; amidst a great number of hypotheses which may be proposed, and a still greater number which may be imagined?

And what shadow of an argument, continued Philo, can you produce, from your hypothesis, to prove the unity of the Deity? A great number of men join in building a house or ship, in rearing a city, in framing a commonwealth: Why may not several

Deities combine in contriving and framing a world? This is only so much greater similarity to human affairs. By sharing the work among several, we may so much farther limit the attributes of each, and get rid of that extensive power and knowledge, which must be supposed in one Deity, and which, according to you, can only serve to weaken the proof of his existence. And if such foolish, such vicious creatures as man can yet often unite in framing and executing one plan; how much more those Deities or Dæmons, whom we may suppose several degrees more perfect?

To multiply causes, without necessity, is indeed contrary to true philosophy: But this principle applies not to the present case. Were one Deity antecedently proved by your theory, who were possessed of every attribute requisite to the production of the universe; it would be needless, I own (though not absurd) to suppose any other Deity existent. But while it is still a question, whether all these attributes are united in one subject, or dispersed among several independent Beings: By what phenomena in nature can we pretend to decide the controversy? Where we see a body raised in a scale, we are sure that there is in the opposite scale, however concealed from sight, some counterpoising weight equal to it: But it is still allowed to doubt, whether that weight be an aggregate of several distinct bodies, or one uniform united mass. And if the weight requisite very much exceeds any thing which we have ever seen conjoined in any single body, the former supposition becomes still more probable and natural. An intelligent Being of such vast power and capacity, as is necessary to produce the universe, or, to speak in the language of ancient philosophy, so prodigious an animal, exceeds all analogy, and even comprehension.

But farther, Cleanthes; men are mortal, and renew their species by generation; and this is common to all living creatures. The two great sexes of male and female, says Milton, animate the world. Why must this circumstance, so universal, so essential, be excluded from those numerous and limited Deities? Behold then the theogony of ancient times brought back upon us.

And why not become a perfect anthropomorphite? Why not assert the Deity or Deities to be corporeal, and to have eyes, a nose, mouth, ears, &c.? Epicurus maintained, that no man had ever seen reason but in a human figure; therefore the gods must have a human figure. And this argument, which is deservedly so much ridiculed by Cicero, becomes, according to you, solid and philosophical.

In a word, Cleanthes, a man, who follows your hypothesis, is able, perhaps, to assert, or conjecture, that the universe, sometime, arose from something like design: But beyond that position he cannot ascertain one single circumstance, and is left afterwards to fix every point of his theology, by the utmost licence of fancy and hypothesis. This world, for aught he knows, is very faulty and imperfect, compared to a superior standard; and was only the first rude essay of some infant Deity, who afterwards abandoned it, ashamed of his lame performance; it is the work only of some dependent, inferior Deity; and is the object of derision to his superiors: it is the production of old age and dotage in some superannuated Deity; and ever since his death, has run on at adventures, from the first impulse and active force, which it received from him. . . . You justly give signs of horror, Demea, at these strange suppositions: But these, and a thousand more of the same kind, are Cleanthes's suppositions, not mine. From the moment the attributes of the Deity are supposed finite, all these have place. And I cannot, for my part, think, that so wild and unsettled a system of theology is, in any respect, preferable to none at all.

. . .

In subjects, adapted to the narrow compass of human reason, there is commonly but one determination, which carries probability or conviction with it; and to a man of sound judgment, all other suppositions, but that one, appear entirely absurd and chimerical. But in such questions as the present, a hundred contradictory views may preserve a kind of imperfect analogy; and invention has here full scope to exert itself. Without any great effort of thought, I believe that I could, in an instant, propose other systems of cosmogony, which would have some faint appearance of truth; though it is a thousand, a million to one, if either yours or any one of mine be the true system.

For instance; what if I should revive the old Epicurean hypothesis? This is commonly; and I believe, justly, esteemed the most absurd system, that has yet been proposed; yet, I know not, whether, with a few alterations, it might not be brought to bear a faint appearance of probability. Instead of supposing matter infinite, as Epicurus did; let us suppose it finite. A finite number of particles is only susceptible of finite transpositions: And it must happen, in an eternal duration, that every possible order or position must be tried an infinite number of times. This world, therefore, with all its events, even the most minute, has before been produced and destroyed, and will again be produced and destroyed, without any bounds and limitations. No one, who has a conception of the powers of infinite, in comparison of finite, will ever scruple this determination.

But this supposes, said Demea, that matter can acquire motion, without any voluntary agent or first mover.

And where is the difficulty, replied Philo, of that supposition? Every event, before experience, is equally difficult and incomprehensible; and every event, after experience, is equally easy and intelligible. Motion, in many instances, from gravity, from elasticity, from electricity, begins in matter, without any known voluntary agent; and to suppose always, in these cases, an unknown voluntary agent, is mere hypothesis; and hypothesis attended with no advantages. The beginning of motion in matter itself is as conceivable *a priori* as its communication from mind and intelligence.

Besides, why may not motion have been propagated by impulse through all eternity, and the same stock of it, or nearly the same, be still upheld in the universe? As much as is lost by the composition of motion, as much is gained by its resolution. And whatever the causes are, the fact is certain, that matter is, and always has been in continual agitation, as far as human experience or tradition reaches. There is not probably, at present, in the whole universe, one particle of matter at absolute rest.

And this very consideration too, continued Philo, which we have stumbled on in the course of the argument, suggests a new hypothesis of cosmogony, that is not absolutely absurd and improbable. Is there a system, an order, an œconomy of things, by which matter can preserve that perpetual agitation, which seems essential to it, and yet maintain a constancy in the forms, which it produces? There certainly is such an œconomy: For this is actually the case with the present world. The continual motion of matter, therefore, in less than infinite transpositions, must produce this œconomy or order; and by its very nature, that order, when once established, supports itself, for many ages, if not to eternity. But wherever matter is so poised, arranged, and adjusted as to continue in perpetual motion, and yet preserve a constancy in the forms, its situation must, of necessity, have all the same appearance of art and contrivance which we observe at present. All the parts of each form must have a relation to each other, and to the whole: And the whole itself must have a relation to the other parts of the universe; to the element, in which the form subsists; to the materials, with which it repairs its waste and decay; and to every other form, which is hostile or friendly. A defect in any of these particulars destroys the form; and the matter, of which it is composed, is again set loose, and is thrown into irregular motions and fermentations, till it unite itself to some other regular form. If no such form be prepared to receive it, and if there be a great quantity of this corrupted matter in the universe, the universe itself is entirely disordered; whether it be the feeble embryo of a world in its first beginnings, that is thus destroyed, or the rotten carcass of one, languishing in old age and infirmity. In either case, a chaos ensues; till finite, though innumerable revolutions produce at last some forms, whose parts and organs are so adjusted as to support the forms amidst a continued succession of matter.

Suppose (for we shall endeavour to vary the expression), that matter were thrown into any position, by a blind, unguided force; it is evident that this first position must in all probability be the most confused and most disorderly imaginable, without any resemblance to those works of human contrivance, which, along with a symmetry of parts, discover an adjustment of means to ends and a tendency to self-preservation. If the actuating force cease after this operation, matter must remain for ever in disorder, and continue an immense chaos, without any proportion or activity. But suppose, that the actuating force, whatever it be, still continues in matter, this first position will immediately give place to a second, which will like-wise in all probability be as disorderly as the first, and so on, through many successions of changes and revolutions. No particular order or position ever continues a moment unaltered. The original force, still remaining in activity, gives a perpetual restlessness to matter. Every possible situation is produced, and instantly destroyed. If a glimpse or dawn of order appears for a moment, it is instantly hurried away, and confounded, by that never-ceasing force, which actuates every part of matter.

Thus the universe goes on for many ages in a continued succession of chaos and disorder. But is it not possible that it may settle at last, so as not to lose its motion and active force (for that we have supposed inherent in it), yet so as to preserve an uniformity of appearance, amidst the continual motion and fluctuation of its parts? This we find to be the case with the universe at present. Every individual is perpetually changing, and every part of every individual, and yet the whole remains, in appearance, the same. May we not hope for such a position, or rather be assured of it, from the eternal revolutions of unguided matter, and may not this account for all the appearing wisdom and contrivance which is in the universe? Let us contemplate the subject a little, and we shall find, that this adjustment, if attained by matter, of a seeming stability in the forms, with a real and perpetual revolution or motion of parts, affords a plausible, if not a true solution of the difficulty.

It is in vain, therefore, to insist upon the uses of the parts in animals or vegetables, and their curious adjustment to each other. I would fain know how an animal could subsist, unless its parts were so adjusted? Do we not find, that it immediately perishes whenever this adjustment ceases, and that its matter corrupting tries some new form? It happens, indeed, that the parts of the world are so well adjusted, that some regular form immediately lays claim to this corrupted matter: And if it were not so, could the world subsist? Must it not dissolve as well as the animal, and pass through new positions and situations; till in a great, but finite succession, it fall at last into the present or some such order?

It is well, replied Cleanthes, you told us, that this hypothesis was suggested on a sudden, in the course of the argument. Had you had leisure to examine it, you would soon have perceived the insuperable objections, to which it is exposed. No form, you: say, can subsist, unless it possess those powers and organs, requisite for its subsistence: Some new order or œconomy must be tried, and so on, without intermission; till at last some order, which can support and maintain itself, is fallen upon. But according to this hypothesis, whence arise the many conveniences and advantages which men and all animals possess? Two eyes, two ears, are not absolutely necessary for the subsistence of the species. Human race might have been propagated and preserved, without horses, dogs, cows, sheep, and those innumerable fruits and products which serve to our satisfaction and enjoyment. If no camels had been created for the use of man in the sandy deserts of Africa and Arabia, would the world have been dissolved? If no loadstone had been framed to give that wonderful and useful direction to the needle, would human society and the human kind have been immediately extinguished? Though the maxims of nature be in general very frugal, yet instances of this kind are far from being rare; and any one of them is a sufficient proof of design, and of a benevolent design, which gave rise to the order and arrangement of the universe.

At least, you may safely infer, said Philo, that the foregoing hypothesis is so far incomplete and imperfect; which I shall not scruple to allow. But can we ever reasonably expect greater success in any attempts of this nature? Or can we ever hope to erect a system of cosmogony, that will be liable to no exceptions, and will contain no circumstance repugnant to our limited and imperfect experience of the analogy of nature? Your theory itself cannot surely pretend to any such advantage; even though you have run into *anthropomorphism*, the better to preserve a conformity to common experience. Let us once more put it to trial. In all instances which we have ever seen, ideas are copied from real objects, and are ectypal, not archetypal, to express myself in learned terms: You reverse this order, and give thought the precedence. In all instances which we have ever seen, thought has no influence upon matter, except where that matter is so conjoined with it, as to have an equal reciprocal influence upon it. No animal can move immediately any thing but the members of its own body; and indeed, the equality of action and re-action seems to be an universal law of nature: But your theory implies a contradiction to this experience. These instances, with many more, which it were easy to collect (particularly the supposition of a mind or system of thought that is eternal, or in other words, an animal ingenerable and immortal), these instances, I say, may teach, all of us, sobriety in condemning each other, and let us see, that as no system of this kind ought ever to be received from a slight analogy, so neither ought any to be rejected on account of a small incongruity. For that is an inconvenience from which we can justly pronounce no one to be exempted.

All religious systems, it is confessed, are subject to great and insuperable difficulties. Each disputant triumphs in his turn; while he carries on an offensive war, and exposes the absurdities, barbarities, and pernicious tenets of his antagonist. But all of them, on the whole, prepare a complete triumph for the sceptic; who tells them, that no system ought ever to be embraced with regard to such subjects: For this plain reason, that no absurdity ought ever to be assented to with regard to any subject. A total suspense of judgment is here our only reasonable resource. And if every attack, as is commonly observed, and no defence, among theologians, is successful; how complete must be *his* victory, who remains always, with all mankind, on the offensive; and has himself no fixed station or abiding city, which he is ever, on any occasion, obliged to defend?

Chapter 26

The limits of design arguments

Immanuel Kant

THIS world presents to us so immeasurable a stage of variety, order, purposiveness, and beauty, as displayed alike in its infinite extent and in the unlimited divisibility of its parts, that even with such knowledge as our weak understanding can acquire of it, we are brought face to face with so many marvels immeasurably great, that all speech loses its force, all numbers their power to measure, our thoughts themselves all definiteness, and that our judgment of the whole resolves itself into an amazement which is speechless, and only the more eloquent on that account. Everywhere we see a chain of effects and causes, of ends and means, a regularity in origination and dissolution. Nothing has of itself come into the condition in which we find it to exist, but always points to something else as its cause, while this in turn commits us to repetition of the same enquiry. The whole universe must thus sink into the abyss of nothingness unless, over and above this infinite chain of contingencies, we assume something to support it—something which is original and independently self-subsistent, and which as the cause of the origin of the universe secures also at the same time its continuance. What magnitude are we to ascribe to this supreme cause—admitting that it is supreme in respect of all things in the world? We are not acquainted with the whole content of the world, still less do we know how to estimate its magnitude by comparison with all that is possible. But since we cannot, as regards causality, dispense with an ultimate and supreme being, what is there to prevent us ascribing to it a degree of perfection that sets it *above everything else that is possible*? This we can easily do—though only through the slender outline of an abstract concept—by representing this being to ourselves as combining in itself all possible perfection, as in a single substance. This concept is in conformity with the demand of our reason for parsimony of principles; it is free from self-contradiction, and is never decisively contradicted by any experience; and it is likewise of such a character that it contributes to the extension of the employment of reason within experience, through the guidance which it yields in the discovery of order and purposiveness.

This proof always deserves to be mentioned with respect. It is the oldest, the clearest, and the most accordant with the common reason of mankind. It enlivens the study of nature, just as it itself derives its existence and gains ever new vigour from that source. It suggests ends and purposes, where our observation would not

Immanuel Kant 'Critique of Pure Reason' from Immanuel Kant, *Critique of Pure Reason*, translated by Norman Kemp Smith (St Martin's Press, 1965).

have detected them by itself, and extends our knowledge of nature by means of the guiding-concept of a special unity, the principle of which is outside nature. This knowledge again reacts on its cause, namely, upon the idea which has led to it, and so strengthens the belief in a supreme Author [of nature] that the belief acquires the force of an irresistible conviction.

But although we have nothing to bring against the rationality and utility of this procedure, but have rather to commend and to further it, we still cannot approve the claims, which this mode of argument would fain advance, to apodeictic certainty and to an assent founded on no special favour or support from other quarters. It cannot hurt the good cause, if the dogmatic language of the overweening sophist be toned down to the more moderate and humble requirements of a belief adequate to quieten our doubts, though not to command unconditional submission.

The chief points of the physico-theological proof are as follows: (1) In the world we everywhere find clear signs of an order in accordance with a determinate purpose, carried out with great wisdom; and this in a universe which is indescribably varied in content and unlimited in extent. (2) This purposive order is quite alien to the things of the world, and only belongs to them contingently; that is to say, the diverse things could not of themselves have co-operated, by so great a combination of diverse means, to the fulfilment of determinate final purposes, had they not been chosen and designed for these purposes by an ordering rational principle in conformity with underlying ideas. (3) There exists, therefore, a sublime and wise cause (or more than one), which must be the cause of the world not merely as a blindly working all-powerful nature, by *fecundity*, but as intelligence, through *freedom*. (4) The unity of this cause may be inferred from the unity of the reciprocal relations existing between the parts of the world, as members of an artfully arranged structure—inferred with certainty in so far as our observation suffices for its verification, and beyond these limits with probability, in accordance with the principles of analogy.

We need not here criticise natural reason too strictly in regard to its conclusion from the analogy between certain natural products and what our human art produces when we do violence to nature, and constrain it to proceed not according to its own ends but in conformity with ours—appealing to the similarity of these particular natural products with houses, ships, watches. Nor need we here question its conclusion that there lies at the basis of nature a causality similar to that responsible for artificial products, namely, an understanding and a will; and that the inner possibility of a self-acting nature (which is what makes all art, and even, it may be, reason itself, possible) is therefore derived from another, though superhuman, art—a mode of reasoning which could not perhaps withstand a searching transcendental criticism. But at any rate we must admit that, if we are to specify a cause at all, we cannot here proceed more securely than by analogy with those purposive productions of which alone the cause and mode of action are fully known to us. Reason could never be justified in abandoning the causality which it knows for grounds of explanation which are obscure, of which it does not have any know-ledge, and which are incapable of proof.

On this method of argument, the purposiveness and harmonious adaptation of so much in nature can suffice to prove the contingency of the form merely, not of the matter, that is, not of the substance in the world. To prove the latter we should have to demonstrate that the things in the world would not of themselves be capable of such order and harmony, in accordance with universal laws, if they were not *in their substance* the product of supreme wisdom. But to prove this we should require quite other grounds of proof than those which are derived from the analogy with human art. The utmost, therefore, that the argument can prove is an *architect* of the world who is always very much hampered by the adaptability of the material in which he works, not a *creator* of the world to whose idea everything is subject. This, however, is altogether inadequate to the lofty purpose which we have before our eyes, namely, the proof of an all-sufficient primordial being. To prove the contingency of matter itself, we should have to resort to a transcendental argument.

The inference, therefore, is that the order and purposiveness everywhere observ-able throughout the world may be regarded as a completely contingent arrange-ment, and that we may argue to the existence of a cause *proportioned* to it. But the concept of this cause must enable us to know something quite *determinate* about it, and can therefore be no other than the concept of a being who possesses all might, wisdom, etc., in a word, all the perfection which is proper to an all-sufficient being. For the predicates—'very great', 'astounding', 'immeasurable' in power and excellence—give no determinate concept at all, and do not really tell us what the thing is in itself. They are only relative representations of the magnitude of the object, which the observer, in contemplating the world, compares with himself and with his capacity of comprehension, and which are equally terms of eulogy whether we be magnifying the object or be depreciating the observing subject in relation to that object. Where we are concerned with the magnitude (of the perfection) of a thing, there is no determinate concept except that which comprehends all possible perfection; and in that concept only the allness (*omnitudo*) of the reality is com-pletely determined.

Now no one, I trust, will be so bold as to profess that he comprehends the relation of the magnitude of the world as he has observed it (alike as regards both extent and content) to omnipotence, of the world order to supreme wisdom, of the world unity to the absolute unity of its Author, etc. Physico-theology is therefore unable to give any determinate concept of the supreme cause of the world, and cannot therefore serve as the foundation of a theology which is itself in turn to form the basis of religion.

To advance to absolute totality by the empirical road is utterly impossible. None the less this is what is attempted in the physico-theological proof.

Chapter 27

God, regularity, and David Hume

R. G. Swinburne

THE object of this paper is to show that there are no valid formal objections to the argument from design, so long as the argument is articulated with sufficient care. In particular I wish to analyse Hume's attack on the argument in *Dialogues Concerning Natural Religion* and to show that none of the formal objections made therein by Philo have any validity against a carefully articulated version of the argument

The argument from design is an argument from the order or regularity of things in the world to a god or, more precisely, a very powerful free non-embodied rational agent, who is responsible for that order. By a body I understand a part of the material universe subject, at any rate partially, to an agent's direct control, to be contrasted with other parts not thus subject. An agent's body marks the limits to what he can directly control; he can only control other parts of the universe by moving his body. An agent who could directly control any part of the universe would not be embodied. Thus ghosts, if they existed, would be non-embodied agents, because there are no particular pieces of matter subject to their direct control, but any piece of matter may be so subject. I use the word 'design' in such a way that it is not analytic that if anything evinces design, an agent designed it, and so it becomes a synthetic question whether the design of the world shows the activity of a designer.

The argument, taken by itself, as was admitted in the *Dialogues* by Cleanthes the proponent of the argument, does not show that the designer of the world is omnipotent, omniscient, totally good, etc. Nor does it show that he is the God of Abraham, Isaac, and Jacob. To make these points, further arguments would be needed. The isolation of the argument from design from the web of Christian apologetic is perhaps a somewhat unnatural step, but necessary in order to analyse its structure. My claim is that the argument does not commit any formal fallacy, and by this I mean that it keeps to the canons of argument about matters of fact and does not violate any of them. It is, however, an argument by analogy. It argues from an analogy between the order of the world and the products of human art to a god responsible for the former, in some ways similar to man who is responsible for the latter. And even if there are no formal fallacies in the argument, one unwilling to admit the conclusion might still claim that the analogy was too weak and remote for him to have to admit it, that the argument gave only negligible support to the

Richard Swinburne 'The Argument of Design' from *Philosophy*, vol. 43 (1968), reprinted by permission of the author.

conclusion which remained improbable. In defending the argument I will leave to the objector this way of escape from its conclusion.

I will begin by setting forward the argument from design in a more careful and precise way than Cleanthes did.

There are in the world two kinds of regularity or order, and all empirical instances of order are such because they evince one or other or both kinds of order. These are the regularities of co-presence or spatial order, and regularities of succession, or temporal order. Regularities of co-presence are patterns of spatial order at some one instant of time. An example of a regularity of co-presence would be a town with all its roads at right angles to each other, or a section of books in a library arranged in alphabetical order of authors. Regularities of succession are simple patterns of behaviour of objects, such as their behaviour in accordance with the laws of nature—for example, Newton's law of gravitation, which holds universally to a very high degree of approximation, that all bodies attract each other with forces proportional to the product of their masses and inversely proportional to the square of their distance apart.

Many of the striking examples of order in the world evince an order which is the result both of a regularity of co-presence and of a regularity of succession. A working car consists of many parts so adjusted to each other that it follows the instructions of the driver delivered by his pulling and pushing a few levers and buttons and turning a wheel to take passengers whither he wishes. Its order arises because its parts are so arranged at some instant (regularity of co-presence) that, the laws of nature being as they are (regularity of succession), it brings about the result neatly and efficiently. The order of living animals and plants likewise results from regularities of both types.

Men who marvel at the order of the world may marvel at either or both of the regularities of co-presence and of succession. The men of the eighteenth century, that great century of 'reasonable religion,' were struck almost exclusively by the regularities of co-presence. They marvelled at the design and orderly operations of animals and plants; but since they largely took for granted the regularities of succession, what struck them about the animals and plants, as to a lesser extent about machines made by men, was the subtle and coherent arrangement of their millions of parts. Paley's *Natural Theology* dwells mainly on details of comparative anatomy, on eyes and ears and muscles and bones arranged with minute precision so as to operate with high efficiency, and Hume's Cleanthes produces the same kind of examples: 'Consider, anatomise the eye, survey its structure and contrivance, and tell me from your own feeling, if the idea of a contriver does not immediately flow in upon you with a force like that of sensation.'[1]

Those who argue from the existence of regularities of copresence other than those produced by men to the existence of a god who produced them are, however, in many respects on slippery ground when compared with those who rely for their

1. David Hume, *Dialogues Concerning Natural Religion*, ed. H. D. Aiken (New York, 1948), p. 28.

premises on regularities of succession. We shall see several of these weaknesses later in considering Hume's objections to the argument, but it is worthwhile noting two of them at the outset. First, although the world contains many striking regularities of co-presence (some few of which are caused by human agency), it also contains many examples of spatial disorder. The uniform distribution of the galactic clusters is a marvellous example of spatial order, but the arrangement of trees in an African jungle is a marvellous example of spatial disorder. Although the proponent of the argument may then proceed to argue that in an important sense or from some point of view (e.g., utility to man) the order vastly exceeds the disorder, he has to argue for this in-no-way-obvious proposition.

Secondly the proponent of the argument runs the risk that the regularities of co-presence may be explained in terms of something else by a normal scientific explanation[2] in a way that the regularities of succession could not possibly be. A scientist could show that a regularity of co-presence R arose from an apparently disordered state D by means of the normal operation of the laws of nature. This would not entirely 'explain away' the regularity of co-presence, because the proponent of this argument from design might then argue that the apparently disordered state D really had a latent order, being the kind of state which, when the laws of nature operate, turns into a manifestly ordered one. As long as only few of the physically possible states of apparent disorder were states of latent order, the existence of many states of latent order would be an important contingent fact which could form a premiss for an argument from design. But there is always the risk that scientists might show that most states of apparent disorder were states of latent order, that is, that if the world lasted long enough considerable order must emerge from whichever of many initial states it began. If a scientist showed that, he would have explained by normal scientific explanation the existence of regularities of co-presence in terms of something completely different. The eighteenth-century proponents of the argument from design did not suspect this danger, and hence the devastating effect of Darwin's Theory of Evolution by Natural Selection on those who accepted their argument. For Darwin showed that the regularities of co-presence of the animal and plant kingdoms had evolved by natural processes from an apparently disordered state and would have evolved equally from many other apparently disordered states. Whether all regularities of co-presence can be fully explained in this kind of way no one yet knows, but the danger remains for the proponent of an argument from design of this kind that they can be.

However, those who argue from the operation of regularities of succession other than those produced by men to the existence of a god who produces them do not run into either of these difficulties. Regularities of succession (other than those

---

2. I understand by a 'normal scientific explanation' one conforming to the pattern of deductive or statistical explanation utilised in paradigm empirical sciences such as physics and chemistry, elucidated in recent years by Hempel, Braithwaite, Popper, and others. Although there are many uncertain points about scientific explanation, those to which I appeal in the text are accepted by all philosophers of science.

produced by men), unlike regularities of co-presence, are all-pervasive. Simple natural laws rule almost all successions of events. Nor can regularities of succession be given a normal scientific explanation in terms of something else. For the normal scientific explanation of the operation of a regularity of succession is in terms of the operation of a yet more general regularity of succession. Note too that a normal scientific explanation of the existence of regularities of co-presence in terms of something different, if it can be provided, is explanation in terms of regularities of succession.

For these reasons the proponent of the argument from design does much better to rely for his premiss more on regularities of succession. St. Thomas Aquinas, wiser than the men of the eighteenth century, did just this. He puts forward an argument from design as his fifth and last way to prove the existence of God, and gives his premiss as follows:

'The fifth way is based on the guidedness of nature. An orderedness of actions to an end is observed in all bodies obeying natural laws, even when they lack aware-ness. For their behaviour hardly ever varies, and will practically always turn out well; which shows that they truly tend to a goal, and do not merely hit it by accident.'[3] If we ignore any value judgment in 'practically always turn out well,' St. Thomas' argument is an argument from regularities of succession.

The most satisfactory premiss for the argument from design is then the opera-tion of regularities of succession other than those produced by men, that is, the operation of natural laws. Almost all things almost always obey simple natural laws and so behave in a strikingly regular way. Given the premiss, what is our justifica-tion for proceeding to the conclusion that a very powerful free non-embodied rational agent is responsible for their behaving in that way? The justification which Aquinas gives is that 'Nothing . . . that lacks awareness tends to a goal, except under the direction of someone with awareness and with understanding; the arrow, for example, requires an archer. Everything in nature, therefore, is directed to its goal by someone with understanding, and this we call "God".'[4] A similar argument has been given by many religious apologists since Aquinas, but clearly as it stands it is guilty of the grossest *petitio principii*. Certainly *some* things which tend to a goal, tend to a goal because of a direction imposed upon them by someone 'with aware-ness and with understanding.' Did not the archer place the arrow and pull the string in a certain way the arrow would not tend to its goal. But whether *all* things which tend to a goal tend to a goal for this reason is the very question at issue, and that they do cannot be used as a premiss to prove the conclusion. We must therefore reconstruct the argument in a more satisfactory way.

The structure of any plausible argument from design can only be that the exist-ence of a god responsible for the order in the world is a hypothesis well-confirmed on the basis of the evidence—viz., that contained in the premiss which we have now

---

3. St. Thomas Aquinas, *Summa Theologiae*, Ia.2.3. Trans. Timothy McDermott, o.p. (London, 1964).
4. *Ibid.*

stated, and better confirmed than any other hypothesis. I shall begin by showing that there can be no other possible explanation for the operation of natural laws than the activity of a god, and then see to what extent the hypothesis is well confirmed on the basis of the evidence.

Almost all phenomena can, as we have seen, be explained by a normal scientific explanation in terms of the operation of natural laws on preceding states. There is, however, one other way of explaining natural phenomena, and that is explaining in terms of the rational choice of a free agent. When a man marries Jane rather than Anne, becomes a solicitor rather than a barrister, kills rather than shows mercy after considering arguments in favour of each course, he brings about a state of the world by his free and rational choice. To all appearances this is an entirely different way whereby states of the world may come about than through the operation of laws of nature on preceding states. Someone may object that it is necessary that physiological or other scientific laws operate in order for the agent to bring about effects. My answer is that certainly it is necessary that such laws operate in order for effects brought about directly by the agent to have ulterior consequences. But unless there are some effects which the agent brings about directly without the operation of scientific laws' acting on preceding physical states bringing them about, then these laws and states could fully explain the effects and there would be no need to refer in explaining them to the rational choice of an agent. True, the apparent freedom and rationality of the human will *may* prove an illusion. Many may have no more option what to do than a machine and be guided by an argument no more than is a piece of iron. But this has never yet been shown, and, in the absence of good philosophical and scientific argument to show it, I assume, what is apparent, that when a man acts by free and rational choice, his agency is the operation of a different kind of causality from that of scientific laws. The free choice of a rational agent is the only way of accounting for natural phenomena other than the way of normal scientific explanation, which is recognised as such by all men and has not been reduced to normal scientific explanation.

Almost all regularities of succession are the result of the normal operation of scientific laws. But to say this is simply to say that these regularities are instances of more general regularities. The operation of the most fundamental regularities clearly cannot be given a normal scientific explanation. If their operation is to receive an explanation and not merely to be left as a brute fact, that explanation must therefore be in terms of the rational choice of a free agent. What, then, are grounds for adopting this hypothesis, given that it is the only possible one?

The grounds are that we can explain some few regularities of succession as produced by rational agents and that the other regularities cannot be explained except in this way. Among the typical products of a rational agent acting freely are regularities both of co-presence and of succession. The alphabetical order of books on a library shelf is the result of the activity of the librarian who chose to arrange them thus. The order of the cards of a pack by suits and seniority in each suit is the result of the activity of the card-player who arranged them thus. Among examples of regularities of succession produced by men are the notes of a song sung by a singer or the movements of a dancer's body when he performs a dance in time with the accompanying instrument. Hence, knowing that some regularities of succession have such a cause, we postulate that they all have. An agent produces the celestial harmony like a man who sings a song. But at this point an obvious difficulty arises. The regularities of succession, such as songs which are produced by men, are produced by agents of comparatively small power, whose bodies we can locate. If an agent is responsible for the operation of the laws of nature, he must act directly on the whole universe, as we act directly on our bodies. Also he must be of immense power and intelligence compared with men. Hence he can only be somewhat similar to men, having, like them, intelligence and freedom of choice, yet unlike them in the degree of these and in not possessing a body. For a body, as I have distinguished it earlier, is a part of the universe subject to an agent's direct control, to be contrasted with other parts not thus subject. The fact that we are obliged to postulate on the basis of differences in the effects, differences in the causes, men and the god, weakens the argument. How much it weakens it depends on how great these differences are.

Our argument thus proves to be an argument by analogy and to exemplify a pattern common in scientific inference. As are caused by Bs, A*s are similar to As. Therefore—given that there is no more satisfactory explanation of the existence of A*s—they are produced by B*s similar to Bs. B*s are postulated to be similar in all respects to Bs except in so far as shown otherwise, viz., except in so far as the dissimilarities between As and A*s force us to postulate a difference. A well-known scientific example of this type of inference is as follows. Certain pressures (As) on the walls of containers are produced by billiard balls (Bs) with certain motions. Similar pressures (A*s) are produced on the walls of containers which contain not billiard balls but gases. Therefore, since we have no better explanation of the existence of the pressures, gases consist of particles (B*s) similar to billiard balls except in certain respects—e.g., size. By similar arguments, scientists have argued for the existence of many unobservables. Such an argument becomes weaker in so far as the properties which we are forced to attribute to the B*s because of the differences between the As and the A*s become different from those of the Bs. Nineteenth-century physicists postulated the existence of an elastic solid, the aether, to account for the propagation of light. But the way in which light was propagated turned out to have such differences (despite the similarities) from the way in which waves in solids are normally propagated that the physicists had to say that if there was an aether it had very many peculiar properties not possessed by normal liquids or solids. Hence they concluded that the argument for its existence was very weak. The proponent of the argument from design stresses the similarities between the regularities of succession produced by man and those which are laws of nature and so between men and the agent which he postulates as responsible for the laws of nature. The opponent of the argument stresses the dissimilarities. The degree of support which the conclusion obtains from the evidence depends on how great the similarities are.

The degree of support for the conclusion of an argument from analogy does not, however, depend merely on the similarities between the types of evidence but on the degree to which the resulting theory makes explanation of empirical matters more simple and coherent. In the case of the argument from design, the conclusion has an enormous simplifying effect on explanations of empirical matters. For if the conclusion is true, if a very powerful non-embodied rational agent is responsible for the operation of the laws of nature, then normal scientific explanation would prove to be personal explanation. That is, explanation of some phenomenon in terms of the operation of a natural law would ultimately be an explanation in terms of the operation of an agent. Hence (given an initial arrangement of matter) the principles of explanation of phenomena would have been reduced from two to one. It is a basic principle of explanation that we should postulate as few as possible kinds of explanation. To take a more mundane example—if we have as possible alternatives to explain physical phenomena by the operation of two kinds of force, the electromagnetic and the gravitational, and to explain physical phenomena in terms of the operation of only one kind of force, the gravitational, we ought always—*ceteris paribus*—to prefer the latter alternative. Since, as we have seen, we are obliged, at any rate at present, to use explanation in terms of the free choice of a rational agent in explaining many empirical phenomena, then if the amount of similarity between the order in the universe not produced by human agents and that produced by human agents makes it at all plausible to do so, we ought to postulate that an agent is responsible for the former as well as for the latter. So then in so far as regularities of succession produced by the operation of natural laws are similar to those produced by human agents, to postulate that a rational agent is responsible for them would indeed provide a simple unifying and coherent explanation of natural phenomena. What is there against taking this step? Simply that celebrated principle of explanation—*entia non sunt multiplicanda praeter necessitatem*—do not add a god to your ontology unless you have to. The issue turns on whether the evidence constitutes enough of a *necessitas* to compel us to multiply entities. Whether it does depends on how strong the analogy is between the regularities of succession produced by human agents and those produced by the operation of natural laws. I do not propose to assess the strength of the analogy but only to claim that everything turns on it. I claim that the inference from natural laws to a god responsible for them is of a perfectly proper type for inference about matters of fact, and that the only issue is whether the evidence is strong enough to allow us to affirm that it is probable that the conclusion is true.

Now that I have reconstructed the argument from design in what is, I hope, a logically impeccable form, I turn to consider Hume's criticisms of it, and I shall argue that all his criticisms alleging formal fallacies in the argument do not apply to it in the form in which I have stated it. This, we shall see, is largely because the criticisms are bad criticisms of the argument in any form but also in small part because Hume directed his fire against that form of the argument which used as its premiss the existence of regularities of co-presence other than those produced by men, and did not appeal to the operation of regularities of succession. I shall begin by considering one general point which he makes only in the *Enquiry* and then consider in turn all the objections which appear on the pages of the *Dialogues*.

1. The point which appears at the beginning of Hume's discussion of the argument in section XI of the *Enquiry* is a point which reveals the fundamental weakness of Hume's sceptical position. In discussing the argument, Hume puts forward as a general principle that 'when we infer any particular cause from an effect, we must proportion the one to the other, and can never be allowed to ascribe to the cause any qualities but what are exactly sufficient to produce the effect.'[5] Now, it is true that Hume uses this principle mainly to show that we are not justified in inferring that the god responsible for the design of the universe is totally good, omnipotent, and omniscient. I accept, as Cleanthes did, that the argument does not by itself lead to that conclusion. But Hume's use of the principle tends to cast doubt on the validity of the argument in the weaker form in which I am discussing it, for it seems to suggest that although we may conclude that whatever produced the regularity of the world was a regularity-producing object, we cannot go further and conclude that it is an agent who acts by choice, etc., for this would be to suppose more than we need in order to account for the effect. It is, therefore, important to realise that the principle is clearly false on our normal understanding of what are the criteria of inference about empirical matters. For the universal adoption of this celebrated principle would lead to the abandonment of science. Any scientist who told us only that the cause of E and E-producing characteristics would not add an iota to our knowledge. Explanation of matters of fact consists in postulating on reasonable grounds that the cause of an effect has certain characteristics other than those sufficient to produce the effect.

2. Two objections seem to be telescoped in the following passage of the *Dialogues*. 'When two *species* of objects have always been observed to be conjoined together, I can *infer* by custom the existence of one wherever I *see* the existence of the other; and this I call an argument from experience. But how this argument can have place where the objects, as in the present case, are single, individual, without parallel or specific resemblance, may be difficult to explain.'[6] One argument here seems to be that we can only infer from an observed A to an unobserved B when we have frequently observed As and Bs together, and that we cannot infer to a B unless we have actually observed other Bs. Hence we cannot infer from regularities of succession to an unobserved god on the analogy of the connection between observed regularities and human agents, unless we have observed at other times other gods. This argument, like the first, reveals Hume's inadequate appreciation of

5. David Hume, *An Enquiry Concerning Human Understanding*, ed. L. A. Selby-Bigge (2nd edn, 1902), p. 136.
6. *Dialogues*, p. 23.

scientific method. As we saw in the scientific examples which I cited, a more developed science than Hume knew has taught us that when observed As have a relation R to observed Bs, it is often perfectly reasonable to postulate that observed A*s, similar to As, have the same relation to unobserved and unobservable B*s similar to Bs.

3. The other objection which seems to be involved in the above passage is that we cannot reach conclusions about an object which is the only one of its kind, and, as the universe is such an object, we cannot reach conclusions about the regularities characteristic of it as a whole.[7] But cosmologists are reaching very well-tested scientific conclusions about the universe as a whole, as are physical anthropologists about the origins of our human race, even though it is the only human race of which we have knowledge and perhaps the only human race there is. The principle quoted in the objections is obviously wrong. There is no space here to analyze its errors in detail, but suffice it to point out that it becomes hopelessly confused by ignoring the fact that uniqueness is relative to description. Nothing describable is unique under all descriptions (the universe is, like the solar system, a number of material bodies distributed in empty space), and everything describable is unique under some description.

4. The next argument which we meet in the *Dialogues* is that the postulated existence of a rational agent who produces the order of the world would itself need explaining. Picturing such an agent as a mind, and a mind as an arrangement of ideas, Hume phrases the objection as follows: 'a mental world or Universe of ideas requires a cause as much as does a material world or Universe of objects.'[8] Hume himself provides the obvious answer to this—that it is no objection to explaining X by Y that we cannot explain Y. But then he suggests that the Y in this case, the mind, is just as mysterious as the ordered universe. Men never 'thought it satisfactory to explain a particular effect by a particular cause which was no more to be accounted for than the effect itself.'[9] On the contrary, scientists have always thought it reasonable to postulate entities merely to explain effects, so long as the postulated entities accounted simply and coherently for the characteristics of the effects. The existence of molecules with their characteristic behaviour was 'no more to be accounted for' than observable phenomena, but the postulation of their existence gave a neat and simple explanation of a whole host of chemical and physical phenomena, and that was the justification for postulating their existence.

5. Next, Hume argues that if we are going to use the analogy of a human agent we ought to go the whole way and postulate that the god who gives order to the universe is like men in many other respects. 'Why not become a perfect anthropomorphite? Why not assert the deity or deities to be corporeal, and to have eyes, a

7. For this argument see also *Enquiry*, pp. 147 f.
8. *Dialogues*, p. 33.
9. *Ibid.*, p. 36.

nose, mouths, ears, etc.'[10] The argument from design is, as we have seen, an argument by analogy. All analogies break down somewhere; otherwise they would not be analogies. In saying that the relation of A to B is analogous to a relation of A* to a postulated B*, we do not claim that B* is in all respects like B, but only in such respects as to account for the existence of the relation and also in other respects except in so far as we have contrary evidence. For the activity of a god to account for the regularities, he must be free, rational, and very powerful. But it is not necessary that he, like men, should only be able to act on a limited part of the universe, a body, and by acting on that control the rest of the universe. And there is good reason to suppose that the god does not operate in this way. For, if his direct control was confined to a part of the universe, scientific laws outside his control must operate to ensure that his actions have effects in the rest of the universe. Hence the postulation of the existence of the god would not explain the operations of those laws: yet to explain the operation of all scientific laws was the point of postulating the existence of the god. The hypothesis that the god is not embodied thus explains more and explains more coherently than the hypothesis that he is embodied. Hume's objection would, however, have weight against an argument from regularities of co-presence which did not appeal to the operation of regularities of succession. For one could suppose an embodied god just as well as a disembodied god to have made the animal kingdom and then left it alone, as a man makes a machine, or, like a landscape gardener, to have laid out the galactic clusters. The explanatory force of such an hypothesis is as great as that of the hypothesis that a disembodied god did these things, and argument from analogy would suggest the hypothesis of an embodied god to be more probable. Incidentally, a god whose prior existence was shown by the existence of regularities of co-presence might now be dead, but a god whose existence was shown by the present operation of regularities of succession could not be, since the existence of an agent is contemporaneous with the temporal regularities which he produces.

6. Hume urges: why should we not postulate many gods to give order to the universe, not merely one? 'A great number of men join in building a house or a ship, in rearing a city, in framing a commonwealth, why may not several deities combine in framing a world?'[11] Hume again is aware of the obvious counter-objection to his suggestion—'To multiply causes without necessity is . . . contrary to true philosophy.'[12] He claims, however, that the counter-objection does not apply here, because it is an open question whether there is a god with sufficient power to put the whole universe in order. The principle, however, still applies whether or not we have prior information that a being of sufficient power exists. When postulating entities, postulate as few as possible. Always suppose only one murderer, unless the evidence forces you to suppose a second. If there were more than one deity respon-

10. *Ibid.*, p. 40.
11. *Ibid.*, p. 39.
12. *Ibid.*, p. 40.

sible for the order of the universe, we should expect to see characteristic marks of the handiwork of different deities in different parts of the universe, just as we see different kinds of workmanship in the different houses of a city. We should expect to find an inverse square law of gravitation obeyed in one part of the universe, and in another part a law which was just short of being an inverse square law—without the difference's being explicable in terms of a more general law. But it is enough to draw this absurd conclusion to see how ridiculous the Humean objection is.

7. Hume argues that there are in the universe other things than rational agents which bestow order. 'A tree bestows order and organisation on that tree which springs from it, without knowing the order, an animal in the same manner on its offspring.'[13] It would, therefore, Hume argues, be equally reasonable if we are arguing from analogy, to suppose the cause of the regularities in the world 'to be something similar or analogous to generation or vegetation.'[14] This suggestion makes perfectly good sense if it is the regularities of co-presence which we are attempting to explain. But as analogous processes to explain regularities of succession, generation or vegetation will not do, because they only produce regularities of co-presence—and those through the operation of regularities of succession outside their control. The seed only produces the plant because of the continued operation of the laws of biochemistry.

8. The last distinct objection which I can discover in the *Dialogues* is the following. Why should we not suppose, Hume urges, that this ordered universe is a mere accident among the chance arrangements of eternal matter? In the course of eternity, matter arranges itself in all kinds of ways. We just happen to live in a period when it is characterised by order, and mistakenly conclude that matter is always ordered. Now, as Hume phrases this objection, it is directed against an argument from design which uses as its premiss the existence of the regularities of co-presence. 'The continual motion of matter . . . in less than infinite transpositions must produce this economy or order, and by its very nature, that order, when once established supports itself for many ages if not to eternity.'[15] Hume thus relies here partly on chance and partly on the operation of regularities of succession (the preservation of order) to account for the existence of regularities of co-presence. In so far as it relies on regularities of succession to explain regularities of co-presence, such an argument has, as we saw earlier, some plausibility. But in so far as it relies on chance, it does not—if the amount of order to be accounted for is very striking. An attempt to attribute the operation of regularities of succession to chance would not thus be very plausible. The claim would be that there are no laws of nature which always apply to matter; matter evinces in the course of eternity all kinds of patterns of behaviour; it is just chance that at the moment the states of the universe

13. *Ibid.*, p. 50.
14. *Ibid.*, p. 47.
15. *Ibid.*, p. 53.

are succeeding each other in a regular way. But if we say that it is chance that in 1960 matter is behaving in a regular way, our claim becomes less and less plausible as we find that in 1961 and 1962 and so on it continues to behave in a regular way. An appeal to chance to account for order becomes less and less plausible, the greater the order. We would be justified in attributing a typewritten version of collected works of Shakespeare to the activity of monkeys typing eternally on eternal type-writers if we had some evidence of the existence of an infinite quantity of paper randomly covered with type, as well as the collected works. In the absence of any evidence that matter behaved irregularly at other temporal periods, we are not justified in attributing its present regular behaviour to chance.

In addition to the objections which I have stated, the *Dialogues* contain a lengthy presentation of the argument that the existence of evil in the world shows that the god who made it and gave it order is not both totally good and omnipotent. But this does not affect the argument from design which, as Cleanthes admits, does not purport to show that the designer of the universe does have these characteristics. The eight objections which I have stated are all the distinct objections to the argument from design which I can find in the *Enquiry* and in the *Dialogues*, which claim that in some formal respect the argument does not work. As well as claiming that the argument from design is deficient in some formal respect, Hume makes the point that the analogy of the order produced by men to the other order of the universe is too remote for us to postulate similar causes.[16] I have argued earlier that if there is a weakness in the argument it is here that it is to be found. The only way to deal with this point would be to start drawing the parallels or stressing the dissimilarities, and these are perhaps tasks more appropriate for the preacher and the poet than for the philosopher. The philosopher will be content to have shown that though perhaps weak, the argument has some force. How much force depends on the strength of the analogy.

16. See, for example, *Dialogues*, pp. 18 and 37.

Chapter 28

Can design arguments be defended today?

Robert Hambourger

Part I

A⊤ the beginning, I would like to distinguish two sorts of argument from design. Arguments of both sorts start with the fact that many natural phenomena look *as if* they might have been produced by design and try to show that such phenomena really *were* designed, and from this they hope that it will be concluded that the universe as a whole was produced by the intentional actions of a single being. But then, the arguments conclude, since the universe appears to be good, and since it would take an extraordinarily wise and powerful being to design and create it, the universe must have been created by a wise, powerful, and good being, and this is God.

Now I think it is clear that any argument of this type will face difficulties when it tries to conclude, from the claim that many natural phenomena were designed, that the universe as a whole was produced by the design of a single being. For it seems possible that the universe itself was not a product of design, even if many important parts of it were, and, further, even if we are willing to grant that the universe as a whole was designed, it still will not follow that it was created by the design of a single being.

This, however, does not seem to be the most serious objection facing the argument from design. For one thing, even if it is granted, the objection will not rob the argument entirely of its power. It would be a significant achievement to prove that certain natural phenomena were results of intentional action, even if one could not prove that the entire universe was created by a single being, and this achievement, by itself, would be enough to show that something was seriously wrong with the atheist's standard picture of the universe. Also, though, even if a demonstration that important portions of the universe were created by design would not actually entail the hypothesis that God exists, it would seem that, nonetheless, it would render that hypothesis more plausible than any competing one. In a contest with polytheism, monotheism is likely to prevail, and one who comes to hold that many natural phenomena were created intentionally probably will come to believe in God. This objection, then, does not seem to me to be a crucial one, and I shall not

Robert Hambourger 'The Argument from Design' from *Intention and Intentionality* edited by Cora Diamond and Jenny Teichmann (Harvester Press, 1979), reprinted by permission of the author.

deal with it further in what follows. Instead, I shall be concerned with attempts by arguments from design to show that certain features of the natural world are products of design, and it is in the ways that they try to do this that the two sorts of argument I wish to distinguish here differ.

Arguments of the first of the sorts I want to discuss are true analogical arguments. One begins by pointing to ways in which certain natural phenomena resemble human artifacts. An animal's eye, for example, is much like a fine machine. And even where the likeness is not so direct, natural phenomena often share with artifacts what Cleanthes, in Hume's *Dialogues*, calls 'the curious adapting of means to ends'.[1] That is, in the case of numerous natural phenomena, as in the case of human artifacts, states of affairs which plausibly could be desired as ends are brought about by phenomena that themselves might reasonably have been intended as means to those ends.

Once such resemblances are noted, arguments of the sort I have in mind proceed straightforwardly by induction. Certain natural phenomena have features in common with human artifacts. However, in many cases, namely, in cases of artifacts, phenomena with these features have been discovered to result from the intentional actions of intelligent beings. Further, in no cases have phenomena with the features been discovered not to result from such a cause; for we have not discovered that natural phenomena with the features are *not* ultimately the result of God's design, and human artifacts all are designed. But then, by induction, we can conclude that all phenomena with the relevant features are products of design and, so, that many natural phenomena are results of intentional action.

This argument, however, I think, must fail. One important principle of inductive reasoning is that, in making inductive inferences, one should not extrapolate from cases of one sort to others that differ too widely from them. For example, if one has studied a great many horses but no other mammals with respect to a certain anatomical feature and has found that all mammals studied have had the feature, one still cannot properly conclude that all mammals and, thus, all dogs have the feature. For the difference between horses and dogs is too great. The point here is not that one can never make inductive inferences from one sort of case to another. If one has examined many animals of numerous mammalian species, though no dogs, with respect to a given feature, and if all mammals studied have had the feature, then it might well be proper to conclude that dogs have the feature, even though there are significant differences between a dog and any of the animals studied. For here the animals that have been studied vary as greatly among themselves as they do from dogs. But when all the cases one has examined for a property are alike in significant respects, and all differ in those respects from a new case that is being considered, then one can have little confidence that the new case will be like the others.

---

1. D. Hume, *Dialogues Concerning Natural Religion*, ed. Norman Kemp Smith (Bobbs-Merrill, Indianapolis, 1947) Part II, p. 143.

This, however, I think, is exactly the situation in which we find ourselves, if we attempt to infer—from the fact that human artifacts have been designed, and natural phenomena have not been proven not to result from design—that natural phenomena that resemble human artifacts have been designed. It is not that there are not clear analogies between artifacts and some natural phenomena. I think there are. But there are also important respects in which natural phenomena do not resemble artifacts. Consider, for example, the eye. One difference between an eye and a machine is the materials out of which the two are made. But I do not think this is the crucial difference. Suppose that a 'mad scientist' some day should construct eyes exactly like natural ones out of flesh and blood. This, I think, would make us no more inclined than we would be otherwise to think that our own eyes were produced by design, nor would we conclude that the analogy between natural phenomena and artifacts was finally close enough for the argument from design to go through.

What seems to me a more important difference is this. Human artifacts, even in cases of automated production, result quite *directly* from intentional actions. Our eyes, on the other hand, while we were developing in the womb, originated from genetically controlled processes that themselves had natural causes, and so on, back as far as we can determine. These processes might have been the results of design, but, if so, the design seems, so to speak, to have been woven into the fabric of nature. And, it would seem, a similar disanalogy can be found in all cases between human artifacts and those natural phenomena that look as if they were produced by design.

This difference between natural phenomena and human artifacts, then, which involves the very features of natural phenomena to which a proponent of the argument from design would be most likely to point to justify his belief that such phenomena, if designed, must have been designed by a divine being, is, I suspect, a sufficiently great difference to block analogical versions of the argument from design. At any rate, I shall not pursue the attempt to work out such a version here. There is, however, another sort of argument from design which is not an analogical argument; and though it also faces serious difficulties, in the end, I think, much can be said for it. Indeed, the version of the argument I shall offer later might be classified as one of this sort.

Arguments of this second sort begin with the claim that, in numerous cases, desirable features of the universe have been brought about by complex states of affairs whose occurrences might seem totally fortuitous, if they were not produced by design. The fact that conditions on earth, for example, were suitable for the development of life probably depended on precise details of the planet's composition and the positioning of its orbit about the sun, and the earth might well have been lifeless, if these had been even slightly different as the planet developed.

Again, basic features of the physical world depend on the fact that bodies of the sort that exist will interact as they do, given the laws of nature that hold. If either the bodies or the laws had been sufficiently unlike what they are, the universe probably would have been quite different and, very possibly, less interesting than it is. Consider, as an example, the forces that bind particles together into bodies and physical systems, for example, the forces binding atoms to form molecules or the force of gravitational attraction. If these forces had been much weaker than they are, matter could not easily have been formed into stable configurations, and the universe might have been little more than a system of particles in flux. On the other hand, if the forces were significantly stronger than they are, it would seem that things would have been overly stable, and discrete, changeable bodies might be at a premium.

It seems, then, not to be a matter of course that the universe is as impressive a place as it is. In many cases, desirable features of the universe would not have come about, unless seemingly unconnected states of affairs had come together in the right sort of way. But, also, one would think, it could not simply have been an accident that, in so many cases, things came together in ways that had such impressive results. Cases of this kind need explanation. However, someone who presents an argument of the sort I am describing would argue that such cases could not be explained unless they were results of design or, at any rate, that they could be better explained in this way than in any other. And if this is true, it would seem that we can conclude that in many noteworthy cases features of the universe were created by design.

Arguments of this second sort, notice, are not analogical arguments. They do not claim that the natural phenomena they hold to have resulted from design are very much like human artifacts. Instead, they hope to show on other grounds that the phenomena need explanation but can only be explained properly as results of design. Thus, these arguments seem to sidestep the problems that beset analogical versions of the argument from design. Nonetheless, arguments of this new sort are open to serious objections, and before presenting my own version of the argument from design I shall mention three that I think are the most serious:

(i) Arguments from design of the second sort depend on the view that certain natural phenomena have features that make it appropriate to explain them as results of intentional action, quite apart from any analogies that hold between them and phenomena that have previously been discovered to be products of design. But this would seem untrue. When we first come by the family of notions that are connected with intending, we are not, it seems, taught logical criteria that allow us to determine whether a state of affairs was brought about intentionally. Instead, we begin by learning to recognize cases of intentional *behaviour*, and, once we know what it is for a person to act intentionally, it would seem that we come to learn that states of affairs of certain sorts are brought about intentionally, only because we frequently find such states to result from actions we recognize as intentional. That is, it seems that there are no inherent features of a state of affairs that show it to have been produced by design. Rather, we can only know a state to have been brought about intentionally either by knowing directly that it was produced by intentional actions or by knowing it to be sufficiently like states that we have discovered to result from such actions. But if this is true, then the only sorts of argument from design that can succeed are analogical arguments, and we have already seen reasons to think that analogical arguments fail.

(ii) We can reach this same conclusion from more general considerations about causation. A justly celebrated feature of Hume's theory of causation is the thesis that there are no *a priori* connections between cause and effect. One cannot by reason alone discover the cause of any state of affairs. One can only do this by having observed similar states to have been preceded by a given sort of occurrence in repeated instances. But then it will follow, again, that we can only know a state of affairs to have been caused by intentional actions if it is sufficiently like states we have already discovered to have had such causes, and if, as seems likely, the most general features of the universe are too dissimilar from those occurrences whose causes we have discovered for us to be able to reason by analogy from one to the other, then we will have to remain in ignorance about the ultimate causes in nature. These two objections, together with the objection against analogical arguments from design I presented earlier, seem to me to constitute the most serious challenge to the argument from design, and it should be noted that they challenge far more than just this single argument. Indeed, they call into question whether reason ever could provide adequate grounds for believing in the existence of God. For suppose one had adequate reason to believe in God. Then one would thereby have adequate reason to believe that the universe was caused by design. But if either objections (i) or (ii) succeed, one could not have such reason unless one had discovered states of affairs that both sufficiently closely resemble the universe as a whole and are known to have been produced by design. And, given the difficulties we saw with analogical arguments from design, it would seem that one could not do this.

(iii) Finally, non-analogical versions of the argument from design ask us to conclude that certain phenomena were produced by design, simply because no other adequate explanations seem to be available. However, even apart from the difficulties above, one should be suspicious of arguments of this form. It might, after all, be that alternative explanations are available but that we just have not been able to think of them. Indeed, it would seem that alternative explanations of many suggestive natural phenomena are available by using the sorts of devices employed by the theory of evolution in biology. For that theory seems to show a way in which purely natural processes can result in the most highly organized and impressive sorts of creatures.

Of course, the theory of evolution applies directly only to examples of seeming design in biological organisms. Nonetheless, the theory counts against the argument from design in two ways. First, it seems to rob the argument of many of its best examples. Using the theory, for example, one can explain why the various parts of the eye developed in just the way that would best promote good vision, without having to make reference to a designer. Second, even where evolutionary explanations cannot be employed directly, they seem to provide a model for explanations of phenomena that look as if they were designed. For it would seem that purely random processes could result in a universe filled with highly organized and, therefore, one would expect, impressive structures, as long as such structures came about on rare occasions and, once in existence, tended to remain in existence, while less highly organized structures tended to be less stable and more short lived.

I shall attempt to answer these three objections in Part III below. However, for now I shall set them aside and turn to the version of the argument from design I wish to offer.

Part II

The version of the argument from design I shall present here trades heavily on a distinction that is very similar to one worked out by Elizabeth Anscombe in a brief, unpublished paper, entitled 'Cause, chance, and hap', and to a great extent it grew from thoughts stimulated by Miss Anscombe's paper. In 'Cause, chance, and hap' Miss Anscombe distinguishes what she calls 'mere hap' from a sense of 'chance' she defines as 'the unplanned crossing of causes'. When an event occurs by mere hap, there is an element of randomness in its coming about; it might not have occurred, even if all of the conditions relevant to its production had been the same. To use Miss Anscombe's example, the wind might carry a sycamore seed to a certain spot and let it down, though, perhaps, it could have carried the seed just a bit further without anything relevant having been different. And if so, we can say that it merely happened that the seed dropped where it did and not a bit further on. Notice that in this case we will have a violation of the doctrine of determinism, and indeed determinism might be expressed simply as the thesis that nothing ever occurs by mere hap.

There are other sorts of cases, though, where we would say that something happened by chance, though there need be no violation of determinism. To use another example from 'Cause, chance, and hap', a plane might jettison a bomb which hits a boulder as it rolls down a slope. And here Miss Anscombe will say that it was by chance that the bomb hit the boulder, if it was not intended that it should, even though it may be that no randomness was involved. Perhaps, given sufficient information about the path of the boulder and the manner in which the bomb was jettisoned, one could predict with certainty that the bomb was going to hit the boulder or, at least, that it would if nothing intervened.

The distinction on which the argument I shall present below depends is one between Miss Anscombe's sense of 'mere hap' and a notion of chance quite similar to that of an unplanned or unintended crossing of causes. Consider as an example a typical case in which one would say that it was by chance that a friend and I met in a restaurant. One would not mean, in calling this a chance occurrence, that our meeting had no connexion with antecedent causal factors. It might well be that various occurrences brought it about that my friend was at the restaurant when he was and that others brought it about that I was there at the same time. If you wish, it might have been determined, perhaps it even always had been determined, that we would meet. None of this seems to be ruled out when one says that we met by chance. For if it were ruled out, it would be far easier than it is to refute determinism, or, rather, one would not be able to say that cases of this sort occurred by chance, unless one had refuted determinism.

What one does seem to mean in saying that it was by chance that my friend and I met, I think, is that there was no *common* cause of our meeting. I came for whatever reasons I did, and my friend for whatever reasons he did. There was nothing in common to the causal chains that got us there. Thus, if we met at the restaurant because we planned to meet, or if one of us went because he heard the other would be there, our meeting would not be a chance one. And, again, if we both went to the restaurant because a great chef was to give a one-night demonstration or because everyone in our circle of friends was there to celebrate a certain occasion, then, even if we had not intended to meet, one would not be inclined to say that we met by chance. These last two examples show, I think, that it need not be intended that two states of affairs occur together for their co-occurrence not to be by chance. It is enough if the causal chains by which the two come about contain a significant part in common.

In what follows I shall use the term 'chance' in the sense I have described here. More precisely, I shall say that the co-occurrence of two states of affairs comes about by chance when neither is a significant part of the cause of the other, and no third state is a significant part of the cause of both; that is, when the two do not come about by causal chains that have a significant part in common. Also, corresponding to the distinction between mere hap and this sense of 'chance', I shall find it useful to distinguish two ways in which one might explain conjunctions of states of affairs.

Suppose that I happen by chance to be standing up at the moment you read this sentence. Can one then hope to explain why I stand as you read? I think it would be natural to answer in the negative. There is no reason why I was standing as you read; things just happened to work out that way. However, someone who takes seriously the principle of sufficient reason, that every truth has an explanation, will not accept this reply as the last word. Rather, I think, he will want to say that all one has to do to explain the occurrence in question in the sense *he* has in mind is to conjoin explanations of why, at a certain time, I was standing and why, at the same time, you were reading the sentence you were. Corresponding to these two possible answers, let me say that a conjunction of two or more states of affairs, or the co-occurrence of the states of affairs, has a *basic explanation* when and only when each state in the conjunction has an explanation, and I shall say that a basic explanation of a conjunction is a conjunction of explanations of its conjuncts. Further, let me say that the states in a conjunction of two or more states of affairs have an *explanation in common* when and only when explanations of any two states in the conjunction contain a significant part in common. That is, the co-occurrence of a group of states of affairs will be guaranteed a basic explanation whenever no state in the group occurs by mere hap, and the states in the group will have an explanation in common if and only if no two occur together by chance.

Now there are two points I would like to make using these distinctions. First, there would seem to be no logical guarantee that two logically independent states of affairs will have an explanation in common. Things often happen by chance, and a supporter of the principle of sufficient reason can hope for no more than that every conjunction will have a basic explanation. Secondly, however, there are cases in which, as an epistemological matter of fact, we simply would not believe that certain states of affairs had occurred together by chance. And it is on this second point that the argument I shall present is based. For I believe there are natural phenomena which it would be extremely hard to believe occurred together by chance but which, it would seem, could only have an explanation in common if at least some of them were created by design. And thus, I think, by a two-step argument we might be able to prove that some natural phenomena are created intentionally.

I shall not offer an example of the sort of phenomena I have in mind until later. First, let me illustrate the reasoning I hope to use with a fictitious example which, if my memory has not deceived me, is adapted from one I was given a number of years ago by Miss Anscombe.

Suppose that one day a perfect picture, say, of a nativity scene were formed by the frost on someone's window. I think we almost certainly would believe that this occurrence was brought about by design, though not necessarily by the design of a divine being. And if we were asked why, I think we would probably respond that if this were not so, there would be no way to explain why ice formed on the window in the pattern it did. However, if by an explanation, we have in mind a basic explanation, this might well not be true.

Supposedly, in normal cases, various facts about weather conditions, the make-up of a pane of glass, the temperature and humidity in the room in which the pane is installed and the like, cause ice to form in the way it does on a window pane. And also, supposedly, there are possible conditions which, if they were to obtain, might cause ice to form a nativity scene on a given pane. Of course, these conditions might be very strange, but we do not know this. Suppose, in fact, that the nativity scene in our example arose by natural means from conditions that appeared quite normal, that those conditions themselves arose from normal-seeming conditions, etc. Then we can imagine that scientists could give a perfectly good basic explanation of why the pattern formed by the ice in our example was one that constituted a nativity scene.

First, one would explain why ice formed in the pattern it did on the relevant window in the way that one might hope to do so in normal cases, that is, by explaining why ice crystals of various sorts formed on various spots of the window. Then one would explain why the pattern that was formed made up a nativity scene, using facts about geometry, about basic human perceptual mechanisms, perhaps, and the like. The result would be a basic explanation of why the pattern that formed was a nativity scene.

What I think is interesting here, though, is this. If we were given such an explanation of the nativity scene in our example, we would still, I think, be no less inclined than before to believe that it resulted from design. If anything, by showing that the scene arose from processes that were, so to speak, part of the course of nature, such an explanation would make us more inclined to believe that it was designed by a being deserving of our worship and not merely by someone who had made a technological breakthrough over ice.[2]

The question, then, I think, is: what reasoning do we use when we conclude that the nativity scene in our example was produced by design? And the answer, I believe, is the following. First, I think, we believe that ice could not form a nativity scene on a window merely by chance. That is, in our example, there must be an explanation in common of the fact that ice formed the pattern it did on a certain window and the fact that that pattern constitutes a nativity scene. Why we believe this is not completely clear. Ice very often forms beautiful patterns on window panes, and yet we are content to accept that it is by chance that the patterns that are formed are ones that strike us as beautiful. However, that we would not be content to hold similarly that a nativity scene resulted from chance I think is clear.

But if this is true, then the fact that the ice formed a certain pattern on the pane in our example and the fact that that pattern constitutes a nativity scene must share a significant part of their causes in common. And, therefore, either one of the facts is a significant part of the cause of the other, or a third state of affairs is a significant part of the cause of both. However, the fact that a certain pattern forms a nativity scene is a very general one. It results from facts about geometry, about what counts as a nativity scene, and, perhaps, about what patterns we see when we encounter various sorts of objects. And many of these facts are not caused at all, while the remainder, it would seem, as an empirical matter of fact, could be caused neither by the fact that ice formed in a certain pattern on a particular pane of glass nor by the sort of facts, for example, about local weather conditions and the make-up of a pane, that would cause ice to form in such a pattern. And, therefore, it seems that neither the fact that ice formed in a certain pattern nor causes of that fact could be significant parts of what caused the pattern to be a nativity scene.

However, in this case it must be that the fact that a certain pattern constitutes a nativity scene was an important part of what brought it about that the pattern appeared on the window in our example. And this, again as an empirical matter, seems to be something that could not happen unless the pattern was produced by design. For the fact that a pattern forms a nativity scene could give a designer reason to bring it about that it appeared on a window and, thus, play a significant role in an explanation of such a fact. However, if the pattern in our example was not

2. It should be noted that an analogous point could be made about the argument from design. Someone holding that certain natural phenomena were designed need not deny that the phenomena resulted from a chain of purely natural causes extending indefinitely far in the past. And, again, if a natural phenomenon one believes to have been produced by design turns out to have resulted from such a chain of causes, that fact may count as evidence for the eminence of its designer.

brought about by design, then it seems out of the question to think that the fact that it constitutes a nativity scene might have been an important part of the cause of the very specific conditions holding in and around a particular piece of glass on a particular night that caused it to be formed in ice. And, thus, it seems that the nativity scene in our example must have been produced by design.

The case of the nativity scene, of course, is fictitious, but I believe that similar reasoning might well be able to show that in many actual cases natural phenomena have been produced by design. For in many cases complex states of affairs have come together in ways that have produced noteworthy features of the universe, and one might argue that it could not simply be by chance that they came together in ways that had such impressive results. That is, one might think that there must be an explanation in common of the facts that certain states of affairs have occurred and that, by having done so, they have produced the impressive results they have. However, the fact that various states of affairs would produce impressive results, if they occurred together, cannot, it would seem, be explained by the fact that the states actually did occur, nor by the sort of facts that would cause them to occur. And, therefore, the only alternative is that the fact that the states would produce impressive results helps to explain their occurrence. But, again, it would seem that this could not happen unless the states were caused to occur by a designer acting to produce their impressive results.

This, then, in brief, is the version of the argument from design I wish to put forward, and I want to claim that the reasoning employed in it gains plausibility from the fact that similar reasoning explains our intuitions in the case of the nativity scene. However, I think one might want to dispute this last claim. For, first, it might be thought that our intuitions about the example of the nativity scene are based, not on the complex argument I suggested, but on simple analogical reasoning. That is, one might think that, unlike the sorts of natural phenomena to which arguments from design appeal, the nativity scene in our example is sufficiently like works of art created by human beings for one to reason simply by analogy that it too must have been designed

And, secondly, one might want to argue that even if our intuitions about the nativity scene can be explained by the reasoning I proposed, that reasoning itself is only a disguised form of analogical reasoning. For it might seem that there is only one way in which one can discover that a group of phenomena have an explanation in common, assuming that one has not discovered this directly by first having discovered the causes of the various members of the group, and that is to find sufficient similarities between the group and others whose members are already known to have explanations in common. But in this case, it might be thought that the conjunctions of phenomena to which an argument from design points differ enough from those whose origins we have been able to discover to block an argument by analogy that their members have explanations in common.

I think, however, that these two objections fail. First of all, it is true that in many respects the nativity scene in our example closely resembles works of art we know to have been designed by human beings. Indeed, the image formed in the example can be supposed to look just like the sort of image artists put on canvas. Nonetheless, there are also ways in which the nativity scene differs from works of art. Most importantly, the process by which the scene came to be on its window differs greatly from that by which paint comes to be on a canvas, and this is just the sort of difference that earlier made us conclude that we could not claim that eyes were produced by design merely because they resemble machines.

That the similarities between our nativity scene and human works of art are not enough to permit a simple argument by analogy for the design of the scene can be shown, I think, by the following consideration. Frequently frost forms beautiful, symmetrical 'snowflake' patterns on window panes, and these patterns often resemble man-made geometrical designs just as closely as the nativity scene in our example might be supposed to resemble works of art. Yet no one would conclude straight away that such frost patterns are produced by design. More than resemblance to works of art, then, is needed to show that the nativity scene in our example would have to have been created intentionally.

Secondly, it might be true that one can infer that phenomena whose causes are not known have an explanation in common, *only* if one does so by analogy from cases that already have been discovered to have such explanations, though shortly I shall suggest that this is not true. But even if it is true, it does not follow that one cannot infer that a group of phenomena have an explanation in common unless there are no significant disanalogies between that group and others that have been discovered to have explanations in common. For it must be remembered that we know phenomena of many different sorts to have explanations in common and, as a result, if a new group of phenomena has important features in common with those groups that have been discovered to have explanations in common, and if the differences between the new group and the other groups seem no more relevant than the differences between some of the other groups themselves, then one should be able to reason by analogy that the members of the new group have an explanation in common. That is, in this case our inference will be more like one which concludes that dogs have a certain feature from the fact that all mammals studied from a wide range of species do, than it will be like one which concludes that dogs have a feature because horses do and because no other mammals have been studied.

At any rate, the fact that the natural phenomena to which arguments from design point are not enough like human artifacts for one to argue by simple analogy that they came about by design is not sufficient to show that one cannot conclude that there must be an explanation in common of the facts that they took place as they did and that, by doing so, they brought about impressive states of affairs. Again, a case in point here is the eye. We cannot argue by simple analogy to machines that our eyes were designed, but it would be preposterous to maintain that the development of the various parts of the eye could be explained without bringing in the fact that they allow one to see. Indeed, one of the most attractive features of the theory of evolution is that it can provide explanations that meet this sort of requirement.

Earlier I suggested that when we infer that two states of affairs have an explanation in common, we might not be reasoning by analogy. In fact, I am inclined to think that the judgement that certain states of affairs have an explanation in common is not dependent on but, rather, is presupposed by inductive reasoning, and I think it might well be the case that it is certain inherent features of states of affairs that make us judge them to have explanations in common, and, further, that we are justified in doing so, if we are justified in reasoning by induction.

Consider a case in which a coin is tossed 100 times and comes up heads each time. One would, no doubt, conclude from this both that the coin had been rigged and that it was almost certain to come up heads on future tosses. And what I think is important here is that these two judgements are connected. In particular, if one thought it was merely by chance that the coin came up the same way on each toss, then it would be as irrational to conclude, by induction, that future tosses would be like previous ones as it would be to conclude, by the gambler's fallacy, that a string of heads must be followed by one of tails. In each new toss the probability would still be one in two that the coin would land heads.

And this, I think, is true in general of inductive inferences. We can sensibly hold that unobserved cases will be like observed ones only when we believe the observed cases have had a significant part of their causes in common. Thus, if we do not believe observed emeralds have been green because of general features of the process by which they were formed, then it would not be reasonable to conclude that unobserved emeralds are green. But if this is true, then it seems that we must be able to make judgements that various phenomena have explanations in common before we can reason by induction and, therefore, it seems that such judgements are not based on induction.

Part III

Let me now turn to the three objections against the argument from design that I mentioned at the end of Part I. Objections (i) and (ii) from Part I tried to show that one could come to know that a state of affairs was brought about by design only directly or by straightforward analogical reasoning. However, if my remarks about our example of the nativity scene were correct, one could know that that scene was produced by design but could not do so in either of these ways. Further, even if I am mistaken, and one could infer by analogy that the scene in our example was designed, still, I think, one could also come to know that it was by the more complex reasoning I described, and such reasoning might let one know that a state of affairs was produced by design, even when this could not be shown by analogy.

Objections (i) and (ii), then, fail, and that they do, I think, should not come as too great a surprise. For the two objections hold, plausibly enough, that one cannot know *a priori* that any given state of affairs was brought about by intentional action.

But it does not follow from this that one could know such a thing only directly or by analogy. The objections, then, do not show that there could not be a line of empirical reasoning that is not straightforwardly analogical but that, nonetheless, might allow one to infer that a state of affairs had been brought about by intention. They simply assume that there could be no such line. However, if I am correct, the reasoning I proposed to explain our intuitions about the nativity scene on the window is just such a bit of reasoning, and if the reasoning seems plausible, then objections (i) and (ii) should not stand in its way.

Let me move on, then, to objection (iii). I think many people today are taken by a certain picture of the origin of life in which the theory of evolution plays a large part. As things are represented by this picture, it was simply a matter of good fortune that the earth came to provide an environment suitable for living creatures, though the good fortune here was not particularly surprising. For in a universe as vast as ours there are many stars like the sun, and—often enough—such stars should have planets whose size, composition, and orbit are similar to those of the earth. Then, once the earth afforded the proper environment, the first primitive organisms came into existence as results of what, it is hoped, were not too improbable series of chemical reactions. Again, here, it was simply by chance that the chemical processes that occurred were ones that produced living creatures. Finally, once the first organisms were in existence, it is thought that the theory of evolution can account for the rest and that the mechanisms of chance mutation and natural selection embodied in the theory led to the development of more and more highly developed creatures until, finally, beings evolved that were capable of reason.

This picture of the origin of life seems to be widely held today. Indeed, I believe its popularity is an important feature of the intellectual history of the present age. Nonetheless, I think the picture is flawed. For one thing, we might believe that various chemical processes could produce very simple living creatures, even if the fact that they produced such creatures had nothing to do with the fact that the processes came about. But we would not accept that very complex creatures could come about in this way. However, as Geach has noted,[3] the process of natural selection itself seems to presuppose the existence of creatures with highly developed genetic mechanisms and, so, cannot be used to explain their origin. And, therefore, we must find another plausible account of the origin of these mechanisms.

Natural selection can only take place among creatures that bear offspring that closely resemble their parents without resembling them too closely. For if offspring are exactly like their parents, then natural selection can occur only among characteristics already in existence and, thus, will not lead to the development of new characteristics. On the other hand, if offspring do not closely resemble their parents, then even if certain parents have highly adaptive characteristics and bear many more children than others, their children will not be very likely to inherit the characteristics, and the process will stop.

3. P. T. Geach, 'An irrelevance of omnipotence', *Philosophy* vol. 48, No. 186 (1973), 327–33.

Of course, in fact creatures do have genetic mechanisms that facilitate natural selection, but the mechanisms are very complicated, and though they might themselves have evolved to some extent by natural selection, it would seem that any mechanism that led to offspring that resembled their parents closely enough but not too closely would have to be very complicated. And so, one would have to ask how they could come about, if not by design. As Geach writes:

There can he no origin of *species*, as opposed to an Empedoclean chaos of varied monstrosities, unless creatures reproduce pretty much after their kind; the elaborate and ostensibly teleological mechanism of this reproduction logically cannot be explained as a product of evolution by natural selection from among chance variations, for unless the mechanism is presupposed there cannot be any evolution.[4]

Thus, there is much that is noteworthy about the development of living beings that cannot be explained by the theory of evolution. But even if this problem can be surmounted without recourse to a designer, there is a second difficulty.

Simplified accounts of the theory of evolution might make it appear inevitable that creatures evolved with the sorts of impressive and obviously adaptive features that might otherwise be thought to have been designed. For over a sufficient period, one might think, a few individuals would develop such features by chance mutation, and once some creatures had them, the obvious desirability of the features would be enough to explain their proliferation. However, this impression of inevitability, I think, is quite misleading.

Evolutionary change generally proceeds very slowly. We can be confident, for example, that no ancestors of birds suddenly came by wings in a single step and, likewise, that no ancestor of man came to have a brain capable of reason because of one chance mutation. Instead, these sorts of noteworthy and obviously adaptive features come about only as results of long series of evolutionary changes, each of which has to be adaptive and has to become dominant among members of a species, and the noteworthy features themselves cannot come about unless all the others do. Further, these smaller evolutionary changes cannot be counted on to be obviously adaptive, nor always to be adaptive for the same reasons that the larger, more noteworthy changes are. And most importantly, as the term 'adaptive' itself suggests, very often these small changes will be adaptive only because of fine details of, and changes in, the relationship between members of a species and their environment.

Consider the following passage from a recent biology textbook, for example:

There is . . . good evidence that during the period in which *Australopithecus* lived there existed considerable expanses of lush savannah with scattered shrubs, trees, and grasses. There were berries and roots in abundance, and because such areas were suitable for grazing, these savannahs were well stocked with game. These areas provided new habitats, abundant in food, and so we surmise the australopithecines came down from the trees in which their own apelike ancestors lived in order to avail themselves of these new sources of food. . . .

4. P. T. Geach, *ibid.* p. 330.

Although descent from the trees does not always result in evolution of upright posture in primates . . . through a lucky combination of anatomy and habits, these ape-men became bipedal. Being bipedal meant that the hands were freed from locomotor function and could be employed in manipulative skills such as carrying and dragging objects, fashioning tools and weapons, and so on.[5]

This, in turn, led to improvements in the primitive tool-making that had preceded upright posture. And finally, 'with the advent of toolmaking, hunting for big game became a possibility, and the brain and the hand were now subject to the molding force of natural selection'.[6]

Now whether the precise details of the picture presented in this passage turn out to be true is not important here. What is important is that something of this sort almost certainly was true. Had not the grass in a certain area grown to the proper height, had not a certain food source become available or unavailable, had not various predators been present or absent, had not climatic conditions been what they were, etc. as ancestors of man developed, human beings would not have come into existence. And if they had not, there seems to be no reason to think other beings capable of reason would have evolved instead. After all, useful as intelligence is, no other species has come into existence with such a high level of it.

Furthermore, seemingly chance occurrences like these did not play a role only in the final stages of the evolution of human beings. It is likely that, at nearly every step in the evolutionary chain that led from the most primitive of creatures to people, similar sorts of occurrences played a role. In fact, without specific evidence one cannot assume even that it was inevitable that mammals, vertebrates, or even multi-celled creatures would evolve.

But then, one might ask, again, whether it could have been simply by chance that so many seemingly unconnected occurrences came together in just the way that would lead to the evolution of creatures capable of reason, and I think that one might well conclude that it could not have been. At least, it would be very strange, if the myriad occurrences needed to produce human beings came about in just the right way simply by chance and equally strange if the occurrences had an explanation in common, but the fact that they would produce intelligent beings had nothing to do with the fact that they came about. However, one might wonder how so many different sorts of occurrences could have an explanation in common and, indeed, have an explanation in common with the fact that they would lead to the evolution of beings capable of reason, unless they were produced by design?

5. I. W. Sherman and V. G. Sherman, *Biology: A Human Approach* (OUP, New York, 1975), p. 456.
6. I. W. Sherman and V. G. Sherman, *ibid.* p. 456.

Questions for discussion

1. What might be meant by calling something 'designed'?
2. How can we decide if something has a purpose?
3. Can design arguments ever establish the existence of something other than a finite being?
4. Does the world contain order in itself, or is order a creation of the human mind?
5. Have design arguments been refuted by developments in science?

Advice on further reading

For two clearly written book-length treatments of design arguments, see Robert H. Hurlbutt III, *Hume, Newton, and the Design Argument* (Lincoln, Nebraska, 1965) and Thomas McPherson, *The Argument from Design* (London, 1972). For briefer discussions, see the introductions to philosophy listed in the General Introduction's further reading section (all of them contain sections on design arguments). For an account of some medieval design arguments, see Herbert A. Davidson, *Proofs for Eternity, Creation and the Existence of God in Medieval Islamic and Jewish Philosophy* (New York and Oxford, 1987), pp. 216–36. For an impressive defence of a design argument not mentioned above, see F. R. Tennant, *Philosophical Theology*, vol. 2 (New York and Cambridge, 1930). Also see Richard Taylor, *Metaphysics* (3rd edn, Englewood Cliffs, NJ, 1983), ch. 10.

Aquinas on God as a final cause is expounded and discussed by Leo J. Elders, *The Philosophical Theology of St Thomas Aquinas* (Leiden, 1990), ch. III, and by Anthony Kenny, *The Five Ways* (London, 1969), ch. VI. For a more technical treatment, see Jan Aertsen, *Nature and Creature: Thomas Aquinas's Way of Thought* (Leiden, 1988), ch. 8. With great lucidity, Kenny also discusses final causation in 'The Argument from Design', reprinted in Anthony Kenny, *Reason and Religion* (Oxford, 1987).

A fine introduction to Boyle on religion is Jan W. Wojcik, *Robert Boyle and the Limits of Reason* (Cambridge, 1997). For introductions to Hume on design arguments, see J. C. A. Gaskin, 'Hume on Religion', in David Fate Norton (ed.), *The Cambridge Companion to Hume* (Cambridge, 1993), and J. C. A. Gaskin, *Hume's Philosophy of Religion* (2nd edn, London, 1988), chs 2 and 7. For an introduction to and discussion of Hume's *Dialogues* as a whole, see Stanley Tweyman (ed.), *David Hume Dialogues Concerning Natural Religion in Focus* (London and New York, 1991). For a collection of discussions on Hume on religion (including discussions of Hume on design arguments), see Stanley Tweyman (ed.), *David Hume: Critical Assessments*, vol. 5 (London and New York, 1995).

A good source book to consult with reference to Paley and Darwin is Tess Cosslett (ed.), *Science and Religion in the Nineteenth Century* (Cambridge, 1984). Did Darwin undermine design arguments? For helpful discussions of this question, see Peter Geach, *Providence and Evil* (Cambridge, 1977), ch. 4, and James A. Sadowsky, 'Did Darwin Destroy the Design Argument?', *International Philosophical Quarterly* XXVIII (1988). See also Kenny's 'The Argument from Design', cited above.

Kant's thinking on design arguments is best understood with an eye on what he is arguing overall in the *Critique of Pure Reason*. For a recent introductory guide to this, see Sebastian Gardner, *Kant and the Critique of Pure Reason* (London and New York, 1999). For a commentary on the text from Kant printed in Chapter 26, see Norman Kemp Smith, *A Commentary to Kant's 'Critique of Pure Reason'* (2nd edn, London and Basingstoke, 1979).

Richard Swinburne has written fairly extensively on design arguments. In addition to Chapter 27, see:

'The Argument from Design—A Defence', *Religious Studies*, 8 (1972).

Evidence for God (Oxford, 1986).

Is There a God? (Oxford and New York, 1986), ch. 4.

The Existence of God (revised edn, Oxford, 1991), ch. 8.

In recent years, there has been much discussion of contemporary scientific findings which indicate that the origin and evolution of intelligent life on earth depends on the fact that the universe is 'fine-tuned' for its production. This discussion is relevant to those with interests in design arguments. Its relevance to them is considered by Swinburne in Appendix B to the revised edition of *The Existence of God*. For scientific matters, see John D. Barrow and Frank J. Tipler, *The Anthropic Cosmological Principle* (Oxford, 1986). For more on their relevance to design arguments, see William Lane Craig, 'The Teleological Argument and the Anthropic Principle', in William Lane Craig and M. McLeod (eds), *The Logic of Rational Theism* (Lewiston, NY, 1990), and (for a different approach) R. Dawkins, *The Blind Watchmaker* (Harlow, 1986). See also John Leslie, *Universes* (London and New York, 1989).

For a somewhat original defence of an argument from design which concentrates on beauty and goodness in the world, see Mark Wynn, *God and Goodness* (London and New York, 1999).

Ontological arguments

Introduction

What is an 'ontological argument'?

In the *Critique of Pure Reason*, Kant asserts that 'there are only three possible ways of proving the existence of God by means of speculative reason'.[1] One way argues 'completely a priori, from mere concepts, to the existence of a supreme cause'. Kant calls it the 'ontological' argument, and the name has stuck. But it is now commonly used by philosophers to refer to what we find in texts which actually take significantly different positions. There is no such thing as 'the' ontological argument. Rather there is a family of related arguments which may be thought of as 'ontological' since, as we may put it, they take their stand on a concept rather than on the fact that the world exists or that the world has a certain nature.

The concept here is the concept of God.[2] Common to all ontological arguments is the suggestion that once we understand what this amounts to, we will see that God exists. And not only that. Ontological arguments maintain that God *cannot possibly fail to exist*, or that there is some intrinsic absurdity in denying God's existence. To put things another way, they hold that God is a *necessary being*. Once we understand what the word 'triangle' means, we can see, straight off, that 'There are four-sided triangles' cannot possibly be true (is necessarily false). According to ontological arguments, once we take note of the meaning of the word 'God', we can see (maybe not straight off, but with a little thought) that 'God does not exist' also cannot possibly be true (is necessarily false).

Anselm and the beginnings of ontological arguments

Though it was Kant who invented the phrase 'the ontological argument', it is usually agreed that the kind of thinking he had in mind when using it originated as far back as the eleventh century. For the father of ontological arguments is generally reckoned to be Anselm of Canterbury. And it is his first contribution to the history of these arguments

---

1. *Critique of Pure Reason* A591/B619. Note that many would disagree with Kant's assertion here.
2. As I have noted, one has to reckon with the fact that people have understood the word 'God' in a variety of ways. Fortunately, however, defenders of ontological arguments always indicate what sense of 'God' they have in mind. Indeed, they have to in order to develop their arguments.

which you can find in Chapter 29. It comes from his *Proslogion*, the work he published after writing the *Monologion* (cf. Chapter 13).

What is Anselm trying to say in this extract? One problem of interpretation concerns the unity of the argument. The extract comprises chapters 2 and 3 of the *Proslogion*. Are these to be taken as offering one single argument? Or do they offer two distinct arguments for two different conclusions? Some have said that *Proslogion* 2 is designed to prove that God exists and that *Proslogion* 3 is designed separately to argue that God cannot possibly fail to exist. Others have said that *Proslogion* 2 effectively argues that God cannot possibly fail to exist and that *Proslogion* 3 adds little of substance to what precedes it. Yet others have viewed *Proslogion* 2 and 3 as comprising one single argument which Anselm thought to be over only at the end of *Proslogion* 3. In reading the extract from Anselm, these matters of interpretation are ones you should bear in mind.[3]

Another problem of interpretation concerns what seem to be two crucial sentences in *Proslogion* 2. The chapter begins with Anselm challenging the statement 'There is no God' and seeking to show why it is foolish to assert it.[4] He then homes in on the idea that the word 'God' can be taken to signify 'something-than-which-nothing-greater-can-be-thought' (*aliquid quo nihil maius cogitari possit*). We cannot, says Anselm, doubt that people have an idea or some notion of God (that, as Anselm puts it, God exists 'in the mind' (*in intellectu*), as a picture exists 'in the mind' of a painter before he has painted it). But we must also, says Anselm, concede that God exists 'in reality' (*in re*), as, for example, does a finished painting. But why? Here we come to the sentences to which I just referred.

In Latin they read: '*Et certe id quo maius cogitari nequit non potest esse in solo intellectu. Si enim vel in solo intellectu est potest cogitari esse et in re quod maius est.*' But these sentences can be translated in significantly different ways. We could (as the translation of Anselm below does) render them: 'And surely that-than-which-a-greater-cannot-be-thought cannot exist in the mind alone. For if it exists solely in the mind, it can be thought to exist in reality also, which is greater.' This would leave us with Anselm saying that God must exist since existing in reality is a perfection which we cannot think of as lacking in that-than-which-a-greater-cannot-be-thought. But the sentence can also be translated: 'And surely that-than-which-a-greater-cannot-be thought cannot exist in the mind alone. For if it is only in the mind, what is greater can be thought to be in reality as well.' And, if this is what Anselm is saying, he is not thinking of existing in reality as a perfection. Rather, he is suggesting that we can think of something which is greater than something existing only in the mind, implying that that-than-which-a-greater-cannot-be thought cannot exist only in the mind.

Anselm is usually taken to be arguing that God must exist in reality since nothing corresponding to the notion of God could fail to lack the perfection of real existence. And maybe he is. But one might seriously doubt that this is his line of thought chiefly because it does not occur either in *Proslogion* 3 or in his reply to the *Proslogion*'s first

---

3. For help in doing so, see 'Advice on further reading' for this section of the book.
4. Here Anselm is alluding to Psalm 14: 1, which he would have read as giving divine warrant for the claim that it is, indeed, foolish to deny the existence of God.

published critic. However you think of the relationship between *Proslogion* 2 and 3, it is clear that their arguments are thought of by Anselm as connected with each other. Yet there is nothing in *Proslogion* 3 about real existence being a perfection.[5] Nor is there anything about it being so in what Anselm says to Gaunilo, which brings us to chapters 30 and 31.

Anselm and Gaunilo

After the appearance of the *Proslogion*, Anselm received a critical response to chapters 2 and 3. This came from Gaunilo, a Benedictine monk of the Abbey of Marmoutiers. Anselm was impressed by Gaunilo's comments. He replied to them at length. He also directed that they should be copied in all subsequent editions of the *Proslogion*. At the same time, however, he was also unhappy with what Gaunilo had to say.

What did that amount to? To start with, Gaunilo suggests that the fact that we have a notion of something does not show that there is anything in reality which corresponds to it. We can have all sorts of unreal objects in our understanding. In any case, so Gaunilo adds, we do not understand what God is. And, so he goes on to say, if Anselm is right, then absurd consequences follow. For if Anselm has succeeded in proving God's existence, has he not also provided reason to believe in the existence of what nobody takes to exist? For what about the mythical notion of a most perfect island? It would, says Gaunilo, be absurd to argue:

1. They say that island X (the most perfect island) exists.
2. If X does not exist, it would be less perfect than any island you care to mention.
3. So X exists.

And yet, so Gaunilo suggests, Anselm's *Proslogion* argument is basically like this one.

But is it? In his reply to Gaunilo Anselm distinguishes between the notion of a most perfect such and such and the notion of that-than-which-a-greater-cannot-be-thought. And, so he observes, it is the latter notion with which he is concerned in the *Proslogion*. So he takes the 'perfect island' objection as failing to engage with what he is saying there. He also goes on to defend himself in various other ways. He argues, for example, that to think of that-than-which-a-greater-cannot-be-thought is to think of something without a beginning, and that something without a beginning cannot be thought of as not existing since something which does not exist can be thought of as being able to begin to exist. Among other things, he also argues:

1. Something which is able to be, but which does not exist, could, if it existed, be able not to be either in the mind or outside it. But something able not to be either in

<hr />

5. One might find this unsurprising since one might take *Proslogion* 3 to be arguing, not that God exists, but that God exists necessarily. On the other hand, *Proslogion* 2 is arguing that it is 'impossible' that God should fail to exist 'in reality' and one might read *Proslogion* 3 as merely giving further reason as to why this is so. In that case, one might wonder why the notion of existence in reality being a perfection simply does not feature in *Proslogion* 3.

the mind or outside it would not be that-than-which-a-greater-cannot-be-thought.

2. Suppose there is something which exists at some time and in some place, though not at all times and all places. Such a thing can be thought of as not existing at any time or at any place. Also suppose that there is something bits of which do not exist at the time and place its other parts exist. Such a thing can also be thought of as not existing at any time or at any place. And what is composed of parts can be thought of as able to be broken up and, hence, as not existing at some time and place. But that-than-which-a-greater-cannot-be-thought cannot be thought not to exist, if it does exist, and must exist as a whole at every time and every place.

3. We can conceive of something existing only in the mind. But we can also conceive of something greater which is not just in the mind. So, if God is that-than-which-a-greater-cannot-be-thought, it cannot be that God exists only in the mind.

Is Anselm here trading on the notion that God must exist since existence is a perfection which that-than-which-a-greater-cannot-be-thought must have? He does not seem to be. Yet many defenders of ontological arguments explicitly take this notion to be important when it comes to proving that God exists. Perhaps the most famous example is Descartes.

Descartes on God as 'supremely perfect'

In the Middle Ages, ontological arguments met with a varied reaction. Some, such as St Bonaventure, applauded them. According to him: 'Since it is true that that which cannot be thought not to be is more true than that which can be thought not to be, therefore, if God is that than which nothing greater can be conceived, God cannot be thought not to be?'[6] But other medieval thinkers rejected such reasoning, a notable example being Aquinas, who, in *Summa Theologiae*, Ia. 2. 1, after citing an argument very similar to Bonaventure's, replies that though we may give the word 'God' any meaning we please, nothing follows from this when it comes to the real existence of God. Or, in his words:

Someone hearing the word *God* may very well not understand it to mean *that than which nothing greater can be thought* ... And even if the word *God* were generally recognized to have that meaning, nothing would thereby be granted existence in the world of fact, but merely in thought. Unless one is given that something in fact exists than which nothing greater can be thought—and this nobody denying God's existence would grant—the conclusion that God in fact exists does not follow.[7]

Though he thinks that there is a sense in which God's non-existence is unthinkable (see

---

6. Cf. Bonaventure, *Disputed Questions on the Mystery of the Trinity*, Question 1, Article 1. For a translation, see Zachary Hayes (trans.), *Saint Bonaventure's 'Disputed Questions on the Mystery of the Trinity'* (St Bonaventure, New York, 1979).

7. *Summa Theologiae*, Ia. 2. 1 ad 2.

Part IV, chapter 50), Aquinas also argues that we lack sufficient knowledge of God to provide us with an understanding on the basis of which we can move from an account of what God is to the conclusion that God exists.

I maintain then that the proposition *God exists* is self-evident in itself, since its subject and predicate are identical ... But because what it is to be God is not evident to us the proposition is not self-evident to us.[8]

Yet ontological arguments came to be seriously considered in subsequent times, and Descartes stands as a major influence in this connection. His contribution to discussion of ontological arguments comes in Chapter 32, and in Chapter 33, in which he replies to some of his critics.

Descartes's argument may be laid out formally as follows:

1. The idea of God is the idea of 'a supremely perfect being'.
2. A supremely perfect being has all perfections.
3. Existence is a perfection.
4. So a supremely perfect being has the perfection of existence.
5. So one cannot think of God except as existing.
6. So God exists.

But does this argument work? Some of Descartes's contemporaries thought not. Pierre Gassendi (1592–1655) attacked it, arguing that 'existence is not a perfection either in God or in anything else'. He also suggested that no thoughts as to what God might be like can serve to establish that there actually is a God. Johannes Caterus (a Catholic theologian from Holland) suggested that Descartes's argument falls foul of Aquinas's criticism of the ontological argument.

Yet Descartes, as you can read below, remained convinced that the notion of God implies God's existence. And his conviction was shared by some notable philosophers in the years after his death. A significant figure to note here is Leibniz. According to him, Descartes's ontological argument is a good piece of reasoning if the idea of a wholly perfect being 'is possible and does not imply a contradiction'. And, since Leibniz maintained that it *is* possible and that it does not imply a contradiction, he defended Descartes's argument.[9]

Kant and 'the ontological argument'

But might it not be said that authors such as Gassendi and Caterus were effectively drawing attention to some pretty serious weaknesses in Descartes's argument? This question brings us to chapter 34, which is an extract from Kant's *Critique of Pure Reason*. One of the most famous discussions of ontological arguments in the history of philosophy, it purports definitively to show that we simply cannot prove God's existence in the way that Descartes thought.

8. *Ibid.*
9. Cf. G. W. Leibniz, *New Essays on Human Understanding*, Book IV, ch. X.

What is Kant's case against ontological arguments? It is not an easy one to follow, but it chiefly seems to be twofold.[10] Kant seems to be saying (1) that there is no contradiction involved in saying 'God does not exist', and (2) that existence is not a property or attribute which can be listed when stating what God is like (that, in Kant's language, '"*Being*" is obviously not a real predicate').

Descartes holds that to deny God's existence is like denying that triangles have three sides. But for Kant 'God does not exist' could be true, since to define something is only to say that if anything matches the definition or the description of the thing, then it will be as the definition states.

Descartes thinks that to understand God's perfections is to see that they include the perfection of existing. Kant's view, however, is that existing is no perfection in anything since it cannot be listed in a description of anything.

Is Kant's assessment right here? Many philosophers have been persuaded as to the truth of his first claim. Like Kant, they would say that 'Whatever, and however much, our concept of an object may contain, we must go outside it, if we are to ascribe existence to the object'—that, in effect, you cannot define things into existence. As for Kant's point about existence and description: that, too, has found pretty widespread acceptance among philosophers, particularly among those influenced by Frege and Russell, who may be thought of as refining and defending Kant's assertion that 'Being' is not a 'real predicate'.[11] But plenty of philosophers continue to insist that we do learn something about things when learning that they exist, and that existing is a property which can be thought of as entering into an account of what something is. So the issues at stake between Kant and people like Descartes are still alive, as are ontological arguments in general.

Ontological arguments since Kant

The Anselmian ontological argument, for instance, has been spoken of favourably by Elizabeth Anscombe, who attempts to rescue it from the charge of supposing that existence is a perfection.[12] In a well-known paper published in 1960, Norman Malcolm does the same, focusing on *Proslogion* 3. Here, so Malcolm suggests, Anselm argues that God must exist, not because existence is a perfection but because *necessary existence* is one. And, so Malcolm goes on to say, the argument is a good one. He writes:

10. The *Critique of Pure Reason* is a notoriously difficult text to read, as philosophers frequently observe. Kant himself admitted that it lacks literary merit.
11. Frege argues that statements of existence are statements of number and do not tell us what something is like any more than 'Horses are numerous' describes a particular horse. See Gottlob Frege, *The Foundations of Arithmetic* (trans. J. L. Austin, Oxford, 1980), pp. 59 ff. Russell argues that one can understand existence statements without understanding that there are particular individuals with actual properties or attributes, from which he concludes that existence statements are logically different from descriptions of things. See Bertrand Russell, *Logic and Knowledge* (London and New York, 1950), p. 228 ff.
12. G. E. M. Anscombe, 'Why Anslem's Proof in the *Proslogion* Is Not an Ontological Argument', *The Thoreau Quarterly* 17 (1985). Anscombe's treatment of Anselm, of course, presupposes a reading of his writings which not everyone would share.

If God, a being a greater than which cannot be conceived, does not exist then He cannot *come* into existence. For if He did He would either have been *caused* to come into existence or have *happened* to come into existence, and in either case He would be a limited being, which by our conception of Him He is not. Since He cannot come into existence, if He does not exist His existence is impossible. If He does exist He cannot have come into existence . . . nor can He cease to exist, for nothing could cause him to cease to exist nor could it just happen that He ceased to exist. So if God exists His existence is necessary. Thus God's existence is either impossible or necessary. It can be the former only if the concept of such a being is self-contradictory or in some way logically absurd. Assuming that this is not so, it follows that He necessarily exists.[13]

Is that right, however? Many have found Malcolm's position somewhat unconvincing, but it has been taken up, developed, and ultimately defended by Alvin Plantinga, as you can see in chapter 35. Plantinga's approach turns on the notion that if God possibly exists, then God necessarily exists. His augmentation of Malcolm's argument has become something of a classic in twentieth-century philosophy, and it has given rise to much discussion. It depends heavily on the notion of 'possible worlds' introduced into philosophy by Leibniz and much developed by twentieth-century philosophers working in the area of what is called 'modal logic'. Some philosophers would suggest that it is a notion to be treated with a large degree of suspicion, especially as employed in defending ontological arguments. But it has certainly proved to be a fertile one. And it cannot be denied that its application to ontological arguments currently presents philosophers of religion with a lot to think about.

13. Norman Malcolm, 'Anselm's Ontological Arguments', *The Philosophical Review* 69 (1960), pp. 49 f.

Chapter 29

Anselm argues that God cannot be thought not to exist

Anselm of Canterbury

That God truly exists

W ELL then, Lord, You who give understanding to faith, grant me that I may understand, as much as You see fit, that You exist as we believe You to exist, and that You are what we believe You to be. Now we believe that You are something than which nothing greater can be thought. Or can it be that a thing of such a nature does not exist, since 'the Fool has said in his heart, there is no God' [Ps. 4: 1]? But surely, when this same Fool hears what I am speaking about, namely, 'something-than-which-nothing-greater-can-be-thought', he understands what he hears, and what he understands is in his mind, even if he does not understand that it actually exists. For it is one thing for an object to exist in the mind, and another thing to understand that an object actually exists. Thus, when a painter plans beforehand what he is going to execute, he has [the picture] in his mind, but he does not yet think that it actually exists because he has not yet executed it. However, when he has actually painted it, then he both has it in his mind and understands that it exists because he has now made it. Even the Fool, then, is forced to agree that something-than-which-nothing-greater-can-be-thought exists in the mind, since he understands this when he hears it, and whatever is understood is in the mind. And surely that-than-which-a-greater-cannot-be-thought cannot exist in the mind alone. For if it exists solely in the mind, it can be thought to exist in reality also, which is greater. If then that-than-which-a-greater-cannot-be-thought exists in the mind alone, this same that-than-which-a-greater-*cannot*-be-thought is that-than-which-a-greater-*can*-be-thought. But this is obviously impossible. Therefore there is absolutely no doubt that something-than-which-a-greater-cannot-be-thought exists both in the mind and in reality.

That God cannot be thought not to exist

And certainly this being so truly exists that it cannot be even thought not to exist. For something can be thought to exist that cannot be thought not to exist, and this

Anselm of Canterbury 'Proslogion', translated by M. Charlesworth, copyright © Oxford University Press 1965, from *Anselm of Canterbury The Major Works* edited with an introduction and notes by Brian Davies and G. R. Evans (Oxford World's Classics, 1998), editorial matter copyright © Brian Davies and G. R. Evans 1998, reprinted by permission of Oxford University Press.

is greater than that which can be thought not to exist. Hence, if that-than-which-a-greater-cannot-be-thought can be thought not to exist, then that-than-which-a-greater-cannot-be-thought is not the same as that-than-which-a-greater-cannot-be-thought, which is absurd. Something-than-which-a-greater-cannot-be-thought exists so truly then, that it cannot be even thought not to exist.

And You, Lord our God, are this being. You exist so truly, Lord my God, that You cannot even be thought not to exist. And this is as it should be, for if some intelligence could think of something better than You, the creature would be above its Creator and would judge its Creator—and that is completely absurd. In fact, everything else there is, except You alone, can be thought of as not existing. You alone, then, of all things most truly exist and therefore of all things possess existence to the highest degree; for anything else does not exist as truly, and so possesses existence to a lesser degree. Why then did 'the Fool say in his heart, there is no God' [Ps. 13: 1; 52: 1] when it is so evident to any rational mind that You of all things exist to the highest degree? Why indeed, unless because he was stupid and a fool?

Chapter 30

Gaunilo argues that Anselm is wrong

Gaunilo of Marmoutiers

1

To one doubting whether there is, or denying that there is, something of such a nature than which nothing greater can be thought, it is said here [in the *Proslogion*] that its existence is proved, first because the very one who denies or doubts it already has it in his mind, since when he hears it spoken of he understands what is said; and further, because what he understands is necessarily such that it exists not only in the mind but also in reality. And this is proved by the fact that it is greater to exist both in the mind and in reality than in the mind alone. For if this same being exists in the mind alone, anything that existed also in reality would be greater than this being, and thus that which is greater than everything would be less than some thing and would not be greater than everything, which is obviously contradictory. Therefore, it is necessarily the case that that which is greater than everything, being already proved to exist in the mind, should exist not only in the mind but also in reality, since otherwise it would not be greater than everything.

2

But he [the Fool] can perhaps reply that this thing is said already to exist in the mind only in the sense that I understand what is said. For could I not say that all kinds of unreal things, not existing in themselves in any way at all, are equally in the mind since if anyone speaks about them I understand whatever he says? Unless perhaps it is manifest that this being is such that it can be entertained in the mind in a different way from unreal or doubtfully real things, so that I am not said to think of or have in thought what is heard, but to understand and have it in mind, in that I cannot really think of this being in any other way save by understanding it, that is to say, by grasping by certain knowledge that the thing itself actually exists. But if this is the case, first, there will be no difference between having an object in mind (taken as preceding in time), and understanding that the object actually exists (taken as following in time), as in the case of the picture which exists first in the mind of the painter and then in the completed work. And thus it would be scarcely conceivable that, when this object had been spoken of and heard, it could not be thought not to exist in the same way in which God can [be thought] not to exist. For if He cannot, why put forward this whole argument against anyone denying or doubting that there is something of this kind? Finally, that it is such a thing that, as soon as it is thought of, it cannot but be certainly perceived by the mind as indubitably existing, must be proved to me by some indisputable argument and not by that proposed, namely, that it must already be in my mind when I understand what I hear. For this is in my view like [arguing that] any things doubtfully real or even unreal are capable of existing if these things are mentioned by someone whose spoken words I might understand, and, even more, that [they exist] if, though deceived about them as often happens, I should believe them [to exist]—which argument I still do not believe!

3

Hence, the example of the painter having the picture he is about to make already in his mind cannot support this argument. For this picture, before it is actually made, is contained in the very art of the painter and such a thing in the art of any artist is nothing but a certain part of his very understanding, since as St Augustine says [*In Iohannem*, tract. 1, n. 16], 'when the artisan is about actually to make a box he has it beforehand in his art. The box which is actually made is not a living thing, but the box which is in his art is a living thing since the soul of the artist, in which these things exist before their actual realization, is a living thing.' Now how are these things living in the living soul of the artist unless they are identical with the knowledge or understanding of the soul itself? But, apart from those things which are known to belong to the very nature of the mind itself, in the case of any truth perceived by the mind by being either heard or understood, then it cannot be doubted that this truth is one thing and that the understanding which grasps it is another. Therefore even if it were true that there was something than which nothing greater could be thought, this thing, heard and understood, would not, however, be the same as the not-yet-made picture is in the mind of the painter.

4

To this we may add something that has already been mentioned, namely, that upon hearing it spoken of I can so little think of or entertain in my mind this being (that which is greater than all those others that are able to be thought of, and which it is said can be none other than God Himself) in terms of an object known to me either by species or genus, as I can think of God Himself, whom indeed for this very reason I can even think does not exist. For neither do I know the reality itself, nor can I form an idea from some other things like it since, as you say yourself, it is such that nothing could be like it. For if I heard something said about a man who was completely unknown to me so that I did not even know whether he existed, I could nevertheless think about him in his very reality as a man by means of that specific or generic notion by which I know what a man is or men are. However, it could happen that, because of a falsehood on the part of the speaker, the man I thought of did not actually exist, although I thought of him nevertheless as a truly existing object—not this particular man but any man in general. It is not, then, in the way that I have this unreal thing in thought or in mind that I can have that object in my mind when I hear 'God' or 'something greater than everything' spoken of. For while I was able to think of the former in terms of a truly existing thing which was known to me, I know nothing at all of the latter save for the verbal formula, and on the basis of this alone one can scarcely or never think of any truth. For when one thinks in this way, one thinks not so much of the word itself, which is indeed a real thing (that is to say, the sound of the letters or syllables), as of the meaning of the word which is heard. However, it [that which is greater than everything] is not thought of in the way of one who knows what is meant by that expression— thought of, that is, in terms of the thing [signified] or as true in thought alone. It is rather in the way of one who does not really know this object but thinks of it in terms of an affection of his mind produced by hearing the spoken words, and who tries to imagine what the words he has heard might mean. However, it would be astonishing if he could ever [attain to] the truth of the thing. Therefore, when I hear and understand someone saying that there is something greater than every- thing that can be thought of, it is agreed that it is in this latter sense that it is in my mind and not in any other sense. So much for the claim that that supreme nature exists already in my mind.

5

That, however, [this nature] necessarily exists in reality is demonstrated to me from the fact that, unless it existed, whatever exists in reality would be greater than it and consequently it would not be that which is greater than everything that undoubt- edly had already been proved to exist in the mind. To this I reply as follows: if something that cannot even be thought in the true and real sense must be said to exist in the mind, then I do not deny that this also exists in my mind in the same way. But since from this one cannot in any way conclude that it exists also in reality, I certainly do not yet concede that it actually exists, until this is proved to me by an indubitable argument. For he who claims that it actually exists because otherwise it would not be that which is greater than everything does not consider carefully enough whom he is addressing. For I certainly do not yet admit this greater [than everything] to be any truly existing thing; indeed I doubt or even deny it. And I do not concede that it exists in a different way from that—if one ought to speak of 'existence' here—when the mind tries to imagine a completely unknown thing on the basis of the spoken words alone. How then can it be proved to me on that basis that that which is greater than everything truly exists in reality (because it is evident that it is greater than all others) if I keep on denying and also doubting that this is evident and do not admit that this greater [than everything] is either in my mind or thought, not even in the sense in which many doubtfully real and unreal things are? It must first of all be proved to me then that this same greater than everything truly exists in reality somewhere, and then only will the fact that it is greater than everything make it clear that it also subsists in itself.

6

For example: they say that there is in the ocean somewhere an island which, because of the difficulty (or rather the impossibility) of finding that which does not exist, some have called the 'Lost Island'. And the story goes that it is blessed with all manner of priceless riches and delights in abundance, much more even than the Happy Isles, and, having no owner or inhabitant, it is superior everywhere in abundance of riches to all those other lands that men inhabit. Now, if anyone tell me that it is like this, I shall easily understand what is said, since nothing is difficult about it. But if he should then go on to say, as though it were a logical consequence of this: You cannot any more doubt that this island that is more excellent than all other lands truly exists somewhere in reality than you can doubt that it is in your mind; and since it is more excellent to exist not only in the mind alone but also in reality, therefore it must needs be that it exists. For if it did not exist, any other land existing in reality would be more excellent than it, and so this island, already conceived by you to be more excellent than others, will not be more excellent. If, I say, someone wishes thus to persuade me that this island really exists beyond all doubt, I should either think that he was joking, or I should find it hard to decide which of us I ought to judge the bigger fool—I, if I agreed with him, or he, if he thought that he had proved the existence of this island with any certainty, unless he had first convinced me that its very excellence exists in my mind precisely as a thing existing truly and indubitably and not just as something unreal or doubtfully real.

7

Thus first of all might the Fool reply to objections. And if then someone should assert that this greater [than everything] is such that it cannot be thought not to exist (again without any other proof than that otherwise it would not be greater than everything), then he could make this same reply and say: When have I said that there truly existed some being that is 'greater than everything', such that from this it could be proved to me that this same being really existed to such a degree that it could not be thought not to exist? That is why it must first be conclusively proved by argument that there is some higher nature, namely that which is greater and better than all the things that are, so that from this we can also infer everything else which necessarily cannot be wanting to what is greater and better than everything. When, however, it is said that this supreme being cannot be *thought* not to exist, it would perhaps be better to say that it cannot be *understood* not to exist nor even to be able not to exist. For, strictly speaking, unreal things cannot be *understood*, though certainly they can be *thought* of in the same way as the Fool *thought* that God does not exist. I know with complete certainty that I exist, but I also know at the same time nevertheless that I can not-exist. And I *understand* without any doubt that that which exists to the highest degree, namely God, both exists and cannot not exist. I do not know, however, whether I can *think* of myself as not existing while I know with absolute certainty that I do exist; but if I can, why cannot [I do the same] with regard to anything else I know with the same certainty? If however I cannot, this will not be the distinguishing characteristic of God [namely, to be such that He cannot be thought not to exist].

Chapter 31

Anselm replies to Gaunilo

Anselm of Canterbury

S INCE it is not the Fool, against whom I spoke in my tract, who takes me up, but one who, though speaking on the Fool's behalf, is an orthodox Christian and no fool, it will suffice if I reply to the Christian.

1

You say then—you, whoever you are, who claim that the Fool can say these things—that the being than-which-a-greater-cannot-be-thought is not in the mind except as what cannot be thought of, in the true sense, at all. And [you claim], moreover, that what I say does not follow, namely, that 'that-than-which-a-greater-cannot-be-thought' exists in reality from the fact that it exists in the mind, any more than that the Lost Island most certainly exists from the fact that, when it is described in words, he who hears it described has no doubt that it exists in his mind. I reply as follows: If 'that-than-which-a-greater-cannot-be-thought' is neither understood nor thought of, and is neither in the mind nor in thought, then it is evident that *either* God is not that-than-which-a-greater-cannot-be-thought *or* is not understood nor thought of, and is not in the mind nor in thought. Now my strongest argument that this is false is to appeal to your faith and to your conscience. Therefore 'that-than-which-a-greater-cannot-be-thought' is truly understood and thought and is in the mind and in thought. For this reason, [the arguments] by which you attempt to prove the contrary are either not true, or what you believe follows from them does not in fact follow.

Moreover, you maintain that, from the fact that that-than-which-a-greater-cannot-be-thought is understood, it does not follow that it is in the mind, nor that, if it is in the mind, it therefore exists in reality. I insist, however, that simply if it can be thought it is necessary that it exists. For, 'that-than-which-a-greater-cannot-be-thought' cannot be thought save as being without a beginning. But whatever can be thought as existing and does not actually exist can be thought as having a beginning of its existence. Consequently, 'that-than-which-a-greater-cannot-be-thought' cannot be thought as existing and yet not actually exist. If, therefore, it can be thought as existing, it exists of necessity.

Further: even if it can be thought of, then certainly it necessarily exists. For no one who denies or doubts that there is something-than-which-a-greater-cannot-be-thought, denies or doubts that, if this being were to exist, it would not be capable of not-existing either actually or in the mind—otherwise it would not be that-than-which-a-greater-cannot-be-thought. But, whatever can be thought as existing and does not actually exist, could, if it were to exist, possibly not exist either actually or in the mind. For this reason, if it can merely be thought, 'that-than-which-a-greater-cannot-be-thought' cannot not exist. However, let us suppose that it does not exist even though it can be thought. Now whatever can be thought and does not actually exist would not be, if it should exist, 'that-than-which-a-greater-cannot-be-thought'. If, therefore, it were 'that-than-which-a-greater-cannot-be-thought' it would not be that-than-which-a-greater-cannot-be-thought, which is completely absurd. It is, then, false that something-than-which-a-greater-cannot-be-thought does not exist if it can merely be thought; and it is all the more false if it can be understood and be in the mind.

I will go further: It cannot be doubted that whatever does not exist in any one place or at any one time, even though it does exist in some place or at some time, can however be thought to exist at no place and at no time, just as it does not exist in some place or at some time. For what did not exist yesterday and today exists can thus, as it is understood not to have existed yesterday, be supposed not to exist at any time. And that which does not exist here in this place, and does exist elsewhere can, in the same way as it does not exist here, be thought not to exist anywhere. Similarly with a thing some of whose particular parts do not exist in the place and at the time its other parts exist—all of its parts, and therefore the whole thing itself, can be thought to exist at no time and in no place. For even if it be said that time always exists and that the world is everywhere, the former does not, however, always exist as a whole, nor is the other as a whole everywhere; and as certain particular parts of time do not exist when other parts do exist, therefore they can be even thought not to exist at any time. Again, as certain particular parts of the world do not exist in the same place where other parts do exist, they can thus be supposed not to exist anywhere. Moreover, what is made up of parts can be broken up in thought and can possibly not exist. Thus it is that whatever does not exist as a whole at a certain place and time can be thought not to exist, even if it does actually exist. But 'that-than-which-a-greater-cannot-be-thought' cannot be thought not to exist if it does actually exist; otherwise, if it exists it is not that-than-which-a-greater-cannot-be-thought, which is absurd. In no way, then, does this being not exist as a whole in any particular place or at any particular time; but it exists as a whole at every time and in every place.

Do you not consider then that that about which we understand these things can to some extent be thought or understood, or can exist in thought or in the mind? For if it cannot, we could not understand these things about it. And if you say that, because it is not completely understood, it cannot be understood at all and cannot be in the mind, then you must say [equally] that one who cannot see the purest light of the sun directly does not see daylight, which is the same thing as the light of the sun. Surely then 'that-than-which-a-greater-cannot-be-thought' is understood and is in the mind to the extent that we understand these things about it.

2

I said, then, in the argument that you criticize, that when the Fool hears 'that-than-which-a-greater cannot-be-thought' spoken of he understands what he hears. Obviously if it is spoken of in a known language and he does not understand it, then either he has no intelligence at all, or a completely obtuse one.

Next I said that, if it is understood it is in the mind; or does what has been proved to exist necessarily in actual reality not exist in any mind? But you will say that, even if it is in the mind, yet it does not follow that it is understood. Observe then that, from the fact that it is understood, it does follow that it is in the mind. For, just as what is thought is thought by means of a thought, and what is thought by a thought is thus, as thought, *in* thought, so also, what is understood is understood by the mind, and what is understood by the mind is thus, as understood, *in* the mind. What could be more obvious than this?

I said further that if a thing exists even in the mind alone, it can be thought to exist also in reality, which is greater. If, then, it (namely, 'that-than-which-a-greater-cannot-be-thought') exists in the mind alone, it is something than which a greater *can* be thought. What, I ask you, could be more logical? For if it exists even in the mind alone, cannot it be thought to exist also in reality? And if it can [be so thought], is it not the case that he who thinks this thinks of something greater than it, if it exists in the mind alone? What, then, could follow more logically than that, if 'that-than-which-a-greater-*cannot*-be-thought' exists in the mind alone, it is the same as that-than-which-a-greater-*can*-be-thought? But surely 'that-than-which-a-greater-*can*-be-thought' is not for any mind [the same as] 'that-than-which-a-greater-*cannot*-be-thought'. Does it not follow then, that 'that-than-which-a-greater-*cannot*-be-thought', if it exists in anyone's mind, does not exist in the mind alone? For if it exists in the mind alone, it is that-than-which-a-greater-*can*-be-thought, which is absurd.

3

You claim, however, that this is as though someone asserted that it cannot be doubted that a certain island in the ocean (which is more fertile than all other lands and which, because of the difficulty or even the impossibility of discovering what does not exist, is called the 'Lost Island') truly exists in reality since anyone easily understands it when it is described in words. Now I truly promise that if anyone should discover for me something existing either in reality or in the mind alone—except 'that-than-which-a-greater-cannot-be-thought'—to which the logic of my argument would apply, then I shall find that Lost Island and give it, never more to be lost, to that person. It has already been clearly seen, however, that 'that-than-which-a-greater-cannot-be-thought' cannot be thought not to exist, because it exists as a matter of such certain truth. Otherwise it would not exist at all. In short, if anyone says that he thinks that this being does not exist, I reply that, when he thinks of this, either he thinks of something than which a greater cannot be thought, or he does not think of it. If he does not think of it, then he does not think that what he does not think of does not exist. If, however, he does think of it, then indeed he thinks of something which cannot be even thought not to exist. For if it could be thought not to exist, it could be thought to have a beginning and an end—but this cannot be. Thus, he who thinks of it thinks of something that cannot be thought not to exist; indeed, he who thinks of this does not think of it as not existing, otherwise he would think what cannot be thought. Therefore 'that-than-which-a-greater-cannot-be-thought' cannot be thought not to exist.

4

You say moreover, that when it is said that this supreme reality cannot be *thought* not to exist, it would perhaps be better to say that it cannot be *understood* not to exist or even to be able not to exist. However, it must rather be said that it cannot be *thought*. For if I had said that the thing in question could not be *understood* not to exist, perhaps you yourself (who claim that we cannot understand—if this word is to be taken strictly—things that are unreal) would object that nothing that exists can be understood not to exist. For it is false [to say that] what exists does not exist, so that it is not the distinguishing characteristic of God not to be able to be understood not to exist. But, if any of those things which exist with absolute certainty can be understood not to exist, in the same way other things that certainly exist can be understood not to exist. But, if the matter is carefully considered, this objection cannot be made apropos [the term] 'thought'. For even if none of those things that exist can be *understood* not to exist, all however can be *thought* as not existing, save that which exists to a supreme degree. For in fact all those things (and they alone) that have a beginning or end or are made up of parts and, as I have already said, all those things that do not exist as a whole in a particular place or at a particular time can be thought as not existing. Only that being in which there is neither beginning nor end nor conjunction of parts, and that thought does not discern save as a whole in every place and at every time, cannot be thought as not existing.

Know then that you can think of yourself as not existing while yet you are absolutely sure that you exist. I am astonished that you have said that you do not know this. For we think of many things that we know to exist, as not existing; and [we think of] many things that we know not to exist, as existing—not judging that it is really as we think but imagining it to be so. We *can*, in fact, think of something as not existing while knowing that it does exist, since we can [think of] the one and know the other at the same time. And we *cannot* think of something as not existing if yet we know that it does exist, since we cannot think of it as existing and not existing at the same time. He, therefore, who distinguishes these two senses of this assertion will understand that [in one sense] nothing can be thought as not existing while yet it is known to exist, and that [in another sense] whatever exists, save that-than-which-a-greater-cannot-be-thought, can be thought of as not existing even when we know that it does exist. Thus it is that, on the one hand, it is the distinguishing characteristic of God that He cannot be thought of as not existing, and that, on the other hand, many things, the while they do exist, cannot be thought of as not existing. In what sense, however, one can say that God can be thought of as not existing I think I have adequately explained in my tract.

5

As for the other objections you make against me on behalf of the Fool, it is quite easy to meet them, even for one weak in the head, and so I considered it a waste of time to show this. But since I hear that they appear to certain readers to have some force against me, I will deal briefly with them.

First, you often reiterate that I say that that which is greater than everything exists in the mind, and that if it is in the mind, it exists also in reality, for otherwise that which is greater than everything would not be that which is greater than everything. However, nowhere in all that I have said will you find such an argument. For 'that which is greater than everything' and 'that-than-which-a-greater-cannot-be-thought' are not equivalent for the purpose of proving the real existence of the thing spoken of. Thus, if anyone should say that 'that-than-which-a-greater-cannot-be-thought' is not something that actually exists, or that it can possibly not exist, or even can be thought of as not existing, he can easily be refuted. For what does not exist can possibly not exist, and what can not exist can be thought of as not existing. However, whatever can be thought of as not existing, if it actually exists, is not that-than-which-a-greater-cannot-be-thought. But if it does not exist, indeed even if it should exist, it would not be that-than-which-a-greater-cannot-be-thought. But it cannot be asserted that 'that-than-which-a-greater-cannot-be-thought' is not, if it exists, that-than-which-a-greater-cannot-be-thought, or that, if it should exist, it would not be that-than-which-a-greater-cannot-be-thought. It is evident, then, that it neither does not exist nor can not exist or be thought of as not existing. For if it does exist in another way it is not what it is said to be, and if it should exist [in another way] it would not be [what it was said to be].

However it seems that it is not as easy to prove this in respect of what is said to be greater than everything. For it is not as evident that that which can be thought of as not existing is not that which is greater than everything, as that it is not that-than-which-a-greater-cannot-be-thought. And, in the same way, neither is it indubitable that, if there is something which is 'greater than everything', it is identical with 'that-than-which-a-greater-cannot-be-thought'; nor, if there were [such a being], that no other like it might exist—as this is certain in respect of what is said to be 'that-than-which-a-greater-cannot-be-thought'. For what if someone should say that something that is greater than everything actually exists, and yet that this same being can be thought of as not existing, and that something greater than it can be thought, even if this does not exist? In this case can it be inferred as evidently that [this being] is therefore not that which is greater than everything, as it would quite evidently be said in the other case that it is therefore not that-than-which-a-greater-cannot-be-thought? The former [inference] needs, in fact, a premiss in addition to this which is said to be 'greater than everything'; but the latter needs nothing save this utterance itself, namely, 'that-than-which-a-greater-cannot-be-thought'. Therefore, if what 'that-than-which-a-greater-cannot-be-thought' of itself proves concerning itself cannot be proved in the same way in respect of what is said to be 'greater than everything', you criticize me unjustly for having said what I did not say, since it differs so much from what I did say.

If, however, it can [be proved] by means of another argument, you should not have criticized me for having asserted what can be proved. Whether it can [be proved], however, is easily appreciated by one who understands that it can [in respect of] 'that-than-which-a-greater-cannot-be-thought'. For one cannot in any way understand 'that-than-which-a-greater-cannot-be-thought' without [understanding that it is] that which alone is greater than everything. As, therefore, 'that-than-which-a-greater-cannot-be-thought' is understood and is in the mind, and is consequently judged to exist in true reality, so also that which is greater than everything is said to be understood and to exist in the mind, and so is necessarily inferred to exist in reality itself. You see, then, how right you were to compare me with that stupid person who wished to maintain that the Lost Island existed from the sole fact that being described it was understood.

6

You object, moreover, that any unreal or doubtfully real things at all can equally be understood and exist in the mind in the same way as the being I was speaking of. I am astonished that you urge this [objection] against me, for I was concerned to prove something which was in doubt, and for me it was sufficient that I should first show that it was understood and existed in the mind *in some way or other*, leaving it to be determined subsequently whether it was in the mind alone as unreal things are, or in reality also as true things are. For, if unreal or doubtfully real things are understood and exist in the mind in the sense that, when they are spoken of, he who hears them understands what the speaker means, nothing prevents what I have spoken of being understood and existing in the mind. But how are these [assertions] consistent, that is, when you assert that if someone speaks of unreal things you would understand whatever he says, and that, in the case of a thing which is not entertained in thought in the same way as even unreal things are, you do not say that you think of it or have it in thought upon hearing it spoken of, but rather that you understand it and have it in mind since, precisely, you cannot think of it save by understanding it, that is, knowing certainly that the thing exists in reality itself?

How, I say, are both [assertions] consistent, namely that unreal things are understood, and that 'to understand' means knowing with certainty that something actually exists? You should have seen that nothing [of this applies] to me. But if unreal things are, in a sense, understood (this definition applying not to every kind of understanding but to a certain kind) then I ought not to be criticized for having said that 'that-than-which-a-greater-cannot-be-thought' is understood and is in the mind, even before it was certain that it existed in reality itself.

7

Next, you say that it can hardly be believed that when this [that-than-which-a-greater-cannot-be-thought] has been spoken of and heard, it cannot be thought not to exist, as even it can be thought that God does not exist. Now those who have attained even a little expertise in disputation and argument could reply to that on my behalf. For is it reasonable that someone should therefore deny what he understands because it is said to be [the same as] that which he denies since he does not understand it? Or if that is denied [to exist] which is understood only to some extent and is the same as what is not understood at all, is not what is in doubt more easily proved from the fact that it is in some mind than from the fact that it is in no mind at all? For this reason it cannot be believed that anyone should deny 'that-than-which-a-greater-cannot-be-thought' (which, being heard, he understands to some extent), on the ground that he denies God whose meaning he does not think of in any way at all. On the other hand if it is denied on the ground that it is not understood completely, even so is not that which is understood in some way easier to prove than that which is not understood in any way? It was therefore not wholly without reason that, to prove against the Fool that God exists, I proposed 'that-than-which-a-greater-cannot-be-thought', since he would understand this in some way, [whereas] he would understand the former [God] in no way at all.

8

In fact, your painstaking argument that 'that-than-which-a-greater-cannot-be-thought' is not like the not-yet-realized painting in the mind of the painter is beside the point. For I did not propose [the example] of the foreknown picture because I wanted to assert that what was at issue was in the same case, but rather that so I could show that something not understood as existing exists in the mind.

Again, you say that upon hearing of 'that-than-which-a-greater-cannot-be-thought' you cannot think of it as a real object known either generically or specifically or have it in your mind, on the grounds that you neither know the thing itself nor can you form an idea of it from other things similar to it. But obviously this is not so. For since everything that is less good is similar in so far as it is good to that which is more good, it is evident to every rational mind that, mounting from the less good to the more good we can from those things than which something greater can be thought conjecture a great deal about that-than-which-a-greater-cannot-be-thought. Who, for example, cannot think of this (even if he does not believe that what he thinks of actually exists) namely, that if something that has a beginning and end is good, that which, although it has had a beginning, does not, however, have an end, is much better? And just as this latter is better than the former, so also that which has neither beginning nor end is better again than this, even if it passes always from the past through the present to the future. Again, whether something of this kind actually exists or not, that which does not lack anything at all, nor is forced to change or move, is very much better still. Cannot this be thought? Or can we think of something greater than this? Or is not this precisely to form an idea of that-than-which-a-greater-cannot-be-thought from those things than which a greater can be thought? There is, then, a way by which one can form an idea of 'that-than-which-a-greater-cannot-be-thought'. In this way, therefore, the Fool who does not accept the sacred authority [of Revelation] can easily be refuted if he denies that he can form an idea from other things of 'that-than-which-a-greater-cannot-be-thought'. But if any orthodox Christian should deny this let him remember that 'the invisible things of God from the creation of the world are clearly seen through the things that have been made, even his eternal power and Godhead' [Rom. 1: 20].

9

But even if it were true that [the object] that-than-which-a-greater-cannot-be-thought cannot be thought of nor understood, it would not, however, be false that [the formula] 'that-than-which-a-greater-cannot-be-thought' could be thought of and understood. For just as nothing prevents one from saying 'ineffable' although one cannot specify what is said to be ineffable; and just as one can think of the inconceivable—although one cannot think of what 'inconceivable' applies to—so also, when 'that-than-which-a-greater-cannot-be-thought' is spoken of, there is no doubt at all that what is heard can be thought of and understood even if the thing itself cannot be thought of and understood. For if someone is so witless as to say that there is not something than-which-a-greater-cannot-be-thought, yet he will not be so shameless as to say that he is not able to understand and think of what he was speaking about. Or if such a one is to be found, not only should his assertion be condemned, but he himself condemned. Whoever, then, denies that there is something than-which-a-greater-cannot-be-thought, at any rate understands and thinks of the denial he makes, and this denial cannot be understood and thought about apart from its elements. Now, one element [of the denial] is 'that-than-which-a-greater-cannot-be-thought'. Whoever, therefore, denies this understands and thinks of 'that-than-which-a-greater-cannot-be-thought'. It is evident, moreover, that in the same way one can think of and understand that which cannot not exist. And one who thinks of this thinks of something greater than one who thinks of what can not exist. When, therefore, one thinks of that-than-which-a-greater-cannot-be-thought, if one thinks of what can not exist, one does not think of that-than-which-a-greater-cannot-be-thought. Now the same thing cannot at the same time be thought of and not thought of. For this reason he who thinks of that-than-which-a-greater-cannot-be-thought does not think of something that can not exist but something that cannot not exist. Therefore what he thinks of exists necessarily, since whatever can not exist is not what he thinks of.

10

I think now that I have shown that I have proved in the above tract, not by a weak argumentation but by a sufficiently necessary one, that something-than-which-a-greater-cannot-be-thought exists in reality itself, and that this proof has not been weakened by the force of any objection. For the import of this proof is in itself of such force that what is spoken of is proved (as a necessary consequence of the fact that it is understood or thought of) both to exist in actual reality and to be itself whatever must be believed about the Divine Being. For we believe of the Divine Being whatever it can, absolutely speaking, be thought better to be than not to be. For example, it is better to be eternal than not eternal, good than not good, indeed goodness-itself than not goodness-itself. However, nothing of this kind cannot but be that-than-which-a-greater-cannot-be-thought. It is, then, necessary that 'that-than-which-a-greater-cannot-be-thought' should be whatever must be believed about the Divine Nature.

Chapter 32

Descartes defends an ontological argument

René Descartes

CERTAINLY, the idea of God, or a supremely perfect being, is one which I find within me just as surely as the idea of any shape or number. And my understanding that it belongs to his nature that he always exists is no less clear and distinct than is the case when I prove of any shape or number that some property belongs to its nature. Hence, even if it turned out that not everything on which I have meditated in these past days is true, I ought still to regard the existence of God as having at least the same level of certainty as I have hitherto attributed to the truths of mathematics.

At first sight, however, this is not transparently clear, but has some appearance of being a sophism. Since I have been accustomed to distinguish between existence and essence in everything else, I find it easy to persuade myself that existence can also be separated from the essence of God, and hence that God can be thought of as not existing. But when I concentrate more carefully, it is quite evident that existence can no more be separated from the essence of God than the fact that its three angles equal two right angles can be separated from the essence of a triangle, or than the idea of a mountain can be separated from the idea of a valley. Hence it is just as much of a contradiction to think of God (that is, a supremely perfect being) lacking existence (that is, lacking a perfection), as it is to think of a mountain without a valley.

However, even granted that I cannot think of God except as existing, just as I cannot think of a mountain without a valley, it certainly does not follow from the fact that I think of a mountain with a valley that there is any mountain in the world; and similarly, it does not seem to follow from the fact that I think of God as existing that he does exist. For my thought does not impose any necessity on things; and just as I may imagine a winged horse even though no horse has wings, so I may be able to attach existence to God even though no God exists.

But there is a sophism concealed here. From the fact that I cannot think of a mountain without a valley, it does not follow that a mountain and valley exist anywhere, but simply that a mountain and a valley, whether they exist or not, are

Rene Descartes extract from 'Meditation 5' of 'Meditations on First Philosophy' from vol. 2 of *The Philosophical Writings of Descartes* translated and edited by J. Cottingham, R. Stoothoff and D. Murdoch (Cambridge University Press, 1984), reprinted by permission of the publisher and the editors.

mutually inseparable. But from the fact that I cannot think of God except as existing, it follows that existence is inseparable from God, and hence that he really exists. It is not that my thought makes it so, or imposes any necessity on any thing; on the contrary, it is the necessity of the thing itself, namely the existence of God, which determines my thinking in this respect. For I am not free to think of God without existence (that is, a supremely perfect being without a supreme perfection) as I am free to imagine a horse with or without wings.

And it must not be objected at this point that while it is indeed necessary for me to suppose God exists, once I have made the supposition that he has all perfections (since existence is one of the perfections), nevertheless the original supposition was not necessary. Similarly, the objection would run, it is not necessary for me to think that all quadrilaterals can be inscribed in a circle; but given this supposition, it will be necessary for me to admit that a rhombus can be inscribed in a circle—which is patently false. Now admittedly, it is not necessary that I ever light upon any thought of God; but whenever I do choose to think of the first and supreme being, and bring forth the idea of God from the treasure house of my mind as it were, it is necessary that I attribute all perfections to him, even if I do not at that time enumerate them or attend to them individually. And this necessity plainly guarantees that, when I later realize that existence is a perfection, I am correct in inferring that the first and supreme being exists. In the same way, it is not necessary for me ever to imagine a triangle; but whenever I do wish to consider a rectilinear figure having just three angles, it is necessary that I attribute to it the properties which license the inference that its three angles equal no more than two right angles, even if I do not notice this at the time. By contrast, when I examine what figures can be inscribed in a circle, it is in no way necessary for me to think that this class includes all quadrilaterals. Indeed, I cannot even imagine this, so long as I am willing to admit only what I clearly and distinctly understand. So there is a great difference between this kind of false supposition and the true ideas which are innate in me, of which the first and most important is the idea of God. There are many ways in which I understand that this idea is not something fictitious which is dependent on my thought, but is an image of a true and immutable nature. First of all, there is the fact that, apart from God, there is nothing else of which I am capable of thinking such that existence belongs to its essence. Second, I cannot understand how there could be two or more Gods of this kind; and after supposing that one God exists, I plainly see that it is necessary that he has existed from eternity and will abide for eternity. And finally, I perceive many other attributes of God, none of which I can remove or alter.

But whatever method of proof I use, I am always brought back to the fact that it is only what I clearly and distinctly perceive that completely convinces me. Some of the things I clearly and distinctly perceive are obvious to everyone, while others are discovered only by those who look more closely and investigate more carefully; but once they have been discovered, the latter are judged to be just as certain as the former. In the case of a right-angled triangle, for example, the fact that the square on the hypotenuse is equal to the square on the other two sides is not so readily apparent as the fact that the hypotenuse subtends the largest angle; but once one has seen it, one believes it just as strongly. But as regards God, if I were not overwhelmed by preconceived opinions, and if the images of things perceived by the senses did not besiege my thought on every side, I would certainly acknowledge him sooner and more easily than anything else. For what is more self-evident than the fact that the supreme being exists, or that God, to whose essence alone existence belongs, exists?

Chapter 33

Descartes replies to critics

Pierre Gassendi, Johannes Caterus, René Descartes

Pierre Gassendi: reply to Descartes

You next attempt to demonstrate the existence of God, and the thrust of your argument is contained in the following passage:

When I concentrate, it is quite evident that existence can no more be separated from the essence of God than the fact that its three angles equal two right angles can be separated from the essence of a triangle, or than the idea of a mountain can be separated from the idea of a valley. Hence it is just as much of a contradiction to think of God (that is, a supremely perfect being) lacking existence (that is, lacking a perfection) as it is to think of a mountain without a valley.

But we must note here that the kind of comparison you make is not wholly fair.

It is quite all right for you to compare essence with essence, but instead of going on to compare existence with existence or a property with a property, you compare existence with a property. It seems that you should have said that omnipotence can no more be separated from the essence of God than the fact that its angles equal two right angles can be separated from the essence of a triangle. Or, at any rate, you should have said that the existence of God can no more be separated from his essence than the existence of a triangle can be separated from its essence. If you had done this, both your comparisons would have been satisfactory, and I would have granted you not only the first one but the second one as well. But you would not for all that have established that God necessarily exists, since a triangle does not necessarily exist either, even though its essence and existence cannot in actual fact be separated. Real separation is impossible no matter how much the mind may separate them or think of them apart from each other—as indeed it can even in the case of God's essence and existence.

Next we must note that you place existence among the divine perfections, but do not place it among the perfections of a triangle or mountain, though it could be said that in its own way it is just as much a perfection of each of these things. In fact, however, existence is not a perfection either in God or in anything else; it is that without which no perfections can be present.

Pierre Gassendi, Johannes Caterus, and René Descartes 'Objections to Descartes's "Fifth Meditation" with Replies by Descartes' from René Descartes; *Meditations on First Philosophy* translated and edited by John Cottingham (Cambridge University Press, 1986), reprinted by permission of the publisher and John Cottingham.

For surely, what does not exist has no perfections or imperfections, and what does exist and has several perfections does not have existence as one of its individual perfections; rather, its existence is that in virtue of which both the thing itself and its perfections are existent, and that without which we cannot say that the thing possesses the perfections or that the perfections are possessed by it. Hence we do not say that existence 'exists in a thing' in the way perfections do; and if a thing lacks existence, we do not say it is imperfect, or deprived of a perfection, but say instead that it is nothing at all.

Thus, just as when you listed the perfections of the triangle you did not include existence or conclude that the triangle existed, so when you listed the perfections of God you should not have included existence among them so as to reach the conclusion that God exists, unless you wanted to beg the question . . .

You say that you are not free to think of God without existence (that is, a supremely perfect being without a supreme perfection) as you are free to imagine a horse with or without wings. The only comment to be added to this is as follows. You are free to think of a horse not having wings without thinking of the existence which would, according to you, be a perfection in the horse if it were present; but, in the same way, you are free to think of God as having knowledge and power and other perfections without thinking of him as having the existence which would complete his perfection, if he had it. Just as the horse which is thought of as having the perfection of wings is not therefore deemed to have the existence which is, according to you, a principal perfection, so the fact that God is thought of as having knowledge and other perfections does not therefore imply that he has existence. This remains to be proved. And although you say that both existence and all the other perfections are included in the idea of a supremely perfect being, here you simply assert what should be proved, and assume the conclusion as a premiss. Otherwise I could say that the idea of a perfect Pegasus contains not just the perfection of his having wings but also the perfection of existence. For just as God is thought of as perfect in every kind of perfection, so Pegasus is thought of as perfect in his own kind. It seems that there is no point that you can raise in this connection which, if we preserve the analogy, will not apply to Pegasus if it applies to God, and *vice versa*.

Descartes's reply to Gassendi

Here I do not see what sort of thing you want existence to be, nor why it cannot be said to be a property just like omnipotence—provided, of course, that we take the word 'property' to stand for any attribute, or for whatever can be predicated of a thing; and this is exactly how it should be taken in this context. Moreover, in the case of God necessary existence is in fact a property in the strictest sense of the term, since it applies to him alone and forms a part of his essence as it does of no other thing. Hence the existence of a triangle should not be compared with the existence of God, since the relation between existence and essence is manifestly quite different in the case of God from what it is in the case of the triangle.

To list existence among the properties which belong to the nature of God is no more 'begging the question' than listing among the properties of a triangle the fact that its angles are equal to two right angles.

Again, it is not true to say that in the case of God, just as in the case of a triangle, existence and essence can be thought of apart from one another; for God is his own existence, but this is not true of the triangle. I do not, however, deny that possible existence is a perfection in the idea of a triangle, just as necessary existence is a perfection in the idea of God; for this fact makes the idea of a triangle superior to the ideas of chimeras, which cannot possibly be supposed to have existence. Thus at no point have you weakened the force of my argument in the slightest.

Johannes Caterus: reply to Descartes

Let us then concede that someone does possess a clear and distinct idea of a supreme and utterly perfect being. What is the next step you will take from here? You will say that this infinite being exists, and that his existence is so certain that 'I ought to regard the existence of God as having at least the same level of certainty as I have hitherto attributed to the truths of mathematics. Hence it is just as much of a contradiction to think of God (that is, a supremely perfect being) lacking existence (that is, lacking a perfection), as it is to think of a mountain without a valley.' This is the lynchpin of the whole structure; to give in on this point is to be obliged to admit defeat. But since I am taking on an opponent whose strength is greater than my own, I should like to have a preliminary skirmish with him, so that, although I am sure to be beaten in the end, I may at least put off the inevitable for a while.

I know we are basing our argument on the reason alone and not on appeals to authority. But to avoid giving the impression that I am wilfully taking issue with such an outstanding thinker as M. Descartes, let me nevertheless begin by asking you to listen to what St Thomas says. He raises the following objection to his own position:

As soon as we understand the meaning of the word 'God', we immediately grasp that God exists. For the word 'God' means 'that than which nothing greater can be conceived'. Now that which exists in reality as well as in the intellect is greater than that which exists in the intellect alone. Hence, since God immediately exists in the intellect as soon as we have understood the word 'God', it follows that he also exists in reality. (*Summa Theologiae*, P1, Q2, art. 1)

This argument may be set out formally as follows. 'God is that than which nothing greater can be conceived. But that than which nothing greater can be conceived includes existence. Hence God, in virtue of the very word or concept of "God", contains existence; and hence he cannot lack, or be conceived of as lacking, existence.' But now please tell me if this is not the selfsame argument as that produced by M. Descartes? St Thomas defines God as 'that than which nothing greater can be conceived'. M. Descartes calls him 'a supremely perfect being'; but of course nothing greater than this can be conceived. St Thomas's next step is to say 'that than which nothing greater can be conceived includes existence', for otherwise something greater could be conceived, namely a being conceived of as also including existence. Yet surely M. Descartes' next step is identical to this. God, he says, is a supremely perfect being; and a supremely perfect being includes existence, for otherwise it would not be a supremely perfect being. St. Thomas's conclusion is that 'since God immediately exists in the intellect as soon as we have understood the word "God", it follows that he also exists in reality'. In other words, since the very concept or essence of 'a being than which nothing greater can be conceived' implies existence, it follows that this very being exists. M. Descartes' conclusion is the same: 'From the very fact that I cannot think of God except as existing, it follows that existence is inseparable from God and hence that he really exists.' But now let St Thomas reply both to himself and to M. Descartes. 'Let it be granted', he says,

that we all understand that the word 'God' means what it is claimed to mean, namely 'that than which nothing greater can be thought of'. However, it does not follow that we all understand that what is signified by this word exists in the real world. All that follows is that it exists in the apprehension of the intellect. Nor can it be shown that this being really exists unless it is conceded that there really is something such that nothing greater can be thought of; and this premiss is denied by those who maintain that God does not exist.

My own answer to M. Descartes, which is based on this passage, is briefly this. Even if it is granted that a supremely perfect being carries the implication of existence in virtue of its very title, it still does not follow that the existence in question is anything actual in the real world; all that follows is that the concept of existence is inseparably linked to the concept of a supreme being. So you cannot infer that the existence of God is anything actual unless you suppose that the supreme being actually exists; for then it will actually contain all perfections, including the perfection of real existence.

Pardon me, gentlemen: I am now rather tired and propose to have a little fun. The complex 'existing lion' includes both 'lion' and 'existence', and it includes them essentially, for if you take away either element it will not be the same complex. But now, has not God had clear and distinct knowledge of this composite from all eternity? And does not the idea of this composite, as a composite, involve both elements essentially? In other words, does not existence belong to the essence of the composite 'existing lion'? Nevertheless the distinct knowledge of God, the distinct knowledge he has from eternity, does not compel either element in the composite to exist, unless we assume that the composite itself exists (in which case it will contain all its essential perfections including actual existence). Similarly even if I have distinct knowledge of a supreme being, and even if the supremely perfect being includes existence as an essential part of the concept, it still does not follow that the existence in question is anything actual, unless we suppose that the supreme being exists (for in that case it will include actual existence along with all its other perfections). Accordingly we must look elsewhere for a proof that the supremely perfect being exists.

Descartes's reply to Caterus

St Thomas asks whether the existence of God is self-evident as far as we are concerned, that is, whether it is obvious to everyone; and he answers, correctly, that it is not. The argument which he then puts forward as an objection to his own position can be stated as follows. 'Once we have understood the meaning of the word "God", we understand it to mean "that than which nothing greater can be conceived". But to exist in reality as well as in the intellect is greater than to exist in the intellect alone. Therefore, once we have understood the meaning of the word "God" we understand that God exists in reality as well as in the understanding.' In this form the argument is manifestly invalid, for the only conclusion that should have been drawn is: 'Therefore, once we have understood the meaning of the word "God" we understand that what is conveyed is that God exists in reality as well as in the understanding.' Yet because a word conveys something, that thing is not therefore shown to be true. My argument however was as follows: 'That which we clearly and distinctly understand to belong to the true and immutable nature, or essence, or form of something, can truly be asserted of that thing. But once we have made a sufficiently careful investigation of what God is, we clearly and distinctly understand that existence belongs to his true and immutable nature. Hence we can now truly assert of God that he does exist.' Here at least the conclusion does follow from the premisses. But, what is more, the major premiss cannot be denied, because it has already been conceded that whatever we clearly and distinctly understand is true. Hence only the minor premiss remains, and here I confess that there is considerable difficulty. In the first place we are so accustomed to distinguishing existence from essence in the case of all other things that we fail to notice how closely existence belongs to essence in the case of God as compared with that of other things. Next, we do not distinguish what belongs to the true and immutable essence of a thing from what is attributed to it merely by a fiction of the intellect. So, even if we observe clearly enough that existence belongs to the essence of God, we do not draw the conclusion that God exists, because we do not know whether his essence is immutable and true, or merely invented by us.

But to remove the first part of the difficulty we must distinguish between possible and necessary existence. It must be noted that possible existence is contained in the concept or idea of everything that we clearly and distinctly understand; but in no case is necessary existence so contained, except in the case of the idea of God. Those who carefully attend to this difference between the idea of God and every other idea will undoubtedly perceive that even though our understanding of other things always involves understanding them as if they were existing things, it does not follow that they do exist, but merely that they are capable of existing. For our understanding does not show us that it is necessary for actual existence to be conjoined with their other properties. But, from the fact that we understand that actual existence is necessarily and always conjoined with the other attributes of God, it certainly does follow that God exists.

To remove the second part of the difficulty, we must notice a point about ideas which do not contain true and immutable natures but merely ones which are invented and put together by the intellect. Such ideas can always be split up by the same intellect, not simply by an abstraction but by a clear and distinct intellectual operation, so that any ideas which the intellect cannot split up in this way were clearly not put together by the intellect. When, for example, I think of a winged horse or an actually existing lion, or a triangle inscribed in a square, I readily understand that I am also able to think of a horse without wings, or a lion which does not exist, or a triangle apart from a square, and so on; hence these things do not have true and immutable natures. But if I think of a triangle or a square (I will not now include the lion or the horse, since their natures are not transparently clear to us), then whatever I apprehend as being contained in the idea of a triangle—for example that its three angles are equal to two right angles—I can with truth assert of the triangle. And the same applies to the square with respect to whatever I apprehend as being contained in the idea of a square. For even if I can understand what a triangle is if I abstract the fact that its three angles are equal to two right angles, I cannot deny that this property applies to the triangle by a clear and distinct intellectual operation—that is, while at the same time understanding what I mean by my denial. Moreover, if I consider a triangle inscribed in a square, with a view not to attributing to the square properties that belong only to the triangle, or attributing to the triangle properties that belong to the square, but with a view to examining only the properties which arise out of the conjunction of the two, then the nature of this composite will be just as true and immutable as the nature of the triangle alone or the square alone. And hence it will be quite in order to maintain that the square is not less than double the area of the triangle inscribed within it, and to affirm other similar properties that belong to the nature of this composite figure.

But if I were to think that the idea of a supremely perfect body contained existence, on the grounds that it is a greater perfection to exist both in reality and in the intellect than it is to exist in the intellect alone, I could not infer from this that the supremely perfect body exists, but only that it is capable of existing. For I can see quite well that this idea has been put together by my own intellect which has linked together all bodily perfections; and existence does not arise out of the other bodily perfections because it can equally well be affirmed or denied of them. Indeed, when I examine the idea of a body, I perceive that a body has no power to create itself or maintain itself in existence; and I rightly conclude that necessary existence—and it is only necessary existence that is at issue here—no more belongs to the nature of a body, however perfect, than it belongs to the nature of a mountain to be without a valley, or to the nature of a triangle to have angles whose sum is greater than two right angles. But instead of a body, let us now take a thing— whatever this thing turns out to be—which possesses all the perfections which can exist together. If we ask whether existence should be included among these perfections, we will admittedly be in some doubt at first. For our mind, which is finite, normally thinks of these perfections only separately, and hence may not immediately notice the necessity of their being joined together. Yet if we attentively examine whether existence belongs to a supremely powerful being, and what sort of existence it is, we shall be able to perceive clearly and distinctly the following facts. First, possible existence, at the very least, belongs to such a being, just as it belongs to all the other things of which we have a distinct idea, even to those which are put together through a fiction of the intellect. Next, when we attend to the immense power of this being, we shall be unable to think of its existence as possible without also recognizing that it can exist by its own power; and we shall infer from this that this being does really exist and has existed from eternity, since it is quite evident by the natural light that what can exist by its own power always exists. So we shall come to understand that necessary existence is contained in the idea of a supremely powerful being, not by any fiction of the intellect, but because it belongs to the true and immutable nature of such a being that it exists. And we shall also easily perceive that this supremely powerful being cannot but possess within it all the other perfections that are contained in the idea of God; and hence these perfections exist in God and are joined together not by any fiction of the intellect but by their very nature.

Chapter 34

A classic repudiation of ontological arguments

Immanuel Kant

The impossibility of an ontological proof of the existence of God

IN all ages men have spoken of an *absolutely necessary* being, and in so doing have endeavoured, not so much to understand whether and how a thing of this kind allows even of being thought, but rather to prove its existence. There is, of course, no difficulty in giving a verbal definition of the concept, namely, that it is something the non-existence of which is impossible. But this yields no insight into the conditions which make it necessary to regard the non-existence of a thing as absolutely unthinkable. It is precisely these conditions that we desire to know, in order that we may determine whether or not, in resorting to this concept, we are thinking anything at all. The expedient of removing all those conditions which the understanding indispensably requires in order to regard something as necessary, simply through the introduction of the word *unconditioned*, is very far from sufficing to show whether I am still thinking anything in the concept of the unconditionally necessary, or perhaps rather nothing at all.

Nay more, this concept, at first ventured upon blindly, and now become so completely familiar, has been supposed to have its meaning exhibited in a number of examples; and on this account of all further enquiry into its intelligibility has seemed to be quite needless. Thus the fact that every geometrical proposition, as, for instance, that a triangle has three angles, is absolutely necessary, has been taken as justifying us in speaking of an object which lies entirely outside the sphere of our understanding as if we understood perfectly what it is that we intend to convey by the concept of that object.

All the alleged examples are, without exception, taken from *judgments*, not from *things* and their existence. But the unconditioned necessity of judgments is not the same as an absolute necessity of things. The absolute necessity of the judgment is only a conditioned necessity of the thing, or of the predicate in the judgment. The above proposition does not declare that three angles are absolutely necessary, but that, under the condition that there is a triangle (that is, that a triangle is given),

Immanuel Kant 'Critique of Pure Reason' from Immanuel Kant, *Critique of Pure Reason*, translated by Norman Kemp Smith (St Martin's Press, 1965).

three angles will necessarily be found in it. So great, indeed, is the deluding influence exercised by this logical necessity that, by the simple device of forming an *a priori* concept of a thing in such a manner as to include existence within the scope of its meaning, we have supposed ourselves to have justified the conclusion that because existence necessarily belongs to the object of this concept—always under the condition that we posit the thing as given (as existing)—we are also of necessity, in accordance with the law of identity, required to posit the existence of its object, and that this being is therefore itself absolutely necessary—and this, to repeat, for the reason that the existence of this being has already been thought in a concept which is assumed arbitrarily and on condition that we posit its object.

If, in an identical proposition, I reject the predicate while retaining the subject, contradiction results; and I therefore say that the former belongs necessarily to the latter. But if we reject subject and predicate alike, there is no contradiction; for nothing is then left that can be contradicted. To posit a triangle, and yet to reject its three angles, is self contradictory; but there is no contradiction in rejecting the triangle together with its three angles. The same holds true of the concept of an absolutely necessary being. If its existence is rejected, we reject the thing itself with all its predicates; and no question of contradiction can then arise. There is nothing outside it that would then be contradicted, since the necessity of the thing is not supposed to be derived from anything external; nor is there anything internal that would be contradicted, since in rejecting the thing itself we have at the same time rejected all its internal properties. 'God is omnipotent' is a necessary judgment. The omnipotence cannot be rejected if we posit a Deity, that is, an infinite being; for the two concepts are identical. But if we say, 'There is no God', neither the omnipotence nor any other of its predicates is given; they are one and all rejected together with the subject, and there is therefore not the least contradiction in such a judgment.

We have thus seen that if the predicate of a judgment is rejected together with the subject, no internal contradiction can result, and that this holds no matter what the predicate may be. The only way of evading this conclusion is to argue that there are subjects which cannot be removed, and must always remain. That, however, would only be another way of saying that there are absolutely necessary subjects; and that is the very assumption which I have called in question, and the possibility of which the above argument professes to establish. For I cannot form the least concept of a thing which, should it be rejected with all its predicates, leaves behind a contradiction; and in the absence of contradiction I have, through pure *a priori* concepts alone, no criterion of impossibility.

Notwithstanding all these general considerations, in which every one must concur, we may be challenged with a case which is brought forward as proof that in actual fact the contrary holds, namely, that there is one concept, and indeed only one, in reference to which the not-being or rejection of its object is in itself contradictory, namely, the concept of the *ens realissimum*. It is declared that it possesses all reality, and that we are justified in assuming that such a being is possible (the fact that a concept does not contradict itself by no means proves the possibility of its object: but the contrary assertion I am for the moment willing to allow). Now (the argument proceeds) 'all reality' includes existence; existence is therefore contained in the concept of a thing that is possible. If, then, this thing is rejected, the internal possibility of the thing is rejected—which is self-contradictory.

My answer is as follows. There is already a contradiction in introducing the concept of existence—no matter under what title it may be disguised—into the concept of a thing which we profess to be thinking solely in reference to its possibility. If that be allowed as legitimate, a seeming victory has been won; but in actual fact nothing at all is said: the assertion is a mere tautology. We must ask: Is the proposition that *this or that thing* (which, whatever it may be, is allowed as possible) *exists*, an analytic or a synthetic proposition? If it is analytic, the assertion of the existence of the thing adds nothing to the thought of the thing; but in that case either the thought, which is in us, is the thing itself, or we have presupposed an existence as belonging to the realm of the possible, and have then, on that pretext, inferred its existence from its internal possibility—which is nothing but a miserable tautology. The word 'reality', which in the concept of the thing sounds other than the word 'existence' in the concept of the predicate, is of no avail in meeting this objection. For if all positing (no matter what it may be that is posited) is entitled reality, the thing with all its predicates is already posited in the concept of the subject, and is assumed as actual; and in the predicate this is merely repeated. But if, on the other hand, we admit, as every reasonable person must, that all existential propositions are synthetic, how can we profess to maintain that the predicate of existence cannot be rejected without contradiction? This is a feature which is found only in analytic propositions, and is indeed precisely what constitutes their analytic character.

I should have hoped to put an end to these idle and fruitless disputations in a direct manner, by an accurate determination of the concept of existence, had I not found that the illusion which is caused by the confusion of a logical with a real predicate (that is, with a predicate which determines a thing) is almost beyond correction. Anything we please can be made to serve as a logical predicate; the subject can even be predicated of itself; for logic abstracts from all content. But a *determining* predicate is a predicate which is added to the concept of the subject and enlarges it. Consequently, it must not be already contained in the concept.

'*Being*' is obviously not a real predicate; that is, it is not a concept of something which could be added to the concept of a thing. It is merely the positing of a thing, or of certain determinations, as existing in themselves. Logically, it is merely the copula of a judgment. The proposition, 'God is omnipotent', contains two concepts, each of which has its object—God and omnipotence. The small word 'is' adds no new predicate, but only serves to posit the predicate *in its relation* to the subject. If, now, we take the subject (God) with all its predicates (among which is omnipotence) and say 'God is', or 'There is a God', we attach no new predicate to the concept of God, but only posit the subject in itself with all its predicates, and indeed posit it as being an *object* that stands in relation to my *concept*. The content of both must be one and the same; nothing can have been added to the concept, which expresses merely what is possible, by my thinking its object (through the expression 'it is') as given absolutely. Otherwise stated, the real contains no more than the merely possible. A hundred real thalers do not contain the least coin more than a hundred possible thalers. For as the latter signify the concept, and the former the object and the positing of the object, should the former contain more than the latter, my concept would not, in that case, express the whole object, and would not therefore be an adequate concept of it. My financial position is, however, affected very differently by a hundred real thalers than it is by the mere concept of them (that is, of their possibility). For the object, as it actually exists, is not analytically contained in my concept, but is added to my concept (which is a determination of my state) synthetically; and yet the conceived hundred thalers are not themselves in the least increased through thus acquiring existence outside my concept.

By whatever and by however many predicates we may think a thing—even if we completely determine it—we do not make the least addition to the thing when we further declare that this thing *is*. Otherwise, it would not be exactly the same thing that exists, but something more than we had thought in the concept; and we could not, therefore, say that the exact object of my concept exists. If we think in a thing every feature of reality except one, the missing reality is not added by my saying that this defective thing exists. On the contrary, it exists with the same defect with which I have thought it, since otherwise what exists would be something different from what I thought. When, therefore, I think a being as the supreme reality, without any defect, the question still remains whether it exists or not. For though, in my concept, nothing may be lacking of the possible real content of a thing in general, something is still lacking in its relation to my whole state of thought, namely, (in so far as I am unable to assert) that knowledge of this object is also possible *a posteriori*. And here we find the source of our present difficulty. Were we dealing with an object of the senses, we could not confound the existence of the thing with the mere concept of it. For through the concept the object is thought only as conforming to the *universal conditions* of possible empirical knowledge in general, whereas through its existence it is thought as belonging to the context of experience as a whole. In being thus connected with the *content* of experience as a whole, the concept of the object is not, however, in the least enlarged; all that has happened is that our thought has thereby obtained an additional possible perception. It is not, therefore, surprising that, if we attempt to think existence through the pure category alone, we cannot specify a single mark distinguishing it from mere possibility.

Whatever, therefore, and however much, our concept of an object may contain, we must go outside it, if we are to ascribe existence to the object. In the case of objects of the senses, this takes place through their connection with some one of our perceptions, in accordance with empirical laws. But in dealing with objects of pure thought, we have no means whatsoever of knowing their existence, since it would have to be known in a completely *a priori* manner. Our consciousness of all existence (whether immediately through perception, or mediately through inferences which connect something with perception) belongs exclusively to the unity of experience; any [alleged] existence outside this field, while not indeed such as we can declare to be absolutely impossible, is of the nature of an assumption which we can never be in a position to justify.

The concept of a supreme being is in many respects a very useful idea; but just because it is a mere idea, it is altogether incapable, by itself alone, of enlarging our knowledge in regard to what exists. It is not even competent to enlighten us as to the *possibility* of any existence beyond that which is known in and through experience. The analytic criterion of possibility, as consisting in the principle that bare positives (realities) give rise to no contradiction, cannot be denied to it. But since the realities are not given to us in their specific characters; since even if they were, we should still not be in a position to pass judgment; since the criterion of the possibility of synthetic knowledge is never to be looked for save in experience, to which the object of an idea cannot belong, the connection of all real properties in a thing is a synthesis, the possibility of which we are unable to determine *a priori*. And thus the celebrated Leibniz is far from having succeeded in what he plumed himself on achieving—the comprehension *a priori* of the possibility of this sublime ideal being.

The attempt to establish the existence of a supreme being by means of the famous ontological argument of Descartes is therefore merely so much labour and effort lost; we can no more extend our stock of (theoretical) insight by mere ideas, than a merchant can better his position by adding a few noughts to his cash account.

Chapter 35

A contemporary defence of ontological arguments

Alvin Plantinga

The argument restated

LET'S look once again at our initial schematization of the argument. I think perhaps it is step (2)

(2) Existence in reality is greater than existence in the understanding alone

that is most puzzling here. Earlier we spoke of the properties in virtue of which one being is greater, just as a being, than another. Suppose we call them *great-making properties*. Apparently Anselm means to suggest that *existence* is a great-making property. He seems to suggest that a nonexistent being would be greater than in fact it is, if it did exist. But how can we make sense of that? How could there be a nonexistent being anyway? Does that so much as make sense?

Perhaps we can put this perspicuously in terms of possible worlds. An object may exist in some possible worlds and not others. There are possible worlds in which you and I do not exist; these worlds are impoverished, no doubt, but are not on that account impossible. Furthermore, an object can have different properties in different worlds. In the actual world Paul J. Zwier is not a good tennis player; but surely there are worlds in which he wins the Wimbledon Open. Now if a person can have different properties in different worlds, then he can have different degrees of greatness in different worlds. In the actual world Raquel Welch has impressive assets; but there is a world RW_f in which she is fifty pounds overweight and mousy. Indeed, there are worlds in which she does not so much as exist. What Anselm means to be suggesting, I think, is that Raquel Welch enjoys very little greatness in those worlds in which she does not exist. But of course this condition is not restricted to Miss Welch. What Anselm means to say, more generally, is that for any being x and worlds W and W' if x exists in W but not in W' then x's greatness in W exceeds x's greatness in W'. Or more modestly, perhaps he means to say that if a being x does not exist in a world W (and there is a world in which x does exist), then *there is at least one world* in which the greatness of x exceeds the greatness of x in W. Suppose Raquel Welch does not exist in some world W. Anselm means to say that there is at least one possible world in which she has a degree of greatness that exceeds the

Alvin Plantinga 'Defence of the Ontological Argument' from *God, Freedom and Evil* (Harper and Row, 1975), reprinted by permission of the author.

degree of greatness she has in that world W. (It is plausible, indeed, to go much further and hold that she has no *greatness at all* in worlds in which she does not exist.)

But now perhaps we can restate the whole argument in a way that gives us more insight into its real structure. Once more, use the term 'God' to abbreviate the phrase 'the being than which it is not possible that there be a greater.' Now suppose

(13) God does not exist in the actual world

Add the new version of premise (2):

(14) For any being *x* and world *W* if *x* does not exist in *W* then there is a world *W'* such that the greatness of *x* in *W'* exceeds the greatness of *x* in *W*.

Restate premise (3) in terms of possible worlds:

(15) There is a possible world in which God exists.

And continue on:

(16) If God does not exist in the actual world, then there is a world *W'* such that the greatness of God in *W'* exceeds the greatness of God in the actual world. (from (14))
(17) So there is a world *W'* such that the greatness of God in *W'* exceeds the greatest of god in the actual world. ((13) and (16))
(18) So there is a possible being *x* and a world *W'* such that the greatness of *x* in *W'* exceeds the greatness of God in actuality. ((17))
(19) Hence it's possible that there be a being greater than God is. ((18))
(20) So it's possible that there be a being greater than the being than which it's not possible that there be a greater. (19), replacing 'God' by what it abbreviates.

But surely

(21) It's not possible that there be a being greater than the being than which it's not possible that there be a greater.

So (13) (with the help of premises (14) and (15)) appears to imply (20), which, according to (21), is necessarily false. Accordingly, (13) is false. So the actual world contains a being than which it's not possible that there be a greater—that is, God exists.

Now where, if anywhere, can we fault this argument? Step (13) is the hypothesis for *reductio*, the assumption to be reduced to absurdity, and is thus entirely above reproach. Steps (16) through (20) certainly look as if they follow from the items they are said to follow from. So that leaves only (14), (15), and (20). Step (14) says only that it is possible that God exists. Step (15) also certainly seems plausible: if a being doesn't even *exist* in a given world, it can't have much by way of greatness in that world. At the very least it can't have its *maximum* degree of greatness—a degree of greatness that it does not excel in any other world—in a world where it doesn't exist. And consider (20): surely it has the ring of truth. How could there be a being greater than the being than which it's not possible that there be a greater? Initially, the argument seems pretty formidable.

Its fatal flaw

But there is something puzzling about it. We can see this if we ask what sorts of things (14) is supposed to be *about*. It starts off boldly: 'For any being *x* and world *W*, . . .' So (14) is talking about worlds and beings. It says something about each world-being pair. And (16) follows from it, because (16) asserts of *God* and *the actual world* something that according to (14) holds of every being and world. But then if (16) follows from (14), God must be a *being*. That is, (16) follows from (14) only with the help of the additional premise that God is a being. And doesn't this statement—that God is a being—imply that *there is* or *exists* a being than which it's not possible that there be a greater? But if so, the argument flagrantly begs the question; for then we can accept the inference from (14) to (16) only if we already know that the conclusion is true.

We can approach this same matter by a slightly different route. I asked earlier what sorts of things (14) was *about;* the answer was: beings and worlds. We can ask the same or nearly the same question by asking about the *range* of the *quantifiers—* 'for any being,' 'for any world'—in (14). What do these quantifiers range over? If we reply that they range over possible worlds and beings—*actually existing* beings— then the inference to (16) requires the additional premise that God is an actually existing being, that there *really is* a being than which it is not possible that there be a greater. Since this is supposed to be our conclusion, we can't very gracefully add it as a *premise*. So perhaps the quantifiers don't range just over actually existing beings. But what else is there? Step (18) speaks of a *possible being*—a thing that may not in fact exist, but *could* exist. Or we could put it like this. A possible being is a thing that exists in some possible world or other; a thing *x* for which there is a world *W*, such that if *W* had been actual, *x* would have existed. So (18) is really about worlds and *possible beings*. And what it says is this: take any possible being *x* and any possible world *W'*. If *x* does not exist in *W*, then there is a possible world *W'* where *x* has a degree of greatness that surpasses the greatness that it has in *W*. And hence to make the argument complete perhaps we should add the affirmation that God is a *possible being*.

But *are* there any possible beings—that is, *merely* possible beings, beings that don't in fact exist? If so, what sorts of things are they? Do they have properties? How are we to think of them? What is their status? And what reasons are there for supposing that there are any such peculiar items at all?

These are knotty problems: Must we settle them in order even to consider this argument? No. For instead of speaking of *possible beings* and the worlds in which they do or don't exist, we can speak of *properties* and the worlds in which they do or don't *have instances*, are or are not *instantiated* or *exemplified*. Instead of speaking of a possible being named by the phrase, 'the being than which it's not possible that there be a greater,' we may speak of the property *having an unsurpassable degree of greatness*—that is, *having a degree of greatness such that it's not possible that there exist a being having more.* And then we can ask whether this property is instantiated in this or other possible worlds. Later on I shall show how to restate the argument this way. For the moment please take my word for the fact that we can speak as freely as we wish about possible objects; for we can always translate ostensible talk about such things into talk about properties and the worlds in which they are or are not instantiated.

The argument speaks, therefore, of an unsurpassably great being—of a being whose greatness is not excelled by any being in any world. This being has a degree of greatness so impressive that no other being in any world has more. But here we hit the question crucial for this version of the argument. *Where* does this being have that degree of greatness? I said above that the same being may have different degrees of greatness in different worlds; in which world does the possible being in question have the degree of greatness in question? All we are really told, in being told that God is a possible being, is this: among the possible beings there is one that in some world or other has a degree of greatness that is nowhere excelled.

And this fact is fatal to this version of the argument. I said earlier that (21) has the ring of truth; a closer look (listen?) reveals that it's more of a dull thud. For it is ambiguous as between

(21′) It's not possible that there be a being whose greatness surpasses that enjoyed by the unsurpassably great being *in the worlds where its greatness is at a maximum*

and

(21″) It's not possible that there be a being whose greatness surpasses that enjoyed by the unsurpassably great being *in the actual world.*

There is an important difference between these two. The greatest possible being may have different degrees of greatness in different worlds. Step (21′) points to the worlds in which this being has its maximal greatness; and it says, quite properly, that the degree of greatness this being has in those worlds is nowhere excelled. Clearly this is so. The greatest possible being is a possible being who in some world or other has unsurpassable greatness. Unfortunately for the argument, however, (21′) does not contradict (20). Or to put it another way, what follows from (13) (together with (14) and (15)) is not the denial of (21′). If that *did* follow, then the *reductio* would be complete and the argument successful. But what (20) says is not that there is a possible being whose greatness exceeds that enjoyed by the greatest possible being *in a world where the latter's greatness is at a maximum*; it says only that there is a possible being whose greatness exceeds that enjoyed by the greatest possible being *in the actual world*—where, for all we know, its greatness is *not* at a maximum. So if we read (21) as (21′), the *reductio* argument falls apart.

Suppose instead we read it as (21″). Then what it says is that there couldn't be a being whose greatness surpasses that enjoyed by the greatest possible being in Kronos, the actual world. So read, (21) does contradict (20). Unfortunately, however, we have *no* reason, so far, for thinking that (21″) is true at all, let alone necessarily true. If, among the possible beings, there is one whose greatness *in some world or other* is absolutely maximal—such that no being in any world has a degree of greatness surpassing it—then indeed there couldn't be a being that was greater than *that* . But it doesn't follow that this being has that degree of greatness in the *actual* world. It has it *in some world or other* but not necessarily in Kronos, the actual world. And so the argument fails. If we take (21) as (21′), then it follows from the assertion that God is a possible being; but it is of no use to the argument. If we take it as (21″), on the other hand, then indeed it is useful in the argument, but we have no reason whatever to think it true. So this version of the argument fails.[1]

A modal version of the argument

But of course there are many other versions; one of the argument's chief features is its many-sided diversity. The fact that *this* version is unsatisfactory does not show that *every* version is or must be. Professors Charles Hartshorne[2] and Norman Malcolm[3] claim to detect two quite different versions of the argument in Anselm's work. In the first of these versions *existence* is held to be a perfection or a great-making property; in the second it is *necessary existence*. But what could *that* amount to? Perhaps something like this. Consider a pair of beings *A* and *B* that both do in fact exist. And suppose that *A* exists in every other possible world as well—that is, if any other possible world has been actual, *A* would have existed. On the other hand, *B* exists in only some possible worlds; there are worlds *W* such that had any of *them* been actual, *B* would not have existed. Now according to the doctrine under consideration, *A* is so far greater than *B*. Of course, on *balance* it may be that *A* is not greater than *B;* I believe that the number seven, unlike Spiro Agnew, exists in every possible world; yet I should be hesitant to affirm on that account that the number seven is greater than Agnew. Necessary existence is just one of several great-making properties, and no doubt Agnew has more of some of these others than does the number seven. Still, all this is compatible with saying that necessary existence is a great-making property. And given this notion, we can restate the argument as follows:

(22) It is possible that there is a greatest possible being.

(23) Therefore, there is a possible being that in some world W^1 or other has a

1. This criticism of this version of the argument essentially follows David Lewis, 'Anselm and Actuality,' *Nous* 4 (1970): 175–88. See also Alvin Plantinga, *The Nature of Necessity* (Oxford: Clarendon Press, 1974), pp. 202–5.

2. Charles Hartshorne, *Man's Vision of God* (New York: Harper and Row, 1941). Portions reprinted in Alvin Plantinga, *The Ontological Argument* (Garden City, New York, 1965), pp. 123–35.

3. Norman Malcolm, 'Anselm's Ontological Arguments,' *Philosophical Review* 69 (1960)

maximum degree of greatness—a degree of greatness that is nowhere exceeded.

(24) A being B has the maximum degree of greatness in a given possible world W only if B *exists in every possible world.*

(22) and (24) are the premises of this argument; and what follows is that if W' had been actual, B would have existed in every possible world. That is, if W' had been actual, B's nonexistence would have been impossible. But logical possibilities and impossibilities do not vary from world to world. That is to say, if a given proposition or state of affairs is impossible in at least one possible world, then it is impossible in every possible world. There are no propositions that in fact are possible but could have been impossible; there are none that are in fact impossible but could have been possible.[4] Accordingly, B's nonexistence is impossible in every possible world; hence it is impossible in *this* world; hence B exists and exists necessarily.

A flaw in the ointment

This is an interesting argument, but it suffers from at least one annoying defect. What it shows is that if it is possible that there be a greatest possible being (if the idea of a greatest possible being is coherent) and if that idea includes necessary existence, then in fact there is a being that exists in every world and in *some* world has a degree of greatness that is nowhere excelled. Unfortunately it doesn't follow that the being in question has the degree of greatness in question in Kronos, the actual world. For all the argument shows, this being might *exist* in the actual world but be pretty insignificant here. In some world or other it has maximal greatness; how does this show that it has such greatness in Kronos?

But perhaps we can repair the argument. J. N. Findlay once offered what can only be called an ontological *disproof* of the existence of God.[5] Findlay begins by pointing out that God, if He exists, is an 'adequate object of religious worship.' But such a being, he says, would have to be a *necessary* being; and, he adds, this idea is incredible 'for all who share a contemporary outlook.' 'Those who believe in necessary truths which aren't merely tautological think that such truths merely connect the *possible* instances of various characteristics with each other; they don't expect such truths to tell them whether there *will* be instances of any characteristics. This is the outcome of the whole medieval and Kantian criticism of the ontological proof.'[6] I've argued above that 'the whole medieval and Kantian criticism' of Anselm's argument may be taken with a grain or two of salt. And certainly most

4. See Plantinga, 'World and Essence,' *Philosophical Review* 79 (October 1970): 475; and Plantinga, *The Nature of Necessity,* chap. 4, sec. 6.
5. J. N. Findlay, 'Can God's Existence Be Disproved?' *Mind* 57 (1948): 176–83.
6. P. 119. Mr. Findlay no longer endorses this sentiment. See the preface to his *Ascent to the Absolute* (London, 1970).

philosophers who believe that there are necessary truths, believe that *some* of them *do* tell us whether there will be instances of certain characteristics; the proposition *there are no married bachelors* is necessarily true, and it tells us that there will be no instances whatever of the characteristic *married bachelor*. Be that as it may what is presently relevant in Findlay's piece is this passage:

Not only is it contrary to the demands and claims inherent in religious attitudes that their object should *exist* 'accidentally'; it is also contrary to these demands that it should *possess its various excellences* in some merely adventitious manner. It would be quite unsatisfactory from the religious stand point, if an object merely *happened* to be wise, good, powerful, and so forth, even to a superlative degree . . . And so we are led on irresistibly, by the demands inherent in religious reverence, to hold that an adequate object of our worship must possess its various excellences *in some necessary manner*.[7]

I think there is truth in these remarks. We could put the point as follows. In determining the greatness of a being B in a world W, what counts is not merely the qualities and properties possessed by B in W; what B is like in *other* worlds is also relevant. Most of us who believe in God think of Him as a being than whom it's not possible that there be a greater. But we don't think of Him as a being who, had things been different, would have been powerless or uninformed or of dubious moral character. God doesn't *just happen* to be a greatest possible being; He couldn't have been otherwise.

Perhaps we should make a distinction here between *greatness* and *excellence*. A being's excellence in a given world W, let us say, depends only upon the properties it has in W; its *greatness* in W depends upon these properties but also upon what it is like in other worlds. Those who are fond of the calculus might put it by saying that there is a function assigning to each being in each world a degree of excellence; and a being's *greatness* is to be computed (by someone unusually well informed) by integrating its excellence over all possible worlds. Then it is plausible to suppose that the maximal degree of greatness entails *maximal excellence in every world*. A being, then, has the maximal degree of *greatness* in a given world W only if it has *maximal excellence in every possible world*. But *maximal excellence* entails *omniscience, omnipotence*, and *moral perfection*. That is to say, a being B has maximal excellence in a world W only if B has omniscience, omnipotence, and moral perfection in W—only if B would have been omniscient, omnipotent, and morally perfect if W had been actual.

The argument restated

Given these ideas, we can restate the present version of the argument in the following more explicit way.

(25) It is possible that there be a being that has maximal greatness.

---

7. J. N. Findlay, 'Can God's Existence Be Disproved?' p. 117.

(26) So there is a possible being that in some world *W* has maximal greatness.

(27) A Being has maximal greatness in a given world only if it has maximal excellence in every world.

(28) A being has maximal excellence in a given world only if it has omniscience, omnipotence, and moral perfection in that world.

And now we no longer need the supposition that necessary existence is a perfection; for obviously a being can't be omnipotent (or for that matter omniscient or morally perfect) in a given world unless it *exists* in that world. From (25), (27), and (28) it follows that there actually exists a being that is omnipotent, omniscient, and morally perfect; this being, furthermore, exists and has these qualities in every other world as well. For (26), which follows from (25), tells us that there is a possible world *W′* let's say, in which there exists a being with maximal greatness. That is, had *W′* been actual, there would have been a being with maximal greatness. But then according to (27) this being has maximal excellence in every world. What this means, according to (28), is that in *W′* this being has omniscience, omnipotence, and moral perfection *in every world.* That is to say, if *W′* had been actual, there would have existed a being who was omniscient and omnipotent and morally perfect and who would have had these properties in every possible world. So if *W′* had been actual, it would have been *impossible* that there be no omnipotent, omniscient, and morally perfect being. But while *contingent* truths vary from world to world, what is logically impossible does not. Therefore, in every possible world *W* it is impossible that there be no such being; each possible world *W* is such that if it had been actual, it would have been impossible that there be no such being. And hence it is impossible in the *actual* world (which is one of the possible worlds) that there be no omniscient, omnipotent, and morally perfect being. Hence there really does exist a being who is omniscient, omnipotent, and morally perfect and who exists and has these properties in every possible world. Accordingly these premises, (25), (27), and (28), entail that God, so thought of, exists. Indeed, if we regard (27) and (28) as consequences of a *definition*—a definition of maximal greatness—then the only premise of the argument is (25).

But now for a last objection suggested earlier (p. 101). What about (25)? It says that there is a *possible being* having such and such characteristics. But what *are* possible beings? We know what *actual* beings are—the Taj Mahal, Socrates, you and I, the Grand Teton—these are among the more impressive examples of actually existing beings. But what is a *possible* being? Is there a possible mountain just like Mt. Rainier two miles directly south of the Grand Teton? If so, it is located at the same place as the Middle Teton. Does that matter? Is there another such possible mountain three miles east of the Grand Teton, where Jenny Lake is? Are there possible mountains like this all over the world? Are there also possible oceans at all the places where there are possible mountains? For any place you mention, of course, it is *possible* that there be a mountain there; does it follow that in fact *there is* a possible mountain there?

These are some questions that arise when we ask ourselves whether there are merely possible beings that don't in fact exist. And the version of the ontological argument we've been considering seems to make sense only on the assumption that there are such things. The earlier versions also depended on that assumption; consider for example, this step of the first version we considered:

(18) So there is a possible being x and a world W' such that the greatness of x in W' exceeds the greatness of God in actuality

This possible being, you recall, was God Himself, supposed not to exist in the actual world. We can make sense of (18), therefore, only if we are prepared to grant that there are possible beings who don't in fact exist. Such beings exist in other worlds, of course; had things been appropriately different, they would have existed. But in fact they don't exist, although nonetheless there *are* such things.

I am inclined to think the supposition that there are such things—things that are possible but don't exist—is either unintelligible or necessarily false. But this doesn't mean that the present version of the ontological argument must be rejected. For we can restate the argument in a way that does not commit us to this questionable idea. Instead of speaking of *possible beings* that do or do not exist in various possible worlds, we may speak of *properties* and the worlds in which they are or are not *instantiated*. Instead of speaking of the possible fat man in the corner, noting that he doesn't exist, we may speak of the property *being a fat man in the corner*, noting that it isn't instantiated (although it could have been). Of course, the *property* in question, like the property *being a unicorn*, exists. It is perfectly good property which exists with as much equanimity as the property of equininity, the property of being a horse. But it doesn't happen to apply to anything. That is, in *this* world it doesn't apply to anything; in other possible worlds it does.

The argument triumphant

Using this idea we can restate this last version of the ontological argument in such a way that it no longer matters whether there are any merely possible beings that do not exist. Instead of speaking of the possible being that has, in some world or other, a maximal degree of greatness, we may speak of *the property of being maximally great* or *maximal greatness*. The premise corresponding to (25) then says simply that maximal greatness is possibly instantiated, i.e., that

(29) There is a possible world in which maximal greatness is instantiated.

And the analogues of (27) and (28) spell out what is involved in maximal greatness:

(30) Necessarily, a being is maximally great only if it has maximal excellence in every world

and

(31) Necessarily, a being has maximal excellence in every world only if it has omniscience, omnipotence, and moral perfection in every world.

Notice that (30) and (31) do not imply that there are possible but nonexistent beings—any more than does, for example,

(32) Necessarily, a thing is a unicorn only if it has one horn.

But if (29) is true, then there is a possible world *W* such that if it had been actual, then there would have existed a being that was omnipotent, omniscient, and morally perfect; this being, furthermore, would have had these qualities in every possible world. So it follows that if *W* had been actual, it would have been *impossible* that there be no such being. That is, if *W* had been actual,

(33) There is no omnipotent, omniscient, and morally perfect being

would have been an impossible proposition. But if a proposition is impossible in at least one possible world, then it is impossible in every possible world; what is impossible does not vary from world to world. Accordingly (33) is impossible in the *actual* world, i.e., impossible *simpliciter*. But if it is impossible that there be no such being, then there actually exists a being that is omnipotent, omniscient, and morally perfect; this being, furthermore, has these qualities essentially and exists in every possible world.

   What shall we say of this argument? It is certainly valid; given its premise, the conclusion follows. The only question of interest, it seems to me, is whether its main premise—that maximal greatness *is* possibly instantiated—is *true*. I think it *is* true; hence I think this version of the ontological argument is sound.

   But here we must be careful; we must ask whether this argument is a successful piece of natural theology, whether it *proves* the existence of God. And the answer must be, I think, that it docs not. An argument for God's existence may be *sound*, after all, without in any useful sense proving God's existence.[8] Since I believe in God, I think the following argument is sound:

Either God exists or $7 + 5 = 14$
It is false that $7 + 5 = 14$
Therefore God exists.

But obviously this isn't a *proof*; no one who didn't already accept the conclusion, would accept the first premise. The ontological argument we've been examining isn't just like this one, of course, but it must be conceded that not everyone who understands and reflects on its central premise—that the existence of a maximally great being is *possible*—will accept it. Still, it is evident, I think, that there is nothing *contrary to reason* or *irrational* in accepting this premise.[9] What I claim for this

8. See George Mavrodes, *Belief in God* (New York: Macmillan Co., 1970), pp. 22 ff.
9. For more on this see Plantinga, *The Nature of Necessity*, chap. 10, sec. 8.

argument, therefore, is that it establishes, not the *truth* of theism, but its rational acceptability. And hence it accomplishes at least one of the aims of the tradition of natural theology.

Questions for discussion

1. What is Anselm arguing in *Proslogion* 2 and 3?
2. Even if I have the best dictionary definition of the word 'W', why should I suppose that the definition alone allows me to conclude that there is something in reality to which 'W' latches on?
3. Is there an absurdity in saying 'Something which cannot fail to exist might not exist'?
4. Do we have a sufficient understanding of what God is to argue that existence belongs to him by nature?
5. Is it right to say that existence is a property of some kind?

Advice on further reading

For a short book-length treatment of ontological arguments, see Jonathan Barnes, *The Ontological Argument* (London, 1972). For an extremely comprehensive analysis and discussion of a large range of ontological arguments (from Anselm to the present), a basic reference work is Graham Oppy, *Ontological Arguments and Belief in God* (Cambridge, 1995). For helpful essays introducing the topic of ontological arguments, see Clement Dore, 'Ontological Arguments' in Philip Quinn and Charles Taliaferro (eds), *A Companion to Philosophy of Religion* (Oxford, 1997) and Peter Van Inwagen, 'Ontological Arguments', *Nous* 11 (1977). For a Reader on ontological arguments, see John Hick and Arthur McGill (eds), *The Many Faced Argument* (London, 1967).

For an introduction to interpretations of Anselm on ontological arguments, see M. J. Charlesworth, *St Anselm's Proslogion* (Oxford, 1965), pp. 3–46; Jasper Hopkins, *A Companion to the Study of St Anselm* (Minneapolis, 1972), ch. III; Jasper Hopkins, *A New, Interpretative Translation of St Anselm's Monologion and Proslogion* (Minneapolis, 1986), pp. 3–42. For a critique of Anselm as interpreted by Anscombe, see C. J. F. Williams, 'Russelm' *The Philosophical Quarterly* 43 (1993), which also contains a response from Anscombe herself ('Russelm or Anselm?'). For a helpful discussion of Gaunilo, see Nicholas Wolterstorff, 'In Defence of Gaunilo's Defense of the Fool', in C. Stephen Evans and Merold Westphal (eds), *Christian Perspectives on Religious Knowledge* (Grand Rapids, 1993).

There is a certain amount of disagreement when it comes to interpreting Descartes's defence of ontological arguments. For an introduction to this, see Anthony Kenny, *Descartes* (New York, 1968), ch. 7, and Bernard Williams, *Descartes: The Project of Pure Enquiry* (Harmondsworth, 1978), ch. 5. For a commentary on the above extract from Kant, see Norman Kemp Smith, *A Commentary to Kant's 'Critique of Pure Reason'* (2nd edn, London and Basingstoke, 1979), pp. 527–31. See also James Van Cleve, *Problems from Kant* (New York and Oxford, 1999), ch. 12 and S. Morris Engel, 'Kant's "Refutation" of the Ontological Argument', in Robert Paul Wolff (ed.), *Kant: A Collection of Critical Essays* (London and Melbourne, 1968).

Kant's claim about existence and predication has generated a lot of literature. For a survey and discussion of it, see chapter 10 of Graham Oppy's *Ontological Arguments and Belief in God*. A most impressive introduction to the topic of existence and predication (which ends up defending Kant via Frege) is C. J. F. Williams, *What is Existence?* (Oxford, 1981). See also, C. J. F. Williams, *Being, Identity and Truth* (Oxford, 1992), chs I and IX.

You shall be helped in understanding Plantinga's defence of ontological arguments if you know something about modal logic and the notion of 'possible worlds'. For an introduction to modal logic, see Kenneth Konyndyk, *Introductory Modal Logic* (Notre Dame, 1986). For a more advanced introduction, see G. E. Hughes and M. J. Cresswell, *A New Introduction to Modal Logic* (London and New York, 1996). For 'possible worlds', see Robert C. Stalnaker, 'Possible Worlds', in Ted Honderich and Myles Burnyeat (eds), *Philosophy As It Is* (London, 1979).

Plantinga presents a more detailed account of his ontological argument in Alvin Plantinga, *The Nature of Necessity* (Oxford, 1974). For a brief critique of Plantinga's argument, see William Rowe, 'Modal Versions of the Ontological Argument', in Louis P. Pojman (ed.), *Philosophy of Religion: An Anthology* (3rd edn, Belmont CA, 1998).

Ontological arguments all seem to conclude that God's existence is strongly necessary (that God exists of necessity). The notion of 'necessary existence' has been subject to a lot of philosophical debate which is worth pursuing with an eye on ontological arguments. Good, introductory discussions include: Robert M. Adams, 'Has It Been Proved That All Real Existence Is Contingent?' and 'Divine Necessity', in Robert M. Adams, *The Virtue of Faith* (Oxford, 1987), and Anthony Kenny, 'God and Necessity' and 'Necessary Being', in Anthony Kenny, *Reason and Religion* (Oxford, 1987).

God and human experience

Introduction

Knowing by experience

How do we defend our claims to know that something or other is the case? How do we attempt to justify beliefs which we have? We often appeal to what we have been told, as when we say that an event has occurred because we have read about it in a newspaper or have heard it reported on television. But we also do other things. Sometimes we appeal to an abstract process of inference of a purely logical or mathematical kind. We also appeal to inference from empirical data, as detectives often do when attempting to identify a criminal.

Frequently, however, we defend what we assert by referring to what we have directly encountered. Suppose we have all been informed that Fred is dead. And suppose I then meet him. 'He's alive!', I tell everyone. 'How do you know?', they ask. 'I've seen him', I reply. Here I am not relying on anyone's testimony. Nor am I indulging in purely logical inference. I do not seem to be indulging in inference at all. I am reporting how things directly seem to me. I am drawing on personal experience. And this is something which people do continually. Ask New Yorkers how they know that their city is crowded. They will probably tell you about the huge numbers of people they see there daily. Ask people from Minnesota how they know that it gets cold there in the winter. They will probably tell you to try spending a winter in Minnesota.

Defenders of cosmological, design, and ontological arguments are evidently seeking to show that we have inferential reason for supposing that God exists. But might it not be said that people can know of God's existence in something like the way I might come to know, from meeting him, that Fred is still alive? Might there be knowledge of God's existence (or belief that God exists) which is solidly or reliably grounded in personal experience of God? Should we not take seriously the notion that God can be directly encountered, perceived, or seen?

Experience and God

The author of the Gospel of John roundly declares 'No one has ever seen God'.[1] But there is a lot of talk about seeing God in the Old Testament. For instance, we are told that Jacob said: 'I have seen God face to face.'[2] In the book of Exodus we are informed that 'the Lord used to speak to Moses face to face, as a man speaks to his friend'.[3] In the book Deuteronomy, the children of Israel cry out: 'Behold the Lord our God has shown us his glory and greatness, and we have heard his voice . . . we have this day seen God speak with man and man still live.'[4] And the prophet Isaiah writes: 'In the year that King Uzziah died I saw the Lord sitting upon a throne, high and lifted up.'[5]

Interpreting such texts is doubtless a difficult matter. On the surface, however, they seem to be supposing that God can somehow be directly encountered (as opposed to inferred). And this supposition has been employed by some philosophers when arguing that belief in God has rational support. If I have met the living Fred, then I am surely rationally warranted in claiming that Fred is as real as me. By the same token, so it has been suggested, there is, or there could be, rational warrant for belief in the existence of the living God from the fact that God has been directly encountered, perceived, or seen in some way.

Hence, for example, according to John Baillie (d. 1960): 'There is no reality by which we are more directly confronted than we are by the Living God.'[6] Baillie, who is referred to in Chapter 36, vigorously opposes the notion that knowledge of God is arrived at by inference. We must, he says, acknowledge God to be 'of all realities, that by which we are most directly and immediately confronted'.[7] According to Baillie, human beings have four 'subjects' of knowledge: 'ourselves, our fellows, the corporeal world, and God'.[8] And, so he argues, God is an object of human knowledge in something like the way our fellows are. On Baillie's account, our knowledge of people is knowledge of realities which are neither perceived by the senses nor arrived at by means of inference. He writes:

There is an element of immediacy in our knowledge of one another. Our knowledge of other minds is not merely a derivative from our knowledge of other bodies or of our own minds or of both together, but is itself a primary and original mode of consciousness of equal right with these others and having, like them, a character *sui generis*.[9]

And, so Baillie thinks, there is consciousness of God as a personal '*object* of our cognition'. Or, as he puts it: 'From the beginning God meets us, not as one among the many objects of our knowledge, but as another Knower by whom both they and we ourselves

1. John 1: 18.
2. Genesis 32: 30.
3. Exodus 33: 11.
4. Deuteronomy 5: 24.
5. Isaiah 6: 1.
6. John Baillie, *Our Knowledge of God* (New York, 1959), p. 166. Note that Baillie's position seems to be very similar to that developed by Plantinga in Chapter 4.
7. Ibid., p. 175.
8. Ibid., p. 178.
9. Ibid., p. 213.

are known.'[10] In developing his account, Baillie insists that we must allow for the existence in people of 'perceptive (or intuitive) reason' as opposed to 'discursive' reason.[11]
According to him, there can be a simple apprehension of the fact that something is the
case, one which is immediate and not arrived at by inference. And, so he thinks, the
reality of God is something which (at least some) people can simply apprehend.

Is Baillie saying that God can be directly experienced? He seems to be, for he calls the
'consciousness of God' an 'experience of God'.[12] And other philosophers have suggested
that we might have reason to believe in God on the basis of direct experience. Two
notable recent examples include Richard Swinburne and William Alston.

Swinburne takes his stand on what he calls 'the principle of credulity'. Am I justified in
supposing that something is present just because it seems to me that the thing is there?
According to Swinburne, I am. It is, he suggests, 'a principle of rationality that (in the
absence of special considerations) if it seems (epistemically) to a subject that x is present,
then probably x is present; what one seems to perceive is probably so.'[13] And, so Swinburne suggests, this principle allows one reasonably to hold that God exists on the basis
of experience. 'If it seems to me that I have a glimpse of Heaven, or a vision of God', he
argues, 'that is grounds for me and others to suppose that I do.'[14]

And this is basically what Alston maintains. In *Perceiving God* he suggests that experience of God can be thought of as 'a functioning, socially established, perceptual doxastic
practice [i.e. a way of forming beliefs and epistemically evaluating them] with distinctive
experiential inputs, distinctive input–output functions, a distinctive conceptual scheme,
and a rich, internally justified overrider system'.[15] As such, Alston argues, it 'possesses a
prima facie title to being rationally engaged in, and its outputs are thereby prima facie
justified, *provided we have no sufficient reason to regard it as unreliable or otherwise
disqualified for rational acceptance*'.[16]

Evaluating claims to experience of God

But can an (ostensible) experience of God really provide good grounds for believing that
God exists? Baillie, Swinburne, and Alston have provided some of the strongest philosophical cases for saying that it can.[17] But many philosophers have been sceptical of the
claim that the existence of God can be known on the basis of experience. Why? Here are
some reasons which have been given:

---

10. Ibid., p. 220.
11. Ibid., p. 226.
12. Ibid., p. 224.
13. Richard Swinburne, *The Existence of God* (revised edn, Oxford, 1991), p. 254. The word 'epistemic-
    ally' means 'pertaining to knowledge'. The word derives from the Greek term which has also led to
    the English word 'epistemology': the study of the nature and/or grounds of human knowledge
    Epistemology has long been a major branch of philosophy.
14. Ibid., p. 260.
15. William Alston, *Perceiving God* (Ithaca, New York, and London, 1991).
16. Ibid.
17. For some other significant defenders of the notion that God can be experienced, see further 'Advice
    on reading' below.

1.   There could not be a God, so there could not be experience of God.[18]
2.   Human experience is limited to experience of material things. Since God is not supposed to be a material thing, there can be no human experience of God.[19]
3.   God is a reality which defies human understanding. So, even if God accounts for the experiences we have, we cannot be in any position explicitly to recognize that any object of our experience is God.[20]
4.   When I say that I have encountered or perceived something, I am merely reporting how things seem to me. I am offering a piece of self-description. But its seeming to someone that such and such is the case (a psychological state) does not guarantee that it *is* the case (its seeming to Fred that-P does not entail that-P). So claims to have experienced God may fail to square with what is actually the case.
5.   Experience can often present false impressions. It looks as though the sun moves round the earth, but it does not. You may think you heard Elizabeth, though it was actually Margaret. People suffering from various kinds of drug addiction may genuinely believe that the world contains fifty-foot penguins and the like. But it does not. So experience can carry little weight when it comes to the question of God's existence.
6.   The occurrence of what people take to be experience of God may admit of a purely natural explanation. Perhaps it is due to (or identical with) a physical process in the human body. Perhaps it is due to matters which a psychoanalyst might be able to uncover, matters which do not need to be accounted for in theological terms.[21]

Yet are these good reasons for concluding that one cannot be right when claiming that one has encountered God directly? Those who think that they are not have typically responded to them by arguing along the following lines:

1.   There is no good reason to suppose that 'God exists' is somehow meaningless, or contradictory, or not possibly true. So one should not reject claims to experience of God by rejecting the whole idea of God.[22]

18. This is what the Logical Positivists would have argued. And it is what would be suggested by anyone arguing that there is reason for supposing that belief in God involves some intrinsic incoherence or impossibility, as, for example, Anthony Kenny does in *The God of the Philosophers* (Oxford, 1979).
19. One may attribute this view to Aquinas. His view of human knowledge effectively restricts it to what can be derived from sense experience. Cf. *Summa Theologiae*, Ia. 84–8.
20. This view has been defended over many centuries, chiefly by a variety of theologians in the Jewish and Christian traditions. Aquinas, again, is a good example. Cf. *Summa Theologiae*, Ia. 2. 1 and Ia. 12. 1–4 and Ia. 12. 11. It is not surprising that Baillie, for instance, sees Aquinas as a major opponent of what he wants to say. Cf. *Our Knowledge of God*, ch. III, §9. But also see, for example, J. L. Mackie, *The Miracle of Theism* (Oxford, 1982), p. 182: 'Nothing in an experience as such could reveal a creator of the world, or omnipotence, or omniscience, or perfect goodness, or eternity, or even that there is just one God.'
21. The psychologist Sigmund Freud (1856–1939) famously took religious belief to be explicable in non-religious terms. Many other psychologists, though not sharing Freud's approach to psychology, have taken a similar view. For an introduction to them, and to Freud, see David M. Wulff (ed.), *Psychology of Religion: Classic and Contemporary Views* (New York, 1991).
22. Hence, for example, Swinburne's defence of experience of God in *The Existence of God* is preceded by, and presupposes all that he has to say, in *The Coherence of Theism*.

2. It is wrong to say that we have no experience of things which are not material. For what of other people? These are things with minds. Yet minds are not objects of sensory experience, though we can obviously know of them in a direct or immediate way.[23]

3. God does not completely defy human understanding and there is no reason in principle why people should not be able correctly to identify an object of their experience as divine.[24]

4. When I say that I have encountered or perceived something, I am reporting how things seem to me. But experience can give us grounds for supposing that things really are as we take them to be. We can acquire knowledge by experience. And we can acquire knowledge of God by experience.[25]

5. In claiming that physical objects exist we have to rely on experience. So why can we not rely on experience when it comes to the existence of God?

6. The fact that people can make mistakes when describing how things are does not mean that they are always mistaken in the way they take them to be. Experience can sometimes give us knowledge. And it can give us knowledge of God.[26]

7. Naturalistic attempts to write off experience of God fail since they do not take account of those who rightly claim to experience God. While some claims to have experienced God may come from people whose beliefs do not derive from a genuine experience of God, it does not follow that all do.[27]

So how should we think? Should we accept that there is experience of God which gives grounds for believing in God? Or should we take another view? In Chapter 36 C. B. Martin suggests that when people say that they know God by experience they are best thought of as reliably informing us only of how things *seem to them*. They cannot, he argues, be thought of as reliably informing us of God's existence. And, in Chapter 37,

23. As we have seen, Baillie makes much of the analogy between experience of God and our knowledge of each other. So does H. P. Owen in *The Christian Knowledge of God* (London, 1969), ch. 6. Note, however, that both Baillie and Owen are relying on a notion of people which sees them as essentially incorporeal, a notion which many philosophers would reject. For more on this, see Part VII.

24. Cf. Swinburne, *The Existence of God*, pp. 256 f.: ' "God", like "centaur", is defined in terms of properties of which most of us have had experience. He is defined as a "person" without a "body" who is unlimited in his "power", "knowledge", and "freedom", and in terms of other similar properties, of all of which we have had mundane experience.' Cf. also Alston, *Perceiving God*, ch. 1. Swinburne and Alston, of course, are working with an understanding of the word 'God' which not all would share.

25. A philosopher who has done more than most to press this argument is Illtyd Trethowan. See his books *Certainty: Philosophical and Theological* (London, 1948), *The Basis of Belief* (London, 1961), *Absolute Value* (London and New York, 1970), and *Mysticism and Theology* (London, 1975).

26. This position again is something which authors like Trethowan defend at length.

27. Trethowan argues in this way. The argument is implicit in what Swinburne and Alston say about experience of God. Cf. Alston, *Perceiving God*, p. 240: 'No theories of human nature and behaviour sweeping enough to generate conflicts with religious belief are, or have any prospects of becoming, well enough established scientifically to give cause for concern'. By 'concern' Alston means concern for religious (specifically, Christian) believers. But he clearly sees his claim as one which could be fruitfully developed in response to naturalistic explanations of what people take to be experience of God.

Peter Donovan gives further reasons for being cautious of claims to know God by experience. In Chapter 38, however, William Alston offers a resounding defence of the view that God can be known as an object of experience. Reading these authors should help to give you a sense of ways in which one might seek to evaluate the idea that God can be thought of as an object of experience. Following up the reading suggestions below, and reflecting on what I have written above, should help you to take your thinking further.

Chapter 36

Why 'knowing God by experience' is a notion open to question

C. B. Martin

SOME theologians support their claim to knowledge of the existence of God on the basis of direct experience of God. The alleged theological way of knowing may be described as follows.

'I have direct experience (knowledge, acquaintance, apprehension) of God, therefore I have valid reason to believe that God exists.'

A. By this it may be meant that the statement 'I have had direct experience of God, but God does not exist' is contradictory. Thus, the assertion that 'I have had direct experience of God' commits one to the assertion that God exists. From this it follows that 'I have had direct experience of God' is more than a psychological statement, because it claims more than the fact that I have certain sensations—it claims that God exists. Thus as it stands this is a correct form of deductive argument. The assertion 'I have direct experience of God' includes the assertion 'God exists' thus, the conclusion 'therefore, God exists' follows tautologically.

B. Unfortunately, this deduction is useless. The addition of the existential claim 'God exists' to the psychological claim of having religious experiences must be shown to be warrantable. It cannot be shown to be warrantable by any deductive argument, because psychological statements of the form

1. I feel as if an unseen person were interested in (willed) my welfare.
2. I feel an elation quite unlike any I have ever felt before.
3. I have feelings of guilt and shame at my sinfulness.
4. I feel as if I were committed to bending all of my efforts to living in a certain way, etc., etc.,

can make the claim only that I have these complex feelings and sensations. Nothing else follows deductively. No matter what the existential statement might be that is added to the psychological statement, it is always logically possible for future psychological statements to call this existential claim in doubt. The only thing that I can establish beyond correction on the basis of having certain feelings and sensations is that I have these feelings and sensations. No matter how unique an experience may be claimed to be, it cannot do the impossible.

C. Neither is the addition of the existential claim 'God exists' to the psycho-

C. B. Martin 'A Religious Way of Knowing' from *Mind*, vol. 61 (1952), reprinted by permission of Oxford University Press.

logical claim made good by any inductive argument. There are no tests agreed upon to establish genuine experience of God and distinguish it decisively from the ungenuine. Indeed, many theologians deny the possibility of any such test or set of tests. Nor is there any increased capacity for prediction produced in the Christian believer which we cannot explain on a secular basis. However, just such a capacity is implied by those who talk of religious experience as if it were due to some kind of sixth sense.

1. The believer may persuade us that something extraordinary has happened by saying, 'I am a changed man since 6.37 p.m., 6th May, 1939'. This is a straightforward empirical statement. We can test this by noticing whether or not he has given up bad habits, etc. We may allow the truth of the statement, even if he has not given up bad habits, etc., because we may find evidence of bad conscience, selfsearchings and remorse that had not been present before that date.

2. However, if the believer says, 'I had a direct experience of God at 6.37 p.m., 6th May, 1939', this is not an empirical statement in the way that the other statement is. The checking procedure is very far from clear. No matter how much or how little his subsequent behaviour such as giving up bad habits, etc., is affected, it could never prove or disprove his statement.

D. The way in which many theologians talk would seem to show that they think of knowing God as something requiring a kind of sixth sense.

1. The Divine Light is not merely of a colour usually visible only to eagles and the Voice of God is not merely of a pitch usually audible only to dogs. No matter how much more keen our senses became, we should be no better off than before. This sixth sense, therefore, must be very different from the other five.

(a) This supposed religious sense has no vocabulary of its own, but depends upon metaphors drawn from the other senses. There are no terms which apply to it and it alone. There is a vocabulary for what is sensed but not for the sense. We 'see' the Holy, the Numinous, the Divine, etc. This linguistic predicament may be compared with the similar one of the intuitionists when they talk of 'seeing' a logical connexion. It also may be compared with 'hearing' the Voice of Conscience.

(b) The intuitionists seldom differ from the rest of us in the number of facts referred to in describing how we come to understand logical statements and their relations. The intuitionist, however, emphasizes the fact that often we come to understand the point of an argument or problem in logic very suddenly. We mark this occurrence by such phrases as 'the light dawned', 'understood it in a flash'. Such events are usually described in terms of a complete assurance that one's interpretation is correct and a confidence that one will tend to be able to reproduce or recognize the argument or problem in various contexts in the future. A vitally important distinction between this 'seeing' and the religious 'seeing' is that there is a checking procedure for the former, but not for the latter. If the intuitionist finds that his boasted insight was wrong, then he says, 'I couldn't really have "seen" it'. No matter how passionate his claim he cannot have 'seen' that $2 + 2 = 5$.

The religious way of knowing is described as being unique.

A. No one can deny the existence of feelings and experiences which the believer calls 'religious' and no one can deny their power. Because of this and because the way of knowing by direct experience is neither inductive nor deductive, theologians have tried to give this way of knowing a special status. One way in which this has been done has been to claim that religious experience is unique and incommunicable. There is a sense in which this is true. This sense may be brought out by a list such as the following.

1. You don't know what the experience of God is until you have had it.
2. You don't know what a blue sky is until you have been to Naples.
3. You don't know what poverty is until you have been poor.

Professor John Baillie, in likening our knowledge of God to our knowledge of other minds, says that it is

like our knowledge of tridimensional space and all other primary modes of knowledge, something that cannot be imagined by one who does not already possess it, since it cannot be described to him in terms of anything else than itself. (*Our Knowledge of God*, p. 217)

What Professor Baillie does not see is that according to his criteria anything can qualify as a primary mode of knowledge. Each one of the statements in the above list is unique and incommunicable in just this way. You must go to Naples and not just to Venice. A postcard is no substitute.

B. That this sort of uniqueness is not to the point in supporting the existential claim 'God exists' can be seen by examining the following two examples.

1. You don't know what the experience of God is until you have had it.
2. You don't know what the colour blue is until you have seen it.

Professor H. M. Farmer says, 'All the basic elements in our experience are incommunicable. Who could describe light and colour to one who has known nothing but darkness?' (*Towards Belief in God*, p. 41). Just in so far as the experience of God is unique and incommunicable in this way, then just so far is it not to the point in supporting the existential claim 'God exists'.

All that this proves is that a description of one group of sensations A in terms of another set of sensations B is never sufficient for knowing group A. According to this definition of 'know', in order to know one must have those sensations. Thus, all that is proved is that in order to know what religious experience is one must have a religious experience. This helps in no way at all to prove that such experience is direct apprehension of God and helps in no way to support the existential claim 'God exists'.

C. Professor Farmer makes the point that describing the experience of God to an unbeliever is like describing colour to a blind man. So it is, in the sense that the believer has usually had experiences which the unbeliever has not. However, it is also very much unlike. The analogy breaks down at some vital points.

1. The blind man may have genuine though incomplete knowledge of colour. He

may have an instrument for detecting wave lengths, etc. Indeed, he may even increase our knowledge of colour. More important still, the blind man may realize the differences in powers of prediction between himself and the man of normal eyesight. He is well aware of the fact that, unlike himself, the man of normal eyesight does not have to wait to hear the rush of the bull in order to be warned.

2. This point is connected with the problem of how we are to know when someone has the direct experience of God or even when we ourselves have the direct experience of God. It was shown above how the situation is easier in the case of the blind man. It is easy also, in the case of knowing a blue sky in Naples. One can look at street signs and maps in order to be sure that this is the really blue sky in question. It is only when one comes to such a case as knowing God that the society of tests and check-up procedures that surround other instances of knowing, completely vanishes. What is put in the place of these tests and checking procedures is an immediacy of knowledge that is supposed to carry its own guarantee.

D. It is true that the man of normal vision has a way of knowing colour which the blind man does not have. Namely, he can see coloured objects. However, as we have seen, it would be wrong to insist that this is the only way of knowing colour and that the blind man has *no* way of knowing colour. There is a tendency to deny this and to maintain that having colour sensations is *the* way of knowing colour. Perhaps Professor Farmer has this in mind when he tries to make an analogy between the incommunicability of the believer's direct knowledge of God to the unbeliever and the incommunicability of the normal man's knowledge of colour to the blind man. The analogy is justified if 'knowing colour' is made synonymous with 'having colour sensations'.

1. On this account, no matter how good his hearing and reliable his colour-detecting instruments, etc., the blind man could not know colour and the man of normal vision could not communicate to him just what this knowledge would be like.

2. The believer has had certain unusual experiences which, presumably, the unbeliever has not had. If 'having direct experience of God' is made synonymous with 'having certain religious experiences', and the believer has had these and the unbeliever has not, then we may say that the believer's knowledge is incommunicable to the unbeliever in that it has already been legislated that in order to know what the direct experience of God is one must have had certain religious experiences. Reading theological text-books and watching the behaviour of believers is not sufficient.

E. The theologian has made the above analogy hold at the cost of endangering the existential claim about God which he hoped to establish.

1. If 'knowing colour' is made synonymous with 'having colour sensations' and 'having direct experience of God' is made synonymous with 'having certain religious experiences', then it is certainly true that a blind man cannot 'know colour' and that a non-religious man cannot 'have direct experience of God'. By definition, also, it is true that the blind man and the non-religious man cannot

know the meaning of the phrases 'knowing colour' and 'having direct experience of God', because it has been previously legislated that one cannot know their meaning without having the relevant experiences.

2. If this analogy is kept then the phrases 'knowing colour' and 'having direct experience of God' seem to make no claim beyond the psychological claims about one's colour sensations and religious feelings.

3. If this analogy is not kept then there is no sense in the comparison between the incommunicability between the man of normal vision and the blind man and the incommunicability between the believer and the unbeliever.

4. If 'knowing colour' is to be shaken loose from its purely psychological implications and made to have an existential reference concerning certain features of the world then a whole society of tests and check-up procedures which would be wholly irrelevant to the support of the psychological claim about one's own colour sensations become relevant. E.g. what other people see and the existence of light waves and the description of their characteristics needing the testimony of research workers and scientific instruments.

F. Because 'having direct experience of God' does not admit the relevance of a society of tests and checking procedures it places itself in the company of the other ways of knowing which preserve their self-sufficiency, 'uniqueness' and 'incommunicability' by making a psychological and not an existential claim. E.g. 'I seem to see a blue piece of paper'. This statement requires no further test or checking procedure in order to be considered true. Indeed, if A makes the statement 'I seem to see a blue piece of paper', then not only does A need no further corroboration, but there could be no disproof of his statement for him, for, if B says to A, 'It does not seem to me as if I were now seeing a blue piece of paper', then B's statement does *not* call A's statement in doubt for A though it does for B. However, if A makes the statement, 'I see a piece of blue paper', and B says in the same place and at the same time, 'I do not see a piece of blue paper', then B's statement *does* call A's statement in doubt for A. Further investigation will then be proper and if no piece of paper can be felt and other investigators cannot see or feel the paper and photographs reveal nothing, then A's statement will be shown to have been false. A's only refuge will be to say, 'Well, I certainly seem to see a piece of blue paper'. This is a perfect refuge because no one can prove him wrong, but its unassailability has been bought at the price of making no claim about the world beyond the claim about his own state of mind.

G. Another way of bringing out the closeness of the religious statement to the psychological statement is the following.

1. When A wishes to support the assertion that a certain physical object exists, the tests and checking procedures made by A himself are not the only things relevant to the truth of his assertion. Testimony of what B, C, D, etc. see, hear, etc. is also relevant. That is, if A wanted to know whether it was really a star that he saw, he could not only take photographs, look through a telescope, etc., but also ask others if they saw the star. If a large proportion of a large number of people denied seeing

the star, A's claim about the star's existence would be weakened. Of course, he might still trust his telescope. However, let us now imagine that A does not make use of the tests and checking procedures (photographs and telescopes) but is left with the testimony of what he sees and the testimony of others concerning what they see. In this case, it is so much to the point if a large number of people deny seeing the star, that A will be considered irrational or mad if he goes on asserting its existence. His only irrefutable position is to reduce his physical object claim to an announcement concerning his own sensations. Then the testimony of men and angels cannot disturb his certitude. These sensations of the moment he knows directly and immediately and the indirect and non-immediate testimony of men and angels is irrelevant. Absolute confidence and absolute indifference to the majority judgment is bought at the price of reducing the existential to the psychological.

2. The religious claim is similar to, though not identical with, the above case in certain important features. We have seen that there are no tests or checking procedures open to the believer to support his existential claim about God. Thus, he is left with the testimony of his own experience and the similar testimony of the experience of others. And, of course, he is not left wanting for such testimony, for religious communities seem to serve just this sort of function.

3. Let us imagine a case comparable to the one concerning the existence of a physical object. In this case A is a professor of Divinity and he believes that he has come to know of the existence of God through direct experience of God. In order to understand the intricate character of what Professor A is asserting we must imagine a highly unusual situation. The other members of the faculty and the members of Professor A's religious community suddenly begin sincerely to deny his and what has been their assertion. Perhaps they still attend church services and pray as often as they used to do, and perhaps they claim to have the same sort of experiences as they had when they were believers, but they refuse to accept the conclusion that God exists. Whether they give a Freudian explanation or some other explanation or no explanation of their experiences, they are agreed in refusing to accept the existential claim (about God) made by Professor A. How does this affect Professor A and his claim? It may affect Professor A very deeply—indeed, he may die of broken-hearted disappointment at the loss of his fellow-believers. However, the loss of fellow-believers may not weaken his confidence in the truth of his assertion or in the testimony of his experience. In this matter his experience may be all that ultimately counts for him in establishing his confidence in the truth of his claim about the existence of God. It has been said that religious experience carries its own guarantee and perhaps the above account describes what is meant by this.

H. It is quite obvious from the examples given above that the religious statement ('I have direct experience of God') is of a different status from the physical object statement ('I see a star') and shows a distressing similarity to the psychological statement ('I seem to see a star'). The bulk of this paper has been devoted to showing some of the many forms this similarity takes. Does this mean then that the religious statement and its existential claim concerning God amount to no more than a reference to the complex feelings and sensations of the believer?

I. Perhaps the best way to answer this last question is to take a typical psychological statement and see if there is anything which must be said of it and all other psychological statements which cannot be said of the religious statement.

1. One way of differentiating a physical object statement from a psychological statement is by means of prefixing the phrase 'I seem . . .'. For instance, the statement 'I see a star' may be transformed from a statement concerning the existence of a certain physical object to a statement concerning my sensations by translating it into the form 'I seem to see a star'. The first statement involves a claim about the existence of an object as well as an announcement concerning my sensations and therefore subjects itself to the risk of being wrong concerning that further claim. Being wrong in this case is determined by a society of tests and checking procedures such as taking photographs and looking through telescopes and by the testimony of others that they see or do not see a star. The second statement involves no claim about the existence of an object and so requires no such tests and no testimony of others; indeed, the sole judge of the truth of the statement is the person making it. If no existential claim is lost by the addition of this phrase to a statement then the statement is psychological. For instance, the statement 'I feel pain' loses nothing by the addition 'I seem to feel pain'.

2. In the case of the religious statement 'I have direct experience of God' the addition of the phrase is fatal to all that the believer wants to assert. 'I seem to be having direct experience of God' is a statement concerning my feelings and sensations of the moment and as such it makes no claim about the existence of God. Thus, the original statement 'I have direct experience of God' is not a psychological statement. This should not surprise us. We should have known it all along, for isn't it an assertion that one comes to know something, namely God, by means of one's feelings and sensations and this something is not reducible to them? The statement is not a psychological one just because it is used to assert the existence of something. Whether this assertion is warranted and what exactly it amounts to is quite another question.

3. The statement 'I seem to be having direct experience of God' is an eccentric one. It is eccentric not only because introspective announcements are unusual and because statements about God have a peculiar obscurity, but for a further and more important reason. This peculiarity may be brought out by comparing this statement with others having the same form. A first formulation of this may be put in the following way. In reference to things other than our sensations of the moment knowledge is prior to seeming as if.

The statement 'I seem to be looking directly at a chair' has a meaning only in so far as I already *know* what it is like to look directly at a chair. The statement 'I seem to be listening to a choir' has a meaning only in so far as I already *know* what it is like to be listening to a choir. The assumption of knowledge in both of these cases is one which all normal people are expected to be able to make and do in fact make.

The statement 'I seem to be having direct experience of God' does not lend itself so easily to the criterion for meaning exemplified in the above, because if this statement has meaning only in so far as one already *knows* what it is like to have direct experience of God, then the assumption of such knowledge is certainly not one which all normal people may be expected to be able to make or do in fact make.

Chapter 37

Can we know God by experience?

Peter Donovan

'WHY all this talk about arguing from religious experience?' someone may be asking. 'If you really experience God you don't have to argue, you *know* he's real, and that's all there is to it.' So if we are trying to do justice to the varieties of religious experience, we must take very seriously this particular type, the sense of knowledge arising from inner conviction.

It is a risky business, of course, to claim to know something and to act as though one knows for sure, if one can't give much in the way of reasons for one's claim. People have claimed to 'just *know*' (as they put it) all sorts of things. Even the most irrational and misguided things have been said and done at times with apparent certainty and complete conviction by tyrants and dictators, and by ordinary people confused by ignorance or blinded by prejudice. To have no doubts at all about one's beliefs may sometimes be more a symptom of insanity or arrogant irresponsibility than of sound thinking. Yet believers, aware of all these risks, may still feel they have a right to say they know because they experience God's reality for themselves.

We laugh about the person who says, 'I know I'm right; don't confuse me with arguments'. And yet there are times when we find ourselves wanting to say that too. For there *are* situations in which we feel sure that we know something, even though if asked to give a good argument to back up our claim we are at a loss to know quite how to do so. 'I *know* you're the person I spoke to on the bus yesterday.' 'I *know* I have two hands.' 'I *know* it is wrong to let that child starve.' 'I *know* that six minus four leaves two.' Our experience of being confident that we are right in cases like those is often called *intuition*. Intuitive knowing seems to be a direct, convincing way of knowing, which needs no further argument. And it is a perfectly ordinary, everyday occurrence as those examples show.

Are there such things as intuitions in religious matters too? Does a similar feeling of conviction in cases of religious experience also give us the right to say we *know*, even without having to produce any further reasons or offer any additional arguments?

Peter Donovan extract from *Interpreting Religious Experience* (Sheldon Press, 1979), reprinted by permission of the publisher.

Knowledge from intuition

A number of mid-twentieth-century theologians and philosophers of religion maintained, in more or less similar ways, that religious experience is a source of religious knowledge, and that the way such knowledge arises is not from reasoning or argument, but from *intuition*. God (the primary object of religious knowledge for these thinkers) is known through finite things—events and experiences in time and space. (Human beings could not otherwise have any contact with God.) But he is known directly, in and through such media. His reality is not arrived at merely as the conclusion of an argument based upon them.

The writers who presented this position began by drawing attention to the important part played by direct, intuitive awareness in other areas of our knowledge, areas that are well established and beyond dispute. They then argued that an intuitive awareness arising through religious interpretations of experience can also be claimed as a way of knowing, though in this case it is knowledge of God that the intuition grasps.

The argument was very thoroughly presented by H. P. Owen, for instance, in *The Christian Knowledge of God.*[1] Owen argued that intuition is necessary for our grasp of the material world through the experiences our sense organs give us. It is present also when we experience other people not just as visible, tangible, moving bodies, but as conscious selves with minds and feelings like our own. There are several similarities, Owen suggests, between our intuitive awareness of other people and the believer's intuitive knowledge of God. They can be summed up thus:

(a) Just as a human person reveals their inner nature through their outer acts, so God reveals himself to us in the created order.

(b) Just as there are special moments in which another person's inner self stands out and challenges our attention, so God is known most clearly by his special revelation in Christ.

(c) Just as a human person's acts reveal both their existence as a self and something of their character, so through God's signs in nature and within our experience we learn both of his existence and, to some extent, of his character.

(d) Just as we intuitively grasp that another person is a subject and agent who brings about both physical and spiritual (or mental) effects, so we apprehend God who creates both material and spiritual realities.

In all these respects, our intuition of the reality of God, like our intuition of other selves, has a 'mediated immediacy'. It is not the product of reasoning or inference, but is none the less mediated by finite things and experiences: in the one case bodily

1. Athlone Press 1969. See also H. D. Lewis, *Our Experience of God* (Allen and Unwin 1959), Fontana edn 1970, and Illtyd Trethowan, *Mysticism and Theology* (Geoffrey Chapman 1975).

movements, words, behaviour—in the other, general features of the natural world suggesting a divine creator, and particular religiously significant experiences.

Of course the intellectual activity of the mind, as well as the intuitive, has its part to play. It may clear the way for the intuition and provide suitable concepts (names, descriptions, interpretations, etc.) so as to make it expressible and able to be related to a wider body of knowledge. But first and foremost, none the less, it is by intuition through religious experience that God is known.

The basic form of Christian experience is the apprehension of God to which I have given the names of 'intuition' and 'faith'. All forms of experience are modes of this one fundamental form; they are all expressions of this primary awareness.[2]

Having taken care of the basic issue of knowledge by appealing to an intuition of the reality of God, Owen treats all cases of genuine religious experiences as forms of that knowledge. (In a similar way, once we have accepted that there *are* other people, the sense of their reality persists in all our experiencing of their bodily actions without argument or reasoning being needed to justify it.)

The sense of God's reality, in Owen's view, underlies all other Christian experience, i.e. experience under Christian interpretations. The basic intuition of God may arise in many ways.

The sense of God's reality can occur in various contexts. It can be produced by the contemplation of beauty and order in nature, by meditation on the words of Scripture, by participation in the Church's liturgy, by some event within our personal existence. Yet it may not have any assignable cause or channel; it may come uninvited. And although it is more likely to occur in moods of quiet recollection, it can also occur when our minds are troubled by the secular pressures of life.[3]

The idea of knowing God by intuition through religious experience is an attractive one for Christians, and it seems quite consistent with the teachings of the Bible about how God is known. Throughout the Bible God is viewed as personal, as one who communicates, draws near, and seeks fellowship with humanity, making himself known through natural things and in the lives and experiences of people. The world is the medium of his revealing activity, and by his gracious activity (the initiative he takes in approaching humanity for its own good) natural things and experiences become signs and symbols through which he is known. As one theologian put it:

Because nature is God's and He is its creator, it lends itself to His use, and He can make its natural elements to speak sacramentally to us; not in the sense of a 'natural theology' which can *prove* the purpose of God from a mere contemplation of nature, but in the sense that God by His Word can use, and therefore we by our faith can use, natural objects . . . as sacramental expressions of His mercy and faithfulness.[4]

2. Owen, *op. cit.*, p. 191.
3. Owen, *op. cit.*, pp. 192–3.
4. D. M. Baillie, *The Theology of the Sacraments* (Faber 1964 edn), pp. 45–6.

Not only does the knowledge-of-God-by-intuition approach fit well with biblical views of the ways God reveals himself, it also enables an account to be given of the human response to God, which is usually called *faith*. Faith, on this view, becomes a way of knowing as an intuitive response. It is not a kind of stretched belief, or assent to a set of dogmas without sufficient evidence. It is the basic intuitive awareness of God experienced as actively approaching humanity and seeking the human response of acknowledgement and trust. Another noted Christian theologian set out the relation between revelation and faith in this way:

The essential content of revelation is . . . God Himself, and not general truths about God or the universe or immortality or the way of duty; though such truths are implicit in the divine self-giving, as this is mediated ever more richly to the responsive soul in the changing situations of life, and are capable of reflective formulation.

And the proper response to revelation is . . . faith, faith being not an intellectual assent to general truths, but the decisive commitment of the whole person in active obedience to, and quiet trust in, the divine will apprehended as rightfully sovereign and utterly trustworthy at one and the same time.[5]

The knowledge a believer has of God, on this view, is a living awareness of a direct, intuitive kind. It may arise in different situations and be kept alive by many different kinds of experience, but for the person who has it, it requires no further argument or support.

Feeling certain and being right

Despite its careful presentation by writers such as Farmer, Lewis, and Owen and its wide appeal in popular Christian thinking, the position considered in the previous section has seemed particularly unconvincing to some of its contemporary philosophical critics.[6] This is not to be put down simply to their scepticism about things religious. Rather, it relates to the fatal weakness, in their eyes, of reliance on *intuition* as a way of knowledge that can be appealed to in the case of God or the objects of religious belief.

The criticism of this position often begins with the making of a distinction between two kinds of certainty, which are sometimes called *psychological* certainty and *rational* certainty. Certainty is a much-disputed notion in philosophy. But we can get at the main point, for our purposes, simply by comparing the difference between 'feeling certain' and 'being right'.

It is obvious, after a moment's thought, that one can feel certain without being right. I may, for instance, feel certain that it is half past three, after looking at my watch (which is usually right). But I won't go on feeling certain if I discover that for

5. H. H. Farmer, *The World and God* (Nisbet 1935), Fontana edn 1963, p. 85.
6. In particular, see R. W. Hepburn, *Christianity and Paradox* (Watts 1958); C. B. Martin, 'A Religious Way of Knowing', in *New Essays in Philosophical Theology*, ed. Antony Flew and Alasdair MacIntyre (SCM Press 1955); Antony Flew, *God and Philosophy* (Hutchinson 1966), ch. 6.

once the watch has stopped. In other words, I can check the appropriateness of my feeling of certainty against the rightness of the watch. But I can't check the rightness of the watch against my feeling of certainty. The feel of certainty is not what makes us right, even though we may often have a feel of certainty when we *are* right.

Being right then is not a matter of having some recognizable state of mind, a sense or feeling of certainty. It is a matter of our beliefs and states of mind standing in some appropriate relation to various states of affairs.

Many of the problems associated with 'feeling certain' go also with the idea of having intuitive knowledge. The sense of 'having an intuition that such-and-such is the case' may possess a quality of clarity or conviction or a peculiar directness in some circumstances. I may feel very strongly, for instance, that I am being watched, or that something disastrous or momentous is about to happen. Perhaps these feelings turn out to be justified at times. What we felt certain about, intuitively, was actually so. Such cases, taken along with the everyday cases of intuitive knowing mentioned above, may tempt us to conclude that *having an intuition* has a recognizable feel about it, that can be taken as a reliable sign of being right, whatever the circumstances.

But then the following question arises. If you have *only* the intuitive feeling of certainty to go on, how do you know in a given case that you are having *that* feeling (i.e. the one that counts as a sign of intuitions)? Perhaps your memory of 'the intuitive feel' is letting you down this time. It is not enough to say you feel certain that your memory is right; for that is just repeating the process—using an intuition to check intuition itself. And if *whatever* seems right can be right, what does 'getting it right (or wrong)' mean?

The reliability of our 'sense of intuition' is not something to be taken for granted, then, as an independent guide to genuine knowledge. There's no doubt that we have reliable intuitions in some situations. But it is the situation, not the feeling of intuition, that determines whether or not intuition is a reliable way of knowing in these cases. Even in the case of our intuitive knowledge of other people (on which the argument for religious intuition so heavily relies) the feeling that we have profound and certain knowledge may be quite false. As Bertrand Russell once wrote,

One of the most notable examples of intuition is the knowledge people believe themselves to possess of those with whom they are in love. The wall between different personalities seems to become transparent, and people think they see into another soul as into their own. Yet deception in such cases is constantly practised with success; and even where there is no intentional deception, experience gradually proves, as a rule, that the supposed insight was illusory, and that the slower more groping methods of the intellect are in the long run more reliable.[7]

Those are some of the difficulties which face anyone who argues from what

7. *Mysticism and Logic* (Longmans Green & Co. 1919), p. 16.

seems to be an intuitive awareness, in religious experience, to the conclusion that there really is knowledge of God. It is not enough to emphasize the sense of certainty or directness of the basic religious experience by giving it descriptions like 'awareness', 'encounter', 'apprehension', or 'response'. For those terms take it for granted that there *is* a genuine object of experience, beyond the experiencer's own mental states. But that is the very question at issue.

Nor does it seem sufficient to point out, as Owen does, that we accept intuitive, non-inferential knowledge in such everyday areas as sense perception, or awareness of other minds. For the case of sense perception is a special one. Our knowledge of the workings of sense organs, and the range of tests and checking procedures which surround the experiences they give us, all contribute to the context in which our intuitive perceptions take place and help us to justify them. Similarly with our awareness of other people as being conscious, and not as mere moving bodies. For we have, after all, a body ourselves. And while our awareness of others may at times be largely intuitive it is capable of being backed up with a strong argument from analogy, from our knowledge of ourselves as conscious beings.

But when we turn to some other areas in which people rely on intuitions (gardening, investment, archaeological exploration, or fortune-telling, for instance) it is much more difficult to say whether the sense of having such-and-such an intuition is a sure sign of knowing or being right. The nature of those subjects is such that rules for making sound judgements and ways of avoiding self-deception are far less well established. How can appealing to intuition make up for those deficiencies? And is religion any better off, with all its variety and openness to disagreement? The idea of knowing purely by intuition seems to become less and less plausible the more the fact of religious diversity is faced. Aren't there just too many different intuitions being had, by too many people, for intuition on its own to be a reliable guide to the truth?

Just because we have *some* acceptable cases of knowing by intuition (sense perception, other minds, simple arithmetic) it does not follow that there is an intuitive 'way of knowing' open to be used in other cases as well. To assume that is like assuming that because someone is able to read road-signs and to read newspapers, they will also be able to read palms. But what counts as being able to read palms is not an agreed-upon matter, in the way the reading of road-signs and newspapers is; and therefore it is quite unclear whether the other kinds of reading abilities have anything in common with palm-reading at all. Similarly, what counts as having knowledge of God is so much in doubt and dispute that until agreement is reached on that question there is no sound basis for deciding whether such knowledge could or could not be arrived at through intuitions, even if intuitions *are* reliable in certain other cases of knowledge.

Of course Owen, Lewis, and the other thinkers who appeal to intuitive knowledge of God have not intended to produce a short-cut argument for the truth of Christianity based on the view that the believer simply *knows* and that's all there is to it. There is far more in their position than that. They offer very comprehensive accounts of the interplay of experiences, interpretations, doctrines, traditions, imagination, and action which make up religious life as a whole. Their aim is to describe and analyse the total Christian enterprise in such a way that it commends itself as an interpretation of the world and the experiences of human life.

But the central place given to a basic, not-argued-for intuition of God in their overall position does invite serious criticisms from philosophers for whom intuition seems a very weak straw to be clutching at.

Yet for all the possible criticisms, it doesn't follow at all that what people think are experiences of God must all be illusory. Nor has it been shown that the person who says 'I know he lives—he lives within my heart' is talking simple-minded nonsense. If a religion like Christianity is true, it is very likely that there are situations in which people are directly aware of God's reality and activity, within the experiences and situations of life. But it is the *if*, in the previous sentence, that highlights the difficulty, for the philosopher at least. While *that* question is still open, how can one decide whether people's impressions that they are intuitively aware of God should be regarded as reliable?

Knowledge about and experience of

Theologians who argue that God is known by immediate encounter rather than by inference and argument rest their claim on a view of the special features of person-to-person knowledge. Meeting someone at first hand, they remind us, is very different from merely knowing about them. And encountering someone as another conscious person seems to involve a rather special kind of knowledge quite different from our knowledge of them as an object or thing.

The religious philosopher Martin Buber in his book *I and Thou* has given a widely influential account of that difference. He begins:

The world is twofold for man in accordance with his twofold attitude.
The attitude of man is twofold in accordance with the two basic words he can speak
The basic words are not single words but word pairs.
One basic word is the pair I–You
The other basic word is the pair I–It.[8]

I–You relationships are direct, reciprocal, person-to-person. They contain no reasoning or reflection and though deeply profound are fragile and impermanent. The world of It—of objectivity, reasoning, analysis—is unavoidable and human beings cannot live without it. But whoever lives only in the world of It, Buber tells us, does not become truly human.

Buber and other personalistic thinkers have encouraged theologians to point also to the biblical tradition in which, as we have seen, God is personal and seeks person-to-person relations with human beings whom he has created. If God is

---

8. *I and Thou*, a new tr. by Walter Kaufmann (Scribners 1970), p. 53.

conceived of as personal, then we must think in I–You rather than I–It terms in seeking to experience God, they say. So great stress is placed in theology on the difference between thinking or arguing about God on the one hand, and experiencing God in personal existential encounter on the other.

That contrast is easily related to other familiar contrasts in Christian thought. For instance, belief *in* is taken to be better than belief *about*. Faith is recommended, rather than speculation, in approaching God. Involvement and trust are encouraged, rather than detachment and theorizing. A wealth of religiously suggestive parallels can be drawn, all resting on the basic distinction between knowledge *about* God (an I–It matter) and experience *of* God (an I–You experience).

A further feature of I–You, rather than I–It, relationships is the impression that much of what we know in a personal encounter can't be put into words. This inexpressibility at the heart of an interpersonal relationship supports the view that if God is to be known, relationships with him will inevitably have features appropriate to an I–You rather than an I–It encounter. Why should we expect genuine knowledge of God to be any more capable of analysis, description, or reasoned argument than genuine person-to-person knowledge is? Questions of reasoning or analysis have no application to the profound experiences of meeting and encounter, we are told. Indeed, if one attempts in a moment of encounter to describe or analyse the person encountered, the I–You relation is immediately broken and the other party experienced only as an It.

Because the idea of encountering God in religious experience is so familiar a notion to Christian believers and so consistent with the biblical ways of speaking, anyone relying on this way of speaking needs to be very much aware of the philosophical problems it raises. For as in the case of the supposed intuitive knowledge of God, this closely-related idea of knowledge through encounter has been subjected to some telling criticisms. Arising from the criticisms, three points need to be discussed.

(i)   The sense that an encounter is taking place may be mistaken.
(ii) Having 'experience of' presupposes having knowledge about.
(iii) 'Experience of' is not in itself knowledge.

(i) The 'sense of encounter' may be mistaken This is similar to the problem about intuition and the feeling of certainty. It is not that our sense of such things is *never* reliable. But the surrounding of possible checks and tests that show it to be reliable in one context may simply not be there in another context, and then the mere impression of certainty is no guide at all for us to go by.

As Bertrand Russell reminded us, our apparent intuitions about other people can be wildly astray. The same is true of the sense of a 'genuine I–You encounter'. We all have experiences of shared awareness with close friends, in which 'knowledge about' fades into the background, and person-to-person communion or *rapport* is achieved. At such times neither person seems to be treated as an It. Each may think they have genuinely become a You in the eyes of the other. Yet how do we know when such an encounter has really been achieved? Is the impression that it is taking place enough to go on?

Standard situations in plays or television dramas remind us how easily what seems to be a genuine I–You relationship can turn out to be something quite different. A caller discovers they are conversing with a computer. A spy reveals secrets to a trusted friend who is an unsuspected double agent. In classic cases of disguise such as those in *Twelfth Night* or *The Marriage of Figaro*, everybody but the victim of the deception knows what the real facts are. Misinterpreted encounters, then, far from being impossible, are not at all rare.

Up to this point the critic's position may not amount to much more than the caution, 'You may not be as right as you think you are', in treating what seems to be an encounter as a genuine experience of God. The fact that some supposed encounter with God could possibly be mistaken won't much worry believers if they are convinced that they are right in fact. There is more to the sceptic's position, however, as appears in the next point we must consider.

(ii) Having 'experience of' presupposes having 'knowledge about' Preachers and theologians often point out that 'know', in the biblical and religious sense, is a much richer notion than simply 'possess knowledge about'. It involves an I–You, not an I–It relationship. Thus when Adam 'knew his wife Eve' (Genesis 4. 1) there was a good deal more to it than simply his possessing the information that such-and-such a female person existed. Religious knowing, like person-to-person knowing, is not just a possession of facts or information. It is an experience of total involvement.

Knowledge in the biblical sense of the word is not theoretical contemplation but an entering into subjective relations as between person and person—relations of trust, obedience, respect, worship, love, fear, and so on. It is knowledge in the sense of our knowledge of other persons rather than of our knowledge of objects, 'existential' rather than 'scientific' knowledge.[9]

If believers genuinely do have a direct encounter with God, then, it is quite inappropriate to try to force that experience into the mould of scientific information or knowledge about—expecting them to provide accurate descriptions or meet objective tests. Surely we know well enough from our experience of personal knowledge that such an approach is bound to be negative and fruitless.

But even granting that scientific, impersonal 'knowledge about' isn't the most important thing in interpersonal relations, we must not conclude that it is quite irrelevant and can be done without. After all, Adam's knowledge about Eve is there in the background all the time, so to speak. It may not seem very important to him when she is right beside him, and his interest is in something more I–You than mere

9. Alan Richardson, *An Introduction to the Theology of the New Testament* (SCM Press, 1958), p. 40.

factual information. But suppose Adam has never actually met Eve, and has only the odd trace (a slender footprint, a strand or two of hair) to go by, in deciding whether there is anyone other than himself in the world. The possibility of external, objective information will then be by far the more important question for him. For without Eve's existence as an It being established, there is no question at all of her being encountered as a You.

So 'mere factual knowledge' is by no means as unimportant to personal, existential knowledge as the contrast between I–You and I–It may suggest. In the same way, it is too easily taken for granted, in making a contrast between knowing about God and personally encountering him, that 'knowledge about' is largely unproblematic and readily available, and that its only defect is that it lacks immediacy and depth by contrast with genuine, interpersonal experience of God.

To the philosophical onlooker at least, knowledge about God is the very thing that is in question. It is largely because it might be a source of knowledge about God, that religious experience is being investigated at all. So even though the preacher or believer may not rate 'knowledge about' as highly as 'experience of', the philosopher would be more than content if even the former could be established for certain.

That is not to say, of course, that the philosopher demands objective, scientific knowledge of God before contemplating the possibility that anyone might have a direct, interpersonal awareness of God. If a certain religious tradition holds that God is not to be thought of as an It, then it is up to the philosopher to respect that feature of the concept of God. But isn't it on this very point that encounters with God differ so much from encounters with people? For at least so far as establishing their existence goes, people *are* open to being investigated and known about as Its, however much we may prefer (at times) to be encountering them as Yous.

In the case of people we certainly can have I–It relationships without I–You ones. But could we have an I–You encounter that did not seriously depend on a background of I–It knowledge? (Who would we take the 'You' we were experiencing to be, if we knew nothing about them?) Similarly in the case of a religious experience believed to be an I–You encounter with God, unless the believer was in a position to supplement the experience with a good deal of already available knowledge about God (that he is creator of the world, for instance, judge of all people, father of Jesus Christ, etc.) their belief 'I am personally encountering God' would mean no more than 'I am experiencing a profound personal encounter with someone I know not who'. Without knowledge about what is being experienced, experience *of* points no more towards God than towards any other possible person.

(iii) 'Experience of' is not in itself knowledge Suppose it were indisputable that God is genuinely experienced in some form of first-hand awareness. It does not follow that such first-hand experience or encounter, *on its own*, would count as knowledge at all. The point can be put this way. We generally think that someone who has experienced something for themselves is in a better position to know the truth about it than someone who has not. Yet why should that be so? What does first-hand experience add, that all available second-hand knowledge cannot supply?

There are obviously some cases in which a lack of first-hand experience is unimportant, so long as there is good second-hand knowledge. A male doctor, for instance, simply cannot have first-hand experience of being pregnant; yet his knowledge about pregnancy may be far greater than that of some uninformed woman patient who is experiencing pregnancy at first hand yet understands little of what is taking place. She might still feel inclined to say that her doctor doesn't *really* know what pregnancy is, whereas she does. But what does she mean?

Perhaps a clearer case would be to compare equally well trained and experienced doctors, one a man and one a woman, the latter of whom has also given birth. Surely then we should say that the woman doctor has a better knowledge of what pregnancy is than the man. Well, perhaps we should—but is it merely the *experience* of pregnancy that the man lacks? There seems to be more to it than that. For what the woman doctor gains from having been pregnant is not just an additional experience, but a whole set of impressions and memories and items of information that can only be learnt by having the experience oneself.

It is the additional knowledge *about* pregnancy that being pregnant makes available, rather than the mere experience *of* pregnancy, that makes the woman doctor better off than the man. The extra knowledge she now has, though it can only be gained by having first-hand experience, is certainly not *the same thing as* that experience. Furthermore, without all her other knowledge (which she and the male doctor have acquired through training, practice, etc.) the additional lessons learnt through actually having the experience would mean nothing much to her. If she had no prior knowledge at all about pregnancies, the experience she went through would not even be recognized as a pregnancy by her, and might merely seem to be a rather lengthy and uncomfortable bodily process, ending in the surprise arrival of a baby.

First-hand experience is important then not because it *is* knowledge but because it may put us in a position to increase our knowledge. Knowledge, in other words, is not merely a matter of experiences or kinds of awareness. It consists as well in what one can do with or make of those experiences in relation to the rest of one's knowledge and experience. To treat *experience of* something as itself a kind of knowing is to confuse the means by which we may gain knowledge with the content of the knowledge itself.

At this point someone may object that too much emphasis is being placed on learning, or gaining knowledge. Surely we do not seek close personal encounters with people simply for the sake of learning from those experiences more facts about them, which we could not find out so well in other ways. Our I–You encounters are for the sake of company, enjoyment, fellowship, sharing, and love. 'Knowledge about', even if we do presuppose it, is a secondary matter. And if God exists, the same is true of religious experiences taken to be I–You encounters with him. They are sought for the sake of love, worship, fellowship, not as aids to knowledge (even if knowledge may be increased through them).

The objection is a sound one. If there are encounters between God and people they may be chiefly for those non-intellectual interpersonal reasons, and not for the sake of acquiring knowledge. It is only if a claim to *know* is based on experiences taken as encounters with God, and on them alone, that the philosophical difficulties considered above apply. And the fact is that believers often do try to argue that they have knowledge of God purely on the strength of such experiences. The effect of the philosophical criticisms has been simply to show how inadequate that kind of argument is.

The criticisms do nothing at all to show that awareness of God is illusory. They simply suggest that even if it is genuine it cannot, by itself, solve all the problems about whether or not we have good reason for belief in God.

The sense of knowing God

Awareness of God, oneness with God, the sense of his presence, the inner conviction of his reality—the situations and experiences which lead people to talk in these ways are vital for religious belief. They have kept it alive in the past and continue to make it plausible for millions of people today. What such experiences do is to generate a *sense of knowing God*.

The philosophical difficulties of intuitions, encounters, mystical experiences, and other sources of that sense do not detract from its importance for religion. Religious people may conclude, 'If philosophy isn't very impressed with the sense of God, then so much the worse for philosophers. They have obviously hardened their hearts and refused to be open to God.'

But it is a mistake to react in that way. For one thing, a fair number of modern philosophers are religious believers and regard the sense of God as a central fact in their own lives. That makes it all the more important for them to give it the most careful philosophical attention. For they will not want so important an experience to be discredited by being used in weak arguments or doubtful reasoning.

The chief point of the philosophical criticisms of 'knowing God by experience' amounts to this. Where popular religious reasoning falls down is not in taking the sense of God too seriously, but in trying to treat it as a form of knowledge, of a self-certifying kind, immediately available to those who have it. Knowledge, the philosophers point out, is just not like that—whether it is knowledge of God or of anything else. The *sense* of knowing is never on its own a sufficient sign of knowledge. (That distinction is a key to many of the philosophical difficulties in claims to know God by experience.)

But if the *sense of God* fails, in the end, to count as knowledge of God, what is to be said about it? Is it of no further philosophical interest and to be discarded, like a pricked balloon, as being simply a great illusion?

Nothing that has been said here leads to that conclusion. There is no justification for taking such an all-or-nothing view of religious experience (even though at times both philosophical critics and religious thinkers are inclined to do so).

Chapter 38

Why should there *not* be experience of God?

William P. Alston

A<small>N</small> argument from religious experience that is parallel to the cosmological and design arguments would start with a kind of experience that is specified purely subjectively, in terms of its qualitative character, and then argue that it can only be adequately explained in terms of divine agency. But that is not the way people who base a belief in God's existence on experience typically think of the matter. Rather than supposing they need this, or any other, *argument* for the existence of God, they take themselves, or others, to have been directly aware of God. And just as actually perceiving a certain tree is the best way of knowing the tree exists, so it is here. This is the kind of basis for belief in God's existence that I will be considering.

The term 'religious experience' can be applied to any experiences one has in connection with one's religious life, including a sense of guilt or release, joys, longings, and a sense of gratitude. But the usual philosophical concern is with experiences taken by the subject to be an awareness of God. To cast the net as widely as possible, let's understand 'God' to range over any *supreme reality*, however construed.

Here is an anonymous report of such an experience.

All at once I . . . felt the presence of God—I tell of the thing just as I was conscious of it—as if his goodness and his power were penetrating me altogether . . . Then, slowly, the ecstasy left my heart; that is, I felt that God had withdrawn the communion which he had granted . . . I asked myself if it were possible that Moses on Sinai could have had a more intimate communication with God. I think it well to add that in this ecstasy of mine God had neither form, color, odor, nor taste; moreover, that the feeling of his presence was accompanied by no determinate localization . . . But the more I seek words to express this intimate intercourse, the more I feel the impossibility of describing the thing by any of our usual images. At bottom the expression most apt to render what I felt is this: God was present, though invisible; he fell under no one of my senses, yet my consciousness perceived him.

This report is typical in several respects.

1. The awareness of God is *experiential*, as contrasted with thinking of God or reasoning about God. Like sense experience it seems to involve a *presentation* of the object.

William P. Alston 'God and the Religious Experience' from *Philosophy of Religion: A Guide to the Subject* edited by Brian Davies (Cassell, 1998), reprinted by permission of Continuum International Publishing Group Ltd and the author.

2. The experience is *direct*. It seems to the subject that she is *immediately* aware of God rather than through being aware of something else. It seems to be analogous to seeing another human being in front of you, rather than seeing that person on television. But there are more indirect experiences of God. For example:

There was a mysterious presence in nature ... which was my greatest delight, especially when as happened from time to time, *nature became lit up from inside* with something that came from beyond itself. (Timothy Beardsworth, *A Sense of Presence* (Oxford, 1997) p. 19)

3. The experience is lacking in sensory content. It is a *non-sensory presentation* of God. But there are also experiences of God that involve sense perception.

I awoke and looking out of my window saw what I took to be a luminous star which gradually came nearer, and appeared as a soft slightly blurred white light. I was seized with violent trembling, but had no fear. I knew that what I felt was great awe. This was followed by a sense of overwhelming love coming to me, and going out from me, then of great compassion from this Outer Presence. (Beardsworth, op. cit., p. 30)

4. It is a *focal* experience, one in which the awareness of God attracts one's attention so strongly as to blot out everything else. But there are also milder experiences that persist over long periods of time as a *background* to everyday experiences.

God surrounds me like the physical atmosphere. He is closer to me than my own breath. In him literally I live and move and have my being. (William James, *The Varieties of Religious Experience* (New York, 1982), p. 71)

This discussion will be limited to *direct, non-sensory, focal* experiences, since they involve the most striking claims to be experientially aware of God.

Much of the literature on this subject concentrates on *mystical experience*, understood as a state in which all distinctions are transcended, even the distinction between subject and object. The person is aware only of a seamless unity. This falls under our general category, for it is typically taken by the mystic to be a direct non-sensory awareness of supreme reality. But experiences like this pose special problems of their own. In what follows I will be thinking of more moderate cases like the ones I have cited, in which the subject does not seem to lose her own identity. Nevertheless, I will use the term *mystical experience* to designate what is taken by the subject to be a direct experience of God. And since these subjects suppose themselves to be aware of God in a way analogous to that in which one is aware of things in one's environment through sense perception, I will also use the term *mystical perception* in this connection. (See William Alston, *Perceiving God* (Ithaca, NY, 1991), ch. 1 for a defence of the use of the term perception in this application.)

Our specific concern here is with the idea that mystical experience is a source of knowledge about God, more specifically the knowledge that God exists. Since the subject of the experience takes herself to be perceiving God, she naturally takes it that God exists. One cannot genuinely perceive something that does not exist. But, of course, the fact that she supposes this does not guarantee that it is so. Even with sense experience one can be deceived as to what, if anything, one is perceiving. One can suppose that one saw, at dusk, that there was a car in the distance when it was actually a cow that one saw. And one can even be subject to complete hallucinations, as when Macbeth falsely takes there to be a dagger in front of him. With both sense experience and mystical experience contradictions between reports prevent us from taking all of them to be veridical. Reports of automobile accidents provide many examples for sense experience. As for mystical experience, there are cases of someone supposing that God told him to murder as many people of a certain sort as possible, in contrast to awarenesses of God as supremely loving. The people in question can't be genuinely perceiving God in both cases. Thus the main issue to be addressed in assessing the claim that mystical experience enables us to know that God exists is this. *Are mystical experiences ever, or significantly often, genuine experiences of God?*

In discussing this question I will first look at reasons there are for a positive answer, and then consider reasons for a negative answer together with responses to those reasons by supporters of mystical perception.

The most important philosophical positive reason is this. Any supposition that one perceives something to be the case—that there is a zebra in front of one or that God is strengthening one—is *prima facie* justified. That is, one is justified in supposing this unless there are strong enough reasons to the contrary. In the zebra case these would include reasons for thinking that there is no zebra in the vicinity and reasons for supposing oneself to be subject to hallucinations because of some drug. According to this position, beliefs formed on the basis of experience possess an initial credibility by virtue of their origin. They are innocent until proven guilty.

This position has been widely advocated for sense perception, e.g. in Roderick M. Chisholm, *Theory of Knowledge* (2nd edn; Englewood Cliffs, NJ, 1977), chapter 4. (See the references there to other advocates.) It is applied to mystical perception in Richard Swinburne, *The Existence of God* (Oxford, 1979), chapter 13, where it is termed 'The Principle of Credulity'. In Alston (op. cit.) it is given a more social twist. The claim is that any socially established belief-forming practice is to be accepted as a source of (generally) true beliefs unless there are sufficient reasons against its reliability. The main argument for the 'innocent until proven guilty' position is that unless we accord a *prima facie* credibility to experiential reports, we can have no sufficient reason to trust *any* experiential source of beliefs. This is the only alternative to a thoroughgoing scepticism about experience.

On the negative side a number of arguments have been put forward, most of which turn on alleged differences between sense experience and mystical experience. They are critically discussed in Alston (op. cit.), chapters 5–7 and William Wainwright, *Mysticism* (Brighton, UK, 1981), chapter 3.

1. Most obviously, there are many striking differences between sensory and mystical experience. (1) Sense experience is a common possession of mankind, while mystical experience is not. (2) Sense experience is continuously and unavoidably present during all our waking hours, whereas for most people mystical experience is, at best, enjoyed rarely. (3) Sense experience, especially visual, is vivid and richly

detailed, while mystical experience is meagre and obscure. These differences certainly show that mystical experience provides much less information than its sensory analogue, but why suppose that it does not give one knowledge of the existence of God?

2. A frequent charge is that since mystical experience can be completely explained in terms of this-worldly factors, we cannot suppose that it constitutes a genuine awareness of anything supernatural. It is a basic principle of perception that we cannot be perceiving anything that does not make a causal contribution to the experience involved. If a dog is on the other side of a solid wall from me, then I can't actually see the dog, whatever my experience is like. But if mystical experience can be completely explained without mentioning God, then God is not among the causes of the experience.

There is more than one response to this. (1) We are not actually in possession of any purely naturalistic explanation of mystical experience. At most there are programmatic suggestions of the form such explanations might take. (2) The strongest response is this. The case of sense perception shows us that the object perceived need not be among the *proximate* causes of experience. Those causes are all within the subject's brain, which is not itself perceived. What we sensorily perceive is located further back along the causal chain leading to the experience. Hence even if the proximate causes of mystical experience are all within the natural world, the possibility remains that God figures further back among the causes of the experience in such a way as to be perceived in having that experience.

3. An important difference between sensory and mystical perception is that there are effective intersubjective tests for accuracy for the former but not for the latter. When someone claims to have seen a certain person at a party at a certain time, there are procedures that can, in favourable cases, yield a conclusive verdict on that claim. We can look into whether qualified observers who were at the party at that time saw the person. If guests signed a guest register, we can check that. But nothing like this is available for mystical perception. There *are* checks that are commonly applied in mystical communities, e.g. conformity with the background system of religious doctrine and conducivity to spiritual development. But they are far from yielding comparable results. And there is nothing like the check of other observers we have for sense-perceptual reports. If I claim to have been aware of God's sustaining me in being, there are no conditions such that if someone else who satisfies those conditions is not (at that time or at any other time) aware of God's sustaining her in being, I will take that as showing that I was mistaken. The critic argues that this discredits the claim of the mystic to be aware of an objective reality. If my claims to perceive something objective cannot be validated by intersubjective agreement, they have no standing.

The best response of the mystic is to charge the critic with *epistemic imperialism*, subjecting the outputs of one belief-forming practice to the requirements of another. The critic's complaint is that a mystical perception cannot lay claim to putting its subject into effective touch with objective reality because she cannot validate this status in the way she can with sense perceptions. Note that there are unproblematic sources of belief that work quite differently from sense experience in this respect. Consider introspection, one's awareness of one's own conscious states. My report that I feel upset cannot be validated by considering whether someone else, who satisfies certain conditions, feels upset (mine or his). But it would be absurd to reject introspection as a source of knowledge because of the unavailability of such tests. Unless the critic can give a convincing reason for supposing that the criteria available for sense perception constitute a necessary condition for *any* experiential access to objective reality, he is guilty of epistemic *chauvinism* (to change the metaphor) in rejecting mystical perception for this reason. Epistemic chauvinism is also exhibited by criticism 1, as I, in effect, pointed out in asking why one should suppose that a mode of experience different from sense experience in the ways specified should be less likely to be a source of knowledge.

Questions for discussion

1. How would you set about determining whether what seems to you to be the case is, in fact, the case?
2. Should we suppose that things are as they seem to us to be? If so, why? If not, why not?
3. Does the claim 'I am aware of God' raise problems which are not raised by claims to be aware of the existence of what is not divine?
4. How could one know that an object of one's experience is God and not something else?
5. Are there good reasons for supposing that the conviction of having experienced God can always be explained in terms which involve no reference to God?

Advice on further reading

The notion of experience of God is frequently discussed by philosophers under the heading 'Religious Experience'. For a classic treatment, see William James, *The Varieties of Religious Experience*. Originally published in 1901–2, the best edition of this text is now Volume 15 of the Harvard series *The Works of William James* (Cambridge, Massachusetts, and London, 1985). For a recent attempt to categorize and comment on 'religious experiences', see Caroline Franks Davis, *The Evidential Force of Religious Experience* (Oxford, 1989). For a general, philosophical discussion of the notion of 'religious experience', see T. R. Miles, *Religious Experience* (London, 1972). For an unusually sophisticated and sustained treatment of the notion, see Simon Tugwell, 'Faith and Experience I–XII', *New Blackfriars* (August 1978–February 1980). For a collection of essays, see S. Hook, *Religious Experience and Truth* (New York, 1961). A very influential and much quoted text on the notion of religious experience is Rudolf Otto, *The Idea of the Holy* (trans. John W. Harvey, 2nd edn, London, Oxford, and New York, 1950).

The notion of experience of God is also frequently discussed under the heading 'Mysticism'. For attempts to explain what mysticism is, see:

Cuthbert Butler, *Western Mysticism* (3rd edn, London, 1967).

W. T. Stace, *Mysticism and Philosophy* (London, 1960).

Evelyn Underhill, *Mysticism* (London, 1977).

William Wainwright, *Mysticism* (Brighton, 1981).

R. C. Zaehner, *Mysticism, Sacred and Profane* (London, 1957).

For a very useful selection of philosophical essays on mysticism, see Steven T. Katz, *Mysticism and Philosophical Analysis* (London, 1978).

The topic of experience of God is discussed in all of the introductions to philosophy of religion noted above. For another book-length treatment which complements that of Alston, see Keith E. Yandell, *The Epistemology of Religious Experience* (Cambridge, 1995). For some other notable discussions of the topic see:

John Bowker, *The Sense of God* (Oxford, 1973).

Antony Flew, *God and Philosophy* (London, 1966), ch. 6.

Richard M. Gale, *On the Nature and Existence of God* (Cambridge, 1991), ch. 8.

N. Horsburgh, 'The Claims of Religious Experience', *Australasian Journal of Philosophy* 35 (1957).

Anthony Kenny, 'Mystical Experience: St John of the Cross', in Anthony Kenny, *Reason and Religion* (Oxford, 1987).

H. D. Lewis, *Our Experience of God* (London, 1959).

Wayne Proudfoot, *Religious Experience* (Los Angeles, 1985).

In 1 Corinthians, 13: 12, St Paul writes: 'Now we see in a mirror dimly, but then face to face. Now I know in part, then I shall understand fully, even as I have been fully understood.' As Christians after Paul reflected on his words, they came to teach that the blessed, in heaven, enjoy the vision of God (the 'beatific vision'). This teaching seems to be something which ought to be of interest to anyone with an eye on the topic of experience of God. But how is it to be understood? And does it make sense? There is no contemporary philosophical literature on the beatific vision to which I can direct you. For a medieval discussion of it, see Thomas Aquinas, *Summa Theologiae*, Ia. 12.

As you try to think about the topic of God and human experience, you should do something to familiarize yourself with what philosophers have said about human knowledge in general (what is it? how do we acquire it?). In the jargon of contemporary philosophers, you should read in the field of 'epistemology'. For excellent recent introductions to this area of philosophical inquiry, see Robert Audi, *Epistemology* (London and New York, 1998) and John Greco and Ernest Sosa (eds), *The Blackwell Guide to Epistemology* (Oxford, 1999). See also Jennifer Trusted, *An Introduction to the Philosophy of Knowledge* (Basingtoke, 1981). For a useful reader on the subject, see Kenneth G. Lucey (ed.), *On Knowing and the Known* (Amherst NY, 1996).

Part IV

What is God?

Introduction

'Does God exist?' and 'what is God?'

JUST before *Summa Theologiae*, Ia. 3, Aquinas writes: 'Having recognized that a certain thing exists, we have still to investigate the way in which it exists, that we may come to understand what it is that exists.' This is a curious remark since, so one might think, one can hardly discover that something exists without simultaneously learning something about its nature. Suppose I say 'I've found it' and you reply 'Found what?' You would probably be puzzled if I then said nothing but 'It'. 'How', you might ask, 'can you know that it's there if you know nothing of what it's like?'

And yet, of course, one can know that something is present without knowing much about it. Suppose I try to push a door open, and suppose that it moves only so far, presses against something, and stops. Here I will say 'Well, something is certainly in the way'. But I may be much in the dark as to what, precisely, the 'something' in question is. Is it a ton of leaves? Is it an elephant? Is it someone playing a practical joke on me? I may have no idea. And it is this kind of scenario which Aquinas has in mind as he distinguishes between (a) recognizing that a certain thing exists and (b) investigating the way in which it exists. The remark from him just quoted comes after he has claimed to prove that there is a God and before he starts inquiring into what can and cannot be asserted of God. It is a way of setting the scene for a discussion of what God is.

Philosophers of religion have frequently distinguished between the questions 'Does God exist?' and 'What is God?'. And they have, in consequence, often treated them separately. Abstracting from the question 'Is there a God?', they have frequently focused on assertions of the form 'God is X'. They have then asked what such assertions can mean and whether we ought to accept them. Or, as some would say, they have taken 'the attributes of God' to be a topic distinct from 'the existence of God'.

But is it? Arguably not. For how can one sensibly decide what something is like with no reference to why one takes it to be there in the first place? Nobody would assume that one should offer an account of what tigers are which abstracts from our first-hand knowledge of tigers. So why should one suppose that one can profitably consider what God is with no reference to reasons for believing that there is a God?

Yet one can note some of the assertions which people have made when seeking to say what God is. And one can consider whether, and in what sense, they are ones worth accepting. And this is what this part of the book is designed to help you to do. Those who believe in God have commonly wanted to insist that God is omnipotent, omniscient, and eternal. Some have thought it important to declare that God is 'simple'. What do they mean? And are they right? The following extracts contain responses to these questions. Those who believe in God normally want to stress that God, above all, is good. For the topic of God's goodness, however, you will need to proceed to Parts V and VI below.

A warning to bear in mind when reading what follows

On what basis should we begin to think about the question 'What is God?'? Some would say: 'Start with what is said about God in the Bible, or the Koran, or the creeds and official documents published by the Catholic Church, or by other Christian denominations.' Others would say. 'Consider the findings of natural theology', or 'Consider what people have said when explaining what they mean by the word "God"'.

All of these answers can be happily taken on board by philosophers. The trouble is that, taken together, they provide no clear agenda when it comes to the task of pondering the question 'What is God?'. They do not point us to a single, generally agreed upon, notion of divinity.

As I have stressed above, the word 'God' has been understood in different ways. So you should not assume that contributors to discussions as to what God is are always proceeding on a set of shared assumptions when it comes to the nature of the divine. You should recognize that some people who talk about what God is begin by assuming things to be true which others, who also talk of what God is, reject. Philosophical discussions of the divine nature have never proceeded from an account of what 'God' means coming down from heaven on a cloud. They have proceeded from a variety of views about God influenced by a range of different reasons, traditions, and ways of thinking developed over many centuries.

Advice on further reading

For a general description and discussion of the various notions of God which people have subscribed to, see H. P. Owen, *Concepts of Deity* (London and Basingstoke, 1971). For a brief history of Christian thinking concerning God's nature, see Christopher B. Kaiser, *The Doctrine of God* (London, 1982).

For helpful general philosophical treatments of the question 'What is God?', the following are all much worth consulting:

J. Collins, *God in Modern Philosophy* (Chicago, 1959).

Steven T. Davis, *Logic and the Nature of God* (London, 1983).

Brian Davies, *Thinking About God* (London, 1985).

R. Garrigou-Lagrange, *God: His Existence and Nature* (2 vols, St Louis, Missouri, 1934).

Gerard Hughes, *The Nature of God* (London and New York, 1995).

Anthony Kenny, *The God of the Philosophers* (Oxford, 1979).

H. P. Owen, *Concepts of Deity* (London, 1971).

E. L. Mascall, *He Who Is* (London, 1945).

Gareth Moore, *Believing in God* (Edinburgh, 1989).

Thomas V. Morris (ed.), *The Concept of God* (Oxford, 1987).

Thomas V. Morris, *Our Idea of God* (Notre Dame, Indiana, and London, 1991).

Ronald H. Nash, *The Concept of God* (Grand Rapids, Michigan, 1983).

Edward R. Wierenga, *The Nature of God* (Ithaca, New York, 1969).

Omnipotent

Introduction

The notion of omnipotence

What can God do? In the Gospel of Luke, the angel Gabriel tells the Virgin Mary: 'With God nothing will be impossible.'[1] And in the Gospel of Matthew, Jesus says: 'With God all things are possible.'[2] But how are we to understand these teachings. Can God go jogging? Can God forget what day of the week it is? Can God bring the dead to life? Can God fall in love? Can God choose to act differently? Can God order us to hate him? Could God have made a different world from ours?

Those who believe in God have always insisted that God certainly has power. But they have differed in their ways of thinking about it. Biblical authors typically speak of God's power as a mastery over nature. For them, God has power chiefly as the orderer and ruler of the created world. God is its Lord, and it is subject to him. He has power *over* it. But should it not also be said that God must have power in a somewhat stronger sense—not just power *over* things, but power of an unlimited or infinite kind (power God possesses intrinsically)? Many have said that power such as this should also be attributed to God and that God should therefore be called omnipotent ('all powerful').

Yet what might one mean by calling God omnipotent? Philosophers have given different answers to this question. The trouble is that most of their answers seem to raise further questions. According to some thinkers, God is omnipotent since he can do even what seems logically impossible. But does this mean that, for example, God can make circles to be square? Some have said that God is omnipotent since God can perform any logically possible feat. But does this mean that, for example, God can commit suicide? Some definitions of omnipotence take it to be the ability to bring about the existence of any conceivable thing, event, or state of affairs. But are there not things which cannot intelligibly be thought of as being brought about by God? What, for example, of human free choices?

Can the notion of divine omnipotence be explicated in any satisfactory way? Or is it fundamentally incoherent? In Chapter 39 Thomas Morris provides a lucid discussion of these questions together with a defence of the claim that God is omnipotent. In doing so, he reports on a large range of ways in which philosophers have thought about

---

1. Luke 1: 37.
2. Matthew 19: 26.

omnipotence. So even if you disagree with his main conclusions, you will learn much from him about the history of debates concerning divine omnipotence.

You will also learn much about philosophical questions arising from the notion of omnipotence when reading Chapter 40, in which Aquinas offers a classic analysis of divine power. Like Morris, he considers a range of objections to the claim that God is omnipotent. He also addresses the question 'Why should one want to call God omnipotent?'. As you will see, his basic answer to this question places him among those who think of omnipotence as God's ability to bring about the existence of any conceivable thing, event, or state of affairs. Distinguishing between passive power (as in 'I can be shot') and active power (as in 'I can sing'), Aquinas argues that God is omnipotent since he can make (active power) anything to exist which can be thought of as (absolutely speaking) able to be. He argues that God is omnipotent in the sense that there is no definite limited range of possibilities in what he can bring about. Things belonging to a distinct genus and species are limited in what they can bring about, for they can only produce effects which are characteristic of things in that genus and species. According to Aquinas, however, God is not limited in this way. A man and a woman can bring it about that something is a human being. Two dogs can bring it about that something is a dog. But God can bring it about that something is, *period*. So, says Aquinas, if it *could be*, then God can bring it about. In arguing in this way, Aquinas is drawing on his teaching that God is the cause of the existence (*esse*) of things. So, in reading Chapter 40, you should bear in mind what you find him saying in Chapters 12 and 14 above. Even if you find Aquinas on omnipotence no more convincing than Morris, he will help you to get a sense of the philosophical questions to which the concept of omnipotence gives rise. He will also help you to see how one might set about reflecting on them.

Miracles

In a great deal of religious thinking, belief in God's omnipotence has been closely tied to belief in miracles. What are these supposed to be? Some philosophers have thought of them merely as remarkable occurrences which may, for various reasons, be thought of as of special religious significance. But, though religious believers have always thought of miracles as events of religious significance, they have also normally viewed them as more than remarkable occurrences. Suppose that all the people in the major London airports at 5.00 p.m. on a particular Friday evening turn out to be bald men aged fifty-three. That would be very remarkable. But even if it could somehow be deemed to have religious significance, it would not count as what most religious believers have thought of when using the word 'miracle'. For those who believe in miracles have normally taken them to be events which cannot be explained naturalistically and which can only be produced by God.[3] They have often described them as 'violations' of 'laws of nature'.[4] Hence the link between omnipotence and miracles.

3. I take it that there are fairly mundane reasons which could account for the remarkable coincidence of all the people in the airports being bald men of the same age.
4. Cf. John Mackie, *The Miracle of Theism* (Oxford, 1982), pp. 19 f. Cf. also Richard Swinburne, 'Miracles', *Philosophical Quarterly* 18 (1968).

But could we ever have reason to affirm that a miracle has occurred? We might prefer to sidestep the question by noting that we are still relatively ignorant when it comes to understanding what can and cannot happen in the world (when it comes, you might say, to knowing what the laws of nature are). At one time people would have refused to believe that someone in London could hold a conversation with someone in Australia. But we know that nothing is easier. You just have to pick up a phone and dial. Such facts, we might say, should make us pause before roundly taking stands on what can and cannot happen in nature.

Yet what should we say if told that a person clinically dead for two weeks had suddenly got up and walked around in a state of perfect health? What should we say if told that the Empire State Building left the ground and safely came to earth a million miles away? What should we say if told that someone in the last stages of bowel cancer recovered in a minute? Most of us would probably deny such happenings might possibly occur in the course of nature. Most of us would be likely to view them as events which, should they occur, could never be explained in scientific terms.

But are miracles possible? And might we reasonably believe that any have occurred? Many people who believe that there is an omnipotent God would confidently assert that miracles might occur. For, so they would say, there is nothing to stop God bringing events about directly, without natural causes. If God can make a world from nothing, they would ask, why cannot God bring about events which lack scientific explanation, events which are God's doing and not the doing of anything else?[5] And even philosophers with no belief in God sometimes agree that events might occur which cannot be explained in terms of the powers of things in nature. For, so they would say, the occurrence of such events is logically possible. It is logically impossible for 'Paris is in France' to be simultaneously true and false. 'Paris is and is not in France' is a statement which self-destructs. But can this be said of, for example, 'Fred died on 1 June and was then alive on 20 June' or 'The Empire State Building has just landed in Australia'? Even many non-religious philosophers would tend to reply 'No' and, in this sense, would accept that miracles are possible.[6]

Yet there are also philosophers who would argue that miracles are impossible if thought to be violations of natural laws. For they would question the claim that there are such laws. Others, again, would say that if there are laws of nature they cannot be violated. According to Alastair McKinnon, for instance:

The idea of a suspension of natural law is self-contradictory. This follows from the meaning of the term. Natural law is not, as has been widely supposed, a kind of code for nature having legislative and, perhaps particularly, prohibitive force. This is an outdated, untenable, and completely unscientific view. Natural laws bear no similarities to civil codes and they do not in any way constrain the course of nature. They exert no opposition or resistance to anything, not even to the odd or exceptional. They are simply highly generalized shorthand descriptions of how things do in fact

5. In Jewish, Islamic, and Christian thinking, God is regularly thought of as creating 'from nothing'. The idea is not that 'nothing' is the name of something which God works on when creating. The suggestion is that God makes things to be, but not out of anything.
6. Yet how are we to decide when a suggestion contains a logical contradiction? Here you might care to reflect on some of the points made by Anscombe in Chapter 21.

happen . . . Hence there can be no suspensions of natural law rightly understood. Or . . . *Miracle* contains a contradiction in terms.[7]

But is McKinnon right? Chapter 41 should help you to reflect on this question. For in it, Richard Swinburne asks what a law of nature is and whether it makes sense to suppose that one has been violated. Yet to read perhaps the most famous philosophical discussion of miracles you need to turn to Chapter 42, from Hume's *Enquiry Concerning Human Understanding*.

Hume on miracles

Hume accepts the approach to miracles which sees them as violations of natural laws. 'A miracle', he says, 'may be accurately defined, *a transgression of a law of nature by a particular volition of the Deity or by the interposition of some invisible agent.*' But what precisely is Hume arguing in Chapter 42? His readers have often been unsure, since some of his statements seem to pull in opposite directions. At times he seems to allow that miracles could occur, while, at other times, he seems to be suggesting that they are plainly impossible. One thing, however, seems evident. This is that Hume thinks that we could never be justified in believing on the basis of *testimony* that any miracle has occurred.

According to Hume, 'A wise man proportions his belief to the evidence'. And, so he adds, the evidence against miracles occurring is enormous. He writes:

A miracle is a violation of the laws of nature; and as a firm and unalterable experience has established these laws, the proof against a miracle, from the very nature of the fact, is as entire as any argument from experience can possibly be imagined. Why is it more than probable, that all men must die; that lead cannot, of itself, remain suspended in the air; that fire consumes wood, and is extinguished by water; unless it be, that these events are found agreeable to the laws of nature, and there is required a violation of these laws, or in other words, a miracle to prevent them?

Hume allows that many witnesses may testify that a miraculous event has occurred. But, he continues:

No testimony is sufficient to establish a miracle unless the testimony be of such kind, that its falsehood would be more miraculous, than the fact, which it endeavours to establish; and even in that case there is a mutual destruction of arguments, and the superior only gives us assurance to that degree of force, which remains, after deducting the inferior.

Here, the suggestion seems to be that reports of miracles are intrinsically such that we *always* have more reason to reject them than to accept them. The argument seems to be like that propounded by John Mackie when he observes that, when someone reports the occurrence of a miracle,

this event must, by the miracle advocate's own admission, be contrary to a genuine, not merely a supposed law of nature, and therefore maximally improbable. It is this maximal improbability that the weight of the testimony would have to overcome . . . Where there is some plausible testimony about the occurrence of what would appear to be a miracle, those who accept this as a miracle have

---

7. Alastair McKinnon, 'Miracle and Paradox', *American Philosophical Quarterly* 4 (1967).

the double burden of showing both that the event took place and that it violated the laws of nature. But it will be very hard to sustain this double burden. For whatever tends to show that it would have been a violation of a natural law tends for that very reason to make it most unlikely that it actually happened.[8]

In Hume's words: 'Nothing is esteemed a miracle, if it ever happens in the common course of nature ... There must, therefore, be a uniform experience against every miraculous event, otherwise the event would not merit that appellation'. Miracles, Hume seems to be saying, are 'events' which we have overwhelming *advance* reason to believe to be impossible on the basis of experience. And, so Hume also suggests, we have overwhelming reason to disbelieve reports of miracles when we consider the sources from which they come. Why? Because, says Hume, miracles only get reported by people who should be considered untrustworthy or by people belonging to religions with conflicting truth claims.

Does Hume's discussion of miracles definitively show that we have no reason to believe in their occurrence? Its critics have raised several questions in response to it. In particular, they have asked:

1. Is it true that we should only believe that for which we have personal evidence?
2. Is it true that reports of miracles always come from dubiously reliable sources?
3. Does the fact that reports of miracles come from people who have conflicting beliefs mean that none of these reports should be taken seriously?
4. Are miracles as intrinsically improbable as Hume makes them out to be?

Some of Hume's critics have also even wondered whether what is contrary to a law of nature might actually be more probable than not with respect to our evidence. An example here is Alvin Plantinga, who writes:

Suppose (as has been the case for various groups of people at various times in the past) we knew nothing about whales except what can be garnered by rather distant visual observation. Now it might be a law of nature that whales have some property P (mammalian construction, for example) that can be detected only by close examination; but it might also be the case that we know that most things that look and behave more or less like whales do not have this property P. Then the proposition *S is a whale and does not have P* could very well be more probable than not with respect to our evidence, even though it is contrary to a law of nature.[9]

But is Plantinga right? And is Hume to be refuted as his other critics suggest? You need to consider such questions as you ruminate on what Hume has to say. The works listed in 'Advice on further reading' should help you as you do so.

8. *The Miracle of Theism*, pp. 25 ff.
9. 'Is Theism Really a Miracle?', *Faith and Philosophy* 3 (1986), pp. 112 f.

Chapter 39

A modern discussion of divine omnipotence

Thomas V. Morris

Iɴ the book of Jeremiah, the prophet reports that in one prayer to God he said: 'Ah, Lord God! Behold, Thou has made the heavens and the earth by Thy great power and by Thine outstretched arm! Nothing is too difficult for Thee' (Jer. 32: 17). He also recounts that God answered his prayer, saying, 'Behold, I am the Lord, the God of all flesh; is anything too difficult for Me?' (Jer. 32: 27). In the circumstances, the point about God's power obviously bore repeating. The absoluteness of that power is an important theme in the Old Testament and into the New, where Jesus is quoted as having said that 'with God all things are possible' (Math. 19: 26). The religious importance of this theme is impossible to overestimate. In both testaments, God is believed to have made his people certain promises, grand promises concerning eternity. If he is perfectly good, we know he will endeavor to keep those promises. But unless he is sufficiently powerful, we cannot be confident that he will succeed. To think of God as creator of our world, though, is to think of him as having immense power on an almost inconceivable scale. To think of him as the greatest possible being is to think of that power as perfect. And the greatest possible power can surely sustain the grandest imaginable promises. Thus we can see that the theistic attempt to understand the magnitude or scope of God's power is far from being just an exercise in speculative theorizing. It is connected up with vital human religious concerns which affect the way we think of ourselves and our future.

The magnitude of divine power

Picking up on many passages in the Bible, Christians throughout the centuries have characterized God as 'almighty' and 'all powerful.' Philosophers and theologians have sought to register the magnitude of divine power by saying that God is *omnipotent*. They have also put a great deal of effort into trying to explain precisely what this means. What exactly is it to be perfectly powerful?

Philosophers have explored two ways of explicating the concept of omnipotence. There is first of all, and most commonly, the attempt to specify the magnitude of

Thomas V. Morris edited extract from *Our Idea of God* (University of Notre Dame Press, 1991), chapter 4, reprinted by permission of the author.

omnipotence by indicating the range of things an omnipotent being can do—the range of acts he can perform, tasks he can accomplish, or states of affairs he can bring about. This sort of analysis usually begins with the simple, commonplace religious assertion that:

(1) God can do everything,

and proceeds to test its initially unrestricted universality ('everything') against various logical, metaphysical and theological intuitions which seem to call for more cautious qualification. For example, it is often pointed out that if 'everything' is meant to encompass the logically impossible as well as the logically possible, then (1) entails that God can create spherical cubes, and married bachelors, as well as bring about states of affairs in which he both does and does not exist at one and the same time. But to say that God is so powerful that he can do the logically impossible is not pious or reverential; it is just confused. For logically impossible tasks are not just particularly esoteric and unusually difficult tasks—when you have attempted to describe an act or task and end up with the expression of a logical impossibility, you end up with nothing that can even be a candidate for power ascriptions. To put it vividly, in many such descriptions we can say that one half of the description just cancels the other half out, and vice versa. For instance, if we ask God to create a 'married bachelor,' each of the two terms cancels the other out. It is as if we were to write something down and then immediately erase it—the net result being nothing at all, no task specified. Now, not all impossibility can be thought of in even roughly this way. But the general point is that if we insist that God can do the logically impossible, we find that if we were to attempt to describe the results of his so doing, we violate the conditions under which, and under which alone, we are able to engage in coherent discourse capable of describing reality. So, most philosophers suggest that (1) be qualified accordingly, resulting in something like:

(2) God can do everything logically possible,

which is still quite an extraordinary claim. For the rest of us, there is a tremendous disparity between what is logically possible and what we can do. For God, (2) tells us, there is no such gap.

But even (2) seems insufficiently cautious, many philosophers have urged. For, assuming that each of us has free will, it is logically possible for us to do something not done by God. But we do not want to say that God can do something not done by God. That is to say, we do not want to commit ourselves to holding, because of what (2) stipulates, that God could possibly do something which would be such that, once done, it would properly bear the description 'Not done by God.' This, again, is just confused. So perhaps we need to be a little more careful still and express the range of God's power by saying that:

(3) Anything which it is logically possible for God to do, he can do.

And this is a phrasing which does not commit us to holding that God can do things 'not done by God,' or make things not made by God. It is impossible that God make a table thereafter properly described as 'Not made by God,' and so (3) does not locate such a task within the range of divine omnipotence. But (3) still expresses an extraordinary conception of divine power. It is logically possible for me to bench-press eight hundred pounds, but I can't do it. There is a tremendous disparity between what is logically possible *for me* and what is in my power. And (3) assures us that there is no such disparity faced by God.

But certain features of (3) can still be seen as problematic. The content of (3) leaves open the possibility that God could be by nature weak in numerous ways, that he could be such that many basic tasks are impossible for him, and yet by the conditions expressed in (3) still qualify as omnipotent. Any weakness that was essential to God, such that overcoming it would be logically impossible for him, would be compatible with calling him omnipotent. But do we want to allow this? Surely, some further rephrasing is called for. Perhaps:

(4) Anything that it is logically possible for a perfect being to do, God can do

would solve our problems. For any weakness is surely an imperfection. And an essential weakness would be an even greater imperfection. (4), accordingly, does not allow what (3) would seem to allow, namely, the compatibility between essential weaknesses and omnipotence.

The informativeness of (4), however, depends on our having some prior sense of what it is logically possible for a perfect being to do. And if part of perfection is omnipotence, we seem to confront here a sort of circularity that should at least give us pause. The philosopher Peter Geach once concluded that this avenue of searching for an adequate account of the magnitude of divine power is a dead end, and stated:

When people have tried to read into 'God can do everything' a signification not of Pious Intention but of Philosophical Truth, they have only landed themselves in intractable problems and hopeless confusions; no graspable sense has ever been given to this sentence that did not lead to self-contradiction or at least to conclusions manifestly untenable from the Christian point of view.[1]

Geach's recommendation was to give up the ascription of omnipotence to God and to characterize him instead as 'almighty,' a word Geach reserved to mean 'having power *over* all things.' In other words, Geach believed it was hopeless to try to understand God's power in terms of things God can do, which he took to be the only way of explicating omnipotence, and so he attempted to distinguish conceptually a different way of understanding divine power altogether, which he labeled 'almightiness.' Not many philosophers have followed Geach in his abandonment of the concept of omnipotence, but it must be said that those who have persevered along the lines we have explored have found themselves faced with increasing

1. Peter Geach, *Providence and Evil* (Cambridge: Cambridge University Press, 1977), p. 4.

complexity.[2] There is an alternative, however. We can seek to explore the notion of omnipotence not in terms of the range of *things God can do*, but a bit more abstractly, and at the same time, at least potentially, more simply, in terms of *powers God possesses*.

The idea of a power is a very basic, fundamental idea. It is such a basic idea that it is very difficult to analyze or explain, since analysis and explanation typically break up the complex into the simple, or illuminate the unfamiliar by reference to the familiar. We normally give an account of one idea by explaining it in terms of more basic ideas. But the idea of a power is so basic in our conceptualization of the world that it is hard to find much to say in elucidation of it. But we can say a few things that are helpful for getting our bearings.

Our first acquaintance with power is, presumably, our experience of the power of personal agency. Other people act upon us, and we act upon them, as well as upon the world around us. When a small child wants a toy, he reaches for it and moves it closer to where he sits. He has exercised his power upon the world around him to get what he wants, to effect the satisfaction of his desires. He finds that he does not just have desires caused in him by things in the world; he finds that he himself can form intentions and cause changes in the world in response to those desires. He experiences, in his own small way, power—causal power.

This is arguably the most fundamental, or at least is closely related to the most fundamental, kind of power. The most fundamental sort of power, in the sense of ultimacy, would be the power to create *ex nihilo* ('from nothing'), the sheer power to bring into existence things which are not brought into being merely by the arrangement of previously existing things. Some philosophers categorize this as a kind of causal power—the power to cause being. Others divide the conceptual terrain a bit differently, and think of causal power as power which can only be exercised upon previously existing things, in accordance with causal laws which are already in place. Regardless of whether creative and causal power are distinguished as basically different kinds of power, or whether the former is treated as just the ultimate instance of the latter, both are metaphysical forms of power and are thus relevant to our understanding of the power of God.

In this regard, creative and causal power are to be distinguished from what we refer to as 'political power' and 'legal power.' When we talk of political power we often mean to refer to no more than the entrenchment or institutionalization of personal influence or group influence with respect to matters of political governance. In legal matters, the power of attorney is just an authority, duly conferred upon one, to act for another person in business dealings or kindred actions. Political and legal power are powers defined in terms of, and dependent upon,

---

2. See, for example, Thomas P. Flint and Alfred J. Freddoso, 'Maximal Power,' in *The Existence and Nature of God*, ed. Alfred J. Freddoso (Notre Dame: University of Notre Dame Press, 1983), pp. 81–113; and Edward R. Wierenga, *The Nature of God: An Inquiry into Divine Attributes* (Ithaca, NY: Cornell University Press, 1989), pp. 12–35.

406 THOMAS V. MORRIS

previously existing rules or practices forming human social activity. If I am not a participant rightly placed in the appropriate practices or institutions, I cannot be said to have various powers of this sort. As God is not a creature participating in such creaturely institutions, he is not said to have power in these senses, but rather always in the more fundamental metaphysical sense.

Some further distinctions can be drawn to help us better understand the role of causal power in our conceptualization of the world. In our thought and talk about the world, we often attribute power, or the lack of certain powers, to objects and people. We often say what someone 'can' or 'cannot' do, and we sometimes assume that such talk always can be translated into talk about powers. But if I say of some task *x* that Jones cannot do *x*, I do not necessarily ascribe to Jones any lack of power at all. The little word 'can' can serve many different functions; the word 'cannot' cannot always be assumed to mean the same thing. Can-locutions sometimes attribute power. Often they do not. Likewise, cannot-locutions sometimes attribute lack of power. But often they do not. When I say 'Jones cannot do *x*,' I may mean that Jones lacks the *power* necessary for doing *x*. Or, again, I may grant him the power and the skill, but believe that he lacks the *opportunity* for drawing on that power, by means of that skill, in the circumstances in which he finds himself. But even with all the requisite power, skill and opportunity, poor Jones may lack the *practical knowledge* of his situation—of his power, skill and opportunity, as well as of how they could come together for the performance of *x*—necessary for the doing of *x*. And it may be *this* lack I mean to convey, or which I have in mind, when I say 'Jones cannot do *x*.'

One other distinction can be drawn here, one relating to questions of moral character. Suppose that a young boy with a precociously obnoxious personality and a proclivity to mischief lives down the street from old Jones. He bothers Jones daily in extremely irritating ways. A neighbor who witnesses this regular harassment comments to a mutual friend, 'If I were Jones, I'd throttle the kid. Why doesn't he just catch him, wrap his hands around that loud, whiny windpipe, and give it a good long squeeze?' The friend might reply, 'Jones could not possibly do anything like that. He's not capable of such behavior.' The friend need not be attributing to Jones any lack of physical power, skill, opportunity or practical knowledge here. In fact, he's probably not. Often, when we say that a certain person is not 'capable' of a morally dubious or improper line of action, what we mean to indicate is that doing such a thing would be contrary to a firmly entrenched character that person has, that the desire or inclination to perform the action is not within the range of his possible desires and inclinations, or that a serious intention to engage in the action is prohibited by a stable moral stance characteristic of that person. And this is a very different matter from anything having to do with power, skill, opportunity or practical knowledge. We can somewhat stipulatively refer to this matter as a consideration of 'moral capability,' or just *capability*, to set it apart from the other factors we have identified as determinative with respect to what a person can or cannot do.

We can think of power, skill, opportunity and practical knowledge as comprising one cluster of factors concerning what an individual can or cannot do, and capability as defining the moral dimension relevant to this. But there is often one final factor potentially involved in action, and it is difficult to know whether to classify it with the larger cluster of factors which we can refer to as 'the ability-cluster,' or rather with the moral dimension of capability. What I have in mind is often called 'will power,' and is just the element of determination or persistence in pursuing a line of action which takes either time or effort to attain or complete. A person may have the requisite ability-cluster, as already identified, for *x*, and it may be that doing *x* is consistent with the person's settled values, but the individual cannot do *x* because of a lack of will power or determination. This can be viewed as something more akin to a lack of power, or as something more like a moral weakness. Perhaps we can allot to it an intermediate status, as in the diagram:

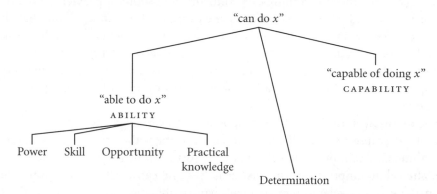

Our informal, colloquial uses of 'can' and 'cannot' irregularly convey many different things. They do not always convey convictions about power. We can understand the conceptual terrain that our idea of power in the metaphysical sense is meant to cover only if we keep it distinct from these other many different ideas with which it is often confused when we talk simply of what an individual can or cannot do. This, in part, is what makes any explication of omnipotence in terms of what God can do such a complicated business. And it is this which, when kept in mind, will help us to understand and defend the simpler conception of omnipotence in terms of powers possessed.

So, what is the magnitude of divine power? In his book *The God of the Philosophers*, Anthony Kenny says: 'A being is omnipotent if it has every power which it is logically possible to possess'.[3] He goes on to explain: 'It is logically possible to possess a power, I suggest, if, the exercise of the power does not *as such* involve any logical impossibility.'[4] And he further specifies that by this, he means that:

---

3. Anthony Kenny, *The God of the Philosophers* (Oxford: Oxford University Press, 1979), p. 96.
4. Ibid.

there is no incoherence in the description of what it is to exercise that power. For a power to be a logically possible power, it is not necessary that every exercise of it should be coherently conceivable, but only that some exercise of it should be.

Along these lines, it can be said that when we describe God as omnipotent, we commit ourselves to his having every power which it is logically possible to possess. This is a very simple account of omnipotence, and seems clearly to present a view sufficiently exalted to accord with the perspective of perfect being theology. Indeed, it is a view which looks tailor-made for this perspective, for it is impossible to imagine coherently any greater account of perfect power.

Problems for divine power

Many critics of theism have alleged that calling God omnipotent, or perfect in power, lands the theist in a number of difficult philosophical problems. One particularly renowned problem is known as 'the paradox of the stone.' Somewhat akin to the form of argument known as the *reductio ad absurdum* ('reduction to absurdity'), the stone paradox arises in the asking and answering of a question. With this question-and-answer dynamic, the critic is trying to show that the ascription of omnipotence to God is self-defeating, or that the notion itself of omnipotence is incoherent.

The question is this: If God is omnipotent, then can he create a stone which he cannot lift (cause to rise)? If the answer is 'no' then, the critic reasons, there is something God cannot do, namely, create the sort of stone in question, and so he is not, after all, omnipotent. If the answer is 'yes', he can create such a stone, then again there is a task he cannot perform, namely, lift the stone once created, and therefore again he is not omnipotent. Regardless of which answer is given to the question, the conclusion follows that God is not omnipotent. But we were assuming that he is. So the supposition that God is omnipotent must be ultimately self-defeating or incoherent. Therefore, there cannot be such a being. This is the critic's argument.

First, it should be noted that the critic is assuming throughout that if there is something specifiable that God cannot do, it follows that he lacks omnipotence. But if omnipotence is understood as perfect power along the lines suggested by Kenny, this is too quick an inference. For if it is true to say with respect to some particular act-description that God cannot perform the sort of act described, then it seems to follow only that God lacks either the power, the skill, the opportunity, the determination or the moral capability to exercise his power in that way. It does not directly follow that there is some power that God lacks. And if the act-description itself is incoherent, such as 'create a married bachelor,' it does not follow that God lacks anything at all, save perhaps the opportunity to exercise his perfect power in response to the act-description with which he is presented, since an incoherent act-description does not present even a possible candidate for action. And, remembering Kenny's stricture on what can count as a power, we can see that from the fact that God cannot act in such a way as to satisfy all the requirements of an incoherent act-description A, we cannot infer under any conditions that there is a power-to-A which God thus lacks. The relevance of all this should now be explained.

The critic is asking whether God can create a certain kind of stone—a stone which is such that he, a being who by supposition is omnipotent, cannot lift it, or cause it to rise. What is the relevant act-description here? It seems to be 'creating a stone that even a being with every logically possible power can't lift.' But what would such a stone be like? What, for example, would it weigh? If God is omnipotent, then, presumably, he can create stones of any possible weight. But if he is omnipotent, then, presumably as well, for any possible weight n, he can lift stones of weight n. Realizing this has led some philosophers to one of the simplest solutions which has been offered to the stone paradox. They have just claimed that 'creating a stone which even an omnipotent being can't lift,' and all its analytical equivalents, is just an incoherent act-description. And since the phrase 'the power to create a stone which even an omnipotent being can't lift' does not designate a logically possible power, it does not follow from the fact that God cannot create such a stone that God lacks any power required for omnipotence, or that he lacks in any other respect. This solution maintains that the proper answer to our original question is no, but that does not cause any problems for the ascription of omnipotence to God.

Other philosophers remain unconvinced that we have here an incoherent act-description. They suggest that even if it is impossible to specify the weight or size of a stone that would render it unliftable by an omnipotent being, there still might be a possible form or source of immobility which can't be overcome even by God. One suggestion is that if God is supposed to be truly omnipotent, why couldn't he create a stone which was endowed with the property of being essentially unliftable, though not because of its weight, or size, or any such distinct feature. Why couldn't there just be a stone which directly, not because of or through other properties, has the property of being impossible to lift or move? And if such a stone is possible, then surely the creation of such a stone is possible as well. So if God cannot create it, then he lacks a power it is possible to have.

It may be difficult to imagine how something could be a physical object and have the property of being necessarily immobile or unliftable. What would account for such a property? How would it work? By means of what possible laws could it operate? But even if such a property is in the end inconceivable, such philosophers could suggest, couldn't God just create an ordinary stone and promise never to move it, thereby rendering it true that he subsequently cannot lift it? And, implausible as such a scenario might be, if it is possible, then the answer to our question is not no after all but rather yes: God can create a stone he cannot lift.

But any action from which God is debarred by having made a promise is not, in virtue of its inaccessibility to him, thereby indicative of a lack of *power*. This would clearly be a case in which God lacks not a certain *ability* but a *moral capability* of doing the evil of breaking his promise. So there is a potential threat to omnipotence only from the less likely, or more perplexing, possibility of a stone he brought into existence with the essential property of unliftability, or immobility.

Suppose for a moment that God could create and did create such a stone S. Should we then say that God lacks the power to lift S? Is there a discrete power properly individuated as 'the power to lift S'? Well, in Kenny's sense, there is no such possible power, for if S is essentially unliftable, there can be no single exercise of a 'power to lift S.' Thus, lacking a power to lift S is not lacking a possible power, a power possible to have, and so no such lack would detract from God's being omnipotent.

I shall not argue for just one of these two possible solutions to the paradox of the stone. Either will suffice. If we choose to say that God *cannot* create a stone he can't lift, we can block the inference to his lacking omnipotence and explain the apparent divine inability by characterizing the act-description here as incoherent. If we choose to say that he *can* create such a stone which, once created, he cannot lift, we can block the inference to his lacking omnipotence by explaining that the subsequent inability to lift cannot be thought of as reflecting the lack of any power it is possible to have. But by either strategy the claim of omnipotence for God is defended.

What can seem at first to be such a trivial puzzle, a silly little brain-teaser, can thus force us to clarify for ourselves much about the logic of act-descriptions, powers and ascriptions of perfection to God. The stone paradox shows that sometimes, regardless of what reasonable theistic stand we take, there is a plausible defense available for the claim that God is perfect in some respect, in this case with respect to his power.

Many critics of theism in the recent past have prematurely announced the demise of rational belief in God precisely because they have not understood the conceptual dynamics of the Christian idea of God. At the core of our idea of God is the conception of a greatest possible creator. This core conception is highly abstract and in itself very difficult to attack directly. It is the focus of the Christian's theistic convictions, as I understand them. This is the inner ring of secure conceptual commitment. But then there are the various possible developments, or elaborations, of that core conception by means of value intuitions and metaphysical argument. These more specific elaborations of the divine attributes which comprise God's perfection constitute a second level of conceptual commitment, a more fluid level of conviction. A theist very sure about his core concept of God can be much more tentative, open-minded and unsure about various possible detailed explications of the attributes of deity. But it is at this level of greater specificity that critical arguments usually arise. The critic believes he has created a problem for some attempted specification of a divine attribute, such as omnipotence, and consequently announces that the concept of God is flawed or that the attribute of omnipotence is incoherent. The arguments of critics can be very helpful to theists, because if they are good they can steer us away from faulty specifications of the nature of divine perfection; whereas, if they are themselves flawed, our effort required to see their flaws can help us to understand better the nature of the truth at which we have arrived. The paradox of the stone allows us to see how the understanding of omnipotence in terms of powers possessed works, and the existence of two possible ways of solving it allows us to see the conceptual room available to the theist, who need not make detailed commitments on all relevant matters in order to defend his view and come to understand it better.

In the last few years another problem relating to omnipotence has emerged. A number of philosophers have suggested that necessary goodness is incompatible with omnipotence. The argument goes like this: If God is supposed to be omnipotent, he is supposed to have every power it is logically possible to possess. Now, surely, it is logically possible to possess the power to sin. This is a power all too common among human beings. So it is a power which should be ascribed to an omnipotent being, in accordance with the definition or explication of omnipotence we are using. But one cannot have the power to perform a certain type of action *A* unless it is possible for one to perform actions of this type. Possibility is required for power. But it is proper for the perfect being theologian to think of God as necessarily good, as being such that it is impossible for him to sin. On the perspective of perfect being theology, then, God must lack the power to sin. And so, on this way of thinking, he cannot be ascribed omnipotence after all.

There are two possible ways of responding to this objection. First, we could acknowledge that there is a special, discrete power to sin, a power humans have and God lacks. Along these lines, we would then have to revise our conception of the magnitude of divine power. We might still want to call God 'omnipotent,' but we would then have to qualify Kenny's account of what this means and offer something like the more restrictive gloss:

(P) God has every power it is logically possible for a being perfect in every other respect to possess.

This strategy for reconciling ascriptions of perfect goodness and omnipotence to God might be judged effective as long as three important theistic beliefs about God's power were respected by any such restriction:

(1) There can be no independent, externally determined constraints on God's power.

God is sovereign in the world. He is not hemmed in by any other competitive power. If moral principles are then thought of as constraints on God's power, morality cannot be thought of as independent of, or external to, God.

(2) The internally determined structure and scope of God's possibilities of action (the limits on divine action set by God's own nature and decisions) are not, and cannot be, such that he lacks any power which otherwise would be ingredient in perfection.

Neither God's nature, in its other facets, nor his decisions can have a negative impact on the perfection of the power available to him. Perfection is not self-destructive or self-undermining. Finally,

(3) God is the sole source of all the power there is or could be.

This assurance, along with a strong conception of divine goodness and wisdom, disallows the implication following from the restricted account of divine power that there could even possibly be a being with all the power God does have *plus* a power to sin, a being independent of God who could possibly, through the having of this greater total array of power, ultimately thwart God's purposes and plans. With all this in mind, a restricted account of God's power could be a usable solution to the problem raised by the apparent existence of a power to sin.

But the best solution to this problem, I think, will involve denying that there is a discrete causal power to sin. If we hold that God is necessarily good, we do believe that it is impossible that God sin. This can be stated by saying that God cannot sin. But it may be sheer carelessness to think that this is the same as saying, or that it even implies, that God lacks some power, namely, what has been, so far, loosely referred to as 'the power to sin.'

How do we identify discrete powers? The idea of a power is a very fundamental notion. We typically identify powers with a certain standard locution, employing the infinitives of verbs along with verb phrases. We speak, for example, of 'the power to lift one hundred pounds,' 'the power to communicate through an earthly language,' 'the power to create a stone.' Now there are, no doubt, many sorts of powers of which we have no conception and for which we have no ready-made power locutions of this type. But in another respect, our language is much richer than the underlying metaphysical realities having to do with power. For consider the two phrases (power locutions):

(A) the power to lift a blue two-ounce pencil
(B) the power to lift a yellow two-ounce pencil.

I have whatever power is designated by (A). I have whatever power is designated by (B). The power locutions (A) and (B) are two distinct locutions. It doesn't follow that they express two different powers, or that by being able to lift blue and yellow pencils I should be credited with two different powers. There is, presumably, only one basic power referred to differently by these two different power phrases.

So, distinct power locutions are no guarantee of correspondingly distinct powers. Nor is the mere existence of a power locution of the appropriate form any guarantee that there is a discrete power referred to by the phrase. Consider as an extreme instance: 'the power to see to it that there never were any powers at all.' There cannot be a discrete power referred to by this phrase. And whatever power is referred to by (A) and (B) has absolutely nothing intrinsically to do with anything regarding color. The surface grammar of power locutions can be misleading in numerous ways.

Following an example once presented by St Anselm, we can see that to say of a certain man that 'he cannot lose in battle' is not to attribute to him any lack of power. It attributes any real lack only to his enemies.[5] Likewise, to say of God that he cannot sin, should not be taken to imply on God's part any lack of power. It only indicates a necessarily firm directedness in the way in which God will *use* his unlimited power.

I would like to suggest that there is no discrete power referred to by the phrase 'the power to sin.' There are many powers necessary for sinning in various ways, but there is no single, distinct power to sin exercised in addition to all other powers exercised on any and every occasion of the intentional doing of evil. Suppose Jones wrongfully hits Smith in the face, intending to cause him pain. Jones must have and exercise the power to make a fist, the power to swing and aim his fist, and so forth, in order to commit the deed. Does he need an additional causal power once he has all those physical powers, a distinct power to sin? I do not think so. Drawing upon the chart presented earlier in this chapter, we could say that Jones is capable of using his power in a way a more saintly person would not, and in a way a perfect person could not. The difference is not in the powers possessed, but in the moral capacity for employing those powers.

To account for why it is that a certain person cannot perform a certain kind of act we need not, and should not, always suppose that a lack of power is what is involved. In the present case, to account for why God cannot do evil we need not, and should not, attribute this divine guarantee to inability or lack of power. It is due, rather, entirely to God's perfection of character. There is no power to sin which God lacks. So there is here no exception to his being thought of as altogether omnipotent after all.

But the following problem could be raised. Even if it is granted that there is no incoherence about the ascription of omnipotence to God, and even if there is no glaring counterexample to the claim that God has every power it is logically possible to possess, how can the positive ascription of omnipotence ever be justified? To defend omnipotence against objections is not yet to provide any positive ground for thinking of God as omnipotent. And it can be thought that the provision of a positive ground would be impossible.

How do we justify power ascriptions? Typically, on the basis of observation. We see a person perform an action or range of actions and ascribe to him whatever kind or degree of power would be necessary for the performance we have witnessed. But under what conditions could any finite number of observations of divine conduct warrant or justify the ascription of omnipotence to God? Suppose God somehow were observed performing extraordinary miracles, in whatever

---

5. This is to be found in *Cur Deus Homo*. I have discussed it more fully in *Anselmian Explorations*, chapter four.

mode of observation is appropriate. Would any number of such dramatic actions legitimate the claim that God has every power it is logically possible to possess? Suppose we know God to have created the entire existent universe. Would even *that* piece of astounding information call for the postulation of omnipotence, and nothing less? It is hard to see how any finite observations and data could ever demand, or even justify, so extreme an ascription of power as that ingredient in the attribution of omnipotence. And if this is so, one recent writer has suggested, not only could *we* never know or justifiably believe that God is omnipotent, he himself could not know or justifiably believe it. For, no matter how many tough tasks he proposed to himself and accomplished without the least effort, the literal ascription, or self-ascription, of omnipotence would go beyond the theoretical demands of explaining the observations made.[6] Omnipotence is that extreme a notion.

The answer to this challenge is actually simple. First, God does not come to know himself inferentially, from making observations about his own conduct and extrapolating from those observations to their best theoretical explanations. God knows himself directly, as St Thomas Aquinas taught us.[7] Second, we do not have to rely upon observation and inference for all our ascriptions of properties to God. We hold that God is literally omnipotent because of the requirements of perfect being theology, as it encapsulates and extends the data of revelation. We derive the belief in strict omnipotence as a divine attribute not inductively from observation, but deductively from the conceptual and intuitive resources of perfect being theology. As a perfect being, God is perfect in power. We are justified in thinking of God as perfect in this respect, as in every other, unless there is well-attested revelation or credible human experience to the contrary. Observation is a constraint upon, but not the sole source of our ideas about God.

6. Richard Creel, 'Can God Know That He Is God?' *Religious Studies* 16 (June 1980): 195–201.
7. *Summa Contra Gentiles*, Anton C. Pegis, trans. (Notre Dame: University of Notre Dame Press, 1975), chapter 57.

Chapter 40

Why think of God as omnipotent?

Thomas Aquinas

God's power

Is there power in God?

THE FIRST POINT: 1. It seems not. For bare matter is in terms of potentiality like God, who is first cause, in terms of actuality. Of itself bare matter is completely devoid of actuality. And therefore God is without potentiality.

2. Moreover, according to Aristotle, *to act is better than the power to act*. For, as being its purpose, form is more real than matter, and activity more real than the ability to be active. All in God is best, for all there is God, as we have shown. So God has no power to act.

3. In other words, power is the principle of activity. Yet what God does is what God is, since in God there are no qualities. And what God is has no principle. Therefore there is no power in God.

ON THE OTHER HAND it says in the *Psalms, Thou art powerful, O God, and thy truth is round about thee.*

REPLY: There are two kinds of power, namely passive and active. The first is not at all in God, but the second is his supremely.

Precisely as being actual and complete, each thing shows itself an active principle of something, and as being wanting and incomplete a passive principle. God is sheer actuality, simply and wholly complete, and not wanting for anything. Hence his it is above all to be a principle of activity and in no way to be a passive principle. To be an active principle directly spells active power. Active power is a principle of acting on another, while passive power is a principle of being acted on by another, as Aristotle explains. We are left with the conclusion that in God supremely there is active power.

HENCE: 1. Active power springs from actuality, and is not contrasted with it as an

Thomas Aquinas extracts from *Summa Theologiae* from Volume 5 of the Blackfriars edition of *Summa Theologiae* edited by Thomas Gilby (Eyre and Spottiswoode and McGraw Hill, 1967).

opposite, for a thing acts inasmuch as it is actual. Whereas passive potentiality and actuality, however, are counter-divisions, for a thing undergoes activity inasmuch as it is potential. It is this that we rule out in God, but not active power.

2. Whenever activity is distinct from the power of acting then it must also be real at a higher pitch. God's activity, however, is not distinct from his power; each is the divine essence, identical with the divine existence. The prospect does not arise, therefore, of anything more highly real than divine power.

3. Power or ability in created things is not only the source of an action, but also of an effect. It is in the last sense that we justify the meaning of power in God, not as being the principle of divine acting, which is identical with his being, but as the principle of an effect.

Unless, perhaps, the first sense is applicable according to human notions, and as follows: we can conceive of the divine being, which in itself possesses and anticipates every value there is in created things in terms of both activity and power, as also we can as both substantial and essential.

Is God's power infinite?

THE SECOND POINT: 1. It would seem not. According to Aristotle, anything boundless is incomplete. Since it is not imperfect, God's power is not boundless.

2. Besides, every power is manifested through its effect, otherwise it would be pointless. Were God's power infinite it could produce an infinite effect: which is impossible.

ON THE OTHER HAND Hilary says that God's strength is unmeasured, living and mighty.

REPLY: As already noted, we attribute active power to God in that he is actual. His existence is infinite because not limited by anything receiving it. It demonstrably follows that God's active power is infinite. For in all efficient causality you find this, the more perfectly a cause possesses the form whereby it acts the more powerful its acting: the hotter a thing the more fiercely it can heat, and were its heat unlimited so also would be its power of heating. Since the divine essence itself, through which God acts, is infinite, it follows that his power has no limits.

HENCE: 1. Aristotle is there speaking of the boundless with regard to matter unshaped by form; this is infinity imagined in terms of quantity. God's essence is not indefinite in this sense, and consequently neither is his power. We cannot infer, therefore, that it is imperfect.

2. An effect of a univocal agent exhaustively manifests its power; the begetting of a man tells us all about human generative power as such. The power of a non-univocal agent, however, is not entirely displayed in the production of an effect;

thus the sun has resources not revealed in the heat which generates an animal from decaying matter. That God is not a univocal cause is evident; he is not in a class with anything, neither in genus nor species, as we have shown. We are left with the conclusion that his effects are always less than his power.

To contend that God's infinite power should be shown by his producing an infinite effect has no basis in reason. Even if it produced no effect his power would not be pointless, which means being set on an end which is not reached. God's power is not subordinate to its effect as to its end, but is rather itself the end of the effect.

Is God omnipotent?

THE THIRD POINT: 1. It would seem that he is not. All things can be moved and acted upon. But not God; for he is changeless. He is not, therefore, capable of everything.

2. Moreover, to commit sin is to do something. God, however, is not able to sin or deny himself, according to II *Timothy*. Therefore God is not omnipotent.

3. Furthermore, a collect says that God's almighty power is best shown by sparing and having mercy. This, then, is his ultimate. Yet there are much greater works, for instance creating another world or the like. Therefore God is not in fact almighty.

ON THE OTHER HAND there is what is said in Luke, *With God no word shall be impossible.*

REPLY: By common profession God is almighty. Yet it seems hard to lay one's finger on the reason, because of the doubt about what is meant by 'all' when you say that God can do all. Yet looked at aright, when you say God has the power for everything, you are most correctly interpreted as meaning this: that since power is relative to what is possible, divine power can do everything that is possible, and on this account is God called omnipotent.

According to Aristotle the possible can be taken in two senses, relative and absolute. The first is with respect to some particular power, thus what comes under human power is termed possible for us. Now God should not be called all-powerful because he can do all things that are possible to created natures, for his power extends to many more. Yet if you say that God is all-powerful because he can do everything possible to his power, your explanation of omnipotence goes round in a circle, repeating no more than that God is almighty because he can do all that he can do.

We are left with the alternative, that he is almighty because he can do everything that is absolutely possible: this is the second sense of the word possible. Something is judged to be possible or impossible from the implication of the terms: possible when the Predicate is compatible with the Subject, for instance, that Socrates is seated; impossible when it is not compatible, for instance, that man is a donkey.

Consider this: since every agent enacts its like, every active power has a possible objective corresponding to the nature of that activity which the active power is for; thus the power of heating supposes that things can be heated. The divine being, on which the notion of divine power is founded, is infinite existence, not limited to any kind of being, but holding within itself and anticipating the perfection of the whole of existence. Whatever can have the nature of being falls within the range of things that are absolutely possible, and it is with respect to these that God is called all-powerful.

Nothingness, and only that, contradicts the real meaning of being. Now it is incompatible with the meaning of the absolutely possible that anything involving the contradiction of simultaneously being and not being should fall under divine omnipotence. Such a contradiction is not subject to it, not from any impotence in God, but because it simply does not have the nature of being feasible or possible. Whatever does not involve a contradiction is in that realm of the possible with respect to which God is called omnipotent. Whatever involves a contradiction is not held by omnipotence, for it just cannot possibly make sense of being possible. Better, however, to say that it cannot be done, rather than God cannot do it. Nor is this against the angel's saying, *With God no word shall be impossible.* For a contradiction in terms cannot be a word, for no mind can conceive it.

HENCE: 1. As we have shown, God is called omnipotent with regard to active power, not passive power. That he cannot be in motion or undergo action does not disagree with omnipotence.

2. To sin is to fall short of full activity. Hence to be able to sin is to be able to fail in doing, which cannot be reconciled with omnipotence. It is because God is omnipotent that he cannot sin. True, Aristotle says that *God and the cautious person can go wrong.* His language, however, can be interpreted in several ways. First, as a conditional statement conditional on a clause that is impossible, as though to say, if he wanted to, God could do wrong. A conditional argument can be valid when both the antecedent and consequent are false, for instance, if man is a donkey he has four legs. Or secondly he can be taken to mean that God could do things that seem crooked now, nevertheless if he were to do them they would not be so. Or he is adopting the common usage of the heathen, who spoke of men in the guise of gods, like Jupiter or Mercury.

3. Omnipotence is specially manifested in God's sparing and having mercy, for that he forgives sins freely declares his supreme power; he who is bound by the law of a superior is not free to forgive offences against it. Again, by sparing and having pity on men he brings them to share the infinite good, which is the crowning effect of God's power. Then again, as we have seen, the carrying out of divine mercy is at the root of all God's works; we are entitled to nothing except on the basis of what has come from God in the first place as a sheer gift. Here above all divine omnipotence is discovered, for it lays the first foundation of all good things.

Can God make what had been not to have been?

THE FOURTH POINT: 1. It seems that he can, for what is impossible in itself is much more impossible than what is impossible under the circumstances. God can do what is impossible in itself, like giving sight to a blind man, or raising a corpse to life. Much more, therefore, can he do what is impossible under the circumstances. For a thing in the past not to have happened is impossible under the circumstances or incidentally; for instance, that Socrates happened not to have run from the fact that he did. So God can make what has happened not to have happened.

2. Moreover, whatever God could have done he can do now, since his power has not diminished. But God could have seen to it that before Socrates was going to run he would not run. Therefore after he had run God could effect that he had not run.

3. Furthermore, charity is a virtue greater than virginity. God can restore charity that has been lost, and so also virginity. Therefore he can make what was damaged not to have been damaged.

ON THE OTHER HAND there is Jerome saying, *Though God can do everything, he cannot make the unspoilt from the spoilt.* For the same reason he cannot make something that has been not to have been.

REPLY: As we have seen, anything that implies a contradiction does not fall under God's omnipotence. For the past not to have been implies a contradiction; thus to say that Socrates is and is not seated is contradictory, and so also to say that he had and had not been seated. To affirm that he had been seated is to affirm a past fact, to affirm that he had not been is to affirm what was not the case. Hence for the past not to have been does not lie under divine power. This is what Augustine says, *Whoever declares that if God is all-powerful let him make the things that have been done not to have been done is not aware that he is asserting that if God is all-powerful let him make things that are true because they are true also to be false.* And Aristotle speaks to the same effect, *This alone is lacking in God, the power to make undone the things that once have been done.*

HENCE: 1. If you think of a past event, for instance that Socrates once ran, merely as a contingent event, then it is only incidentally impossible that it did not take place, but if you think of it as a past event and definitively so, then it is not only in itself but also absolutely impossible that it did not take place, for it implies a contradiction. As such it is more impossible than the raising of the dead to life, which implies no contradiction, and is called impossible only according to natural power. Impossibilities of this sort are subject to divine power.

2. As for the perfection of his power, God can do everything; some fancies, however, cannot be submitted to his power because they are outside the realm of the possible. If we look at the changelessness of divine power, whatever God could do he still can do. Nevertheless some things were in the realm of the merely possible

when they remained yet to be done, but now when they have been done they have ceased to be possible. Now they cannot be undone, and therefore, so we say, not even by God.

3. God can take away all corruption, mental and physical, from a woman who has lost her integrity, but he cannot remove the fact that once she did lose it. Similarly the fact that a sinner did lapse from divine friendship.

Can God do what he does not do?

THE FIFTH POINT: 1. The answer, it seems, is no. For God cannot do except what he has foreseen and pre-ordained he was going to do. This is just what he does do. Therefore he cannot do otherwise.

2. Moverover, God cannot do except what he ought to do and what is right. Yet there is no ought about the doing of what God does not do, nor right about the making of what he does not make. Therefore he cannot do what he does not do.

3. Or put it like this, God cannot do except what is good and fitting for the things he makes. That they should be other than what they are is neither good nor fitting. Consequently he cannot do what he does not do.

ON THE OTHER HAND is the text in *Matthew, Thinkest thou I cannot pray to my Father, and he will presently give me more than twelve legions of angels?* But our Lord did not ask, nor did the Father summon them to repulse back the Jews. Therefore God can do what he does not do.

REPLY: Two mistakes have been made on this point.

Some have held that God acts as though from natural determinism, so that as from the action of natural things effects cannot proceed other than as they do, thus men come from human seed, and olive trees from olives, so likewise from God's working there cannot proceed effects or an arrangement of effects other than those in the present economy.

However, God does not act from necessity of nature, but his will is the cause of all things, and there is no natural drive that necessitates and determines and makes his will produce them. Hence the present course of things does not proceed from his will by such necessity that other arrangements could not have been made.

Others have held that God's power is restricted to the present course of events because the plan of his wisdom and justice, without which he does nothing, requires it.

Now since God's power, which is his essence, is not other than his wisdom, it may be fairly said that they are commensurate, for divine wisdom covers the whole range of power. Nevertheless the order of the world established by divine wisdom, on which, so we have taught, the meaning of justice stands, is not such an adequate expression that divine wisdom is enclosed within its boundaries.

Clearly the whole reason for an arrangement set up by a wise man in the things he does is drawn from his end. When an end is proportionate to the things made in order to achieve it then the maker's wisdom is committed to a determinate pattern.

Now the divine goodness is an end immeasurably surpassing created things; hence divine wisdom is not limited to one fixed system in such a manner that no other course of things could flow from it. In consequence we should declare quite simply that God can make other things than the things he does make.

HENCE: 1. In us our substance and power are distinct from our actual understanding and willing, and our mind is distinct from our wisdom and our will from our justice, with the result that some things lie within our power which are not within a wise understanding or a just will. With God, however, substance and power and understanding and willing and wisdom and justice are all identical. Therefore nothing can be within divine power which is not held in the wisdom and justice of his mind and will.

All the same, since his will is not bound of necessity to this or that particular objective, except incidentally on a supposition, neither is his wisdom and justice committed to any one particular economy, consequently there is no reason why something should not be within divine power which God does not will, and which is no part of the present order he has established. We conceive of understanding and wisdom as directing, will as commanding, and power as executing; as for what lies within power as such, God is said to be able to do it by his absolute power. And this, as we have noticed, covers everything that is consonant with the meaning of being real. As for what lies within his power as carrying out the command of his just will, he is said to be able to do it by his ordinate power.

Accordingly we should state that by his absolute power God can do things other than those he foresaw that he would do and pre-ordained to do. Nevertheless nothing can come to pass that he has not foreseen and pre-ordained; for his doing falls under his foreknowing and pre-ordaining, not the power of his doing, for that is his nature, not his choice. Why he does something is because he wills to do it; why he is able to do it is because such he is by nature, not because he wills it.

2. God owes nothing to anyone other than himself. So that when you speak of his not being able to do except what he ought to do you only mean that he cannot do other than what for him is fitting and fair. Can do only what is fitting and fair—the phrase can be taken in two ways, with the first emphasis either on 'is' or 'can'. When you stress the verb 'is', you tighten the sense to stand for the present course of things, and so refer to the exercise of power; you mean that God cannot do except what now is fitting and fair: and then the phrase is false. But if you bring in the verb 'can' and lay the first stress there, which has the force of opening out the meaning, afterwards bringing in the verb 'is', you refer to what lies before us without pinning yourself down to a particular fact; you mean that God cannot do except what is fitting and fair if he does it: then the phrase is true.

3. Though the present course of things is prescribed by the things that now exist it does not enclose God's wisdom and power. Granted that no other arrangement would be right and appropriate to things as they exist at present, nevertheless God could make other things and under another constitution.

Chapter 41
Miracles and laws of nature
Richard Swinburne

Laws of nature

THE task of the theoretical scientist is to set forth the laws of nature (which may be physical, chemical, biological or psychological laws, or laws of any other science). In any field he will have a number of observational results. He seeks the most natural generalisation or extrapolation of those results, or, as I shall put it, the simplest formula from which the past results can be deduced.

In a primitive way ordinary people generalise their observations in the most natural or simple way to obtain general statements about how things behave, from which they can deduce how things will behave in future. Thus, to take a well-worn example, suppose that swans had not previously been observed and then we observe in different parts of England a number of swans and find them all to be white. We might set forward a hypothesis 'all swans are white'. This allows us to infer of each past swan observed that it was white, and predicts of each future swan which will be observed that it will be white. Another formula equally compatible with observations to date, but making different predictions is 'all swans in England are white, but elsewhere are black'. Yet this would never be seriously proposed because it is so obviously less simple than, a less natural extrapolation from the data than, the alternative formula.

The task of the scientist may thus be compared to that of a man finding a formula governing the occurrence of points on a graph. Compatible with any finite set of data, there will always be an infinite number of possible formulae from which the data can be predicted. We can rule out many by further tests, but however many tests we make we shall still have only a finite number of data and hence an infinite number of formulae compatible with them. Yet some of these formulae will be highly complex relative to the data so that no scientist would consider that the data provided evidence that those formulae were laws of nature. Others are very simple formulae such that the data can be said to provide evidence that they are laws of nature. Thus suppose the scientist finds marks at $(1,1)$, $(2,2)$, $(3,3)$, and $(4,4)$, the first number of each pair being the x-coordinate and the second the y-coordinate. One formula which would predict these marks is $x = y$. Another one is $(x - 1)(x - 2)$ $(x - 3)(x - 4) + x = y$. But clearly we would not regard the data as supporting the

Richard Swinburne extract from *The Concept of Miracle* (Macmillan Ltd, 1970), reprinted by permission of the publisher and the author.

second formula. It is too clumsy a formula to explain four observations. Among simple formulae supported by the data, the simplest is the best supported and regarded, provisionally, as correct. If the formula survives further tests, that increases the evidence in its favour as a law.

What counts as a formula of sufficient simplicity to be adopted as a law and so used for prediction in the absence of simpler formulae is a matter of the quantity and variety of the data on the basis of which it is constructed. While

$$(x-1)(x-2)(x-3)(x-4) + x = y$$

would not do if supported only by the four cited data, it could reasonably be put forward on the basis of four hundred data. Einstein's field equations of General Relativity could hardly be put forward solely on the basis of observations of the movement of Mercury's perihelion (observations compatible with those equations) but could be put forward on the basis of an enormous number of terrestrial and planetary motions and of optical phenomena, previously accounted for by Newtonian mechanics or the Special Theory of Relativity, and of certain further phenomena (such as the movement of Mercury's perihelion) not compatible with the latter theories.

Often, unlike in my two initial examples, a number of different formulae of similar simplicity (no one clearly simpler than the rest) are equally compatible with past data, yet, being different formulae, make different predictions for the future. An artificial example of this would be if we had a number of points on a graph which could be fitted on to hyperbolic curves of different eccentricity but not on to any simpler curves (e.g. a straight line). More complicated real-life examples are provided by current cosmological theories, e.g. 'big bang' and 'steady state' theories. They all take account of the same data of astronomy and mechanics, yet integrate these in different ways so as to get different predictions. Yet many of them seem equally simple, no one a more natural extrapolation from the data than the others. In such cases, in so far as he can, a scientist will test between conflicting predictions and reject those formulae which yield incorrect predictions. If he can do this and is left with only one formula compatible with the data of observation, then he will adopt that.

Sometimes the scientist will be able to see no simple formula, that is formula of sufficient simplicity, compatible with a collection of data in some field, and in that case will not feel justified in adopting any one formula and making predictions on the basis of it. If in our studies of swans we had observed in England several white, several black, and several red ones with no obvious pattern of geographical distribution, we would not be able to produce any simple formula covering these data which would enable us to predict the colours of future swans. In so far as a formula is simple and the simplest known formula compatible with observations, we regard it—provisionally—as a law of nature. Any proposed law of nature will be corrigible—that is, future observations could show the proposed law not to be a true law. But in so far as a formula survives further tests that increases the evidence in its favour as a true law.

Another example of these points is provided by Kepler's work on planetary motion. Studying the positions of planets observed during the previous thirty years, Kepler sought formulae from which those results could be deduced. But not any formulae would do; the formulae would have to be formulae of fairly simple curves, describing each planet as having travelled along a curve of that type, in order for us to be justified in supposing that the formulae described the future as well as the past behaviour of planets. If the formulae were simply records of past positions with unrelated predictions attached, we would not, despite the fact that they accurately recorded past positions, think ourselves justified in believing the future predictions yielded by them. Only if they were the formulae of simple curves which fitted the past positions would we think that we could predict from them. Kepler eventually fitted the positions of each planet on to an ellipse, having the Sun at one focus. The neat fit of the past positions on to this curve justified men in supposing that planets in future would travel in elliptical paths.

The general points of the last few pages would, I believe—with qualifications and additions—be accepted by most philosophers of science. Philosophers of science today are very concerned to bring out clearly and explicitly the criteria for choosing between alternative theories equally compatible with observations obtained so far, criteria which, in common with many philosophers of science, I have termed criteria of simplicity. But although philosophers may still disagree about exactly what those criteria are, they agree that such criteria operate, and they agree in many particular cases when two different theories equally compatible with observations obtained to date are constructed which of the two is to be preferred.

The upshot of all this is that laws of nature do not just describe what happens ('the actual course of events'). They describe what happens in a regular and predictable way. When what happens is entirely irregular and unpredictable, its occurrence is not something describable by natural laws.

Meaning of 'Violation of a law of nature'

Given this understanding of a law of nature, what is meant by a violation of a law of nature? I think that those who, like Hume, have used this or a similar expression have intended to mean by it an occurrence of a non-repeatable counter-instance to a law of nature. The use of the definiens and of the definiendum, violation of a law of nature, both assume that the operation of a law of nature is logically compatible with the occurrence of an exception to its operation. This point will be developed below.

Clearly, as we have noted, events contrary to predictions of formulae which we had good reason to believe to be laws of nature often occur. But if we have good reason to believe that they have occurred and good reason to believe that similar events would occur in similar circumstances, then undoubtedly we have good reason to believe that the formulae which we previously believed to be the laws of nature were not in fact such laws. For then the real laws of nature will, we can best suppose, be the old purported laws with a modification for the circumstances in question. There cannot be repeatable counter-instances to genuine laws of nature, that is, counter-instances which would be repeated in similar circumstances. Repeatable counter-instances to purported laws only show those purported laws not to be genuine laws.

But what are we to say if we have good reason to believe that an event E has occurred contrary to predictions of a formula L which otherwise we have good reason to believe to be a law of nature, and we have good reason to believe that events similar to E would not occur in circumstances as similar as we like in any respect to those of the occurrence of E? E would then be a non-repeatable counter-instance to L. In this case we could say *either* (as before) that L cannot be the law of nature operative in the field, since an exception to its operation has occurred, *or* that L is the law of nature operative in the field, but that an exceptional non-repeatable counter-instance to its occurrence has occurred. The advantage of saying the former is particularly obvious where universal laws are involved. As a universal law has the form 'so-and-sos always do such and such', it seems formally incompatible with a counter-instance reported by 'this is a so-and-so, and did not do such-and-such'. Both statements cannot be true together, the argument goes; evidence in favour of the exception is evidence against the purported law. The advantage of saying the latter is however this. The evidence shows that we cannot replace L by a more successful law allowing us to predict E as well as other phenomena supporting L. For any modified formula which allowed us to predict E would allow us to predict similar events in similar circumstances and hence, *ex hypothesi*, we have good reason to believe, would give false predictions. Whereas if we leave the formula L unmodified, it will, we have good reason to believe, give correct predictions in all other conceivable circumstances. Hence if we are to say that any law of nature is operative in the field in question we must say that it is L. The only alternative is to say that no law of nature operates in the field. Yet saying this does not seem to do justice to the (in general) enormous success of L in predicting occurrences in the field.

For these latter reasons it seems not unnatural to describe E as a non-repeatable counter-instance to a law of nature L. If we do say this we have to understand the operation of a universal law of the form 'so-and-so's always do such-and-such' as logically compatible with 'this is a so-and-so and does not do such-and-such'. To say that a certain such formula is a law is to say that in general its predictions are true and that any exceptions to its operation cannot be accounted for by another formula which could be taken as a law (by the criteria discussed earlier). One must thus distinguish between a formula being a law *and* a formula being (universally) true or being a law which holds without exception.

I believe this second account of the way to describe the relation between a formula which otherwise we have good reason to believe to be a law of nature, and an isolated exception to it, to be more natural than the first, that is, to do more justice to the way in which most of us ordinarily talk about these matters. However that may be, it is clearly a coherent way of talking, and it is the way adopted by those who talk of violations of natural laws. For if any exception to its operation was incompatible with a law being a true law, there appears to be no ready sense which could be given to 'a violation of a law of nature'. Hence I shall in future presuppose the second account. Since the second account is a possible account, the concept of a violation of a law of nature is coherent, and we must reject the views of those who claim that it is not logically possible that a law of nature be violated.

If, as seems natural, we understand by the physically impossible what is ruled out by a law of nature, then our account of laws of nature suggests that it makes sense to suppose that on occasion the physically impossible occurs. (If this seems too para-doxical a thing to say we shall have to give a different sense to the 'physically impossible'.) Substantially the same conclusion is reached by R. F. Holland ('The Miraculous', in D. Z. Phillips (ed.), *Religion and Understanding*, Oxford, 1967). For Holland a violation of a law of nature is a 'conceptual impossibility'. He terms it this because the supposition that there is an object behaving in a way other than that laid down by laws of nature is the supposition that there is an object behav-ing in ways other than the ways embodied in our normal understanding of it, and so, in wide senses of 'involved' and 'concept', involved in our ordinary concept of it. Therefore, having shown that it makes sense to suppose a law of nature vio-lated, Holland argues that in such a case the conceptually impossible would occur. That being so, he concludes, one cannot deduce from a thing having happened that it is a possible occurrence—*ab esse ad posse non valet consequentia*. (When assessing Holland's conclusion, we should remember what he means by 'conceptual impossibility'. He does not mean what most philosophers mean by that expression—viz. something the description of which involves a self-contradiction—but merely something the occurrence of which is ruled out by our ordinary (and with this exception basically correct) understanding of the way objects behave.)

Evidence as to which events, if they occurred, would be violations of laws of nature

The crucial question however is what would be good reason for believing that an event E, if it occurred, was a non-repeatable as opposed to a repeatable counter-instance to a formula L which we have on all other evidence good reason to believe to be a law of nature. The evidence that E is a repeatable counter-instance would be that a new formula L^1 better confirmed than L as a law of nature can be set up, which, unlike L, predicted E. A formula is confirmed by data, it will be recalled, in so far as the data obtained so far are predicted by the formula, new predictions are successful, and the formula is a simple one relative to the collection of data (viz. a natural extrapolation from the data). Now L^1 will be better confirmed than L if it, like L, predicts the data so far obtained, other than E; unlike L, predicts E; and is no more complex than L. If it is considerably more complex than L, that counts against it and might perhaps balance the fact that it, unlike L, predicts E. And if it is so much more complicated than L that it is not of sufficient simplicity relative to the data (see our earlier discussion) to be a law of nature, it will clearly have to be rejected. In so far as there is a doubt whether any proposed law L^1 is more satisfactory than L, clearly the scientist will, if he can, test between the further predictions of the two laws. If, for matters where they make conflicting predictions, L^1 predicts successfully and L unsuccessfully, L^1 will be preferred, and vice versa. It follows from all this that L will have to be retained as a law of nature and E regarded as a non-repeatable counter-instance to it, if any proposed rival formula L^1 were too much more complicated than L without giving better new predictions, or predicted new phenomena unsuccessfully where L predicted successfully. L^1 would certainly be too much more complicated if it were not of sufficient simplicity relative to the data to be a law of nature at all (see our earlier discussion). L would have to be abandoned if some proposed rival formula L^1 which predicted E were not much more complicated than L, or predicted new phenomena successfully where L predicted unsuccessfully.

Here is an example. Suppose E to be the levitation (i.e. rising into the air and remaining floating on it, in circumstances where no known forces other than gravity (e.g. magnetism) are acting) of a certain holy person. E is thus a counter-instance to otherwise well-substituted laws of nature L (viz. the laws of mechanics, electro-magnetism etc.) which together purport to give an account of all the forces operating in nature. We could show E to be a repeatable counter-instance if we could construct a formula L^1 which predicted E and also successfully predicted other divergencies from L, as well as all other tested predictions of L; *or* if we could construct L^1 which was comparatively simple relative to the data and predicted E and all the other tested predictions of L, but predicted divergencies from L which had not yet been tested. L^1 might differ from L in postulating the operation of an entirely new kind of force, e.g. that under certain circumstances bodies exercise a gravitational repulsion on each other, and those circumstances would include the circumstances in which E occurred. If L^1 satisfied either of the above two conditions, we would adopt it, and we would then say that under certain circumstances people do levitate and so E was not a counter-instance to a law of nature. However it might be that any modification which we made to the laws of nature to allow them to predict E might not yield any more successful predictions than L and they might be so clumsy that there was no reason to believe that their predictions not yet tested would be successful. Under these circumstances we would have good reason to believe that the levitation of the holy person violated the laws of nature.

If the laws of nature are statistical and not universal, as Quantum Theory suggests, it is not in all cases so clear what counts as a counter-instance to them. A universal law is a law of the form 'all so-and-sos do such-and-such', and a counter-instance is therefore a so-and-so which does not do such-and-such. The occurrence of such a counter-instance is the occurrence of an exception to the law. A statistical law is a law of the form 'n% of so-and-sos do such-and-such'. But here however many so-and-sos are observed which do not do such-and-such, their occurrence is not completely ruled out by the theory. The theory tells us the proportion of so-and-sos which do such-and-such in an infinite class, and however many so-and-sos are found not to do such-and-such in a finite class, this finite class may be just an unrepresentative selection from the infinite class. It *may* be. But if something occurs which, given the truth of the law, is highly unlikely, that counts against the law, is counter-evidence to it, even if not formally ruled out by it. If the proportion of so-and-sos which do such-and-such in one of the very few, albeit large, finite classes studied is vastly different from that stated to hold in the law, that is counter-evidence to the law. Such an event is therefore not unnaturally described as an exception to a statistical law and the question can therefore be discussed whether it is a repeatable or a non-repeatable exception. It is formally compatible with the currently accepted statistical version of the second law of thermodynamics that a kettle of water put on a fire freeze instead of boiling. But it is vastly improbable that such an event will ever happen within human experience. Hence if it does happen, it is not unnaturally described as an exception to the law. If the evidence does not lead to our adopting a rival law, the event can then be described as a violation of the second law of thermodynamics. Any who speak of a violation of statistical laws would presumably mean the occurrence of a non-repeatable counter-instance to such laws, in the above sense of counter-instance.

All claims about what are the laws of nature are corrigible. However much support any purported law has at the moment, one day it may prove to be no true law. So likewise will be all claims about what does or does not violate the laws of nature. When an event apparently violates such laws, the appearance may arise simply because no one has thought of the true law which could explain the event, or, while they have thought of it, it is so complex relative to the data as rightly to be dismissed before even being tested, or too complex to be adopted without further testing and the tests too difficult in practice to carry out. New scientific knowledge may later turn up which forces us to revise any such claims about what violates laws of nature. But then all claims to knowledge about the physical world are corrigible, and we must reach provisional conclusions about them on the evidence available to us. We have to some extent good evidence about what are the laws of nature, and some of them are so well established and account for so many data that any modifications to them which we could suggest to account for the odd counter-instance would be so clumsy and *ad hoc* as to upset the whole structure of science. In such cases the evidence is strong that if the purported counter-instance occurred it was a violation of the law of nature. There is good reason to believe that the following events, if they occurred, would be violations of the laws of nature: levitation; resurrection from the dead in full health of a man whose heart has not been beating for twenty-four hours and who was dead also by other currently used criteria; water turning into wine without the assistance of chemical apparatus or catalysts; a man getting better from polio in a minute. We know quite enough about how things behave to be reasonably certain that, in the sense earlier delineated, these events are physically impossible.

Chapter 42
Why we should disbelieve in miracles

David Hume

Part I

I FLATTER myself, that I have discovered an argument of a like nature, which, if just, will, with the wise and learned, be an everlasting check to all kinds of superstitious delusion, and consequently, will be useful as long as the world endures. For so long, I presume, will the accounts of miracles and prodigies be found in all history, sacred and profane.

Though experience be our only guide in reasoning concerning matters of fact; it must be acknowledged, that this guide is not altogether infallible, but in some cases is apt to lead us into errors. One, who in our climate, should expect better weather in any week of June than in one of December, would reason justly, and conformably to experience; but it is certain, that he may happen, in the event, to find himself mistaken. However, we may observe, that, in such a case, he would have no cause to complain of experience; because it commonly informs us beforehand of the uncertainty, by that contrariety of events, which we may learn from a diligent observation. All effects follow not with like certainty from their supposed causes. Some events are found, in all countries and all ages, to have been constantly conjoined together: Others are found to have been more variable, and sometimes to disappoint our expectations; so that, in our reasonings concerning matter of fact, there are all imaginable degrees of assurance from the highest certainty to the lowest species of moral evidence.

A wise man, therefore, proportions his belief to the evidence. In such conclusions as are founded on an infallible experience, he expects the event with the last degree of assurance, and regards his past experience as a full *proof* of the future existence of that event. In other cases, he proceeds with more caution: He weighs the opposite experiments: He considers which side is supported by the greater number of experiments: to that side he inclines, with doubt and hesitation; and when at last he fixes his judgement, the evidence exceeds not what we properly call *probability*. All probability, then, supposes an opposition of experiments and observations, where the one side is found to overbalance the other, and to produce a degree of evidence,

David Hume 'Of Miracles' from *Enquiries Concerning Human Understanding and Concerning the Principles of Morals*, revised edition by P. H. Nidditch (OUP, 1975), copyright © Oxford University Press 1975, reprinted by permission of the publisher.

proportioned to the superiority. A hundred instances or experiments on one side, and fifty on another, afford a doubtful expectation of any event; though a hundred uniform experiments, with only one that is contradictory, reasonably beget a pretty strong degree of assurance. In all cases, we must balance the opposite experiments, where they are opposite, and deduct the smaller number from the greater, in order to know the exact force of the superior evidence.

A miracle is a violation of the laws of nature; and as a firm and unalterable experience has established these laws, the proof against a miracle, from the very nature of the fact, is as entire as any argument from experience can possibly be imagined. Why is it more than probable, that all men must die; that lead cannot, of itself, remain suspended in the air; that fire consumes wood, and is extinguished by water; unless it be, that these events are found agreeable to the laws of nature, and there is required a violation of these laws, or in other words, a miracle to prevent them? Nothing is esteemed a miracle, if it ever happen in the common course of nature. It is no miracle that a man, seemingly in good health, should die on a sudden: because such a kind of death, though more unusual than any other, has yet been frequently observed to happen. But it is a miracle, that a dead man should come to life; because that has never been observed in any age or country. There must, therefore, be a uniform experience against every miraculous event, otherwise the event would not merit that appellation. And as a uniform experience amounts to a proof, there is here a direct and full *proof*, from the nature of the fact, against the existence of any miracle; nor can such a proof be destroyed, or the miracle rendered credible, but by an opposite proof, which is superior.

The plain consequence is (and it is a general maxim worthy of our attention), 'That no testimony is sufficient to establish a miracle, unless the testimony be of such a kind, that its falsehood would be more miraculous, than the fact, which it endeavours to establish; and even in that case there is a mutual destruction of arguments, and the superior only gives us an assurance suitable to that degree of force, which remains, after deducting the inferior.' When anyone tells me, that he saw a dead man restored to life, I immediately consider with myself, whether it be more probable, that this person should either deceive or be deceived, or that the fact, which he relates, should really have happened. I weigh the one miracle against the other; and according to the superiority, which I discover, I pronounce my decision, and always reject the greater miracle. If the falsehood of his testimony would be more miraculous, than the event which he relates; then, and not till then, can he pretend to command my belief or opinion.

Part II

In the foregoing reasoning we have supposed, that the testimony, upon which a miracle is founded, may possibly amount to an entire proof, and that the falsehood of that testimony would be a real prodigy: But it is easy to shew, that we have been a great deal too liberal in our concession, and that there never was a miraculous event established on so full an evidence.

For *first*, there is not to be found, in all history, any miracle attested by a sufficient number of men, of such unquestioned good-sense, education, and learning, as to secure us against all delusion in themselves; of such undoubted integrity, as to place them beyond all suspicion of any design to deceive others; of such credit and reputation in the eyes of mankind, as to have a great deal to lose in case of their being detected in any falsehood; and at the same time, attesting facts performed in such a public manner and in so celebrated a part of the world, as to render the detection unavoidable: All which circumstances are requisite to give us a full assurance in the testimony of men.

Secondly. We may observe in human nature a principle which, if strictly examined, will be found to diminish extremely the assurance, which we might, from human testimony, have, in any kind of prodigy. The maxim, by which we commonly conduct ourselves in our reasonings, is, that the objects, of which we have no experience, resemble those, of which we have; that what we have found to be most usual is always most probable; and that where there is an opposition of arguments, we ought to give the preference to such as are founded on the greatest number of past observations. But though, in proceeding by this rule, we readily reject any fact which is unusual and incredible in an ordinary degree; yet in advancing farther, the mind observes not always the same rule; but when anything is affirmed utterly absurd and miraculous, it rather the more readily admits of such a fact, upon account of that very circumstance, which ought to destroy all its authority. The passion of *surprise* and *wonder*, arising from miracles, being an agreeable emotion, gives a sensible tendency towards the belief of those events, from which it is derived. And this goes so far, that even those who cannot enjoy this pleasure immediately, nor can believe those miraculous events, of which they are informed, yet love to partake of the satisfaction at second-hand or by rebound, and place a pride and delight in exciting the admiration of others.

With what greediness are the miraculous accounts of travellers received, their descriptions of sea and land monsters, their relations of wonderful adventures, strange men, and uncouth manners? But if the spirit of religion join itself to the love of wonder, there is an end of common sense; and human testimony, in these circumstances, loses all pretensions to authority. A religionist may be an enthusiast, and imagine he sees what has no reality: he may know his narrative to be false, and yet persevere in it, with the best intentions in the world, for the sake of promoting so holy a cause: or even where this delusion has not place, vanity, excited by so strong a temptation, operates on him more powerfully than on the rest of mankind in any other circumstances; and self-interest with equal force. His auditors may not have, and commonly have not, sufficient judgement to canvass his evidence: what judgement they have, they renounce by principle, in these sublime and mysterious subjects: or if they were ever so willing to employ it, passion and a heated imagination disturb the regularity of its operations.

Their credulity increases his impudence: and his impudence overpowers their credulity.

The many instances of forged miracles, and prophecies, and supernatural events, which, in all ages, have either been detected by contrary evidence, or which detect themselves by their absurdity, prove sufficiently the strong propensity of mankind to the extraordinary and the marvellous, and ought reasonably to beget a suspicion against all relations of this kind. This is our natural way of thinking, even with regard to the most common and most credible events. For instance: There is no kind of report which rises so easily, and spreads so quickly, especially in country places and provincial towns, as those concerning marriages; insomuch that two young persons of equal condition never see each other twice, but the whole neighbourhood immediately join them together. The pleasure of telling a piece of news so interesting, of propagating it, and of being the first reporters of it, spreads the intelligence. And this is so well known, that no man of sense gives attention to these reports, till he find them confirmed by some greater evidence. Do not the same passions, and others still stronger, incline the generality of mankind to believe and report, with the greatest vehemence and assurance, all religious miracles?

Thirdly. It forms a strong presumption against all supernatural and miraculous relations, that they are observed chiefly to abound among ignorant and barbarous nations; or if a civilized people has ever given admission to any of them, that people will be found to have received them from ignorant and barbarous ancestors, who transmitted them with that inviolable sanction and authority, which always attend received opinions. When we peruse the first histories of all nations, we are apt to imagine ourselves transported into some new world; where the whole frame of nature is disjointed, and every element performs its operations in a different manner, from what it does at present. Battles, revolutions, pestilence, famine and death, are never the effect of those natural causes, which we experience. Prodigies, omens, oracles, judgements, quite obscure the few natural events, that are intermingled with them. But as the former grow thinner every page, in proportion as we advance nearer the enlightened ages, we soon learn, that there is nothing mysterious or supernatural in the case, but that all proceeds from the usual propensity of mankind towards the marvellous, and that, though this inclination may at intervals receive a check from sense and learning, it can never be thoroughly extirpated from human nature.

I may add as a *fourth* reason, which diminishes the authority of prodigies, that there is no testimony for any, even those which have not been expressly detected, that is not opposed by an infinite number of witnesses; so that not only the miracle destroys the credit of testimony, but the testimony destroys itself. To make this the better understood, let us consider, that, in matters of religion, whatever is different is contrary; and that it is impossible the religions of ancient Rome, of Turkey, of Siam, and of China should, all of them, be established on any solid foundation. Every miracle, therefore, pretended to have been wrought in any of these religions (and all of them abound in miracles), as its direct scope is to establish the particular system to which it is attributed; so has it the same force, though more indirectly, to overthrow every other system. In destroying a rival system, it likewise destroys the credit of those miracles, on which that system was established; so that all the prodigies of different religions are to be regarded as contrary facts, and the evidences of these prodigies, whether weak or strong, as opposite to each other. According to this method of reasoning, when we believe any miracle of Mahomet or his successors, we have for our warrant the testimony of a few barbarous Arabians: And on the other hand, we are to regard the authority of Titus Livius, Plutarch, Tacitus, and, in short, of all the authors and witnesses, Grecian, Chinese, and Roman Catholic, who have related any miracle in their particular religion; I say, we are to regard their testimony in the same light as if they had mentioned that Mahometan miracle and had in express terms contradicted it, with the same certainty as they have for the miracle they relate. This argument may appear over subtle and refined; but is not in reality different from the reasoning of a judge, who supposes, that the credit of two witnesses, maintaining a crime against any one, is destroyed by the testimony of two others, who affirm him to have been two hundred leagues distant, at the same instant when the crime is said to have been committed.

Upon the whole, then, it appears, that no testimony for any kind of miracle has ever amounted to a probability, much less to a proof; and that, even supposing it amounted to a proof, it would be opposed by another proof; derived from the very nature of the fact, which it would endeavour to establish. It is experience only, which gives authority to human testimony; and it is the same experience, which assures us of the laws of nature. When, therefore, these two kinds of experience are contrary, we have nothing to do but substract the one from the other, and embrace an opinion, either on one side or the other, with that assurance which arises from the remainder. But according to the principle here explained, this substraction, with regard to all popular religions, amounts to an entire annihilation; and therefore we may establish it as a maxim, that no human testimony can have such force as to prove a miracle, and make it a just foundation for any such system of religion.

I beg the limitations here made may be remarked, when I say, that a miracle can never be proved, so as to be the foundation of a system of religion. For I own, that otherwise, there may possibly be miracles, or violations of the usual course of nature, of such a kind as to admit of proof from human testimony; though, perhaps, it will be impossible to find any such in all the records of history. Thus, suppose, all authors, in all languages, agree, that, from the first of January 1600, there was a total darkness over the whole earth for eight days: suppose that the tradition of this extraordinary event is still strong and lively among the people: that all travellers, who return from foreign countries, bring us accounts of the same tradition, without the least variation or contradiction: it is evident, that our present philosophers, instead of doubting the fact, ought to receive it as certain, and ought to search for the causes whence it might be derived. The decay, corruption, and dissolution of nature, is an event rendered probable by so many analogies, that any phenomenon, which seems to have a tendency towards that catastrophe, comes within the reach of human testimony, if that testimony be very extensive and uniform.

But suppose, that all the historians who treat of England, should agree, that, on the first of January 1600, Queen Elizabeth died; that both before and after her death she was seen by her physicians and the whole court, as is usual with persons of her rank; that her successor was acknowledged and proclaimed by the parliament; and that, after being interred a month, she again appeared, resumed the throne, and governed England for three years: I must confess that I should be surprised at the concurrence of so many odd circumstances, but should not have the least inclination to believe so miraculous an event. I should not doubt of her pretended death, and of those other public circumstances that followed it: I should only assert it to have been pretended, and that it neither was, nor possibly could be real. You would in vain object to me the difficulty, and almost impossibility of deceiving the world in an affair of such consequence; the wisdom and solid judgement of that renowned queen; with the little or no advantage which she could reap from so poor an artifice: All this might astonish me; but I would still reply, that the knavery and folly of men are such common phenomena, that I should rather believe the most extraordinary events to arise from their concurrence, than admit of so signal a violation of the laws of nature.

Questions for discussion

1. Are there reasons for supposing that there is an omnipotent God?
2. How might we decide what God can and cannot do?
3. Is the power of God limited by logical considerations? If so, why? If not, why not?
4. Are miracles intrinsically impossible?
5. What would convince you that a miracle had actually occurred?

Advice on further reading

Especially helpful discussions of omnipotence can be found in the volumes by Davis, Hughes, and Wierenga cited on p. 571. For a scholarly exposition and discussion of some early ways of thinking about God's power, the book to read is Lawrence Moonan, *Divine Power: The Medieval Power Distinction up to its Adoption by Albert, Bonaventure, and Aquinas* (Oxford, 1994). This, however, is a very technical study. Moonan offers a brief treatment of omnipotence in Part 3(c) of Brian Davies (ed.), *Philosophy of Religion: A Guide to the Subject* (London, 1998). For a book-length treatment of omnipotence which discusses the topic from a contemporary philosophical perspective, see G. van den Brink, *Almighty God: A Study of the Doctrine of Divine Omnipotence* (Kampen, 1993).

There are lots of good philosophical articles on divine omnipotence. Ones which are especially worth looking at when approaching the subject for the first time (since they cover a lot of ground and are all clearly written) include:

Harry H. Frankfurt, 'The Logic of Omnipotence', *The Philosophical Review* 74 (1964).

Peter Geach, 'Omnipotence', *Philosophy* 48 (1973).

George I. Mavrodes, 'Some Puzzles Concerning Omnipotence', *Philosophical Review* 72 (1963).

Thomas P. Flint and Alfred J. Freddoso, 'Maximal Power', in Alfred J. Freddodo (ed.), *The Existence and Nature of God* (Notre Dame, Indiana, 1983).

For a splendid anthology of texts on the topic of miracles, see Richard Swinburne (ed.), *Miracles* (New York and London, 1989). For historical accounts of understandings of miracles, see:

C. F. D. Moule (ed.), *Miracles* (London, 1965).

R. M. Grant, *Miracle and Natural Law in Graeco-Roman and Early Christian Thought* (Amsterdam, 1952).

J. A. Hardon, 'The Concept of Miracle from St Augustine to Modern Apologetics', *Theological Studies* 15 (1954).

For two notable book-length treatments of miracles, see C. S. Lewis, *Miracles* (revised edn, London, 1960) and Richard Swinburne, *The Concept of Miracle* (London, 1970).

To understand what Hume is saying in his discussion of miracles, it helps to know something of the context in which he wrote. For this, see R. M. Burns, *The Great Debate on Miracles: From Joseph Granville to David Hume* (London and Toronto, 1981). Also see J. C. A. Gaskin, *Hume's Philosophy of Religion* (2nd edn, Basingstoke, 1988), ch. 8. The Swinburne anthology, *Miracles*, and the volume by Gaskin will lead you to many other works seeking to evaluate Hume's discussion.

Belief in God's omnipotence has led to the belief that God can do what we ask him to do as we pray. I say nothing of this above, and it is not touched on in the foregoing extracts, but for some philosophical treatments of prayer, see:

D. Bassinger, 'Why Petition an Omnipotent, Omniscient, Wholly Good God?', *Religious Studies* 19 (1983).

Vincent Brümmer, *What Are We Doing When We Pray? A Philosophical Inquiry* (London, 1984).

Brian Davies, 'What Happens When You Pray?', *New Blackfriars* 61 (1980).

Peter Geach, 'Praying for Things to Happen', in Peter Geach, *God and the Soul* (London, 1969).

Herbert McCabe, 'Prayer', *Doctrine and Life* 20 (1970).

Eleonore Stump, 'Petitionary Prayer', *American Philosophical Quarterly* 16 (1979).

Knowing

Introduction

The knowing God

In Book XII of his *Metaphysics*, Aristotle says that the object of divine thought must be nothing but the best thing there is, namely itself. It must be divinity alone. But in the major Western theistic traditions God's knowledge has been thought of as much more extensive. Hence, for example, one Old Testament author writes:

> O Lord, thou hast searched me and known me!
> Thou knowest when I sit down and when I rise up;
> though discernest my thoughts from afar.
> Thou searchest out my path and my lying down,
> and art acquainted with all my ways.
> Even before a word is on my tongue, Lo O Lord, thou knowest it altogether[1]

For the (unknown) author of these words, God knows more than himself. He knows people through and through. And this is a teaching reiterated in New Testament texts, where we find it said that God's knowledge extends not only to people, but to every living non-human thing, and even to the number of the hairs on our heads.[2]

The Bible contains nothing that we could call a philosophical treatise on God's knowledge. But if we take the word 'omniscient' in its literal sense (if we take it to mean 'all-knowing', without specifying what, precisely, is to be thought of by 'all'), then we can read the Bible as teaching that God is omniscient. And even if we prefer to say that it only takes God to have a high degree of knowledge, the idea that God's knowledge amounts to omniscience has been unequivocally taught by many post-biblical Jewish and Christian thinkers, not to mention Islamic ones.[3] Hence, for example, St Anselm roundly declares:

---

1. *Ps.* 139: 1–4.
2. Cf. Matt. 10: 29 and Luke 12: 6–7. Cf. also John 16: 30 where, given the theology of the Gospel as a whole, it seems to be implied that Jesus's divinity is the reason why he knows 'all things'.
3. God's omniscience seems to be asserted in chapter 34 of the Koran: 'Praise be to Allah, to whom belongs all that the earth contain! . . . He is the Wise One, the All-knowing. He has knowledge of all that goes into the earth and all that springs up from it; all that comes down from heaven and all that ascends to it'. Cf. *The Koran*, translated with notes by N. J. Dawood (4th revised edn, Harmondsworth, 1974).

'You are supremely perceptive, in the sense that You know supremely all things and not in the sense in which an animal knows through a bodily sense-faculty.'[4] Here, Anselm is saying that God's knowledge is infinite or unlimited. He is also saying that it is direct, that it is not acquired by any medium on which God depends for it.

Why think of God as knowing?

Yet why should it be supposed that God has any knowledge? Some philosophers have challenged the very idea of a knowing God since they find it implausible to suppose that there could be a God at all (cf. Chapter 9). Others have fought shy of the notion of a knowing God because of the natural association between 'knowing' and 'having a mind'. The word 'God' normally signifies 'something non-material'. But our understanding of mind at work seems much limited to our knowledge and understanding of people, who are not immaterial. Can we make sense of 'mind-talk' when it is used to refer to what is not material? It has been argued that we cannot, and that, as a consequence, we can make little sense of the notion of God as a knower.[5]

But those who think that there is a knowing God have given a number of reasons in defence of their position.[6] We can summarize some of them as follows:

1. God is wholly perfect. He cannot be this if he lacks knowledge.[7] So God has knowledge.
2. The order in the world can only be accounted for in terms of something with knowledge.[8]
3. God is the Creator of the universe. But creating is an act of intelligence. So God has knowledge.
4. Knowledge is something which exists in the world. Since God accounts for all that exists in the world, and since this must reflect what God is, knowledge is something we can ascribe to God.[9]

Also worth highlighting is a view of divine knowledge which is not too commonly defended today, but which is an interesting one to reflect on in the light of the view that God cannot know if God is immaterial. For it holds that God knows precisely because he *is* immaterial. You can find it represented at the outset of Chapter 43, from Aquinas.

---

4. *Proslogion* 6.
5. For more on 'mind' and 'matter', see Part VII below.
6. Here I am referring to philosophers who think that there is philosophical reason to think of God as knowing. Many people, of course, would simply say that God has knowledge since the Bible or some other religious authority says so. Some, such as D. Z. Phillips, would say that 'God knows' is what we have to say as we seek to explain what belief in God means.
7. St Anselm defends this line of thinking in his *Proslogion*. You can find it in many other writers, however (e.g. Aquinas).
8. Hence, defenders of design arguments for God's existence commonly take themselves to be arguing for the existence of a knower.
9. Aquinas uses this argument as part of his case for thinking of God as knowing. For the ideas behind the argument, see the Introduction to Part II above.

To understand what Aquinas says here you need to realize that he always insists that we must sharply distinguish between knowledge (or understanding) and sensation. Sensations, he thinks, are particular occurrences in distinct physical organisms. They are private property. My sensations are mine, not yours (as my hands are mine, not yours). Yet, so Aquinas adds, knowledge is something we can literally share. There is nothing private about it. On his account, if I know that cats are mammals, and if you know that cats are mammals, then exactly the same thing can be ascribed to us: the knowledge that cats are mammals.

According to Aquinas, human knowing only occurs as sensations (particular physical events which, in themselves, lack significance or intelligibility) are taken up and transformed into an understanding which is not identifiable with any individual physical process, not even a brain process, since that is an individual occurrence, while knowledge is something we can share with each other as we cannot share our brain processes. For Aquinas, to say that knowledge occurs can never be to say that some identifiable physical process has occurred. It is to say that the physical has been transcended. It is to say that you and I, though different physical individuals, can share something which is not physical.

For Aquinas, therefore, knowledge and immateriality go together. And on this basis he argues that the only way to think of a wholly immaterial God is to think of him as being what knowledge essentially is: what you get when you have immateriality or liberation from particular material objects and processes. For him, the notion of knowledge must be immediately associated with God as soon as it is admitted that God is immaterial.[10]

What and how does God know?

But what, exactly, might we take God to know? And in what way might we take God to exist as a knower? These are the questions which have most preoccupied philosophers reflecting on the topic of God's knowledge. Yet those who believe that God has knowledge extending beyond himself have varied in their answers. Even those subscribing to the formula 'God is omniscient' have given different accounts as to how to understand it.

According to some, for instance, God's knowledge extends to every historical object and event, including those which lie in the future. For some thinkers God knows all that was, is, and will be.

But how does God know all this? Is it by a simple awareness akin to what we normally take ourselves to have when we look at the world around us? Or is it by understanding that a series of propositions or statements are true, as (without literally looking at anything) we might understand that '2 + 2 = 4' is true or that 'Caesar was murdered' is true or that 'Today is Wednesday' is true. Both answers have been defended.

Yet might it not be wrong to suppose in the first place that God knows all that was, is, and will be? While emphasizing the range of God's knowledge, some have thought that it would be wrong to suppose this. For what of the future? Should we not agree that one

---

10. Aquinas, you should note, does not take this conclusion to imply that we should think of God as being exactly like human knowers. Cf. Part II above. Also cf. Chapter 50.

can only know what is the case or what is now true? Yet can the future be said to be now the case? And can future tensed statements be thought of as now true? How can the future be an object of knowledge? How can it be an object even of God's knowledge?

Some have argued that reflecting on questions such as these ought to leave us denying that God knows the future. Or they have argued that talk about God doing so should be explicated so as to avoid seeming to refer to the future as there before God as objects of sensory perception are there before us. While accepting that God can somehow be thought of as knowing the future, others have denied that he can be rightly thought of as knowing all of it. God's knowledge of the future, they argue, is real, but restricted. Why? Because, so it has been argued, there are certain events which cannot, in principle, be known ahead of time. Some things can only be known by us as they come to pass in time. And, so it has been claimed, this means that God's knowledge has to be thought of as somehow developing or increasing, as human knowledge does.

But can we intelligibly think of God as containing any development? If we cannot, then it will be wrong to think of God's knowledge as being added to or modified as time goes on. And many philosophers have thoroughly rejected all talk of God developing in any sense. Why? Because they take God to be the source of all change, something which cannot, therefore, be something which changes. On their account, God's knowledge (as with everything attributable to God) is unchanging and even unchangeable. It admits of no variation. According to some philosophers, it is outside time. It is timeless knowledge.

God's knowledge of future contingents

Many of the views just noted emerge with particular clarity in discussions of what has, perhaps, been the most debated question of all when it comes to God's knowledge. We can call it 'The Problem of Future Contingents'. And we can state it as follows:

1. If X knows that-*p*, it follows that-*p*. For example, if you know that John is a thief, then John *is* a thief.
2. So if God knows that something will come to pass, it will come to pass.
3. But what if God knows that I will freely perform some action tomorrow? What, for example, if he knows that tomorrow I will freely brush my teeth?
4. From 1 and 2, it looks as though it is already settled that I will brush my teeth. For if God knows that I will brush my teeth tomorrow, then it is certain that I will brush my teeth tomorrow.
5. But freely occurring actions are ones which people might or might not perform. They are contingent (as opposed to necessary). They are not events which are certain in advance to come about.
6. In that case, however, how can God know that I will freely brush my teeth tomorrow? How, indeed, can he know about *any* future contingent event?

In other words, if God knows what is to come, how can the future be anything but predetermined or unpreventable?

How might we respond to this question? Some philosophers have argued that there is a serious conflict between the claim that God knows the future in advance and the claim that some events (e.g. human actions) are contingent or not predetermined. According to Richard Sorabji, for instance:

If God were not *infallible* in his judgment of what we would do, then we might be able so to act that his prediction turned out *wrong*. But this is not even a possibility, for to call him infallible is to say not merely that he *is* not, but that he *cannot* be wrong, and correspondingly we *cannot* make him wrong ... The restriction on freedom arises not from God's infallibility alone, but from that coupled with the *irrevocability* of the past. If God's infallible knowledge of our doing exists *in advance*, then we are *too late* so to act that God will have had a different judgement about what we are going to do. His judgement exists *already*, and the past *cannot* be affected.[11]

This view is also defended by Nelson Pike in Chapter 45. According to Pike, if God at time 1 knew that Jones would mow his lawn at time 10, then Jones can only mow his lawn freely at time 10 by achieving the impossible—by changing the past.[12]

But other philosophers have taken a different line. For, according to them, God's knowledge cannot by itself make any event to be either contingent or necessary. What God knows is determined by how things are. So if he knows, for instance, that event E will occur, and that E is contingent, this can only be because E will occur as contingent. Hence, for example, according to William Lane Craig:

The reason God foreknows that Jones will mow his lawn is the simple fact that Jones will mow his lawn. Jones is free to refrain, and were he to do so, God would have foreknown that he would refrain. Jones is free to do whatever he wants, and God's foreknowledge logically follows Jones's action like a shadow, even if chronologically the shadow precedes the coming of the event itself.[13]

Another approach to the problem of future contingents rejects what seems to be a crucial premise needed in order to state it. For the problem arises on the supposition that God and his knowledge exist in time. It seems to arise on the assumption that God has *fore*knowledge. But why should we suppose that this is so? And might we not suggest that even if there is a conflict between the notion of God foreknowing some event and the event being contingent, there is no threat to contingency if God's knowledge is construed not as foreknowledge, but as the knowledge of one who does not exist at any time? My knowing that-*p* does not entail that *p* is a truth which cannot be false. John may know that Mary is his wife. But this does not mean that Mary is not freely wedded to John. Suppose, then, we say that God's knowledge is always a matter of God simply knowing, though not at any time. Can we on this basis argue that omniscience and contingency are compatible notions?

11. Richard Sorabji, *Time, Creation and the Continuum* (London, 1983), p. 255.
12. For a similar argument coming from a famous Protestant theologian, see Jonathan Edwards (1703–58), *Freedom of the Will* (1754), Section 12. Here, Edwards writes: 'If there be a full, certain and infallible foreknowledge of the future existence of the volitions of moral agents, then there is a certain infallible and indissoluble connection between those events and that foreknowledge: ... those events are necessary events; being infallibly and indissolubly connected with that whose existence already is, and so is now necessary, and can't but have been.' See Jonathan Edwards, *The Freedom of the Will* (ed. Paul Ramsey, New Haven and London, 1957), p. 258.
13. William Lane Craig, *The Only Wise God* (Grand Rapids, 1987), p. 74.

Many philosophers have suggested that we can. The most famous example is Boethius, whose views on God's knowledge can be found in Chapter 44.[14] According to him, God is 'eternal'. What is eternity? For Boethius it is 'the whole, simultaneous and perfect possession of boundless life'. According to Boethius, therefore, God's knowledge is not best thought of as foreknowledge. It should rather be thought of as 'knowledge of a never passing instant', in that God sees future things 'present to him just such as in time they will at some future point come to be'. For Boethius, God does not foreknow. God simply knows. And though this fact, says Boethius, allows to conclude that 'If God knows that-*p*, then *p*' is necessarily true, it also allows us to deny that God knows nothing except that which cannot fail to be.

Boethius's way of dealing with the problem of future contingents is probably the most historically influential one. You can find echoes of it in the writings of philosophers such as Anselm, Aquinas, and Leibniz. It has been defended in various ways by contemporary philosophers such as Paul Helm, Brian Leftow, Norman Kretzmann, and Eleonore Stump. But in much recent writings a different approach to the problem of future contingents has been defended, one based on the thought of the sixteenth-century Jesuit theologian Luis de Molina (1536–1600).

Focusing on human free actions, Molina argues that God creates in the light of his knowledge as to *how things would go if*. On his account, God knows how uncreated (possible) people would freely act *if* created. According to Molina, therefore, God's knowledge does not interfere with my freedom. Suppose I play the flute at 5.00 p.m. on 27 June 2000. According to Molina I could do so freely even though God knows of me doing what I do. How? Because my freely playing the flute is something which God brings into existence in the light of his 'middle knowledge' (*scientia media*), a knowledge of how I would freely act given certain circumstances. God knows how I would act *if*. Then he creates me with all my options and free choices in place. And many contemporary philosophers have found this way of thinking of God and future contingents to be wholly congenial. Hence, for example, William Lane Craig has written:

The doctrine of middle knowledge is a doctrine of remarkable theological fecundity. Molina's scheme would resolve in a single stroke most of the traditional difficulties concerning divine providence and human freedom. Molina defines providence as God's ordering of things to their ends, either directly or mediately through secondary agents. By His middle knowledge God knows an infinity of orders which He could instantiate because He knows how the creatures in them would in fact freely respond given the various circumstances. He then decides by the free act of His will how He would respond in these various circumstances and simultaneously wills to bring about one of these orders. He directly causes certain circumstances to come into being and others indirectly by causally determined secondary causes. Free creatures, however, He allows to act as He knew they would when placed in such circumstances, and He concurs with their decisions in producing in being the effects they desire. Some of these effects God desired unconditionally and so wills positively that they occur, but others He does not unconditionally desire, but nevertheless permits due to His overriding desire to allow creaturely freedom and knowing that even these sinful acts will fit into the overall scheme

14. Note that this consists of part of Boethius's *Consolation of Philosophy*, which is mostly written in the form of a dialogue between Boethius and a personification of philosophy ('Lady Philosophy'). The *Consolation* was drafted by Boethius while he was in prison towards the end of his life.

of things, so that God's ultimate ends in human history will be accomplished. God has thus providentially arranged for everything that happens by either willing or permitting it, yet in such a way as to preserve freedom and contingency. Molinism thus effects a dramatic reconciliation between divine sovereignty and human freedom.[15]

Does it? Some would say it does not, since they are suspicious of the notion of middle knowledge. Hence, for example, Elizabeth Anscombe writes:

As a result of my teen-age conversion to the Catholic Church . . . I read a work called *Natural Theology* by a nineteenth-century Jesuit . . . and found it all convincing except for two things. One was the doctrine of *scientia media*, according to which God knew what anybody would have done if, e.g., he hadn't died when he did . . . I found I could not believe this doctrine: it appeared to me that there was not, quite generally, any such thing as what would have happened if what did happen had not happened, and that in particular there was no such thing, generally speaking, as what someone would have done if . . . and certainly that there was no such thing as how someone would have spent his life if he had not died as a child.[16]

Yet appeal to God's middle knowledge, or to something like this, forms the basis of many contemporary discussions of the problem of future contingents. It is, you might say, very much a contemporary concern among philosophers of religion.[17]

As you may have surmised, the notion that God has middle knowledge does not require one to take sides on the question of whether or not God exists in time. Some of its contemporary advocates clearly find problems with the suggestion that God is outside time. But Molina himself did not. On his account, God's middle knowledge is not to be thought of as something which God has at some stage in his life. He did not think of God as something the existence of which can be measured by time. As you may also have surmised, however, one's view of some approaches to the problem of future contingents is inevitably going to depend on how one thinks about God and time. If you think that there cannot be a timeless God, then you will have little sympathy for what Boethius maintains about God's knowledge. If you think that God must be timeless, then you will have little time for the arguments of authors such as Pike. In this sense, the topic of God's omniscience naturally leads to the topic of God's relation to time, which is the subject-matter of the section 'Eternal'.

15. William Lane Craig, 'Creation, Providence and Miracle', in Brian Davies (ed.), *Philosophy of Religion: A Guide to the Subject* (London, 1998).
16. G. E. M. Anscombe, *Collected Philosophical Papers*, vol. II (Oxford, 1981), p. vii.
17. The idea of divine middle knowledge has proved especially popular with some contemporary philosophers who like to draw heavily on the notion of possible worlds, to which I refer in the section in Part III on ontological arguments.

Chapter 43

Why ascribe knowledge to God?

Thomas Aquinas

On God's knowledge

Is there knowledge in God?

THE FIRST POINT: 1. It would seem that there is no knowledge in God. For knowledge is a disposition, which God cannot have since it is intermediate between potentiality and actuality. Therefore there is no knowledge in God.

2. Further, since 'science' is knowledge of conclusions, it is a kind of knowledge that is caused by something else, namely from knowing principles. But in God there is nothing caused. Therefore there is no knowledge in God.

3. Further, all knowledge is either universal or particular. But in God there is not universal and particular, as is clear from what we have said above. Therefore there is no knowledge in God.

ON THE OTHER HAND we have the words of St Paul, *O the depth of the riches of the wisdom and knowledge of God.*

REPLY: God has knowledge, and that in the most perfect way. This will become evident if we note that the difference between knowing and non-knowing subjects is that the latter have nothing but their own form, whereas a knowing subject is one whose nature it is to have in addition the form of something else; for the likeness of the thing known is in the knower. Thus, clearly, the nature of a non-knowing subject is more confined and limited by comparison with knowing subjects; the latter have a greater scope and extension; hence Aristotle says that *the soul is in a manner all things.* Now form is limited by matter: for which reason we said above that the freer forms are from matter the more they approach to a kind of infinity. It is clear, then, that a thing's freedom from matter is the reason why it is able to know; and the capacity to know is in proportion to the degree of freedom from matter. Thus plants are said to have no knowledge because of their materiality. But the senses are able to know because they are able to receive the likenesses of things without the matter; and intellect is still more capable of knowing because it is freer from matter and unmixed, as we read in Aristotle. Hence since God is immaterial in

Thomas Aquinas extracts from *Summa Theologiae* from Volume 4 of the Blackfriars edition of the *Summa Theologiae* edited by Thomas Gornall SJ (Eyre and Spottiswoode and McGraw Hill, 1964).

the highest degree, as is clear from what we have said above, it follows that he has knowledge in the highest degree.

HENCE: 1. The perfections which go out from God into creatures are in God in a higher way, as we have said above; therefore whenever a description taken from any perfection of a creature is attributed to God, we must eliminate from its meaning all that pertains to the imperfect way in which it is found in the creature. Hence knowledge in God is not a quality nor an habitual capacity, but substance and pure actuality.

2. Perfections found in creatures in a state of division and multiplicity exist in God without division and in unity, as we have said above. In man different objects of knowledge imply different kinds of knowledge: in knowing principles he is said to have 'understanding', in knowing conclusions 'science', in knowing the highest cause 'wisdom', in knowing human actions 'counsel' or 'prudence'. But all these things God knows by one simple knowledge, as will be shown below. Hence God's simple knowledge may be called by all these names, provided that in using any of them of God we exclude from their meaning all that implies imperfection and retain only what implies perfection. It is in this sense that we find the words, *With him is wisdom and strength; he has counsel and understanding.*

3. Knowledge depends on the capacity of the knower; for what is known is in the knower according to the measure of his capacity. And therefore since the divine nature exists in a manner higher than that by which creatures exist, divine knowledge is not measured by the manner of created knowledge, so as to be universal or particular, or to be habitual or potential, or to be similarly qualified.

Does God understand himself?

THE SECOND POINT: 1. It would seem that God does not understand himself. For it is stated in the *Book on Causes* that *every knower who knows his own essence is in the condition of returning on his essence by a complete returning.* But God does not go forth outside his essence, nor does he move in any way; and thus it is impossible for him to return to his essence. Therefore he does not understand himself

2. Further, to understand is a kind of passivity and movement, as Aristotle states; also knowledge is an assimilation to the thing known; and further, the thing as known is a perfecting of the knower. But nothing is moved or is passive or is perfected under its own agency; *nor is a thing its own likeness,* as Hilary says. Therefore God does not know himself.

3. Further, our likeness to God is chiefly in our intellect: it is in our mind that we are made in the image of God, as Augustine says. But our intellect does not understand itself except as it understands other things, as we read in Aristotle. Therefore God does not understand himself, except perhaps in understanding other things.

ON THE OTHER HAND we have the words: *The things that are of God no one knows but the Spirit of God.*

REPLY: God knows himself through himself. This will become evident if we note that whereas in activities which produce an external effect the object of the activity, its end or terminus, is something outside the agent, in activities which take place in the agent the object which is the end of the activity is in the agent itself: the object in the agent is the activity actually taking place. Thus we read in Aristotle that the sensible actualized is the sense in activity, and the intelligible actualized is the intellect in activity. We have actual sensation or actual knowledge because our intellect or our senses are informed by the species or likeness of the sensible or intelligible object. Sense or intellect is other than the sensible or the intelligible only to the extent that all of themselves are in a condition of potentiality.

Since, therefore, God has no potentiality but is pure actuality, in him intellect and what is known must be identical in every way: thus he is never without the knowledge-likeness, as our intellect is when it is only potentially knowing; and in him the knowledge-likeness is not different from the substance of the divine intellect, as in ourselves the knowledge-likeness is different from the substance of our intellect when we are actually knowing; but in him the knowledge-likeness itself is the divine intellect itself. And thus he knows himself through himself.

HENCE: 1. For a thing to 'return on its own essence' is simply for it to be self-subsistent. A form, when it completes the matter by giving it existence, in a certain sense spreads itself out over the matter; but in so far as it has existence in itself, it returns on itself. Therefore those powers of knowing which are not subsistent but are the acts of certain organs, do not know themselves, as is clear in the case of each of the senses. But powers of knowing which are subsistent do know themselves. Hence the statement in the book *On Causes* that *the knower who knows his own essence returns upon his own essence.* But to be self-subsistent belongs to God in the highest degree; so that if we use that manner of speaking, he 'returns to his own essence', and knows himself, in the highest degree.

2. When the act of understanding is called a kind of movement or passivity, the expressions 'to move' and 'to be passive' are used equivocally, as we read in Aristotle. For the act of knowing is not a movement in the sense of the actualization of something incompletely actualized, and passing from one subject to another; it is the act of something completely actualized, taking place within the agent itself. And similarly, for an intellect to be perfected by the intelligible, or assimilated to it, is proper to an intellect which is at some time in the state of potentiality; because by being by itself potential it differs from the intelligible, and is assimilated to it by the knowledge-species which is the likeness of the thing known; and the intellect as potentiality is completed by it as by actuality. But the divine intellect, which is in no way in the condition of potentiality, is not completed by the intelligible, nor assimilated to it, but is its own completeness and its own intelligible object.

3. The existence of a natural body is not attributed to prime matter, which of

itself is potential except in so far as it is brought to actuality by the form. Now, in ourselves the passive intellect has, in the order of knowing, the same condition as that of prime matter in the order of natural bodies; it is in potency to receive intelligible forms as prime matter is to receive natural forms. Hence our passive intellect can have an activity which it can know, only when it is completed by the knowledge-likeness of some thing. In that way it knows itself through a knowledge-likeness, as it does other things: for evidently in knowing the intelligible it knows its own act of knowing, and knows the power of knowing through the act of knowing. But God's condition is that of pure actuality both in the order of existence and in that of knowledge; and therefore he knows himself through himself.

Does God know things other than himself?

THE FIFTH POINT: 1. It would seem that God does not know things other than himself. For whatever is other than God is external to him. But Augustine says that *God does not behold anything external to himself.* Therefore he does not know things other than himself.

2. Further, the thing known is the perfection or completion of the knower. If, therefore, God knew things other than himself, something other would be the completion of God and of greater worth than he: which is impossible.

3. Further, the act of knowing is given its specific content by the intelligible object, just as every other act is by its object; hence the excellence of the act of knowing is in proportion to that of the object known. But God is his own act of knowing, as is clear from what has been said. If, then, God knew something other than himself, God himself would receive a specific characteristic from something different from himself: which is impossible. Therefore he does not know things other than himself.

ON THE OTHER HAND, we have the words: *All things are naked and open to his eyes.*

REPLY: God must know things other than himself. For evidently he knows himself perfectly: otherwise his being would not be perfect, since his being is his act of knowledge. But if something is known perfectly, its power must be known perfectly. Now the power of a thing cannot be known perfectly unless the objects to which the power extends are known. Hence, since the divine power extends to other things by being the first cause which produces all beings, as is clear from what has been said above, God must know things other than himself. And this will be still more evident if we add that the very being of God, the first efficient cause, is his act of knowing. Hence whatever effects pre-exist in God as in the first cause must be in his act of knowledge; and everything there must be in the condition of intelligibility; for all that is in another is therein according to the condition of that in which it is.

To understand in what way God knows things other than himself we must note that a thing can be known in two ways: in itself, or in another. A thing is known in itself when it is known through a likeness proper to the thing itself, co-terminous with the thing known, as when the eye sees a man through the likeness of a man. A thing is seen in another when it is seen through the likeness of what contains it, as when the part is seen in the whole through the knowledge-likeness of the whole, or when a man is seen in a mirror through the likeness of the mirror, and so of other ways in which one thing is known in another.

Thus we must say that God sees himself in himself, because he sees himself through his essence. Things other than himself he sees not in themselves but in himself, because his essence contains the likeness of things other than himself.

HENCE: 1. The saying of Augustine that God 'does not behold anything external to himself' is not to be understood as meaning that he does not behold anything that is external to himself, but as meaning that what is external to himself he beholds only in himself, as we have just said.

2. It is not the substance of the thing known that is the completion of the knower, but its likeness, by which it is in the intellect as the latter's form and completion: *the stone is not in the soul, but its likeness*, as we read in Aristotle. Things other than God are known by God because his essence contains their likeness, as we have just said. So it does not follow that something other than the essence of God is the completion of the divine intellect.

3. The act of knowledge is not specified by an object known in another, but by the primary object, in which other things are known. The specific content of an act of knowledge derives from its object just because the knowledge-form is the source of the activity of knowing; for every activity is specified by the form which is the source of the activity, as heating is by heat. Hence intellectual activity is specified by the knowledge-form which makes the intellect to be actually knowing; and this form is the knowledge-likeness of the principal object known; which likeness in God is no other than his essence, in which all the intelligible natures of things are included. Thus there is no question of the divine act of knowledge, or rather God himself, being specified by anything other than the divine essence.

Is God's knowledge discursive?

THE SEVENTH POINT: 1. It would seem that God's knowledge is discursive. For God's knowing is not a matter of being able to call up knowledge but of actually knowing. Now according to Aristotle the condition of being able to call up knowledge covers many objects at the same time, while actual knowledge covers only one object. Since, therefore, God knows many things—both himself and other things, as has been shown—it would seem that he does not know everything at once, but passes from one object to another.

2. Further, to know effect through cause is discursive knowledge. But God knows other things through himself, as effect through cause. Therefore his knowledge is discursive.

3. Further, God knows every creature more completely than we do. But we know created effects in created causes, and thus pass discursively from causes to effects. So it would seem that God does likewise.

ON THE OTHER HAND we have the words of Augustine that God *sees all things not piecemeal or one at a time, as though turning his gaze this way and that; he sees them all at once.*

REPLY: In God's knowledge there is no discursiveness. This is clear from the consideration that in our knowledge there is a twofold discursiveness: (i) that of mere succession, as when after actually knowing one thing we turn to another thing; (ii) the discursiveness that involves causality, as when we come to know conclusions through principles. The first of these cannot be in God. We know a number of things successively when taken one at a time, which we know all at once if we know them in a unity: thus we can know the parts in the whole, or see different things in a mirror. But God sees everything in one, that is, in himself, as we have concluded. Hence he sees everything at once and not successively. Similarly the second kind of discursiveness cannot be in God; firstly, because the second kind presupposes the first: for when we pass from principles to conclusions we are not considering both at the same time. Secondly, because this kind of discursiveness passes from known to unknown. So it is clear that when we know the first we are still ignorant of the second. Thus we do not know the second *in* the first, but *from* the first. And the process comes to an end when the second *is* seen in the first and the effects are found in their causes; at which point the discursive process ceases. Therefore, since God sees his effects in himself as in their cause, his knowledge is not discursive.

HENCE: 1. Although an act of knowledge in itself is one, it is possible all the same to know many things in one thing, as we have said.

2. God does not know through a cause in such a way that the cause is known first and the effects unknown; he knows the effects in the cause. His knowledge, then, is not discursive, as we have said.

3. God does see the effects of created causes in the causes, much better than we do; but not in such a way that knowledge of the effects is caused in him from knowledge of created causes, as happens in ourselves. Hence his knowledge is not discursive.

Is God's knowledge the cause of things?

THE EIGHTH POINT: 1. It would seem that God's knowledge is not the cause of things. For Origen says: *A thing will not happen in the future because God knows it will happen, but because it is going to happen therefore it is known by God before it does happen.*

2. Further, to posit the cause is to posit the effect. But God's knowledge is eternal.

If, then, God's knowledge is the cause of created things, it would seem that creatures exist from eternity.

3. Further, the knowable is prior to knowledge and is its measure, as we read in the *Metaphysics*, But that which is posterior and measured cannot be a cause. Therefore God's knowledge is not the cause of things.

ON THE OTHER HAND we have the words of Augustine: *God does not know all creatures, spiritual and corporeal, because they exist; but because he knows them therefore they exist.*

REPLY: God's knowledge is the cause of things. For God's knowledge stands to all created things as the artist's to his products. But the artist's knowledge is the cause of his products, because he works through his intellect; and so the form in his intellect must be the principle of his activity, as heat is of the activity of heating. But we may note that a natural form, merely as the form remaining in the thing to which it gives existence, does not indicate a principle of activity; it does so only in so far as it has an inclination towards producing an effect. And similarly an intelligible form does not indicate a principle of activity merely as it is in the knower, unless it is accompanied by an inclination towards producing an effect; this is supplied by the will. A knowledge-form is indifferent to opposite courses, since one and the same knowledge covers contraries; therefore the form would not produce a determined effect if it were not determined to one course by desire, as we read in the *Metaphysics*. Now it is clear that God causes things through his intellect, since his existence is his act of knowing. His knowledge, therefore, must be the cause of things when regarded in conjunction with his will. Hence God's knowledge as the cause of things has come to be called the 'knowledge of approbation'.

HENCE: 1. Origen in the passage quoted is taking knowledge in the sense in which it is not formally a cause except in conjunction with the will, as we have said. His saying that God foreknows certain things because they are going to happen, is to be understood of the causality of logical consequence, not of the causality which produces existence. For it follows logically that if certain things are going to happen, God foreknows them; but the things that are going to happen are not themselves the cause of God's knowledge.

2. Knowledge is the cause of things in accordance with the way things are in the knowledge. But it was no part of God's knowledge that things should exist from eternity. Hence, although God's knowledge is eternal, it does not follow that creatures exist from eternity.

3. Natural things mediate between God's knowledge and ours; for we get our knowledge from natural things, of which God is the cause through his knowledge. Hence, just as the knowable things of nature are prior to our knowledge, and are its measure, so God's knowledge is prior to natural things, and is their measure. In the same way a house mediates between the knowledge of the architect who made it

and that of one who gets his knowledge of the house from the house itself once it is made.

Has God knowledge of contingent future events?

THE THIRTEENTH POINT: 1. It would seem that God has not knowledge of contingent future events. For from a necessary cause there proceeds a necessary effect. But God's knowledge is the cause of the things he knows, as we have said above. Since, then, his knowledge is necessary, it follows that what he knows is necessary. Therefore God does not know contingent events.

2. Further, in a conditional proposition, if the antecedent is absolutely necessary the consequent is absolutely necessary; for the antecedent stands to the consequent as premises to conclusion. But from necessary premises, only a necessary conclusion can follow, as is proved in the *Posterior Analytics*. Now the following is a conditional that is true: *If God knew that this is going to happen it will happen*—because knowledge is only of what is true. And its antecedent is absolutely necessary: first, because it is eternal, and also because it is expressed as having taken place. Therefore the consequent is absolutely necessary. Therefore whatever is known by God is necessary; and thus God has no knowledge of contingent events.

3. Further, all that is known by God must necessarily be; because everything known even by us must necessarily be, and God's knowledge is more certain than ours. But no contingent future event must necessarily be. Therefore no contingent future event is known by God.

ON THE OTHER HAND we have the words: *He who has fashioned the hearts of every one of them*, namely of men, and *knows all their works*. Now the works of men are contingent, as being subject to free choice. Therefore God knows contingent future events.

REPLY: From what we have shown above, namely, that God knows all things, not only those which exist in actuality, but those which are in the potency of himself or of a creature, and some of these are contingent events in our future, it follows that God knows contingent future events.

To see this we must observe that a contingent event can be considered in two ways: (i) in itself, as already in the state of actuality. Thus regarded it is not future but present; and not indifferent to different effects, but determined to one effect. Hence in that condition it can be the object of certain and infallible knowledge, as a thing seen is to vision, as when I see Socrates sitting down. (ii) A contingent event can be considered as it is in its cause. Thus it is taken as going to happen, as a contingent event not yet determined to one effect; because a contingent cause is indifferent to opposite effects. In this latter condition a contingent event is not a subject of which there is any certain knowledge. Therefore anyone who knows a contingent effect in its cause only has no more than a conjectural knowledge of it. But God knows all contingent events not only as they are in their causes but also as each of them is in actual existence in itself.

Now although contingent events come into actual existence successively, God does not, as we do, know them in their actual existence successively, but all at once; because his knowledge is measured by eternity, as is also his existence; and eternity, which exists as a simultaneous whole, takes in the whole of time, as we have said above. Hence all that takes place in time is eternally present to God, not merely, as some hold, in the sense that he has the intelligible natures of things present in himself, but because he eternally surveys all things as they are in their presence to him.

It is clear, then, that contingent events are known infallibly by God because they are the objects of the divine gaze in their presence to him; while on the other hand they are *future* contingent events in relation to their proximate causes.

HENCE: 1. A first cause can be necessary and yet its effects contingent because of a contingent proximate cause; thus the sprouting of a plant is contingent because of a contingent proximate cause, although the first cause, the motion of the sun, is necessary. In the same way things known by God are contingent because of their contingent causes, though the first cause, God's knowledge, is necessary.

2. Some hold that the antecedent, 'God knew this contingent future event', is not necessary but contingent: because though it is past, yet it refers to the future.—That, however, does not take away its necessity; because what had in fact a reference to a future event must have had it, even though the future is sometimes not realized.

Others take the line that the antecedent in question is contingent because it is made up of necessary and contingent, as the proposition 'Socrates is a white man' is contingent.—But that does not help either; because in the proposition, 'God knew something to be a contingent future event', the word 'contingent' is merely part of the matter of the proposition and not a principal part; so that its contingence or necessity makes no difference to the necessity or contingence, truth or falsity, of the proposition. Thus e.g. it can be just as true that I said 'a man is an ass' as that I said 'Socrates is running' or 'God exists': and the same applies to the words 'necessary' and 'contingent'.

Therefore we must hold that the antecedent in question is absolutely necessary. Some however go on to say that it does not follow that the consequent is absolutely necessary, because the antecedent is only the remote cause of the consequent, which is contingent because of its proximate cause. But that will not do; because a conditional whose antecedent was a remote necessary cause, and its consequent a contingent effect, would be false: e.g. 'if the sun is moving, the grass will grow'.

Therefore we must take a different line and say that when the antecedent contains something that pertains to a mental act, the consequent is to be understood not as it exists in itself but as it exists in the soul: for the existence of a thing in itself is not the same as its existence in the soul. For example, if we say, 'Whatever the soul knows is immaterial', the word 'immaterial' is to be understood of the thing's existence in the mind, not of its existence in itself. Similarly if one said, 'If God knew something, it will happen', the consequent is to be understood in its condition as an object of the divine knowledge, namely, in the existence it has in its presence to him. And thus it has the same necessity as the antecedent has, *because that which is, when it is, must necessarily be*, as we read in *De Interpretatione*.

3. Things which are brought to the state of actuality in the time-series are known by us in time successively, but by God in eternity, which is above time. Hence future contingents cannot be certain to us, because we know them *as* future contingents; they can be certain only to God, whose act of knowledge is in eternity, above time. In the same way a man going along a road does not see those who come behind him; but the man who sees the whole road from a height sees all together those who are passing along the road. Therefore what is known by us must be necessary even in itself; because things in themselves contingent and future cannot be known by us. But the objects of God's knowledge must be necessary in their condition as such, as we have said; yet not absolutely necessary considered as existing in their own causes.

Accordingly the proposition, 'All that God knows must necessarily be', is usually distinguished: it can apply either to the thing or to the statement. Understood of the thing, the proposition is taken independently of the fact of God's knowing, and false, giving the sense, 'Every thing that God knows is a necessary thing'. Or it can be understood of the statement, and thus it is taken in conjunction with the fact of God's knowing, and true, giving the sense, 'The statement, *a thing known by God is*, is necessary'.

Some however object that this distinction is in place only in the case of forms that can be separated from their subject, as in 'it is possible for white to be black', which is false of the words but true of a thing: a white thing *can* be black, but the words 'white is black' can never be true. They say moreover that in the case of forms that cannot be separated from the subject, the distinction can have no place, as e.g. in 'it is possible for a black crow to be white', which is false in both senses. Now, 'to be known by God' is inseparable from the thing, because what is known by God cannot be not known.—This objection would be relevant if the expression 'thing known' referred merely to a disposition belonging to a subject. However since it refers to the knower's act of knowing, the thing itself that is known, even if it is always known, can be characterized in its own independent existence in a way it cannot be characterized in its condition as part of the act of knowing; thus materiality is attributed to the stone in its own physical condition but not in its intelligible condition in the mind.

Chapter 44

Omniscience and human freedom: a classical discussion

Boethius

III

THEN, I said: 'See, I am again confused, with a still more difficult doubt.'
'What is that?' she asked. 'Tell me, for I already guess what troubles you.'

'It seems,' I said, 'much too conflicting and contradictory that God foreknows all things *and* that there is any free will. For if God foresees all and cannot in any way be mistaken, then that must necessarily happen which in his providence he foresees will be. And therefore if he foreknows from all eternity not only the deeds of men but even their plans and desires, there will be no free will; for it will be impossible for there to be any deed at all or any desire whatever except that which divine providence, which cannot be mistaken, perceives beforehand. For if they can be turned aside into a different way from that foreseen, then there will no longer be firm foreknowledge of the future, but rather uncertain opinion, which I judge impious to believe of God.

For neither do I agree with that argument according to which some believe that they can solve this knotty question. For they say that a thing is not going to happen because providence has foreseen that it will be, but rather to the contrary, that since something is going to be, it cannot be hidden from divine providence, and in this way the necessity slips over to the opposite side. For, they say, it is not necessary that those things happen which are foreseen, but it is necessary that those things that will happen are foreseen; as if indeed our work were to discover which is the cause of which, foreknowledge of future things' necessity, or future things' necessity of providence, and as if we were not striving to show this, that whatever the state of the ordering of causes, the outcome of things foreknown is necessary, even if that foreknowledge were not to seem to confer on future things the necessity of occurring.

For indeed, if anyone sit, then the opinion that thinks that he sits must be true; and conversely also, if the opinion about any man be true, that he sits, then he must be sitting. There is thus a necessity in both cases: in the latter, he must be sitting, but in the former, the opinion must be true. But a man does not sit because the opinion

Boethius edited extract from 'The Consolation of Philosophy' from *The Consolation of Philosophy* translated by S. J. Tester (Loeb Classical Library, Harvard University Press, 1973).

about him is true, but rather that opinion is true because that someone is sitting happened first. So that although the cause of truth proceeds from the one part, yet there is in both a common necessity.

Obviously the same reasoning holds with regard to providence and future events: for even if the reason they are foreseen is that they *are* future events, yet they do not happen simply because they are foreseen; and yet nevertheless things either must be foreseen by God because they are coming or happen because they are foreseen, and that alone is enough to destroy the freedom of the will. But now how upside-down it is that it should be said that the cause of eternal foreknowledge is the occurrence of temporal things! But what else is it, to think that God foresees future things because they are going to happen, than to think that those things, once they have happened, are the cause of his highest providence? Furthermore, just as when I know that something is, then that necessarily is so, so when I know something will be, then that necessarily will be so; and so it happens that the occurrence of a thing foreknown cannot be avoided. Lastly, if a man think a thing to be otherwise than it is, that is not only not knowledge, but it is a mistaken opinion very different indeed from the truth of knowledge. And therefore if something is future in such a way that its occurrence is not certain or necessary, how will it be possible for it to be foreknown that it will occur? For just as real knowledge is unmixed with falsity, so that which is grasped by knowledge cannot be otherwise than as it is grasped. For the real reason why knowledge lacks any falsehood is that every single thing must necessarily be just as knowledge comprehends it to be.

Well then, how does God foreknow that these uncertain things shall be? For if he thinks those things will inevitably occur which it is yet possible may not occur, he is mistaken, which it is not only impious to think but still more impious to say aloud. But if he sees that those future things are just as indeed they are, so that he knows that they can equally either happen or not happen, what sort of foreknowledge is this, that grasps nothing certain, nothing stable? And in what will divine providence be better than the opinions of men, if it judges in the way men do those things to be uncertain the occurrence of which is uncertain? But if in him, the most certain fount of all things, there can be nothing uncertain, then the occurrence is certain of those things which he firmly foreknows will be.

And therefore there is no freedom in human intentions or actions, which the divine mind, foreseeing all without mistaken error binds and constrains to one actual occurrence. This once accepted, it is clear what a great collapse of human affairs follows! For it is vain to propose for good and evil men rewards or punishments which no free and voluntary act of their minds has deserved. And that very thing will seem most unjust of all which now is judged most just, that either the wicked are punished or the good rewarded, since they have not been brought by their own wills but driven by the certain necessity of what shall be to one or other end. And therefore there would be no vices nor virtues, but rather a mixed-up and indistinguishable confusion of all deserts, and—than which nothing more wicked can be conceived!—since the whole ordering of things proceeds from providence and nothing is really possible to human intentions, it follows that even our vices are to be referred to the author of all things good. And therefore there is no sense in hoping for anything or in praying that anything may be averted; for what even should any man hope for or pray to be averted when an inflexible course links all that can be desired?'

IV

Then she said: 'That is the old complaint about providence, one powerfully dealt with by Cicero when he was classifying kinds of divination, and a matter for a very long time and deeply investigated by yourself; but it has so far been by no means sufficiently carefully or steadfastly developed by any of you. The cause of this obscurity is that the movement of human reasoning cannot approach the simplicity of divine foreknowledge; if that could by any means be conceived, no doubt whatever will remain. And I shall try to make clear and explain this only when I have first considered those things by which you are now troubled. For I ask, why do you think that explanation of those solving the problem less than effectual which, since it considers that foreknowledge is not the cause of any necessity for future events, thinks the freedom of the will not at all restricted by foreknowledge? For you, surely, do not produce proof of the necessity of future things other than from the fact that those things that are foreknown cannot not happen? Then if foreknowledge imposes no necessity on future things, which you did indeed admit a little while ago, what is the reason why the outcome of those things dependent on the will should be forced to end in a certain result?

Now for the sake of argument, that you may see what follows, let us suppose that there is no foreknowledge. In such a case, those things that depend upon the will would not be forced into any necessity, would they?'

'Not at all.'

'Again, let us suppose that there is foreknowledge, but that it enjoins no necessity on things; there will remain, I think, that same freedom of the will, whole and absolute. But foreknowledge, you will say, although it does not constitute a necessity for future things, of their happening, yet it is a sign that they will necessarily come to be. In this way, then, even had there been no foreknowledge, it would be agreed that the outcome of future things is necessary; for every sign only points to what is, but does not cause to be what it signifies. Wherefore it must first be demonstrated that nothing happens except of necessity, that foreknowledge may be seen to be the sign of that necessity; otherwise, if there is no necessity, nor then will foreknowledge be able to be a sign for that which does not exist. But it is agreed that a proof supported by firm reasoning must be drawn not from signs nor from arguments fetched from outside the subject, but from relevant and necessary causes.

But how could it be that those things should not happen which are foreseen to be future? Just as if we were to believe that those things which providence foreknows will happen were not going to happen, and did not rather think that although they do happen, yet they have of their nature no necessity that they must happen. Which you may easily gather from this for many things, while they are happening, we look at set out before our eyes, as for example those things which charioteers are watched doing in guiding and turning their teams, and other things of a similar kind. Now surely no necessity compels any of these things to happen as it does?'

'Not at all; for the exercise of skill would be useless if all things moved under compulsion.'

'Therefore things which, while they are happening, lack any necessity of being so, these same things, before they happen, are future without any necessity. And therefore there are some things going to happen the occurrence of which is free from all necessity. For I do not think that any man would say this, that those things which are happening now were not "going to happen" before they happened; therefore of these, even foreknown, the occurrence is free. For just as knowledge of present things introduces no necessity into those things which are happening, so the foreknowledge of future things introduces none into those things which are to come. But this, you say, is exactly what is in doubt, whether there can be any foreknowledge of those things which do not have necessary outcomes. For these two (foreknowledge and not-necessary outcomes) seem to be incompatible, and you think that if things are foreseen, necessity is a consequence, and if there is no necessity, they cannot be foreknown at all, and nothing can be grasped by knowledge except what is certain. But if those things which are of uncertain outcome are foreseen as if they were certain, that is really the obscurity of opinion, not the truth of knowledge; for you believe thinking things to be other than as they are to be alien to the integrity of knowledge. The cause of this mistake is that each thinks that all that he knows is known simply by the power and nature of those things that are known. Which is altogether otherwise for everything which is known is grasped not according to its own power but rather according to the capability of those who know it. For—that this may become clear by a brief example—the same roundness of a body sight recognizes in one way and touch in another; the former sense remaining at a distance looks at the whole at once by the light of its emitted rays, while the latter, being united and conjoined to the round body, going right round its circuit, grasps the roundness by parts.

Man himself also, sense, imagination, reason and intelligence look at in different ways. For sense examines the shape set in the underlying matter, imagination the shape alone without the matter while reason surpasses this too, and examines with a universal consideration the specific form itself, which is present in single individuals. But the eye of intelligence is set higher still; for passing beyond the process of going round the one whole, it looks with the pure sight of the mind at the simple form itself. And herein the greatest consideration is to be given to this: for the higher power of comprehension embraces the lower, while the lower in no way rises to the higher. For neither can sense attain to anything outside matter, nor does imagination look at universal specific forms, nor reason grasp the simple Form: but the intelligence, as it were looking down from above, by conceiving the Form distinguishes all the things subject to that Form, but only because of the way it comprehends the Form itself, which could not be known to anything else. For it knows the reason's universal, and the imagination's shape, and what is materially sensible, but without using reason, imagination or the senses, but by the one stroke of the mind, Formally, so to speak, looking forth on all these things together. Reason, too, when it regards some universal, without using imagination or the senses grasps the imaginable and sensible aspects. For reason it is which defines the universal it has conceived thus: man is a rational, bipedal animal. And although this is a universal idea, at the same time no-one is ignorant that it is an imaginable and sensible thing which the reason is considering, not by means of imagination or sense, but in its rational conceiving. Imagination also, although it has taken its beginning of seeing and forming shapes from the senses, yet with sense removed surveys all sensible things not by a sensible manner of examining them but by an imaginative one. Do you therefore see that in knowing, all these use their own capability rather than that of those things which are known? Nor is this wrong for since every judgement is the act of one judging, it must be that each performs his task not from some other's power but from his own.

V

Now if in perceiving corporeal things, although qualities presented from without affect the apparatus of the senses, and the emotive movement of the body precedes the activity of the active mind, a movement which calls forth upon itself the action of the mind and stirs up the forms previously lying at rest within; if, I say, in perceiving corporeal things, the mind is not marked by that movement, but of its own power judges that movement, which is a quality of the body, then how much the more do those things which are quite separate from all bodily affections, in the act of judgement not follow things presented from without, but set in motion the action of the mind to which they belong! And so on this principle many kinds of knowledge belong to different and diverse substances. For sense alone without any other kind of knowledge belongs to living things that do not move, such as are sea shells and such other things as feed clinging to rocks; but imagination belongs to beasts that move, which seem already to have in them some disposition to flee or to seek out things. But reason belongs only to human kind, as intelligence only to the divine. So it is that that kind of knowledge is better than the rest which of its own nature knows not only its own object but the subjects of other kinds of knowledge also.

What, then, if sense and imagination gainsay reasoning, saying that that universal which reason thinks she perceives, is nothing at all? For that which is the object of sense and imagination cannot, they say, be universal; therefore either the judgement of reason is true, and there is nothing sensible, or, since they know that many things are objects of the senses and imagination, reason's concept is empty, since she thinks of that which is sensible and singular as if it were some kind of universal. Further, if reason rejoins to this that she does indeed see both the object of sense and the object of imagination under the aspect of their universality, but that they cannot aspire to the knowledge of universality since their knowledge cannot go beyond corporeal shapes, but we must give credence rather to the more firm, and perfect judgement concerning the knowledge of things: in this sort of argument, then, should we not, we who have in us the power of reasoning as well as those of imagination and sense; should we not rather judge in favour of reason's case? It is similar when human reason thinks that the divine intelligence does not see future things except in the same manner as she herself knows them. For this is how you argue: if any things seem not to have certain and necessary occurrences, those things cannot be certainly foreknown as going to occur. Therefore of these things there is no foreknowledge, and if we think there is foreknowledge in these matters, there will be nothing which does not happen from necessity. Now if just as we have a share in reason, so we could possess the judgement belonging to the divine mind, then just as we have judged that imagination and sense ought to give way to reason, so we should think it most just that human reason should submit to the divine mind. Wherefore let us be raised up, if we can, to the height of that highest intelligence; for there reason will see that which she cannot look at in herself, and that is, in what way even those things which have no certain occurrence a certain and definite foreknowledge yet does see, neither is that opinion, but rather the simplicity, shut in by no bounds, of the highest knowledge.

VI

Since, then, as was shown a little while ago, everything which is known is known not according to its own nature but according to the nature of those comprehending it, let us now examine, so far as is allowable, what is the nature of the divine substance, so that we may be able to recognize what kind of knowledge his is. Now that God is eternal is the common judgement of all who live by reason. Therefore let us consider, what is eternity; for this makes plain to us both the divine nature and the divine knowledge. Eternity, then, is the whole, simultaneous and perfect possession of boundless life, which becomes clearer by comparison with temporal things. For whatever lives in time proceeds in the present from the past into the future, and there is nothing established in time which can embrace the whole space of its life equally, but tomorrow surely it does not yet grasp, while yesterday it has already lost. And in this day to day life you live no more than in that moving and transitory moment. Therefore whatever endures the condition of time, although, as Aristotle thought concerning the world, it neither began ever to be nor ceases to be, and although its life is drawn out with the infinity of time, yet it is not yet such that it may rightly be believed to be eternal. For it does not simultaneously comprehend and embrace the whole space of its life, though it be infinite, but it possesses the future not yet, the past no longer. Whatever therefore comprehends and possesses at once the whole fullness of boundless life, and is such that neither is anything future lacking from it, nor has anything past flowed away, that is rightly held to be eternal, and that must necessarily both always be present to itself, possessing itself in the present, and hold as present the infinity of moving time.

And therefore those are not right who, when they hear that Plato thought this world neither had a beginning in time nor would have an end, think that in this way the created world is made co-eternal with the Creator. For it is one thing to be drawn out through a life without bounds, which is what Plato attributes to the world, but it is a different thing to have embraced at once the whole presence of boundless life, which it is clear is the property of the divine mind. Nor should God seem to be more ancient than created things by some amount of time, but rather by his own simplicity of nature. For this present nature of unmoving life that infinite movement of temporal things imitates, and since it cannot fully represent and equal it, it fails from immobility into motion, it shrinks from the simplicity of that present into the infinite quantity of the future and the past and, since it cannot possess at once the whole fullness of its life, in this very respect, that it in some way never ceases to be, it seems to emulate to some degree which it cannot fully express, by binding itself to the sort of present of this brief and fleeting moment, a present which since it wears a kind of likeness of that permanent present, grants to what-soever things it touches that they should seem to be. But since it could not be permanent, it seized on the infinite journeying of time, and in that way became such that it should continue by going on a life the fullness of which it could not embrace by being permanent. And so if we should wish to give things names befitting them, then following Plato we should say that God indeed is eternal, but that the world is perpetual.

Since then every judgement comprehends those things subject to it according to its own nature, and God has an always eternal and present nature, then his know-ledge too, surpassing all movement of time, is permanent in the simplicity of his present, and embracing all the infinite spaces of the future and the past, considers them in his simple act of knowledge as though they were now going on. So if you should wish to consider his foreknowledge, by which he discerns all things, you will more rightly judge it to be not foreknowledge as it were of the future but knowledge of a never-passing instant. And therefore it is called not prevision (*praevidentia*) but providence (*providentia*), because set far from the lowest of things it looks forward on all things as though from the highest peak of the world. Why then do you require those things to be made necessary which are scanned by the light of God's sight, when not even men make necessary those things they see? After all, your looking at them does not confer any necessity on those things you presently see, does it?'

'Not at all.'

'But if the comparison of the divine and the human present is a proper one, just as you see certain things in this your temporal present, so he perceives all things in his eternal one. And therefore this divine foreknowledge does not alter the proper nature of things, but sees them present to him just such as in time they will at some future point come to be. Nor does he confuse the ways things are to be judged, but with one glance of his mind distinguishes both those things necessarily coming to be and those not necessarily coming to be, just as you, when you see at one and the same time that a man is walking on the ground and that the sun is rising in the sky, though the two things are seen simultaneously, yet you distinguish them, and judge the first to be voluntary, the second necessary. So then the divine perception looking down on all things does not disturb at all the quality of things that are present indeed to him but future with reference to imposed conditions of time. So it is that it is not opinion but a knowledge grounded rather upon truth, when he knows that something is going to happen, something which he is also aware lacks all necessity of happening

If at this point you were to say that what God sees is going to occur cannot not occur, and that what cannot not occur happens from necessity, and so bind me to this word "necessity," I will admit that this is a matter indeed of the firmest truth, but one which scarcely anyone except a theologian could tackle. For I shall say in answer that the same future event, when it is related to divine knowledge, is necessary, but when it is considered in its own nature it seems to be utterly and absolutely free. For there are really two necessities, the one simple, as that it is necessary that all men are mortal; the other conditional, as for example, if you know that someone is walking, it is necessary that he is walking. Whatever anyone knows cannot be otherwise than as it is known, but this conditional necessity by no means carries with it that other simple kind. For this sort of necessity is not caused by a thing's proper nature but by the addition of the condition; for no necessity forces him to go who walks of his own will, even though it is necessary that he is going at the time when he is walking. Now in the same way, if providence sees anything as present, that must necessarily be, even if it possesses no necessity of its nature. But God beholds those future events which happen because of the freedom of the will, as present; they therefore, related to the divine perception, become necessary through the condition of the divine knowledge, but considered in themselves do not lose the absolute freedom of their nature. Therefore all those things which God foreknows will come to be, will without doubt come to be, but certain of them proceed from free will, and although they do come to be, yet in happening they do not lose their proper nature, according to which, before they happened, they might also not have happened. What then does it matter that they are not necessary, since on account of the condition of the divine knowledge it will turn out in all respects like necessity? Surely as much as those things I put before you a moment ago, the rising sun and the walking man while these things are happening, they cannot not happen, but of the two one, even before it happened, was bound to happen, while the other was not. So also, those things God possesses as present, beyond doubt will happen, but of them the one kind is consequent upon the necessity of things, the other upon the power of those doing them. So therefore we were not wrong in saying that these, if related to the divine knowledge, are necessary, if considered in themselves, are free from the bonds of necessity, just as everything which lies open to the senses, if you relate it to the reason, is universal, if you look at it by itself, is singular.

But if, you will say, it lies in my power to change my intention, I shall make nonsense of providence, since what providence foreknows, I shall perhaps have changed. I shall reply that you can indeed alter your intention, but since the truth of providence sees in its present both that you can do so, and whether you will do so and in what direction you will change, you cannot avoid the divine prescience, just as you could not escape the sight of an eye that was present, even though of your own free will you changed to different courses of action. What then will you say? Will the divine knowledge be changed by my disposition, so that, since I want to do this at one time and that at another, it too alternates from this kind of knowledge to that? Not at all. For the divine perception runs ahead over every future event and turns it back and recalls it to the present of its own knowledge, and does not alternate, as you suggest, foreknowing now this, now that, but itself remaining still anticipates and embraces your changes at one stroke. And God possesses this present instant of comprehension and sight of all things not from the issuing of future events but from his own simplicity. In this way that too is resolved which you suggested a little while ago, that it is not right that our future actions should be said to provide the cause of the knowledge of God. For the nature of his knowledge as we have described it, embracing all things in a present act of knowing, establishes a measure for everything, but owes nothing to later events. These things being so, the freedom of the will remains to mortals, inviolate, nor are laws proposing rewards and punishments for wills free from all necessity unjust. There remains also as an observer from on high foreknowing all things, God, and the always present eternity of his sight runs along with the future quality of our actions dispensing rewards for the good and punishments for the wicked. Nor vainly are our hopes placed in God, nor our prayers, which when they are right cannot be ineffectual. Turn away then from vices, cultivate virtues, lift up your mind to righteous hopes, offer up humble prayers to heaven. A great necessity is solemnly ordained for you if you do not want to deceive yourselves, to do good, when you act before the eyes of a judge who sees all things.'

Chapter 45

Problems for the notion of divine omniscience

Nelson Pike

IN Book V, sec. 3 of his *Consolatio Philosophiae*, Boethius entertained (though he later rejected) the claim that if God is omniscient, no human action is voluntary. This claim seems intuitively false. Surely, given only a doctrine describing God's *knowledge*, nothing about the voluntary status of human actions will follow. Perhaps such a conclusion would follow from a doctrine of divine omnipotence or divine providence, but what connection could there be between the claim that God is *omniscient* and the claim that human actions are determined? Yet Boethius thought he saw a problem here. He thought that if one collected together just the right assumptions and principles regarding God's knowledge, one could derive the conclusion that if God exists, no human action is voluntary. Of course, Boethius did not think that all the assumptions and principles required to reach this conclusion are true (quite the contrary), but he thought it important to draw attention to them nonetheless. If a theologian is to construct a doctrine of God's knowledge which does not commit him to determinism, he must first understand that there is a way of thinking about God's knowledge which would so commit him.

In this paper, I shall argue that although his claim has a sharp counterintuitive ring, Boethius was right in thinking that there is a selection from among the various doctrines and principles clustering about the notions of knowledge, omniscience, and God which, when brought together, demand the conclusion that if God exists, no human action is voluntary. Boethius, I think, did not succeed in making explicit all of the ingredients in the problem. His suspicions were sound, but his discussion was incomplete. His argument needs to be developed. This is the task I shall undertake in the pages to follow. I should like to make clear at the outset that my purpose in rearguing this thesis is not to show that determinism is true, nor to show that God does not exist, nor to show that either determinism is true or God does not exist. Following Boethius, I shall not claim that the items needed to generate the problem are either philosophically or theologically adequate. I want to concentrate attention on the implications of a certain set of assumptions. Whether the assumptions are themselves acceptable is a question I shall not consider.

Nelson Pike edited extract from 'Divine Omniscience and Voluntary Action' from *The Philosophical Review*, vol. 74 (1965), reprinted by permission of the author.

I

A. Many philosophers have held that if a statement of the form 'A knows X' is true, then 'A believes X' is true and 'X' is true. As a first assumption, I shall take this partial analysis of 'A knows X' to be correct. And I shall suppose that since this analysis holds for all knowledge claims, it will hold when speaking of God's knowledge. 'God knows X' entails 'God believes X' and ' "X" is true.'

Secondly, Boethius said that with respect to the matter of knowledge, God 'cannot in anything be mistaken.'[1] I shall understand this doctrine as follows. Omniscient beings hold no false beliefs. Part of what is meant when we say that a person is omniscient is that the person in question believes nothing that is false. But, further, it is part of the 'essence' of God to be omniscient. This is to say that any person who is not omniscient could not be the person we usually mean to be referring to when using the name 'God.' To put this last point a little differently: if the person we usually mean to be referring to when using the name 'God' were suddenly to lose the quality of omniscience (suppose, for example, He came to believe something false), the resulting person would no longer be God. Although we might call this second person 'God' (I might call my cat 'God'), the absence of the quality of omniscience would be sufficient to guarantee that the person referred to was not the same as the person formerly called by that name. From this last doctrine it follows that the statement 'If a given person is God, that person is omniscient' is an a priori truth. From this we may conclude that the statement 'If a given person is God, that person holds no false beliefs' is also an a priori truth. It would be conceptually impossible for God to hold a false belief. ' "X" is true' follows from 'God believes X.' These are all ways of expressing the same principle—the principle expressed by Boethius in the formula 'God cannot in anything be mistaken.'

A second principle usually associated with the notion of divine omniscience has to do with the scope or range of God's intellectual gaze. To say that a being is omniscient is to say that he knows everything. 'Everything' in this statement is usually taken to cover future, as well as present and past, events and circumstances. In fact, God is usually said to have had foreknowledge of everything that has ever happened. With respect to anything that was, is, or will be the case, God knew, *from eternity*, that it would be the case.

The doctrine of God's knowing everything from eternity is very obscure. One particularly difficult question concerning this doctrine is whether it entails that with respect to everything that was, is, or will be the case, God knew *in advance* that it would be the case. In some traditional theological texts, we are told that God is *eternal* in the sense that He exists 'outside of time,' that is, in the sense that He bears no temporal relations to the events or circumstances of the natural world.[2] In a

---

1. Boethius, *Consolatio Philosophiae*, Bk. V, sec. 3, par. 6.
2. This position is particularly well formulated in St Anselm's *Proslogium*, ch. xix, and *Monologium*, chs. xxi–xxii; and in Frederich Schleiermacher's *The Christian Faith*, Pt. I, sec. 2, par. 51. It is also explicit in Boethius, *Consolatio*, secs. 4–6, and in St Thomas Aquinas's *Summa Theologicae*, Pt. I q. 10.

theology of this sort, God could not be said to have known that a given natural event was going to happen before it happened. If God knew that a given natural event was going to occur *before* it occurred, at least one of God's cognitions would then have occurred before some natural event. This, surely would violate the idea that God bears no temporal relations to natural events.[3] On the other hand, in a considerable number of theological sources, we are told that God *has always* existed—that He existed long *before* the occurrence of any natural event. In a theology of this sort, to say that God is eternal is not to say that God exists 'outside of time' (bears no temporal relations to natural events); it is to say, instead, God has existed (and will continue to exist) at each moment.[4] The doctrine of omniscience which goes with this second understanding of the notion of eternity is one in which it is affirmed that God *has always* known what was going to happen in the natural world. John Calvin wrote as follows:

When we attribute foreknowledge to God, we mean that all things have ever been and perpetually remain before, his eyes, so that to his knowledge nothing is future or past, but all things are present; and present in such manner, that he does not merely conceive of them from ideas formed in his mind, as things remembered by us appear to our minds, but really he holds and sees them as if (*tanquam*) actually placed before him.[5]

All things are 'present' to God in the sense that He 'sees' them as if (*tanquam*) they were actually before Him. Further, with respect to any given natural event, not only is that event 'present' to God in the sense indicated, it has *ever been and has perpetually remained* 'present' to Him in that sense. This latter is the point of special interest. Whatever one thinks of the idea that God 'sees' things as if 'actually placed before him,' Calvin would appear to be committed to the idea that God has *always known* what was going to happen in the natural world. Choose an event (E) and a time (t_2) at which E occurred. For any time (t_1) prior to t_2 (say, five thousand, six hundred, or eighty years prior to t_2), God knew at t_1 that E would occur at t_2. It will follow from this doctrine, of course, that with respect to any human action, God knew well in advance of its performance that the action would be performed. Calvin says, 'when God created man, He foresaw what would happen concerning him.' He adds, 'little more than five thousand years have elapsed since the creation of the world.'[6] Calvin seems to have thought that God foresaw the outcome of every human action well over five thousand years ago.

In the discussion to follow, I shall work only with this second interpretation of God's knowing everything *from eternity*. I shall assume that if a person is omnis-

---

3. This point is explicit in Boethius, *Consolatio*, secs. 4–6.
4. This position is particularly well expressed in William Paley's *Natural Theology*, ch. xxiv. It is also involved in John Calvin's discussion of predestination, *Institutes of the Christian Religion*, Bk. III, ch. xxi; and in some formulations of the first cause argument for the existence of God, e.g., John Locke's *An Essay Concerning Human Understanding*, Bk. IV, ch. x.
5. Calvin, *Institutes of the Christian Religion*, Bk. III, ch. xxi; this passage trans. by John Allen (Philadelphia, 1813), II, p. 145.
6. Ibid., p. 144.

cient, that person has always known what was going to happen in the natural world—and, in particular, has always known what human actions were going to be performed. Thus, as above, assuming that the attribute of omniscience is part of the 'essence' of God, the statement 'For any natural event (including human actions), if a given person is God, that person would always have known that that event was going to occur at the time it occurred' must be treated as an a priori truth. This is just another way of stating a point admirably put by St Augustine when he said: 'For to confess that God exists and at the same time to deny that He has fore-knowledge of future things is the most manifest folly . . . One who is not prescient of all future things is not God.'[7]

B. Last Saturday afternoon, Jones mowed his lawn. Assuming that God exists and is (essentially) omniscient in the sense outlined above, it follows that (let us say) eighty years prior to last Saturday afternoon, God knew (and thus believed) that Jones would mow his lawn at that time. But from this it follows, I think, that at the time of action (last Saturday afternoon) Jones was not *able*—that is, it was not *within Jones's power*—to refrain from mowing his lawn.[8] If at the time of action, Jones had been able to refrain from mowing his lawn, then (the most obvious conclusion would seem to be) at the time of action, Jones was able to do something which would have brought it about that God held a false belief eighty years earlier. But God cannot in anything be mistaken. It is not possible that some belief of His was false. Thus, last Saturday afternoon, Jones was not able to do something which would have brought it about that God held a false belief eighty years ago. To suppose that it was would be to suppose that, at the time of action, Jones was able to do something having a conceptually incoherent description, namely something that would have brought it about that one of God's beliefs was false. Hence, given that God believed eighty years ago that Jones would mow his lawn on Saturday, if we are to assign Jones the power on Saturday to refrain from mowing his lawn, this power must not be described as the power to do something that would have rendered one of God's beliefs false. How then should we describe it vis-à-vis God and His belief? So far as I can see, there are only two other alternatives. First, we might try describing it as the power to do something that would have brought it about that God

---

7. Augustine, *City of God*, Bk. V, sec. 9.
8. The notion of someone being *able* to do something and the notion of something being *within one's power* are essentially the same. Traditional formulations of the problem of divine foreknowledge (e.g., those of Boethius and Augustine) made use of the notion of what is (and what is not) *within one's power*. But the problem is the same when framed in terms of what one is (and one is not) *able* to do. Thus, I shall treat the statements 'Jones was able to do X,' 'Jones had the ability to do X,' and 'It was within Jones's power to do X' as equivalent. Richard Taylor, in 'I Can,' *The Philosophical Review*, 69 (1960): 78–89, has argued that the notion of ability or power involved in these last three statements is incapable of philosophical analysis. Be this as it may, I shall not here attempt such an analysis. In what follows I shall, however, be careful to affirm only those statements about what is (or is not) within one's power that would have to be preserved on any analysis of this notion having even the most distant claim to adequacy.

believed otherwise than He did eighty years ago; or, secondly, we might try describing it as the power to do something that would have brought it about that God (Who, by hypothesis, existed eighty years earlier) did not exist eighty years earlier—that is, as the power to do something that would have brought it about that any person who believed eighty years ago that Jones would mow his lawn on Saturday (one of whom was, by hypothesis, God) held a false belief, and thus was not God. But again, neither of these latter can be accepted. Last Saturday afternoon, Jones was not able to do something that would have brought it about that God believed otherwise than He did eighty years ago. Even if we suppose (as was suggested by Calvin) that eighty years ago God knew Jones would mow his lawn on Saturday in the sense that He 'saw' Jones mowing his lawn as if this action were occurring before Him, the fact remains that God knew (and thus believed) eighty years prior to Saturday that Jones would mow his lawn. And if God held such a belief eighty years prior to Saturday, Jones did not have the power on Saturday to do something that would have made it the case that God did not hold this belief eighty years earlier. No action performed at a given time can alter the fact that a given person held a certain belief at a time prior to the time in question. This last seems to be an a priori truth. For similar reasons, the last of the above alternatives must also be rejected. On the assumption that God existed eighty years prior to Saturday, Jones on Saturday was not able to do something that would have brought it about that God did not exist eighty years prior to that time. No action performed at a given time can alter the fact that a certain person existed at a time prior to the time in question. This, too, seems to me to be an a priori truth. But if these observations are correct, then, given that Jones mowed his lawn on Saturday, and given that God exists and is (essentially) omniscient, it seems to follow that at the time of action, Jones did not have the power to refrain from mowing his lawn. The upshot of these reflections would appear to be that Jones's mowing his lawn last Saturday cannot be counted as a voluntary action. Although I do not have an analysis of what it is for an action to be *voluntary*, it seems to me that a situation in which it would be wrong to assign Jones the *ability* or *power* to do *other* than he did would be a situation in which it would also be wrong to speak of his action as voluntary. As a general remark, if God exists and is (essentially) omniscient in the sense specified above, no human action is voluntary.[9]

As the argument just presented is somewhat complex, perhaps the following schematic representation of it will be of some use.

---

9. In Bk. II, ch. xxi, secs. 8–11 of *An Essay*, Locke says that an agent is not free with respect to a given action (i.e., that an action is done 'under necessity') when it is not within the agent's power to do otherwise. Locke allows a special kind of case, however, in which an action may be *voluntary* though done under necessity. If a man chooses to do something without knowing that it is not within his power to do otherwise (e.g., if a man chooses to stay in a room without knowing that the room is locked), his action may be voluntary though he is not free to forbear it. If Locke is right in this (and I shall not argue the point one way or the other), replace 'voluntary' with (let us say) 'free' in the above paragraph and throughout the remainder of this paper.

1. 'God existed at t_1' entails 'If Jones did X at t_2, God believed at t_1 that Jones would do X at t_2.

2. 'God believes X' entails '"X" is true.'

3. It is not within one's power at a given time to do something having a description that is logically contradictory.

4. It is not within one's power at a given time to do something that would bring it about that someone who held a certain belief at a time prior to the time in question did not hold that belief at the time prior to the time in question.

5. It is not within one's power at a given time to do something that would bring it about that a person who existed at that earlier time did not exist at the earlier time.

6. If God existed at t_1 and if God believed at t_1 that Jones would do X at t_2, then if it was within Jones's power at t_2 to refrain from doing X, then (1) it was within Jones's power at t_2 to do something that would have brought it about that God held a false belief at t_1, or (2) it was within Jones's power at t_2 to do something which would have brought it about that God did not hold the belief He held at t_1, or (3) it was within Jones's power at t_2, to do something that would have brought it about that any person who believed at t_1 that Jones would do X at t_2 (one of whom was, by hypothesis, God) held a false belief and thus was not God—that is, that God (who by hypothesis existed at t_1) did not exist at t_1.

7. Alternative 1 in the consequent of item 6 is false. (from 2 and 3)

8. Alternative 2 in the consequent of item 6 is false. (from 4)

9. Alternative 3 in the consequent of item 6 is false. (from 5)

10. Therefore, if God existed at t_1 and if God believed at t_1 that Jones would do X at t_2, then it was not within Jones's power at t_2 to refrain from doing X. (from 6 through 9)

11. Therefore, if God existed at t_1, and if Jones did X at t_2 it was not within Jones's power at t_2 to refrain from doing X. (from 1 and 10)

In this argument, items 1 and 2 make explicit the doctrine of God's (essential) omniscience with which I am working. Items 3, 4, and 5 express what I take to be part of the logic of the concept of ability or power as it applies to human beings. Item 6 is offered as an analytic truth. If one assigns Jones the power to refrain from doing X at t_2 (given that God believed at t_1 that he would do X at t_2), so far as I can see, one would have to describe this power in one of the three ways listed in the consequent of item 6. I do not know how to argue that these are the only alternatives, but I have been unable to find another. Item 11, when generalized for all agents and actions, and when taken together with what seems to me to be a minimal condition for the application of 'voluntary action,' yields the conclusion that if God exists (and is essentially omniscient in the way I have described) no human action is voluntary.

C. It is important to notice that the argument given in the preceding paragraphs avoids use of two concepts that are often prominent in discussions of determinism.

In the first place, the argument makes no mention of the *causes* of Jones's action. Say (for example, with St Thomas)[10] that God's foreknowledge of Jones's action was, itself, the cause of the action (though I am really not sure what this means). Say, instead, that natural events or circumstances caused Jones to act. Even say that Jones's action had no cause at all. The argument outlined above remains unaffected. If eighty years prior to Saturday, God believed that Jones would mow his lawn at that time, it was not within Jones's power at the time of action to refrain from mowing his lawn. The reasoning that justifies this assertion makes no mention of a causal series preceding Jones's action.

Secondly, consider the following line of thinking. Suppose Jones mowed his lawn last Saturday. It was then *true* eighty years ago that Jones would mow his lawn at that time. Hence, on Saturday, Jones was not able to refrain from mowing his lawn. To suppose that he was would be to suppose that he was able on Saturday to do something that would have made false a proposition that was *already true* eighty years earlier. This general kind of argument for determinism is usually associated with Leibniz, although it was anticipated in chapter ix of Aristotle's *De Interpretatione*. It has been used since, with some modification, in Richard Taylor's article, 'Fatalism.'[11] This argument, like the one I have offered above, makes no use of the notion of causation. It turns, instead, on the notion of its being *true eighty years ago* that Jones would mow his lawn on Saturday.

I must confess that I share the misgivings of those contemporary philosophers who have wondered what (if any) sense can be attached to a statement of the form 'It was true at t_1 that E would occur at t_2.'[12] Does this statement mean that had someone believed, guessed, or asserted at t_1 that E would occur at t_2, he would have been right?[13] (I shall have something to say about this form of determinism later in this paper.) Perhaps it means that at t_1 there was sufficient evidence upon which to predict that E would occur at t_2.[14] Maybe it means neither of these. Maybe it means

10. Aquinas, *Summa Theologicae*, Pt. I, q. 14, a. 8.

11. Richard Taylor, 'Fatalism,' *The Philosophical Review*, 71 (1962): 56–66. Taylor argues that if an event E fails to occur at t_2, then at t_1 it was true that E would fail to occur at t_2. Thus, at t_1 a necessary condition of anyone's performing an action sufficient for the occurrence of E at t_2 is missing. Thus at t_1, no one could have the power to perform an action that would be sufficient for the occurrence of E at t_2. Hence, no one has the power at t_1 to do something sufficient for the occurrence of an event at t_2 that is not going to happen. The parallel between this argument and the one recited above can be seen very clearly if one reformulates Taylor's argument, pushing back the time at which it was true that E would not occur at t_2.

12. For a helpful discussion of difficulties involved here, see Rogers Albritton's 'Present Truth and Future Contingency,' a reply to Richard Taylor's 'The Problem of Future Contingency,' both in *The Philosophical Review*, 66 (1957): 1–28.

13. Gilbert Ryle interprets it this way. See 'It Was to Be,' in *Dilemmas* (Cambridge, Engl., 1954).

14. Richard Gale suggests this interpretation in 'Endorsing Predictions,' *The Philosophical Review*, 70 (1961): 37–85.

nothing at all.[15] The argument presented above presupposes that it makes straight-forward sense to suppose that God (or just anyone) held a true belief eighty years prior to Saturday. But this is not to suppose that *what* God believed *was true eighty years prior to Saturday*. Whether (or in what sense) it was true eighty years ago that Jones would mow his lawn on Saturday is a question I shall not discuss. As far as I can see, the argument in which I am interested requires nothing in the way of a decision on this issue.

15. This view is held by John Turk Saunders in 'Sea Fight Tomorrow?,' *The Philosophical Review*, 67 (1958): 367–78.

Questions for discussion

1. Should we distinguish between knowing and believing? If so, what does one have when one knows which one lacks when one believes?
2. Can something which is not embodied know? If so, how?
3. Is 'knowledge' the name for a material object or process? If so, why? If not, why not?
4. To what extent should God's knowledge be understood as being like human knowledge?
5. Under what conditions, if any, can someone be thought of as knowing what is going to happen?

Advice on further reading

For some helpful introductory discussions of divine knowledge, see the relevant chapters of: Steven T. Davis, *Logic and the Nature of God* (London, 1983); Gerard Hughes, *The Nature of God* (London and New York, 1995); Thomas V. Morris, *Our Idea of God* (Notre Dame, Indiana, and London, 1991); Edward R. Wierenga, *The Nature of God* (Ithaca, New York, 1969). Also see George J. Mavrodes, 'Omniscience', in Philip L. Quinn and Charles Taliaferro (eds), *A Companion to the Philosophy of Religion* (Oxford, 1997). For a discussion of God's knowledge which pays special attention to the notion of 'the Future', see P. T. Geach, *Providence and Evil* (Cambridge, 1977), ch. 3.

There are a number of recently published books entirely devoted to the topic of God's knowledge. Ones especially worth consulting include:

William Lane Craig, *The Only Wise God* (Grand Rapids, Michigan, 1987).

Jonathan L. Kvanvig, *The Possibility of an All-Knowing God* (London, 1986).

John C. Moskop, *Divine Omniscience and Human Freedom* (Macon, Georgia, 1984).

Robert Young, *Freedom, Responsibility and God* (London, 1975).

Linda Zagzebski, *The Dilemma of Freedom and Foreknowledge* (New York, 1991).

Among the many published articles on divine knowledge published in recent years, the following stand out as particularly worthy of note:

Hector Neri Castaneda, 'Omniscience and Indexical Reference', *Journal of Philosophy* 64 (1967).

Anthony Kenny, 'Divine Foreknowledge and Human Freedom', in Anthony Kenny (ed.), *Aquinas: A Collection of Critical Essays* (London, 1969).

Norman Kretzmann, 'Omniscience and Immutability', *Journal of Philosophy* 63 (1966).

Alvin Plantinga, 'On Ockham's Way Out', *Faith and Philosophy* III (1986).

Alvin Plantinga, 'Divine Knowledge', in C. Stephen Evans and Merold Westphal (eds), *Christian Perspectives on Religious Knowledge* (Grand Rapids, Michigan, 1993).

A. N. Prior, 'The Formalities of Omniscience', in A. N. Prior, *Papers on Time and Tense* (Oxford, 1968).

For a brief account of Aquinas on knowledge in general and on God's knowledge in particular, see Brian Davies, *The Thought of Thomas Aquinas* (Oxford, 1992), ch. 7. See also Scott MacDonald, 'Theory of Knowledge', in Norman Kretzmann and Eleonore Stump (eds), *The Cambridge Companion to Aquinas* (Cambridge, 1993). For a detailed exposition of Aquinas on God's knowledge (one which places it against the background of authors to whom Aquinas was indebted), see Vivian Boland, *Ideas in God According to Saint Thomas Aquinas* (Leiden, New York, and Koln, 1996).

For an introduction to Boethius which includes discussion of Boethius on God's knowledge, see Edmund Reiss, *Boethius* (Boston, 1982). For a more detailed treatment, see Henry Chadwick, *Boethius: The Consolations of Music, Logic, Theology, and Philosophy* (Oxford, 1981).

Molina's views on God's knowledge can best be studied in a recently published translation into English of a part of his work *De Concordia*. See Luis de Molina, *On Divine Foreknowledge*, translated, with an introduction and notes, by Alfred J. Freddoso (Ithaca and London, 1988). For a trenchant contemporary defence of Molina on middle knowledge, see

Thomas P. Flint, *Divine Providence* (Ithaca, New York, 1998). For a short introduction to Molina, see Thomas P. Flint, 'Two Accounts of Providence', in Thomas V. Morris (ed.), *Divine and Human Action* (Ithaca, New York, and London, 1988).

Eternal

Introduction

What might we mean by 'God is eternal'?

In *The Consolation of Philosophy* Boethius writes: 'That God is eternal is the common judgment of all who live by reason.' The statement is obviously false, since plenty of reasonable people do not believe that there is a God at all. But almost all who describe themselves as believing in God, or as believing that there is a God, would agree that God is indeed eternal. And not surprisingly. In English translations of the Bible, God is frequently called eternal.[1] The teaching that God is eternal has been repeatedly affirmed by ecclesiastical councils and legions of theologians. It seems to be a fundamental part of anything we might call 'theism' or 'theistic belief'.

But how should it be construed? What does it mean to call God eternal? Two main answers have been given. According to the first, 'God is eternal' means that God is non-temporal or timeless. According to the second, it only means that God has no beginning and no end, that God has always existed and will continue to exist forever.

We have already encountered the first answer in the extract from Boethius given in Chapter 44, according to whom eternity 'is the whole, simultaneous and perfect possession of boundless life'. On Boethius's acount, God certainly lacks beginning and end. But, so he thinks, God also lacks a life lived from moment to moment. As Boethius sees it, God's mode of being involves no 'before' or 'after', and no 'earlier than' or 'later than'. It is completely without successiveness. It comprises nothing that we could recognize as a history or biography. Or as Anselm of Canterbury (addressing God from a Boethian perspective on eternity) puts it:

You were not, therefore, yesterday, nor will You be tomorrow, but yesterday and today and tomorrow You *are*. Indeed You exist neither yesterday nor today nor tomorrow but are absolutely outside all times (*es extra omne tempus*). For yesterday and today and tomorrow are completely in time; however, You, though nothing can be without You, are nevertheless not in place or time but all things are in You. For nothing contains You, but You contain all things.[2]

---

1. Cf., for example, the RSV translations of Deuteronomy 33: 27, and Isaiah 57: 15.
2. *Proslogion* 19.

This understanding of divine eternity has been defended by generations of philosophers and theologians. So one might call it 'the classical view of divine eternity'.[3]

For a supporter of the second view of eternity (which we may call 'the temporal view'), we can refer to Richard Swinburne. According to him:

> If a creator of the universe exists now, he must have existed at least as long as there have been other logically contingent existing things . . . However, traditionally theists believe not merely that this spirit, God, exists now or has existed as long as created things, but that he is an eternal being. This seems to mean, firstly, that he has always existed—that there was no time at which he did not exist . . . Let us put this point by saying that they believe that he is backwardly eternal. The supposition that a spirit of the above kind is backwardly eternal seems to be a coherent one . . . The doctrine that God is eternal seems to involve, secondly, the doctrine that the above spirit will go on existing for ever . . . I will put this point by saying that he is forwardly eternal. This too seems to be a coherent suggestion.[4]

In Swinburne's judgement, it is incoherent to suppose that God is outside time. But it is coherent to suppose that God has always existed and always will.

Debating the senses of 'God is eternal'

The two main approaches to 'God is eternal' are clearly very different. Those who subscribe to the classical view have an understanding of God which is quite at odds with that of those who embrace the temporal one. And their disparate conclusions have implications which leave them more in disagreement than one might initially think. Those who say that God is timeless seem, among other things, committed to the view that God is both changeless and impassible.[5] But divine immutability and impassibility is not entailed by the temporal view of divine eternity. According to most of its defenders, it is strictly incompatible with a view of God which sees him as immutable and impassible. Then again, a timeless God must be vastly different from people. Such a God can, for example, have no thoughts which succeed each other. And such a God can have no memories, expectations, or emotions. But if God exists in time, then he might be thoroughly mutable. And, like people, he might have thoughts which come after each other. God might also have memories, expectations, and emotions. He might be much like us, as defenders of the temporal view of eternity often seem to take him to be.

In short: different views of divine eternity have major repercussions for thinking of God in general.[6] And, largely for this reason, they have led to a lot of philosophical discussion. For the most part, this has consisted of (a) attempts to argue that God must be eternal in the classical sense, (b) attempts to argue that the classical view of eternity is somehow

---

3. So you can find it defended by authors such as Augustine, Anselm, Aquinas, Descartes, Calvin, and Leibniz. Contemporary defenders of it are mentioned in 'Advice on further reading' below.
4. Richard Swinburne, *The Coherence of Theism* (Oxford, 1977), p. 221. For reference to authors sharing Swinburne's temporalist approach to divine eternity, see 'Advice on further reading' below.
5. A timeless God clearly cannot undergo change, including change induced in him by something else. So a timeless God must be immutable and impassible.
6. For someone briefly emphasizing this fact, see Paul Helm, 'Eternity', in Brian Davies (ed.), *Philosophy of Religion: A Guide to the Subject* (London, 1998).

open to objection, and (c) responses to purported refutations of the classical view.[7] But how have the arguments gone? They have been many and varied on both sides.

Some of the ones most frequently advanced in defence of the classical view can be summarized thus:

1. God is the cause of all change. But change and time are inseparably connected. So God cannot be something existing in time.[8]
2. God is the Creator who accounts for the existence of the universe. But one can only make sense of things existing in time insofar as one thinks of them as parts of the universe. So God cannot be something existing in time.[9]
3. God is perfect and unlimited. But nothing in time can be this. Among other things, temporal existence always implies loss. Things in time lose what they once had, because things in time are subject to change. And they are always vulnerable to what the future might bring. But something which is perfect and unlimited cannot lose what it has or be vulnerable to what might come.[10]
4. 'God exists' is necessarily true. So everything about God is necessarily existent. God is all that he *can* be, for any reality he lacks but could possess would need grounding in something else. So God must be changeless and unchangeable. And if God is this, then God must be timeless.[11]
5. Things in time occupy space. But God does not. So God is outside of time.[12]
6. If God exists necessarily, and if God is essentially temporal, then time exists necessarily. But temporal things do not exist of necessity. So God should not be thought of as a temporal thing.[13]

Those who have defended the non-classical view of divine eternity have mostly tended to argue along one or more of the following lines:

1. The notion that God is timeless is completely at odds with the fact that God is a person. Nothing timeless can be a person.[14]
2. God is living and acting. But nothing timeless can be this. Life and action can only be intelligibly ascribed to what exists in time.[15]

7. In terms of the history of philosophical debate, the temporal view of God's eternity can be viewed chiefly as a reaction to the classical one, though the reaction began as long ago as the Middle Ages. Ockham, for instance, denied that God is timeless. See William Ockham, *Predestination, God's Foreknowledge, and Future Contingents*, translated with an Introduction, Notes, and Appendices by Marilyn McCord Adams and Norman Kretzmann (New York, 1969).
8. Augustine of Hippo argues along these lines in *Confessions* XI, vii.
9. Cf. ibid., XI, xii.
10. Cf. Anselm, *Proslogion* 18–22.
11. Cf. Thomas Aquinas, *Summa Theologiae*, Ia. 3. 1 and 6.
12. Cf. Brian Leftow, *Time and Eternity* (Ithaca and London, 1991), ch. 12, pp. 271 ff.
13. Cf. ibid., p. 273.
14. Cf. J. R. Lucas, *A Treatise on Space and Time* (London, 1973), p. 200. Cf. also, Nelson Pike, *God and Timelessness* (London, 1970), ch. 7.
15. Cf. Alan Richardson and John Bowden (eds), *A New Dictionary of Christian Theology* (London, 1983), p. 573. Cf. also, Pike, *God and Timelessness*, pp. 106 ff. and Swinburne, *The Coherence of Theism*, p. 221.

3. God is one who loves. But love implies emotion or change on the part of the lover. So nothing which is timeless can be God.[16]

4. On some accounts of divine timelessness, all temporal events are present to God. But they cannot be. If they were, they would be simultaneous, while they are, in fact, temporally distinct. So at least some accounts of divine timelessness contain incoherence.[17]

5. It has been argued that God must be timeless since God is immutable. But something can be in time even if it does not change. There can be time without change.[18]

6. The notion of God as timeless is completely at odds with the biblical picture of God.[19]

And defenders of the classical view have, in turn, tended to argue as follows in response to their critics. In response to the six arguments noted above, for instance, they have offered replies such as these:

1. God is not a person as human beings are persons. So the formula 'God is a person' should not be regarded as relevant when it comes to discussions of divine eternity.[20]

2. The life and action of creatures takes place in time. It also involves change. But it is not part of the meaning of 'living' and 'acting' that something which lives and acts should be located in time or should undergo change.[21]

3. God can be said to love without implying that God literally undergoes emotion or change. God can be said to love creatures, for example, since he brings about what is good for them without himself changing.[22]

4. Even those accounts of divine timelessness which speak of temporal events as present to God come with the insistence that 'being present to God' does not mean 'existing at some time'. So defenders of God's timelessness are not

---

16. Cf. Jon Sobrino, *Christology at the Crossroads* (London, 1978), p. 197. Cf. also Jürgen Moltmann, *The Crucified God* (London, 1974).

17. Cf. Anthony Kenny, *The God of the Philosophers* (Oxford, 1979), pp. 38 ff. Cf. also, Anthony Kenny, 'Divine Foreknowledge and Human Freedom', in Anthony Kenny (ed.), *Aquinas: A Collection of Critical Essays* (London and Melbourne, 1969).

18. Cf. Richard Swinburne, *Space and Time* (2nd edn, London, 1981), pp. 172 ff.

19. Cf. John Lucas, *The Future* (Oxford, 1989), p. 214. Cf. also Swinburne, *The Coherence of Theism*, pp. 214 ff.

20. Cf. Brian Davies, *An Introduction to the Philosophy of Religion* (2nd edn, Oxford and New York, 1993), chs 3 and 8.

21. Cf. Herbert McCabe, *God Matters* (London, 1987), ch. 4. Cf. also Paul Helm, *Eternal God* (Oxford, 1988), ch. 4.

22. Cf. Brian Davies, 'How is God Love?', in Luke Gormally (ed.), *Moral Truth and Moral Tradition: Essays in Honour of Peter Geach and Elizabeth Anscombe* (Dublin and Portland Oregon, 1994). This article also draws attention to the significance of the Christian doctrine of the Trinity when it comes to discussions of what it might mean to say that God loves (something not often considered in much philosophical discussions of the notion of God as a lover).

      committed to supposing that temporally distinct events are actually simultaneous.[23]

5. We have no reason to suppose that there can be time without change. Quite the contrary.[24]

6. The Bible contains no explicitly philosophical teaching to the effect that God is timeless. But reflecting on what the Bible says of God in general, and bearing in mind what it makes sense to affirm of God apart from what is taught in Scripture, we have no option but to regard the classical view of eternity as most consonant with biblical teaching.[25]

In short, the topic of divine eternity has led to quite a significant number of divergent arguments. And the extracts below introduce you to some significant samples of them at first hand.

The following extracts

The first is what we might call a 'classical' defence of the classical view of eternity. Here, Aquinas (one of its most notable medieval exponents) argues that time and eternity differ and that God must therefore be thought of as non-temporal. As you shall see, Aquinas strongly supports what Boethius says about eternity. He also relies heavily on a view of time which sees it as inseparable from change, one which he shares with Aristotle.[26] Critics of the classical view of eternity sometimes regard it as describing God as inert or static. Its defenders have frequently replied by stressing that they are attempting, not to *describe* God, but to insist on what God *cannot be*. They have emphasized that they are mostly engaging in *negative* theology.[27] And this seems much to be what Aquinas is doing in the extract in Chapter 46. Eternity, he chiefly argues, has no beginning or end. He also argues that it has no successiveness and no aspects which are essential to things which exist in time.

    But is the classical view of eternity compatible with the Biblical understanding of God? In Chapter 47 Nicholas Wolterstorff suggests that it is not. And in developing his thesis he provides one of the most sophisticated and articulate recent critiques of the classical view of divine eternity. Yet the authors of Chapters 48 and 49 argue in defence of the classical view, though they disagree with each other in philosophically interesting ways. In Chapter 48 Eleonore Stump and Norman Kretzmann offer a careful articulation of Boethius's teaching on eternity. They then go on to consider what it might mean to speak of something existing non-temporally and to defend the notion that God is something which exists in this way. In doing so, they introduce the idea of simultaneity ('ET-simultaneity') that can obtain between what is eternal and what is temporal. They suggest that any eternal event can be thought of as ET-simultaneous with any temporal

---

23. Cf. Helm, *Eternal God*. ch. 1. Cf. also, Davies, *An Introduction to the Philosophy of Religion*, pp. 153 ff.
24. Cf. David Braine, *The Reality of Time and the Existence of God* (Oxford, 1988), ch. II.
25. Cf. Aquinas, *Summa Theologiae*, Ia. 9–10.
26. For Aristotle on time and change, see Aristotle, *Physics*, Book IV.
27. Cf. McCabe, *God Matters*, p. 41.

event. They also suggest that, unlike simple simultaneity, ET-simultaneity is not transitive, since in order for ET-simultaneity to apply there must be either an eternal or a temporal standpoint from which such simultaneity is observed. In Chapter 49, however, Paul Helm, while defending the notion of divine timelessness, thinks that one can do so without recourse to the proposals of Stump and Kretzmann. Indeed, so he argues, the line on eternity taken by them is both obscure and unhelpful when it comes to addressing the most important issues raised by the classical view of divine eternity.

Who is right? Is it Aquinas? Is it Wolterstorff? Is it Stump and Kretzmann? Is it Helm? Or do all of these authors stand in need of correction? Could it be that they are all partly right in what they say, while also partly wrong? These are questions for you now to think about.

Chapter 46
Why call God 'eternal'?
Thomas Aquinas

Eternity

What is eternity?

IT seems that Boethius' definition of eternity won't do: For (1) he defined eternity as *the simultaneously whole and complete possession of endless life*. Now *endless* is a negative term such as belongs only in the definition of defective things; eternity, however, is no defect. So the word *endless* is out of place in a definition of eternity.

Moreover, (2) *eternity* names a sort of duration, and duration measures existence rather than life. So the word *existence* should be used in the definition in place of *life*.

Moreover, (3) the word *whole* describes something having parts. Now eternity is simple and has no parts. So *whole* won't do.

Moreover, (4) several days or times can't be simultaneous. But in speaking of eternity we talk of *days* and *times* in the plural. For Micah 5 (2) says *his going forth is from the beginning, from the days of eternity*, and St Paul in Romans 16 (25) talks of *the revealing of the mystery kept secret through times eternal*. Eternity then is not simultaneously whole.

Moreover, (5) wholeness and perfection are the same. Given then that eternity is whole it is redundant to add that it is perfect.

Moreover, (6) possession has nothing to do with duration, and eternity is a sort of duration. So eternity is not a possession.

IN REPLY: Just as we derive our knowledge of simple things from composite ones so we derive our knowledge of eternity from time, which is *the measure of before and after in change*. For in all change there is successiveness, one part coming after another, and from our numbering antecedent and consequent parts of change there arises the notion of time, which is simply the numberedness of before and after in change. Now something that lacks change and never varies its mode of existence will not display a before and after. So just as numbering before and after in change produces the notion of time, so awareness of invariability in something altogether free from change produces the notion of eternity. A further point: time is said by

Thomas Aquinas extract from *Thomas Aquinas Selected Philosophical Writings* selected and translated with an introduction and notes by Timothy McDermott (Oxford World's Classics, 1993) copyright © Timothy McDermott 1993, reprinted by permission of Oxford University Press.

Aristotle to measure things that begin and end in time, and that is because you can always find a beginning and an end in changing things. But things altogether unchangeable can no more have a beginning than show successiveness.

Two things then characterize eternity: firstly, things existing in eternity are *endless*, lacking both beginning and end (for both may be called *ends*); and secondly, eternity itself exists as a *simultaneous whole*, lacking successiveness.

HENCE: To 1: We often use negations to define simple things, saying points have no parts, for example. This is not because they are negative in substance but because our minds first grasp composite things and only come to know simple things by denying compositeness of them.

To 2: That which exists in eternity is, in fact, also alive. Moreover, life covers activity too, which existence doesn't, and the flow of duration is more apparent in activity than in existence: time, for example, measures changes.

To 3: Eternity is called whole not because it has parts but because it has nothing lacking to it.

To 4: Just as scripture described God metaphorically in bodily terms though he is not a body, so it describes eternity in temporal and successive terms though it exists simultaneously.

To 5: Note two things about time: time itself is actualized successively, in a present instant which is never complete. So to deny that eternity is time Boethius calls it *simultaneously whole*, and to deny that it is temporal instantaneity he calls it *complete*.

To 6: To possess something is to hold it firmly and unmovingly. So to signify eternity's unchangeableness and constancy Boethius used the word *possession* . . .

Does eternity differ from the aeon and time?

Eternity doesn't seem to differ from time: For (1) two measures of duration can only exist simultaneously if one is part of the other: thus two days or hours can't occur simultaneously, but an hour and a day can, since an hour is part of a day. Now eternity and time, both of which signify some sort of measure of duration, exist simultaneously. So since eternity is not a part of time but exceeds and contains it, time must seemingly be a part of eternity and not differ from it.

Moreover, (2) according to Aristotle the present moment of time persists unchanged throughout time. But the nature of eternity seems to consist precisely in remaining unbrokenly the same throughout the whole course of time. Eternity then must be the present moment of time. But the present moment of time is in substance identical with time itself. So eternity must be in substance identical with time.

Moreover, (3) Aristotle says the measure of the most fundamental change measures all other changes. In the same way it seems that the measure of the most fundamental existence should measure all other existences. But eternity measures God's existence, which is the most fundamental existence; so it should measure all existence. Now the existence of perishable things is measured by time. So time is either eternity or part of eternity.

BUT AGAINST THAT: Eternity is simultaneously whole, while in time there is before and after. So time and eternity differ.

IN REPLY: Time clearly differs from eternity. But some people say the reason for the difference is that time began and will end, whereas eternity doesn't begin or end. Now this is an accidental difference, not an intrinsic one, for even if time had always existed and will always exist—as those hold who think the heavens will go on revolving for ever—there would still be the difference Boethius pointed out between time and eternity: that eternity is simultaneously whole, while time is not, eternity measuring abiding existence and time measuring change.

If, however, the suggested difference is applied to the things being measured rather than to the measures themselves, then it has some justification, for, as Aristotle says, time measures only those things that begin and end in time. So, even if the heavens did rotate for ever, time would measure not the whole duration of the movement—since the infinite is immeasurable—but each revolution separately as it began and ended in time.

Or we could justify applying the difference to the measures themselves if we talked of potential beginnings and ends. For even if time lasted for ever it would always be possible to mark off beginnings and ends in it by dividing it into parts, in the way we talk of days and years beginning and ending; and this would not apply to eternity.

However, these differences are secondary. The primary intrinsic difference of time from eternity is that eternity exists as a simultaneous whole and time doesn't.

HENCE: To 1: This would be a valid argument if time and eternity were measures of the same kind, but when one considers the different things they measure, they clearly aren't.

To 2: The present moment persistently underlies time, altering state continuously; just as time corresponds to movement (of the heavens), the present corresponds to what moves, which remains in substance the same throughout time though it alters its position, first here and then there, and, by altering its position, moves. Time consists in the passing of the present moment as it alters state. Eternity, however, remains unchanged both in substance and in state, and thus differs from the present of time.

To 3: Just as eternity is the proper measure of existence as such, so time is the proper measure of change. In so far then as some existence falls short of permanence in its existing and is subject to change, so will it fall short of eternity and be subject to time. So the existence of perishable things, being changeable, is measured by time and not by eternity. For time measures not only the actually changing but also the potentially changeable. It measures, therefore, not only movement but also rest, the state of the movable when not moving.

Chapter 47

God is 'everlasting', not 'eternal'

Nicholas Wolterstorff

Aᴌᴌ Christian theologians agree that God is without beginning and without end. The vast majority have held, in addition, that God is *eternal*, existing outside of time. Only a small minority have contended that God is *everlasting*, existing within time.[1] In what follows I shall take up the cudgels for that minority, arguing that God as conceived and presented by the biblical writers is a being whose own life and existence is temporal.

The biblical writers do not present God as some passive factor within reality but as an agent in it. Further, they present him as acting within *human* history. The god they present is neither the impassive god of the Oriental nor the nonhistorical god of the Deist. Indeed, so basic to the biblical writings is their speaking of God as agent within history that if one viewed God as only an impassive factor in reality, or as one whose agency does not occur within human history, one would have to regard the biblical speech about God as at best one long sequence of metaphors pointing to a reality for which they are singularly inept, and as at worst one long sequence of falsehoods.

More specifically, the biblical writers present God as a redeeming God. From times most ancient, man has departed from the pattern of responsibilities awarded him at his creation by God. A multitude of evils has followed. But God was not content to leave man in the mire of his misery. Aware of what is going on, he has resolved, in response to man's sin and its resultant evils, to bring about renewal. He has, indeed, already been acting in accord with that resolve, centrally and decisively in the life, death, and resurrection of Jesus Christ.

What I shall argue is that if we are to accept this picture of God as acting for the renewal of human life, we must conceive of him as everlasting rather than eternal. God the Redeemer cannot be a God eternal. This is so because God the Redeemer is a God who *changes*. And any being which changes is a being among whose states there is temporal succession. Of course, there is an important sense in which God as presented in the Scriptures is changeless: he is steadfast in his redeeming intent and ever faithful to his children. Yet, *ontologically*, God cannot be a redeeming God without there being changeful variation among his states.

Nicholas Wolterstorff 'God Everlasting' from *God and the Good Essays in Honor Henry Steb* edited by J. Orlebeke and Lewis B. Smedes (Eerdmans, 1975). Reprinted with permission of the author.

1. The most noteworthy contemporary example is Oscar Cullmann, *Christ and Time* (Eng. tr., Philadelphia, 1950).

If this argument proves correct the importance of the issue here confronting us for Christian theology can scarcely be exaggerated. A theology which opts for God as eternal cannot avoid being in conflict with the confession of God as redeemer. And given the obvious fact that God is presented in the Bible as a God who redeems, a theology which opts for God as eternal cannot be a theology faithful to the biblical witness.

Our line of argument will prove to be neither subtle nor complicated. So the question will insistently arise, why have Christian theologians so massively con-tended that God is eternal? Why has not the dominant tradition of Christian theology been that of God everlasting?

Our argument will depend heavily on taking with seriousness a certain feature of temporality which has been neglected in Western philosophy. But the massiveness of the God eternal tradition cannot, I am persuaded, be attributed merely to philo-sophical oversight. There are, I think, two factors more fundamental. One is the feeling, deep-seated in much of human culture, that the flowing of events into an irrecoverable and unchangeable past is a matter for deep regret. Our bright actions and shining moments do not long endure. The gnawing tooth of time bites all. And our evil deeds can never be undone. They are forever to be regretted. Of course, the philosopher is inclined to distinguish the mere fact of temporality from the actual pattern of the events in history and to argue that regrets about the latter should not slosh over into regrets about the former. The philosopher is right. The regrettable-ness of what transpires in time is not good ground for regretting that there is time. Yet where the philosopher sees the possibility and the need for a distinction, most people have seen none. Regrets over the pervasive pattern of what transpires within time have led whole societies to place the divine outside of time—freed from the 'bondage' of temporality.

But I am persuaded that William Kneale is correct when he contends that the most important factor accounting for the tradition of God eternal within Christian theology was the influence of the classical Greek philosophers on the early theo-logians.[2] The distinction between eternal being and everlasting being was drawn for the first time in the history of thought by Plato (*Timaeus* 37–8), though the lan-guage he uses is reminiscent of words used still earlier by Parmenides. Plato does not connect eternity and divinity, but he does make clear his conviction that eternal being is the highest form of reality. This was enough to influence the early Christian theologians, who did their thinking within the milieu of Hellenic and Hellenistic thought, to assign eternity to God. Thus was the fateful choice made.

A good many twentieth-century theologians have been engaged in what one might call the dehellenization of Christian theology. If Kneale's contention is cor-rect, then in this essay I am participating in that activity. Of course, not every bit of dehellenization is laudatory from the Christian standpoint, for not everything that the Greeks said is false. What is the case, though, is that the patterns of classical

---

2. William Kneale, 'Time and Eternity in Theology,' *Proceedings of the Aristotelian Society* (1961).

Greek thought are incompatible with the pattern of biblical thought. And in facing the issue of God everlasting versus God eternal we are dealing with the fundamental pattern of biblical thought. Indeed, I am persuaded that unless the tradition of God eternal is renounced, fundamental dehellenizing will perpetually occupy itself in the suburbs, never advancing to the city center. Every attempt to purge Christian theology of the traces of incompatible Hellenic patterns of thought must fail unless it removes the roadblock of the God eternal tradition. Around this barricade there are no detours.

I

Before we can discuss whether God is outside of time we must ask what it would be for something to be outside of time. That is, before we can ask whether God is eternal we must ask what it would be for something to be eternal. But this in turn demands that we are clear on what it would be for something to be a temporal entity. We need not be clear on all the features which something has by virtue of being temporal—on all facets of temporality—but we must at least be able to say what is necessary and sufficient for something's being in time.

For our purposes we can take as the decisive feature of temporality the exemplification of the temporal ordering-relations of precedence, succession, and simultaneity. Unless some entities did stand to each other in one or the other of these relations, there would be no temporal reality. Conversely, if there is temporal reality then there are pairs of entities whose members stand to each other in the relation of one occurring before (precedence) or one occurring after (succession) or one occurring simultaneously with (simultaneity) the other.

We must ask in turn what sort of entity is such that its examples can stand to each other in the relations of precedence, succession, and simultaneity. For not every sort of entity is such. The members of a pair of trees cannot stand in these relations. The golden chain tree outside my back door neither occurs before nor after nor simultaneously with the shingle oak outside my front door. Of course, *the sprouting of the former* stands in one of these relations to *the sprouting of the latter*; and so too does *the demise of the latter* to *the demise of the former*. But the trees themselves do not. They do not occur at all.

We have in this example a good clue, though, as to the sort of entity whose examples can stand in the relations of precedence, succession, and simultaneity. It is just such entities as *the demise of my golden chain tree* and *the sprouting of my shingle oak*. It is, in short, what I shall call events that stand in these relations.

As I conceive of an event, it consists in something's actually having some property, or something's actually performing some action, or something's actually standing in some relation to something. Events as I conceive them are all actual occurrences. They are not what *can have* occurrences. They are, rather, themselves occurrences. Furthermore, as I conceive of events, there may be two or more events consisting in a given entity's having a given property (or performing a given action). For example, my golden chain tree flowered last spring and is flowering again this spring. So there are two events each consisting in the flowering of my golden chain tree. One began and ended last year. The other began and will end this year.

Such events as I have thus far offered by way of example are all temporally limited, in the sense that there are times at which the event is not occurring. There are times at which it has not yet begun or has already ended. Last year's flowering of my golden chain tree is such. It began at some time last spring and has now for about a year or so ceased. But there are other events which are not in this way temporally limited; 3's *being prime*, for example. If time itself begins and ends, then this event, too, occurs wholly within a finite interval. Yet even then there is no time at which it does not occur.

I said that every event consists in something's actually having some property, actually performing some action, or actually standing in some relation to something. So consider some event *e* which consists in some entity *a* having some property or performing some action or standing in some relation. Let us call *a*, a *subject* of *e*. And let us call *e* an *aspect* of *a*. A given event may well have more than one subject. For example, an event consisting of my sitting under my shingle oak has both me and the shingle oak as subjects. Indeed, I think it can also be viewed as having the relation of *sitting under* as subject. I see nothing against regarding an event consisting of my sitting under my shingle oak as identical with an event consisting of the relation of *sitting under* being exemplified by me with respect to my shingle oak.

Now consider that set of a given entity's aspects such that each member bears a temporal order-relation to every member of the set and none bears a temporal order-relation to any aspect not a member of the set. Let us call that set, provided that it is not empty, the *time-strand* of that entity. I assume it to be true that every entity has at most one time-strand. That is, I assume that no entity has two or more sets of temporally interrelated aspects such that no member of the one set bears any temporal order-relation to any member of the other. I do not, however, assume that each of the aspects of every entity which has a time-strand belongs to the strand. And as to whether every entity has at least one time-strand—that of course is involved in the question as to whether anything is eternal.

Consider, next, a set of events such that each member stands to every member in one of the temporal order-relations, and such that no member stands to any event which is not a member in any of these relations. I shall call such a set a *temporal array*. A temporal array is of course just the union of a set of time-strands such that every member of each member strand bears some temporal order-relation to every member of every other member strand, and such that no member of any member strand bears any temporal order-relation to any member of any strand which is not a member of the set. In what follows I assume that there is but one temporal array. I assume, that is, that every member of every time-strand bears a temporal order-relation to every member of every time-strand.

Now suppose that there is some entity all of whose aspects are such that they are to be found in no temporal array whatsoever. Such an entity would be, in the most radical way possible, outside of time. Accordingly, I shall define 'eternal' thus:

Def. 1: x is eternal if and only if x has no aspect which is a member of the temporal array.

An alternative definition would have been this: 'x is eternal if and only if x has no time-strand.' The difference between the two definitions is that, on the latter, an entity is eternal if none of its aspects bears any temporal order-relation to any of those events which are *its* aspects; whereas on the former, what is required of an entity for it to be eternal is that none of its aspects be related by any temporal order-relation to *any event whatsoever*. Of course, if every event which bears any temporal order-relation to any event whatsoever is also simultaneous with itself, then everything which fails to satisfy the 'temporal array' definition of 'eternal' will also fail to satisfy the 'time-strand' definition.

At this point, certain ambiguities in the concepts of precedence, succession, and simultaneity should be resolved. By saying that event e_1 occurs *simultaneously with* event e_2, I mean that there is some time at which both e_1 and e_2 are occurring. I do *not* mean—though indeed this might reasonably also have been meant by the words—that there is *no* time at which one of e_1 and e_2 is occurring and the other is not. When two events stand in that latter relation I shall say that they are *wholly simultaneous*. By saying that e_1 *precedes* e_2, I mean that there is some time at which e_1 but not e_2 is occurring, which precedes all times at which e_2 is occurring. I do not mean that every time at which e_1 occurs precedes every time at which e_2 occurs. When e_1 stands to e_2 in this latter relationship, I shall say that *it wholly precedes* e_2. Lastly, by saying that e_1 *succeeds* e_2, I mean that there is some time at which e_1 but not e_2 is occurring which succeeds all times at which e_2 is occurring. This, as in the case of precedence, allows for overlap. And, as in the case of precedence, an over-lapping case of succession may be distinguished from a case in which one event *wholly succeeds* another.

When 'simultaneity,' 'precedence,' and 'succession' are understood thus, they do not stand for exclusive relations. An event e_1 may precede, occur simultaneously with, and succeed, another event e_2. But of course e_1 cannot *wholly* precede e_2 while also being *wholly* simultaneous with it, and so forth for the other combinations.

Reflecting on the consequences of the above definitions and explanations, someone might protest that the definition of eternal is altogether too stringent. For consider, say, the number 3. This, no doubt, was referred to by Euclid and also by Cantor. So, by our explanation of 'aspect,' 3's *being referred to by Euclid* was an aspect of the number 3, and 3's *being referred to by Cantor* was another aspect thereof. And of course the former preceded the latter. So, by our definition, 3 is not eternal. But—it may be protested—the fact that something is successively referred to should not be regarded as ground for concluding that it is not eternal. For after all, successive references to something do not produce any change in it. Although they produce variation among its aspects, they do not produce a changeful variation among them.

In response to this protest it must be emphasized that the concept of an eternal being is not identical with the concept of an unchanging being. The root idea behind the concept of an eternal being is not that of one which does not change but rather that of one which is outside of time. And a question of substance is whether an unchanging being may fail to be eternal. The most thoroughgoing and radical way possible for an entity to be outside of time is that which something enjoys if it satisfies our definition of 'eternal.' And it must simply be acknowledged that if an entity is successively referred to, then it is not in the most thoroughgoing way outside of time. There is temporal succession among its aspects.

However, the idea of change could be used by the protester in another way. It is indeed true that not every variation among the aspects of an entity constitutes change therein. Only variation among some of them— call them its *change-relevant* aspects—does so. So on the ground that the change-relevant aspects of an entity are more basic to it, we might distinguish between something being *fundamentally* noneternal and something being *trivially* noneternal. Something is *fundamentally* noneternal if it fails to satisfy the concept of being eternal by virtue of some of its change-relevant aspects. Something is *trivially* noneternal if its failure to satisfy the concept of being eternal is not by virtue of any of its change-relevant aspects.

Now in fact it will be change-relevant aspects of God to which I will appeal in arguing that he is not eternal. Thus my argument will be that God is *fundamentally* noneternal.

II

In order to present our argument that God is fundamentally noneternal we must now take note of a second basic feature of temporality; namely, that all temporal reality comes in the three modes of past, present, and future.[3]

An important fact about the temporal array is that some events within it are *present*: they *are occurring*; some are *past*: they *were occurring*; some are *future*: they *will be occurring*. Indeed, every event is either past or present or future. And not only *is* this the case now. It always was the case in the past that every event was either past or present or future. And it always will be the case in the future that every event is either past or present or future. Further, every event in the array is such that it either was present or is present or will be present. No event can be past unless it was present. No event can be future unless it will be present. Thus the present is the most basic of the three modes of temporality. To be past is just to have

---

3. There are two other basic features of temporality: one is the phenomenon of temporal location— the fact that events occur at or within intervals. The other is the phenomenon of temporal duration—the fact that intervals have lengths. In our preceding discussion we repeatedly made appeal to the phenomenon of temporal location without calling attention to our doing so.

been present. To be future is just to be going to be present. Further, if an event is past, it *presently* is past. If an event is future, it *presently* is future. In this way, too, the present is fundamental.

The reason every event in the temporal array is either past, present, or future is as follows: in order to be in the array at all, an event must occur either before or after or at the same time as some other event. But then, of course, it must occur sometime. And when an event is occurring it is present. So consider any event *e* which is to be found in the temporal array. If *e* is occurring, *e* is present. If, on the other hand, *e* is not occurring, then *e* either precedes or succeeds what is occurring. For *some* event is presently occurring. And every event in the array either precedes or succeeds or is wholly simultaneous with every other. But if *e* were wholly simultaneous with what is occurring, *e* itself would be occurring. So *e* either succeeds or precedes what is occurring if it is not itself occurring. Now for any event *x* to precede any event *y* is just for *x* sometime to be past when *y* is not past. So if *e* precedes what is occurring and is not itself occurring, then *e* is past. On the other hand, for any event *x* to succeed any event *y* is just for *x* sometime to be future when *y* is not future. So if *e* succeeds what is occurring and is not itself occurring, then *e* is future. Hence everything to be found in the temporal array is either past, present, or future.

In contemporary Western philosophy the phenomenon of temporal modality has been pervasively neglected or ignored in favor of the phenomena of temporal order-relationships, temporal location, and temporal duration. Thus time has been 'spatialized.' For though space provides us with close analogues to all three of these latter phenomena, it provides us with no analogue whatever to the past/present/future distinction.[4]

Perhaps the most fundamental and consequential manifestation of this neglect is to be found in the pervasive assumption that all propositions expressed with tensed sentences are mode-indifferent and dated. Consider for example the tensed sentence 'My golden chain tree is flowering.' The assumption is that what I would assert if I now (June 5, 1974) assertively uttered this sentence with normal sense is *that my golden chain tree is or was or will be flowering on June 5, 1974*. And that the proposition I would be asserting if I assertively uttered the same sentence on June 4, 1975, is *that my golden chain tree is or was or will be flowering on June 4, 1975*. And so forth.

In order to see clearly what the assumption in question comes to, it will be helpful to introduce a way of expressing tenses alternative to that found in our natural language.[5] We begin by introducing the three tense operators, *P*, *T*, and *F*.

---

4. A recent example of the neglect of temporal modality in favor of temporal location is to be found in David Lewis, 'Anselm and Actuality,' *Noûs*, 4 (May 1970). Concluding several paragraphs of discussion he says, 'If we take a timeless view and ignore our own location in time, the big difference between the present time and other times vanishes.'

5. See the writings of Arthur Prior, especially *Time and Modality* (Oxford, 1957); *Past, Present and Future* (Oxford, 1967); and *Time and Tense* (Oxford, 1968).

These are to be read, respectively, as 'it was the case that,' 'it is the case that,' and 'it will be the case that.' They are to be attached as prefixes either to sentences in the present tense which lack any such prefix,[6] or to compound sentences which consist of sentences in the present tense with one or more such prefixes attached. And the result of attaching one such operator to a sentence is to yield a new sentence. For example: P (my golden chain tree is flowering), to be read as, '*it was the case that my golden chain tree is flowering.*' And: F[P (my golden chain tree is flowering)], to be read as: '*it will be the case that it was the case that my golden chain tree is flowering.*'

So consider any sentence *s* which is either a present tense sentence with no operators prefixed or a compound sentence consisting of a present tense sentence with one or more operators prefixed. The proposition expressed by $P(s)$ is true if and only if the proposition expressed by *s* was true (in the past). The proposition expressed by $T(s)$ is true if and only if the proposition expressed by *s* is true (now, in the present).[7] And the proposition expressed by $F(s)$ is true if and only if the proposition expressed by *s* will be true (in the future).

Any proposition expressed by a tensed sentence from ordinary speech can be expressed by a sentence in this alternative language. Thus 'My golden chain tree was flowering' has as its translational equivalent 'P (my golden chain tree is flowering).' And 'My golden chain tree will have been flowering' has as its translational equivalent 'F[P (my golden chain tree is flowering)].'

Let us now introduce a fourth tense operator, *D*, defining this one in terms of the preceding three thus:

Def. 2:   D(. . .), if and only if P(. . .) or T(. . .) or F(. . .).

And let us read it as: 'It was or is or will be the case that. . . .' Let us call this the *tense-indifference* tense operator. And, correspondingly, let us call a sentence which has at least one tense operator and all of whose tense operators are tense-indifferent, a *wholly tense-indifferent* sentence. Furthermore, as the ordinary language counterpart to the tense-indifferent operator let us use the verb in its present tense with a bar over it, thus: 'My golden chain tree is flowering.' Or 'My golden chain tree flowers.'

Finally, let us add to our linguistic stock a certain set of modifiers of these tense operators—modifiers of the form 'at *t*,' 'before *t*,' and 'after *t*,' where *t* stands in for some expression designating a time which is such that that expression can be used to designate that time no matter whether that time is in the past, present, or future. These modifiers are to be attached to our tense operators, thus: *P at 1974* (. . .). The result of attaching one to an operator is to yield an operator of a new form—what one might call a *dated* tense operator. The proposition expressed by a sentence of

6. This reflects the fact that the past is what was *present*; the future what will be *present*.
7. Thus, strictly speaking, the *T* operator is unnecessary. Attaching *T* to any sentence *s* always yields a sentence which expresses the same proposition as does s by itself. This reflects the fact that what is past is *presently* past, what is future is *presently* future, and, of course, what is present is *presently* present.

the form *P at t(s)* is true if and only if the proposition expressed by *s* was true at or within time *t*. The proposition expressed by *T at t(s)* is true if and only if the proposition expressed by *s* is true at or within time *t*. And the proposition expressed by *F at t(s)* is true if and only if the proposition expressed by *s* will be true at or within time *t*. Thus the proposition expressed by 'P at 1973 (my golden chain tree is flowering)' is true if and only if my golden chain tree was flowering at or within 1973. Similarly, the proposition expressed by a sentence of the form *P before t(s)* is true if and only if the proposition expressed by *s* was true before *t*; likewise for *T before t(s)* and *F before t(s)*. And the proposition expressed by a sentence of the form *P after t(s)* is true if and only if the proposition expressed by *s* was true after *t*; likewise for *T after t(s)* and *F after t(s)*. Let us call a sentence which has tense operators and all of whose tense operators are dated ones, a *fully dated* sentence.

The assumption underlying a great deal of contemporary philosophy can now be stated thus: every proposition expressed by a sentence which is not wholly tense-indifferent and not fully dated is a proposition which can be expressed by some sentence which is wholly tense-indifferent and fully dated. Consider, for example, the sentence 'T (my golden chain tree is flowering)'—the translational equivalent of the ordinary sentence, 'My golden chain tree is flowering.' Suppose that I assertively utter this sentence on June 5, 1974. The assumption is that the proposition I assert by uttering this sentence is that which is expressed by 'D at June 5, 1974 (my golden chain tree is flowering).' And in general, where *s* is some present tense sentence, the assumption is that the proposition asserted by assertively uttering *s* at time *t* is just that which would be asserted by assertively uttering D *at t(s)*. Similarly, it is assumed that the proposition asserted by assertively uttering *P(s)* at time *t* is that which would be asserted by assertively uttering *D before t(s)*. And it is assumed that the proposition asserted by assertively uttering *F(s)* at time *t* is that which would be asserted by assertively uttering *D after t(s)*.

On this view, tense-committed sentences are characteristically used to assert different propositions on different occasions of use. For example, if the sentence 'My golden chain tree is flowering' is assertively uttered on June 5, it is being used to assert that it is or was or will be the case on June 5 that my golden chain tree is flowering; whereas, if uttered on June 4, it is being used to assert that it is or was or will be the case on June 4 that my golden chain tree is flowering. Whether this view is correct will be considered shortly. If it is, then tense-committed sentences are in that way different from wholly tense-indifferent sentences. For these latter are used to assert the same proposition on all occasions of utterance.

I think we now have the assumption in question clearly enough before us to weigh its acceptability. It is in fact clearly false. To see this, suppose that I now (June 5, 1974) assertively utter the sentence 'My golden chain tree is flowering' and 'D at June 5, 1974 (my golden chain tree is flowering).' The proposition asserted with the former entails that the flowering of my golden chain tree is something that *is* occurring, *now*, *presently*. But the latter does not entail this at all. In general, if someone assertively utters a present tense sentence *s* at *t*, what he asserts is true if and only if the proposition 'D at $t(s)$' is true. Yet 's' and 'D at $t(s)$' are distinct propositions. So also, if I now assertively utter 'My golden chain tree was flowering,' what I assert entails that the flowering of my golden chain tree is something that *did* take place, in the past. Whereas the proposition asserted with 'D before June 5, 1974 (my golden chain tree is flowering)' does not entail this. And this nonidentity of the propositions holds even though it is the case that if someone assertively utters $P(s)$ at t, what he asserts is true if and only if the proposition D *before* $t(s)$ is true.

Just as a wholly tense-indifferent sentence is used to assert the same proposition no matter what the time of utterance, so, too, the proposition asserted with such a sentence does not vary in truth value. If it is ever true, it is always true, that D *at June 5, 1974* (*my golden chain tree is flowering*). And if it is ever false, it is always false. Such a proposition is constant in its truth value. But an implication of the failure of the contemporary assumption is that the same cannot be said for the propositions expressed by tense-committed sentences. At least some of these are such that they are sometimes true, sometimes false. They are variable in their truth value. For example, 'My golden chain tree is flowering' is now true; but two weeks ago it was false.

So the situation is not that in successively uttering a tense-committed sentence we are asserting distinct propositions, each of which is constant in truth value and each of which could also be expressed with wholly tense indifferent, fully dated, sentences. The situation is rather that we are repeatedly asserting a proposition which is variable in its truth value. Contemporary philosophers, along with assuming the dispensability of the temporal modes, have assumed that all propositions are constant in truth value. Plato's lust for eternity lingers on.

Though philosophers have ignored the modes of time in their theories, we as human beings are all aware of the past/present/future distinction. For without such knowledge we would be lost in the temporal array. Suppose one knew, for each event x, which events $\overline{\text{occur}}$ simultaneously with x, which $\overline{\text{occur}}$ before x, and which $\overline{\text{occur}}$ after x. (Recall the significance of the bar over a present-tense verb.) Then with respect to, say, Luther's posting of his theses, one would know which events $\overline{\text{occur}}$ simultaneously therewith, which $\overline{\text{occur}}$ before it, and which $\overline{\text{occur}}$ after it. And so forth, for all other temporal interrelations of events. There would then still be something of enormous importance which one would not on that account know. One would not know where we are in the array of temporally ordered events. For one would not know which events are occurring, which were occurring, and which will be occurring. To know this it is not sufficient to know, with respect to every event, which events $\overline{\text{occur}}$ simultaneously therewith, which $\overline{\text{occur}}$ before, and which $\overline{\text{occur}}$ after.

Nor, as we have seen above, is such knowledge gained by knowing what $\overline{\text{occurs}}$ at what time. If all I know with respect to events $e_1 \ldots e_n$ is that they all $\overline{\text{occur}}$ at the time, say, of the inauguration of the first post-Nixon President, then I do not yet know whether those events are in the past, in the present, or in the future. And if all my knowledge with respect to every event and every interval is of that deficient sort, I do not know where we are in the temporal array. For I do not know which events are present, which are past, and which are future.

III

It might seem obvious that God, as described by the biblical writers, is a being who changes, and who accordingly is fundamentally noneternal. For God is described as a being who *acts*—in creation, in providence, and for the renewal of mankind. He is an agent, not an impassive factor in reality. And from the manner in which his acts are described, it seems obvious that many of them have beginnings and endings, that accordingly they stand in succession relations to each other, and that these successive acts are of such a sort that their presence and absence on God's time-strand constitutes changes thereon. Thus it seems obvious that God is fundamentally noneternal.

God is spoken of as calling Abraham to leave Chaldea and later instructing Moses to return to Egypt. So does not the event of *God's instructing Moses* succeed that of *God's calling Abraham?* And does not this sort of succession constitute a change on God's time-strand—not a change in his 'essence,' but nonetheless a change on his time-strand? Again, God is spoken of as leading Israel through the Red Sea and later sending his Son into the world. So does not his doing the latter succeed his doing the former? And does not the fact of this sort of succession constitute a change along God's time-strand?

In short, it seems evident that the biblical writers regard God as having a time-strand of his own on which actions on his part are to be found, and that some at least of these actions vary in such a way that there are changes along the strand. It seems evident that they do not regard changes on time-strands as confined to entities in God's creation. The God who acts, in the way in which the biblical writers speak of God as acting, seems clearly to change.

Furthermore, is it not clear from how they speak that the biblical writers regarded many of God's acts as bearing temporal order-relations to events which are not aspects of him but rather aspects of the earth, of ancient human beings, and so forth? The four cited above, for example, seem all to be described thus. It seems obvious that God's actions as described by the biblical writers stand in temporal order-relations to all the other events in our own time-array.

However, I think it is not at all so obvious as on first glance it might appear that the biblical writers do in fact describe God as changing. Granted that the language they use suggests this. It is not at once clear that this is what they wished to say with this language. It is not clear that this is how they were describing God. Let us begin to see why this is so by reflecting on the following passage from St Thomas Aquinas:

Nor, if the action of the first agent is eternal, does it follow that His effect is eternal, . . . God acts voluntarily in the production of things, . . . God's act of understanding and willing is, necessarily, His act of making. Now, an effect follows from the intellect and the will according to the determination of the intellect and the command of the will. Moreover, just as the intellect determines every other condition of the thing made, so does it prescribe the time of its making; for art determines not only that this thing is to be such and such, but that it is to be at this particular time, even as a physician determines that a dose of medicine is to be drunk at such and such a particular time, so that, if his act of will were of itself sufficient to produce the effect, the effect would follow anew from his previous decision, without any new action on his part. Nothing, therefore, prevents our saying that God's action existed from all eternity, whereas its effect was not present from eternity, but existed at that time when, from all eternity, He ordained it (*Summa Contra Gentiles* II.35; cf. II.36, 4).

Let us henceforth call an event which neither begins nor ends an *everlasting event*. And let us call an event which either begins or ends, a *temporal* event. In the passage above, St Thomas is considering God's acts of bringing about temporal events. So consider some such act; say, that of God's bringing about Israel's deliverance from Egypt. The temporal event in question, Israel's deliverance from Egypt, occurred (let us say) in 1225 BC. But from the fact that what God brought about occurred in 1225 it does not follow, says Aquinas, that God's act of bringing it about occurred in 1225. In fact, it does not follow that this act had any beginning or ending whatsoever. And in general, suppose that God brings about some temporal event *e*. From the fact that *e* is temporal it does not follow, says Aquinas, that God's act of bringing about *e*'s occurrence is temporal. The temporality of the event which God brings about does not infect God's act of bringing it about. God's act of bringing it about may well be everlasting. This can perhaps more easily be seen, he says, if we remember that God, unlike us, does not have to 'take steps' so as to bring about the occurrence of some event. He need only will that it occur. If God just wants it to be the case that *e* occur at *t*, *e* occurs at *t*.

Thus God can bring about changes in our history without himself changing. The occurrence of the event of Israel's deliverance from Egypt constitutes a change in our history. But there is no counterpart change among God's aspects by virtue of his bringing this event about.

Now let us suppose that the four acts of God cited above—instructing Moses, calling Abraham, leading Israel through the Red Sea, and sending his Son into the world—regardless of the impression we might gain from the biblical language used to describe them, also have the structure of God's bringing about the occurrence of some temporal event. Suppose, for example, that God's leading Israel through the Red Sea has the structure of God's bringing it about that Israel's passage through the Red Sea occurs. And suppose Aquinas is right that the temporality of Israel's passage does not infect with temporality God's act of bringing about this passage. Then what is strictly speaking the case is not that God's leading Israel through the Red Sea occurs in 1225. What is rather the case is that Israel's passage through the Red Sea occurs during 1225, and that God brings this passage about. And the temporality of the passage does not entail the temporality of God's bringing it about. This latter may be everlasting. So, likewise, the fact that the occurrence of this passage marks a change in our history does not entail that God's bringing it about marks a change among God's aspects. God may unchangingly bring about historical changes.

It is natural, at this point, to wonder whether we do not have in hand here a general strategy for interpreting the biblical language about God acting. Is it not perhaps the case that all those acts of God which the biblical writers speak of as beginning or as ending really consist in God performing the everlasting event of bringing about the occurrence of some temporal event?

Well, God does other things with respect to temporal events than bringing about their occurrence. For example, he also *knows* them. Why then should it be thought that the best way to interpret all the temporal-event language used to describe God's actions is by reference to God's action of bringing about the occurrence of some event? May it not be that the best way to interpret what is said with some of such language is by reference to one of those other acts which God performs with respect to temporal events? But then if God is not to change, it is not only necessary that the temporality of *e* not infect God's act of *bringing about* the occurrence of *e*, but also that *every* act of God such that he performs it with respect to *e* not be infected by the temporality of *e*. For example, if God *knows* some temporal event *e*, his knowledge of *e* must not be infected by the temporality of *e*.

So the best way of extrapolating from Aquinas' hint would probably be along the lines of the following theory concerning God's actions and the biblical speech about them. All God's actions are everlasting. None has either beginning or ending. Of these everlasting acts, the structure of some consists in God's performing some action with respect to some event. And at least some of the events that God acts with respect to are temporal events. However, in no case does the temporality of the event that God acts with respect to infect the event of his acting. On the contrary, his acting with respect to some temporal event is itself invariably an everlasting event. So whenever the biblical writers use temporal-event language to describe God's actions, they are to be interpreted as thereby claiming that God acts with respect to some temporal event. They are not to be interpreted as claiming that God's acting is itself a temporal event. God as described by the biblical writers is to be interpreted as acting, and as acting with respect to temporal events. But he is not to be interpreted as changing. All his acts are everlasting.

This, I think, is a fascinating theory. If true, it provides a way of harmonizing the fundamental biblical teaching that God is a being who acts in our history, with the conviction that God does not change. How far the proposed line of biblical inter-pretation can be carried out, I do not know. I am not aware of any theologian who has ever tried to carry it out, though there are a great many theologians who might have relieved the tension in their thought by developing and espousing it. But what concerns us here is not so much what the theory can adequately deal with as what it cannot adequately deal with. Does the theory in fact provide us with a wholly satisfactory way of harmonizing the biblical presentation of God as acting in his-tory with the conviction that God is fundamentally eternal?

Before we set about looking for a refutation of the theory it should be observed, though, that even if the theory were true God would still not be eternal. For consider God's acts of bringing about Abraham's leaving of Chaldea and of bringing about Israel's passage through the Red Sea. These would both be, on the theory, *everlasting* acts. Both are always occurring. Hence they occur simultaneously. They stand to each other in the temporal order-relation of simultaneity. And since both are aspects of God, God accordingly has a time-strand on which these acts are to be found. Hence God is not eternal. Further, these are surely change-relevant aspects of God. Hence God is fundamentally noneternal.[8]

Though I myself think that this argument is sound, it would not be decisive if presented to Aquinas. For Aquinas held that God is simple. And an implication of this contention on his part is that all aspects of God are identical. Hence in God's case there are no two aspects which are simultaneous with each other; for there are no two aspects at all.

A reply is possible. For consider that which is, on Aquinas' theory, God's single aspect; and refer to it as you will—say, as *God's being omnipotent.* This aspect presumably occurs at the same time as itself. Whenever it occurs, it is itself occurring. It is simultaneous with itself. Furthermore, it occurs simultaneously with every temporal event whatsoever. Since God's being omnipotent is always occurring, it 'overlaps' all temporal events whatsoever. So once again we have the conclusion: God is noneternal, indeed, he is fundamentally noneternal,

It is true, though, that even if Aquinas were to accept this last argument he would not *say*, in conclusion, that God was noneternal. For Aquinas defined an eternal being as one which is without beginning and without end, and which has no *succession* among its aspects (*Summa Theologica*, i.i q 10 a 1). Thus as Aquinas defined eternal, an eternal being may very well have aspects which stand to each other in the temporal order-relation of simultaneity. What Aquinas ruled out was just aspects standing in the temporal order-relation of succession. Our own definition of 'eternal,' which disallows simultaneity as well as succession, is in this way more thoroughgoing than is Aquinas'. For a being at least one of whose aspects occurs simultaneously with some event is not yet, in the most radical way possible, outside of time. However, in refutation of the extrapolated Thomistic theory sketched out above I shall now offer an argument against God's being eternal which establishes that there is not only simultaneity but succession among God's aspects, and not just succession but *changeful* succession. This argument will be as relevant to the issue of God's being eternal on Aquinas' definition of eternal as it is on my own definition.

To refute the extrapolated Thomistic theory we would have to do one or the other of two things. We would have to show that some of the temporal-event language the biblical writers use in speaking of God's actions cannot properly be

8. By a similar argument the number 3 can be seen to be fundamentally noneternal. Surely 3*'s being old* and 3*'s being prime* are both change-relevant aspects of 3. If either of these were for a while an aspect of 3 and then for a while not, we would conclude that 3 had changed. But these two aspects occur simultaneously with each other. They stand to each other in the temporal order-relation simultaneity. Hence 3 is fundamentally noneternal.

construed in the suggested way—that is, cannot be construed as used to put forth the claim that God acts in some way with respect to some temporal events. Or, alternatively, we would have to show that some of the actions that God performs with respect to temporal events are themselves temporal, either because they are infected by the temporality of the events or for some other reason.

One way of developing this latter alternative would be to show that some of God's actions must be understood as a response to the free actions of human beings—that what God does he sometimes does in response to what some human being does. I think this is in fact the case. And I think it follows, given that all human actions are temporal, that those actions of God which are 'response' actions are temporal as well. But to develop this line of thought would be to plunge us deep into questions of divine omniscience and human freedom. So I shall make a simpler, though I think equally effective objection to the theory, arguing that in the case of certain of God's actions the temporality of the event that God acts on infects his own action with temporality.

Three such acts are the diverse though similar acts of knowing about some temporal event that it is occurring (that it is *present*), of knowing about some temporal event that it was occurring (that it is *past*), and of knowing about some temporal event that it will be occurring (that it is *future*). Consider the first of these. No one can know about some temporal event *e* that it is occurring except when it is occurring. Before *e* has begun to occur one cannot know that it is occurring, for it is not. Nor after *e* has ceased to occur can one know that it is occurring, for it is not. So suppose that *e* has a beginning. Then P's knowing about *e* that it is occurring cannot occur until *e* begins. And suppose that *e* has an ending. Then P's knowing about *e* that it is occurring cannot occur beyond *e*'s cessation. But every temporal event has (by definition) either a beginning or an ending. So every case of knowing about some temporal event that it is occurring itself either begins or ends (or both). Hence the act of knowing about *e* that it is occurring is infected by the temporality of *e*. So also, the act of knowing about *e* that it *was* occurring, and the act of knowing about *e* that it *will be* occurring, are infected by the temporality of *e*.

But God, as the biblical writers describe him, performs all three of these acts, and performs them on temporal events. He knows what is happening in our history, what has happened, and what will happen. Hence, some of God's actions are themselves temporal events. But surely the nonoccurrence followed by the occurrence followed by the nonoccurrence of such knowings constitutes a change on God's time-strand. Accordingly, God is fundamentally noneternal.[9]

9. This line of argument is adumbrated by Arthur Prior here and there in his essay 'Formalities of Omniscience,' in *Time and Tense*. It is also adumbrated by Norman Kretzmann, 'Omniscience and Immutability,' *Journal of Philosophy*, 63 (1966). The essence of the argument is missed in discussions of Kretzmann's paper by Hector Castaneda, 'Omniscience and Indexical Reference,' *Journal of Philosophy*, 64 (1967); and Nelson Pike, *God and Timelessness* (New York, 1970), ch. 5. Castaneda and Pike fail to take the *modes* of time with full seriousness; as a partial defense of them it should perhaps be admitted as not wholly clear that Kretzmann himself does so.

It is important, if the force of this argument is to be discerned, that one distinguish between, on the one hand, the act of knowing about some event *e* that it $\overline{occurs}$ at some time *t* (recall the significance of the bar) and, on the other hand, the act of knowing about *e* that it is occurring or of knowing that it was occurring or of knowing that it will be occurring. Knowing about *e* that it $\overline{occurs}$ at *t* is an act not infected by the temporality of the event known. *That Calvin's flight from Geneva $\overline{occurs}$ in 1537* is something that can be known at any and every time whatsoever. For it is both true, and constant in its truth value. But *that Calvin's flight from Geneva is occurring* is variable in its truth value. It once was true, it now is false. And since one can know only what is true, this proposition cannot be known at every time. It cannot be known now. God can know, concerning every temporal event whatsoever, what time that event $\overline{occurs}$ at, without such knowledge of his being temporal. But he cannot know concerning any temporal event whatsoever that it is occurring, or know that it was occurring, or know that it will be occurring, without that knowledge being itself temporal.

Similarly, we must distinguish between, on the one hand, the act of knowing about some temporal event *e* that it $\overline{occurs}$ simultaneously with events $e_1 \ldots e_n$, after events $f_1 \ldots f_n$, and before events $g_1 \ldots g_n$, and, on the other hand, the act of knowing about *e* that it is occurring or of knowing that it was occurring or of knowing that it will be occurring. Knowledge of the former sort is not infected by the temporality of the event whose temporal order-relationships are known. Knowledge of the latter sort is. I know now that Calvin's flight from Geneva $\overline{occurs}$ after Luther's posting of his theses $\overline{occurs}$. But once again, I do not and cannot now know that Calvin's flight *is* occurring. Because it is not. So too, God once knew that Calvin's flight from Geneva was occurring. But he no longer knows this. For he, too, does not know that which is not so. Thus, in this respect his knowledge has changed. But God always knows that Calvin's flight from Geneva $\overline{occurs}$ after Luther's posting of his theses $\overline{occurs}$. Only if time lacked modes and only if propositions were all constant in truth value could God's knowledge be unchanging— assuming that God's knowledge comprises temporal as well as everlasting events.

The act of *remembering* that *e* has occurred is also an act infected by the temporality of *e* (remembering is, of course, a species of knowing). For one can only remember that *e* has occurred after *e* has occurred. 'P remembers that *e* $\overline{occurs}$' entails that *e* has occurred. So if *e* is an event that has a beginning, then the act of remembering that *e* has occurred has a beginning. But some events with beginnings are such that God remembers their occurrence. Consequently this act on God's part is also a temporal event. It too cannot be everlasting.

God is also described by the biblical writers as planning that he would bring about certain events which he does. This, too, is impossible if God does not change. For consider some event which someone brings about, and suppose that he planned to bring it about. His planning to bring it about must occur before the planned event occurs. For otherwise it is not a case of planning.

So in conclusion, if God were eternal he could not be aware, concerning any temporal event, that it is occurring nor aware that it was occurring nor aware that it will be occurring; nor could he remember that it has occurred; nor could he plan to bring it about and do so. But all of such actions are presupposed by, and essential to, the biblical presentation of God as a redeeming God. Hence God as presented by the biblical writers is fundamentally noneternal. He is fundamentally in time.

IV

As with any argument, one can here choose to deny the premisses rather than to accept the conclusion. Instead of agreeing that God is fundamentally noneternal because he changes with respect to his knowledge, his memory, and his planning, one could try to save one's conviction that God is eternal by denying that he knows what is or was or will be occurring, that he remembers what has occurred, and that he brings about what he has planned. It seems to me, however, that this is clearly to give up the notion of God as a redeeming God; and in turn it seems to me that to give this up is to give up what is central to the biblical vision of God. To sustain this latter claim would of course require an extensive hermeneutical inquiry. But lest someone be tempted to go this route of trying to save God's eternity by treating all the biblical language about God the redeemer as either false or misleadingly meta-phorical, let me observe that if God were eternal he could not be the object of any human action whatsoever.

Consider, for example, my act of referring to something, *X*. The event consisting of *my referring to X* is a temporal event. It both begins and ends, as do all my acts. Now the event of *my referring to X* is identical with the event of *X's being referred to by me*. And this event is an aspect both of *X* and of me. So if *X* is a being which lasts longer than my act of referring to *X* does, then for a while *X* has this aspect and for a while not. And thus *X* would have *succession* on its time-strand. And so *X* would not be eternal. Thus if God were eternal, no human being could ever refer to him — or perform any other temporal act with respect to him. If he were eternal, one could not know him. In particular, one could not know that he was eternal, or even believe that he was. Indeed, if God were eternal one could not predicate of him that he is eternal. For predicating is also a temporal act. So this is the calamitous consequence of claiming of God that he is eternal: if one predicates of him that he is eternal, then he is not.

V

I have been arguing that God as described by the biblical writers is a being who changes. That, we have seen, is not self-evidently and obviously so, though the mode of expression of the biblical writers might lead one to think it was. Yet it is so nonetheless.

But are there not explicit statements in the Bible to the effect that God does not change? If we are honest to the evidence, must we not acknowledge that on this matter the biblical writers contradict each other? Let us see.

Surprisingly, given the massive Christian theological tradition in favor of God's ontological immutability, there are only two passages (to the best of my knowledge) in which it is directly said of God that he does not change. One of these is Malachi 3: 6. The prophet has just been saying to the people that God is wearied by their hypocrisy; however (he goes on), God will send his messenger to clear a path before him; and 'he will take his seat, refining and purifying.' As a result of this cleansing, the 'offerings of Judah and Jerusalem shall be pleasing to the Lord as they were in days of old.' And then comes this assurance: 'I am the Lord, unchanging; and you, too, have not ceased to be sons of Jacob. From the days of your forefathers you have been wayward and have not kept my laws. If you will return to me, I will return to you, says the Lord of Hosts' (NEB).

Surely it would be a gross misinterpretation to treat the prophet here as claiming that God is ontologically immutable. What he says, on the contrary, is that God is faithful to his people Israel—that he is unchanging in his fidelity to the covenant he has made with them. All too often theologians have ontologized the biblical message. Malachi 3: 6 is a classic example of a passage which, cited out of context, would seem to support the doctrine of God's ontological immutability. Read in context, however, it supports not that but rather the doctrine of God's unswerving fidelity. No ontological claim whatever is being made.

The other passage in which it is said of God that he is unchanging is to be found in Psalm 102: 27. Again we must set the passage in its context:

> My strength is broken in mid course;
> the time allotted me is short.
> Snatch me not away before half my days are done,
> for thy years last through all generations.
> Long ago thou didst lay the foundations of the earth,
> and the heavens were thy handiwork.
>
> They shall pass away, but thou endurest;
> like clothes they shall all grow old;
> thou shalt cast them off like a cloak,
> and they shall vanish;
> but thou art the same and thy years shall have no end;
> thy servants' children shall continue,
> and their posterity shall be established in thy presence. (NEB)

Here, too, it would be a gross misinterpretation to regard the writer as teaching that God is ontologically immutable. The Psalmist is making an ontological point of sorts, though even so the ontological point is set within a larger context of religious reflection. He is drawing a contrast between God on the one hand and his transitory creation on the other. And what he says about God is clearly that God is without end—'Thy years shall have no end.' He does not say that God is ontologically immutable.

In short, God's ontological immutability is not a part of the explicit teaching of the biblical writers. What the biblical writers teach is that God is faithful and without beginning or end, not that none of his aspects is temporal. The theological tradition of God's ontological immutability has no explicit biblical foundation.[10]

VI

The upshot of our discussion is this: the biblical presentation of God presupposes that God is everlasting rather than eternal. God is indeed without beginning and without end. But at least some of his aspects stand in temporal order-relations to each other. Thus God, too, has a time-strand. His life and existence is itself temporal. (Whether his life and existence always was and always will be temporal, or whether he has taken on temporality, is a question we have not had time to consider.) Further, the events to be found on God's time-strand belong within the same temporal array as that which contains our time-strands. God's aspects do not only bear temporal order-relations to each other but to the aspects of created entities as well. And the aspects and succession of aspects to be found on God's time-strand are such that they constitute *changes* thereon. God's life and existence incorporates changeful succession.

Haunting Christian theology and Western philosophy throughout the centuries has been the picture of time as bounded, with the created order on this side of the boundary and God on the other. Or sometimes the metaphor has been that of time as extending up to a horizon, with all creaturely reality on this side of the horizon and God on the other. All such metaphors, and the ways of thinking that they represent, must be discarded. Temporality embraces us along with God.

This conclusion from our discussion turns out to be wholly in accord with that to be found in Oscar Cullmann's *Christ and Time*. From his study of the biblical words for time Cullmann concluded that, in the biblical picture, God's 'eternity' is not qualitatively different from our temporality. Cullmann's line of argument (though not his conclusion) has been vigorously attacked by James Barr on the ground that from the lexicographical patterns of biblical language we cannot legitimately make inferences as to what was being said by way of that language.[11] Verbal similarities may conceal differences in thought, and similarities in thought may be clothed with verbal differences. Barr's objection is *apropos*. But though we have traveled a very different route from Cullmann's we have come out at the same place. We have not engaged in any word studies. Yet, by seeing that God's temporality is presupposed by the biblical presentation of God as redeemer, we too have reached

10. 'I am that I am' (Exod. 3: 13) has also sometimes been used to support the doctrine of God's immutability. However, this is one of the most cryptic passages in all of Scripture; and—to understate the point—it is not in the least clear that what is being proclaimed is God's ontological immutability. There is a wealth of exegetical material on the passage, but see especially the comments by J. C. Murray, *The Problem of God* (New Haven, 1967), ch. 1.

11. *Biblical Words for Time* (London, 1962).

the conclusion that we share time with God. The lexicographical and philosophical cases coincide in their results.

Though God is within time, yet he is Lord of time. The whole array of contingent temporal events is within his power. He is Lord of what occurs. And that, along with the specific pattern of what he does, grounds all authentically biblical worship of, and obedience to, God. It is not because he is outside of time—eternal, immutable, impassive—that we are to worship and obey God. It is because of what he can and does bring about within time that we mortals are to render him praise and obedience.

Chapter 48

A modern defence of divine eternity

Eleonore Stump and Norman Kretzmann

THE concept of eternity makes a significant difference in the consideration of a variety of issues in the philosophy of religion, including, for instance, the apparent incompatibility of divine omniscience with human freedom, of divine immutability with the efficacy of petitionary prayer, and of divine omniscience with divine immutability; but, because it has been misunderstood or cursorily dismissed as incoherent, it has not received the attention it deserves from contemporary philosophers of religion. In this paper we expound the concept as it is presented by Boethius (whose definition of eternity was the *locus classicus* for medieval discussions of the concept), analyze implications of the concept, examine reasons for considering it incoherent, and sample the results of bringing it to bear on issues in the philosophy of religion.

Eternality—the condition of having eternity as one's mode of existence—is misunderstood most often in either of two ways. Sometimes it is confused with limitless duration in time—sempiternality—and sometimes it is construed simply as atemporality, eternity being understood in that case as roughly analogous to an isolated, static instant. The second misunderstanding of eternality is not so far off the mark as the first, but a consideration of the views of the philosophers who contributed most to the development of the concept shows that atemporality alone does not exhaust eternality as they conceived of it, and that the picture of eternity as a frozen instant is a radical distortion of the classic concept.

1 Boethius's definition

Boethius discusses eternity in two places: *The Consolation of Philosophy*, Book V, Prose 6, and *De trinitate*, chapter 4.[1] The immediately relevant passages are these:

CP That God is eternal, then, is the common judgment of all who live by reason. Let us therefore consider what eternity is, for this makes plain to us both the divine nature and knowledge. Eternity, then, is the complete possession all at once of illimitable life. This becomes clearer by comparison with temporal things. For whatever lives in time

Eleonore Stump and Norman Kretzman 'Eternity' from *The Journal of Philosophy*, vol. 78 (1981), reprinted by permission of The Journal of Philosophy and the authors.

1. E. K. Rand, ed., in H. F. Stewart, E. K. Rand, and S. J. Tester, *Boethius: The Theological Tractates and The Consolation of Philosophy* (London: Heinemann; Cambridge, Mass.: Harvard, 1973).

proceeds as something present from the past into the future, and there is nothing placed in time that can embrace the whole extent of its life equally. Indeed, on the contrary, it does not yet grasp tomorrow but yesterday it has already lost; and even in the life of today you live no more fully than in a mobile, transitory moment. . . . Therefore, whatever includes and possesses the whole fullness of illimitable life at once and is such that nothing future is absent from it and nothing past has flowed away, this is rightly judged to be eternal, and of this it is necessary both that being in full possession of itself it be always present to itself and that it have the infinity of mobile time present [to it]. (422.5–424.31)

DT What is said of God, [namely, that] he is always, indeed signifies a unity, as if he had been in all the past, is in all the present—however that might be—[and] will be in all the future. That can be said, according to the philosophers, of the heaven and of the imperishable bodies; but it cannot be said of God in the same way. For he is always in that for him *always* has to do with present time. And there is this great difference between the present of our affairs, which is *now*, and that of the divine: our now makes time and sempiternity, as if it were running along; but the divine now, remaining, and not moving, and standing still, makes eternity. If you add '*semper*' to 'eternity,' you get sempiternity, the perpetual running resulting from the flowing, tireless now. (20.64–22.77)

The definition Boethius presents and explains in CP and elucidates in the earlier DT is not original with him, nor does he argue for it in those passages. Similarly, we mean to do no more in this section of our paper than to present and explain a concept that has been important in Christian and pre-Christian theology and metaphysics. We will not argue here, for instance, that there is an eternal entity or even that God must be eternal if he exists. It is a matter of fact that many ancient and medieval philosophers and theologians were committed to the doctrine of God's eternality in the form in which Boethius presents it, and our purpose in this section of the paper is simply to elucidate the doctrine they held.

Boethius's definition is this: *Eternity is the complete possession all at once of illimitable life.*

We want to call attention to four ingredients in this definition. It is clear, first of all, that anything that is eternal has life. In this sense of 'eternal,' then, it will not do to say that a number, a truth, or the world is eternal, although one might want to say of the first two that they are atemporal and of the third that it is sempiternal— that it has beginningless, endless temporal existence.

The second and equally explicit element in the definition is illimitability: the life of an eternal being cannot be limited; it is impossible that there be a beginning or an end to it. The natural understanding of such a claim is that the existence in question is infinite duration, unlimited in either 'direction.' But there is another interpretation that must be considered in this context despite its apparent unnaturalness. Conceivably the existence of an eternal entity is said to be illimitable in the way in which a point or an instant may be said to be illimitable: what cannot be extended cannot be limited in its extent. There are passages that can be read as suggesting that this second interpretation is what Boethius intends. In CP eternal existence is expressly contrasted with temporal existence described as extending from the past through the present into the future, and what is eternal is described contrastingly as possessing its entire life *at once*. Boethius's insistence in DT that the eternal now is unlike the temporal now in being fixed and unchanging strengthens that hint with the suggestion that the eternal present is to be understood in terms of the present instant 'standing still.' Nevertheless, there are good reasons, in these passages themselves and in the history of the concept of eternity before and after Boethius, for rejecting this less natural interpretation. In the first place, some of the terminology Boethius uses would be inappropriate to eternity if eternity were to be conceived as illimitable in virtue of being unextended. He speaks in CP more than once of the *fullness* of eternal life. In DT and in *The Consolation of Philosophy* immediately following our passage CP he speaks of the eternal present or an eternal entity as *remaining* and *enduring*. And he claims in DT that it is correct to say of God that he is *always*, explaining the use of 'always' in reference to God in such a way that he can scarcely have had in mind a life illimitable in virtue of being essentially durationless. The more natural reading of 'illimitable,' then, also provides the more natural reading of these texts. In the second place, the weight of tradition both before and after Boethius strongly favors interpreting illimitable life as involving infinite duration, beginningless as well as endless. Boethius throughout the *Consolation* and especially in passage CP is plainly working in the Platonic tradition, and both Plato and Plotinus understand eternal existence in that sense.[2] Medieval philosophers after Boethius, who depend on him for their conception of eternity, also clearly understand 'illimitable' in this way.[3] So, for both these sets of reasons, we understand this part of Boethius's definition to mean that the life of an eternal entity is characterized by beginningless, endless, infinite duration.

The concept of duration that emerges in the interpretation of 'illimitable life' is the third ingredient we mean to call attention to. Illimitable life entails duration of a special sort, as we have just seen, but it would be reasonable to think that any mode of existence that could be called a life must involve duration, and so there may seem to be no point in explicitly listing duration as an ingredient in Boethius's concept of eternity. We call attention to it here, however, because of its importance as part of the background against which the fourth ingredient must be viewed.

The fourth ingredient is presented in the only phrase of the definition still to be considered: 'The complete possession all at once.' As Boethius's explanation of the definition in CP makes clear, he conceives of an eternal entity as atemporal, and he thinks of its atemporality as conveyed by just that phrase in the definition. What he says shows that something like the following line of thought leads to his use of

---

2. See Plato, *Timaeus* 37D–38C; Plotinus, *Enneads* III 7.
3. See e.g., Thomas Aquinas, *Summa theologiae* I, q. 10. Augustine, who is an earlier and in general an even more important source for medieval philosophy and theology than Boethius and who is even more clearly in the Platonist tradition, understands and uses this classic concept of eternity (see, e.g., *Confessions*, book XI, ch. 11; *The City of God*, book XI, ch. 21); but his influence on the medieval discussion of eternity seems not to have been so direct or important as Boethius's.

those words. A living temporal entity may be said to possess a life, but, since the events constituting the life of any temporal entity occur sequentially, some later than others, it cannot be said to possess all its life *at once*. And since everything in the life of a temporal entity that is not present is either past and so no longer in its possession, or future and so not yet in its possession, it cannot be said to have the *complete* possession of its life. So whatever has the complete possession of all its life at once cannot be temporal. The life that is the mode of an eternal entity's existence is thus characterized not only by duration but also by atemporality.

With the possible exception of Parmenides, none of the ancients or medievals who accepted eternity as a real, atemporal mode of existence meant thereby to deny the reality of time or to suggest that all temporal experiences are illusory. In introducing the concept of eternity, such philosophers, and Boethius in particular, were proposing two separate modes of real existence. Eternity is a mode of existence that is, on Boethius's view, neither reducible to time nor incompatible with the reality of time.

In the next two sections of this paper, we will investigate the apparent incoherence of this concept of eternity. We will begin with a consideration of the meaning of atemporality in this connection, including an examination of the relationship between eternity and time; and we will go on to consider the apparent incoherence generated by combining atemporality with duration and with life.

2 The atemporality of an eternal entity: presentness and simultaneity

Because an eternal entity is atemporal, there is no past or future, no earlier or later, *within* its life; that is, the events constituting its life cannot be ordered sequentially from the standpoint of eternity. But, in addition, no temporal entity or event can be earlier or later than or past or future with respect to the whole life of an eternal entity, because otherwise such an eternal life or entity would itself be part of a temporal series. Here it should be evident that, although the stipulation that an eternal entity completely possesses its life all at once entails that it is not part of any sequence, it does not rule out the attribution of presentness or simultaneity to the life and relationships of such an entity, nor should it. In so far as an entity *is*, or *has* life, completely or otherwise, it is appropriate to say that it has present existence in some sense of 'present'; and unless its life consists in only one event or it is impossible to relate an event in its life to any temporal entity or event, we need to be able to consider an eternal entity or event as one of the *relata* in a simultaneity relationship. We will consider briefly the applicability of presentness to something eternal and then consider in some detail the applicability of simultaneity.

If anything exists eternally, it exists. But the existing of an eternal entity is a duration without succession, and, because eternity excludes succession, no eternal entity has existed or will exist; it *only* exists. It is in this sense that an eternal entity is said to have present existence. But since that present is not flanked by past and future, it is obviously not the temporal present. And, furthermore, the eternal, pastless, futureless present is not instantaneous but extended, because eternity entails duration. The temporal present is a durationless instant, a present that cannot be extended conceptually without falling apart entirely into past and future intervals. The eternal present, on the other hand, is by definition an infinitely extended, pastless, futureless duration.

Simultaneity is of course generally and unreflectively taken to mean existence or occurrence at one and the same time. But to attribute to an eternal entity or event simultaneity with anything we need a coherent characterization of simultaneity that does not make it altogether temporal. It is easy to provide a coherent characterization of a simultaneity relationship that is not temporal in case both the *relata* are eternal entities or events. Suppose we designate the ordinary understanding of temporal simultaneity *T-simultaneity*:

(T) T-simultaneity = existence or occurrence at one and the same time.

Then we can easily enough construct a second species of simultaneity, a relationship obtaining between two eternal entities or events:

(E) E-simultaneity = existence or occurrence at one and the same eternal present.

What really interests us among species of simultaneity, however, and what we need for our present purposes, is not E-simultaneity so much as a simultaneity relationship between two *relata* of which one is eternal and the other temporal. We have to be able to characterize such a relationship coherently if we are to be able to claim that there is any connection between an eternal and a temporal entity or event. An eternal entity or event cannot be earlier or later than, or past or future with respect to, any temporal entity or event. If there is to be any relationship between what is eternal and what is temporal, then, it must be some species of simultaneity.

Now in forming the species T-simultaneity and E-simultaneity, we have in effect been taking the genus of those species to be something like this:

(G) Simultaneity = existence or occurrence at once (i.e. together).

And we have formed those two species by giving specific content to the broad expression 'at once.' In each case, we have spelled out 'at once' as meaning at one and the same *something*—time, in the case of T-simultaneity; eternal present, in the case of E-simultaneity. In other words, the *relata* for T-simultaneity occur together at the same time, and the *relata* for E-simultaneity occur together at the same eternal present. What we want now is a species of simultaneity—call it *ET-simultaneity* (for eternal-temporal simultaneity)—that can obtain between what is eternal and what is temporal. It is only natural to try to construct a definition for ET-simultaneity as we did for the two preceding species of simultaneity, by making the broad 'at once' in (G) more precise. Doing so requires starting with the phrase 'at one and the same——' and filling in the blank appropriately. To fill in that blank appropriately, however, would be to specify a single mode of existence in which the two *relata* exist or occur together, as the *relata* for T-simultaneity co-exist (or co-occur) in time and the *relata* for E-simultaneity co-exist (or co-occur) in eternity. But, on the view we are explaining and defending, it is theoretically impossible to specify a single mode of existence for two *relata* of which one is eternal and the other temporal. To do so would be to reduce what is temporal to what is eternal (thus making time illusory) or what is eternal to what is temporal (thus making eternity illusory) or both what is temporal and what is eternal to some *third* mode of existence; and all three of these alternatives are ruled out. The medieval adherents of the concept of eternity held that both time and eternity are real and that there is no mode of existence besides those two.

Against this background, then, it is not conceptually possible to construct a definition for ET-simultaneity analogous to the definitions for the other two species of simultaneity, by spelling out 'at once' as 'at one and the same——' and filling in the blank appropriately. What is temporal and what is eternal can coexist, on the view we are adopting and defending, but not within the same mode of existence; and there is no single mode of existence that can be referred to in filling in the blank in such a definition of ET-simultaneity.

The significance of this difficulty and its implications for a working definition of ET-simultaneity can be better appreciated by returning to the definition of T-simultaneity for a closer look. Philosophers of physics, explaining the special theory of relativity, have taught us to be cautious even about the notion of temporal simultaneity; in fact, the claim that temporal simultaneity is relative rather than absolute is fundamental to the special theory of relativity.

For all ordinary practical purposes and also for our theoretical purposes in this paper, time can be thought of as absolute, along Newtonian lines. But, simply in order to set the stage for our characterization of ET-simultaneity, it will be helpful to look at a standard philosophical presentation of temporal simultaneity along Einsteinian lines. Imagine a train traveling very fast, at 6/10ths the speed of light. One observer (the 'ground observer') is stationed on the embankment beside the track; another observer (the 'train observer') is stationed on the train. Suppose that two lightning bolts strike the train, one at each end, and suppose that the ground observer sees those two lightning bolts simultaneously. The train observer also sees the two lightning bolts, but, since he is traveling toward the light ray emanating from the bolt that strikes the front of the train and away from the bolt that strikes the rear of the train, he will see the lightning bolt strike the front of the train before he sees the other strike the rear of the train. 'This, then, is the fundamental result: events occurring at different places which are simultaneous in one frame of reference will not be simultaneous in another frame of reference which is moving with respect to the first. This is known as *the relativity of simultaneity*'.

We want to leave to one side the philosophical issues raised by this example and simply accept it for our present purposes as a standard example illustrating Einstein's notion of the relativity of temporal simultaneity. According to this example, the very same two lightning flashes are simultaneous (with respect to the reference frame of the ground observer) and not simultaneous (with respect to the reference frame of the train observer). If we interpret 'simultaneous' here in accordance with our definition of T-simultaneity, we will have to say that the same two lightning flashes occur at the same time and do not occur at the same time; that is, it will be both true and false that these two lightning flashes occur at the same time. The incoherence of this result is generated by filling in the blank for the definition of T-simultaneity with a reference to one and the same time, where time is understood as one single uniform mode of existence. The special theory of relativity takes time itself to be relative and so calls for a more complicated definition of temporal simultaneity than the common, unreflective definition given in (T), such as this relativized version of temporal simultaneity:

(RT) RT-simultaneity = existence or occurence at the same time within the reference frame of a given observer.

This relativizing of time to the reference frame of a given observer resolves the apparent incoherence in saying that the same two lightning flashes occur and do not occur at one and the same time. They occur at the same time in the reference frame of one observer and do not occur at the same time in the reference frame of a different observer.

Once this is understood, we can see that, if we persist in asking whether or not the two lightning bolts are *really* simultaneous, we are asking an incoherent question, one that cannot be answered. The question is asked about what is assumed to be a feature of reality, although in fact there is no such feature of reality; such a question is on a par with 'Is Uris Library *really* to the left of Morrill Hall?' There is no absolute state of being temporally simultaneous with, any more than there is an absolute state of being to the left of. We determine the obtaining of the one relationship as we determine the obtaining of the other, by reference to an observer and the observer's point of view. The two lightning flashes, then, are RT-simultaneous in virtue of occurring at the same time within the reference frame of the ground observer and not RT-simultaneous in virtue of occurring at different times within the reference frame of the train observer. And, Einstein's theory argues, there is no privileged observer (or reference frame) such that with respect to it we can determine whether the two events are *really* simultaneous; simultaneity is irreducibly relative to observers and their reference frames, and so is time itself. Consequently, it would be a mistake to think that there is one single uniform mode of existence that can be referred to in specifying 'at once' in (G) in order to derive a definition of temporal simultaneity.

These difficulties in spelling out even a very crude acceptable definition for temporal simultaneity in the light of relativity theory foreshadow and are analogous to the difficulties in spelling out an acceptable definition of ET-simultaneity. More significantly, they demonstrate that the difficulties defenders of the concept of eternity encounter in formulating such a definition are by no means unique to their undertaking and cannot be assumed to be difficulties in the concepts of

ET-simultaneity or of eternity themselves. Finally, and most importantly, the way in which we cope with such difficulties in working out a definition for RT-simultaneity suggests the sort of definition needed for ET-simultaneity. Because one of the *relata* for ET-simultaneity is eternal, the definition for this relationship, like that for E-simultaneity, must refer to one and the same present rather than to one and the same time. And because in ET-simultaneity we are dealing with two equally real modes of existence, neither of which is reducible to any other mode of existence, the definition must be constructed in terms of *two* reference frames and *two* observers. So we can characterize ET-simultaneity in this way. Let '*x*' and '*y*' range over entities and events. Then:

(ET)   For every *x* and for every *y*, *x* and *y* are ET-simultaneous iff
    (i)   either *x* is eternal and *y* is temporal, or vice versa; and
    (ii) for some observer, *A*, in the unique eternal reference frame, *x* and *y* are both present—i.e. either *x* is eternally present and *y* is observed as temporally present, or vice versa; and
    (iii) for some observer, *B*, in one of the infinitely many temporal reference frames, *x* and *y* are both present—i.e. either *x* is observed as eternally present and *y* is temporally present, or vice versa.

Given the concept of eternity, condition (ii) provides that a temporal entity or event observed as temporally present by some eternal observer *A* is ET-simultaneous with every eternal entity or event; and condition (iii) provides that an eternal entity or event observed as eternally present (or simply as eternal) by some temporal observer *B* is ET-simultaneous with every temporal entity or event.

On our definition, if *x* and *y* are ET-simultaneous, then *x* is neither earlier nor later than, neither past nor future with respect to, *y*—a feature essential to any relationship that can be considered a species of simultaneity. Further, if *x* and *y* are ET-simultaneous, *x* and *y* are not temporally simultaneous; since either *x* or *y* must be eternal, it cannot be the case that *x* and *y* both exist *at one and the same time* within a given observer's reference frame. ET-simultaneity is symmetric, of course, but, since no temporal or eternal entity or event is ET-simultaneous with itself, the relationship is not reflexive; and the fact that there are different domains for its *relata* means that it is not transitive. The propositions

(1)   *x* is ET-simultaneous with *y*.

and

(2)   *y* is ET-simultaneous with *z*.

do not entail

(3)   *x* is ET-simultaneous with *z*.

And even if we conjoin with (1) and (2)

(4)   x and *z* are temporal.

(1), (2), and (4) together do not entail

(5) x and z are temporally simultaneous.

   (RT) and the Einsteinian conception of time as relative have served the only purpose we have for them in this paper, now that they have provided an introductory
analogue for our characterization of ET-simultaneity, and we can now revert to a
Newtonian conception of time, which will simplify the discussion without involving any relevant loss of precision. In the first place, at least one of the theological
issues we are going to be discussing—the problem of omniscience and
immutability—depends on the concept of an absolute present, a concept that is
often thought to be dependent on a Newtonian conception of absolute time. But
the concept of an absolute present which is essential to our discussion is not
discredited by relativity theory. Every conscious temporal observer has an undeniable, indispensable sense of the absolute present, *now*, and that thoroughly pervasive feature of temporal consciousness is all we need. We do not need and we will
not try to provide a philosophical justification for the concept of an absolute
present; we will simply assume it for our present purposes. And if it must he said
that the absolute present is absolute only within a given observer's reference frame,
that will not affect our use of the concept here. In the second place, in ordinary
human circumstances, all human observers may be said—*should* be said—to share
one and the same reference frame, and distinguishing individual reference frames
for our discussion of time in the rest of this paper would be as inappropriate as
taking an Einsteinian view of time in a discussion of historical chronology.

3 Implications of ET-simultaneity

If x and z are temporal entities, they co-exist if and only if there is some time during
which both x and z exist. But if anything exists eternally, its existence, although
infinitely extended, is fully realized, all present at once. Thus the entire life of any
eternal entity is co-existent with any temporal entity at any time at which that
temporal entity exists. From a temporal standpoint, the present is ET-simultaneous
with the whole infinite extent of an eternal entity's life. From the standpoint of
eternity, every time is present, co-occurrent with the whole of infinite atemporal
duration.

   We can show the implications of this account of ET-simultaneity by considering
the relationship between an eternal entity and a future contingent event. Suppose
that Richard Nixon will die at noon on August 9, 1990, precisely sixteen years after
he resigned the Presidency. Nixon's death some years from now *will be* present to
those who will be at his deathbed, but it *is* present to an eternal entity. It cannot be
that an eternal entity has a vision of Nixon's death before it occurs; in that case an
eternal event would be earlier than a temporal event. Instead, the actual occasion of
Nixon's dying is present to an eternal entity. It is not that the future pre-exists
somehow, so that it can be inspected by an entity that is outside time, but rather

that an eternal entity that is wholly ET-simultaneous with August 9, 1974, and with today, is wholly ET-simultaneous with August 9, 1990, as well. It is *now* true to say 'The whole of eternity is ET-simultaneous with the present'; and of course it was true to say just the same at noon of August 9, 1974, and it will be true to say it at noon of August 9, 1990. But since it is one and the same eternal present that is ET-simultaneous with each of those times, there is a sense in which it is now true to say that Nixon at the hour of his death is present to an eternal entity; and in that same sense it is now true to say that Nixon's resigning of the Presidency is present to an eternal entity. If we are considering an eternal entity that is omniscient, it is true to say that that entity is *at once* aware of Nixon resigning the Presidency and of Nixon on his deathbed (although of course an omniscient entity understands that those events occur sequentially and knows the sequence and the dating of them); and it is true to say also that for such an entity both those events are present at once.

Such an account of ET-simultaneity suggests at least a radical epistemological or even metaphysical relativism, and perhaps plain incoherence. We *know* that Nixon is now alive. An omniscient eternal entity *knows* that Nixon is now dead. Still worse, an omniscient eternal entity also *knows* that Nixon is now alive, and so Nixon is apparently both alive and dead at once in the eternal present.

These absurdities appear to be entailed partly because the full implications of the concept of eternity have not been taken into account. We have said enough to induce caution regarding 'present' and 'simultaneous,' but it is not difficult to overlook the concomitant ambiguity in such expressions as 'now' and 'at once.' To say that we know that Nixon is now alive although an eternal entity knows that Nixon is now dead does not mean that an eternal entity knows the opposite of what we know. What we know is that:

(6) Nixon is alive in the temporal present.

What eternal entity knows is that

(7) Nixon is dead in the eternal present.

and (6) is not incompatible with (7). Still, this simple observation does nothing to dispel the appearance of incompatibility between (7) and

(8) Nixon is alive in the eternal present.

and, on the basis of what has been said so far, both (7) and (8) are true. But Nixon is temporal, not eternal, and so are his life and death. The conjunction of (7) and (8), then, cannot be taken to mean that the temporal entity Nixon exists in eternity, where he is simultaneously alive and dead, but rather something more nearly like this. One and the same eternal present is ET-simultaneous with Nixon's being alive and is also ET-simultaneous with Nixon's dying; so Nixon's life is ET-simultaneous with and hence present to an eternal entity, and Nixon's death is ET-simultaneous with and hence present to an eternal entity, although Nixon's life and Nixon's death are themselves neither eternal nor simultaneous.

These considerations also explain the appearance of metaphysical relativism inherent in the claim that Nixon's death is really future for us and really present for an eternal entity. It is not that there are two objective realities, in one of which Nixon's death is really future and in the other of which Nixon's death and life are really present; that *would* be incoherent. What the concept of eternity implies instead is that there is one objective reality that contains two modes of real existence in which two different sorts of duration are measured by two irreducibly different sorts of measure: time and eternity. Given the relations between time and eternity spelled out in section 2 of this paper, Nixon's death is really future or not depending on which sort of entity, temporal or eternal, it is being related to. An eternal entity's mode of existence is such that its whole life is ET-simultaneous with each and every temporal entity or event, and so Nixon's death, like every other event involving Nixon, is really ET-simultaneous with the life of an eternal entity. But when Nixon's death is being related to *us*, on [today's date], then, given our location in the temporal continuum Nixon's death is not simultaneous (temporally or in any other way) with respect to us, but really future.

4 Atemporal duration and atemporal life

With this understanding of the atemporality of an eternal entity's existence, we want to consider now the apparent incoherence generated by combining atemporality with duration and with life in the definition of eternity.

The notion of atemporal duration is the heart of the concept of eternity and, in our view, the original motivation for its development. The most efficient way in which to dispel the apparent incoherence of the notion of atemporal duration is to consider, even if only very briefly, the development of the concept of eternity. The concept can be found in Parmenides, we think, but it finds its first detailed formulation in Plato, who makes use of it in working out the distinction between the realms of being and becoming; and it receives its fullest exposition in pagan antiquity in the work of Plotinus. The thought that originally stimulated this Greek development of the concept of eternity was apparently something like this. Our *experience* of temporal duration gives us an impression of permanence and persistence which an *analysis* of time convinces us is an illusion or at least a distortion. Reflection shows us that contrary to our familiar but superficial impression, temporal duration is only apparent duration, just what one would expect to find in the realm of becoming. The existence of a typical existent temporal entity, such as a human being, is spread over years of the past, through the present, and into years of the future; but the past is not, the future is not, and the present must be understood as no time at all, a durationless instant, a mere point at which the past is continuous with the future. Such radically evanescent existence cannot be the foundation of existence. Being, the persistent, permanent, utterly immutable actuality that seems required as the bedrock underlying the evanescence of becoming, must be characterized by genuine duration, of which temporal duration is only the flickering image. Genuine duration is fully realized duration—not only extended existence (even *that* is theoretically impossible in time) but also existence *none* of which is already gone and *none* of which is yet to come—and such fully realized duration must be atemporal duration. Whatever has atemporal duration as its mode of existence is 'such that nothing future is absent from it and nothing past has flowed away,' whereas of everything that has temporal duration it may be said that from it *everything* future is absent and *everything* past has flowed away. What has temporal duration 'does not yet grasp tomorrow but yesterday it has already lost'; even today it exists only; 'in a mobile, transitory moment,' the present instant. To say of something that it is future is to say that it is not (yet), and to say of something that it is past is to say that it is not (any longer). Atemporal duration is duration none of which is not—none of which is absent (and hence future) or flowed away (and hence past). Eternity, not time, is the mode of existence that admits of fully realized duration.

The ancient Greek philosophers who developed the concept of eternity were using the word *aiōn*, which corresponds in its original sense to our word 'duration,' in a way that departed from ordinary usage in order to introduce a notion which, however counter-intuitive it may be, can reasonably be said to preserve and even to enhance the original sense of the word. It would not be out of keeping with the tradition that runs through Parmenides, Plato, and Plotinus into Augustine, Boethius, and Aquinas to claim that it is only the discovery of eternity that enables us to make genuinely literal use of words for duration, words such as 'permanence' and 'persistence,' which in their ordinary, temporal application turn out to have been unintended metaphors. 'Atemporal duration,' like the ancient technical use of *aiōn* itself, violates established usage; but an attempt to convey a new philosophical or scientific concept by adapting familiar expressions is not to be rejected on the basis of its violation of ordinary usage. The apparent incoherence in the concept is primarily a consequence of continuing to think of duration only as 'persistence *through time.*'

Since a life is a kind of duration, some of the apparent incoherence in the notion of an atemporal life may be dispelled in rendering the notion of atemporal duration less readily dismissible. But life is in addition ordinarily associated with processes of various sorts, and processes are essentially temporal, and so the notion of an atemporal entity that has life seems incoherent. Now what Aquinas, for example, is thinking of when he attributes life to eternal God is the doctrine that God is a mind. (Obviously what is atemporal cannot consist of physical matter; we assume for the sake of the argument that there is nothing incoherent in the notion of a wholly immaterial, independently existent mind.) Since God is atemporal, the mind that is God must be different in important ways from a temporal, human mind. Considered as an atemporal mind, God cannot deliberate, anticipate, remember, or plan ahead, for instance; all these mental activities essentially involve time, either in taking time to be performed (like deliberation) or in requiring a temporal viewpoint as a prerequisite to performance (like remembering). But it is clear that there are other mental activities that do not require a temporal interval or viewpoint. Knowing seems to be the paradigm case; learning, reasoning, inferring take time, as knowing does not. In reply to the question 'What have you been doing for the past two hours?' it makes sense to say 'Studying logic' or 'Proving theorems,' but not 'Knowing logic.' Similarly, it makes sense to say 'I'm learning logic,' but not 'I'm knowing logic.' And knowing is not the only mental activity requiring neither a temporal interval nor a temporal viewpoint. Willing, for example, unlike wishing or desiring, seems to be another. Perceiving is impossible in any literal sense for a mind that is disembodied, but nothing in the nature of incorporeality or atemporality seems to rule out the possibility of awareness. And though *feeling* angry is impossible for an atemporal entity—if feelings of anger are essentially associated, as they seem to be, with bodily states—we do not see that anything prevents such an entity from *being* angry, a state the components of which might be, for instance, being aware of an injustice, disapproving of it, and willing its punishment. It seems, then, that the notion of an atemporal mind is not incoherent, but that, on the contrary, it is possible that such a mind might have a variety of faculties or activities. Our informal, incomplete consideration of that possibility is not even the beginning of an argument for such a conclusion, but it is enough for our purposes here to suggest the line along which such an argument might develop. The notion of an atemporal mind is not *prima facie* absurd, and so neither is the notion of an atemporal life absurd; for any entity that has or is a mind must be considered to be *ipso facto* alive, whatever characteristics of other living beings it may lack. . . .

Omniscience and immutability

The doctrine that God is eternal is obviously of critical importance in the consideration of any issue involving the relationship of God to temporal entities or events. We will conclude our exploration of the concept of eternity by sampling its effect on three such issues concerning either God's knowledge or God's power in connection with the future, the past, and the present, respectively.

First, the short answer to the question whether God can foreknow contingent events is no. It is impossible that any event occur later than an eternal entity's present state of awareness, since every temporal event is ET-simultaneous with that state, and so an eternal entity cannot *fore* know anything. Instead, such an entity considered as omniscient knows—is aware of—all temporal events, including those which are future with respect to our current temporal viewpoint; but, because the times at which those future events will be present events are ET-simultaneous with the whole of eternity an omniscient eternal entity is aware of them as they are present.[4]

---

4. What we present here is essentially Boethius's line against the suggestion that divine omniscience and human freedom are incompatible, a line in which he was followed by many medievals, especially Aquinas. On Aquinas's use of the Boethian solution, see Anthony Kenny, 'Divine Foreknowledge and Human Freedom,' in Kenny (ed.), *Aquinas: Collection of Critical Essays* (Garden City, NY: Doubleday Anchor, 1969), pp. 255–70; 264.

Second, the short answer to the question whether God can change the past is no. But it is misleading to say, with Agathon, that not even God can change the past;[5] God *in particular* cannot change the past. The impossibility of *God's* changing the past is a consequence not of the fact that what is past is over and done with but rather of the fact that the past is solely a feature of the experience of temporal entities. It is just because no event can be past with respect to an eternal entity that an eternal entity cannot alter a *past* event.[6] An omnipotent, omniscient, eternal entity can affect temporal events, but it can affect events only as they are actually occurring. As for a past event, the time at which it was actually occurring is the time at which it is present to such an entity; and so the battle of Waterloo is present to God, and God can affect the battle. Suppose that he does so. God can bring it about that Napoleon wins, though we know that he does not do so, because whatever God does at Waterloo is over and done with as we see it. So God cannot alter the past, but he can alter the course of the battle of Waterloo.[7]

5. Aristotle, *Nicomachean Ethics* VI, 2.

6. Although the concept of *the* past, dependent on the concept of the absolute temporal present, has no application for an eternal entity, for an omniscient eternal entity there is the awareness of your past, your present, your future as of January 1, 1970, and of your past, your present, your future as of January 1, 1980, and so on for every temporal entity as of any date in its duration.

7. These observations regarding God's relationship to the past might suggest further issues regarding petitionary prayer. It is obviously absurd to pray in 1980 that Napoleon win at Waterloo when one knows what God does not bring about at Waterloo, but it might not seem absurd—at least not in the same way—to pray in 1980 that Napoleon lose at Waterloo. After all, your prayer and the battle are alike present to God; why should your prayer not be efficacious in bringing about Napoleon's defeat? But, as a petition addressed to the will of God, a prayer is also an expression of the will of the one who prays it, and any temporal entity who prays in 1980, 'Let Napoleon lose at Waterloo,' is to that extent pretending to have atemporal knowledge and an atemporal will. The only appropriate version of that prayer is 'Let Napoleon have lost at Waterloo,' and for one who knows the outcome of the battle more than a hundred and fifty years ago, that prayer is pointless and in that sense absurd. But a prayer prayed in ignorance of the outcome of a past event is not pointless in that way. (We are thus disagreeing with Peter Geach, when he claims that 'A prayer for something to have happened is simply an absurdity, regardless of the utterer's knowledge or ignorance of how things went' (*God and the Soul* (London: Routledge & Kegan Paul, 1969), p. 90); but we find much else to admire in his chapter 'Praying for Things to Happen.') On the hypothesis that there is an eternal, omniscient, omnipotent God, the praying of such a prayer would indeed qualify as 'the only instance of behavior, on the part of ordinary people whose mental processes we can understand, designed to affect the past and coming quite naturally to us' (Michael Dummett, 'Bringing about the Past,' *The Philosophical Review*, 73; 3 (July 1964), pp. 338–59; p. 341). We are grateful to members of the Sage School of Philosophy at Cornell for pointing out the relevance of Dummett's discussion. Dummett does not draw on the concept of divine eternality, but, if it is acceptable in its own right, its introduction would lead to a modification and strengthening of some of the claims he makes—e.g. 'I am not asking God that, even if my son has drowned, He should *now* make him not to have drowned; I am asking that, at the time of the disaster, He should then have made my son not to drown at that time' (342).

Chapter 49
A different modern defence of divine eternity

Paul Helm

THE rationale for introducing the possibility that God exists in a timeless eternity lies in the fact that this supposition will enable more sense to be made of what would otherwise be difficult, and so to vindicate an unattenuated Christian theism. It is agreed that the idea of timeless eternity is obscure and not fully graspable, but there is nothing novel in the introduction of a concept such as *electron* or *virus* to make sense of data otherwise unaccountable. Yet it would not be appropriate to introduce the idea of timeless eternity, or more precisely of God's timeless eternity, if that idea is not so much obscure as downright incoherent. For if it is incoherent then although numbers and propositions may be timelessly eternal, God could not be.

This chapter addresses the question of the coherence of the idea of God's timeless eternity.

There is no better place to begin than the celebrated account by Boethius:

> That God is eternal, then, is the common judgment of all who live by reason. Let us therefore consider what eternity is, for this makes plain to us both the divine nature and knowledge. Eternity, then, is the complete possession all at once of illimitable life. . . . Therefore, whatever includes and possesses the whole fullness of illimitable life at once and is such that nothing future is absent from it and nothing past has flowed away, this is rightly judged to be eternal, and of this it is necessary both that being in full possession of itself it be always present to itself and that it have the infinity of mobile time present to it.[1]

To say that God is eternal is thus to say that he is not in time. There is for him no past and no future. It makes no sense to ask how long God has existed, or to divide up his life into periods of time. He possesses the whole of his life at once: it is not lived successively.

Prima facie, a timelessly eternal God, an individual, has some relations with individuals who are in time. It is the fact of these positive relations which generates the charge that the idea of divine timeless eternity is immediately incoherent. This problem does not arise for other entities that philosophers have sometimes regarded as timeless, such as propositions and numbers, because they are incapable

1. Quoted by E. Stump and N. Kretzman, 'Eternity', *J. of Philosophy* (1981), 430 (see this volume, pp. 505f.).

of entering into relations with individuals such as you and me. Propositions can be thought about and argued over, but they cannot think or argue. The only relations (and changes) that they are capable of are, in Geach's terminology, 'merely Cambridge' relations and changes. They can be thought about and so they can 'change' only by now being thought about, and now ignored.

But things are different with an allegedly timeless being such as God, who has intelligence and will. He can not only be thought about, he can think, and the relations into which he enters with his creation appear to be real relations even though they cannot issue in any changes in God, since (by definition) God is timeless and changeless. The exploration of this asymmetry between the *relata* of the real relations between God and his creatures—they change but he cannot—will be undertaken later. It is sufficient for the present to note that conceptual problems about God's timelessness cannot be sloughed off by saying that God is like a proposition or a number in being timeless.

More than this, not only does God enter into relations with things in time but we must also suppose that he has some concept of time. For instance, he knows what it means for A to exist in time, or for it to occur before B and C. This much seems to be implicit in the idea of creation. To suppose otherwise would lead to insuperable difficulties. It would be to suppose that God created the universe having features which are likewise timeless, and this would mean that God was incapable of creating anything which changes.

It is more debatable whether having this concept of time, the idea of objects existing in a temporal sequence, God also has the concept of temporal indexicals such as 'yesterday', 'ago', 'now', and 'then'. If he is not in time himself these expressions cannot apply to him; a *fortiori* he cannot apply them to himself. But may not God have the idea of a person who understands that, say, his birthday was so many days ago? Does it follow that if God knows what it is like to have had a birthday ten days ago he must be in time? This does not seem plausible. A bachelor may know what it is like to be married. Is this only because bachelors could be married? But even if an understanding of what is involved in individuals in time applying temporal indexicals to themselves is denied to God this may not matter very much because it has been plausibly argued that the use of such indexicals depends on there being a non-indexical concept of time for their proper employment.[2]

Nor is God having the idea of creatures in time at odds with the idea of divine simplicity. What divine simplicity means is that God is incapable of being divided into parts, either temporal or spatial, and that though the sense of his various attributes is different, 'God is wise' meaning something different from 'God is good', the reference of these predicates is the same, the one supreme moral nature. While God's being in time rules out this simplicity, God's timeless eternity is a necessary condition of it. But proponents of divine simplicity do not extend that

2. See e.g. D. H. Mellor, *Real Time* (Cambridge, 1981), ch. 2.

doctrine to the intentional objects of God's mind. The doctrine of divine simplicity is not logically inconsistent with the idea that there is at least one thing which God has created and knows.

So it is quite consistent with the idea of divine timeless eternity (at least that version of it that will be defended here) that God has the concept of time, and that God has the concept of a multiplicity of individual beings in time even though it is more problematic (though not particularly worrying) whether God has the mastery of temporal indexicals which intelligent individuals in time may employ. We may say, then, that God knows (timelessly) the whole temporal series in rather the way in which for us certain things are known at a glance or in a flash of insight or intuition in which the active recalling of memories or the anticipation of the future plays no part. We may say, then, that God knows *at a glance* the whole of his temporally ordered creation in rather the way in which a crossword clue may be solved in a flash.

Where, then, is the conceptual problem? It may be stated as follows. 'But, on St. Thomas' view, my typing of this paper is simultaneous with the whole of eternity. Again, on this view, the great fire of Rome is simultaneous with the whole of eternity. Therefore, while I type these very words, Nero fiddles heartlessly on.'[3] and further:

The inner incoherence can be seen as follows. God's timelessness is said to consist in his existing at all moments of human time—simultaneously. Thus he is said to be simultaneously present at (and a witness of) what I did yesterday, what I am doing today, and what I will do tomorrow. But if t_1 is simultaneous with t_2 and t_2 with t_3, then t_1 is simultaneous with t_3. So if the instant at which God knows these things were simultaneous with both yesterday, today and tomorrow, then these days would be simultaneous with each other. So yesterday would be the same day as today and as tomorrow—which is clearly nonsense.[4]

As indeed it is.

How can this 'inner incoherence' as Swinburne calls it, be met? The obvious way to avoid it is by placing restrictions upon the idea of simultaneity so that it is not transitive in certain contexts. But there may be another way of meeting the difficulty. Why cannot the use of simultaneity in expressing the relation between the timeless God and individuals in time be abandoned altogether? For the concept of simultaneity is obviously one which implies time. If *A* and *B* are simultaneous they exist or occur at the same time. But God is time*less*. Suppose that there exists (timelessly) a set of propositions expressing the history of some event which is of the form 'A at t_1 and then B at t_2'. The occurrence of *A* is at a different time from the occurrence of *B*. Why should the question of what the temporal relation is between such a set of propositions and what they say about *A* and *B* ever be raised? It could be raised about the inscribing of the sentences, which is an event, but surely

3. Anthony Kenny, *The God of the Philosophers* (Oxford, 1979) pp. 38–9.
4. Richard Swinburne, *The Coherence of Theism* (Oxford, 1977) pp. 220–1.

not about the inscription with a fixed meaning? Call the inscription a record; why does it make any sense to ask whether the record is *simultaneous* with the occurrence of A or B and if so whether A and B must be simultaneous, thus reducing the idea of a timeless record of the events to absurdity? Swinburne objects to timeless eternity because he takes God's timelessness to 'consist in his existing at all moments of human time—simultaneously'.[5] But it is far from clear that this follows from Boethius' account, or from any account of timelessness that is attractive. Why cannot divine timelessness consist in a manner of existence which sustains no temporal relations with human time? If God timelessly exists he is neither earlier nor later nor simultaneous with any event of time. He exists time*less*ly.

One objection to this is that it might be supposed that it makes impossible *any* relation between God existing timelessly and his temporal creation. But why? Let us suppose that in creation God brings into being (timelessly) the whole temporal matrix. He knows (timelessly) all about it. In his mind all events are brought together, but they are not brought together at a time, but timelessly. God is time-free.

It is worth looking at a line of thought about timeless eternity which has effectively ruled this out. In their paper on eternity Stump and Kretzmann say:

Although the stipulation that an eternal entity completely possesses its life all at once entails that it is not part of any sequence, it does not rule out the attribution of presentness or simultaneity to the life and relationships of such an entity, nor should it. Insofar as an entity *is*, or *has* life, completely or otherwise, it is appropriate to say that it has present existence in some sense of 'present'; and unless its life consists in only one event or it is impossible to relate an event in its life to any temporal entity or event, we need to be able to consider an eternal entity or event as one of the *relata* in a simultaneity relationship.[6]

This seems to be a very strange line of argumentation. For on the one hand it is averred that the individual who has eternal life is not a part of any sequence; this obviously follows. It is also quite acceptable to say that such a timeless individual has present existence in some sense of 'present', for the same may be said about a number or proposition. But then follow two claims which are much harder to accept.

The first of these supposes that the life of a timeless individual may not consist of only one event. But how could the life of a timeless being *not* consist of only one event, whether by an 'event' one means something that is simple, like the falling of a leaf, or an event that has complex elements, like the Battle of Waterloo? Surely the life of a timeless being must consist of only one event,[7] however ramified the consequences of that event may be in created time. Because for it to consist of more

---

5. Ibid. p. 220.
6. 'Eternity', 434 (see this volume, p. 508).
7. It could be argued that neither an ontology of events nor of substances is applicable to a timeless being, but even if this is so, it would be of no help to Stump and Kretzmann.

than one event these events would have to be temporally ordered, and this would mean that the supposedly timeless existence of God was in fact a temporally ordered life, albeit a temporal ordering in 'super-time'. So it is hard to see how Stump and Kretzmann can use this consideration as an argument justifying the introduction of the simultaneity relation in connection with timelessness, for that seems to be equivalent to the abandoning of timelessness *stricto sensu*.

The second argument is that the only way in which the life of a timeless being can be related to a temporal sequence is by means of a simultaneity relationship. Otherwise, Stump and Kretzmann say, 'it is impossible to relate an event in its life to any temporal entity or event'. But is this so? Suppose we say 'God (timelessly) knows that Helm is typing on Thursday 19 November 1987'. The question is, granted that there is a sense of 'present' in which God's knowledge is present as I am typing, is God's knowing really simultaneous with my typing? Why should it be? Why is this particular way of thinking inevitable, and not a trap? Suppose it is denied that God's knowledge is simultaneous with my typing, why should it follow from this that God cannot know that I am typing? What is the argument? Of course the proposition has to be present to the mind of God, that is, God has to know it, but something being present to his mind has not to be confused with God being temporally present with anything.

So the force of the Stump and Kretzmann argument here is not clear, and it seems sufficient simply to deny what they allege and to wait for an argument to be produced to support it. The other matter, the sense in which (despite what has just been said) it may be acceptable to say that God's knowing is present will be discussed in due course.

But let us suppose that for some reason not yet uncovered it is impossible to refrain from allowing, as part of an explication of divine timelessness, that God's timeless life is in some sense simultaneous with the events of our lives, that God's life is simultaneous with my typing today. The problem now is, how can the *reductio* proposed by Kenny and Swinburne be avoided? One way, hinted at already in the above quotation from Stump and Kretzmann, is to distinguish between different kinds of simultaneity—divine simultaneity and human simultaneity, for example. A number of analogies come to mind which indicate that this is quite plausible. Stump and Kretzmann themselves mention different temporal frameworks. From the standpoint of someone watching a train pass lightning may strike it simultaneously at front and rear whereas from the standpoint of someone in the train— supposing that it is moving very fast—the lightning is not simultaneous. Thus to ask whether the flashes of lightning are simultaneous is to ask an insufficiently precise question. The question should be: from *A*'s standpoint are the lightning flashes simultaneous? A similar analogy can be constructed using the distinction between author's time and character's time. A question about when a certain event recorded in a novel happens could be a question about the writing of the event, a question as to when, in the author's life, he came to write down that event, or it could be a question about when in the novel the event occurs. It would not follow that two events that occur simultaneously in the novel were written simultaneously, or conceived simultaneously. And it would not follow that two events in the novel which occur one after the other occurred one after the other in the author's writing. In novel-time, they may be generations apart, but simultaneous in author-time. Thus there is no one, straightforward, unambiguous answer to the question, 'are the two events simultaneous or not?'.

These analogies are imperfect. What they show is that it is sometimes necessary to indulge in talk of different frameworks of reference, different standpoints. The analogies are no more than this, because although it is possible to distinguish the framework of the author from the framework of the character in the novel the author still employs time in constructing his novel just as the novel has a temporal sequence in which the events in it unfold. In other words, the analogies indicate how it is possible and natural to talk of two different times, but not how it is possible to talk of the relation between timelessness and time, the timelessness of God's eternity and the time of his creation. The analogies do show, incidentally, how it is possible for an author to have a relation to his work without there being any need, *pace* Stump and Kretzmann, to introduce simultaneity talk. The author is the author of the whole, but it does not make sense to go on to ask whether his writing the novel is simultaneous with any of the events in the work. His writing, being in time, is simultaneous with what he writes, but the act of writing is not simultaneous with any of the events that occur in the work, not even if the author writes himself into the novel.

So illustrations such as the author-novel relation, and that provided by different physical frameworks, only serve as analogies and do not suffice to remove the *reductio* charge against the idea of timeless eternity. Although the events in the author's life are not simultaneous with any of the events in the written work, both the life and the narrative of the work are in time, whereas what is needed is an analogy or model in which one of the *relata* is timeless. Nevertheless, as Stump and Kretzmann stress, an analogy is no more than this.

What of their own proposals for avoiding the *reductio*? These involve the introduction of what they call ET-simultaneity, 'a species of simultaneity that can obtain between what is eternal and what is temporal'.[8] ET-simultaneity is characterized as follows:

(ET) for every x and for every y (where 'x' and 'y' range over entities and events), x and y are ET-simultaneous if:

(i)   either x is eternal and y is temporal, or vice versa; and
(ii) for some observer, A, in the unique eternal frame, x and y are both present—i.e., either x is eternally present and y is observed as temporally present, or vice versa; and
(iii) for some observer, B, in one of the infinitely many temporal reference

8. 'Eternity', 436 (see this volume, p. 509).

frames, x and y are both present i.e. either x is observed as eternally present and y is temporally present, or vice versa.[9]

According to Stump and Kretzmann it follows from this definition that any temporal event is ET-simultaneous with any eternal event and vice versa, where the events in question are observed as present by some appropriately placed temporal or eternal observer.

What is crucial about the notion of ET-simultaneity is that according to Stump and Kretzmann it is not transitive. Thus if x is ET-simultaneous with y, and y is ET-simultaneous with z, it does not follow that x is ET-simultaneous with z. This is because the notion of ET-simultaneity only applies or obtains within appropriate frames of reference—there must be an appropriately placed observer. That is, it is crucial to this account that ET-simultaneity applies not to pairs of events but to pairs of events observed either from an eternal standpoint, or from a temporal standpoint, one of the pairs of which is eternal, the other of which is temporal. So that x and y can only be ET-simultaneous by being observed as such by an appropriate observer; hence no event, *qua* event, is ET-simultaneous with any other event.

Nevertheless, although it avoids the *reductio* of the idea of timeless eternity by making the relevant relation not transitive, it does so at a price. It carries difficulties with it that are sufficient to cast doubt on their procedure and to incline us to the alternative account proposed earlier, the account according to which timelessness is time-freeness, and in which nothing time-free is simultaneous in any sense with anything which occurs in time.

What are the difficulties? There is one central obscurity in Stump and Kretzmann's account connected with the idea of an eternal observer observing an event as temporally present, and the corresponding idea of a temporal observer observing an event as eternally present.[10] What could these expressions mean? According to Stump and Kretzmann what they mean is that to an eternal being two temporal events, say Nixon's becoming president and Nixon's dying, are present. Whereas it is now true that Nixon is alive, and it will be true at some later time that he is dead, to an eternal being Nixon is both alive and dead. But this

cannot be taken to mean that the temporal entity Nixon exists in eternity, where he is simultaneously alive and dead, but rather something more nearly like this. One and the same eternal present is ET-simultaneous with Nixon's being alive and is also ET-simultaneous with Nixon's dying; so Nixon's life is ET-simultaneous with and hence present to an eternal entity, and Nixon's death is ET-simultaneous with and hence present to an eternal entity, although Nixon's life and Nixon's death are themselves neither eternal nor simultaneous.[11]

While this explanation removes the obscurity it does so by merely relocating it. For the solution proposed by Stump and Kretzmann is a purely formal affair. Crucial to

---

9. Ibid., 439 (see this volume, p. 514).
10. See Paul Fitzgerald, 'Stump and Kretzmann on Time and Eternity', *J. of Philosophy* (1985).
11. 'Eternity', 443 (see this volume, p. 514).

it, as we have seen, is the introduction of ET-simultaneity; but while the device of ET-simultaneity 'solves' the alleged *reductio* over timeless eternity, it does so simply by stipulating that the *reductio* will not be allowed rather than by offering an explanation of why it cannot or need not follow. The 'solution' to the problem is found simply by rewording the problem with the help of the device of ET-simultaneity. ET-simultaneity has no independent merit or use, nothing is illuminated or explained by it. Its sole purpose is to avoid the alleged *reductio*, which it does.

For the problem is, how can something which is an event in time be wholly present 'to an eternal entity'? The answer given is that it is ET-wholly present. But this answer is wholly obscure. It is not wholly present as two exactly simultaneous temporal events are wholly present to each other, but wholly present in the sense in which what is eternally existing is wholly present to what is temporally existing. But how can an eternal entity be aware of a temporal entity as present, as Stump and Kretzmann's definition requires? What sort of presentness is the eternal presentness of a temporal entity? And what sort of presentness is it that can have wholly present to it the occurring of two temporally distinct events? Further, it is hard to see how for a temporal observer, two events one of which is temporal and the other eternal can fail to exist at one and the same time in that given observer's temporal reference frame. Surely any event that occurs in a temporal observer's temporal framework is itself temporal?

The introduction of ET-simultaneity, with its attendant difficulties, may only have been possible because Stump and Kretzmann have assumed eternal existence to have (some of the) features of temporal duration, with the idea of an ordered sequence with differently enduring individuals occupying different positions along it.[12] On this view timeless eternity is super-time. The reason for saying that the authors must make such an assumption is because only thus can one make sense of what is crucial to their account, namely an eternal observer observing a temporal event. Put differently, it is only by supposing that eternity has the character of an (endless) duration that there can be an eternal event to be a *relatum* on the eternal side of the ET-simultaneity relation. And at times the authors explicitly commit themselves to the view that eternity has features of a temporal duration.

The eternal, pastless, futureless present is not instantaneous but extended, because eternity entails duration. The temporal present is a durationless instant, a present that cannot be extended conceptually without falling apart entirely into past and future intervals. The eternal present, on the other hand, is by definition an infinitely extended, pastless, futureless duration.[13]

Paul Fitzgerald explicates E-duration in terms of three notions which he regards as revealing the (partial) incoherence of the idea.[14] In the first place he claims that

12. Fitzgerald, 'Stump and Kretzmann', 262–3.
13. 'Eternity', 435 (see this volume, p. 509).
14. 'Stump and Kretzmann', 262–3.

E-duration is incompatible with divine simplicity (even though he himself does not favour divine simplicity). Stump and Kretzmann claim that E-duration is compatible with it. Even if we suppose that it is, and that divine simplicity ought to be defended, it is certainly not the only view of eternity which is compatible with it, since non-durational views of eternity are equally compatible with it.

Secondly, Fitzgerald claims that events can have a different location in E-duration, but Stump and Kretzmann take the opposite view. In their view everything that has E-duration exists 'all at once', occupying the whole of it. This may be granted, but the consequence of granting it is an attenuation of the claim that timeless eternity is a *bona fide* case of duration. It is a whole that cannot have parts, but what kind of duration is that?

Finally, Fitzgerald claims that any duration (including E-duration) is potentially divisible. Once again Stump and Kretzmann deny this, and this eats away further at the meaning of 'duration'. Yet Stump and Kretzmann claim that denying successiveness to E-duration does not mean abandoning it in favour of non-durational accounts.[15]

But if E-duration is qualified in these ways—if there is a duration which has no successiveness and no divisibility—and yet duration is still affirmed, does this not amount simply to saying that the mode of divine eternity is durational, and nothing more? What is the value of introducing a concept and then so paring it away that hardly anything is left? Indeed, what is left except the bare claim?

What is the philosophical point of claiming, as Stump and Kretzmann do, that E-duration is genuinely durational, that eternity is not to be compared to an unextended point, but that nevertheless eternal duration does not have succession?[16] What is it about eternity that requires its explication in terms of E-duration and not in non-durational terms? What is at stake here? In their answer to this question, in reply to Fitzgerald, Stump and Kretzmann claim that eternity is the foundation of temporal existence, and that time-boundedness cannot be a perfect being's mode of existence.[17] This can be readily granted; but why does it follow that in order for this contrast between eternal perfection and temporal imperfection to be maintained a perfect being has to have duration at all, even if it is a temporal duration that is not even conceptually divisible? The answer may be that E-duration is needed because it implies a limitlessness in a way that the idea of eternity does not.

But instantaneousness is not the only alternative, and certainly it is as bad an alternative as E-duration since, if words mean anything, both notions are as time-infected as each other. Rather it is preferable that timeless eternity be explained in terms of time-freeness, where the only questions of simultaneity and non-simultaneity are *quoad nos*, and from which both the notions of duration and instantaneousness are banished.

---

15. 'Atemporal Duration: A Reply to Fitzgerald', *J. of Philosophy* (1987), 219.
16. 'Eternity', 434 (see this volume, p. 508).
17. 'Atemporal Duration: A Reply to Fitzgerald', 218.

If ordinary temporal simultaneity generates a *reductio* of the idea of timeless eternity, and the introduction of ET-simultaneity carries with it the difficulties touched upon above, then it is reasonable to conclude that it makes no sense to speak strictly and philosophically of God's eternal existence as being either at the same time as or at a different time from the existence of some temporal event or state. God's eternal existence has no temporal relations whatever to any particular thing which he creates. This does not mean that there are no relations at all between the eternal God and his creation, only no temporal relations. There is, for example, the relation of knowledge. God knows his creatures. This knowledge is time-free; it is not, for example, foreknowledge, or memory, nor is it contemporaneous knowledge. It is knowledge about which it makes no sense to ask how long the knower has known, or when he came to know. Thus to attempt to raise, in a strict and philosophical manner, questions about the simultaneity and non-simultaneity of the divine will and human wills (for example) is to be guilty of a category mistake. It is like asking for the physical dimensions of a thought. The eternally timeless God is not the sort of individual that can have temporal relations with anything distinct from him. Thus to suppose that what God perfectly knows is (in some philosophically significant sense) temporally present to him is to suppose what is both otiose and misleading. The creation is not temporally present to God in his knowing it. Nor is it distant. God knows, and that is all.

What then are we to say about the theologians' talk of foreknowledge, of an eternal duration, of the claim that God knows now, that God remembers, and the like? Following Fitzgerald it is plausible to suppose that such expressions are the proper and inevitable expressions of someone in time who wishes to speak of his relation to a timeless being. It makes sense to say that God endures all through my life and the history of the universe, but this does not mean that God has the property of eternal duration, or duration of some other kind. Rather it means that as regards individuals in time it makes no sense to say, at any time in their lives, that God does not exist. But to license such expressions is not to imply that God exists in time.

So far in this chapter an account of timelessness has been offered which consists largely of *ad hominem* rebuttals and qualifications of others' strictures on the concept. But there is a more positive argument that can be offered. It might be argued that if God's existence in time requires the occurrence of time before the creation of the universe then this would, by a *reductio*, lead to an overturning of the idea that God is in time. For the idea that God exists in an infinitely backward extending time runs up against the idea of an actual infinite.[18] For such a prospect requires that an infinite number of events must have elapsed before the present moment could arrive. And since it is impossible for an infinite number of events to

18. For a defence of this impossibility see Pamela M. Huby, 'Kant or Cantor? That the Universe, if Real, must be finite in both Space and Time', *Philosophy* (1971), and William Lane Craig, *The Kalām Cosmological Argument*. For a thorough discussion of these issues see Richard Sorabji, *Time, Creation and the Continuum* (London, 1983).

have elapsed, and yet the present moment has arrived, the series of events cannot be infinite. Therefore, either there was a time when God began to exist, which is impossible, or God exists timelessly. Therefore, God exists timelessly.

To this argument the following reply might be made. Those who argue for God's existence in time before the creating of the universe require only that the time before the creation is undifferentiated. Thus there is a difference between the claim that infinite time existed before the creation and the claim that an infinite series of events existed before the creation. And it is only the second claim that generates problems over the actual infinite.[19]

But this reply overlooks the fact that one of the prime reasons for maintaining that God is in time is that only such a conception makes it possible to suppose that God has life. A timelessly existing God or, presumably, a God who existed in undifferentiated time, time without events would be, in Swinburne's words, 'a very lifeless thing'.[20] The full implications of what such divine life in undifferentiated time means are not clear, but presumably one thing that it must mean is that there is a succession of thoughts in the divine mind, a mental life. But if this is so then time could not be undifferentiated before the creation but would be marked by a series of mental events in the divine mind. But then if so either God exists in a timeless eternity or he exists in time with a 'life' which is differentiated by events. But this latter idea is ruled out by the arguments for the impossibility of an actual infinite. Therefore God exists in a timeless eternity.

This chapter began with Boethius' well-known definition of timeless eternity as 'the complete possession all at once of illimitable life'. An attempt has been made to defend this idea against the obvious *reductio* which would make it immediately or directly incoherent, by in effect arguing that divine timeless eternity is not to be understood as involving duration of any kind. Hence God, considered as timeless, cannot have temporal relations with any of his creation. He is time-less in the sense of being time-free. This at once provides an answer to the *reductio* brought by philosophers such as Kenny and Swinburne by denying that what any of us is now doing is taking place at the same time as anything God is doing, and by denying also that there is a relation of ET-simultaneity, as defined by Stump and Kretzmann.

Is this conclusion incompatible with anything that Boethius says about eternity in his celebrated definition with which this chapter began? It is clearly consistent with the idea of divine life, that is, with the idea of God as the creator and sustainer of all that is. Boethius says that this life, in God, is illimitable, and this means not, as Stump and Kretzmann suggest, eternal duration, but a property modifying the other attributes of God—his power, goodness, wisdom, knowledge, and so forth. Each of these attributes is illimitable. Boethius, in the passage in which the definition occurs, seems to be contrasting the possession all at once of illimitable life and the possession in temporal sequence or series of illimitable life: 'Whatever includes

---

19. This distinction is drawn by Craig, *The Kalām Cosmological Argument* (London, 1979), p. 172 n. 170.
20. *The Coherence of Theism*, p. 214.

and possesses the whole fullness of illimitable life at once and is such that nothing future is absent from it and nothing past has flowed on, this is rightly judged to be eternal'.[21] So what Boethius appears to be saying is that nothing in time can be illimitable in character. Hence this aspect of Boethius' definition has nothing to do with duration, and his definition does not require the introduction of the idea of eternal duration at any point. But of course the main thrust of this discussion has been not to make a proposal that Boethius could defend but to make one that is of more general appeal.

21. Cited by Stump and Kretzmann, 'Eternity', 430 (see this volume, p. 506).

Questions for discussion

1. Can there be time without change?
2. Can the universe be thought of as created by something which exists in time?
3. According to the biblical *Letter of James*: 'Every good endowment and every perfect gift is from above, coming down from the Father of lights with whom there is no variation or shadow due to change' (*James* 1: 17). But the Bible also speaks of God as though he is something which undergoes change (cf. Amos 7: 6, Jonah 3: 10). So what might philosophers make of the topic of God and time while anxious to be faithful to what is said of God in the Bible?
4. Is it inconceivable that life, action and love can be truly attributed to what is timelessly eternal?
5. Is timelessness a perfection or an imperfection in something truly described as divine?

Advice on further reading

Brief discussions of divine eternity which can be strongly recommended as springboards for thinking about the topic include:

Stephen T. Davis, *Logic and the Nature of God* (London and Basingstoke, 1993), chs 1 and 3.

Brian Leftow, 'Eternity', in Philip Quinn and Charles Taliaferro (eds), *A Companion to Philosophy of Religion* (Oxford, 1997).

Edward R. Wirenga, *The Nature of God* (Ithaca, New York, and London), ch. 6.

I. M. Crombie, 'Eternity and Omnitemporality', in William J. Abraham and Steven W. Holtzer (eds), *The Rationality of Religious Belief* (Oxford, 1987).

For significant books on divine eternity, see:

F. H. Brabant, *Time and Eternity in Christian Thought* (London, 1937).

Michael J. Dodds, *The Unchanging God of Love: A Study of the Teaching of St Thomas Aquinas on Divine Immutability in View of Certain Contemporary Criticism of this Doctrine* (Fribourg, 1986).

Paul Helm, *Eternal God* (Oxford, 1988).

Brian Leftow, *Time and Eternity* (Ithaca, New York, 1991).

Alan G. Padgett, *God, Eternity and the Nature of Time* (London, 1992).

Nelson Pike, *God and Timelessness* (London, 1970).

John C. Yates, *The Timelessness of God* (New York and London, 1990).

Thomas G. Weinandy, *Does God Change?* (Still River, Massachusetts, 1985).

There is a long history of philosophical thinking relating to the question of divine eternity. For a splendid account of some of this, coupled with some lively philosophical evaluations, see Richard Sorabji, *Time Creation and the Continuum* (London, 1983).

Philosophical discussions of divine eternity frequently invoke reference to the Bible and to what it teaches on the subject. For an expert introduction to this, see the article devoted to the words *aiōn* and *aiōnios* in Gerhard Kittel (ed.), *Theological Dictionary of the New Testament* (Grand Rapids, Michigan, 1964), vol. 1.

Since discussions of divine eternity frequently involve reflection on the notion of time, you are well advised to approach them with some knowledge of how philosophers have written of time in general. Two good readers which shall help you to do this are: Robin Le Poidevin and Murray MacBeath (eds), *The Philosophy of Time* (Oxford, 1993) and J. J. C. Smart (ed.), *Problems of Space and Time* (New York and London, 1964).

Simple

Introduction

The notion of divine simplicity

In Part IV of Hume's *Dialogues Concerning Natural Religion*, Cleanthes finds it strange that Demea 'should still maintain the mysterious, incomprehensible nature of the Deity, and should insist so strenuously that he has no manner of likeness or resemblance to human creatures'. If 'our ideas, so far as they go', he says, 'be not just and adequate, and correspondent to [God's] real nature, I know not what there is in this subject worth insisting on'. According to Cleanthes, Demea is a 'mystic', and his view of God looks suspiciously like the teaching of 'sceptics or atheists, who assert, that the first cause of All is unknown and unintelligible'.[1]

Demea replies to Cleanthes by saying that he would rather be a 'mystic' than an 'anthropomorphite'.[2] And he wonders how Cleanthes's approach to God can be thought of as compatible with 'that perfect immutability and simplicity which all true theists ascribe to the Deity'. For Demea, the teaching that God is simple is true, important, and a needed corrective to what people like Cleanthes say about God. And this is how it has seemed to many philosophers and theologians. For the claim that God is simple is an ancient one. Some have argued that it is implied by certain biblical texts.[3] It is decisively endorsed by several of the early Christian

---

1. David Hume, *Dialogues Concerning Natural Religion* (ed. Norman Kemp Smith, Indianapolis, 1977), p. 158.
2. The term derives from the Greek word for 'man'. Demea is taking Cleanthes to be an anthropomorphite since he takes him to be (wrongly) conceiving of God as being like a human being.
3. For example, both Augustine and Thomas Aquinas take it to be implied by Exodus 3: 14, in which Moses is told that the name of God is 'I am who I am' (אֶהְיֶה אֲשֶׁר אֶהְיֶה). But Augustine and Aquinas also differ significantly in their interpretations of this text. Augustine consistently takes it as teaching that God is simple because immutable. Aquinas normally takes it to teach that God is simple for reasons which go beyond the mere affirmation of divine immutability. Modern biblical scholars seem to be much at odds when it comes to the understanding of Exodus 3: 14 and its phrase 'I am who I am', as may be illustrated with reference to three modern commentaries on Exodus. For Brevard S. Childs, the formula is in part a refusal on God's part to divulge his identity, and indicates that God is 'a self-contained, incomprehensible being . . . God announces that his intentions will be revealed in his future acts, which he now refuses to explain' (*Exodus*, London, 1974, p. 76). For Terence E. Fretheim, such an interpretation is 'a counsel of despair'; the force of the

fathers.[4] It is firmly defended by a variety of medieval Jewish, Christian, and Islamic thinkers.[5] It is defended by many contemporary philosophers and theologians.[6] It is also asserted by Christian ecumenical councils. According, for example, to the Fourth Lateran Council (1215), God is 'one absolutely simple essence'. According to the First Vatican Council (1869–70), God is 'completely simple' (*simplex omnino*).[7]

The meaning of 'God is simple'

But what might it mean to say that God is simple?[8] A famous account of divine simplicity comes in Augustine of Hippo's *The City of God*. Here Augustine says:

There is then one sole Good, which is simple, and therefore unchangeable; and that is God. By this Good all good things were created; but they are not simple, and for that reason they are changeable . . . The reason why a nature is called simple is that it cannot lose any attribute it possesses, that there is no difference between what it *is* and what it *has*, as there is, for example, between a vessel and the liquid it contains, a body and its colour, the atmosphere and its light or heat, the soul and its wisdom. None of these *is* what it contains; the vessel is not the liquid, nor the body the colour, nor the atmosphere the light or heat; nor is the soul the same as its wisdom . . . Further, the soul itself, even though it may be always wise—as it will be, when it is set free for all eternity—will be wise through participation in the changeless Wisdom, which is other than itself. For even if the atmosphere were never bereft of the light which is shed on it, there would still be the difference between its being and the light by which it is illuminated . . . Accordingly, the epithet 'simple' applies to things which are in the fullest and truest sense divine, because in them there is no difference between substance and quality.[9]

For Augustine, God is simple because immutable. But Augustine also thinks that God is simple as not possessing different properties or attributes. According to Augustine,

---

formula is rather: 'not simply that God is or that God is present but that God will be faithfully God for them [Israel]' (*Exodus*, Louisville, Kentucky: 1991, pp. 64 and 63). John I. Durham, provides a third interpretation, understanding the formula as meaning ' "I am the Is-ing One", that is, "the One Who Always Is." Not conceptual being, being in the abstract, but active being, is the intent of this reply' (*Exodus*, Waco, Texas, 1987, p. 39).

4. Cf. G. L. Prestige, *God in Patristic Thought* (London, 1952).
5. Cf. David B. Burrell, *Knowing the Unknowable God: Ibn-Sina, Maimonides, Aquinas* (Notre Dame, Indiana, 1986).
6. See 'Advice on further reading' at the end of this section.
7. Cf. Norman P. Tanner (ed.), *Decrees of the Ecumenical Councils* (London and Georgetown, 1990), vol. I, p. 230 and vol. II, p. 805. For somewhat different accounts of what Vatican I meant when calling God simple, see J. M. A.Vacant, *Études Théologiques sur les Constitutions du Concile du Vatican* (Paris, 1895), vol. 1, pp. 203 ff. and Hermann J. Pottmeyer, *Der Glaube vor dem Anspruch der Wissenschaft* (Freiburg, 1968), pp. 133 ff.
8. In much English usage 'simple' means something like 'plain' or 'stupid'. This, of course, is not what 'simple' means when used to speak of God.
9. Augustine, *The City of God*, XI, 10. I quote from the translation by Henry Bettenson (Harmondsworth, 1984).

expressions such as 'the knowledge of God' or 'the goodness of God' are not names for distinct realities.[10]

And this is what other defenders of divine simplicity have also wished to assert. Hence, for example, according to Anselm of Canterbury: 'The supreme nature is simple: thus all the things which can be said of its essence are simply one and the same thing in it.'[11] Anselm acknowledges that those who believe in God use many different statements when speaking of God's nature. They say, for example, 'God is good', 'God is just', and 'God is wise'. But, so Anselm argues, we should not think of God as something with really distinct attributes. Fred might be tall, dark, and handsome. But what if he shrinks, goes grey, and loses all his looks? Would he still be Fred? Most people would say that Fred can exist over a long period of time even though he undergoes many changes (thereby acquiring and losing many attributes).[12] Why would they say this? Presumably because they would want to distinguish between Fred and the attributes he possesses at any given time. They would want to say that being Fred can be distinguished from (and is distinct from) being tall, dark, and handsome (or whatever else one takes Fred to be). They would want to say that Fred and his attributes are not one and the same thing. According to Anselm, however, this is just what cannot be said of God. For him there is no difference between God and anything we might want to call 'the attributes of God'. For Anselm (and also for Augustine) the various attributes we ascribe to God in sentences of the form 'God is X', 'God is Y', and so on, are not distinct realities in God. They are God.

Some defenders of divine simplicity have, however, also wanted to say more than this. For they have wanted to add that God is also simple in the sense that there is no real distinction between God's nature (or essence) and God's existence. On their account, God is simple since he is immutable and since he has no attributes really distinct from himself. But, so they argue, God is also simple since existence belongs to God by nature. You and I exist, but we cannot claim that it belongs to us by nature to do so. Yet for some defenders of the teaching that God is simple, existence belongs to God by nature. On their account, God is also simple since God is Being or Existence without qualification. Or, as Aquinas famously puts it, God is *Ipsum Esse Subsistens* ('*Subsisting Being Itself*'). Having asked whether *Qui Est* ('*He Who Is*') is the most appropriate name for God, Aquinas replies that it is since, among other reasons, 'it does not signify any particular form, but rather existence itself (*sed ipsum esse*)'. 'Since the existence of God is his essence', says Aquinas, 'and since this is true of nothing else . . . it is clear that this name is especially appropriate to God.'[13] According to Aquinas, God is simple since he is immutable and since he is not a being with different

---

10. For some other places in which Augustine argues that God is simple, see *Confessions* I, vi, 10 and *Confessions* XIII, iii, 4.
11. *Monologion* ch. 17. Cf. also, *Proslogion* 18.
12. Some philosophers have, however, argued that we might reasonably say something like this. See Derek Parfitt, *Reasons and Persons* (Oxford, 1984).
13. *Summa Theologiae*, Ia. 13. 11. For other texts in which Aquinas argues in defence of God's simplicity, see: *Compendium Theologiae*, chs 8–17, *De Potentia* VII, and *Summa Contra Gentiles*, I. 14–18

attributes. For Aquinas, however, God is also simple since he is not a 'composite' of 'essence' and 'existence'.[14]

Is God simple?

Your reaction to the suggestion that God is simple will have enormous repercussions when it comes to your approach to the question of God's existence and nature in general.[15] If you believe that God is simple, you will, for a start, take God to be immutable (which will affect your view of divine knowledge and eternity).[16] But you will also be suspicious of expressions such as 'God is a person' and of their employment as a way of settling the truth of questions concerning God's nature. For if you hold that God is simple you will deny that God's nature is something which he has, as people can be said to have their human nature. Rather, you will say that God *is* his nature, and that he shares it with nothing.[17] If you believe that God is simple, you are also likely to think of God as being very much beyond human understanding. If you reject the teaching that God is simple, however, you might feel happy to think of God on the model of human beings, and you might find it perfectly appropriate to call God a person. Like Cleanthes, you might also think that God is fundamentally open to human understanding, even if you also take God to be somewhat puzzling.

But is there any reason for thinking of God as simple? Should we side with Demea? Or should we agree with Cleanthes? Those who have wanted to say that God is simple have argued for their positions in different ways. And they have not always meant the same when saying 'God is simple'. Let us, however, presume that someone who believes that God is simple agrees with one or all of the following statements:

1.   One cannot think of God as changeable.
2.   One cannot take God to be something with a variety of different attributes.
3.   One cannot think of God as something the existence of which is different from its essence.

On this understanding of divine simplicity, should we be friendly to the teaching that God is simple? Or should we roundly reject it?

Those who have defended it have done so by supporting one or more of the following arguments:

14. It would be wrong to suppose that authors like Augustine and Anselm would have contested what Aquinas seems to be driving at in his teaching that God is simple because God's essence and existence are not distinguishable. But this is not a teaching they explicitly defend as they speak of God as 'simple'. The suggestion that God's simplicity crucially means that his essence is existence seems to be something which only came to be emphasized and defended at length in the thirteenth century.
15. In this respect, the notion of divine simplicity is like the notion of divine immutability (which, as you can see from what Demea says, is included in the notion of simplicity, but which does not imply all that the notion of simplicity does).
16. See sections above.
17. If you believe that God is simple, you shall have more to appeal to than reasons to do with political correctness when objecting to talk of God which uses pronouns such as 'he', 'him', and 'his'.

1. God cannot be thought of as having changeable properties, distinct from himself, since God is the source of all change.
2. God cannot be thought of as having distinct temporal properties; since God, as Creator of the Universe, must transcend time.
3. God is not a material object. So he cannot be thought of as having parts in the way that material objects have parts.
4. Something with differing properties depends for its existence on the existence and conjunction of those properties. But God cannot be something which depends for its existence on anything. God is the reason why anything exists at all.
5. If God and the divine nature are not one and the same reality, then God is an instance of a kind. He belongs to a class of which he is but one member. He is 'a such and such'. If God is this, however, he cannot be the source of the existence of the world. As Creator, God is the reason why there is a universe containing instances of kinds.
6. One cannot distinguish between God and God's existence (or between God's nature and God's existence), since to do so would imply that existence is something which God receives from another. But the being of God is wholly underived.
7. The existence of everything non-simple must derive from God. In this sense, existence (without qualification) is an effect of God. But God's effects must express what he is. So one should think of God as being (rather than having) existence.

These lines of argument are insisting that there must be a dramatic difference between God and creatures. Compositeness, or the lack of simplicity, is very much a feature of things in the world. These are material, temporal, and (if God exists) dependent. How shall we preserve God's transcendence vis-à-vis the created order? For defenders of belief in divine simplicity, one way of doing so is to teach that God is simple.

But others have found this teaching to be open to numerous objections. Some of the main ones levelled against it can be summarized thus:

1. Belief in God's simplicity rests on the assumption that God is changeless and/or timeless, or both. But there are reasons for rejecting this assumption.[18]
2. The teaching that God is simple cannot be squared with biblical teaching concerning God.
3. The teaching that God is simple seems to entail that God is just one single property. But such a view of God is at odds with traditional understandings of God.[19]
4. The teaching that God is simple entails that genuinely different properties are, in God, actually identical. But this conclusion is logically incoherent. Different properties cannot be really identical.
5. Insofar as the teaching that God is simple holds that God's nature is to be thought of as pure existence, or 'Existence Itself', it is mistaken since it misconstrues the

18. See the section above on God's eternity.
19. Cf. Alvin Plantinga, *Does God Have a Nature?* (Milwaukee, Wisconsin, 1980).

logic of statements involving the verb 'to be'. Existence can never be thought of as something with which the nature of anything could be identified.[20]

6.   If God is wholly simple, then God is simply and eternally the Creator of the universe. God's will to create *is* what God is. But those who believe in God normally say that God creates freely, and not from some necessity of his nature. So God might not have created. In that case, God might have been different from what he actually is and therefore cannot be wholly simple.

7.   There are reasons for thinking that God is, or has, a body.[21]

Yet defenders of divine simplicity have attempted to meet these, and other, objections to their thesis. You can explore ways in which they have argued by following up 'Advice on further reading' below, which shall also help you to pursue criticisms of belief in divine simplicity. In the following chapters you can see at first hand how some of the exchanges have gone. The first chapter represents what Eleonore Stump has called 'the culmination of medieval Latin discussions of simplicity'.[22] It is a fairly technical piece of writing. But its main arguments should be clear in the light of explanatory comments on Aquinas which I have provided above and in the light of what I say in Chapter 52, where I seek to defend Aquinas's account of simplicity against a number of its critics. This chapter should give you a sense of how belief in divine simplicity has been called into question. But you also need to read critics of the belief for yourself, and Chapter 51 is an excellent text from which to start. Here, Thomas Morris (writing with great verve and clarity) explains why one should take belief in God's simplicity to be false, confused, and unnecessary.

20.   Those who argue along these lines are chiefly indebted to what authors such as Frege and Bertrand Russell have said about existence. For an example of one, see C. J. F. Williams, 'Being', in Philip L. Quinn and Charles Taliaferro (eds), *A Companion to Philosophy of Religion* (Oxford, 1997). For another example, see Anthony Kenny, *Aquinas* (Oxford, 1980), pp. 49 ff.

21.   This is not a line of thinking which is much developed by contemporary philosophers of religion. But it, or something like it, has been defended over time. For a discussion of it, see William J. Wainwright, 'God's Body', *Journal of the American Academy of Religion* XLII (1974).

22.   Cf. Quinn and Taliaferro, *A Companion to Philosophy of Religion*, p. 253

Chapter 50

A classic defence of divine simplicity

Thomas Aquinas

God's simpleness

Is God a body composed of extended parts?

THE FIRST POINT: 1. God, it would seem, is a body. For anything having three dimensions is a body, and the Scriptures ascribe three dimensions to God: *He is higher than the heaven and what wilt thou do? he is deeper than hell and how wilt thou know? the measure of him is longer than the earth and broader than the sea*. God then is a body.

2. Moreover, only bodies have shape, for shape is characteristic of extended things as such. God however seems to have a shape, for in *Genesis* we read: *Let us make man to our image and likeness*, where image means figure or shape as in *Hebrews*: *who being the brightness of his glory, and the figure* (that is to say, image) *of his substance*. Therefore God is a body.

3. Moreover, the parts of the body can belong only to a body. But Scripture ascribes parts of the body to God, saying in *Job, Have you an arm like God?* and in the psalms, *The eyes of the Lord are toward the righteous*, and *the right hand of the Lord does valiantly*. Therefore God is a body.

4. Only bodies can assume postures. But Scripture ascribes certain postures to God: thus Isaiah *saw the Lord sitting*, and says that *the Lord stands to judge*. Therefore God is a body.

5. Moreover, nothing can act as starting-point or finishing-point of a movement unless it be body or bodily. Now God is referred to in Scripture as the finishing-point of a movement, *Come ye to him and be enlightened*; and again as a starting-point, *They that depart from thee shall be written in the earth*. Therefore God is a body.

ON THE OTHER HAND, John writes: *God is spirit*.

REPLY: In no sense is God a body, and this may be shown in three ways.

Thomas Aquinas extracts from *Summa Theologiae* from vol. 2 of the Blackfriars edition of the *Summa Theologiae* (Eyre and Spottiswoode and McGraw Hill, 1963)

First, experience can offer no example of a body causing change without itself being changed. Now God has been shown above to be the unchanging first cause of change. Clearly then God is not a body.

Secondly, in the first existent thing everything must be actual; there can be no potentiality whatsoever. For although, when we consider things coming to exist, potential existence precedes actual existence in those particular things; nevertheless, absolutely speaking, actual existence takes precedence of potential existence. For what is able to exist is brought into existence only by what already exists. Now we have seen that the first existent is God. In God then there can be no potentiality. In bodies, however, there is always potentiality, for the extended as such is potential of division. God, therefore, cannot be a body.

Thirdly, it is evident from what has been said that God is the most excellent of beings, but no body can be the most excellent of beings. For bodies are either living or non-living, and of these living bodies are clearly the more excellent. Now a living body is not alive simply in virtue of being a body (otherwise all bodies would be living); it is alive because of some other principle, in our case, the soul. Such a principle will be more excellent than body as such. God therefore cannot be a body.

HENCE: 1. We remarked earlier that the Scriptures make use of bodily metaphors to convey truth about God and about spiritual things. In ascribing, therefore, three dimensions to God, they are using bodily extension to symbolize the extent of God's power: depth, for example, symbolizes his power to know what is hidden; height, the loftiness of his power above all other things; length, the lasting quality of his existence; breadth, the universality of his love. Or there is Dionysius' explanation of depth as the incomprehensibility of God's nature, length as the penetration of all things by God's power, and breadth the boundless reach of God's guardianship enveloping all things.

2. Man is said to be to God's image, not because he has a body, but because of his superiority to other animals; and this is why Genesis, after saying, *Let us make man in our image and likeness*, adds, *that he may have dominion over the fishes of the sea*, and so on. This superiority man owes to reason and intellect. So that man is to God's image because of his intellect and reason, which are not bodily characteristics.

3. Parts of the body are ascribed to God in the Scriptures by a metaphor drawn from their functions. Eyes, for example, see, and so, we call God's power of sight his eye, though it is not a sense-power, but intellect. And so with other parts of the body.

4. The ascribing of posture to God is again simply metaphor. Sitting symbolizes his authority and his steadfastness; standing his might triumphing in the face of all opposition.

5. One comes to God and one departs from him not by bodily movement, since he is everywhere, but by movement of the heart. Approaching and drawing away are metaphors which picture being moved in spirit as being moved in space.

Is God composed of 'form' and 'matter'?

THE SECOND POINT: 1. God seems to be composed of 'form' and 'matter'. For since soul is the form of the body, anything with a soul is composed of matter and form. Now the Scriptures ascribe soul to God; thus in *Hebrews* we find quoted as if from the mouth of God: *my righteous one shall live by faith, and if he shrinks back my soul will have no pleasure in him.* God therefore is composed of matter and form.

2. Moreover, according to Aristotle, anger, joy and the like, affect body and soul together. Now the Scriptures ascribe such dispositions to God: *the anger of the Lord*, says the psalm, *was kindled against his people.* God then is composed of matter and form.

3. Moreover, individualness derives from matter. Now God seems to be an individual, and not something common to many individuals. So God must be composed of matter and form.

ON THE OTHER HAND, since dimension is an immediate property of matter, anything composed of matter and form will be a body. Now we have seen that God is not a body. God therefore is not composed of matter and form.

REPLY: God cannot contain matter.

First, because the very existence of matter is a being potential; whilst God, as we have seen, contains no potentiality, but is sheer actuality. God cannot therefore be composed of matter and form.

Secondly, in complexes of form and matter it is the form which gives goodness and perfection. Such complexes therefore are but partakers of goodness, for matter merely partakes of form. Now whatever is good of itself is prior to anything merely partaking goodness; so that God, the first and most perfect good, is no mere partaker of goodness, and thus cannot be composed of matter and form.

Thirdly, an agent acts in virtue of its form, and so the way in which it is an agent will depend upon the way in which it has form. A primary and immediate source of activity must therefore be primarily and immediately form. Now God is the primary source of all activity, since, as we saw, he is the first cause. God then is essentially form, and not composed of matter and form.

HENCE: 1. Soul is ascribed to God by a metaphor drawn from its activity. For since soul is the seat of volition in men, we call what is pleasing to God's will, pleasing to his soul.

2. Anger and the like are ascribed to God by a metaphor drawn from their effects. For it is characteristic of anger that it stimulates men to requite wrong. Divine retribution is therefore metaphorically termed anger.

3. If form be considered in itself, free of extraneous factors, then any form assumed by one material thing can be assumed by more than one; individualness

derives from matter, which, as the primary substrate of form, cannot be assumed by anything else. A form however of the sort that is not assumed by material things, but itself subsists as a thing, cannot be assumed by anything else, and is thus individual of itself. Now God is such a form, and therefore does not require matter.

Is God to be identified with his own essence or nature, with that which makes him what he is?

THE THIRD POINT: 1. It seems that God is not to be identified with his essence or nature. For the essence or nature of God is godhead, and godhead is said to reside in God. Now nothing resides in itself. It seems therefore that God must differ from his essence or nature.

2. Moreover, effects resemble their causes, for what a thing does reflects what it is. Now we do not identify created things with their natures: human nature is not a man. Neither then is godhead God.

ON THE OTHER HAND, God is not only called living, but life: *I am the way, the truth and the life.* Now godhead bears the same relationship to God, as life does to the living. God then is godhead itself.

REPLY: God is to be identified with his own essence or nature.

We shall understand this when we see why things composed of matter and form must not be identified with their natures or essences. Essence or nature includes only what defines the species of a thing: thus human nature includes only what defines man, or what makes man man, for by 'human nature' we mean that which makes man man. Now the species of a thing is not defined by the matter and properties peculiar to it as an individual; thus we do not define man as that which has this flesh and these bones, or is white, or black, or the like. This flesh and these bones and the properties peculiar to them belong indeed to this man, but not to his nature. An individual man then possesses something which his human nature does not, so that a man and his nature are not altogether the same thing. 'Human nature' names, in fact, the formative element in man; for what gives a thing definition is formative with respect to the matter which gives it individuality.

The individuality of things not composed of matter and form cannot however derive from this or that individual matter, and the forms of such things must therefore be intrinsically individual and themselves subsist as things. Such things are thus identical with their own natures.

In the same way, then, God, who, as we have seen, is not composed of matter and form, is identical with his own godhead, with his own life and with whatever else is similarly said of him.

HENCE: 1. In talking about simple things we have to use as models the composite things from which our knowledge derives. Thus when God is being referred to as a subsistent thing, we use concrete nouns (since the subsistent things with which we are familiar are composite); but to express God's simpleness we use abstract nouns. So that when we talk of godhead or life or something of that sort residing in God, the diversity this implies is not to be attributed to God himself; but to the way in which we conceive him.

2. God's effects resemble God as far as they can, but not perfectly. One of the defects in resemblance is that they can reproduce only manifoldly what in itself is one and simple. As a result they are composite, and so cannot be identified with their natures.

Can one distinguish in God nature and existence?

THE FOURTH POINT: 1. It is not, it seems, the nature of God simply to exist. If it were, there would be nothing to specify that existence; and since unspecified existence is existence in general and belongs to everything, the word 'God' would mean an existent in general, and would name anything. Now this is false, as the book of *Wisdom* shows: *they invested stocks and stones with the incommunicable name.* So it is not God's nature simply to exist.

2. Moreover, as we remarked earlier, we can know clearly that there is a God, and yet cannot know clearly what he is. So the existence of God is not to be identified with what God is, with God's 'whatness' or nature.

ON THE OTHER HAND, Hilary writes: *Existence does not add anything to God; it is his very substance.* The substance of God is therefore his existence.

REPLY: That God is his own essence, we have seen; that he is also his own existence can be shown in a number of ways.

First, properties that belong to a thing over and above its own nature must derive from somewhere, either from that nature itself, as do properties to a particular species (for example the sense of humour peculiar to man derives from his specific nature), or from an external cause (as heat in water derives from some fire). If therefore the existence of a thing is to be other than its nature, that existence must either derive from the nature or have an external cause. Now it cannot derive merely from the nature, for nothing with derived existence suffices to bring itself into being. It follows then that, if a thing's existence differs from its nature, that existence must be externally caused. But we cannot say this about God, whom we have seen to be the first cause. Neither then can we say that God's existence is other than his nature.

Secondly, forms and natures are realized by existing: thus, we express actual realization of goodness or human nature by saying that goodness or human nature exists. When a nature is not itself existence, then, it must be potential of existence. Now, as we have seen, God does not contain potentialities, so in him nature must not differ from existence. It is therefore God's very nature to exist.

Thirdly, anything on fire either is itself fire or has caught fire. Similarly, anything that exists either is itself existence or partakes of it. Now, God, as we have seen, exists. If then he is not himself existence, and thus not by nature existent, he will only be a partaker of existence. And so he will not be the primary existent. God therefore is not only his own essence, but also his own existence.

HENCE: 1. 'Unspecified' is an ambiguous word. For it may imply on the one hand that further specification is excluded by definition, as reason is excluded by definition from irrational animals. Or it may imply that further specification is not included in the definition, as reason is not included in the definition of animals in general, though neither is it excluded. Understood in the first way, unspecified existence is divine existence; understood in the second way, unspecified existence is existence in general.

2. The verb 'to be' is used in two ways: to signify the act of existing, and to signify the mental uniting of predicate to subject which constitutes a proposition. Now we cannot clearly know the being of God in the first sense any more than we can clearly know his essence. But in the second sense we can, for when we say that God is we frame a proposition about God which we clearly know to be true. And this, as we have seen, we know from his effects.

Chapter 51
Problems with divine simplicity
Thomas V. Morris

Divine simplicity

Mʏ being is complex in many ways. I exist in an embodied form. I have arms, legs, fingers, toes. I have knowledge, I have emotions. I have desires, hopes, plans, dreams. The power I have to act in the world depends on my mental abilities and the soundness of my body. Consider the property I have of being a philosopher. For many years I lived with no knowledge of philosophy. Through intellectual awakening and hard work I came to exemplify this property, I became a philosopher. But it is a fragile thing and can be lost. A blow to the head, a lack of oxygen to the brain, perhaps an obsessive watching of network television around the clock, could suffice to rob me of this possession, this property so intimately tied to how I think of myself. Even laziness, inattention and simple absorption in the mundane can gradually erode the capacities in which this property resides. What I was, I am not. What I am, I may not continue to be. And what is true of me depends on so many forces outside my control.

Traditionally, many theists have insisted that none of this alterability, fragility or dependency could possibly characterize God. An absolutely perfect creator of all must have what philosophers call *ontological independence,* or *aseity* (existence from his own resources alone, 'from himself,' hence the Latin *a se*). God cannot be dependent on anything, otherwise he would not be a greatest possible being, and could not be such that everything depends *on him.* He cannot have any sort of complexity involving composition, for wholes composed of parts are dependent upon their parts for what they are. And he cannot have the sort of complexity in his being which would consist in his having his own properties or attributes the way a man or woman has possessions which can be acquired or lost. There must be greater stability and simplicity in the divine being than this.

These reflections have led many theists of the past, and some prominent theists of the present, to endorse a striking metaphysical thesis sometimes known as the *doctrine of divine simplicity*, the claim that, in his innermost being, God must be without any sort of metaphysical complexity whatsoever. This is usually understood to involve a threefold denial:

(1) God is without any spatial parts (the thesis of spatial simplicity),

Thomas V. Morris 'Simplicity' from *Our Idea of God* (University of Notre Dame Press, 1991), chapter 6, reprinted by permission of the author.

(2) God is without any temporal parts (the thesis of temporal simplicity),

and

(3) God is without the sort of metaphysical complexity which would be involved in his exemplifying numerous different properties ontologically distinct from himself (the thesis of property simplicity).

The thesis of spatial simplicity is endorsed by the vast majority of traditional Christian theists because of considerations deriving from perfect being theology. God is not a physical object, so he does not have physical, or spatially located, parts.

The thesis of temporal simplicity is endorsed by many theists, but is very controversial, even among Christian philosophers and theologians. This thesis maintains that there is no past, present and future in the life of God, no temporal succession of moments coming to be and passing away. The eternal fullness of divine existence is not divisible into temporal segments as our lives are. God is thus outside of time. We shall at this point focus on the most controversial thesis contained within the doctrine of divine simplicity—the thesis of property simplicity.

Representative simplicity theorists (those who present the doctrine of divine simplicity as an important part of any theoretically adequate philosophical theology) claim that if God were like us in exemplifying properties distinct from himself, then he would depend on those properties for what he is, in violation of divine aseity. The idea here is a bit difficult to grasp, but it is roughly this: All God's creatures have properties distinct from themselves. I have many, many properties characterizing me, the property of being human, of being male, of being a philosopher, of being from North Carolina, of being a father, of being a pet owner, of loving the ocean, and so on. These are all properties whose existence is distinct from my own. These properties existed and were exemplified by others before I existed, thus they exist distinct from me and do not depend on me for what they are like. But I could not be what I am if it were not for those properties being as they are, so I depend on them for what I am. God cannot depend on anything, so he must not have properties distinct from himself

Yet we say that God is good, omnipotent, omniscient. We speak of God's properties or attributes, and simplicity itself surely seems to be a property. Should we then think of it as the discrete property of being such as to have no discrete properties? If so, then it seems we have wandered into nonsense unawares. But simplicity theorists have a reply. When we say that God is good, and that God is omnipotent, we are not properly attributing to him ontologically distinct attributes. We are merely conceptualizing the remarkable unity that is God in different ways. According to a main form of the simplicity doctrine, it would be less misleading to say that God is Perfect Goodness, God is Omnipotence, God is Omniscience, where these are understood as identities rather than as the attributions of separate properties. But if these are identities, then it follows by the laws governing identity that Perfect Goodness is Omnipotence, and Omnipotence just is the same thing as

Omniscience. Another way to try put this might be to say that there is only one divine property—Divinity—and it is identical with God. Thus, within the life of God, there is no complexity of properties God has; there is only the one property God is. Simplicity is not the property of having no properties—it is rather a name for the mysterious way in which the being of God supports our many true characterizations of him without ultimately being divisible into substance and attributes, as are his creatures.

With this claim that there is no complexity of properties had by God, we are in deep waters indeed. This is perhaps the most startling, unusual claim ever made about God's being. And it is one with apparently counterintuitive implications. Yet those who endorse it insist that it is of paramount theological importance. It has been thought of as the best explanation for the stability of God's being, his incorporeality, his eternity and his immutability. It has also been presented as the basis for the best view of the relation between God and morality, among other things. But it is an idea whose untoward implications are difficult to defend and whose advantages can perhaps all be had in other ways. It is also an idea whose precise motivation is not so convincing after all, under close scrutiny.

First, as to motivation: what the simplicity theorist is concerned about is that, given the necessary goodness of God, for example, if goodness is thought of as a property distinct from God, then it is true that

(1) If the property of goodness did not exist, then God would not exist.

But this is just an expression of the idea that God's goodness is essential to him— that God is good in every circumstance in which he exists. But since, on the view we have been developing, it is also true that God exists necessarily, in every possible world, it can also be said of the property of goodness that it is essentially such that it is possessed by God. And this can be seen to support the truth of

(2) If God did not exist, then the property of goodness would not exist.

The simplicity theorist thinks that (1) expresses the dependence of God on the property of goodness. But if it did, (2) would express the dependence of the property of goodness on God. But, presumably, ontological dependence, dependence for being or existence, can only go in one direction—if my parents brought me into existence it cannot also be the case that I brought them into existence. Thus, the mere existence and truth of propositions like (1) and (2) cannot alone be taken to show ontological dependence. Their truth merely reflects the logical relation which holds between propositions about necessarily existent entities, and alone implies nothing about the ontological dependence or independence of those entities.

A view can be developed in accordance with which any necessarily existent entities distinct from God can be viewed as ontologically dependent on God as the divine, ontologically independent source of all else. If this theistically attractive view is true, it will be impossible to motivate the doctrine of divine simplicity from considerations of aseity alone. Moreover, other motivations of divine simplicity will be hard to come by. For in the case of God's possession of his defining, distinctively divine attributes, there is no question of coming-to-be and ceasing-to-be. He possesses these properties in all possible circumstances. There is no fragility or tenuousness to his character. His divinity is neither accidental nor temporary. His properties cannot 'come apart'. The instability and contingency which accompany complexity in our case offer no threat to his exalted status whatsoever. Thus, there is no need to endorse property simplicity to provide for a recognition of God's greatest possible metaphysical stature. The purported benefits of simplicity can be had otherwise.

Finally, there are easily apparent counterintuitive implications of the thesis of property simplicity. First, if God is a property, then either God is an abstract object or some property is a concrete object. Either view seems startlingly counterintuitive, in violation of any standard concrete-abstract distinction. Second, if there is no multiplicity of properties really had by God, it will, I think, be very hard, if not just impossible, to make sense of standard distinctions we make about God. We believe that he is necessarily powerful, but that it is only contingently true of him that he used that power to create our world. He could have created another universe instead, or, perhaps, he could have refrained from creating any physical realm at all. We also believe that it is only contingently, not necessarily, true of God that he called Abram out of Ur, spoke through Moses, and sent the prophets he chose. Moreover, I happen to be wearing a striped shirt today. I could have worn a plain shirt instead. It is a contingent fact that I am garbed in stripes. And God knows this fact. He thus has a belief, or is in a specific state of knowledge, which is contingent He has the property of being in this cognitive state contingently, since its status must mirror the contingent status of the fact known. God necessarily is a knower. God contingently has the knowledge that I have on a striped shirt. Thus, there is both necessity and contingency with respect to God. And there seems to be no other good way to capture this truth than to say that God has both necessary (essential) and contingent properties. But if that is so, then he cannot 'have' just one and only one property, a single property with which he is identical. Nor can he be said to literally have no properties. The thesis of property simplicity therefore must be false.

If one component of the doctrine of divine simplicity is false, the doctrine as a whole is false. Yet it is still possible that the doctrine is an attempt to express a true mystery concerning the real metaphysical unity of God. It is sensible to think there is a special kind of integrity to the being of God. The thesis of property simplicity, as it stands, just fails to capture it. So by rejecting the doctrine of divine simplicity, as presented, I don't mean to be turning my back on any legitimate inklings of divine uniqueness which may ultimately stand behind it. I just mean to indicate that insofar as those inklings can be captured in language, the thesis of property simplicity, and its associated general doctrine, is not what we need for that expression.

Chapter 52

A modern defence of divine simplicity

Brian Davies

I

PEOPLE often suppose that theology is grounded in an understanding of the nature and attributes of God considered as a particular individual. It is, for example, pretty axiomatic among modern philosophers of religion that God is a person, where 'person' means something like a consciousness or mind with beliefs and thoughts.

Yet this line of thinking would have seemed strange to earlier generations of thinkers. Here I am referring to what is sometimes called the tradition of classical theism, by which I mean the doctrine of God which you can find in writers like Augustine, Anselm and Thomas Aquinas. For it is characteristic of classical theism to say that God is incomparable and incomprehensible. *De Deo non possumus scire quid sit*—'It is impossible to know of God what he is'.[1] *De Deo scire non possumus quid sit, sed quid non sit*—'We cannot know what God is, but only what he is not'.[2] These are assertions which classical theists ask us to accept in all seriousness, and in doing so they do not just mean that God is a mysterious sort of thing which we cannot understand because we are not quite clever enough or because our researches are still in their infancy. They mean that God belongs to no class at all and that he defies the conceptual equipment by means of which we identify things and single them out as members of a world.

Thus it is that in the writings of classical theists we come across the doctrine of divine simplicity. God has no nature in any intelligible sense. He is divinity through and through without parts or aspects. On this account, everything that God is *is* God. Or, as some classical theists express it, God *has* no attributes but *is* his attributes. And these are nothing less than God himself. As St Anselm puts it:

You are therefore the very life by which You live, the wisdom by which You are wise, the very goodness by which You are good to both good men and wicked . . . . You are truth, You are goodness, You are blessedness, You are eternity, and You are every true good . . . . There are no parts in You, Lord; neither are You many, but You are so much one and the same with

Brian Davies 'Classical Theism and the Doctrine of Divine Simplicity' from *Language Meaning and God* edited by Brian Davies (Geoffrey Chapman, 1987), reprinted by permission of Continuum International Publishing Group Ltd and the author.

1. Aquinas, *Summa Theologiae*, Ia, 1, 7 ad 1.
2. *Summa Theologiae*, Ia, introduction to q.3.

Yourself that in nothing are You dissimilar with Yourself. Indeed You are unity itself not divisible by any mind. Life and wisdom and the other (attributes), then, are not parts of You, but all are one and each one of them is wholly what You are and what all the others are.[3]

Writing in the same vein, Aquinas argues that we can speak of God either by means of concrete terms (as if 'God' were the name of an individual in the world) or by means of abstract terms (as if it were the name for a non-individuated nature). In his view, 'God is Wisdom' or 'God is Goodness' are just as true as 'God is wise' or 'God is good'. Or, as Aquinas himself says:

God is both simple, like the form, and subsistent, like the concrete thing, and so we sometimes refer to him by abstract nouns to indicate his simplicity and sometimes by concrete nouns to indicate his subsistence and completeness; though neither way of speaking measures up to his way of being, for in this life we do not know him as he is in himself.[4]

By 'form' here Aquinas is alluding to what, for example, is shared by all people when it is truly said that each of them is human. We might call it their common humanity. Aquinas's point then is that though we cannot call particular people 'Humanity' (we cannot say that Mary is Humanity or that Fred is Humanity), we can refer to God by the name signifying his nature. Mary and Fred are not Humanity, but God is Divinity.

Yet is this teaching at all believable? And is it of any theological significance? Edmund Hill has recently called it 'profound theology . . . a mature metaphysics of divine being' which sets us on the road to a proper account of the Trinity.[5] That is a minority view, however. Much more typical of the contemporary verdict is the conclusion of Ronald H. Nash. 'It would appear', says Nash, 'that Christian theologians have no good reason to affirm the doctrine of divine simplicity. It seems doubtful that the doctrine adds anything significant to our understanding of God. . . . Perhaps, like Emil Brunner, we should conclude that the doctrine has no practical value: it is pure speculation "which has nothing at all to do with the God of the Christian Faith".'[6]

II

What is wrong with the doctrine of divine simplicity? Here we might mention two lines of criticism.

(a) First, so it might be said, the doctrine leads to absurdity. This is Alvin Plantinga's chief objection to it.[7] 'If God is identical with each of his properties', says Plantinga, 'then each of his properties is identical with each of his properties,

---

3. *Proslogion* XII and XVIII, trans. M. J. Charlesworth, *St Anselm's Proslogion* (Oxford, 1965).
4. *Summa Theologiae*, Ia, 13, 1.
5. Edmund Hill, *The Mystery of the Trinity* (London, 1985), p. 55.
6. Ronald H. Nash, *The Concept of God* (Grand Rapids, Michigan, 1983), pp. 95 f. The quotation from Brunner comes from *The Christian Doctrine of God* (Philadelphia, 1950), p. 294.
7. Alvin Plantinga, *Does God Have A Nature?* (Milwaukee, 1980).

so that God has but one property.' The conclusion here is false, says Plantinga, because God has several properties. It is, he adds, also false because 'if God is identical with each of his properties, then, since each of his properties is a property, he is a property', while 'if God is a property, then he isn't a person but a mere abstract object; he has no knowledge, awareness, power, love or life'.

Part of Plantinga's worry here is that the doctrine of divine simplicity is incompatible with theism. And others have felt the same. One way of affirming the doctrine is to hold that God is not an individual. Sometimes it is said that God is not a thing or a being. And yet, so it has been asked, how can God exist if he is not an individual? And what is the difference between 'God is not a thing or a being' and 'Nothing whatsoever is God'?

(b) A second possible criticism turns on the notion of existence. Defenders of the doctrine of divine simplicity speak as though they identify God's nature with the fact that God exists. Take, for example, Aquinas. As his treatment of God's simplicity draws to a close, he denies that in God there is a mixture (*compositio*) of *essentia* (essence) and *esse* (existence). According to Aquinas, God *is* existence. He is *suum esse* (his own being) or *ipsum esse subsistens* (subsistent existence itself). But some would now deny this on the ground that it misconstrues the logic of assertions concerning existence.

Why? The likely answer would be that there is no such thing as existence *simpliciter*, and there is nothing which can be it or have it as a property. On this account, existence is what is expressed when it is asserted that a concept has instances. It is a property of concepts or predicates rather than a property of objects or subjects. To say that something exists is not to describe it or to tell us something about it. It is to say of some description or account that it truly applies to something or other.[8] In terms of this position the conclusion would seem to be that, in its Thomist form at any rate, the doctrine of divine simplicity is a piece of nonsense. It tries to tell us what God is by using expressions which could never tell what anything is.

Some would add that it implicitly endorses the so-called Ontological Argument, which Aquinas officially rejects. Critics of the argument have urged that, since existence is not a property of objects, one cannot deduce the existence of God from the concept of God. Some have then gone on to say that, by the same token, Aquinas on divine simplicity is misguided. As Terence Penelhum puts it:

The distinctive character of the concept of existence precludes our saying that there can be a being whose existence follows from his essence; and also precludes the even stronger logical move of *identifying* the existence of anything with its essence. These are the Anselmian errors all over again. . . . Since Aquinas differs from Anselm in holding that God's existence has to be inferred from his effects and not from the mere concept of God, he is traditionally credited with having seen what is wrong with the Ontological Proof. He did see it was wrong, but not *why* it was, for he commits the same error himself. He says that we do not

8. This is a very rough account of an approach associated with writers such as Frege and Russell. For a careful attempt to expound it see C. J. F. Williams, *What Is Existence* (Oxford, 1981).

have the requisite knowledge of the divine nature to deduce God's existence from it; but his own argument leads us from finite beings to a being whose existence does follow from his nature, and this entails that *if* we knew God's nature we could deduce his existence from it— and *this* is the mistake. To say that although God's existence is self-evident in itself it is not to us, is to say that it *is* self-evident in itself, and the error lies here. It is not our ignorance that is the obstacle to explaining God's existence by his nature, but the logical character of the concept of existence.[9]

III

Are these objections decisive, however? To start on a positive note, let us first consider what might be said in their defence.

To begin with, then, if A and B are identical, then A and B might be the same thing. So if the properties of God are identical with each other, they could be the same property, and God could be that property if God is his properties. Yet it seems odd to say that different properties can be the same property, and just as odd to say that God is a property. There must be some sense in which to say, for example, 'God is wise and powerful' is to say two different things about him, that he is wise *and* that he is powerful. It must also be somehow true that if we say 'God is wise and powerful' we say something *about* God and do not simply name him (as if 'is wise and powerful' were a synonym for 'God'). Fred maybe bald, but his baldness is not him. Similarly, it would seem nonsense to hold that God and, say, his wisdom are the same (supposing, that is, that we ascribe wisdom to God, and supposing we say that it is an attribute or property of him).

Then again, is there any clear sense to assertions of the kind 'God is not an individual' or 'God is not a thing'? Neither 'individual' nor 'thing' serve by themselves to pick out one thing rather than another. In Wittgenstein's terms, they are 'formal' concepts as defined in *Tractatus* 4.126–4.12721. One might therefore conclude that being told that God is neither an individual nor a thing is not to be told anything of God at all. Alternatively, one might hold that if God is neither an individual nor a thing (or an object or a being, as is sometimes said), then God is nothing, which anyone can be forgiven for reading as 'God does not exist'.

So arguments like those of Plantinga are clearly on to something. And the force of their drift can surely be appreciated if we remember what is typically said of God—that he acts, for example. To say that something acts is to say that it undergoes a process or that it brings one about. Acting is something that is done. It is ascribable to genuine subjects or agents. And what, one might ask, are subjects or agents if they are not things or individuals? Even Aquinas calls God a *res* (thing). He also concedes that God is an individual in some sense. He ascribes to God the individuality proper to things whose nature is not material.

The argument concerning existence seems likewise to be getting at something

9. Terence Penelhum, 'Divine Necessity', *Mind* 69 (1960), repr. in *The Philosophy of Religion*, ed. Basil Mitchell (Oxford, 1971). I quote from Mitchell's text, pp. 184 f.

important. It is, for instance, hard to believe that if we ask whether God exists, and if we ask what God is, the answer to the second question could be the same as the answer to the first. 'There is a God' does not say what God is. As Aristotle observes, 'There is nothing whose essence it is that there is such a thing, for there is no such kind of thing as *things that there are*'.[10]

The reply might be that to say that something exists is indeed to say something about it and that existence is therefore a property which something can have or with which it can be identified. It might be held that '—— exists' can be what is sometimes called a 'first-level predicate' that it can function like '—— is hot' in 'John is hot'. But there is much to be said against this conclusion. We might define a first-level predicate as an expression which yields a proposition when attached to one or more proper names. Such expressions will do the same if attached to a definite description like 'The Pope who succeeded John Paul I'. But while we get an intelligible proposition by, say, attaching 'The Pope who succeeded John Paul I' to the expression 'eats Polish sausage', we get a curious result by attaching to it 'exists'. What does 'The Pope who succeeded John Paul I exists' mean? And what, outside philosophy, would '——exists' mean if attached to a proper name? If you tell someone out of the blue 'Brian Davies exists', will he not presume that something peculiar is going on? And will he not be right?

Well, maybe not. Some people, at any rate, seem to have no problems with utterances like 'Brian Davies exists'. Yet now there is another point worth mentioning. This is that paradox seems entailed by the suggestion that existence is a property of objects or individuals Are we to suppose that, for example, an existing cat is different from a non-existing one? And what if we deny that such and such exists on the assumption that to do so is to deny that it has a particular property? If we say, for example, 'Honest theologians do not exist', then we purport to be talking about honest theologians, we seem to presuppose that they are there to be talked about, but we also deny that they are real. It therefore seems that assertions like 'Honest theologians do not exist' are implicitly contradictory and that assertions like 'Honest theologians exist' are true of necessity. But that is just unbelievable. There must be an honest theologian somewhere, though no theologian is bound to be honest.

With reference to all this, a useful corrective comes in the work of Frege. According to him, 'the content of a statement of number is an assertion about a concept'.[11] This, says Frege, is perhaps clearest with the number 0.

If I say 'Venus has 0 moons', there simply does not exist any moon or agglomeration of moons for anything to be asserted of; but what happens is that a property is assigned to the *concept* 'moon of Venus', namely that of including nothing under it. If I say 'the King's carriage is drawn by four horses', then I assign the number four to the concept 'horse that draws the King's carriage'.

---

10. *An. Post.* 92b, 13–14.
11. Gottlob Frege, *The Foundations of Arithmetic*, trans. J. L. Austin (Oxford, 1980), p. 59.

There are difficulties here, but we can at least say that Frege looks to be right about one thing. For he goes on to say that 'existence is analogous to number' so that if his analysis of number statements is on the right lines, then that is the right analysis of statements of existence. And the fact is that existence is analogous to number. For statements of existence are statements of number. As C. J. F. Williams puts it:

Statements of number are possible answers to questions of the form 'How many A's are there?' and answers to such questions are no less answers for being relatively vague. In answering the question 'How many A's are there?' I need not produce one of the Natural Numbers. I may just say 'A lot', which is tantamount to saying 'The number of A's is not small', or 'A few', which is tantamount to saying 'The number of A's is not large'. If I say 'There are some A's', this is tantamount to saying 'The number of A's is not o'. Instead of saying 'There are a lot of A's' I may say 'A's are numerous' and instead of saying 'There are some A's' I may say 'A's exist'. All these may be regarded as statements of number.[12]

According to Frege, a proposition like 'There exists no rectangular equilateral rectilinear triangle' states a property of the concept 'rectangular equilateral rectilinear triangle'; it 'assigns to it the number nought'. In that case, something similar is true of 'A rectangular equilateral rectilinear triangle exists', for that is the contradictory of 'There exists no rectangular equilateral rectilinear triangle'. If statements of existence are number statements, therefore, such statements ascribe a property to a concept, not to an object, if statements of number ascribe a property to a concept.

IV

Yet even if we can swallow all that it still seems to me that defenders of the doctrine of divine simplicity need not be unduly alarmed.

(a) To begin with, it is by no means obvious that the expressions we use to refer to God and his properties cannot be the means of referring to one and the same reality. In this sense God might be identical with his properties and they might be identical with each other. A natural tendency here is to construe such a view as saying that properties which are different are not different when God has them and that God is nothing but a property. That is how Plantinga seems to construe it. But another interpretation of the view is possible. Its defender might accept that ascribing different properties to God is done by means of sentences which differ in meaning. In this sense he might agree that God has different properties. But then he might say that the reality to which our talk of God latches on is not something distinct from its properties and not something with distinct properties. As P. T. Geach indicates, there is a comparison available to us here in the light of mathematical functions. ' "The square of ——" and "the double of ——" signify two quite different functions, but for the argument 2 these two function both take the number 4 as their value. Similarly, "the wisdom of ——" and "the power of ——" signify different forms, but the individualizations of these forms in God's case are

12. Williams. *op. cit.*, pp. 54 f.

not distinct from one another; nor is either distinct from God, just as the number 1 is in no way distinct from its own square.'[13] This is no more than an analogy, of course. But it ties up well enough with the doctrine of divine simplicity. Defenders of the doctrine do not deny that, for example, 'God is wise' means something different from 'God is powerful'. In this sense they can be said to accept that God has different properties. What they deny is that what is signified by 'the wisdom of God' is possessed by God as a property distinct from that of being powerful. They also deny that 'the wisdom of God' and 'the power of God' refer to something other than what is signified by means of the word 'God'.

(b) Second, it can be argued that writers like Plantinga and Penelhum misconstrue the doctrine of divine simplicity because they treat it as telling us something about God's properties while the doctrine precisely denies that God has properties, at least in one sense. That sounds paradoxical, but what I am getting at is really quite familiar, at least in some circles. With respect to Aquinas the point has been very effectively made by David Burrell and by earlier writers such as Victor White and Josef Pieper:[14] from first to last the doctrine of divine simplicity is a piece of negative or apophatic theology and not a purported description of God. I should have thought that this fact was obvious from even a casual reading of authors like Augustine and Anselm. It is particularly evident from a reading of Aquinas since he is quite explicit that in saying that God is simple he is giving an account of what God is not. This is clear from texts like the Introduction to *Summa Theologiae*, Ia, 3, where Aquinas describes what follows (of which the first thing is his exposition of divine simplicity) as a consideration of 'the ways in which God does not exist'. What this in turn proves to mean is that Aquinas is not saying that, for example, God's properties are unqualifiedly identical with each other and that God is unqualifiedly identical with all of his properties. To cast things in a more modern idiom, the Thomist doctrine of divine simplicity is an exercise in 'logical grammar'; its aim is to tell us the sort of conclusions about God which are not to be drawn. And one thing being said by it is that God is not to be thought of (cannot be known) as something with properties distinguishable from each other, or as something we can conceive of as distinct from the nature we ascribe to it.

(c) Our third reply follows from this. For now I want to suggest that the conclusion just referred to is not only intelligible but also true. For if there is a God, then he is the Creator. And this truth has implications which we can turn to by reflecting for a moment on the notion of creation.

What does it mean to call God the Creator?

Everyone agrees that it means that God is the source or the cause of all his creatures, that it is by virtue of his action that they are there at all, that creatures are

---

13. G. E. M. Anscombe and P. T. Geach, *Three Philosophers* (Oxford, 1973), p. 122. Cf. P. T. Geach, 'Form and Existence', in *God and the Soul* (London, 1969), pp. 491.
14. David Burrell, *Aquinas, God and Action* (London and Henley, 1979); Victor White, *God the Unknown* (London, 1956); Josef Pieper, *The Silence of Saint Thomas*, trans. John Murray and Daniel O'Connor (Chicago, 1965).

'made' by God. By 'creatures' here I mean everything other than God, everything that can be significantly referred to as an individual or object.

But it is important to stress that, in the full theological sense of the term, to say that God 'creates' is not just to say that he brings it about that things come to be. That could be taken only to mean that he causes them to begin to exist, while to say that God creates is normally to be construed as saying that he is also responsible for the existence of things since they are made to be by him for as long as they exist. He is, as we might put it, the cause not just of becoming but also of being.[15] Hence we find writers who have no difficulty in supposing both that God is the Creator and that the created world never had a beginning. As far as the theological notion of creation goes, it is there being any world at all that matters, not just the fact that the world began to be.

And to this one can add another point.

Causes in the world always operate in the context of the world, and they bring things about by changing the world. But the traditional notion of creation rules this out in the case of God. For it asserts that God is the cause of the existence of everything apart from himself. It also states that creation is out of nothing (*ex nihilo*). In that case it follows that creation (God's creating) is not essentially a matter of change. For there is no pre-existing material to be altered by it. So to say that God exists is to say that there is a Creator who, for as long as his creation exists, is the cause of its being, but not by modification of anything. As one might also put it, the continued existence of anything other than God depends on God as a causal agent, but not as one who causes by acting on anything. God, so we might say, cannot make any difference to anything. And this will not be because he is feeble or distant. It will be because he is present to everything as making it to be for as long as it exists.

But what now follows from this? If we are working within the framework of the doctrine of creation, what might we deduce about God *qua* Creator?

To begin with, of course, we will have to deny that God is something bodily. Otherwise he will simply be part of the world the existence of which is said to depend on him in terms of the doctrine of creation.

This, in turn, means that God cannot be comprehensible in terms of what Aristotle meant by 'genus' and 'species'. God cannot be classified as a member of the world; he will be no possible object of research for biologists, zoologists, physicists and chemists.

Nor can he share with things in the world certain of their essential features. He cannot, for instance, be confined in a space, for that presupposes bodily existence and location. Nor can he be something changing or changeable, where 'change' is ascribable to a thing precisely in virtue of its materiality.

So God cannot move around. Nor can he be altered in other ways that depend on or involve bodily changes. He cannot, in fact, be *altered* by anything. To be altered

---

15. Cf. *Summa Theologiae*, 45. cf. James Ross, 'Creation', *The Journal of Philosophy* 77 (1980).

by something is to be on the receiving end of the causal operation of something. It is to be passive to the action of something else. Yet if God is the cause of his creatures being there at all, he cannot be like that. All of God's creatures will be God's effects in that their whole reality will derive from him and will spring from him as making it to be. In this sense the causal relationship between God and creatures must be asymmetrical. In this sense God cannot be altered by anything.

But not only that. For, in spite of what I said earlier, we can also deny that God is an individual.

By this I do not mean that God is in no sense a subject or an agent. I am not denying the reality of God. But suppose one concentrates on the sense of individual (arguably its most common sense) according to which to call something an individual is to imply that there could always be another of the same kind. In that case, so I am arguing, we would be right to deny that God is an individual. We can deny that he can be thought of as sharing a nature with other things.

For how do we distinguish between individuals sharing a nature? How, for example, do we distinguish between one dog and another?

We cannot, to begin with, distinguish between them in terms of their nature as dogs. Their being canine is something they share. They are dogs in precisely the same sense and we cannot appeal to this fact as a means of distinguishing between them.

But nor can we appeal to what Scholastic writers would have called their accidental attributes—differences which can serve to help us distinguish between things of a kind without putting them into different kinds. I mean, for example, that we cannot distinguish between Fido and Rover by noting that one of them has brown hair and the other has black hair, or that one is in the kennel and the other in the field. For to say that is already to presuppose that we have two and not one, that we have *one* and the *other*. It may indeed be that one dog is brown and the other is black. But such differences cannot make the two dogs to be two. The two dogs could not have these varied fortunes if they were not already distinct.

So how do we distinguish between one and another of the same kind of thing? The question is a hard one, but what seems to be going on, I suggest, is that we distinguish between individuals in the world by pointing to them somehow. In the end, as it seems to me, we distinguish between Fido and Rover not just by describing them (by saying what they are by nature or by saying what they look like exactly or where in fact they are and so on) but by simply recognizing that Fido is *this* thing and Rover is *that* thing, that Fido can be located by nodding at *this* parcel of matter, and Rover by nodding at *that* one.

In other words, we distinguish between individuals in the world because they are material or because they exist in a context of materiality. In this sense to understand something as an individual is to understand it as part of the material world. And in this sense we can deny that God is an individual. For if God is the Creator *ex nihilo*, then, as we have seen, he cannot be anything material.

Another way of putting it is to say that *who* God is cannot be something different from *what* God is. John and Mary are both human beings. But John is not Mary and Mary is not John. They are individual people. And though they are human they do not, as individuals, constitute human nature. Along with many others, they exemplify it. Suppose we express this by saying that they are not as individuals the same as their common nature, that who they are and what they are can be distinguished. Then, so I am arguing, if God is in no way material, who he is and what he is are not distinguishable. We cannot get a purchase on the notion of a class of Gods. In terms of the doctrine of creation, 'God', so we may say, is not the name of any class at all. It has to be construed as the name of a nature, as analogous, that is, to 'Man' and 'Horse' in assertions like 'Man is a rational animal' and 'The horse is a quadruped'.

And to all of this one can add something else. For if everything other than God owes its existence to him, then God owes his existence to nothing. He is underived. If he exists, he is also underivable, for if he could owe his existence to something not himself that thing would have to exist independently of him. And that can be expressed by saying that God and his existence are identical. This is something which it makes sense to say even allowing for the sort of considerations about existence, properties and so on noted earlier. Maybe it is true that existence is not something subsistent. Maybe it is no distinctive property. But if there being a thing depends on its being created (if the existence of x derives from what is not x as creatures are said to derive from God), then the thing and its existence can be distinguished simply on the ground that what the thing is will not suffice to secure its being there. And, by the same token, God can be distinguished from it by saying that this cannot be true with reference to him, or that what he is and the fact that he is are not distinguishable. For if such were not the case, then he too would be created. He too would be such that in the sense just noted he and his existence could be distinguished.

In other words, if we concede the doctrine of creation, there is a case for saying that statements like 'God is his own being' or 'God is subsistent existence itself' are perfectly in order even though at one level they can be challenged. They will serve to remind us that we cannot think of God as something which depends for its existence on the activity of anything outside itself, that God is uncreated and uncreateable.

That, it seems to me, is what Aquinas wants to say. In denying that in God there is *compositio* of *essentia* and *esse* he makes three points in the *Summa Theologiae*. First, he says, the existence of God cannot be 'externally caused'. Second, there is no potentiality in God (i.e. he cannot be changed or produced by anything). Third, God is the 'primary existent' (*primum ens*, the ultimate or first cause of creatures). The upshot would seem to be that, according to Aquinas, to say that God is *esse* is not to assert an identity statement comparable to assertions like 'John Smith is really Bill Jones'. What it seems to be is what, as I have noted, Aquinas says that the whole of his doctrine of divine simplicity is—an account of what God is not. What it says is that God is neither made to be by anything nor able to be made by anything. And, in spite of what writers like Penelhum argue, this is not to hold that the fact of God's existence is deducible from his nature. The second thesis here is a positive one, while Aquinas's, it seems, is negative. Apart from that, in terms of Aquinas's thinking, if God's existence were derivable from his nature, someone could know what it is that is signified by 'God'. He could also see that it includes what is signified in saying that something exists. 'God' would be in principle definable and 'existing' could be recognized as part of its definition. Yet Aquinas rejects this view. 'God' for him is not definable since God belongs to no genus or species. Even if this were not so, he says, the existence of God could still be denied without contradiction. There is nothing for Aquinas in the meaning of 'God' which entails the truth of theism. According to Aquinas we do not really know what we mean when we use the term. What we can know is the world of creatures, or at least part of it. 'God' is the name given to the unknown source of this. Though that is not to say that 'God', for Aquinas, is a piece of gibberish. His position is as Herbert McCabe has expressed it. 'When we speak of God, although we know how to use our words, there is an important sense in which we do not know what they mean. Fundamentally this is because of our special ignorance of God. We know how to talk about shoes and ships because of our understanding of shoes and ships. We know how to talk about God, not because of any understanding of God, but because of what we know about creatures.'[16] That, in a nutshell, is the drift of the famous discussion of analogy and the like, *de nominibus Dei*, q.13 of the *Prima Pars*. A careful reading of it will reveal, I think, that Aquinas does not subscribe to the Ontological Argument even unofficially. Insofar as he holds that God is a 'necessary being', his point is that nothing can or does create God.

(d) But now for another problem. Suppose we concede what I have been urging. Are we not still left with a decisive objection to the doctrine of divine simplicity? For will it not now be true that God is not a *person*? And if we say that God is not a person, should we not also agree with Plantinga after all? Does not the doctrine of divine simplicity leave us with something other than theism?

Well, why should it be thought that it does? If what I have been saying is cogent, the opposite is true. For what is theism if it is not belief in the existence of God the Creator? And that belief, so I have argued, leads to what can be recognized as the doctrine of divine simplicity.

In any case, must a theist agree without demur that God is indeed a person? Does he need to accept the presumption of people like Plantinga here?

There are certainly reasons for saying that to believe in the existence of God is to believe in the existence of a person. It is held, for example, that God has knowledge and will, and these are commonly and naturally associated with people. So if people are our models for persons, and if God has knowledge and will, it would seem that God is a person. That looks like a perfectly sensible thing to say.

---

16. *Summa Theologiae*, Blackfriars ed. (London and New York), vol. 3, trans. Herbert McCabe OP (1964), Appendix 3 ('Signifying Imperfectly'), p. 104.

But this kind of argument can be made to cut both ways. For people are also commonly associated with, for example, bodies and parents and food and drink and sex and society and death. Yet God is said to be above such things. He is said to be bodiless and immortal or eternal. So it also seems appropriate to deny that God is a person. If people are our models for persons, then in an obvious sense God, it would seem, is not a person. And this argument can be developed.

Take, for example, the notion of knowledge. People, we might say, are essentially knowers. Something is wrong with them if they do not know things. But how does it come about that people come to know? They learn, of course. And they do so because they are things in the world on which other things in the world impinge. But God cannot be like this. He is supposed to have made the world, and he is not supposed to be part of it. So God, it would seem, just does not know as people know. And if people are our models for persons, and if this implies that God knows as people know, then God is not a person.

Or consider the question of space. People are in space. So they are here and not there, there and not here. Yet God is supposed to be everywhere, which can be taken to mean that he is also nowhere. So again the point can be pressed. If people are our models for persons, and if this implies that God is what people are, then God is not a person. For God is not anywhere, while people are always somewhere.

And so one might go on. I am not denying that God can be called a person. But it can also be said that he is not a person, not because one wishes to say that God does not exist, but because one can be readily struck by the differences between God and the paradigmatic instances of persons provided by the existence of people. If it seems obviously true that God is a person, it seems no less true that he is no such thing.

Nor does this seem something which has to be denied by those anxious to preserve what we might call an orthodox vocabulary about God. The striking fact here is that the formula 'God is a person' is by no means a traditional one. It does not occur in the Bible. It is foreign to the Fathers and to writers up to and beyond the Middle Ages. Nor does it occur in any of the creeds. In Christian circles, of course, one can appeal to the formula of the Trinity: that God is three persons in one *ousia* or *substantia*. But that formula does not say that God is a person or that he is three persons in one person.

V

So there is much to be said for the doctrine of divine simplicity. And this, in turn, means that there is much to be said for classical theism over and against the alternative which I referred to at the outset.

Yet this conclusion clearly raises some major questions. Classical theism, with its doctrine of divine simplicity, evidently goes with the view that God is deeply mysterious. It is an agnostic conception of divinity. If this conception is valid, therefore, how, for example, are we to account for our talk about God? Or is it that we cannot really speak of God at all? And, as many will want to ask, what about the Bible? How does classical theism fit with what the Bible says? Or is it, perhaps, that the two are incompatible?

Such are some of the problems, and I cannot hope to deal with them adequately here. Broadly speaking, however, I have four main things to say about them.

The first is that theists in general have no a *priori* need to be anxious simply because of the unknowability of God. That has been denied on the ground that 'to say that something transcends the human understanding is to say that it is unintelligible', from which it has been held to follow that 'it is impossible for a sentence both to be significant and to be about God'.[17] But there can surely be more than we can understand. And, if I am right, that is what theists are bound to concede. For it follows from the doctrine of creation, which leads in turn to the view that God is simple. And that view entails that in certain ways he is incomprehensible.

The second point is that much of what gets taken as positive assertion about God can equally (or perhaps more usefully) be read as negation. Take, for example, the classical assertion that God is wholly immutable. Is it to be read as a description of God? I should say 'No'. It can be read as saying what God is not, *and no more.* That, at any rate, is what it says on the lips of a writer like Aquinas, who on this point is often badly misconstrued. He holds that God is changeless because God is the non-material cause of all changing beings. That is frequently read as saying that God is static or frozen or indifferent. Then we are reminded that God is active and loving, and Aquinas is dismissed as unbiblical or un-Christian or both. But that reaction is just unfair. Aquinas's point is that whatever God's life consists in, it cannot consist in him changing in specifiable ways that creatures change. His activity and love is the activity and love of the Creator. To say this is quite different from saying that God is static and so on.

The third point concerns a range of typical positive assertions about God. These, I think, can often be read as positive but inadequate. They are inadequate because they should not be thought to reflect a knowledge of God in himself. But they are positive because they do, in a sense, serve to characterize God.

First the questions of inadequacy. Take, for example, the familiar assertion that God is personal. I have no difficulty with that and I therefore presume that I am committed to saying that God, for instance, has knowledge or will. But I deny that we have a comprehension of something called the personality of God, and I deny that we should talk of God as if he were the man in the next street. Our language for what is personal (and hence our primary understanding of this) comes from our knowledge of human beings. And we ought to be struck by the difference between what it takes to be a human being and what it must take to be God. Consider again the idea of knowing. Our personal lives as knowers are the lives of users of language who come to know as we are acted on by things in the world. But if God is the Creator, his personal life as a knower cannot be this. His knowledge cannot be that

17. A. J. Ayer, *Language, Truth and Logic* (Harmondsworth, Middx, 1971), p. 156.

of someone tied to language, nor can it be something acquired because things have some effect on him and by doing so cause him to know. My knowledge is the knowledge of a creature. But God is what accounts for there being any creatures. And that means that though we can say that, for example, God is personal because he has knowledge, this is not to explain what he is. In this sense 'God is personal' is inadequate.

On the other hand it is a natural thing to say and, in this sense, it is true. For the language of personality is naturally applied to God. Only I think it is this not because we know what God is, but rather because we know what he cannot be and because we can sensibly express that in positive terms. God cannot be bodily by nature, nor can he be something whose action is determined by the action on him of things within the world. If that were not the case he would be part of what I mean by 'the world'. Since he is the Creator, however, we are constrained to say that he brings things about. So in this sense he must be active. How, then, can we help thinking of him except as something personal? Given that we are not to think of him as inanimate and as determined by the action on him of things within the world, what else can we say except that the language of personality is somehow appropriate in talking of him? And what do we say there if not that God is personal?

This, I think, is the proper answer to someone who feels that in speaking of God we can only be saying what he is not and that we are in no way saying what he is. There is a sense in which that conclusion is acceptable, for we talk of God with words which first apply to creatures, and these words can always be regarded as inadequate tools for talking of God because of the difference between God and creatures. But, as has often been observed, if our talk of God is simply read as an account of what God is not, then there seems no particular reason for preferring one way of speaking of him to any other, and there is also the danger of departing too radically from anything that could plausibly be called a traditional belief in God. If, for instance, to call God personal is just to say that he is not inanimate, then why not call him square since this can be read as denying that he is round? And if to call him active is just to deny that he is not active, what do we make of talk about the living God who brings things about? On my account, however, these problems do not arise. In my view we can mean what we say about God and it can matter that we apply this term to him rather than that. It is, for instance, true that God is personal and false that he is canine (though that does not mean that he cannot be significantly spoken of as a dog).

On the other hand, in saying what God is we are not comprehending him. The inadequacy of our ways of describing him is as much a fact about them as their truth. We can, if you like, say more about God than we can mean. That, I think, is the point of those who hold that apophatic theology (negative theology) and cataphatic theology (positive theology) are really two sides of a single coin. Both succeed in saying something because each complements the other.

So l am saying that we can speak truly about God. But I am also saying that there is a sense in which we do not know what he is, what the word 'God' stands for. And, coming now to my final point, I have to add that this view seems to me perfectly consistent with respect to the biblical tradition.

This, of course, is widely denied. The God of the Bible is not the God of classical theism, and so on. And, of course, there is something in that. But what is the biblical God if he is not the inscrutable and mysterious Creator of all things beside whom there is no god and whose ways are truly hidden? 'I am the Lord, and there is no other. . . . To whom will you liken me and make me equal, and compare me, that we may be alike?' Certainly the biblical God is spoken of in the Bible as if he were a creature. But he is also spoken of differently. And a significant thing to note here is the sheer range of the resulting imagery. If my line is right, you would expect to find biblical writers revelling in a myriad of conflicting images for God. And that is just what you do find. God in the Bible is everything from a despotic king to a pregnant woman. He is a father and judge, but also an eagle, a lamb, and a case of dry-rot. And if all that is not a mandate for a strong doctrine of God's transcendence, I do not know what it is.

The reply may be that it is positive description of what God is really like. But I hope it will be clear that I need not dispute that. Nor do I wish to deny that the Bible talks of God in concrete terms and that we should do so too. We can cheerfully concede that God is a pregnant woman because nobody will be misled into looking for her husband. The more concrete our images for God, the less they will be taken as fully adequate and the more they can be allowed to work on us and help us to develop a doctrine of God. But if someone says that these images are the end of the story, then he has a curious way of reading the Bible. He may insist that there is still an enormous gulf between the God of classical theism and the God of the Bible since the former is static and remote while the latter is dynamic and involved. But that seems to me an awful misreading of classical theism. As I have indicated with respect to Aquinas, it is not the view of classical theism that God is static. According to classical theism God is active everywhere and in everything precisely because he is the Creator of everywhere and everything and because this is to be distinguished from him observing, interfering, and so on. Aquinas certainly denies that God is passive with respect to the world, so he denies that God can learn from the world or have it as an object of experience in the empiricist's sense. He also denies that God can be affected by the world. But this does not entail that God, for Aquinas, is not involved. On the contrary, for writers like him God is more involved with things than any created thing can be with another. This is because on their view God does not stand outside creation as an entity over and against his creatures. He is not *other* to creatures as they are to each other.[18]

For some people this view will still seem a long way from what needs to be said about God. It will be argued that God is loving and that stress on him being the

---

18. Herbert McCabe, 'The Involvement of God', *New Blackfriars* 66 (1985), p. 470; repr. as chapter 4 of *God Matters* (London, 1987).

Creator fails to allow for this fact. But that also seems to me wrong. If to love means to be moved by passion as we can sometimes be when we love, then I should certainly agree that God cannot love. We will not understand the love of God by taking as our paradigm the case of the romantic lover. Yet it is false that love must involve passion. As Christians have recognized for centuries, it can just as well be thought of as a matter of willing what is good for people. And, for classical theists, God certainly does that.

Questions for discussion

1. According to some philosophers and theologians, 'God is simple' is an essential element in any true account of what God is. But other philosophers and theologians take it to be absolutely contrary to any sensible thinking about God. What might account for these seriously divergent viewpoints?
2. 'God is never going to be an element, a square centimetre, in any picture, not because God's agency is incalculably greater but because it simply cannot be fitted into the same space' (Rowan Williams, 'Reply: Redeeming Sorrows', in D. Z. Phillips (ed.), *Religion and Morality* New York, 1996, p. 135). Is Williams right? If not, why not? If he is right, does his statement have implications for the teaching that God is simple?
3. Must someone who believes that God is simple also deny that traditional ways of speaking of God (as found, for example, in the Bible) are basically false?
4. Should one think of those who believe that God is simple as ascribing to God the attribute of simplicity?
5. Does it make any sense at all to say that God's nature is to be, or that God is 'Being Itself'?

Advice on further reading

Discussions with a significant bearing on the topic of divine simplicity can be found in the writings of authors concerned with the notion of God in general, the issue of God-Talk and the topics of divine knowledge, immutability, and eternity, in particular. Many of the works listed in 'Advice on further reading' sections given above are relevant when it comes to divine simplicity.

For scholarly accounts of the history of teaching to the effect that God is simple, and for philosophical defence of this teaching, see David Burrell, *Aquinas God and Action* (London, 1979), *Knowing the Unknowable God: Ibn-Sina, Maimonides, Aquinas* (Notre Dame, Indiana, 1986), and *Freedom and Creation in Three Traditions* (Notre Dame, 1993). See also Vivian Boland, *Ideas in God According to Saint Thomas Aquinas: Sources and Synthesis* (Leiden, 1996), and Wayne Hankey, 'Aquinas' First Principle: Being or Unity?', *Dionysius* 4 (1980).

For a recent book which aims to defend the notion of divine simplicity, see Barry Miller, *A Most Unlikely God* (Notre Dame, Indiana, and London, 1996). For a book which offers a full-scale attack on the notion, see Christopher Hughes, *On a Complex Theory of a Simple God* (Ithaca, New York, 1980). For another detailed attack on the notion, see Alvin Plantinga, *Does God Have a Nature?* (Marquette, Milwaukee, 1980).

For some essays defending the teaching that God is simple (or aspects of that teaching), see:

David B. Burrell, 'Distinguishing God from the World', in Brian Davies (ed.), *Language, Meaning and God* (London, 1987).

Brian Davies, 'Aquinas, God and Being', *Philosophical Quarterly* 80 (1997).

John King Farlow, 'Simplicity, Analogy and Plain Religious Lives', *Faith and Philosophy* 1 (1984).

William Mann, 'Divine Simplicity', *Religious Studies* 18 (1982).

William Mann, 'Simplicity and Immutability in God', *International Philosophical Quarterly* 23 (1983).

Timothy O'Connor, 'Simplicity and Creation', *Faith and Philosophy* 16 (1999).

Eleonore Stump and Norman Kretzmann, 'Absolute Simplicity', *Faith and Philosophy* 2 (1985).

James Ross, 'Comments on "Absolute Simplicity"', *Faith and Philosophy* 2 (1985).

Eleonore Stump and Norman Kretzmann, 'Simplicity Made Plainer: A Reply to Ross', *Faith and Philosophy* 4 (1987).

For some essays attacking the teaching that God is simple (or aspects of that teaching), see:

William Hasker, 'Simplicity and Freedom: A Response to Stump and Kretzmann', *Faith and Philosophy* 3 (1986).

Thomas V. Morris, 'On God and Mann: A View of Divine Simplicity', *Religious Studies* 21 (1985).

William J. Wainwright, 'Augustine on God's Simplicity: A Reply', *The New Scholasticism* 53 (1979).

C. J. F. Williams, 'Being', in Philip L. Quinn and Charles Taliaferro (eds), *A Companion to Philosophy of Religion* (Oxford, 1997).

Belief in God's simplicity is often rejected on the grounds that God is a person. For a discussion of the formula 'God is a person', see Keith Ward, 'Is God a Person?', in Gijsbert van den Brink, Luco J. van den Brom, and Marcel Sarot (eds), *Christian Faith and Philosophical Theology* (Kampen, Netherlands, 1992).

Part V

The Problem of Evil

Introduction

God and Evil

WHY is there physical pain? Why do we suffer from anxiety and distress? Why are there people who act badly? These are the questions which have chiefly given rise to what contemporary philosophers call the 'problem of evil'. But what exactly is the problem supposed to be?

If Fred is dying of cancer, I might acknowledge a practical problem. I might ask 'What can I do to make Fred as comfortable as possible?'. And I might have an equally practical problem on my hands when trying to cope with people who are morally wicked. Yet the general nastiness of much that occurs has led some to hold that there is an 'intellectual problem of evil', one which is regularly presented as a problem for those who believe in God. The general idea is that it is hard to see how pain, wickedness, and so on could ever have come to pass given that God is omnipotent, omniscient, and good (or 'wholly good' or 'perfect').

This 'intellectual problem of evil', however, could amount to different problems depending on who raises it. For suppose one believes (or thinks that one knows) that there is, indeed, an omnipotent, omniscient, good God. In that case one's problem might be to fathom the place of evil in a world made by God. One might be trying to penetrate the mystery of the God in whom one believes, and one might feel that this is a difficult job, something in which one might never succeed in this life.

But one might also take a different line. One might say that there is a problem of evil which positively undermines belief in the existence of God. There cannot be a circle which is also square. But can there be a world made by God which also contains evil? Taking it as obvious that the world contains evil, one might conclude that God's non-existence is as certain as that of square circles. Alternatively, one might say that, though 'Evil exists' and 'God exists' are *logically compatible*, the evil that exists is positive or strong *evidence that God does not exist*.

For the most part, when contemporary philosophers of religion speak of 'the problem of evil' they are concerned with evil as proof of God's non-existence or as evidence against God's existence. But how so?

Problems of evil

The charge of contradiction The claim that evil is proof of God's non-existence is crisply stated by J. L. Mackie in Chapter 53. He argues that there is a contradiction between 'God is omnipotent', 'God is wholly good', and 'Evil exists'. This contradiction, Mackie concedes, 'does not arise immediately'. Nevertheless, it does arise, he says, if we assume (a) 'that good is opposed to evil, in such a way that a good thing always eliminates evil as far as it can', and (b) 'that there are no limits to what an omnipotent thing can do'. According to Mackie, 'a good omnipotent thing eliminates evil completely' so that 'the propositions that a good omnipotent thing exists, and that evil exists, are incompatible'.

The evidential problem Sometimes called the 'evidentialist' argument from evil, the view that the existence of evil is evidence against God's existence can be summarized by referring to William Rowe's much discussed article 'The Problem of Evil and Some Varieties of Atheism'.[1]

In general, Rowe allows that evil (e.g. intense human and animal suffering) might be justifiable if it leads to some greater good, one not obtainable without the evil in question. With this allowance made, Rowe's basic argument is that there is unjustifiable evil which is evidence against God's existence. Or, in Rowe's own words:

1. There exist instances of intense suffering which an omnipotent being could have prevented without thereby losing some greater good or permitting some evil equally bad or worse.
2. An omniscient, wholly good being would prevent the occurrence of any intense suffering it could, unless it could not do so without thereby losing some greater good or permitting some evil equally bad or worse.
3. [Therefore] there does not exist an omnipotent, omniscient, wholly good being.

Since Rowe takes this argument to be logically valid, his main concern is to argue for the truth of the first and second premises.

The second premise, says Rowe, 'seems to express a belief that accords with our basic moral principles, principles shared by both theists and non-theists'. For Rowe, therefore, the controversial premise is the first. And he admits that it might be false. Suppose we try to imagine an instance of pointless suffering. Though we may not be able to see that it serves a good which cannot be obtained without it, there might, so Rowe agrees, be such a good. And yet, so Rowe continues, we have *reason* to suppose that there are instances of pointless suffering even if we cannot definitively *prove* that there are such instances.

Take, for example, the case of a fawn dying in agony as a victim of a forest fire. 'Is it reasonable', asks Rowe, 'to believe that there is some greater good so intimately connected to that suffering that even an omnipotent, omniscient being could not have obtained that good without permitting that suffering or some evil at least as bad? Rowe answers: 'It certainly does not appear reasonable to believe this. Nor does it seem reasonable to believe that there is some evil at least as bad as the fawn's suffering such that an omnipotent being simply could not have prevented it without permitting the fawn's suffering.' For the sake of argument, Rowe concedes that perhaps he is wrong with respect to the example of the fawn. But what of the instances of 'seemingly pointless human and animal suffering that occur daily in our world'? Turning to this question, Rowe maintains that the only reasonable conclusion is one unfavourable to the theist.

In the light of our experience and knowledge of the variety and scale of human and animal suffering in our world, the idea that none of this suffering could have been prevented by an omnipotent being

---

1. *American Philosophical Quarterly* 16 (1979).

without thereby losing a greater good or permitting an evil at least as bad seems an extraordinarily absurd idea, quite beyond our belief.

With this point made, Rowe holds that his first premise is a reasonable one and that, given also the reasonableness of his second premise, 'it does seem that we have *rational support* for atheism, that it is reasonable to believe that the theistic God does not exist'.

Some theistic responses

Mackie and Rowe are clearly arguing for non-theistic conclusions.[2] But how have theists responded to the charge that evil is proof of, or good evidence for, the non-existence of God? At the risk of simplifying somewhat, we may say that they have mostly done so by embracing one or more of the following lines of argument, some of which Mackie mentions in Chapter 53.

The 'We know that God exists' argument If I know that it often rains in England, I should rightly assume that something is wrong with any attempt to show either that frequent rain in England is impossible or that there is good evidence against its occurring. In a similar way, so it has been argued, we have grounds for supposing that God's existence is not impossible or subject to doubt even though evil exists. For, so it has been said, we can know not only that evil exists, but also that God exists, from which it follows (a) that something is wrong with any attempt to show that God cannot exist, and (b) that something is wrong with any attempt to show that there is good evidence against God's existence. Defenders of this line of thought sometimes offer arguments for God's existence. Taking *p* to be equivalent to 'There is a good, omnipotent, omniscient God', their suggestion is that there are positive grounds for accepting *p*, grounds which entitle us to hold that the existence of God is logically compatible with the existence of evil, grounds which also entitle us to hold that there is no evidence based on evil which shows that God does not exist.[3]

The unreality of evil argument This argument takes two forms. According to the first, evil is an illusion of some kind. This is the view of Christian Science, according to which, in the words of its founder: 'Sin, disease, whatever seems real to material sense, is unreal . . . All inharmony of mortal mind or body is illusion, possessing neither reality nor identity though seeming to be real and identical.'[4] According to the second form of the argument, evil is unreal since it is no positive thing or quality. Rather, it is an absence or privation of good (*privatio boni*).

2. I focus on Mackie and Rowe since they present in a clear form arguments offered by a variety of non-theistic critics of theism writing with respect to the topic of God and evil.
3. To my knowledge, there is no contemporary author who presses the 'We know that God exists' argument while discussing the topic of God and evil. But the argument is implicit in a great deal of Christian philosophical thinking.
4. Mary Baker Eddy, *Science and Health with a Key to the Scriptures* (Boston, 1971), p. 257. Eddy's account of evil clearly takes 'evil' as equivalent to something like 'pain' or 'human sickness'. As such, it makes no contribution to discussions of evil which have a broader focus.

What is this second view driving at? It can be found Chapter 54, from the writings of Augustine of Hippo. It can also be found in Chapter 56, from the contemporary philosopher Herbert McCabe. And the first thing to say about it (since this is often not appreciated) is that it is *not* siding with the Christian Science position and it is *not* claiming that, for example, there is no pain, or that there are no wicked people or bad actions. Augustine and McCabe acknowledge that people and other animals suffer, and that people can be horribly vicious.

On the other hand, however, they also hold that what makes suffering or wickedness bad is the fact that it always amounts to a lack of some kind. On their account, 'evil' or 'badness' is not the name of some independently existing individual (like a particular human being) or of some positive quality or attribute (like being carnivorous). Rather, it is a word we use to signify a gap between what *is actually there* and what *could be* there (and *should be* there) but *is not*. There can be people, but there cannot, so Augustine and McCabe think, be 'baddities' (things whose nature is captured simply by saying that they are bad). There can be wooden boxes, just as there can be wooden chairs. But, so Augustine and McCabe suggest, while 'wooden' signifies a positive property, shareable by different things (such as boxes and chairs), 'evil' or 'bad' do not. Just as to say 'There is nothing here' is not to say of *something* that *it* is here, so, in Augustine and McCabe's view, to say that *there is* evil is not to say that there is *any real individual or any positive quality*.[5] Augustine and McCabe regard this conclusion as significant with respect to the topic of God and evil since, among other things, they take it to imply that evil cannot be thought of as something caused (creatively) by God. It is, so they think, real enough (in the sense that it would be mad to say that nothing is bad or defective or sinful). But it is not, so they hold, something created. Its 'reality' is always a case of something missing, and it is totally parasitic on the existence of what is good.

The Free Will Defence Another popular move made by theists in the face of evil is commonly referred to as the Free Will Defence. According to this:

1. Much evil is the result of what people freely choose to do.
2. It is good that there should be a world with agents able to act freely, and a world containing such agents would be better than a world of puppets controlled by God.
3. Even an omnipotent God cannot ensure that free people act well (for, if they are free and not puppets controlled by God, what they do is up to them).
4. Therefore, much evil is explicable in terms of God allowing for the possible consequences of him willing a great good.

A contemporary philosopher who argues along these lines is Alvin Plantinga. In his discussion of God and evil, Mackie rejects the Free Will Defence on the ground that an omnipotent God could have made a world in which people always behave well. According to Plantinga, however, we cannot know that this is so. He agrees that there

---

5. For another contemporary defence of the notion that evil is *privatio boni*, see Paul Helm, *The Providence of God* (Leicester, 1993), pp. 168 ff.

is no contradiction involved in someone always behaving well. But, so he adds, whether someone freely behaves well in some actual situation cannot be determined by God. People must freely decide to act well. And they cannot do that if the fact that they act as they do is determined by God. 'Of course,' says Plantinga, 'it is up to God whether to create free creatures at all; but if he aims to produce moral good, then he must create significantly free creatures upon whose co-operation he must depend. Thus is the power of an omnipotent God limited by the freedom he confers upon his creatures.'[6]

It might seem that Plantinga wishes to deny God's omnipotence. But that is not the way he sees it. Theists have frequently denied that divine omnipotence means that God can do what is logically impossible, and Plantinga's basic point is that it is logically impossible for God to create a creature whose actions are both free and determined by God. Plantinga thinks that a free action cannot be caused by anything other than the agent whose action it is. Or, in his words: 'If a person S is free with respect to a given action, then he is free to perform that action and free to refrain; no causal laws and antecedent conditions determine either that he will perform the action, or that he will not. It is within his power, at the time in question, to perform the action, and within his power to refrain.'[7]

But can a free action not be caused by God? Plantinga clearly assumes that the answer to this question must be 'Yes', and many would agree with him.[8] Yet some philosophers have argued that there cannot be a free action which is *not* caused by God. McCabe argues this in Chapter 56. In doing so, he echoes some fairly famous thinkers, notably Aquinas.

The view that all human action is determined is something Aquinas regards as 'anarchic' and as undermining all sensible moral thinking. 'Human beings', he says, 'are masters of their own actions, able to act or not to act. And this can only be so if they can freely choose. So human beings can freely choose their action.'[9] Unlike fans of the Free Will Defence, however, Aquinas finds it unthinkable that any created event, including whatever we take to be there when human choosing occurs, should come to pass without God making it to be. Why? Because he takes seriously the claim that creatures owe their entire being to God. Or, in his words:

God exists in everything; not indeed as part of their substance or as an accident, but as an agent is present to that in which its action is taking place . . . Since it is God's nature to exist, he it must be who properly causes existence in creatures, just as it is fire itself that sets other things on fire. And God is causing this effect in things not just when they begin to exist, but all the time they are maintained in existence . . . Now existence is more intimately and profoundly interior to things than anything else,

6. Alvin Plantinga, *The Nature of Necessity* (Oxford, 1974), p. 190.
7. Ibid., pp. 165 f.
8. Cf., for example, William Alston, according to whom 'It is logically impossible for God to create free beings with genuine freedom of choice and also guarantee that they will always choose the right'. See William Alston, 'The Inductive Argument from Evil', in Daniel Howard-Snyder (ed.), *The Evidential Argument from Evil* (Bloomington and Indianapolis, Indiana, 1996), p. 112.
9. *Quaestio Disputata de malo*, 6.

for everything as we said is potential when compared to existence. So God must exist and exist intimately in everything.[10]

Does God's existence in things extend to his existence in human choices? Aquinas answers 'Yes':

Physical things are acted on in the sense that they are directed to an end by another; they do not act like self-determining agents who shape themselves to a purpose, in the manner of rational creatures who deliberate and choose by free judgement . . . Yet because the very act of free will goes back to God as its cause, we strictly infer that whatever people freely do on their own falls under God's Providence . . . The divine power must needs be present to every acting thing . . . God is the cause of everything's action inasmuch as he gives everything the power to act, and preserves it in being and applies it to action, and inasmuch as by his power every other power acts.[11]

With these points in mind, Aquinas argues in Chapter 57 that human freedom is not something to be thought of as threatened by God's causality. On the contrary. For Aquinas, I am free not *in spite of* God but *because of* God.[12]

(d) The Means and Ends Approach You would probably think me bad if I cut off someone's leg just for the fun of it. But you would probably not think me bad if I were a doctor who amputated a leg as the only way known to me of saving someone with gangrene. Why not? You will probably say something like: 'Because it is not bad to aim for something regrettable if one is working towards a good one ought to aim at (or is justified in aiming at) which cannot be achieved in any other way.' And this thought constitutes the basic thrust of what I am calling the Means and End Approach. Here again we have a line of thought alluded to and rejected by Mackie. But it is one which has found many supporters. According to them, the evil we encounter is a necessary means to a good. Considered as such, it cannot be appealed to as *proof* of God's non-existence. Nor is it *evidence* for this.

   Notable contemporary defences of the Means and End Approach can be found in various writings of Richard Swinburne, including the one given in Chapter 55. To begin with, Swinburne endorses a version of the Free Will Defence. He thinks that it is good that people should be significantly free. He also thinks that God can only allow them to be so by allowing them to act badly. For this reason, Swinburne deems human wrong-doing to be accountable in terms of means to an end (the end being a world of free creatures, the means being God's standing back and allowing them freedom). What, however, of pain and suffering not brought about by people? To this question Swinburne replies by suggesting that these can also be seen as necessary means to a good. For it is good, thinks Swinburne, that people have serious moral choice to harm or help each other. And, so he argues, choice like this can only arise against the background of naturally occurring pain and suffering.

   A line of thinking similar to Swinburne's can be found in John Hick's *Evil and the God of*

10. *Summa Theologiae*, Ia, 8, 1.
11. Ibid., Ia, 22, 2, ad 4; *De Potentia*, 3, 7.
12. For a recent defence of a similar line of reasoning, see William E. Mann, 'God's Freedom, Human Freedom, and God's Responsibility for Sin', in Thomas V. Morris (ed.), *Divine and Human Action* (Ithaca and London, 1988).

Love (a modern classic on the topic of God and evil)[13] Hick also employs the Free Will Defence. Then he endorses a line of thought which he claims to find in the writings of St Irenaeus of Lyon (*c.*140–*c.*202). According to Hick, God cannot create a world in which people can morally mature and eventually enjoy a proper relationship with God (this being thought of as a good) unless he also creates a world in which there are obstacles to overcome. Hick understands evil in the light of God's desire not to coerce people into accepting him. He suggests that people are sin-prone creatures, created as such by God, but able, in a world containing naturally occurring evil, to rise to great heights precisely because they are given the opportunity to become mature in the face of evil.

Let us suppose that the infinite personal God creates finite persons to share in the life which He imparts to them. If He creates them in his immediate presence, so that they cannot fail to be con-scious from the first of the infinite divine being and glory, goodness and love, wisdom, power and knowledge in whose presence they are, they will have no creaturely independence in relation to their Maker. They will not be able to *choose* to worship God, or to turn to Him freely as valuing spirits responding to infinite Value. In order, then, to give them the freedom to come to Him, God . . . causes them to come into a situation in which He is not immediately and overwhelmingly evident to them. Accordingly they come to self-consciousness as parts of a universe which has its own autonomous structures and 'laws' . . . A world without problems, difficulties, perils, and hardships would be mor-ally static. For moral and spiritual growth comes through response to challenges; and in a paradise there would be no challenges.[14]

'No pain, no gain', as the athletes say. And this is basically Hick's position when it comes to God and evil.

The 'We can't see all the picture' argument Another theistic response to arguments such as those of Mackie and Rowe takes the form of suggesting that we just cannot be sure that the evil we know about disproves, or is evidence against, God's existence, since our perspective is limited. Hamlet tells Horatio that 'There are more things in heaven and earth than are dreamt of in your philosophy.' The 'We can't see all the picture' argument suggests that, though we might find it *hard* to see why there is evil in a world made by God, there *might* be a reason.

A prominent contemporary defender of the 'We can't see all the picture' argument is William P. Alston. An opponent of theism might suggest that there exist instances of intense suffering that God could have prevented without thereby losing some greater good (let us call this 'Thesis A'). According to Alston, however, 'the magnitude or com-plexity of the question is such that our powers, access to data, and so on are radically insufficient to provide sufficient warrant for accepting' Thesis A.[15] Hamlet's words to Horatio, says Alston, hit the nail on the head. 'They point to the fact that our cognitions of the world, obtained by filtering raw data through such conceptual screens as we have available for the nonce, acquaint us with only some indeterminable fraction of what there is to be know.'[16] Alston's thesis is that God knows what he is doing (or allowing, or

13. 2nd edn, London, 1977.
14. Ibid., pp. 372 ff.
15. 'The Inductive Argument from Evil', p. 98.
16. Ibid., p. 109.

whatever); and God might have reasons for doing what he does (or allows, or whatever); but we might not be able to understand what God is about as he lives his life.[17]

What kind of world can we expect from God? Those who take evil to be a problem for theists tend to rely on assumptions about the kind of world which God (if God exists) would make. So we should therefore note that many theists have addressed the topic of evil and God by trying to call into question some of these assumptions.

Take, for example, the notion that relief from (or absence of) pain and suffering is an intrinsically good thing, something which God would always lay on for things such as human beings. Many anti-theistic writers seem to embrace this notion, but many theists have not. As we have seen, some hold that pain and suffering can perfect human beings. And some hold that what we may loosely call 'an absence of happiness' is not necessarily a bad state of affairs to be avoided at all costs. Suppose we have a child who is thoroughly retarded but who also seems perfectly content and happy. Suppose furthermore that we can render the child normal and healthy by means of an operation. Shall we operate? By doing so we would release the child to the kind of life most people live, one which will certainly render it liable to varieties of pain and frustration. Yet many (perhaps most) people would vote for the operation. And appealing to the assumptions which seem to lie behind such a vote, many theists argue that we have no reason to suppose that God would not create a world containing unhappiness.

Some critics of theism say that God (if he exists) would create 'the best possible world'. Others say that God would maximize happiness for his creatures. But theists have challenged these suggestions as well. They have said, for example, that talk of a 'best possible world' is as incoherent as talk of a 'greatest prime number'. According to C. J. F. Williams, for example: 'It is a consequence of God's infinite power, wisdom and goodness that, for any world we can conceive him creating, it is possible to conceive him creating a better world. More than that—for this has nothing to do with what we can or cannot conceive—for any world which God can create, there is another, better world which he could also have created.'[18] And, though one might be tempted to suppose that 'Maximize happiness' is an imperative which any decent-minded God could be expected to act on, some theists have challenged the idea that such an imperative is intelligible. Suppose we have a happy human being. This person could, presumably, be happier. Is there, then, a limit to happiness—some stage at which further increased happiness is impossible, some stage which God should have brought about for all from the start? Arguing somewhat along the lines of Williams, George N. Schlesinger suggests that there is no such specifiable limit. We can, he argues, always think of ways in which a person's happiness can be increased, and it is no good objection to belief in God's existence to say that God has made a world in which people are less happy than they could be.[19]

With an eye on the question 'What kind of world can God be expected to make?', we should also note that some theists urge that we can have no reasonable expectations one

---

17. Alston's line of reasoning may be compared with that of Peter Van Inwagen's 'The Problems of Evil, Air, and Silence', in *The Evidential Argument from Evil*, pp. 151 ff.

18. C. J. F. Williams, 'Knowing Good and Evil', *Philosophy* 66 (1991), p. 238.

19. George N. Schlesinger, *New Perspectives on Old-Time Religion* (Oxford, 1988), ch. 2.

way or the other. An example here is Aquinas. As we have seen, he thinks of God as the source of the being (*esse*) of creatures. For him, God alone exists by essence or nature, and anything other than God exists because it is made to be by God. It is not, thinks Aquinas, characteristic of God that he should make things like *this* as opposed to things like *that* (though Aquinas is clear that God has made a world of varied things). Insofar as anything can be deemed to be a 'characteristic effect' of God, says Aquinas, it is being (*esse*)—the fact that there is something rather than nothing, the fact that there is any world at all. And this thought leads Aquinas away from suppositions as to what we can expect in a world created by God. We can, he thinks, expect that Vitamin C will have certain effects when taken by human beings. In general, so he thinks, we can have *lots* of expectations about what will be produced by what (such expectations are, for Aquinas, part of a scientific understanding of the world). Yet, says Aquinas, God is not an object of scientific inquiry, not a part of the world in which science can be developed. For him, God 'is to be thought of as existing outside the realm of existents, as a cause from which pours forth everything that exists in all its variant forms'.[20] If it is logically possible for something to be, then, thinks Aquinas, God can make it to be. But, so Aquinas also thinks, we have no means of determining what logically possible things God will make to be. For Aquinas, we have to start by noting what God has, in fact, made to be. Reflections on the topic of God and evil must, so he thinks, start from that, and not from assumptions we might (on what basis?) have dreamed up concerning what God is or is not likely to create.

God suffers also A survey of theistic responses to those who deny or call into question the existence of God because of the reality of evil would not be complete without mention of a currently very popular angle on the topic of God and evil. According to this, God is also a victim of evil, and he also suffers. Two authors who might be cited as defending this line of thought include the German theologian Jürgen Moltmann and the Latin American liberation theologian Jon Sobrino.

As we have seen, many theists take it for granted that God is utterly changeless. From this belief it follows that God cannot be acted on by anything. It also follows that God cannot undergo suffering (since to suffer is to be passive to the action of something which acts on one to bring about a change of a certain kind). Moltmann and Sobrino, however, deny that God is utterly changeless. According to them, if God is to be acceptable to human beings he must be capable of suffering and, in this sense, must be affected by evil. According to Moltmann, the great thing about Christianity is that it offers us a suffering God revealed as such in the person of Christ. Traditional Christian teaching holds that Christ is God, but it also denies that this implies that we can say, without qualification, 'God suffers'. A distinction is made between what is true of Christ *as man*, and what is true of him *as God*. The conclusion then proposed is that, though Christ could suffer as man, he could not suffer as God. But Moltmann rejects this traditional way of talking. For him, the divinity of Christ means that divinity as such is capable of suffering. And in the light of this point we can, says Moltmann, offer some comfort to suffering human beings (the victims of evil). People in distress can be driven to say that because of their suffering they cannot believe in God. According to Moltmann, however, God and

20. See the extract from Aquinas in Chapter 57.

suffering are not to be thought of as irreconcilable with each other. For God suffers too. And that is what Sobrino also wants to say. As he puts it:

For Saint John, God is love . . . Is that statement real? . . . We must insist that love has to be credible to human beings in an unredeemed world. That forces us to ask ourselves whether God can really describe himself as love if historical suffering does not affect him . . . We must say what Moltmann says: 'We find suffering that is not wished, suffering that is accepted, and the suffering of love. If God were incapable of suffering in all those ways, and hence in an absolute sense, then God would be incapable of loving.'[21]

Recall that for Mackie the problem of evil arises from a perceived contradiction between three claims. Mackie accepts that the problem (in his understanding) disappears if one gives up on the claim that God is omnipotent. Since Moltmann and Sobrino want to conceive of God as passive to the action of creatures and as himself suffering (a notion which seems at odds with traditional theistic accounts of omnipotence), they can fairly be taken as rejecting belief in God's omnipotence and as representing a response to the problem of evil which writers like Mackie would presumably deem to dissolve the problem as conceived by them.

21. Jon Sobrino, *Christology at the Crossroads* (London, 1978). For Moltmann, see his *The Crucified God* (New York, 1974) and *The Trinity and the Kingdom of God* (London, 1981), ch. 2.

Chapter 53
Evil shows that there is no God
J. L. Mackie

THE traditional arguments for the existence of God have been fairly thoroughly
criticized by philosophers. But the theologian can, if he wishes, accept this
criticism. He can admit that no rational proof of God's existence is possible. And he
can still retain all that is essential to his position, by holding that God's existence is
known in some other, non-rational way. I think, however, that a more telling criticism can be made by way of the traditional problem of evil. Here it can be shown,
not that religious beliefs lack rational support, but that they are positively
irrational, that the several parts of the essential theological doctrine are inconsistent
with one another, so that the theologian can maintain his position as a whole only
by a much more extreme rejection of reason than in the former case. He must now
be prepared to believe, not merely what cannot be proved, but what can be *disproved* from other beliefs that he also holds.

The problem of evil, in the sense in which I shall be using the phrase, is a
problem only for someone who believes that there is a God who is both omnipotent
and wholly good. And it is a logical problem, the problem of clarifying and reconciling a number of beliefs: it is not a scientific problem that might be solved by further
observations, or a practical problem that might be solved by a decision or an action.
These points are obvious; I mention them only because they are sometimes ignored
by theologians, who sometimes parry a statement of the problem with such
remarks as 'Well, can you solve the problem yourself?' or 'This is a mystery which
may be revealed to us later' or 'Evil is something to be faced and overcome, not to
be merely discussed.'

In its simplest form the problem is this: God is omnipotent; God is wholly good;
and yet evil exists. There seems to be some contradiction between these three
propositions, so that if any two of them were true the third would be false. But at
the same time all three are essential parts of most theological positions: the theologian, it seems, at once *must* adhere and *cannot consistently* adhere to all three.
(The problem does not arise only for theists, but I shall discuss it in the form in
which it presents itself for ordinary theism.)

However, the contradiction does not arise immediately; to show it we need some
additional premises, or perhaps some quasi-logical rules connecting the terms
'good', 'evil', and 'omnipotent'. These additional principles are that good is
opposed to evil, in such a way that a good thing always eliminates evil as far as it

J. L. Mackie 'Evil and Omnipotence' from *Mind*, vol. 64 (1955), reprinted by permission of Oxford
University Press.

can, and that there are no limits to what an omnipotent thing can do. From these it follows that a good omnipotent thing eliminates evil completely, and then the propositions that a good omnipotent thing exists, and that evil exists, are incompatible.

A. Adequate solutions

Now once the problem is fully stated it is clear that it can be solved, in the sense that the problem will not arise if one gives up at least one of the propositions that constitute it. If you are prepared to say that God is not wholly good, or not quite omnipotent, or that evil does not exist, or that good is not opposed to the kind of evil that exists, or that there are limits to what an omnipotent thing can do, then the problem of evil will not arise for you.

There are, then, quite a number of adequate solutions of the problem of evil, and some of these have been adopted, or almost adopted, by various thinkers. For example, a few have been prepared to deny God's omnipotence, and rather more have been prepared to keep the term 'omnipotence' but severely to restrict its meaning, recording quite a number of things that an omnipotent being cannot do. Some have said that evil is an illusion, perhaps because they held that the whole world of temporal, changing things is an illusion, and that what we call evil belongs only to this world, or perhaps because they held that although temporal things *are* much as we see them, those that we call evil are not really evil. Some have said that what we call evil is merely the privation of good, that evil in a positive sense, evil that would really be opposed to good, does not exist. Many have agreed with Pope that disorder is harmony not understood, and that partial evil is universal good. Whether any of these views is *true* is, of course, another question. But each of them gives an adequate solution of the problem of evil in the sense that if you accept it this problem does not arise for you, though you may, of course, have *other* problems to face.

But often enough these adequate solutions are only *almost* adopted. The thinkers who restrict God's power, but keep the term 'omnipotence', may reasonably be suspected of thinking, in other contexts, that his power is really unlimited. Those who say that evil is an illusion may also be thinking, inconsistently, that this illusion is itself an evil. Those who say that 'evil' is merely privation of good may also be thinking, inconsistently, that privation of good is an evil. (The fallacy here is akin to some forms of the 'naturalistic fallacy' in ethics, where some think, for example, that 'good' is just what contributes to evolutionary progress, and that evolutionary progress is itself good.) If Pope meant what he said in the first line of his couplet, that 'disorder' is only harmony not understood, the 'partial evil' of the second line must, for consistency, mean 'that which, taken in isolation, falsely appears to be evil', but it would more naturally mean 'that which, in isolation, really is evil'. The second line, in fact, hesitates between two views, that 'partial evil' isn't really evil, since only the universal quality is real, and that 'partial evil' is really an evil, but only a little one.

In addition, therefore, to adequate solutions, we must recognize unsatisfactory inconsistent solutions, in which there is only a half-hearted or temporary rejection of one of the propositions which together constitute the problem. In these, one of the constituent propositions is explicitly rejected, but it is covertly re-asserted or assumed elsewhere in the system.

B. Fallacious solutions

Besides these half-hearted solutions, which explicitly reject but implicitly assert one of the constituent propositions, there are definitely fallacious solutions which explicitly maintain all the constituent propositions, but implicitly reject at least one of them in the course of the argument that explains away the problem of evil.

There are, in fact, many so-called solutions which purport to remove the contradiction without abandoning any of its constituent propositions. These must be fallacious, as we can see from the very statement of the problem, but it is not so easy to see in each case precisely where the fallacy lies. I suggest that in all cases the fallacy has the general form suggested above: in order to solve the problem one (or perhaps more) of its constituent propositions is given up, but in such a way that it appears to have been retained, and can therefore be asserted without qualification in other contexts. Sometimes there is a further complication: the supposed solution moves to and fro between, say, two of the constituent propositions, at one point asserting the first of these but covertly abandoning the second, at another point asserting the second but covertly abandoning the first. These fallacious solutions often turn upon some equivocation with the words 'good' and 'evil', or upon some vagueness about the way in which good and evil are opposed to one another, or about how much is meant by 'omnipotence'. I propose to examine some of these so-called solutions, and to exhibit their fallacies in detail. Incidentally, I shall also be considering whether an adequate solution could be reached by a minor modification of one or more of the constituent propositions, which would, however, still satisfy all the essential requirements of ordinary theism.

1. 'Good cannot exist without evil' or 'Evil is necessary as a counterpart to good' It is sometimes suggested that evil is necessary as a counterpart to good, that if there were no evil there could be no good either, and that this solves the problem of evil. It is true that it points to an answer to the question 'Why should there be evil?' But it does so only by qualifying some of the propositions that constitute the problem.

First, it sets a limit to what God can do, saying that God *cannot* create good without simultaneously creating evil, and this means either that God is not omnipotent or that there are *some* limits to what an omnipotent thing can do. It may be replied that these limits are always presupposed, that omnipotence has never meant the power to do what is logically impossible, and on the present view the existence of good without evil would be a logical impossibility. This interpretation of omnipotence may, indeed, be accepted as a modification of our original account which does not reject anything that is essential to theism, and I shall in general assume it in the subsequent discussion. It is, perhaps, the most common theistic view, but I think that some theists at least have maintained that God can do what is logically impossible. Many theists, at any rate, have held that logic itself is created or laid down by God, that logic is the way in which God arbitrarily chooses to think. (This is, of course, parallel to the ethical view that morally right actions are those which God arbitrarily chooses to command, and the two views encounter similar difficulties.) And *this* account of logic is clearly inconsistent with the view that God is bound by logical necessities—unless it is possible for an omnipotent being to bind himself, an issue which we shall consider later, when we come to the Paradox of Omnipotence. This solution of the problem of evil cannot, therefore, be consistently adopted along with the view that logic is itself created by God.

But, secondly, this solution denies that evil is opposed to good in our original sense. If good and evil are counterparts, a good thing will not 'eliminate evil as far as it can'. Indeed, this view suggests that good and evil are not strictly qualities of things at all. Perhaps the suggestion is that good and evil are related in much the same way as great and small. Certainly, when the term 'great' is used relatively as a condensation of 'greater than so-and-so', and 'small' is used correspondingly, greatness and smallness are counterparts and cannot exist without each other. But in this sense greatness is not a quality, not an intrinsic feature of anything; and it would be absurd to think of a movement in favour of greatness and against smallness in this sense. Such a movement would be self-defeating, since relative greatness can be promoted only by a simultaneous promotion of relative smallness. I feel sure that no theists would be content to regard God's goodness as analogous to this—as if what he supports were not the *good* but the *better*, and as if he had the paradoxical aim that all things should be better than other things.

This point is obscured by the fact that 'great' and 'small' seem to have an absolute as well as a relative sense. I cannot discuss here whether there is absolute magnitude or not, but if there is, there could be an absolute sense for 'great'; it could mean of at least a certain size, and it would make sense to speak of all things getting bigger, of a universe that was expanding all over, and therefore it would make sense to speak of promoting greatness. But in *this* sense great and small are not logically necessary counterparts: either quality could exist without the other. There would be no logical impossibility in everything's being small or in everything's being great.

Neither in the absolute nor in the relative sense, then, of 'great' and 'small' do these terms provide an analogy of the sort that would be needed to support this solution of the problem of evil. In neither case are greatness and smallness *both* necessary counterparts *and* mutually opposed forces or possible objects for support or attack.

It may be replied that good and evil are necessary counterparts in the same way as any quality and its logical opposite: redness can occur, it is suggested, only if non-redness also occurs. But unless evil is merely the privation of good, they are not logical opposites, and some further argument would be needed to show that they are counterparts in the same way as genuine logical opposites. Let us assume that this could be given. There is still doubt of the correctness of the metaphysical principle that a quality must have a real opposite: I suggest that it is not really impossible that everything should be, say, red, that the truth is merely that if everything were red we should not notice redness, and so we should have no word 'red'; we observe and give names to qualities only if they have real opposites. If so, the principle that a term must have an opposite would belong only to our language or to our thought, and would not be an ontological principle, and, correspondingly, the rule that good cannot exist without evil would not state a logical necessity of a sort that God would just have to put up with. God might have made everything good, though *we* should not have noticed it if he had.

But, finally, even if we concede that this *is* an ontological principle, it will provide a solution for the problem of evil only if one is prepared to say, 'Evil exists, but only just enough evil to serve as the counterpart of good.' I doubt whether any theist will accept this. After all, the *ontological* requirement that non-redness should occur would be satisfied even if all the universe, except for a minute speck, were red, and, if there were a corresponding requirement for evil as a counterpart to good, a minute dose of evil would presumably do. But theists are not usually willing to say, in all contexts, that all the evil that occurs is a minute and necessary dose.

2. 'Evil is necessary as a means to good' It is sometimes suggested that evil is necessary for good not as a counterpart but as a means. In its simple form this has little plausibility as a solution of the problem of evil, since it obviously implies a severe restriction of God's power. It would be a *causal* law that you cannot have a certain end without a certain means, so that if God has to introduce evil as a means to good, he must be subject to at least some causal laws. This certainly conflicts with what a theist normally means by omnipotence. This view of God as limited by causal laws also conflicts with the view that causal laws are themselves made by God, which is more widely held than the corresponding view about the laws of logic. This conflict would, indeed, be resolved if it were possible for an omnipotent being to bind himself, and this possibility has still to be considered. Unless a favourable answer can be given to this question, the suggestion that evil is necessary as a means to good solves the problem of evil only by denying one of its constituent propositions, either that God is omnipotent or that 'omnipotent' means what it says.

3. 'The universe is better with some evil in it than it could be if there were no evil' Much more important is a solution which at first seems to be a mere variant of the previous one, that evil may contribute to the goodness of a whole in which it is found, so that the universe as a whole is better as it is, with some evil in it, than it would be if there were no evil. This solution may be developed in either of two ways. It may be supported by an aesthetic analogy, by the fact that contrasts heighten beauty, that in a musical work, for example, there may occur discords which somehow add to the beauty of the work as a whole. Alternatively, it may be worked out in connection with the notion of progress, that the best possible organization of the universe will not be static, but progressive, that the gradual overcoming of evil by good is really a finer thing than would be the eternal unchallenged supremacy of good.

In either case, this solution usually starts from the assumption that the evil whose existence gives rise to the problem of evil is primarily what is called physical evil, that is to say, pain. In Hume's rather halfhearted presentation of the problem of evil, the evils that he stresses are pain and disease, and those who reply to him argue that the existence of pain and disease makes possible the existence of sympathy, benevolence, heroism, and the gradually successful struggle of doctors and reformers to overcome these evils. In fact, theists often seize the opportunity to accuse those who stress the problem of evil of taking a low, materialistic view of good and evil, equating these with pleasure and pain, and of ignoring the more spiritual goods which can arise in the struggle against evils.

But let us see exactly what is being done here. Let us call pain and misery 'first order evil' or 'evil (1)'. What contrasts with this, namely, pleasure and happiness, will be called 'first order good' or 'good (1)'. Distinct from this is 'second order good' or 'good (2)' which somehow emerges in a complex situation in which evil (1) is a necessary component—logically, not merely causally, necessary. (Exactly *how* it emerges does not matter: in the crudest version of this solution good (2) is simply the heightening of happiness by the contrast with misery; in other versions it includes sympathy with suffering, heroism in facing danger, and the gradual decrease of first order evil and increase of first order good.) It is also being assumed that second order good is more important than first order good or evil, in particular that it more than outweighs the first order evil it involves.

Now this is a particularly subtle attempt to solve the problem of evil. It defends God's goodness and omnipotence on the ground that (on a sufficiently long view) this is the best of all logically possible worlds, because it includes the important second order goods, and yet it admits that real evils, namely first order evils, exist. But does it still hold that good and evil are opposed? Not, clearly, in the sense that we set out originally: good does not tend to eliminate evil in general. Instead, we have a modified, a more complex pattern. First order good (e.g. happiness) *contrasts with* first order evil (e.g. misery): these two are opposed in a fairly mechanical way; some second order goods (e.g. benevolence) try to maximize first order good and minimise first order evil; but God's goodness is not this, it is rather the will to maximize *second* order good. We might, therefore, call God's goodness an example of a third order goodness, or good (3). While this account is different from our original one, it might well be held to be an improvement on it, to give a more accurate description of the way in which good is opposed to evil, and to be consistent with the essential theist position.

There might, however, be several objections to this solution.

First, some might argue that such qualities as benevolence—and *a fortiori* the third order goodness which promotes benevolence—have a merely derivative value, that they are not higher sorts of good, but merely means to good (1), that is, to happiness, so that it would be absurd for God to keep misery in existence in order to make possible the virtues of benevolence, heroism, etc. The theist who adopts the present solution must, of course, deny this, but he can do so with some plausibility, so I should not press this objection.

Secondly, it follows from this solution that God is not in our sense benevolent or sympathetic: he is not concerned to minimize evil (1), but only to promote good (2), and this might be a disturbing conclusion for some theists.

But, thirdly, the fatal objection is this. Our analysis shows clearly the possibility of the existence of a *second* order evil, an evil (2) contrasting with good (2) as evil (1) contrasts with good (1). This would include malevolence, cruelty, callousness, cowardice, and states in which good (1) is decreasing and evil (1) increasing. And just as good (2) is held to be the important kind of good, the kind that God is concerned to promote, so evil (2) will, by analogy, be the important kind of evil, the kind which God, if he were wholly good and omnipotent, would eliminate. And yet evil (2) plainly exists, and indeed most theists (in other contexts) stress its existence more than that of evil (1). We should, therefore, state the problem of evil in terms of second order evil, and against this form of the problem the present solution is useless.

An attempt might be made to use this solution again, at a higher level, to explain the occurrence of evil (2): indeed the next main solution that we shall examine does just this, with the help of some new notions. Without any fresh notions, such a solution would have little plausibility: for example, we could hardly say that the really important good was a good (3), such as the increase of benevolence in proportion to cruelty, which logically required for its occurrence the occurrence of some second order evil. But even if evil (2) could be explained in this way, it is fairly clear that there would be third order evils contrasting with this third order good: and we should be well on the way to an infinite regress, where the solution of a problem of evil, stated in terms of evil (n), indicated the existence of an evil ($n + 1$), and a further problem to be solved.

4. 'Evil is due to human free will' Perhaps the most important proposed solution of the problem of evil is that evil is not to be ascribed to God at all, but to the independent actions of human beings, supposed to have been endowed by God with freedom of the will. This solution may be combined with the preceding one: first order evil (e.g. pain) may be justified as a logically necessary component in second order good (e.g. sympathy) while second order evil (e.g. cruelty) is not *justified*, but is so ascribed to human beings that God cannot be held responsible for it. This combination evades my third criticism of the preceding solution.

The free will solution also involves the preceding solution at a higher level. To explain why a wholly good God gave men free will although it would lead to some

588   J. L. MACKIE

important evils, it must be argued that it is better on the whole that men should act freely, and sometimes err, than that they should be innocent automata, acting rightly in a wholly determined way. Freedom, that is to say, is now treated as a third order good, and as being more valuable than second order goods (such as sympathy and heroism) would be if they were deterministically produced, and it is being assumed that second order evils, such as cruelty, are logically necessary accompaniments of freedom, just as pain is a logically necessary pre-condition of sympathy.

I think that this solution is unsatisfactory primarily because of the incoherence of the notion of freedom of the will: but I cannot discuss this topic adequately here, although some of my criticisms will touch upon it.

First I should query the assumption that second order evils are logically necessary accompaniments of freedom. I should ask this: if God has made men such that in their free choices they sometimes prefer what is good and sometimes what is evil, why could he not have made men such that they always freely choose the good? If there is no logical impossibility in a man's freely choosing the good on one, or on several occasions, there cannot be a logical impossibility in his freely choosing the good on every occasion. God was not, then, faced with a choice between making innocent automata and making beings who, in acting freely, would sometimes go wrong: there was open to him the obviously better possibility of making beings who would act freely but always go right. Clearly, his failure to avail himself of this possibility is inconsistent with his being both omnipotent and wholly good.

If it is replied that this objection is absurd, that the making of some wrong choices is logically necessary for freedom, it would seem that 'freedom' must here mean complete randomness or indeterminacy, including randomness with regard to the alternatives good and evil, in other words that men's choices and consequent actions can be 'free' only if they are not determined by their characters. Only on this assumption can God escape the responsibility for men's actions; for if he made them as they are, but did not determine their wrong choices, this can only be because the wrong choices are not determined by men as they are. But then if freedom is randomness, how can it be a characteristic of *will*? And, still more, how can it be the most important good? What value or merit would there be in free choices if these were random actions which were not determined by the nature of the agent?

I conclude that to make this solution plausible two different senses of 'freedom' must be confused, one sense which will justify the view that freedom is a third order good, more valuable than other goods would be without it, and another sense, sheer randomness, to prevent us from ascribing to God a decision to make men such that they sometimes go wrong when he might have made them such that they would always freely go right.

This criticism is sufficient to dispose of this solution. But besides this there is a fundamental difficulty in the notion of an omnipotent God creating men with free will, for if men's wills are really free this must mean that even God cannot control them, that is, that God is no longer omnipotent. It may be objected that God's gift of freedom to men does not mean that he *cannot* control their wills, but that he always *refrains* from controlling their wills. But why, we may ask, should God refrain from controlling evil wills? Why should he not leave men free to will rightly, but intervene when he sees them beginning to will wrongly? If God could do this, but does not, and if he is wholly good, the only explanation could be that even a wrong free act of will is not really evil, that its freedom is a value which outweighs its wrongness, so that there would be a loss of value if God took away the wrongness and the freedom together. But this is utterly opposed to what theists say about sin in other contexts. The present solution of the problem of evil, then, can be maintained only in the form that God has made men so free that he *cannot* control their wills.

This leads us to what I call the Paradox of Omnipotence: can an omnipotent being make things which he cannot subsequently control? Or, what is practically equivalent to this, can an omnipotent being make rules which then bind himself? (These are practically equivalent because any such rules could be regarded as setting certain things beyond his control and *vice versa*.) The second of these formulations is relevant to the suggestions that we have already met, that an omnipotent God creates the rules of logic or causal laws, and is then bound by them.

It is clear that this is a paradox: the questions cannot be answered satisfactorily either in the affirmative or in the negative. If we answer 'Yes', it follows that if God actually makes things which he cannot control, or makes rules which bind himself, he is not omnipotent once he has made them: there are *then* things which he cannot do. But if we answer 'No', we are immediately asserting that there are things which he cannot do, that is to say that he is already not omnipotent.

It cannot be replied that the question which sets this paradox is not a proper question. It would make perfectly good sense to say that a human mechanic has made a machine which he cannot control: if there is any difficulty about the question it lies in the notion of omnipotence itself.

This, incidentally, shows that although we have approached this paradox from the free will theory, it is equally a problem for a theological determinist. No one thinks that machines have free will, yet they may well be beyond the control of their makers. The determinist might reply that anyone who makes anything determines its ways of acting, and so determines its subsequent behaviour: even the human mechanic does this by his *choice* of materials and structure for his machine, though he does not know all about either of these: the mechanic thus determines, though he may not foresee, his machine's actions. And since God is omniscient, and since his creation of things is total, he both determines and foresees the ways in which his creatures will act. We may grant this, but it is beside the point. The question is not whether God *originally* determined the future actions of his creatures, but whether he can *subsequently* control their actions, or whether he was able in his original creation to put things beyond his subsequent control. Even on determinist principles the answers 'Yes' and 'No' are equally irreconcilable with God's omnipotence.

Before suggesting a solution of this paradox, I would point out that there is a parallel Paradox of Sovereignty. Can a legal sovereign make a law restricting its own future legislative power? For example, could the British parliament make a law forbidding any future parliament to socialize banking, and also forbidding the future repeal of this law itself? Or could the British parliament, which was legally sovereign in Australia in, say, 1899, pass a valid law, or series of laws, which made it no longer sovereign in 1933? Again, neither the affirmative nor the negative answer is really satisfactory. If we were to answer 'Yes', we should be admitting the validity of a law which, if it were actually made, would mean that parliament was no longer sovereign. If we were to answer 'No', we should be admitting that there is a law, not logically absurd, which parliament cannot validly make, that is, that parliament is not now a legal sovereign. This paradox can be solved in the following way. We should distinguish between first order laws, that is laws governing the actions of individuals and bodies other than the legislature, and second order laws, that is laws about laws, laws governing the actions of the legislature itself. Correspondingly, we should distinguish between two orders of sovereignty, first order sovereignty (sovereignty (1)) which is unlimited authority to make first order laws, and second order sovereignty (sovereignty (2)) which is unlimited authority to make second order laws. If we say that parliament is sovereign we might mean that any parliament at any time has sovereignty (1), or we might mean that parliament has both sovereignty (1) and sovereignty (2) at present, but we cannot without contradiction mean both that the present parliament has sovereignty (2) and that every parliament at every time has sovereignty (1), for if the present parliament has sovereignty (2) it may use it to take away the sovereignty (1) of later parliaments. What the paradox shows is that we cannot ascribe to any continuing institution legal sovereignty in an inclusive sense.

The analogy between omnipotence and sovereignty shows that the paradox of omnipotence can be solved in a similar way. We must distinguish between first order omnipotence (omnipotence (1)), that is unlimited power to act, and second order omnipotence (omnipotence (2)), that is unlimited power to determine what powers to act things shall have. Then we could consistently say that God all the time has omnipotence (1), but if so no beings at any time have powers to act independently of God. Or we could say that God at one time had omnipotence (2), and used it to assign independent powers to act to certain things, so that God thereafter did not have omnipotence (1). But what the paradox shows is that we cannot consistently ascribe to any continuing being omnipotence in an inclusive sense.

An alternative solution to this paradox would be simply to deny that God is a continuing being, that any times can be assigned to his actions at all. But on this assumption (which also has difficulties of its own) no meaning can be given to the assertion that God made men with wills so free that he could not control them. The paradox of omnipotence can be avoided by putting God outside time, but the free will solution of the problem of evil cannot be saved in this way, and equally it remains impossible to hold that an omnipotent God *binds himself* by causal or logical laws.

Conclusion

Of the proposed solutions of the problem of evil which we have examined, none has stood up to criticism. There may be other solutions which require examination, but this study strongly suggests that there is no valid solution of the problem which does not modify at least one of the constituent propositions in a way which would seriously affect the essential core of the theistic position.

Quite apart from the problem of evil, the paradox of omnipotence has shown that God's omnipotence must in any case be restricted in one way or another, that unqualified omnipotence cannot be ascribed to any being that continues through time. And if God and his actions are not in time, can omnipotence, or power of any sort, be meaningfully ascribed to him?

Chapter 54

What is evil?

Augustine of Hippo

III. vii(12)

I WAS unaware of the existence of another reality, that which truly is, and it was as if some sharp intelligence were persuading me to consent to the stupid deceivers when they asked me: 'Where does evil come from? and is God confined within a corporeal form? has he hair and nails? and can those be considered righteous who had several wives at the same time and killed people and offered animals in sacrifice?' In my ignorance I was disturbed by these questions, and while travelling away from the truth I thought I was going towards it. I did not know that evil has no existence except as a privation of good, down to that level which is altogether without being. How could I see this when for me 'to see' meant a physical act of looking with the eyes and of forming an image in the mind? I had not realized God is a Spirit (John 4: 24), not a figure whose limbs have length and breadth and who has a mass. For mass is less in a part than in its whole, and if it is unlimited, it is less in a part defined within a given space than in its unlimited extension. It is not everywhere entire as a Spirit and as God. Moreover, I was wholly ignorant of what it is in ourselves which gives us being, and how scripture is correct in saying that we are 'in God's image' (Gen. 1: 27).

IV. xv(24)

I had not as yet come to see that the hinge of this great subject lies in your creative act, almighty one: you alone do marvellous things (Ps. 71: 8; 135: 4). My mind moved within the confines of corporeal forms. I proposed a definition and a distinction between the beautiful as that which is pleasing in itself, and the fitting as that which pleases because it fits well into something else. I supported this distinction by examples drawn from the body. Moreover, I turned then to examine the nature of mind, but the false opinion which I held about spiritual entities did not allow me to perceive the truth. The truth with great force leapt to my eyes, but I used to turn away my agitated mind from incorporeal reality to lines and colours and physical magnitudes of vast size. Because I could not see any such thing in the mind, I thought I could not see my mind. Furthermore, since in virtue I loved peace and in vice I hated discord, I noted that in virtue there is unity, in vice a kind of division. In the unity I thought I saw the rational mind and the nature of truth and of the highest good; whereas in the division there was some substance of irrational life and the nature of supreme evil. I attributed to this evil not only substance but life. Yet it could have no being without you, my God, from whom all things come (I Cor. 8: 6). My opinion was miserable folly. In regard to virtue, I spoke of the Monad as sexless mind, whereas evil was the Dyad, anger in injurious acts, lust in vicious acts. I did not know what I was talking about. I did not know nor had I learnt that evil is not a substance, nor is our mind the supreme and unchangeable good.

V. x(19–20)

When I wanted to think of my God, I knew of no way of doing so except as a physical mass. Nor did I think anything existed which is not material. That was the principal and almost sole cause of my inevitable error.

For the same reason I also believed that evil is a kind of material substance with its own foul and misshapen mass, either solid which they used to call earth, or thin and subtle, as is the body of air. They imagine it to be a malignant mind creeping through the earth. And since piety (however bizarre some of my beliefs were) forbade me to believe that the good God had created an evil nature, I concluded that there are two opposed masses, both infinite, but the evil rather smaller, the good larger; and of this pestilential beginning other blasphemous notions were the corollary. When my mind attempted to return to the Catholic faith, it was rebuffed because the Catholic faith is not what I thought. My God, to whom your mercies make it possible for me to make confession, I felt it more reverent to believe you infinite in all respects but one, namely the mass of evil opposed to you, than to think you in all parts limited to the shape of the human body. I thought it better to believe that you had created no evil—which in my ignorance I thought not merely some sort of substance but even corporeal, since I did not know how to think of mind except as a subtle physical entity diffused through space—rather than to believe that the nature of evil, as I understood it, came from you.

VII. iii(4)–v(7)

But a problem remained to trouble me. Although I affirmed and firmly held divine immunity from pollution and change and the complete immutability of our God, the true God who made not only our souls but also our bodies, and not only our souls and bodies, but all rational beings and everything, yet I had no clear and explicit grasp of the cause of evil. Whatever it might be, I saw it had to be investigated, if I were to avoid being forced by this problem to believe the immutable God to be mutable. Otherwise I might myself become the evil I was investigating. Accordingly, I made my investigation without anxiety, certain that what the Manichees said was untrue. With all my mind I fled from them, because in my inquiry into the origin of evil I saw them to be full of malice, in that they thought it more acceptable to say your substance suffers evil than that their own substance actively does evil.

I directed my mind to understand what I was being told, namely that the free choice of the will is the reason why we do wrong and suffer your just judgement; but I could not get a clear grasp of it. I made an effort to lift my mind's eye out of the abyss, but again plunged back. I tried several times, but again and again sank back. I was brought up into your light by the fact that I knew myself both to have a will and to be alive. Therefore when I willed or did not will something, I was utterly certain that none other than myself was willing or not willing. That there lay the cause of my sin I was now coming to recognize. I saw that when I acted against my wishes, I was passive rather than active; and this condition I judged to be not guilt but a punishment. It was an effortless step to grant that, since I conceived you to be just, it was not unjust that I was chastised. But again I said: 'Who made me? Is not my God not only good but the supreme Good? Why then have I the power to will evil and to reject good? Is it to provide a reason why it is just for me to undergo punishments? Who put this power in me and implanted in me this seed of bitterness (Heb. 12: 15), when all of me was created by my very kind God? If the devil was responsible, where did the devil himself come from? And if even he began as a good angel and became devil by a perversion of the will, how does the evil will by which he became devil originate in him, when an angel is wholly made by a Creator who is pure goodness?' These reflections depressed me once more and suffocated me. But I was not brought down to that hell of error where no one confesses to you (Ps. 6: 6), because people suppose that evil is something that you suffer rather than an act by humanity.

In this way I made an effort to discover other principles. I had ready established that the incorruptible is better than the corruptible, and so I confessed that whatever you are, you are incorruptible. Nor could there have been or be any soul capable of conceiving that which is better than you, who are the supreme and highest good. Since it is most true and certain that the incorruptible is superior to the corruptible, as I had already concluded, had it been the case that you are not incorruptible I could in thought have attained something better than my God. Therefore, when I saw that the incorruptible is superior to the corruptible, I ought to have looked for you there and to have deduced from that principle the locus of evil, that is, the source of the corruption by which it is impossible for your being to be injured. There is absolutely no way corruption can injure our God—no act of will, no necessity, no unforeseen chance—since he is God and what he wills for himself is good, and he is that same good. Whereas to be corrupted is not good.

Moreover, you cannot be unwillingly compelled to anything: for your will is not greater than your power. It would be greater only if you were greater than yourself. For the will and power of God is God's very self. And what can be unforeseen by you who know all things? No nature exists but you know it. Indeed, why need we say repeatedly 'Why is the being of God not a corruptible substance?' If it were so, that would not be God.

I searched for the origin of evil, but I searched in a flawed way and did not see the flaw in my very search. I placed before my spirit a conspectus of the entire creation—all that we can perceive in it, earth, sea, air, stars, trees and mortal animals, and all that we cannot perceive, the firmament of heaven above, all the angels, and all the spiritual beings. But I imagined these beings to be like bodies which are allocated to particular places. I conceived your creation as a single vast mass differentiated by various types of bodies, whether they were real bodies or whether the bodies with which my imagination invested the spirits. I did not make its size precisely what it is, for that I could not know, but I made it as great as seemed appropriate, but on every side finite. I visualized you, Lord, surrounding it on all sides and permeating it, but infinite in all directions, as if there were a sea everywhere and stretching through immense distances, a single sea which had within it a large but finite sponge; and the sponge was in every part filled from the immense sea. This is the kind of way in which I supposed your finite Creation to be full of you, infinite as you are, and said: 'Here is God and see what God has created. God is good and is most mightily and incomparably superior to these things. But being God, God created good creatures. See how God surrounds and fills them. Then where and whence is evil? How did it creep in? What is its root and what is its seed? Or does it not have any being? Why should we fear and avoid what has no being? If our fear is vain, it is certain that fear itself is evil, and that the heart is groundlessly disturbed and tortured. And this evil is the worse for the fact that it has no being to be afraid of. Yet we still fear. Thus either it is evil which we fear or our fear which is evil. Where then does it come from since the good God made everything good? Certainly the greatest and supreme Good made lesser goods; yet the Creator and all that he created are good. What then is the origin of evil? Is it that the matter from which he made things was somehow evil? He gave it form and order, but did he leave in it an element which he could not transform into good? If so, why? Was he powerless to turn and transform all matter so that no evil remained, even though God is omnipotent? Finally, why did God want to make anything out of such stuff and not rather use his omnipotence to ensure that there was no matter at all? Could it exist contrary to God's will? Or indeed, if matter was eternal, why did God allow it to exist for an infinite period of past time in its unordered state and only much later decided to do something with it? Or if now God willed suddenly to do something, would not the Almighty have preferred to cause it not to exist and to be himself alone the totality of the true, supreme, and infinite good? Or if, because he is good, it would not be well that he should not be making and creating something good, could he not abolish evil matter and reduce it to nothing, and himself make good matter out of which he would create every-thing? He would be less than omnipotent if he could not create something good unless assisted by a matter which he had not himself created.'

Such questions revolved in my unhappy breast, weighed down by nagging anxieties about the fear of dying before I had found the truth. But there was a firm place in my heart for the faith, within the Catholic Church, in your Christ, 'our Lord and Saviour' (2 Pet. 2: 20). In many respects this faith was still unformed and hesitant about the norm of doctrine. Yet my mind did not abandon it, but daily drank in more and more.

VII. vii(11)

I was seeking the origin of evil and here was no solution. But you did not allow fluctuations in my thinking to carry me away from the faith which I held, that you exist and are immutable substance and care for humanity and judge us; moreover, that in Christ your Son our Lord, and by your scriptures commended by the authority of your Catholic Church, you have provided a way of salvation whereby humanity can come to the future life after death. These matters, therefore, were secure and firmly fortified in my mind while I was seeking feverishly for the origin of evil. What torments my heart suffered in mental pregnancy, what groans, my God! And though I did not know it, your ears were there.

VII. ix(13)

Through a man puffed up with monstrous pride, you brought under my eye some books of the Platonists, translated from Greek into Latin . . . .

VII. x(16)–xiii(19)

By the Platonic books I was admonished to return into myself. With you as my guide I entered into my innermost citadel, and was given power to do so because you had become my helper (Ps. 29: 11). I entered and with my soul's eye, such as it was, saw above that same eye of my soul the immutable light higher than my mind—not the light of every day, obvious to anyone, nor a larger version of the same kind which would, as it were, have given out a much brighter light and filled everything with its magnitude. It was not that light, but a different thing, utterly different from all our kinds of light. It transcended my mind, not in the way that oil floats on water, nor as heaven is above earth. It was superior because it made me, and I was inferior because I was made by it. The person who knows the truth knows it, and he who knows it knows eternity. Love knows it. Eternal truth and true love and beloved eternity: you are my God. To you I sigh 'day and night' (Ps. 42: 2). When I first came to know you, you raised me up to make me see that what I saw is Being, and that I who saw am not yet Being. And you gave a shock to the weakness of my sight by the strong radiance of your rays, and I trembled with love and awe. And I found myself far from you 'in the region of dissimilarity', and heard as it were your voice from on high: 'I am the food of the fully grown; grow and you will feed on me. And you will not change me into you like the food your flesh eats, but you will be changed into me.'

And I recognized that 'because of iniquity you discipline man' and 'cause my soul to waste away like a spider's web' (Ps. 38: 14), and I said: 'Surely truth cannot be nothing, when it is not diffused through space, either finite or infinite?' And you cried from far away: 'Now, I am who I am' (Exod. 3: 14). I heard in the way one hears within the heart, and all doubt left me. I would have found it easier to doubt whether I was myself alive than that there is no truth 'understood from the things that are made' (Rom. 1: 20).

And I considered the other things below you, and I saw that neither can they be said absolutely to be or absolutely not to be. They are because they come from you. But they are not because they are not what you are. That which truly is is that which unchangeably abides. But 'it is good for me to stick fast to God' (Ps. 72: 28); for if I do not abide in him, I can do nothing (John 15: 5). But he 'abiding in himself makes all things new' (Wisd. 7: 27). 'You are my Lord because you have no need of my goodness' (Ps. 15: 2).

It was obvious to me that things which are liable to corruption are good. If they were the supreme goods, or if they were not good at all, they could not be corrupted. For if they were supreme goods, they would be incorruptible. If there were no good in them, there would be nothing capable of being corrupted. Corruption does harm and unless it diminishes the good, no harm would be done. Therefore either corruption does not harm, which cannot be the case, or (which is wholly certain) all things that are corrupted suffer privation of some good. If they were to be deprived of all good, they would not exist at all. If they were to exist and to be immune from corruption, they would be superior because they would be permanently incorruptible. What could be more absurd than to say that by losing all good, things are made better? So then, if they are deprived of all good, they will be nothing at all. Therefore as long as they exist, they are good. Accordingly, whatever things exist are good, and the evil into whose origins I was inquiring is not a substance, for if it were a substance, it would be good. Either it would be an incorruptible substance, a great good indeed, or a corruptible substance, which could be corrupted only if it were good. Hence I saw and it was made clear to me that you made all things good, and there are absolutely no substances which you did not make. As you did not make all things equal, all things are good in the sense that taken individually they are good, and all things taken together are very good. For our God has made 'all things very good' (Gen. 1: 31).

For you evil does not exist at all, and not only for you but for your created universe, because there is nothing outside it which could break in and destroy the order which you have imposed upon it. But in the parts of the universe, there are certain elements which are thought evil because of a conflict of interest. These elements are congruous with other elements and as such are good, and are also good in themselves. All these elements which have some mutual conflict of interest are congruous with the inferior part of the universe which we call earth. Its heaven is cloudy and windy, which is fitting for it.

It is far from my mind now to say, 'Would that those things did not exist!' If I were to regard them in isolation, I would indeed wish for something better; but now even when they are taken alone, my duty is to praise you for them. That you are to be praised is shown by dragons on earth, and all deeps, fire, hail, snow, ice, the hurricane and tempest, which perform your word—mountains and all hills, fruitful trees and all cedars, beasts and all cattle, reptiles and winged birds; kings of the earth and all peoples, princes and all judges of the earth, young men and maidens, old men with younger: let them praise your name (Ps. 148: 7–12). Moreover, let these from the heavens praise you: let all your angels praise you in the height, our God all your powers, sun and moon, all stars and light, the heaven of heavens and the waters that are above the heavens: let them praise your name (Ps. 148: 1–5).

I no longer wished individual things to be better, because I considered the totality. Superior things are self-evidently better than inferior. Yet with a sounder judgement I held that all things taken together are better than superior things by themselves.

XII. xi(11)

Already you have said to me, Lord, with a loud voice in my inner ear, that you are eternal. 'You alone have immortality' (1 Tim. 6: 16), for you are changed by no form or movement, nor does your will undergo any variation at different times. For that is not an immortal will which is first one thing and then another. 'In your sight' (Ps. 18: 15) this truth is clear to me. Let it become more and more evident, I pray you, and as it becomes manifest may I dwell calmly under your wings (cf. Ps. 35: 8).

Chapter 55

Evil does not show that there is no God

Richard Swinburne

Gᴏᴅ is, by definition, omniscient, omnipotent, and perfectly good. By 'omnisci-ent' I understand 'one who knows all true propositions'. By 'omnipotent' I understand 'able to do anything logically possible'.[1] By 'perfectly good' I under-stand 'one who does no morally bad action', and I include among actions omis-sions to perform some action. The problem of evil is then often stated as the problem whether the existence of God is compatible with the existence of evil. Against the suggestion of compatibility, an atheist often suggests that the existence of evil entails the nonexistence of God. For, he argues, if God exists, then being omniscient, he knows under what circumstances evil will occur, if he does not act; and being omnipotent, he is able to prevent its occurrence. Hence, being perfectly good, he will prevent its occurrence and so evil will not exist. Hence the existence of God entails the nonexistence of evil. Theists have usually attacked this argument by denying the claim that necessarily a perfectly good being, foreseeing the occurrence of evil and able to prevent it, will prevent it. And indeed, if evil is understood in the very wide way in which it normally is understood in this context, to include physi-cal pain of however slight a degree, the cited claim is somewhat implausible. For it implies that if through my neglecting frequent warnings to go to the dentist, I find myself one morning with a slight toothache, then necessarily, there does not exist a perfectly good being who foresaw the evil and was able to have prevented it. Yet it seems fairly obvious that such a being might well choose to allow me to suffer some mild consequences of my folly—as a lesson for the future which would do me no real harm.

The threat to theism seems to come, not from the existence of evil as such, but rather from the existence of evil of certain kinds and degrees—severe undeserved physical pain or mental anguish, for example. I shall therefore list briefly the kinds of evil which are evident in our world, and ask whether their existence in the degrees in which we find them is compatible with the existence of God. I shall call the man who argues for compatibility the theodicist, and his opponent the

Richard Swinburne 'The Problem of Evil' from *Reason and Religion* edited by Stuart C. Brown (Cornell University Press, 1977), copyright © Royal Institute of Philosophy 1977, reprinted by permission of the publisher and the author.

1. This account of omnipotence will do for present purposes. But a much more careful account is needed to deal with other well-known difficulties. I have attempted to provide such an account in my 'Omnipotence,' *American Philosophical Quarterly*, 10 (1973), 231–7.

antitheodicist. The theodicist will claim that it is not morally wrong for God to create or permit the various evils, normally on the grounds that doing so is providing the logically necessary conditions of greater goods. The antitheodicist denies these claims by putting forward moral principles which have as consequences that a good God would not under any circumstances create or permit the evils in question. I shall argue that these moral principles are not, when carefully examined, at all obvious, and indeed that there is a lot to be said for their negations. Hence I shall conclude that it is plausible to suppose that the existence of these evils is compatible with the existence of God.[2]

Since I am discussing only the compatibility of various evils with the existence of God, I am perfectly entitled to make occasionally some (nonself-contradictory) assumption, and argue that if it was true, the compatibility would hold. For if p is compatible with q, given r (where r is not self-contradictory), then p is compatible with q simpliciter. It is irrelevant to the issue of compatibility whether these assumptions are true. If, however, the assumptions which I make are clearly false, and if also it looks as if the existence of God is compatible with the existence of evil *only* given those assumptions, the formal proof of compatibility will lose much of interest. To avoid this danger, I shall make only such assumptions as are not clearly false—and also in fact the ones which I shall make will be ones to which many theists are already committed for entirely different reasons.

What then is wrong with the world? First, there are painful sensations, felt both by men, and, to a lesser extent, by animals. Second, there are painful emotions, which do not involve pain in the literal sense of this word—for example, feelings of loss and failure and frustration. Such suffering exists mainly among men, but also, I suppose, to some small extent among animals too. Third, there are evil and undesirable states of affairs, mainly states of men's minds, which do not involve suffering. For example, there are the states of mind of hatred and envy; and such states of the world as rubbish tipped over a beauty spot. And fourth, there are the evil actions of men, mainly actions having as foreseeable consequences evils of the first three types, but perhaps other actions as well—such as lying and promise breaking with no such foreseeable consequences. As before, I include among actions, omissions to perform some actions. If there are rational agents other than men and God (if he exists), such as angels or devils or strange beings on distant planets, who suffer and perform evil actions, then evil feelings, states, and actions must be added to the list of evils.

I propose to call evil of the first type physical evil, evil of the second type mental evil, evil of the third type state evil, and evil of the fourth type moral evil. Since there is a clear contrast between evils of the first three types, which are evils that happen to men or animals or the world, and evils of the fourth type which are evils that men do, there is an advantage in having one name for evils of any of the first

---

2. Some of what I have to say will not be especially original. The extensive writing on this subject has of course been well described in John Hick, *Evil and the God of Love* (London, 1966).

three types—I shall call these passive evils.[3] I distinguish evil from mere absence of good. Pain is not simply the absence of pleasure. A headache is a pain, whereas not having the sensation of drinking whiskey is, for many people, mere absence of pleasure. Likewise, the feeling of loss in bereavement is an evil involving suffering, to be contrasted with the mere absence of the pleasure of companionship. Some thinkers have, of course, claimed that a good God would create a 'best of all (logically) possible worlds'[4] (i.e., a world than which no better is logically possible), and for them the mere absence of good creates a problem since it looks as if a world would be a better world if it had that good. For most of us, however, the mere absence of good seems less of a threat to theism than the presence of evil, partly because it is not at all clear whether any sense can be given to the concept of a best of all possible worlds (and if it cannot then of logical necessity there will be a better world than any creatable world) and partly because even if sense can be given to this concept it is not at all obvious that God has an obligation to create such a world[5]—to whom would he be doing an injustice if he did not? My concern is with the threat to theism posed by the existence of evil.

Now much of the evil in the world consists of the evil actions of men and the passive evils brought about by those actions. (These include the evils brought about intentionally by men, and also the evils which result from long years of slackness by many generations of men. Many of the evils of 1975 are in the latter category, and among them many state evils. The hatred and jealousy which many men and groups feel today result from an upbringing consequent on generations of neglected opportunities for reconciliations.) The antitheodicist suggests as a moral principle (P1) that a creator able to do so ought to create only creatures such that necessarily they do not do evil actions. From this it follows that God would not have made men who do evil actions. Against this suggestion the theodicist naturally deploys the free-will defense, elegantly expounded in recent years by Alvin Plantinga.[6] This runs roughly as follows: it is not logically possible for an agent to make another agent such that necessarily he freely does only good actions. Hence if a being G creates a free agent, he gives to the agent power of choice between alternative actions, and how he will exercise that power is something which G cannot control while the agent remains free. It is a good thing that there exist free agents, but a logically necessary consequence of their existence is that their power to choose to do evil actions may sometimes be realized. The price is worth paying,

3. In discussion of the problem of evil, terminology has not always been very clear or consistent. See Gerald Wallace, 'The Problems of Moral and Physical Evil,' *Philosophy*, 46 (1971), 349–51.

4. Indeed they have often made the even stronger claim that a good God would create *the* best of all (logically) possible worlds—implying that necessarily there was just one possible world better than all others. There seem to me no grounds at all for adopting this claim.

5. That he has no such obligation is very well argued by Robert Merrihew Adams, 'Must God Create the Best?' *Philosophical Review*, 81 (1972), 317–32.

6. See Alvin Plantinga, 'The Free Will Defence,' in Max Black, ed., *Philosophy in America* (London, 1965); *God and Other Minds* (Ithaca, N.Y., and London, 1967), chaps. 5 and 6; and *The Nature of Necessity* (Oxford, 1974), chap. 9.

however, for the existence of agents performing free actions remains a good thing even if they sometimes do evil. Hence it is not logically possible that a creator create free creatures 'such that necessarily they do not do evil actions'. But it is not a morally bad thing that he create free creatures, even with the possibility of their doing evil. Hence the cited moral principle is implausible.

The free-will defense as stated needs a little filling out. For surely there could be free agents who did not have the power of moral choice, agents whose only opportunities for choice were between morally indifferent alternatives—between jam and marmalade for breakfast, between watching the BBC 1 or the news on ITV. They might lack this power either because they lacked the power of making moral judgments (i.e., lacked moral discrimination); or because all their actions which were morally assessable were caused by factors outside their control; or because they saw with complete clarity what was right and wrong and had no temptation to do anything except the right.[7] The free-will defense must claim, however, that it is a good thing that there exist free agents with the power and opportunity of choosing between morally good and morally evil actions, agents with sufficient moral discrimination to have some idea of the difference and some (though not overwhelming) temptation to do other than the morally good. Let us call such agents humanly free agents. The defense must then go on to claim that it is not logically possible to create humanly free agents such that necessarily they do not do morally evil actions. Unfortunately, this latter claim is highly debatable, and I have no space to debate it.[8] I propose therefore to circumvent this issue as follows. I shall add to the definition of humanly free agents, that they are agents whose choices do not have fully deterministic precedent causes. Clearly then it will not be logically possible to create humanly free agents whose choices go one way rather than another, and so not logically possible to create humanly free agents such that necessarily they do not do evil actions. Then the free-will defense claims that $(P1)$ is not universally true; it is not morally wrong to create humanly free agents—despite the real possibility that they will do evil. Like many others who have discussed this issue, I find this a highly plausible suggestion. Surely as parents we regard it as a good thing that our children have power to do free actions of moral significance—even if the consequence is that they sometimes do evil actions. This conviction is likely to be stronger, not weaker, if we hold that the free actions with which we are concerned are ones which do not have fully deterministic precedent causes. In this way we show the existence of God to be compatible with the existence of moral evil—but only subject to a very big assumption—men are humanly free agents. If they are not, the compatibility shown by the free-will defense is of little interest. For the agreed exception to $(P1)$ would not then justify a creator making men who did evil

7. In the latter case they would have, in Kant's terminology, holy wills. I argue that God must be such an agent in my 'Duty and the Will of God,' *Canadian Journal of Philosophy*, 4 (1974), 213–27.
8. For the debate see Antony Flew, 'Divine omnipotence and Human Freedom,' in Antony Flew and Alasdair MacIntyre, eds., *New Essays in Philosophical Theology*; John L. Mackie, 'Evil and Omnipotence,' *Mind*, 64 (1955), 200–12; and Plantinga, 'Free Will Defence.'

actions; we should need a different exception to avoid incompatibility. The assumption seems to me not clearly false, and is also one which most theists affirm for quite other reasons. Needless to say, there is no space to discuss the assumption here.

All that the free-will defense has shown so far, however (and all that Plantinga seems to show) is grounds for supposing that the existence of moral evil is compatible with the existence of God. It has not given grounds for supposing that the existence of evil consequences of moral evils is compatible with the existence of God. In an attempt to show an incompatibility, the antitheodicist may suggest instead of $(P1)$, $(P2)$—that a creator able to do so ought always to ensure that any creature whom he creates does not cause passive evils, or at any rate passive evils which hurt creatures other than himself. For could not God have made a world where there are humanly free creatures, men with the power to do evil actions, but where those actions do not have evil consequences, or at any rate evil consequences which affect others—e.g., a world where men cannot cause pain and distress to other men? Men might well do actions which are evil either because they were actions which they believed would have evil consequences or because they were evil for some other reason (e.g., actions which involved promise breaking) without them in fact having any passive evils as consequences. Agents in such a world would be like men in a simulator training to be pilots. They can make mistakes, but no one suffers through those mistakes. Or men might do evil actions which did have the evil consequences which were foreseen but which damaged only themselves. Some philosophers might hold that an action would not be evil if its foreseen consequences were ones damaging only to the agent, since, they might hold, no one has any duties to himself. For those who do not hold this position, however, there are some plausible candidates for actions evil solely because of their foreseeable consequences for the agent—e.g., men brooding on their misfortunes in such a way as foreseeably to become suicidal or misanthropic.

I do not find $(P2)$ a very plausible moral principle. A world in which no one except the agent was affected by his evil actions might be a world in which men had freedom but it would not be a world in which men had responsibility. The theodicist claims that it would not be wrong for God to create interdependent humanly free agents, a society of such agents responsible for each other's well-being, able to make or mar each other.

Fair enough, the antitheodicist may again say. It is not wrong to create a world where creatures have responsibilities for each other. But might not those responsibilities simply be that creatures had the opportunity to benefit or to withhold benefit from each other, not a world in which they had also the opportunity to cause each other pain? One answer to this is that if creatures have only the power to benefit and not the power to hurt each other, they obviously lack any very strong responsibility for each other. To bring out the point by a caricature—a world in which I could choose whether or not to give you sweets, but not whether or not to break your leg or make you unpopular, is not a world in which I have a very strong influence on your destiny, and so not a world in which I have a very full responsibility for you. Further, however, there is a point which will depend on an argument which I will give further on. In the actual world very often a man's withholding benefits from another is correlated with the latter's suffering some passive evil, either physical or mental. Thus if I withhold from you certain vitamins, you will suffer disease. Or if I deprive you of your wife by persuading her to live with me instead, you will suffer grief at the loss. Now it seems to me that a world in which such correlations did not hold would not necessarily be a better world than the world in which they do. The appropriateness of pain to bodily disease or deprivation, and of mental evils to various losses or lacks of a more spiritual kind, is something for which I shall argue in detail a little later.

So then the theodicist objects to ($P2$) on the grounds that the price of possible passive evils for other creatures is a price worth paying for agents to have great responsibilities for each other. It is a price which (logically) must be paid if they are to have those responsibilities. Here again a reasonable antitheodicist may see the point. In bringing up our own children, in order to give them responsibility, we try not to interfere too quickly in their quarrels—even at the price, sometimes, of younger children getting hurt physically. We try not to interfere, first, in order to train our children for responsibility in later life and second because responsibility here and now is a good thing in itself. True, with respect to the first reason, whatever the effects on character produced by training, God could produce without training. But if he did so by imposing a full character on a humanly free creature, this would be giving him a character which he had not in any way chosen or adopted for himself. Yet it would seem a good thing that a creator should allow humanly free creatures to influence by their own choices the sort of creatures they are to be, the kind of character they are to have. That means that the creator must create them immature, and allow them gradually to make decisions which affect the sort of beings they will be. And one of the greatest privileges which a creator can give to a creature is to allow him to help in the process of education, in putting alternatives before his fellows.

Yet though the antitheodicist may see the point, in theory, he may well react to it rather like this. 'Certainly some independence is a good thing. But surely a father ought to interfere if his younger son is really getting badly hurt. The ideal of making men free and responsible is a good one, but there are limits to the amount of responsibility which it is good that men should have, and in our world men have too much responsibility. A good God would certainly have intervened long ago to stop some of the things which happen in our world.' Here, I believe, lies the crux—it is simply a matter of quantity. The theodicist says that a good God could allow men to do to each other the hurt they do, in order to allow them to be free and responsible. But against him the antitheodicist puts forward as a moral principle ($P3$) that a creator able to do so ought to ensure that any creature whom he creates does not cause passive evils as many and as evil as those in our world. He says that in our world freedom and responsibility have gone too far—produced too much physical and mental hurt. God might well tolerate a boy hitting his younger brother, but not Belsen.

The theodicist is in no way committed to saying that a good God will not stop things getting too bad. Indeed, if God made our world, he has clearly done so. There are limits to the amount and degree of evil which are possible in our world. Thus there are limits to the amount of pain which a person can suffer—persons live in our world only so many years and the amount which they can suffer at any given time (if mental goings-on are in any way correlated with bodily ones) is limited by their physiology. Further, theists often claim that from time to time God intervenes in the natural order which he has made to prevent evil which would otherwise occur. So the theodicist can certainly claim that a good God stops too much suffering—it is just that he and his opponent draw the line in different places. The issue as regards the passive evils caused by men turns ultimately on the quantity of evil. To this crucial matter I shall return toward the end of the paper.

We shall have to turn next to the issue of passive evils not apparently caused by men. But, first, I must consider a further argument by the theodicist in support of the free-will defense and also an argument of the antitheodicist against it. The first is the argument that various evils are logically necessary conditions for the occurrence of actions of certain especially good kinds. Thus for a man to bear his suffering cheerfully there has to be suffering for him to bear. There have to be acts which irritate for another to show tolerance of them. Likewise it is often said, acts of forgiveness, courage, self-sacrifice, compassion, overcoming temptation, etc., can be performed only if there are evils of various kinds. Here, however, we must be careful. One might reasonably claim that all that is necessary for some of these good acts (or acts as good as these) to be performed is belief in the existence of certain evils, not their actual existence. You can show compassion toward someone who appears to be suffering, but is not really; you can forgive someone who only appeared to insult you, but did not really. But if the world is to be populated with imaginary evils of the kind needed to enable creatures to perform acts of the above specially good kinds, it would have to be a world in which creatures are generally and systematically deceived about the feelings of their fellows—in which the behavior of creatures generally and unavoidably belies their feelings and intentions. I suggest, in the tradition of Descartes (*Meditations* 4, 5 and 6), that it would be a morally wrong act of a creator to create such a deceptive world. In that case, given a creator, then, without an immoral act on his part, for acts of courage, compassion, etc., to be acts open to men to perform, there have to be various evils. Evils give men the opportunity to perform those acts which show men at their best. A world without evils would be a world in which men could show no forgiveness, no compassion, no self-sacrifice. And men without that opportunity are deprived of the opportunity to show themselves at their noblest. For this reason God might well allow some of his creatures to perform evil acts with passive evils as consequences, since these provide the opportunity for especially noble acts.

Against the suggestion of the developed free-will defense that it would be justifiable for God to permit a creature to hurt another for the good of his or the other's soul, there is one natural objection which will surely be made. This is that it is generally supposed to be the duty of men to stop other men hurting each other badly. So why is it not God's duty to stop men hurting each other badly? Now the theodicist does not have to maintain that it is never God's duty to stop men hurting each other; but he does have to maintain that it is not God's duty in circumstances where it clearly is our duty to stop such hurt if we can—e.g., when men are torturing each other in mind or body in some of the ways in which they do this in our world and when, if God exists, he does not step in.

Now different views might be taken about the extent of our duty to interfere in the quarrels of others. But the most which could reasonably be claimed is surely this—that we have a duty to interfere in three kinds of circumstances—(1) if an oppressed person asks us to interfere and it is probable that he will suffer considerably if we do not, (2) if the participants are children or not of sane mind and it is probable that one or other will suffer considerably if we do not interfere, or (3) if it is probable that considerable harm will be done to others if we do not interfere. It is not very plausible to suppose that we have any duty to interfere in the quarrels of grown sane men who do not wish us to do, unless it is probable that the harm will spread. Now note that in the characterization of each of the circumstances in which we would have a duty to interfere there occurs the word 'probable', and it is being used in the 'epistemic' sense—as 'made probable by the total available evidence'. But then the 'probability' of an occurrence varies crucially with which community or individual is assessing it, and the amount of evidence which they have at the time in question. What is probable relative to your knowledge at t_1 may not be at all probable relative to my knowledge at t_2. Hence a person's duty to interfere in quarrels will depend on their probable consequences relative to that person's knowledge. Hence it follows that one who knows much more about the probable consequences of a quarrel may have no duty to interfere where another with less knowledge does have such a duty—and conversely. Hence a God who sees far more clearly than we do the consequences of quarrels may have duties very different from ours with respect to particular such quarrels. He may know that the suffering that A will cause B is not nearly as great as B's screams might suggest to us and will provide (unknown to us) an opportunity to C to help B recover and will thus give C a deep responsibility which he would not otherwise have. God may very well have reason for allowing particular evils which it is our bounden duty to attempt to stop at all costs simply because he knows so much more about them than we do. And this is no ad hoc hypothesis—it follows directly from the characterization of the kind of circumstances in which persons have a duty to interfere in quarrels.

We may have a duty to interfere in quarrels when God does not for a very different kind of reason. God being our creator, the source of our beginning and continuation of existence, has rights over us which we do not have over fellow-men. To allow man to suffer for the good of his or someone else's soul one has to stand in some kind of parental relationship toward him. I don't have the right to let some stranger Joe Bloggs suffer for the good of his soul or of the soul of Bill Snoggs, but I do have *some* right of this kind in respect of my own children. I may let the younger son suffer *somewhat* for the good of his and his brother's soul. I have this right because in small part I am responsible for his existence, its beginning and continuance. If this is correct, then a fortiori, God who is, ex hypothesi, so much more the author of our being than are our parents, has so many more rights in this respect. God has rights to allow others to suffer, while I do not have those rights and hence have a duty to interfere instead. In these two ways the theodicist can rebut the objection that if we have a duty to stop certain particular evils which men do to others, God must have his duty too.

In the free-will defense, as elaborated above, the theist seems to me to have an adequate answer to the suggestion that necessarily a good God would prevent the occurrence of the evil which men cause—if we ignore the question of the quantity of evil, to which I will return at the end of my paper. But what of the passive evil apparently not due to human action? What of the pain caused to men by disease or earthquake or cyclone, and what too of animal pain which existed before there were men? There are two additional assumptions, each of which has been put forward to allow the free-will defense to show the compatibility of the existence of God and the existence of such evil. The first is that, despite appearances, men are ultimately responsible for disease, earthquake, cyclone, and much animal pain. There seem to be traces of this view in Genesis 3: 16–20. One might claim that God ties the goodness of man to the well-being of the world and that a failure of one leads to a failure of the other. Lack of prayer, concern, and simple goodness lead to the evils in nature. This assumption, though it may do some service for the free-will defense, would seem unable to account for the animal pain which existed before there were men. The other assumption is that there exist humanly free creatures other than men, which we may call fallen angels, who have chosen to do evil, and have brought about the passive evils not brought about by men. These were given the care of much of the material world and have abused that care. For reasons already given, however, it is not God's moral duty to interfere to prevent the passive evils caused by such creatures. This defense has recently been used by, among others, Plantinga. This assumption, it seems to me, will do the job, and is not *clearly* false. It is also an assumption which was part of the Christian tradition long before the free-will defense was put forward in any logically rigorous form. I believe that this assumption may indeed be indispensable if the theist is to reconcile with the existence of God the existence of passive evils of certain kinds, e.g., certain animal pain. But I do not think that the theodicist need deploy it to deal with the central cases of passive evils not caused by men—mental evils and the human pain that is a sign of bodily malfunctioning. Note, however, that if he does not attribute such passive evils to the free choice of some other agent, the theodicist must attribute them to the direct action of God himself, or rather, what he must say is that God created a universe in which passive evils must necessarily occur in certain circumstances, the occurrence of which is necessary or at any rate not within the power of a humanly free agent to prevent. The antitheodicist then naturally claims, that although a creator might be justified in allowing free creatures to produce various evils, nevertheless (P4) a creator is never justified in creating a world in which evil results except by the action of a humanly free agent. Against this the theodicist tries to sketch reasons which a good creator might have for creating a world in which there is evil not brought about by humanly free agents. One reason which he produces is one which we have already considered earlier in the development of the free-will defense. This is the reason that various evils are logically necessary conditions for the occurrence of actions of certain especially noble kinds. This was adduced earlier as a reason why a creator might allow creatures to perform evil acts with passive evils as consequences. It can also be adduced as a reason why he might himself bring about passive evils—to give further opportunities for courage, patience, and tolerance. I shall consider here one further reason that, the theodicist may suggest, a good creator might have for creating a world in which various passive evils were implanted, which is another reason for rejecting (P4). It is, I think, a reason which is closely connected with some of the other reasons which we have been considering why a good creator might permit the existence of evil.

A creator who is going to create humanly free agents and place them in a universe has a choice of the kind of universe to create. First, he can create a finished universe in which nothing needs improving. Humanly free agents know what is right, and pursue it; and they achieve their purposes without hindrance. Second, he can create a basically evil universe, in which everything needs improving, and nothing can be improved. Or, third, he can create a basically good but half-finished universe—one in which many things need improving, humanly free agents do not altogether know what is right, and their purposes are often frustrated; but one in which agents can come to know what is right and can overcome the obstacles to the achievement of their purposes. In such a universe the bodies of creatures may work imperfectly and last only a short time; and creatures may be morally ill-educated, and set their affections on things and persons which are taken from them. The universe might be such that it requires long generations of cooperative effort between creatures to make perfect. While not wishing to deny the goodness of a universe of the first kind, I suggest that to create a universe of the third kind would be no bad thing, for it gives to creatures the privilege of making their own universe. Genesis 1 in telling of a God who tells men to 'subdue' the earth pictures the creator as creating a universe of this third kind; and fairly evidently—given that men are humanly free agents—our universe is of this kind.

Now a creator who creates a half-finished universe of this third kind has a further choice as to how he molds the humanly free agents which it contains. Clearly he will have to give them a nature of some kind, that is, certain narrow purposes which they have a natural inclination to pursue until they choose or are forced to pursue others—e.g., the immediate attainment of food, sleep, and sex. There could hardly be humanly free agents without some such initial purposes. But what is he to do about their knowledge of their duty to improve the world—e.g., to repair their bodies when they go wrong, so that they can realize long-term purposes, to help others who cannot get food to do so, etc.? He could just give them a formal hazy knowledge that they had such reasons for action without giving them any strong inclination to pursue them. Such a policy might well seem an excessively laissez-faire one. We tend to think that parents who give their children no help toward taking the right path are less than perfect parents. So a good creator might well help agents toward taking steps to improve the universe. We shall see that he can do this in one of two ways.

An action is something done for a reason. A good creator, we supposed, will give to agents some reasons for doing right actions—e.g., that they are right, that they will improve the universe. These reasons are ones of which men can be aware and then either act on or not act on. The creator could help agents toward doing right actions by making these reasons more effective causally; that is, he could make agents so that by nature they were inclined (though not perhaps compelled) to pursue what is good. But this would be to impose a moral character on agents, to give them wide general purposes which they naturally pursue, to make them natur-ally altruistic, tenacious of purpose, or strong-willed. But to impose a character on creatures might well seem to take away from creatures the privilege of developing their own characters and those of their fellows. We tend to think that parents who try too forcibly to impose a character, however good a character, on their children, are less than perfect parents.

The alternative way in which a creator could help creatures to perform right actions is by sometimes providing additional reasons for creatures to do what is right, reasons which by their very nature have a strong causal influence. Reasons such as improving the universe or doing one's duty do not necessarily have a strong causal influence, for as we have seen creatures may be little influenced by them. Giving a creature reasons which by their nature were strongly causally influential on a particular occasion on any creature whatever his character, would not impose a particular character on a creature. It would, however, incline him to do what is right on that occasion and maybe subsequently too. Now if a reason is by its nature to be strongly causally influential it must be something of which the agent is aware which causally inclines him (whatever his character) to perform some action, to bring about some kind of change. What kind of reason could this be except the existence of an unpleasant feeling, either a sensation such as a pain or an emotion such as a feeling of loss or deprivation? Such feelings are things of which agents are conscious, which cause them to do whatever action will get rid of those feelings, and which provide reason for performing such action. An itch causally inclines a man to do whatever will cause the itch to cease, e.g., scratch, and provides a reason for doing that action. Its causal influence is quite independent of the agent—saint or sinner, strong-willed or weak-willed, will all be strongly inclined to get rid of their pains (though some may learn to resist the inclination). Hence a creator who wished to give agents some inclination to improve the world without giving them a character, a wide set of general purposes which they naturally pursue, would tie some of the imperfections of the world to physical or mental evils.

To tie desirable states of affairs to pleasant feelings would not have the same effect. Only an existing feeling can be causally efficacious. An agent could be moved to action by a pleasant feeling only when he had it, and the only action to which he could be moved would be to keep the world as it is, not to improve it. For men to have reasons which move men of any character to actions of perfecting the world, a creator needs to tie its imperfections to unpleasant feelings, that is, physical and mental evils.

There is to some considerable extent such tie-up in our universe. Pain normally occurs when something goes wrong with the working of our body which is going to lead to further limitation on the purposes which we can achieve; and the pain ends when the body is repaired. The existence of the pain spurs the sufferer, and others through the sympathetic suffering which arises when they learn of the sufferer's pain, to do something about the bodily malfunctioning. Yet giving men such feelings which they are inclined to end involves the imposition of no character. A man who is inclined to end his toothache by a visit to the dentist may be saint or sinner, strong-willed or weak-willed, rational or irrational. Any other way of which I can conceive of giving men an inclination to correct what goes wrong, and generally to improve the universe, would seem to involve imposing a character. A creator could, for example, have operated exclusively by threats and promises, whispering in men's ears, 'unless you go to the dentist, you are going to suffer terribly', or 'if you go to the dentist, you are going to feel wonderful'. And if the order of nature is God's creation, he does indeed often provide us with such threats and promises—not by whispering in our ears but by providing inductive evidence. There is plenty of inductive evidence that unattended cuts and sores will lead to pain; that eating and drinking will lead to pleasure. Still, men do not always respond to threats and promises or take the trouble to notice inductive evidence (e.g., statistics showing the correlation between smoking and cancer). A creator could have made men so that they naturally took more account of inductive evidence. But to do so would be to impose character. It would be to make men, apart from any choice of theirs, rational and strong-willed.

Many mental evils too are caused by things going wrong in a man's life or in the life of his fellows and often serve as a spur to a man to put things right, either to put right the cause of the particular mental evil or to put similar things right. A man's feeling of frustration at the failure of his plans spurs him either to fulfill those plans despite their initial failure or to curtail his ambitions. A man's sadness at the failure of the plans of his child will incline him to help the child more in future. A man's grief at the absence of a loved one inclines him to do whatever will get the loved one back. As with physical pain, the spur inclines a man to do what is right but does so without imposing a character—without, say, making a man responsive to duty, or strong-willed.

Physical and mental evils may serve as spurs to long-term cooperative research leading to improvement of the universe. A feeling of sympathy for the actual and prospective suffering of many from tuberculosis or cancer leads to acquisition of knowledge and provision of cure for future sufferers. Cooperative and long-term research and cure is a very good thing, the kind of thing toward which men need a spur. A man's suffering is never in vain if it leads through sympathy to the work of others which eventually provides a long-term cure. True, there could be sympathy without a sufferer for whom the sympathy is felt. Yet in a world made by a creator, there cannot be sympathy on the large scale without a sufferer, for whom the sympathy is felt, unless the creator planned for creatures generally to be deceived about the feelings of their fellows; and that, we have claimed, would be morally wrong.

So generally many evils have a biological and psychological utility in producing spurs to right action without imposition of character, a goal which it is hard to conceive of being realized in any other way. This point provides a reason for the rejection of ($P4$). There are other kinds of reason which have been adduced reasons for rejecting ($P4$)—e.g., that a creator could be justified in bringing about evil as a punishment—but I have no space to discuss these now. I will, however, in passing, mention briefly one reason why a creator might make a world in which certain mental evils were tied to things going wrong. Mental suffering and anguish are a man's proper tribute to losses and failures, and a world in which men were immunized from such reactions to things going wrong would be a worse world than ours. By showing proper feelings a man shows his respect for himself and others. Thus a man who feels no grief at the death of his child or the seduction of his wife is rightly branded by us as insensitive, for he has failed to pay the proper tribute of feeling to others, to show in his feeling how much he values them, and thereby failed to value them properly—for valuing them properly involves having proper reactions of feeling to their loss. Again, only a world in which men feel sympathy for losses experienced by their friends, is a world in which love has full meaning.

So, I have argued, there seem to be kinds of justification for the evils which exist in the world, available to the theodicist. Although a good creator might have very different kinds of justification for producing, or allowing others to produce, various different evils, there is a central thread running through the kind of theodicy which I have made my theodicist put forward. This is that it is a good thing that a creator should make a half-finished universe and create immature creatures, who are humanly free agents, to inhabit it; and that he should allow them to exercise some choice over what kind of creatures they are to become and what sort of universe is to be (while at the same time giving them a slight push in the direction of doing what is right); and that the creatures should have power to affect not only the development of the inanimate universe but the well-being and moral character of their fellows, and that there should be opportunities for creatures to develop noble characters and do especially noble actions. My theodicist has argued that if a creator is to make a universe of this kind, then evils of various kinds may inevitably—

at any rate temporarily—belong to such a universe; and that it is not a morally bad thing to create such a universe despite the evils.

Now a morally sensitive antitheodicist might well in principle accept some of the above arguments. He may agree that in principle it is not wrong to create humanly free agents, despite the possible evils which might result, or to create pains as biological warnings. But where the crunch comes, it seems to me, is in the amount of evil which exists in our world. The antitheodicist says, all right, it would not be wrong to create men able to harm each other, but it would be wrong to create men able to put each other in Belsen. It would not be wrong to create backaches and headaches, even severe ones, as biological warnings, but not the long severe incurable pain of some diseases. In reply the theodicist must argue that a creator who allowed men to do little evil would be a creator who gave them little responsibility; and a creator who gave them only coughs and colds, and not cancer and cholera would be a creator who treated men as children instead of giving them real encouragement to subdue the world. The argument must go on with regard to particular cases. The antitheodicist must sketch in detail and show his adversary the horrors of particular wars and diseases. The theodicist in reply must sketch in detail and show his adversary the good which such disasters make possible. He must show to his opponent men working together for good, men helping each other to overcome disease and famine; the heroism of men who choose the good in spite of temptation, who help others not merely by giving them food but who teach them right and wrong, give them something to live for and something to die for. A world in which this is possible can only be a world in which there is much evil as well as great good. Interfere to stop the evil and you cut off the good.

Like all moral arguments this one can be settled only by each party pointing to the consequences of his opponent's moral position and trying to show that his opponent is committed to implausible consequences. They must try, too, to show that each other's moral principles do or do not fit well with other moral principles which each accepts. The exhibition of consequences is a long process, and it takes time to convince an opponent even if he is prepared to be rational, more time than is available in this paper. All that I claim to have *shown* here is that there is no *easy proof* of incompatibility between the existence of evils of the kinds we find around us and the existence of God. Yet my sympathies for the outcome of any more detailed argument are probably apparent, and indeed I may have said enough to convince some readers as to what that outcome would be.

My sympathies lie, of course, with the theodicist. The theodicist's God is a god who thinks the higher goods so worthwhile that he is prepared to ask a lot of man in the way of enduring evil. Creatures determining in cooperation their own character and future, and that of the universe in which they live, coming in the process to show charity, forgiveness, faith, and self-sacrifice is such a worthwhile thing that a creator would not be unjustified in making or permitting a certain amount of evil in order that they should be realized. No doubt a good creator would put a limit on the amount of evil in the world and perhaps an end to the struggle with it after a number of years. But if he allowed creatures to struggle with evil, he would allow them a real struggle with a real enemy, not a parlor game. The antitheodicist's mistake lies in extrapolating too quickly from *our* duties when faced with evil to the duties of a creator, while ignoring the enormous differences in the circumstances of each. Each of us at one time can make the existing universe better or worse only in a few particulars. A creator can choose the kind of universe and the kind of creatures there are to be. It seldom becomes us in our ignorance and weakness to do anything more than remove the evident evils—war, disease, and famine. We seldom have the power or the knowledge or the right to use such evils to forward deeper and longer-term goods. To make an analogy, the duty of the weak and ignorant is to eliminate cowpox and not to spread it, while the doctor has a duty to spread it (under carefully controlled conditions). But a creator who made or permitted his creatures to suffer much evil and asked them to suffer more is a very demanding creator, one with high ideals who expects a lot. For myself I can say that I would not be too happy to worship a creator who expected too little of his creatures. Nevertheless such a God does ask a lot of creatures. A theodicist is in a better position to defend a theodicy such as I have outlined if he is prepared also to make the further additional claim—that God knowing the worthwhileness of the conquest of evil and the perfecting of the universe by men, shared with them this task by subjecting himself as man to the evil in the world. A creator is more justified in creating or permitting evils to be overcome by his creatures if he is prepared to share with them the burden of the suffering and effort.

Chapter 56

God, evil, and divine responsibility

Herbert McCabe

I APPEAR then as though in a lawcourt as a counsel for defence of God against his philosophical accusers. I seek to do no more than to answer *their* arguments.

The prisoner stands accused of wreaking all kinds of murder and mayhem, of running a world full of misery and malice. Evidence for the crimes lies all around us, and the question is whether God is really responsible, whether he should be judged guilty and perhaps whether he should get off on a plea of diminished responsibility due to unsound mind or natural ignorance.

May I say at once that I shall be falling back on that sound principle of English law that a God is innocent until he is proved guilty. It is not my job to prove that God is innocent; I am not going to explain how and why his activities have been good. I am simply going to refute the charges brought against him. I shall be dealing, in fact with what his accusers have said about him.

At the end of this hearing I hope you will agree that God has not been proved guilty, but I expect you will be as puzzled as I am about his innocence. In other words I hope it will remain a mystery to you why God has done what he has done; but you will at least agree that what he has done does not prove his guilt.

First of all what is the charge? The world is full of suffering and sin; and God committed this world; he openly admits to having done so. Nobody else interfered, there is no one else to take the blame from him. You might imagine a defence on the lines that the poor fellow couldn't help it, he's only a God after all. But this cannot be my defence for I hold that he is omnipotent and can do anything he likes that you could mention. (The only reason why you would have to say that he can't make square circles is that you can't mention them; the words cancel each other out so that you haven't said anything.)

But anything you *could* describe or think of God could do, and it is not difficult, surely, to think of a world with less suffering and sin than this one has in it; indeed it is hard *not* to think of such a world.

So here stands the accused, perfectly capable of making a delightful, happy, painless world but instead he has deliberately made this dreadful place. What possible defence can be put up for him?

Before I start my case for the defence may I just say what I will *not* resort to. I have already said that I am not going to make a plea of diminished responsibility on the grounds of incapacity. I am not going to say that God is innocent because he is

Herbert McCabe 'Evil' from *New Blackfriars*, vol. 62 (1981), republished in *God Matters* (Geoffrey Chapman, 1987), reprinted by permission of Continuum International Publishing Group Ltd and the author.

not omnipotent. Secondly I am not going to question the evidence: there are some people who would say that evil is not real, that it is only an illusion and if we look at it the right way it disappears like the ghost at the corner of the stairs. But I shall not be arguing that 'it's all in the mind', that nothing's good or bad, but thinking makes it so. I admit wholeheartedly that when someone says: 'My toothache hurts like mad', or 'that cow is suffering from a disease', or 'Charlie is a wicked and depraved man', he is making quite literal true statements, just as literal and true as the statement that London is in England. So I accept the evidence; evil is real. I shall not be using the 'unreality of evil' defence.

Thirdly, another defence is not open to me. This is the defence that at least some of the evil in the world is not caused by God but by the free actions of people. God, this defence goes, can hardly be held responsible for what men do freely, and a great deal of the awfulness of the world is due to the viciousness of men and women. Now, I hold that all my free acts are caused by God, that I do not act independently of God, and so I can hardly get my client off the hook by putting the blame on someone else.

So I shall not defend God on the grounds that he is incompetent, or that the evidence is phoney or on grounds of mistaken identity—that someone else did it. God is omnipotent, the world he made is full of evils and they were not put there by human beings independently of God.

1. I am going to argue that everything good in the world is brought about by my client.

2. I am going to argue that some kinds of evil—suffering—what I shall call 'evil suffered' is a necessary concomitant of certain kinds of good, and God can only be said, therefore, to have brought it about in the sense that he brought about that good.

3. I am going to argue that another kind of evil—sin—what I shall call 'evil done' is not brought about by God at all. I shall grant that he could have prevented it, but I shall give reasons why this does not make my client guilty by neglect.

So God brings about everything that is good and he does not directly bring about anything that is evil; if this can be shown it seems a sufficient defence, even if it leaves a great deal that we do not understand.

Let us now consider the evidence: and first of all let us ask what it is supposed to be evidence *of*. It is evidence of evil; but what do we mean when we say that something is evil or bad. I am using the words more or less synonymously but I suppose that 'evil' has a rather more sinister ring in English than 'bad'. A bad man and an evil man are much the same, but a bad washing machine wouldn't ordinarily be called evil. Perhaps we usually keep 'evil' for moral evil, for the evil that belongs to human beings or to other creatures that are free and act deliberately, like human beings, devils and such like.

Let us look then, first of all at badness. The charge is made that God made a bad world, when he could have made a better one. Let us see what this means.

First of all, I suppose you will agree that there is no such *thing* as badness just as there is no such thing as redness. There are just bad things, as there are red things. You never get badness unless there is first of all something that exists that is bad, just as you never get redness unless there is first of all something to be red.

Badness is not like milk or chewing gum, something that a cow or a man or God might make, it is the *character* of something that has been made. The charge against God, then, is not that he made something called badness, there is no such thing. The charge is that some of the things he made are bad, just as, some of them are red.

Now what exactly are we saying when we say that a thing is bad? Here we come immediately to a difference between badness and redness. For all red things share a *property* in common, the property of being red. If you know what it is like for an apple to be red then you more or less know what it is like for a pencil or a nose to be red.

But this won't work with badness; if you know what it is like for a deckchair to be a bad deckchair you do not for that reason know what it is like for a grape to be a bad grape. A bad deckchair collapses when you sit down, but the fact that a grape collapses when you sit on it is not what would show it to be a bad grape.

We call something a bad deckchair when it doesn't come up to our expectations for deckchairs, and we call something a bad grape when it doesn't come up to our expectations for grapes. But they are different expectations. And similarly when we say that a thing is a good grape or a good deckchair we mean that they do come up to our respective expectations for grapes and deckchairs. Goodness, like badness, is different from redness in that what it is like for one thing to be good isn't the same as what it is like for another. The fact that wine can be made from good grapes has no tendency at all to suggest that wine can be made from good deckchairs.

Now notice that whenever we say something is bad we are saying that it *doesn't* come up to expectations; we are saying, in fact, something negative about it. A bad washing machine is one that won't wash the clothes properly—notice that this makes badness a good deal less *specific* than goodness. If someone says he has a good washing machine you know pretty well what it is like—it cleans the clothes quickly and efficiently and quietly and cheaply and so on. But if someone just says his washing machine is a bad one, you don't know yet whether it tears the clothes into strips or soaks them in oily water or just doesn't move at all when you switch on, or electrocutes the children when they go near it. It can be bad for an indefinite number of reasons so long as the one negative thing is true: that it doesn't come up to expectations for a washing machine.

So badness is a negative thing. Please notice carefully that this does *not* mean that a bad washing machine always has to have a part missing— it is not negative in that sense. A washing machine may be bad not only because it has too little—as when there is no driving belt on the spin drier, but also because it has too much, as when someone has filled the interior with glue. Badness is negative just in the sense that a bad thing doesn't succeed in measuring up to our expectations. Badness, then, is always a defect, an absence, in this sense.

So not only is there no such thing as badness in the sense that there is no such *thing* as redness (for redness, even if it is not a *thing* is at least a positive quality of a thing); but badness isn't even that, it is the *lack* of some positive quality in a thing—the positive quality of being a clothes-cleaner for example. And do remember that it is a lack of precisely that positive quality which we think is to be *expected* of a thing. We say 'That is a bad bottle' because it won't hold the liquid as we expect bottles to do; we don't say it is bad because it hasn't got a ten-foot neck as we expect giraffes to have. So badness is just a lack, but a particular lack.

Now does this mean that badness is unreal? Certainly not. Things really are bad sometimes and this is because the absence of what is to be expected is just as real as a presence. If I have a hole in my sock, the hole is not anything at all, it is just an absence of wool or cotton or whatever, but it is a perfectly real hole in my sock. It would be absurd to say that holes in socks are unreal and illusory just because the hole isn't made of anything and is purely an absence. *Nothing* in the wrong place can be just as real and just as important as *something* in the wrong place. If you inadvertently drive your car over a cliff you will have nothing to worry about; it is precisely the nothing that you will have to worry about.

So badness is quite real even though it isn't the name of a stuff like milk or even the name of a quality like redness.

Everything I have said about bad washing machines and bottles is just as true of bad men and women. We call a person bad (or in this case sometimes, evil or wicked) just because he or she doesn't measure up to what we think we can expect of human beings. Cruelty, injustice, selfishness, are just dispositions or activities that don't measure up to our idea of what a proper human being should be like, they are not fitting to a human being. We may find it a lot harder to be clear about what *is* fitting to a human being than we are about what is fitting to a washing machine, because all a washing machine has to do, so far as we are concerned, is wash the clothes properly; it is an instrument that we expect to function in a certain way. People, of course, aren't instruments in that way; they are not just good because they do some job well, and so the whole thing is more complicated. But it doesn't matter how we decide this matter and it doesn't matter whether we disagree about *what* makes a human being a proper human being; the thing is that if we call a man bad we mean he doesn't measure up to whatever it is that we expect of a man.

Let us remember that with people, as with washing machines, to say that they are bad is not always to say that they lack some part or other. A washing machine may be bad and defective for very positive reasons like being full of glue, and a man may be bad and defective for very positive reasons like being full of hatred or lust, but what makes us call this bad is that just as the positive glue stops the washing machine washing, so the positive hatred or lust stops the man being human enough.

Now let us also notice that since badness is a defect it is always parasitic on good. I mean by that that you can't have badness unless there is at least some goodness, whereas you can have goodness without any badness. The two are not symmetrical, so to say. I mean that if a washing machine is to be a bad one it must be at least good enough at being a washing machine for us to call it one. If I produce a cup and saucer and complain that it is a useless washing machine because it never gets the clothes clean, you will gently correct me and explain that what I have is not a washing machine at all. So even the worst washing machine must be a little good, otherwise it is not even a washing machine and cannot therefore be a bad one. But it doesn't work the other way round. Goodness does not mean a defect in badness. You could, theoretically, have something that was just very good with no defects at all. You could probably have a perfectly good washing machine with nothing wrong with it at all, were it not for built-in obsolescence and the capitalist modes of production.

So now if we are fairly clear about what, if you want to be pompous, you can call the logic of the words 'bad' and 'good' and 'evil', we can take a look at some of the pieces of evidence against my client, God. There are I think two main exhibits:

There is the badness that *happens to* people and things; that is exhibit A. Then there is the evil that people *do*, that is exhibit B. I think this covers all the evil there is. The first kind is evil that comes to something from outside, as when bacteria attack a healthy horse and it falls sick, or when a lion attacks a lamb and chews it up. The agent that brings about the unpleasantness is separate from the one that suffers.

The second kind of evil is evil that is not brought about by some outside agent but is self-inflicted, and this is moral evil or sin. I mean by this that if a man can show that what he did was not really due to him but was caused by something outside him—he was acting under the influence of drugs or hypnotism or something—then we stop blaming him, we say he hasn't really sinned, we sympathise with him as one who has *suffered* evil rather than as one who himself *inflicts* it.

Let us look first at the evil suffered in the world. Let us be clear that by no stretch of the imagination can this be attributed to the viciousness of men and women, or hardly any of it can. For millions upon millions of years before the human race even appeared, dinosaurs were setting upon each other or upon harmless plants and chewing them up, undoubtedly inflicting evil on them; a plant that has been chewed by a dinosaur is nothing like as good a plant as it was before. The lamb that is attacked by a lion speedily becomes a very defective lamb.

When however, we look into the business of the lion eating the lamb we see that necessarily what is a defect suffered by the lamb is at the same time a fulfilment or achievement for the lion. The lion is being fulfilled, indeed he is being filled, precisely by what damages the lamb and renders it defective. In fact there can never be a defect inflicted on one thing except by another thing that is, in doing so, perfecting itself. When I suffer from a disease it is because the bacteria or whatever are fulfilling themselves and behaving exactly as good bacteria should behave. If we found a bacterium which was not engaged in inflicting disease on me we should have to judge that, like a washing machine that did not wash clothes, it was a defective or sick bacterium. The things that inflict evil on me, therefore, are not themselves evil; on the contrary, it is by being good in their way that they make me bad in my way.

Being eaten by a lion is undoubtedly bad for a lamb; it is not just that it *seems* bad from some point of view; it actually *is* bad from the lamb's point of view. On the other hand, it actually is good from the lion's point of view. Good and bad are relative but they are not just subjective.

Thus if God is to make a lion, and a good lion, he cannot but allow for the defect of the lamb; that is the kind of things that lions and lambs are. It is no reflection on God's omnipotence that he cannot make good lions without allowing for damaged lambs. However omnipotent God may be he cannot compose a string quartet for three instruments or five. It belongs to being a quartet that it is for four instruments; and in a somewhat similar way it belongs to being a lion that it wants to eat lambs.

In general, it seems to me that you cannot make material things that develop in time without allowing for the fact that in perfecting themselves they will damage other material things. Life evolves in the course of the constant interaction of things which includes the damaging and destroying of things. But every occasion of destruction is, of itself an occasion of good for the thing that is doing the destroying—always with the single exception of the free creature which may sometimes while destroying something else be simultaneously destroying itself, but of that more in a moment.

Ordinarily it is by being good little bacteria or good healthy lions that the agents of destruction work, and it is God who makes them to be good bacteria and good lions. He does not directly cause the defectiveness of the sick animals and chewed sheep that are the concomitant of this; for defectiveness as such does not exist, it is a mere absence. But in creating good lions we can certainly say that God brings it about *indirectly* that there shall be evil suffered. He brings it about because it is not possible to bring about this good without allowing for the concomitant defects. None of this, I submit, shows that God is guilty of deliberately proposing and bringing about evil.

You may be tempted to argue that it would be better not to have any lions at all— but if you think along those lines you have to end up thinking that it would be better not to have any material world at all—and indeed I think that some Buddhist thinkers have reached this very conclusion. But then you do have to change the charge against my client; it is not that he has made a bad world but that he has made a material world at all. This does not sound a very damning charge; most people are rather glad that he did so and even sometimes thank him for it.

Now it may be argued that God could have made a material world without *so much* sheer pain in it. But let us look at what is being said if we say this. Ordinarily if I have a headache the doctor will explain what brought it about—it was that fifth whiskey last night. It was the whiskey behaving like good whiskey—as whiskey may be expected to behave—which brought about my headache. There is no mystery about my headache. Similarly with my cancer or my influenza—always there is a natural explanation and always the explanation is in terms of some things, cells or germs or whatever, doing what comes naturally, being good. Sometimes of course and rather more often than he admits, the doctor is baffled. But he puts this down to his own ignorance; he says: 'Well eventually we may hope to find out what is causing this, what things are bringing it about simply by being their good selves, but for the moment we don't know'. What he does *not* say is this: there is no explanation in nature for this, it is an anti-miracle worked by a malignant God.

But that is what he would *have* to say if he thought there was more pain in the world than there need be. More suffering than there need be would be suffering that had no natural cause, this was not the obverse of some good, that was scientifically inexplicable. Now I do not think that any one in a scientific tradition would believe in the existence of such suffering, except perhaps in one case, in the case of evil inflicted by a malignant free cause such as a wicked man or a demon. Given that his acts are free, then they are not caused and thus cannot be explained by the fulfilment of natural things like germs and viruses. But leaving aside for the moment, the pain and agony of the world is just what you would expect to find in a material world—no more and no less. If we think otherwise we do not just give up belief in a good God, we give up belief in the rational scientific intelligibility of the world.

Of course God could have made a kind of material world and then by a series of miraculous interventions prevented any suffering in it. He could have fed the lion miraculously without damaging any lambs, and so on throughout the order of nature. But such a world would have no reason or order within itself. Lions would not do things because they were lions, but simply because of the miraculous action of God. What we mean by the miraculous action of God is indeed simply the non-presence of natural causes and explanations. A miracle is not God intervening in the world—God is always acting in the world—a miracle is when *only* God is acting in the world.

A world without any defects suffered, then, would be a world without any natural order in it. No reasonable person objects to an occasional withdrawal of natural causes, a miracle from time to time; but a world without *any* natural causes, entirely consisting of miracles, would not be a natural material world at all. So the people who would like my client to have made a material world without suffering and defect would have preferred him not to have made a world subject to its own laws, an autonomous scientifically explicable world. But here again I would say most people are pleased that he made such a world which, so to say, runs by itself according to its own scientific laws. The accusation that God made it does not seem very damning.

Perhaps I should add a little note here about pain. You might find some people saying: yes we can see how if lions are to be good lions then lambs will have to die, but why does it all have to be so agonisingly painful? Surely God could have stopped that. Not so; pain is, in fact, a good and necessary thing from one point of view. If the lamb were not hurt by the lion it would not be afraid of it—except maybe by a miracle, and then we are back with the previous discussion. I happen to know of a young girl who is highly intelligent but by some malfunctioning of the brain or nervous system is incapable of feeling pain—she once left her hand in a pan of boiling water and damaged it terribly because she was not warned by pain. She had a special frame strapped to her because of the damage she has done to her limbs by unnoticed collisions and accidents. Her case shows the value of pain, its evolution-ary significance. If pain were unnecessary for our survival we would long ago have discarded it like our tails.

It is true of course that some pain seems to go above and beyond the call of duty—we can understand why it needs to hurt but not why it needs to hurt so much. Take dying of rabies for example. But I think if you investigated the matter, and taking into account that it is not just the human animal but all the other animals and even the rabies virus that has to be considered, you would find that none of this was without scientific explanation. The pain of rabies is not, like the warning pain of boiling water, useful to *us*, but it follows necessarily on what is good and useful for other things. I think, then, that Exhibit A, the pain and suffer-ing of the world, has not sufficed to convict my client, God, of crime in creating this world. Let us then turn to Exhibit B, the wickedness of the world.

Here I am bound to admit, my client faces his most dangerous threat. There are, as I have said, those who think otherwise. For them, wickedness, at least, is not due to God; it is an offence against God which he would rather not have happen. It is due to wicked human wills and the actions of these, being free, are not caused by God. God, they will argue, could have prevented evil, but only by making humans unfree; and just as it is a great glory to have a real material world with its own laws of action even though this has to involve pain and suffering; so it is a great glory to have free creatures even if this involves at least the risk of some sin and wickedness.

This cosy escape route is not, however, open to me. I hold that there is nothing existing in the world that he did not create. There is no being which does not depend on him. All my good acts, are more due to him than they are to me, since it is due to him that they are due to me. He makes me *me*. So what about my bad deeds?

First I think we need to be clear that unlike evil suffered, evil done, sin, is *not* an inevitable concomitant of good in the world. There could not be a material world, developing according to its own laws, without evil suffered but there most certainly could be a material human world without evil done. A world without selfishness and greed and cruelty and domination would obviously be a happier, pleasanter, livelier, more sensuously enjoyable world than the one we have now. Evil suffered is the obverse of good achieved but evil done has no connection with good at all, except accidentally. That is to say God may bring good even out of my evil acts but in themselves they have no good aspect. This is because evil done, moral evil, is self-inflicted. Whereas in evil suffered there are two beings to be considered, the one inflicting the harm and the one suffering it: (for one what is done is good; while for the other, it is evil); in evil done the harm is done to the agent which causes it.

In the case of the lion eating the lamb, what makes this bad for the lamb is that its lambness, so to say, is diminished. It becomes less like what we expect of a lamb; but what brings this about is the lion. But in the case of, say, Fred being unjust what makes this bad for Fred is that his humanity is diminished, he becomes less like what we expect of a man, but what brings this about is Fred himself. In the lamb/ lion encounter at least the perpetrator, the lion, is benefiting, but in Fred's act of injustice the perpetrator, Fred, is precisely the one who suffers.

Perhaps I should make that a little clearer because there may well be those who think that what makes an action morally wrong is the harm it does to others, and they may be a little surprised that I say that what makes an action morally wrong is the harm it does to the perpetrator. An action may be morally wrong *because* it does harm to others, but what we *mean* by saying that it is morally wrong is that it damages the perpetrator. I can after all do a great deal of harm to others without doing morally wrong at all. I may bring with me to a foreign country some deadly infectious disease that I don't know about, so that in a few weeks people are dying in agony because of my arrival. If so, I have certainly harmed them by my arrival but I have not done anything morally wrong. If however I knew about it and went all the same, then you could well say that I was acting unjustly, that I was behaving in an irresponsible way in which no human being should behave, that I was defective in my humanity, that I was committing a moral evil. The moral evil would *consist* in the injustice and the way that I had diminished myself in acting like that.

When I am the cause of frightful things happening to others, the evil suffered is in them and is inflicted by me, but if in doing this I am acting unjustly (as would ordinarily be the case if I did it deliberately) the evil done is in me and consists in the diminishment of my humanity that injustice means. I do not mean by this that acting unjustly has a bad *effect* on me (making me a drearier person or whatever). I mean that acting unjustly *is* a bad effect on me, it *is* a diminishment of me, just as not being able to rinse the clothes *is* a diminishment of the washing machine. And the point is that this diminishment of me is brought about by me. So there is no separate agent to achieve something by diminishing me, as the lion achieves something by diminishing the lamb; evil done is evil to the perpetrator himself. It is a dead loss with no good aspect to it.

Of course morally evil actions may have good *effects*, my injustice may benefit my family, my adultery may give birth to a child, but what we mean when we say they are morally bad, if we think they *are* bad, is the defect that they are in me.

You will remember that when God was accused of damaging lambs, I was able to reply for him that what he was really doing was creating and sustaining lions: this was the good thing he was engaged in doing; the evil to the lamb was merely a necessary concomitant to this. But now in the case of moral evil, no such course is open to me. Moral evil is not the concomitant of some good. It is, as I said, sheer loss.

Of course God may bring good even out of my evil actions, and good may even be the ordinary consequence of my evil action, but that is not the point. The action itself has no good in it, and we cannot exonerate God simply on the grounds that it is for good ends that he uses evil means.

My defence is quite different, it is simply this: since there is no good at all except incidentally, in a morally evil act, in evil done, there is nothing created there, hence no action of God. A morally evil act as such is an absence of something, a failure on my part to live as humanly, as intensely as I might have done. Evidently God does not bring about failure as such, for failure is not there, it is an absence. When, as in the case of the lamb, the failure is brought about by the fulfilment of something else, then indeed God can be said in a Pickwickian way to have brought about the failure, but only because he brought about the fulfilment of the lion. But here there is sheer failure on my part, not brought by the fulfilment of some outside agent, but simply allowed by me. So God has no hand in it at all.

When I do evil I have a choice between what will fulfil me as a human being, as what I truly am, and some lesser good which conflicts with this fulfilment: say I have to choose between being just and being rich. There is no harm in being rich of course, unless, as it usually does, it conflicts with being just. If I then choose the riches unjustly I have failed in being human, and that is moral evil.

I could not, of course, act unjustly unless I existed and were sustained in being by God, I could not do it unless every positive action I took were sustained in being by God. My desire for riches is a positive thing, and a perfectly good positive thing, created by God—the only thing is that it is a *minor* thing. I should desire other things more than this. My failure to seek my true happiness and fulfilment, of course, since it is a failure, an absence, a non-being, is not created or sustained or brought about by God.

There are no such things as evil desires, there is only evil disproportion in our desires; human evil, moral evil lies in sacrificing great things for the sake of trivial things, it lies in the failure to want happiness enough.

It is evident, then, that though it is due to God that any good and positive thing is due to me, it is not due to God that any moral failure is due to me. God does not make absences, non-beings, failures. On this count then my client is fully exonerated and his character has no visible stain on it.

But, and I think this will be the final argument from the prosecution, must we not admit that although God did not, of course, bring about my failure he could, instead, have brought about my success? In fact it was the fact that God did not cause me freely to succeed that brought it about that I freely failed. There can be no doubt, then, that had he wished to do so God could always have prevented me from sinning—without, of course, in any way interfering with my freedom. For freedom does not mean independence of God. It means independence of other creatures. Thus although God does not cause me to fail of choosing the good, he could easily have caused me to choose the good. In what way, asks the prosecutor, is my client's position any different from that of the careless helmsman who fails to steer the ship clear of the rocks? Is he not guilty of neglect in permitting me to sin?

Let me say just once more that there is no question of God *having to* permit me to sin in order to leave me with my freedom. *That* kind of argument belongs to a theory that freedom makes me independent of God. In fact God could have made a world in which nobody ever sinned at all and everyone was perfectly free. In such a world, if it were material and historical, there would certainly have to be suffering as the obverse of the good of material things, but there would be no need whatever for sin. Sin has no useful function in the world except by accident.

Is God, then, guilty by neglect? I think that he is not, for this reason. You can only be guilty by neglect if you have some kind of obligation to do something and you do not do it. It is the helmsman who is accused of neglect, and not the cabin-boy, because it is the helmsman's *job* to steer the ship. Now by no stretch of the imagination is it God's *job* to prevent me from sinning. In his mercy and kindness he frequently does so, and frequently he gives me the grace to repent of the sins I have committed, but this is not his job, his *métier*. There can be no sense in the idea that God has *any* job or is under any obligation; if he were, there would be something greater than God which constrained him. God is no more under an obligation to prevent me from sinning than he was under an obligation to create the world in the first place. He cannot therefore be said to be guilty by neglect.

Chapter 57

God and human freedom

Thomas Aquinas

BUT if God's providence is the cause of everything that happens in the world, or at the very least all good things, it seems that everything *must* happen the way it does: firstly, because he knows it and his knowledge can't be mistaken, so what he knows must necessarily happen; and secondly, because he wills it and his will can't be ineffective, so everything he wills, it seems, must necessarily happen. But these objections depend on thinking of knowledge in God's mind and the working of God's will on the model of such activities in us, when they are in fact very different.

For firstly, in regard to knowledge we should note that a mind contained in some way within time relates differently to the knowing of what happens in time from a mind altogether outside time. A convenient illustration may be drawn from space, since, according to Aristotle, the successiveness of time derives from that of change and movement, and that from extended successiveness in space. So if we imagine many people travelling a road, all those travelling will have knowledge of the people in front and behind them, according to their beforeness and afterness in space. And so each traveller will see the people next to him and the people in front, but not the people behind. But if someone is outside the whole travelling situation, standing in some high tower, for example, from which he can see the whole road, then he will have a bird's-eye of every traveller, not seeing them as in front or behind in relation to his own seeing, but seeing them all together in front and behind each other. Now since our knowing occurs within time, either in itself or incidentally (so that when making propositional connections and disconnections we have to add tense, as Aristotle points out), things are known as present or past or future. Present events are known as actually existing and perceptible to the senses in some way; past events are remembered; and future events are not known in themselves—because they don't yet exist—but can be predicted from their causes: with certainty if their causes totally determine them, as with things that must happen; conjecturally if they are not so determined that they cannot be obstructed, as with things that happen usually; and not at all if they are only possible and not determined to either one side or the other, as with things that *might be either*, for we know things not by their potentialities but by what is realized in them, as Aristotle says. God's knowing, however, is altogether outside time, as if he stands on the summit of eternity where

Thomas Aquinas 'Commentary on Aristotle's *Peri Hermeneias*' from *Thomas Aquinas Selected Philosophical Writings* selected and translated with an introduction and notes by Timothy McDermott (Oxford World's Classics, 1993), copyright © Timothy McDermott 1993, reprinted by permission of Oxford University Press.

everything exists together, looking down in a single simple glance on the whole course of time. So in his one glance he sees everything going on throughout time, and each as it is in itself, not as something future to himself and his seeing and visible only as it exists within its causal situation (although he sees that causal situation). But he sees things altogether eternally, each as it exists in its own time, just as our human eye sees John sitting there himself, not just as something determined by causes. Nor does our seeing John sitting there stop it being an event that might not have been when regarded just in relation to its causes. And yet while he is sitting there we see him sitting there with certainty and without doubt, since when a thing exists in itself it is already determined. In this way then God knows everything that happens in time with certainty and without doubt, and yet the things that happen in time are not things that must exist or must come to exist, but things that might or might not be.

A similar difference must be noted in regard to God's will; for God's will is to be thought of as existing outside the realm of existents, as a cause from which pours forth everything that exists in all its variant forms; Now *what can be* and *what must be* are variants of being, so that it is from God's will itself that things derive whether they must be or may or may not be and the distinction of the two according to the nature of their immediate causes. For he prepares causes that must cause for those effects that he wills must be, and causes that might cause but might fail to cause for those effects that he wills might or might not be. And it is because of the nature of their causes that some effects are said to be effects that must be and others effects that need not be, although all depend on God's will as primary cause, a cause which transcends this distinction between *must* and *might not*. But the same cannot be said of human will or of any other cause, since every other cause exists within the realm of *must* and *might not*. So of every other cause it must be said either that it can fail to cause, or that its effect must be and cannot not be; God's will, however, cannot fail, and yet not all his effects must be, but some can be or not be.

In the same way some people strive to uproot the other root of *may or may not be*—that which Aristotle here identifies with our ability to deliberate—wanting to show that will when it chooses is compelled to move by what it desires. For since the object of willing is what is good, it doesn't seem possible to turn away will from desiring what seems to it good, just as reason can't be turned away from assenting to what seems to it true. And so it seems that any choice consequent on deliberation will always be made under compulsion; so that everything which takes its rise from our deliberation and choice will be done under compulsion. But the answer to this is that goods differ just as truths do. Certain truths like the first unprovable premisses of all proofs are self-evident and compel the assent of mind; but certain truths are not self-evident but evident for other reasons. And there are two sorts of such truth. Some follow necessarily from the premisses, and given the truth of the premisses can't be false, and these are all provable conclusions; the mind must assent to such truths once it has perceived their relation to the premisses, though not before. Other truths don't follow necessarily from the premisses and even given the truth of the premisses they can be false; they are matters of opinion and the mind doesn't have to assent to them, although it may, for some motive or other, incline to one side or the other. Now in the same way there is also a certain good which is desirable for its own sake, namely, happiness, which has the nature of ultimate goal, and the will is compelled to adhere to that good, for there is a sort of natural compulsion on everyone to want to be happy. But there are other goods which are desirable for the sake of the goal, and can be compared to the goal as conclusions are to premisses, in the way Aristotle explains. If then there were goods which were *sine qua nons* of happiness, these too would compel desire, and most of all in a person that perceived the connection: and existence, life, understanding, and the like are perhaps goods like these. But the particular goods to which human activity is directed are not like this, and are not seen as *sine qua nons* of happiness: eating or not eating this food or that, for instance; but something in them attracts desire according to the good we see in them. And so our wills are not compelled to choose them. And it is worthy of notice for this reason that Aristotle identified the root of *might or might not be* in what we do with deliberation, which is concerned with as yet undetermined means to a goal. For, as Aristotle says, when the means are already determined there is no role for deliberation.

Questions for discussion

1. Is there really a problem of evil? If so, how should it be articulated?
2. How should we understand the statement 'God is good'? On what basis can we claim to arrive at a true understanding of what the statement should be taken to mean?
3. Might evil be said to derive from God? If so, why? If not, why not?
4. How might one's understanding of what God is influence one's approach to the problem of evil?
5. Should we say that God is justified in bringing about or permitting the evil we encounter?
6. Could God have made a world in which free people always act well? If so, why? If not, why not?

Advice on further reading

For three excellent readers on the problem of evil, see Marilyn McCord Adams and Robert Merrihew Adams (eds), *The Problem of Evil* (Oxford, 1990); Nelson Pike (ed.), *God and Evil: Readings on the Theological Problem of Evil* (London, 1971); and Daniel Howard-Snyder (ed.) *The Evidential Argument from Evil* (Bloomington and Indianapolis, Indiana, 1996). For a (now slightly outdated) survey of recent discussions of God and evil, see Barry L. Whitney, *What are They Saying About God and Evil?* (New York, 1989).

Significant books on the problem of evil include:

Marylin Adams, *Horrendous Evils and the Goodness of God* (Ithaca and London, 1999).

M. B. Ahern, *The Problem of Evil* (London, 1971).

A. Farrer, *Love Almighty and Ills Unlimited* (London, 1961).

P. T. Geach, *Providence and Evil* (Cambridge, 1977).

John Hick, *Evil and the God of Love* (2nd edn, London, 1975).

E. Madden and P. Hare, *Evil and the Concept of God* (Springfield, Massachusetts,1968).

Kenneth Surin, *Theology and the Problem of Evil* (Oxford, 1986).

Peter Vardy, *The Puzzle of Evil* (London, 1992).

For an introduction to some biblical thinking on God and evil, see James L. Crenshaw, *Theodicy in the Old Testament* (Philadelphia and London, 1983). For an account of Augustine on evil, see G. R. Evans, *Augustine on Evil* (Cambridge, 1982). For an account of Aquinas on God and evil, see Brian Davies, *The Thought of Thomas Aquinas* (Oxford, 1992), ch. 5.

Many discussions of God and evil clearly assume that God (if he exists) must be morally good (or well behaved). This is not what, for example, Augustine or Aquinas would have thought. For discussions of the question 'Is God's goodness moral goodness?', see Brian Davies, 'How is God Love?', in Luke Gormally (ed.), *Moral Truth and Moral Tradition: Essays in Honour of Peter Geach and Elizabeth Anscombe* (Dublin and Portland, Oreg., 1994) and Brian Davies, 'The Problem of Evil', in Brian Davies (ed.), *Philosophy of Religion: A Guide to the Subject* (London, 1998).

Part VI

Morality and religion

Introduction

The moral and the religious

How should we behave? Can we offer rationally grounded judgements on the worth of what people do? Or are our evaluations of people and their behaviour simply ways of expressing our non-rational tastes, likes, and dislikes? Are human actions capable of being intrinsically good? Can they be intrinsically bad? Should we speak of people as having duties or obligations? Are there virtues and vices? Are there rules for human conduct which we need to learn in order to live well or appropriately? Are there goods we should strive for which somehow transcend the material world?

These are some of the major questions posed by moral philosophers. But not only philosophers ask them. Most people tend to raise some or all of them sooner or later. For most people at some time or other wonder about morality or ethics. We cannot avoid acting. And we cannot avoid reacting to the actions of others. So what could be more natural than to seek guidance as we do so? What could be more natural than to ask questions of the kind just listed?

But do moral questions lead to religious ones? Though millions of people would speak of themselves as having moral beliefs, far fewer would describe themselves as having religious ones. Yet can one do justice to moral matters without reference to the notion of religious truth? Might it even be said that reflection on morality should lead us to embrace some religious beliefs? Or should we, perhaps, conclude that correct reflection on morality suggests that we should reject certain religious beliefs? Should we, perhaps, conclude that it should lead us to reject religion altogether?

These questions would have struck many people of earlier times than ours as puzzling in the extreme. For, as H. O. Mounce explains:

> The moral as a distinct or autonomous category is of comparatively recent origin. In earlier cultures, there was no sharp distinction between the moral and the religious. The Ten Commandments of the Ancient Hebrews will serve as an example. The first four concern our duties to God; the remaining six, our duties to our neighbour. Nowadays, it may be said that the last six are moral, the first four religious. But to the Ancient Hebrews there was no such distinction. Throughout, the commands instruct us in our duties to God. Thus the last six do not instruct us in how to serve our neighbour as distinct from serving God. Rather they instruct us in how God wishes us to serve him in our dealings with our neighbour.[1]

And, as some philosophers have held, much that we might today take to be purely moral discourse and belief arguably derives from religious ways of thinking and is unintelligible apart from them.[2] But many philosophers have thought it profitable to distinguish

---

1. H. O. Mounce, 'Morality and Religion', in Brian Davies (ed.), *Philosophy of Religion: A Guide to the Subject* (London, 1998), p. 253.
2. Cf. G. E. M. Anscombe, 'Modern Moral Philosophy', *Philosophy* 33 (1958) and Alasdair MacIntyre, *After Virtue* (Notre Dame, Indiana, 1981).

between moral and religious beliefs and to consider what might be said about their relationship. In particular, they have thought it worth asking whether moral considerations should lead us to conclude that God exists.[3]

From morality to God?

One's approach to this question will much depend on how one conceives of moral thinking and discourse in the first place. Some philosophers have argued that there is no such thing as moral truth. On their account, sentences like 'Henry is a good man' or 'Genocide is wrong' are merely expressions of personal preferences or feelings and have no cognitive content. Hence, for example, according to A. J. Ayer:

In so far as statements of value are significant, they are ordinary 'scientific' statements; and . . . in so far as they are not scientific, they are not in the literal sense significant but are simply expressions of emotion which can be neither true nor false . . . The presence of an ethical symbol in a proposition adds nothing to its factual content. Thus if I say to someone, 'You acted wrongly in stealing that money,' I am not stating anything more than if I had simply said, 'You stole that money.' In adding that this action is wrong I am not making any further statement about it. I am simply evincing my moral disapproval of it. It is as if I had said, 'You stole that money,' in a peculiar tone of horror, or written it with the addition of some special exclamation marks. The tone, or the exclamation marks, adds nothing to the literal meaning of the sentence. It merely serves to show that the expression of it is attended by certain feelings in the speaker . . . In every case in which one would commonly be said to be making an ethical judgement, the function of the relevant ethical word is purely 'emotive'. It is used to express feeling about certain objects, but not to make any assertion about them.[4]

But what if one thinks that what Ayer calls 'statements of value' are either true or false? What if one thinks that it is objectively either true or false that Henry is good (i.e. true or false regardless of how anyone thinks or feels)? What if one thinks that it is objectively either true or false that genocide is wrong? Then, so one might conclude, one has beliefs with serious theological implications.

Such, at any rate, is what Immanuel Kant famously maintains. As you can see from Chapter 58, he argues that, since humanity ought to strive for moral perfection, and since it cannot be successful in this unless helped by divinity, God must exist to ensure that humanity can achieve that for which it must strive.

According to Kant, morality requires us to aim for the Highest Good, which means willing a proper return of happiness to those who pursue moral goodness. For him, therefore, willing the Highest Good means willing a correlation between moral rectitude and happiness. But now comes the snag. For in this life it is impossible to ensure what

---

3. They have also thought it profitable to pursue other questions such as 'Should religious beliefs determine standards for conduct set by political legislation?' and 'Are religious considerations relevant when it comes to questions concerning our treatment of our environment?'. Here, however, I focus on what, historically, has been the most debated philosophical issue with respect to morality and religion. For an introduction to other philosophical questions linking ethical thinking and philosophy of religion, see Philip L. Quinn and Charles Taliafero (eds), *A Companion to Philosophy of Religion* (Oxford, 1997), chs 62–5.

4. A. J. Ayer, *Language Truth and Logic* (Harmondsworth, 1971), pp. 136–43.

morality requires. For we are not omnipotent and bad things happen to good people in spite of our best efforts. So we have a problem on our hands. The Highest Good must be possible; but at one level it seems impossible.

How do we resolve the dilemma? Kant's answer is that we must postulate the existence of God as able to ensure that fidelity to moral requirements is properly rewarded. Why? Because the realization of the Highest Good can only be guaranteed if there is something able to ensure its realization. Or, as Kant puts it, practical reason obliges us to postulate the existence of God.

But this argument is not the only one that has been offered in defence of the view that morality gives us grounds for belief in God. Many writers have argued that one can infer the existence of God from the existence of moral commands or laws. These, it has been said, imply the existence of a moral law-giver or a moral commander. An example of someone arguing in this way is H. P. Owen, whose approach to the question of morality and God can be found in Chapter 59. In Owen's view: 'A clear choice faces us. Either we take moral claims to be self-explanatory modes of impersonal existence or we explain them in terms of a personal God.' In defending this thesis, Owen provides a particularly clear presentation of the view that moral thinking implies the existence of God.

Yet might it not be said that our moral thinking actually puts us in touch with God *directly* rather than *inferentially*? In Chapter 60 Illtyd Trethowan suggests that it does. For Trethowan, God is immediately present to people as they encounter objective goodness or value and as they recognize the claims which these make on us. In Trethowan's view, the most reasonable way of accounting for what we are aware of in morality (or in 'moral experience') is to say that its object is absolute, unconditioned, and the source of all creaturely value, especially that of people. For Trethowan, as for many religious thinkers, God is pure goodness or absolute value. Hence, so he argues, our awareness of goodness and value is nothing less than an awareness of God. In this sense, so Trethowan thinks, morality and religion come together. For him, moral experience is ultimately religious experience.

Moral goodness and God

In that case, however, how are we to think of the relation between God and moral goodness? Should we, for instance, say that God somehow *determines* what is morally good or bad. Or should we think of God as somehow subject to standards of moral goodness distinct from himself?

In Plato's dialogue *Euthyphro* Socrates asks: 'Is the holy loved by the gods because it is holy? Or is it holy because it is loved?' Suppose we change the wording of these questions so as to ask: 'Does God will X because it is morally good? Or is X morally good because God wills it?' If we say that God wills X because it is morally good, we would seem to be understanding moral truths in a very different way from authors such as Owen and Trethowan. For they might be summarized as saying 'The morally good is the will of God.' According to Owen, moral claims, duties, and obligations are divine commands. For Trethowan, moral demands and obligations are a summons from God. But how can that be? Normally, we accept advice on moral matters from people we think of as knowing the difference between good and evil. We do not take them as able to decree what good and evil amount to. So why should we suppose that something is morally good *because* God wills it?

As you will see, Owen addresses these questions as he comments on an important study on ethics and theology by W. G. Maclagan. And his conclusion is that God is the source of the moral imperatives to which we are subject. But many philosophers have felt highly uncomfortable with the suggestion that moral truths should be thought of as depending on God in any sense. For them, we have strong reason to resist any claim which looks remotely like saying 'X is morally good because God wills X'.[5]

Kant is someone who might be cited as thinking along these lines. For him, moral truths are independent of God. On his account, God is significant when it comes to morality only as ensuring that the requirements of morality are met. He says nothing to suggest that 'X is morally good' or 'X is morally obligatory' should be construed as meaning 'X is what it is because of God' or 'X is what it is because it is willed by God'. And many philosophers have agreed with Kant in this respect. A good example is Kai Nielsen, who in Chapter 61 trenchantly attacks the suggestion that morality should be thought of as grounded in anything we might take to be God's nature or will. For Nielsen, sound moral thinking is something *from which* to evaluate religious belief, including belief in God. Or, as he puts it: 'Morality cannot be based on religion. If anything, the opposite is partly true, for nothing can be God unless he or it is an object worthy of worship and it is our own moral insight which must tell us if anything at all could possibly be worthy of worship.'

Are religion and morality at odds?

Nielsen goes on to say that, in his opinion, nothing could be 'an object or being worthy of worship'. Why? Because he seems to think that to worship means to stop thinking and to defer to something other than oneself as determining what is right, wrong, true, or false. A philosopher agreeing with Nielsen on this matter is James Rachels. According to him, belief in God involves a total and unqualified commitment to obey God's commands. And, so Rachels suggests, such a commitment is not appropriate for a moral agent, since 'to be a moral agent is to be an autonomous or self-directed agent . . . The virtuous man is therefore identified with the man of integrity, i.e. the man who acts according to precepts which he can, on reflection, conscientiously approve in his own heart.'[6] With these thoughts in mind, Rachels goes on to maintain that one can actually disprove God's existence. He argues:

---

5. Notice, however, that philosophers sharing the view that moral imperatives can be thought of as deriving from God or from God's will (or commands) have also differed significantly when it comes to explaining and defending themselves. Some (e.g. William of Ockham) have held that God has the power to command absolutely anything and that we are bound to do anything which God commands. But others have argued that, though there are actions which God cannot command, there are some which he can. And others have offered yet other ways of explaining how moral action can be thought of as somehow grounded in God's nature or will.

6. 'God and Human Attitudes', *Religious Studies* 7 (1971), p. 334.

1. If any being is God, it must be a fitting object of worship.
2. No being could possibly be a fitting object of worship, since worship requires the abandonment of one's role as an autonomous moral agent.
3. Therefore, there cannot be any being who is God.

In a somewhat similar vein, Bertrand Russell argues that religious belief is positively inimical to true morality:

Religion prevents our children from having a rational education; religion prevents us from removing the fundamental causes of war; religion prevents us from teaching the ethic of scientific co-operation in place of the old fierce doctrines of sin and punishment. It is possible that mankind is on the threshold of a golden age; but if so, it will be necessary first to slay the dragon that guards the door, and this dragon is religion.[7]

Russell's judgement is probably not one which would be widely defended today among philosophers.[8] But one frequently encounters it in non-philosophical contexts. And its contrast between ethical thinking and religious thinking can also be found in the writings of philosophers who have no desire to denigrate religion as Russell does.

A famous example here is Kierkegaard (1813–55). In *Fear and Trembling* he considers the biblical story of Abraham being told by God to sacrifice Isaac (Genesis 22). He says that Abraham was bound to do what God commanded. 'Here', he adds, 'there can be no question of ethics in the sense of morality ... Ordinarily speaking, a temptation is something which tries to stop a man from doing his duty, but in this case it is ethics itself which tries to prevent him from doing God's will. But what then is duty? Duty is quite simply the expression of the will of God.'[9] In this connection Kierkegaard talks about 'a teleological suspension of the ethical', an idea which can also be traced in the work of D. Z. Phillips, according to whom religious belief provides religious believers with their standard for evaluating actions, a standard which is different from, and may be opposed to, a moral one. He writes:

The religious concept of duty cannot be understood if it is treated as a moral concept. When the believer talks of doing his duty, what he refers to is doing the will of God. In making a decision, what is important for the believer is that it should be in accordance with the will of God. To a Christian, to do one's duty *is* to do the will of God. There is indeed no difficulty in envisaging the 'ethical' as the obstacle to 'duty' in this context.[10]

Yet not all Christians would think of there being an opposition between duty and the 'ethical' in the manner of Kierkegaard and Phillips. Why? Mostly because they would

7. Bertrand Russel, *Why I am not a Christian* (London, 1927), p. 37.
8. But see, for example, Ray Billington, *Living Philosophy: An Introduction to Moral Thought* (2nd edn, London and New York, 1993), p. 189: 'After sixteen years as an ordained minister of the Church, and with several degrees in and books on theology behind me, I have over the ensuing years become increasingly convinced that Christianity, and theism generally, is more a force for harm than for good ... There have been "moral" Christians: but the connection has, I believe, been quite accidental.'
9. *Fear and Trembling*, trans. Robert Payne (London, New York, and Toronto, 1939), pp. 84 f.
10. 'God and Ought', in Ian Ramsey (ed.), *Christian Ethics and Contemporary Philosophy* (London, 1966), pp. 137 f.

deny that there could be any conflict between right moral thinking and right religious thinking. According, for example, to Augustine, God is perfectly good and is intrinsically incapable of willing evil. 'True inward justice', he argues, judges 'by the most righteous law of almighty God' and is unchanging.[11] According to Aquinas, the goodness for which we should always be aiming is nothing less than God himself:

The object of the will, that is the human appetite, is the Good without reserve, just as the object of the mind is the True without reserve. Clearly, then, nothing can satisfy our will except such goodness, which is found, not in anything created, but in God alone. Everything created is a derivative good.[12]

For Aquinas, as for Augustine, all right moral thinking accords with what God is all about. On this basis he famously maintains that human moral goodness is action in accord with an 'Eternal Law', namely God:

Law is nothing but a dictate of practical reason issued by a sovereign who governs a complete community. Granted that the world is ruled by divine Providence . . . it is evident that the whole community of the universe is governed by God's mind. Therefore the ruling idea of things which exists in God as the effective sovereign of them all has the nature of law. Then since God's mind does not conceive in time, but has an eternal concept . . . it follows that this law should be called eternal . . . Through his wisdom God is the founder of the universe of things, and . . . in relation to them he is like an artist with regard to the things he makes . . . [Also] he is the governor of all acts and motions to be found in each and every creature. And so, as being the principle through which the universe is created, divine wisdom means art, or exemplar, or idea, and likewise it also means law, as moving all things to their due ends. Accordingly the Eternal Law is nothing other than the exemplar of divine wisdom as directing the motions and acts of everything.[13]

On Aquinas's account, all things are subject to God and his will. And with this thought in mind he maintains that there is a sense in which rational agents with freedom can participate in God's will for them in a way that non-rational things cannot.

Since all things are regulated and measured by Eternal Law . . . it is evident that all somehow share in it, in that their tendencies to their own proper acts and ends are from its impression. Among them intelligent creatures are ranked under divine Providence the more nobly because they take part in Providence by their own providing for themselves and others. Thus they join in and make their own the Eternal Reason through which they have their natural aptitudes for their due activity and purpose. Now this sharing in the Eternal Law by intelligent creatures is what we call 'natural law'.[14]

But does it really make sense to think along these lines? Or might it not be more reasonable to conclude that morality has no religious significance or that religious belief is irrelevant or inimical to an accurate understanding of morality? The following chapters should help you to start thinking about these questions in a useful way, since they offer some influential answers to them in an accessible form.

11. Cf. *Confessions* III. vii. 13 ff. .
12. *Summa Theologiae*, 1a2ae. 2. 8.
13. Ibid., 1a2ae. 91.1 and 91.3.
14. Ibid., 1a2ae. 91. 2.

Chapter 58

God as a 'postulate' of sound moral thinking

Immanuel Kant

The existence of God as a postulate of pure practical reason

HAPPINESS is the condition of a rational being in the world, in whose whole existence everything goes according to wish and will. It thus rests on the harmony of nature with his entire end and with the essential determining ground of his will. But the moral law commands as a law of freedom through motives wholly independent of nature and of its harmony with our faculty of desire (as incentives). Still, the acting rational being in the world is not at the same time the cause of the world and of nature itself. Hence there is not the slightest ground in the moral law for a necessary connection between the morality and proportionate happiness of a being which belongs to the world as one of its parts and as thus dependent on it. Not being nature's cause, his will cannot by its own strength bring nature, as it touches on his happiness, into complete harmony with his practical principles. Nevertheless, in the practical task of pure reason, i.e., in the necessary endeavor after the highest good, such a connection is postulated as necessary: we *should* seek to further the highest good (which therefore must be at least possible). Therefore also the existence is postulated of a cause of the whole of nature, itself distinct from nature, which contains the ground of the exact coincidence of happiness with morality. This supreme cause, however, must contain the ground of the agreement of nature not merely with a law of the will of rational beings but with the idea of this law so far as they make it the supreme ground of determination of the will. Thus it contains the ground of the agreement of nature not merely with actions moral in their form but also with their morality as the motives to such actions, i.e., with their moral intention. Therefore, the highest good is possible in the world only on the supposition of a supreme cause of nature which has a causality corresponding to the moral intention. Now a being which is capable of actions by the idea of laws is an intelligence (a rational being), and the causality of such a being according to this idea of laws is his will. Therefore, the supreme cause of nature, in so far as it must be presupposed for the highest good, is a being which is the cause (and consequently the author) of nature through understanding and will, i.e., God. As a consequence; the postulate of the possibility of a highest derived

Immanuel Kant extracts from *Critique of Practical Reason* translated by Lewis White Beck (Bobbs-Merrill/Macmillan, 1956), reprinted by permission of Prentice Hall, Inc.

good (the best world) is at the same time the postulate of the reality of a highest original good, namely, the existence of God. Now it was our duty to promote the highest good; and it is not merely our privilege but a necessity connected with duty as a requisite to presuppose the possibility of this highest good. This presupposition is made only under the condition of the existence of God, and this condition inseparably connects this supposition with duty. Therefore, it is morally necessary to assume the existence of God.

It is well to notice here that this moral necessity is subjective, i.e., a need, and not objective, i.e., duty itself. For there cannot be any duty to assume the existence of a thing, because such a supposition concerns only the theoretical use of reason. It is also not to be understood that the assumption of the existence of God is necessary as a ground of all obligation in general (for this rests, as has been fully shown, solely on the autonomy of reason itself). All that here belongs to duty is the endeavor to produce and to further the highest good in the world, the existence of which may thus be postulated though our reason cannot conceive it except by presupposing a highest intelligence. To assume its existence is thus connected with the consciousness of our duty, though this assumption itself belongs to the realm of theoretical reason. Considered only in reference to the latter, it is a hypothesis, i.e., a ground of explanation. But in reference to the comprehensibility of an object (the highest good) placed before us by the moral law, and thus as a practical need, it can be called *faith* and even pure *rational faith*, because pure reason alone (by its theoretical as well as practical employment) is the source from which it springs.

The doctrine of Christianity, even when not regarded as a religious doctrine, gives at this point a concept of the highest good (the Kingdom of God) which is alone sufficient to the strictest demand of practical reason. The moral law is holy (unyielding) and demands holiness of morals, although all moral perfection to which man can attain is only virtue, i.e., a law-abiding disposition resulting from respect for the law and thus implying consciousness of a continuous propensity to transgress it or at least to a defilement, i.e., to an admixture of many spurious (not moral) motives to obedience to the law; consequently, man can achieve only a self-esteem combined with humility. And thus with respect to the holiness required by the Christian law, nothing remains to the creature but endless progress, though for the same reason hope of endless duration is justified. The worth of a character completely accordant with the moral law is infinite, because all possible happiness in the judgment of a wise and omnipotent dispenser of happiness has no other limitation than the lack of fitness of rational beings to their duty. But the moral law does not of itself promise happiness, for the latter is not, according to concepts of any order of nature, necessarily connected with obedience to the law. Christian ethics supplies this defect of the second indispensable component of the highest good by presenting a world wherein reasonable beings single-mindedly devote themselves to the moral law; this is the Kingdom of God, in which nature and morality come into a harmony, which is foreign to each as such, through a holy Author of the world, who makes possible the derived highest good. The holiness of morals is prescribed to them even in this life as a guide to conduct, but the well-being proportionate to this, which is bliss, is thought of as attainable only in eternity. This is due to the fact that the former must always be the pattern of their conduct in every state, and progressing toward it is even in this life possible and necessary, whereas the latter, under the name of happiness, cannot (as far as our own capacity is concerned) be reached in this life and therefore is made only an object of hope. Nevertheless, the Christian principle of morality is not theological and thus heteronomous, being rather the autonomy of pure practical reason itself, because it does not make the knowledge of God and His will the basis of these laws but makes such knowledge the basis only of succeeding to the highest good on condition of obedience to these laws; it places the real incentive for obedience to the law not in the desired consequences of obedience but in the conception of duty alone, in true observance of which the worthiness to attain the latter alone consists.

In this manner, through the concept of the highest good as the object and final end of pure practical reason, the moral law leads to religion. Religion is the recognition of all duties as divine commands, not as sanctions, i.e., arbitrary and contingent ordinances of a foreign will, but as essential laws of any free will as such. Even as such, they must be regarded as commands of the Supreme Being because we can hope for the highest good (to strive for which is our duty under the moral law) only from a morally perfect (holy and beneficent) and omnipotent will; and, therefore, we can hope to attain it only through harmony with this will. But here again everything remains disinterested and based only on duty, without being based on fear or hope as incentives, which, if they became principles, would destroy the entire moral worth of the actions. The moral law commands us to make the highest possible good in a world the final object of all our conduct. This I cannot hope to effect except through the agreement of my will with that of a holy and beneficent Author of the world. And although my own happiness is included in the concept of the highest good as a whole wherein the greatest happiness is thought of as connected in exact proportion to the greatest degree of moral perfection possible to creatures, still it is not happiness but the moral law (which, in fact, sternly places restricting conditions upon my boundless longing for happiness) which is proved to be the ground determining the will to further the highest good.

On the postulates of pure practical reason in general

The postulates of pure practical reason all proceed from the principle of morality, which is not a postulate but a law by which reason directly determines the will. This will, by the fact that it is so determined, as a pure will requires these necessary conditions for obedience to its precept. These postulates are not theoretical dogmas but presuppositions of necessarily practical import; thus, while they do not extend speculative knowledge, they give objective reality to the ideas of speculative reason in general (by means of their relation to the practical sphere), and they justify it in holding to concepts even the possibility of which it could not otherwise venture to affirm.

These postulates are those of immortality, of freedom affirmatively regarded (as the causality of a being so far as he belongs to the intelligible world), and of the existence of God. The first derives from the practically necessary condition of a duration adequate to the perfect fulfilment of the moral law. The second comes from the necessary presupposition of independence from the world of sense and of the capacity of determining man's will by the law of an intelligible world, i.e., the law of freedom itself; the third arises from the necessary condition of such an intelligible world by which it may be the highest good, through the presupposition of the highest independent good, i.e., the existence of God.

The prospect of the highest good, necessary through respect for the moral law and the consequent supposition of its objective reality, thus leads through postulates of practical reason to concepts which the speculative reason only exhibited as problems which it could not solve. It leads first to the problem of immortality, in the solution of which speculative reason could only commit paralogisms, because the marks of permanence, by which the psychological concept of an ultimate subject necessarily ascribed to the soul in self-consciousness, were lacking though they were needed to complete the real conception of a substance. Practical reason, through the postulates of fitness to the moral law in the highest good as the whole end of practical reason, consigns to this subject the requisite duration. Secondly, it leads to the concept which speculative reason contained only as an antinomy, and the solution of which it could base only on a problematical, though thinkable, concept whose objective reality was not provable or determinable by speculative reason. This is the cosmological idea of an intelligible world and the consciousness of our existence in it. It leads to this by means of the postulate of freedom (the reality of which practical reason exhibits in the moral law, at the same time exhibiting the law of an intelligible world, which the speculative reason could only indicate but whose concept it could not define). Thirdly, it gives significance to what speculative reason could indeed think but had to leave indeterminate as a mere transcendental ideal, i.e., to the theological concept of a First Being. This significance is given in a practical point of view, i.e., as a condition of the possibility of the object of a will determined by that law. It is that of a supreme principle of the highest good in an intelligible world having sovereign power in it by means of a moral legislation.

Is our knowledge really widened in such a way by pure practical reason, and is that which was transcendent for speculative reason immanent in practical reason? Certainly, but only from a practical point of view. For we thereby know neither the nature of our soul, nor the intelligible world, nor the Supreme Being as they are in themselves, but have only united the concepts of them in a practical concept of the highest good as the object of our will and have done so entirely a priori through pure reason. We have so united them only by means of the moral law and merely in relation to it, with respect to the object which it commands. But how freedom is possible, and how we should think theoretically and positively of this type of causality, is not thereby discovered. All that is comprehended is that such a causality is postulated through the moral law and for its sake. It is the same with the remaining ideas, whose possibility cannot be fathomed by human understanding, though no sophistry will ever wrest from the conviction of even the most ordinary man an admission that they are not true.

On assent arising from a need of pure reason

A need of pure reason in its speculative use leads only to hypotheses; that of pure practical reason, to postulates. For, in the first case, I may ascend from the result as far as I wish in the series of conditions, and I shall need an ultimate ground not in order to give objective reality to the result (e.g., the causal connection of things and changes in the world) but only in order completely to satisfy my inquiring reason with respect to them. Thus before me I see order and design in nature, and I do not need to go over to speculation in order to assure myself of their reality, though in order to explain them I need to presuppose a Deity as their cause; but since an inference from an effect to a definite cause, especially to one so exactly and perfectly defined as we have to think God to be, is always uncertain and fallible, such a presupposition cannot be brought to a higher degree of certainty than the acknowledgement that it is the most reasonable opinion for us men.

A need of pure practical reason, on the other hand, is based on a duty to make something (the highest good) the object of my will so as to promote it with all my strength. In doing so, I must presuppose its possibility and also its conditions, which are God, freedom, and immortality; for these conditions I am not in a position to prove by my speculative reason, though I cannot disprove them either. This duty is based on an apodictic law, the moral law, which is independent of these presuppositions, and thus needs no further support from theoretical opinions on the inner character of things, on the secret final end of the world order, or on a ruler presiding over it in order to bind us completely to actions unconditionally conformable to the law. But the subjective effect of this law, i.e., the intention which is suitable to this law and which is necessary because of it, the intention to promote the practically possible highest good at least presupposes that the latter is possible. Otherwise it would be practically impossible to strive for the object of a concept, which, at bottom, would be empty and without an object. Now the aforementioned postulates concern only the physical or metaphysical conditions (that is, those lying in the nature of things) of the possibility of the highest good, though not for the sake of some arbitrary speculative design but only for the sake of a practically necessary end of the pure rational will, which does not here choose but rather obeys an inexorable command of reason. This command of reason has its ground objectively in the character of things as they must be universally judged by pure reason and is not based on inclination, which would by no means justify us in assuming the means to be possible or the object to be real for the sake of that which we wish on merely subjective grounds. This is, therefore, an absolutely necessary need and justifies its presupposition not merely as an allowable hypothesis but as a practical postulate. Granted that the pure moral law inexorably binds every man as a command (not as a rule of prudence), the righteous man may say: I will that there be a God, that my existence in this world be also an existence in a pure world of the understanding outside the system of natural connections, and finally that my duration be endless. I stand by this and will not give up this belief, for this is the only case where my interest inevitably determines my judgment because I will not yield anything of this interest; I do so without any attention to sophistries, however little I may be able to answer them or oppose them with others more plausible

In order to avoid all misinterpretations of the use of such an unusual concept as that of pure practical faith, I may add one more remark. It might almost seem as if this rational faith is here decreed as a command to assume as possible the highest good. But faith that is commanded is an absurdity. If one remembers from the preceding analysis what is needed to be presupposed in the concept of the highest good, one will realize that to assume this possibility cannot be commanded, and that no practical disposition to grant it can be demanded, but that speculative reason must admit it without being asked; for no one can affirm that it is impossible of itself that rational beings in the world should at the same time be worthy of happiness in conformity to the moral law and be in possession of happiness proportionate to this worthiness. Now with respect to the first component of the highest good, viz., morality, the moral law merely gives a command, and to doubt the possibility of that ingredient would be the same as to call the moral law itself into question. But with respect to the second component of that object, viz., happiness perfectly proportionate to that worthiness, the assumption of its possibility is not at all in need of a command, for theoretical reason has nothing to say against it. It is only in the way in which we are to think of this harmony of natural laws with laws of freedom that there is anything about which we have a choice, because here theoretical reason does not decide with apodictic certainty, and in this respect there can be a moral interest which turns the scale.

I have said above that in the mere course of nature happiness exactly proportionate to moral worth is not to be expected and is indeed impossible and that therefore the possibility of the highest good from this side cannot be granted except under the presupposition of a moral Author of the world. I intentionally postponed restricting this judgment to the subjective conditions of our reason in order to make use of this restriction only when the manner of the assent had been more precisely defined. In fact, the impossibility mentioned is merely subjective, i.e., our reason finds it impossible to conceive, in the mere course of nature, a connection so exactly proportioned and so thoroughly adapted to an end between natural events which occur according to laws so heterogeneous. But, as with every other purposive thing in nature, it still cannot prove that it is impossible according to universal laws of nature [only], i.e., show this by objectively sufficient reasons.

But now a determining factor of another kind comes into play to turn the scale in this indecision of speculative reason. The command to further the highest good is objectively grounded (in practical reason), and its possibility itself is likewise objectively grounded (in theoretical reason, which has nothing to say against it). But as to the manner in which this possibility is to be thought, reason cannot objectively decide whether it is by universal laws of nature without a wise Author presiding over nature or whether only on the assumption of such an Author. Now a subjective condition of reason enters which is the only way in which it is theoretically possible for it to conceive of the exact harmony of the realm of nature with the realm of morals as the condition of the possibility of the highest good; and it is the only way which is conducive to morality (which is under an objective law of reason). Since the promotion of the highest good and thus the presupposition of its possibility are objectively necessary (though only as a consequence of practical reason), and since the manner in which we are to think of it as possible is subject to our own choice, in which a free interest of pure practical reason is decisive for the assumption of a wise Author of the world, it follows that the principle which here determines our judgment, while subjectively a need, is the ground of a maxim of moral assent, as a means to promoting that which is objectively (practically) necessary; that is, it is a faith of pure practical reason. As a voluntary decision of our judgment to assume that existence and to make it the foundation of further employment of reason, conducing to the moral (commanded) purpose and agreeing moreover with the theoretical need of reason, it is itself not commanded. It rather springs from the moral disposition itself. It can therefore often waver even in the well disposed but can never fall into unbelief.

Chapter 59

Why morality implies the existence of God

H. P. Owen

MORAL claims constitute an independent order of reality. I shall now suggest five reasons for inferring God as their source or ground.

1. Claims, I submit, are not self-explanatory. Their mode of existence is highly puzzling and obscure. We feel their 'pressure'; we are aware of being 'constrained' by them; but on the purely moral plane we are unable to give any further account of their existence. They just 'are'—enigmatic entities in an uncharted sphere. Their enigma consists in the fact that, taken in themselves, they are *im*personal.

In order to perceive this ontological incongruity it is enough to consider ordinary language. The words 'obligation', 'duty', 'claim' always imply a *personal* constraint whenever they refer to an object within the finite world. We say that we are 'under an obligation' to our friend, but not to our computer.[1] Similarly we define justice as 'giving every man his due'; but we should consider it nonsensical to replace 'every man' by 'every*thing*'. The personal overtones of 'claim' are no less obvious.

A personal reference is especially clear in 'law' when this is taken to signify 'command'.[2] It is impossible to think of a command without also thinking of a command*er*. The analogy with positive law makes this plain. Of any such law it can be asked: 'what is its source and authority?' While the source may lie in a remote and unrecorded past, the present authority must be a person or group of persons who act as its interpreters—the Sovereign, Parliament, the judiciary.

A clear choice faces us. Either we take moral claims to be self-explanatory modes of *im*personal existence or we explain them in terms of a personal God. The first of these alternatives cannot be disproved. The idea that claims can exist without any personal ground is not, perhaps, a logical contradiction; for even if in our experience of finite things and persons claims are always personal we cannot demonstrate that they must be personal *per se*. But we can say that if the transcendent and visible

H. P. Owen edited extract from *The Moral Argument for Christian Theism* (George Allen and Unwin, 1965), reprinted by permission of HarperCollins Publishers.

1. The fact that we doubt whether we have duties towards animals (even though we deplore cruelty towards them) is due to their ambiguous status. They are not (as Descartes thought) complex machines; but also they are not persons.

2. For the argument from the moral law to a divine Lawgiver see especially Clement Webb (*Divine Personality and Human Life*, London, 1920, pp. 113–44). Webb acknowledges his debt to Martineau.

orders of morality are not continuous at this vital point—if the *modus essendi* of claims in themselves is totally different from their *modus essendi* when empirically embodied—the moral life is unintelligible.

If moral claims are left in this unintelligible state it is hard for a reflective person to continue believing in them; for belief is always insecure until it is rooted in understanding. While naturalistic explanations of the moral law fail to account for its authority they at least do justice to its *personal* character. The dictates of society cannot explain the absoluteness of the categorical imperative; but in so far as they are personal they have a superficial credibility. On the other hand bare belief in an impersonal order of claims, while it is compatible with their absolute authority, does not provide the personal basis which their imperatival quality requires.[3]

I shall now deal with three objections to my argument.

(a) It has been said that those who argue from the moral law to a divine Law-giver assume too readily that language mirrors facts. It is invalid to say 'because Western languages take the subject-predicate form the world must consist in substances and their attributes'. It is no more valid to say 'because law suggests a lawgiver, a divine lawgiver must exist'.

The example is misleading. The move from subject-predicate to substance-attribute is one from language to reality; but the move from human claimants to a divine Claimant occurs within reality itself. Certainly the belief in a divine lawgiver involves an analogical use of moral terms; but this use is governed by a desire to unify the facts to which these terms refer. The argument is that since within the human realm claims imply a claimant and laws a lawgiver the same implications must be posited within the supra-human order if we are to make morality consistent.

(b) A second objection is that belief in a divine lawgiver is merely the projection of an authoritarian 'father-image'. The Christian illicitly transfers authority from an earthly to a heavenly father when he posits God as the source of the moral law. Once he sees the transference for what it is—a sign of emotional immaturity—he will be able to discard it and give his ethics a purely humanistic foundation.

A full answer would require a critique of the whole Freudian attitude towards religion. Here I shall simply observe that the objection is a gross *petitio principii*. If it is logically possible that the authority ascribed to God is solely a 'projection' it is no less logically possible that the authority of human fathers is derived from that of the divine Father 'from whom every family in heaven and on earth is named'.[4]

(c) It could be objected that the personal source of positive laws does not itself make them valid. Even a technically legitimate ruler forfeits his right to obedience if his mandates do not correspond to moral norms. So John Laird, in rejecting Clement Webb's argument for a divine Lawgiver, wrote: 'it is not apparent that the

3. For a brief, but forceful, statement of the view that the categorical imperative must be a *personal* constraint see A. R. Vidler's *Christian Belief* (London 1950, pp. 20–1). Compare also G. F. Wood's *Theological Explanation* (London 1958, pp. 190–2).
4. Eph. 3. 15.

rightness or *equity* of any juridical law is just what the sovereign commands, and so that if there were no commander there could be no such thing as justice or equity'.[5]

Laird's criticism can be briefly answered. Of course the commands of human rulers may be morally invalid because they may be wicked or foolish men. But God's commands are always right and true because he himself *is* perfect righteousness and truth.

Yet I must clarify (even at the cost of repetition) what I mean by saying that personal theism 'explains' the ontological objectivity of moral claims. There can be no hope of making the ground of duty 'plain' in a form that would imply an intuition of God's essence. The most the theist can maintain is that the idea of a divine Lawgiver elucidates the *modus essendi* of claims according to the limits of analogical predication.

The agnostic, of course, may find the very idea of analogy unacceptable. If we cannot know God 'in himself' how can we invoke him as an *explicans*? But an *explicans* need not be clearer than the *explicandum*, and the obscurity (when understood as the 'mystery') of God is the condition of his capacity to act as a final *explicans*. Two further considerations must be stressed.

Firstly, the main task of metaphysics is to offer ultimate explanations of facts which are not self-explanatory either when taken in themselves or even when related to each other. If someone does not desire this type of explanation he cannot be compelled to seek it. To some people 'ultimate explanations' will always seem gratuitous. The theist has no magic formula for dealing with an anti-metaphysical attitude. His only hope of dispelling it is to show the contradictions it involves. If the atheist is content to acquiesce in these the argument is at an end.

Secondly, since theism is a secondary pursuit it is likely to seem chimerical if it is severed from its experiential roots. When we look at claims theoretically we may not perhaps be over-worried by the problem of their status; but the problem cannot be so easily evaded when we recollect their practical significance. *Theoria* without *praxis* is empty, and *praxis* without *theoria* is blind.

2. The contradiction I have pointed out becomes especially apparent (and distressing) when we consider the *obedience* that the categorical imperative requires. Here we have an additional paradox. On the one hand claims transcend every human person and every personal embodiment. On the other hand we value the personal more highly than the impersonal; so that it is contradictory to assert that impersonal claims are entitled to the allegiance of our wills. The only solution of the paradox is to suppose that the order of claims, while it appears as impersonal from a purely moral point of view, is in fact rooted in the personality of God.

This demand for personality in the object of obedience is confirmed by the manner in which abstract claims are conditioned in their modes of operation by a personal setting. Two modes of conditioning are plain.

In the first place claims are apt to be most stringent when they are personally

5. *Mind and Deity* (London 1941, p. 231).

mediated. Thus for many readers the claims of loyalty in general and promise-keeping in particular are exemplified supremely in their marriage-vows. Conversely the violation of another person's trust incurs universal condemnation. Certainly it is always wrong to break one's word, or even to intend to do so, except in order to observe some other claim. Yet we feel especial guilt when our wrong-doing betrays another person's confidence. From the Christian standpoint all wrongdoing takes this form; for it is, directly or indirectly, a betrayal of God's love.[6]

Secondly, in cases of conflict between claims most of us, I believe, would give preference to the claim which possessed the greater *personal* stringency. At least we should tend to do so. The most quoted instance is the dilemma created by a conflict between the demands of truth-telling and compassion. Many of those who have a high regard for truth would be prepared to tell a lie in order to save a sick friend from harmful, or even unnecessary, distress. Adherence to abstract principles at *any* cost merits the reproach of hardness if not also inhumanity.

3. I have been speaking of the especial weight that we attach to claims when they occur within personal relationships. Yet persons do not merely exemplify abstract claims. They exert claims in their own right because they are persons and not things. Even the atheist admits this truth when he agrees with Kant that each person must be treated as an end and never simply as a means.

It is on this ground that we condemn the subordination of the individual to the State. For certain purposes a person can be viewed in terms of his official role or social class. Yet he also has *intrinsic* worth. He deserves unlimited respect solely because he is a human being. This respect can be neither increased nor diminished by his role or status in society.

An admirable statement of this moral truth from agnostic premises has been given by J. P. Corbett.

I have come to realize clearly, lately at least, that life is intolerable unless you recognize your neighbour as a person who has absolute claims upon you, unless you go about in the world meeting people and seeing in those people something which demands your utmost attention and all the service you can give them. This does not mean that you have to think in terms of any philosophical or religious system so far as I can see. It is just that it is only in unconditional service to the next man, whoever he may be, and under no matter what circumstances you meet him, that you escape from the sense of frustration and incompleteness and doubt which otherwise dogs one's steps.[7]

It is instructive to compare and contrast this passage with another taken from Basil Willey's *Christianity Past and Present.*[8]

Christianity teaches that humanity inevitably becomes subhuman when cut off from the superhuman; that, as Chesterton expressed it, nature becomes unnatural unless redeemed by

6. Hence the words in the greatest of the penitential Psalms (51. 4): 'against thee, thee only, have I sinned, and done this evil in thy sight'.
7. Taken from *The Listener* (January 21st, 1960).
8. Cambridge 1952, pp. 80–1.

the supernatural. It is indeed possible for an atheist to be noble, selfless, devoted to his fellows, and willing to lay down his life for them; we see examples of this around us constantly. But such nobility commonly has unconfessed religious springs, deep and hidden in the man's own heart or in his family history. It is theoretically indefensible except on religious presuppositions.

I am here concerned solely to maintain that the belief in human dignity is 'theoretically indefensible' unless it is derived from theistic premises. Whether it is practically tenable for any length of time without these premises is another question. But one cannot fail to be impressed by the fact (which Willey stresses) that many of the great Victorian humanists (such as T. H. Huxley and Leslie Stephen) were brought up in Christian homes.

There are, I believe, two reasons why human persons cannot *in themselves* exert the absolute claim of which Corbett speaks.

Firstly, each human person is a finite being and so exhibits goodness in a finite form. Most of us have some good qualities to some degree; but they are only partial embodiments of 'the good life'. One man excels in patience, another in courage, another in magnanimity; but none of us excels in all the virtues. Furthermore even if someone did possess all the virtues equally he would still not possess them to an infinite degree. The limitations of finite being would remain. Thus even Socrates exemplified the moral life in a typically Hellenic form. He himself would have said that nothing less than absolute goodness—the Idea of the Good that transcends all finite instances—can possess unconditioned worth.

Secondly, in fact (to anticipate the next stage of my argument) no one ever does exemplify all the virtues even in a finite mode. We are all sinners. How then can we merit reverence? Yet humanitarian sentiment compels the agnostic to treat all men as ends irrespective of their moral state. Hence, for example, he is shocked if the police maltreat a criminal in order to secure a conviction. One cannot evade the dilemma by saying that we are reverencing the 'ideal' of humanity, not the man himself; for firstly (as I shall later show) it is meaningless to speak of reverencing an 'ideal' (considered as a notion in the mind), and secondly we distinguish sharply between the reverence which is due to persons because they are persons and the admiration which we feel for them because they are good.

We are therefore driven to suppose that human persons exert their distinctive claim on account of their relation to a moral Absolute. Yet what can this relation be? There are three possibilities. Firstly we could say (with Hegel and Spinoza) that persons are 'modes' or 'expressions' of the Absolute; but a mode cannot possess the unconditioned nature of the Whole; and in any case the moral consciousness demands a God who transcends all finite selves. Secondly we may follow Kant in affirming that a person has dignity or worth in so far as he obeys (or is able to obey) the moral law. But (as I have already said) we revere persons even when they fail to obey the law and even if they are incapable of obedience.

We must therefore interpret the relation between human persons and the moral Absolute in terms of Christian theism. Their worth consists in the fact that they are created, loved, and destined for eternal life by God. The value we attach to them is the value bestowed on them by God; so that, in A. M. Farrer's words, 'what claims our regard is not simply our neighbour, but God in our neighbour and our neighbour in God'.[9] Human beings are 'sacred' because they are subject to the operations of God's holy will.

4. My fourth argument consists in the analysis of three moral terms: reverence, responsibility, and guilt.

(a) *Reverence.* Philosophers and theologians have often urged that our reverence for the moral law is an unacknowledged adoration of a holy law-giver. Thus Cook-Wilson affirmed that 'it is true that we speak of reverence for the moral law, but I believe no such feeling possible for a mere formula, and that, so far as it exists, it is only possible because we think of the moral law as a manifestation of the nature of the Eternal Spirit'.[10]

Although this argument impressed so acute a thinker as Cook-Wilson I find it, when taken alone, unconvincing. If 'reverence' means a 'sense of the sublime' it need not have a personal object in the moral, any more than in the natural, sphere. Equally if it means a 'sense of the numinous' it could still be compatible with a numinously toned apprehension of the moral law. Cook-Wilson's formulation of the argument appears to be convincing only because he has reduced the moral law to the status of a 'mere formula'.

However, if we take the moral law to mean an order of claims, and if we take reverence to include an attitude of devotion, the argument is a phenomenological form of the one I have already given. One cannot (morally) devote oneself to an object that is less than personal. The word 'reverence' would then describe the feeling-state that accompanies devotion and would not afford any independent evidence for theism.

(b) *Responsibility.* The concept of responsibility has clearer theistic implications. When we call someone 'irresponsible' we can often supply a reference to another human person. He is lacking in responsibility to (for example) his family or employers. To be responsible involves the idea of a person or persons to whom responsibility is due. Frequently 'being responsible' also conveys the sense of 'being answerable to'. Thus a minister of the Crown is answerable, or accountable, to Parliament for his decisions.

Yet we also speak of responsibility when no human persons are in view. Thus a person who wasted his talents could be called 'irresponsible'. Admittedly we may mean that he is irresponsible towards his wife who depends on his income or to his parents who are eager for his success. Yet even if he has no wife or parents, and even if he discharges the duties of his station to the satisfaction of society, we should still regard him as irresponsible if he squandered his gifts. To whom then is he responsible if not to God who bestows all gifts on trust?

9. *Faith and Logic* (London 1957, p. 26). The whole of Farrer's article is an important contribution to the moral argument.
10. *Statement and Inference*, Vol. 2 (Oxford 1926, p. 862).

The only other possibilities are that I am responsible either to myself or to an abstract order of claims. With regard to the first it seems to me plain that the idea of responsibility involves the idea of an 'other' to whom responsibility is due. Can then, this 'other' be a set of impersonal claims? Hardly. Each person must speak for himself. But I, for one, cannot make any sense of the view that such claims, however august and magisterial they may be, can be objects of responsibility. There is even a linguistic impropriety in saying that we are responsible to *it*.

(c) *Guilt.* The theistic implications of guilt were set forth by Newman with incomparable incisiveness as follows:

Inanimate things cannot stir our affections; these are correlative with persons. If, as is the case, we feel responsibility, are ashamed, are frightened, at transgressing the voice of con-science, this implies that there is One to whom we are responsible, before whom we are ashamed, whose claims upon us we fear. If, on doing wrong, we feel the same tearful, broken-hearted sorrow which overwhelms us on hurting a mother; if, on doing right, we enjoy the same sunny serenity of mind, the same soothing, satisfactory delight which follows on our receiving praise from a father, we certainly have within us the image of some person, to whom our love and veneration look, in whose smile we find our happiness, for whom we yearn, towards whom we direct our pleadings, in whose anger we are troubled and waste away. These feelings in us are such as require for their exciting cause an intelligent being: we are not affectionate towards a stone, nor do we feel shame before a horse or a dog; we have no remorse or compunction on breaking mere human law: yet, so it is, conscience excites all these painful emotions, confusion, foreboding, self-condemnation; and on the other hand it sheds upon us a deep peace, a sense of security, a resignation, and a hope, which there is no sensible, no earthly object to elicit. 'The wicked flees, when no one pursueth'; then why does he flee? whence his terror? Who is it that he sees in solitude, in darkness, in the hidden chambers of his heart? If the cause of these emotions does not belong to this visible world, the Object to which his perception is directed must be Supernatural and Divine; and thus the phenomena of Conscience, as a dictate, avail to impress the imagination with the picture of a Supreme Governor, a Judge, holy, just, powerful, all-seeing, retributive, and is the creative principle of religion, as the Moral Sense is the principle of ethics.[11]

Newman intended this to be a persuasive, not a demonstrative, argument. He simply points out that if in the finite and visible sphere our sense of guilt is proportionate to our betrayal of human persons, and if in this sphere we never find the same sense engendered by reflection on our treatment of mere 'things', we may reasonably conclude that our shame at having violated the moral law is due to the fact that we are in the presence of a holy lawgiver.

5. My final argument is based on the fact of moral failure. Many of us find that we are unable to do what the law requires. We are faced with a distressing paradox. On the one hand 'I ought' theoretically implies 'I can'. On the other hand we often find that we can*not*. This inner conflict was described with classical simplicity by St

---

11. *A Grammar of Assent* (London 1901, pp. 109–10). This argument is developed (through an unusually profound analysis of moral guilt) by A. E. Taylor (*The Faith of a Moralist*, London 1930, Vol. 1, chap. 5).

Paul in Romans 7. 19: 'I do not do the good I want, but the evil I do not want is what I do.'

Certainly this conflict sometimes terminates in a moral victory. Thus I may be tempted to 'forget' a promise to attend a tedious meeting; but after a struggle I decide to go. Moreover it is undeniable that the highest acts of heroism can be performed from a sheer sense of duty in defiance of all selfish inclinations. It would be outrageous to set *a priori* limits to the moral possibilities of any particular person on any particular occasion.

Yet can anyone honestly say that he is able to perform the more exacting claims continually with the purity of motive that the moral law requires?[12] Or must we not admit that in our attempts to answer the absolute claim that our neighbour exerts on our regard we are constantly frustrated by a self-centredness that we are power-less to eradicate? If we admit this we posit a contradiction in the highest reaches of the moral life.

It is surely obvious that on the human plane the contradiction is insoluble. If our natures are defective how can they be healed except by aid which is strictly *super-natural*? That such aid (or grace) is given through Christ is the gospel ('the good news') that the New Testament proclaims.

I shall not discuss this argument further for two reasons. Firstly, it is different in kind from my previous arguments which all consist in the theistic implications of the moral law *per se*; and it is on these implications that I wish to rest my case. Secondly, it could (I know) be said that we are obliged to perform only those actions (or cultivate only those attitudes) which lie within our power. We are not obliged to pursue perfection or even to aim at a standard which, though less than perfect, is beyond our grasp.

The argument to a divine Claimant and Lawgiver has recently been criticized in detail by W. G. Maclagan.[13] Maclagan objects to the argument on two grounds.

Firstly, the idea of a divine Lawgiver is meaningless. Maclagan starts with these alternatives. Either an action is right because God commands it or God commands it because it is right. The first alternative is morally, and the second theologically, disastrous; for according to the first an action becomes right or wrong by an arbitrary *fiat*, while according to the second, norms of rightness exist independently of God in whom they are supposed to have their ground. But there is a third possibility. 'God's action, it could be said, ceases to appear arbitrary without being conditioned by anything other than himself if moral distinctions are regarded neither as the product of his will nor as altogether independent of him, but as con-stitutive of his understanding, and as "having reality" only thus' (p. 70). Maclagan rejects this possibility for one reason only. 'What we know and our knowing it

---

12. Note how in Romans 7 St Paul illustrates his point by a commandment that involves an *interior* act—'Thou shalt not covet'. The essence of the moral life consists in the goodness of a *will* that is determined by (or is in accordance with) the moral law.

13. *The Theological Frontier of Ethics* (London, Allen & Unwin, 1961).

are from the human point of view never the same thing, and to claim knowledge that something is the case includes the affirmation that it is the case apart from our knowledge' (p. 70).

However, divine and human understanding are bound to differ at this point. To say that God knows what is absolutely right and good is to say, ultimately, that he knows himself; for he *is* goodness. Moral distinctions are constitutive of his understanding because moral values are constitutive of his being. Of course anyone can deny that essence and existence are identical in God; but the denial undermines Christian theism as a whole and not simply the moral argument.

In the second place Maclagan denies that there is any need to posit a divine Lawgiver. 'What we have to say is, rather, that the moral law is a law without a lawgiver; and to the objection that this is absurd the answer is that it is just a way of saying that to call it "law" at all is only inadequate metaphor for something that is *sui generis*' (p. 73).

To this I would make a three-fold reply.

(a) The metaphor of 'law' is an inevitable way of interpreting morality. Even as children we are aware of 'Thou shalt' (or, more often, 'Thou shalt not') as a mandate that is qualitatively distinct from both our parents' will and our own desires. At the rarefied level of philosophical speculation we have Kant's determinative example. When he came to describe moral 'autonomy'—that which differentiates moral activity from other activities and makes morality (as Maclagan puts it) *sui generis*—he did so through the concept of the 'categorical imperative'. Maclagan himself entitles the chapter from which I have quoted 'The Moral Demand'.

(b) Since the metaphor of law is inevitable is it not better to have it whole than maimed? Kant at any rate thought so when he affirmed that the goal of the practical reason is to see all duties as divine commands. So too Wordsworth called Duty 'the stern daughter of the voice of God'. Unless we posit God's existence the metaphor is defective at the core (not simply in some peripheral association).

(c) Maclagan anyhow misrepresents the theistic case by concentrating on the merely linguistic aspect of the inference to a divine Lawgiver. Even if (as I do not think possible) we discard the metaphor of 'law' we still have to explain the 'pressure' of moral claims. Maclagan does not offer any explanation. He simply leaves us with a mysterious 'demand'. This demand, he says, 'comes to us in the form of a duty—consciousness that imposes an absolute claim on our lives' (p. 53); it has unquestionable authoritativeness' (p. 55). These statements raise metaphysical questions which Maclagan does not even attempt to answer. On the contrary (as we shall see later) he confesses that the moral demand presupposes an 'order of values' concerning which nothing further can be said.

Since Maclagan wishes to reject a theistic inference from moral claims and to retain the possibility of belief in divine existence he is unable to give a satisfactory account of the relation between God and the moral law. Morality does not require a personal God. The moral consciousness can admit the idea of such a God only by equating him with the idea of an impersonal moral law. 'It is the moral experience that interprets to us (that is to say, that contributes to the interpretation of) the term "God", not the other way round' (p. 94). Yet Maclagan admits that religious experience requires a personal God. The only way out of this dilemma is to regard God as personal for some purposes and impersonal for others:

> We must, then, somehow think of God as both personal and impersonal, and in one sense, it would seem, this presents no difficulty. Something very like it is achieved constantly, by all except the most simple-minded, in the very acknowledgement that personality as we know it does not adequately represent the divine nature. Yet when, in reflection, we endeavour to be more explicit, what results seems not to be integration so much as a sort of working conflation of the ideas of the personal and the impersonal, consisting in what remains the blank affirmation of their conjunction together with their use as *alternatives*, according as one or other seems more apt in a particular context. The concept of God (if it can be called a concept) then functions in much the same way as Eddington's notorious concept (if it can be called a concept) of 'wavicle' in the theory of light. Now this procedure may be prag-matically justified; it may be indispensable for the 'practical purposes' of the religious life. Indeed it is, in a manner, preferable even as theory to any one-sided clarity. None the less it is manifestly unsatisfactory. Our working conflation rests on an inattention to the conflict of personal and impersonal conceptions rather than on a transcendence of it. What is needed is that we should, so to put it, replace a 'bi-focal' vision of God by one that is 'uni-focal'. (p. 179).

It seems to me that belief in God on these terms would be metaphysically unjustified even if it is psychologically possible. Divine personality utterly tran-scends its created image. Yet to say that God is more that personal in the finite sense is one thing; but to say that he is impersonal is quite another. Furthermore (with reference to Eddington's 'wavicle') if there is one thing to be learned from empiri-cist critics of religion it is surely that theistic statements become untenable as soon as they are reduced to the pragmatic status of scientific postulates.

Maclagan treats the argument from claims to Claimant similarly. 'Claim', like 'law', is a metaphor that must not be pressed. But in speaking of claims he makes a statement I shall discuss because the misapprehensions it contains may be (at least partly) responsible for the precarious view he holds. 'I maintain,' he writes on p. 75, 'that there is no awareness of any such relationship [sc. between claims and God] inherent in the duty-consciousness itself, and I suggest that those who think there is do so precisely because they are not successfully abstracting from their independent theistic conviction. Their moral phenomenology has, so to put it, been vitiated by infection from beliefs at which they have arrived by a quite different route.'

Two observations must be made.

Firstly, Maclagan fails to observe the distinction (so clearly drawn by Ewing) between entailment and awareness. To say that X entails Y is not to say that I am aware of Y whenever I think of X. Alternatively Maclagan confuses phenomenology with metaphysics and the *ordo cognoscendi* with the *ordo essendi*. Because I am not aware of God when I answer moral claims it does not follow that his existence is not required as their ground.

Secondly, even if we confine ourselves to phenomenology we may well hesitate before accepting Maclagan's dogmatic (and pejoratively coloured) assertion that a theistic view of moral obligation is possible only if the moral consciousness has been vitiated by beliefs acquired by a wholly non-moral route. The assertion is a caricature of Hebrew ethics from which, historically, Maclagan's outlook is derived. The Jews did not first have a secular sense of obligation to which, as a kind of afterthought, they added a 'numinous fringe' engendered by a totally separate 'sense of the divine'. Their morality was conditioned by religious faith throughout their history.

I do not therefore think that Maclagan undermines the argument to God from moral claims. On the contrary he has confirmed it; for his own reasoning has brought us to the frontier of religion; and, once misunderstandings are removed, we have good grounds for an intuitive act of faith.

Lest any misunderstanding should remain—and it is likely that I have sometimes used incautious language in presenting the theistic case—I must stress the following points.

1. Although the believer derives morality from the will of God he need not be aware of the derivation every time he passes a moral judgment or makes a moral choice. In fact he need be aware of it only in special moments (for example when he brings a problem before God in prayer) or when his duties are themselves religious (for example when he resolves to say his prayers even though he may not want to do so).

2. It is again necessary to recall the relative independence of ethics and the distinction between the *ordo essendi* and the *ordo cognoscendi*. Even within the religious life the 'autonomy' of ethics is preserved. Even when a believer consciously identifies an action with God's will he is also simultaneously aware of it as being right in purely moral terms. Indeed he must be antecedently aware of its congruence with the moral law; for otherwise he could not ascribe it to God's will.

Such ethical autonomy is required by the Christian account of divine action both by nature and by grace. God does not act merely from without in discontinuous moments of 'encounter'; he also acts within through the illumination of his Word and Spirit. Having made us in his image he has given us the power to discern the rightness of those actions which are in accordance with his will.

Existentialist theologians do well to stress the transcendence and hiddenness of God; but they often forget (if they do not deny) that God is also immanent; and so they fail to locate his 'hiddenness' in the soul of man. Yet the affirmation of God's hidden presence within all men is necessary if we are to interpret the moral life religiously without obliterating its distinctive nature.

3. The identification of moral claims with God's holy will is not free from ambiguity. On the purely moral plane obligation is self-evident; for there is nothing else through which it can be understood. But when it is equated with the will of God it is not immediately self-evident. That God is holy in himself does not require

any further explanation; but that he requires his creatures to be holy does require one. It is insufficient to reply that he has a right to command because he made us; for the mere fact that he made us cannot constitute an obligation.

Here we must discard the last shreds of naturalism. Even those who would not otherwise speak naturalistically of God are apt to construe his creative act solely in terms of power. That his creativity manifests a unique mode of power is true; but the power is suffused by love; and it is the love that constitutes the final ground of obligation.

Yet we must not think that God's love is separate from his holiness; for his will reflects his character. His holiness *is* love. He made us out of love in order that we might share in the love that is his very being. Just as his will of love is the imperative of the moral law so also his character of love is the exemplar of the moral life.

4. Therefore, while theism 'explains' obligation it does not 'explain it away'. The constraint of God's will and our corresponding duty to perform it are self-authenticating moral facts. Just as the content of the moral law must always be perceived by Christians and non-Christians equally through the autonomous operations of the conscience even when the content is referred to the character of God, so also the form of the law as an unconditional obligation must be autonomously experienced even when it is referred to God's sovereign will. 'Ought' is always irreducible.

It is surely obvious that here we have the highest case of obligation. Even in our finite lives we know that there is no stronger obligation than one imposed by a friend who has showered his gifts on us with self-less generosity; and that correspondingly there is no stronger duty than a debt of gratitude. Therefore morality, so far from being negated, is fulfilled in the belief that the whole life of duty is a debt of gratitude to God for his great love in creating us to share in his perfection.[14]

5. By faith, then, we identify the form and content of the moral law with God's will and character. God wills us to be truthful and compassionate because he possesses these qualities to an infinite degree. Out of love he created us to share his holiness; and our duty to fulfil the moral law is our answer to his love.

Yet on occasions it is hard to know how claims are to be satisfied. Sometimes they conflict. At other times we are uncertain of the *manner* in which they are best fulfilled. How, then, can we be sure that we are doing God's will? I can here only offer a few, brief, observations.

(a) The Christian is used to the idea that he can never perfectly perform God's will. In this life he remains *simul justus et peccator*. Even when his duty is entirely plain (as it very often is) he knows that he is deficient in his inner attitude if not also in his outward acts. It is therefore not surprising if he exhibits deficiency in those choices which require special insight and imagination.

14. W. G. De Burgh wrote that 'love precludes all thought of obligation' (*From Morality to Religion*, London 1938, p. 66). This statement, while applicable to Platonic *eros*, is directly contradicted by the New Testament's formulation of Christian *agape* in such terms as 'Thou *shalt* love thy neighbour as thyself' and 'Beloved, if God so loved us, we *ought* to love one another'.

(b) Yet we can always be sure of doing God's will to some degree so long as we answer claims to the extent that our vision and circumstances here and now permit. Doubtless if we were closer to God our vision would be clearer and our circumstances more propitious. But in every situation we can discover *some* manner of embodying *some* element of the moral law; and so we achieve a degree of approximation to, and co-operation with, God's will.

(c) We must not assume that even in a wholly obedient life God's will is fully known in advance. Even in Gethsemane Jesus hoped that God would spare him crucifixion. Therefore the moral condition even of the saints is often one of *docta ignorantia*. De Caussade stated this painful truth as follows:

It is no doubt a great blow, as of death, to the soul, this loss of the sight of the Divine Will which retires before her eyes to take up a position behind her, as it were, and impels her forward, being no longer her clearly conceived object but becoming her invisible principle.[15]

(d) Therefore in cases of real doubt we cannot invoke the will of God as a *criterion* for moral choice. His will is here a mystery. It cannot become the 'clearly conceived object' that ethical judgment needs. We may *feel* that an action is demanded by God's will for us here and now; but since the feeling can be illusory (as the behaviour of 'enthusiasts' has shown) we are obliged to justify the action on independent moral grounds.

(e) When Christians differ in their attitudes to complex moral problems we need not conclude that the one obeys, and the other disobeys, God's will. Thus in the conditions of our evil world it may be God's will that some Christians should be pacifists and others non-pacifists. It *may* be so. Our ignorance is necessarily complete.

To sum up, we can say that the form of the moral law as a categorical imperative is the personal command of God and that the general precepts of this law constitute the content of his will. But in complex and difficult situations we cannot be sure that we have chosen the course that a *perfect* obedience to his *particular* will for us *here and now* requires. At the same time Christians believe that as they learn to rely on him he will enable them increasingly (often through their very failures) to know and do what is pleasing in his sight. How far we have strayed from his will (both when it is plain and when it seems obscure) is known to him alone; for he alone discerns the thoughts and intents of the heart; and as we fear his judgment so also we trust in his salvation.

15. *Self-Abandonment to Divine Providence* (English trans. by A. Thorold, London 1955, p. 110).

Chapter 60

Moral thinking as awareness of God

Illtyd Trethowan

Iᴛ is a commonplace to say that we know very little about ourselves, and the remark would often be taken to refer, at least in part, to what is called the 'unconscious'. But I am referring to the *obscurity* of our knowledge of ourselves. We are never aware simply of ourselves and of nothing else; our knowledge of ourselves is always, as it were, interfered with by knowledge of something else. This gives it an elusive quality. Hume managed to avoid it altogether, for philosophical purposes, by concentrating upon the succession of sense-impressions and images; he seemed to suppose that the self should present itself, if it existed, in total isolation or, as it were, on a plate. We come across the self *in* an awareness of interacting bodies. Such spatial metaphors as 'in', as I remarked earlier, have to be used when we are talking about mental operations, which are not themselves spatial.

We know our own minds or souls only in their particular activities, but this is not to say that we have no direct knowledge of them. Some philosophers have maintained that the first object of our knowledge is an external body and that we know our own minds only as secondary objects or indirectly. I find it difficult to understand what can be meant by calling knowledge of one's own mind an indirect knowledge as contrasted with our knowledge of bodies. Human awareness, it seems to me, is essentially self-awareness.

Philosophers have been known to protest that to speak of knowing oneself is to speak of a subject which is also an object and that this is unintelligible. It is true that subject and object are distinct in all other circumstances. But our experience compels us to say that in this instance the subject becomes its own object. Once again we find a state of affairs which is a unique one. And why should we not do so? A prejudice against the unique is a frequent by-product of a training in the natural sciences. We do not mean in this instance what we mean when we speak of subject and object in other contexts. But we can point to what we mean, if we need to do so, only by using such language.

We have been pausing on the threshold of human experience. As soon as we step over it, we observe that our experience is very much richer than philosophers in a certain empiricist tradition have tended to suppose. They have commonly assumed that they are disembodied minds. They seem also to regard themselves as just

Illtyd Trethowan edited extract from *Absolute Value* (George Allen & Unwin, 1970), reprinted by permission of Routledge, an imprint of Taylor and Francis Books Ltd.

spectators. In fact we do not find ourselves just looking at things and wondering what, if anything, we know about them. We find ourselves wanting things or wishing them out of the way. We find ourselves in contact with other human beings, some of whom we like or love, some of whom we dislike. We find ourselves always engaged in some sort of plan or project which makes all the difference to the ways in which we react both to persons and to things. Our experience is not only retrospective but also prospective, anticipating the future not only by a process of guessing at its contents by analogy with the past but by an awareness of our own undeveloped capacities which gives us a real insight into what is possible for us if we care to pursue it. We are aware of ourselves in a state of progress—or perhaps of regress.

It is the recognition of this very obvious complexity about human experience which should be considered, I think, the distinguishing mark of the existentialist philosopher. Such a philosopher is in reaction against regarding man simply as a knower. His problem is not the problem of knowledge but the problem of life. The existentialist need not and should not deny that awareness is the distinguishing mark of the human being. But his awareness does not function in a vacuum. It promotes and is profoundly affected by his feelings, his desires, and his choices. It is his *choosing* which usually impresses the existentialist more than anything else. We are in a situation which forces us to choose. It may seem a very odd state of affairs. Sartre, as everyone knows, thinks it an absurd one. But Sartre is, nevertheless, a moralist, holding forth about 'bad faith', for instance. If you once start talking about projects, even if you declare them absurd, you find yourself inevitably facing the question of *value*.

By speaking of the value of anything, it will hardly be contested, we mean what makes it worth while. Let us consider the implications of this notion. I shall suggest that it does more than merely hint at metaphysical questions: it raises the ultimate ones. Someone who disagrees with this may say that what is worth while is for him simply what ministers to his personal convenience. This statement cannot be proved self-contradictory, but it is just as desperate an expedient as the statement 'I am uncertain whether I am uncertain whether I am uncertain *ad infinitum*', which is equally secure against logical attack. On such a view it would have to be maintained that, since most people enjoy certain things, for example, an expensive sort of dinner, our language reflects such common agreement and that thus a language about what is worth while has grown up which we call the language of morality (this is the counterpart in the field of moral theory to the 'conventionalist' view of truth). On such a view, then, 'I ought' will be reduced in meaning to 'If I want something, this is the way to get it' or 'This is what the people around expect of me, and if they don't get it they may make themselves unpleasant'. I have called this a desperate expedient, but it may not be clear that it is so unless a better answer to the question becomes clear. It should be clear already, however, that the answer just mentioned is at least very difficult to justify. It seems to rule out everything which has seemed most worth while to the man in the street and to the philosopher in all ages up to our own, and, in regard at least to the man in the street, including our own, for the great movements of thought (or should I say of feeling?) which are going on among us, movements for the unification of classes and of races, are certainly not based on the philosophy of egoistic hedonism. It will be much more to the point to consider what answer can be given to our question by the secular humanist.

Secular humanism has many different forms, but it always implies the production of some kind of programme for mankind, however vaguely described. The secular humanist is often prepared to go to much trouble in the interests of other people's happiness. How is he going to explain to himself why he regards this as worth while? He will be forced to ask himself the question, it may be, because he wants co-operation in his project but finds that other people do not always regard it as worth while. 'Why', someone may say to him, 'should I have to bother, as you do, about other people's happiness if in fact I am disinclined to do so?' Our humanist may reply that one cannot achieve one's happiness without aiming at that of other people. He will not mean by this what the egoistic hedonist means by it, that you have to use other people as a means to your own happiness. The sort of humanist whom I have in mind, at any rate, will mean that other people's happiness is worth while because other people are worth while in the sense of having value in themselves, and that one cannot be truly happy unless one is aiming at what is worth while. He may not put it in those words, but that must be in fact his position if it is to make sense as something different from egoistic hedonism. He will not be able to gain co-operation for his project in some cases until he can persuade someone to take his view about what 'worth while' ought to mean. And 'ought' now becomes the operative word. The notion of value is bound up with the notion of obligation. To say that people are worth while, that they have value in themselves, is to say that there is something about them which makes a demand upon us, that we *ought* to make them part of our own project, identify ourselves with them in some sort.

Again this is something which has to be *seen*—it cannot be proved by a coercive argument starting from premisses which everyone will accept. But it is not possible to deny it, I should wish to say, without making nonsense of human living. Our humanist might try to avoid talking about moral obligation because he might feel (and rightly) that it does not fit into a view of things which is purely secular. He will perhaps say that, although things are valuable in themselves in some mysterious way, some people see them as such and some people do not. Some people find fulfilment in giving themselves up, so to say, to aesthetic objects, to works of art, other people in giving themselves up to moral objects, to various causes. They just happen to be sensitive to the cause of social justice or whatever. Naturally you like people to co-operate with you for the causes which you espouse, but there need be no question of anyone's having any *obligation* to do anything. It should be obvious that the humanist is now slipping into the position of the egoistic hedonist. In the end, he will find himself saying, it is just a question of what you personally happen to like. But some secular humanists, at any rate, will not fall back on this position.

They are ready to devote themselves to the interests of future generations, to give up their comfort and convenience for the happiness of those whom they will never see. They will have to say that it is the acknowledgement of what is worth while, simply as such, which is the motive force of their lives. But nothing can be a motive force for us unless it makes an appeal to us, unless it is something that we *want*. I propose to say that the awareness of obligation is an awareness of God from which, unless we reject it, happiness derives and not only beyond the grave but on this side of it. It is hardly necessary to say that happiness then proves to mean something very different from material comfort and convenience.

So sudden an introduction of the name of God may seem startling and gratuitous. It will not seem justified, perhaps, until other aspects of the general problem of human experience have been investigated. The point which I want to repeat for a start is that the secular humanist of the self-sacrificing kind seems to be asserting an absolute unconditional obligation in fact whether or not he cares to describe what he is doing in those terms. He declares by his actions that the welfare of others (however one may envisage it) *ought* to be aimed at, whatever the cost. And can we regard the acknowledgement of moral obligation, absolute and unconditional obligation, as just a brute fact which requires no explanation or as a fact which can be explained in a naturalistic, non-religious way? If I found myself faced with it as a brute fact I should find it such an odd one that I should take it to a psychiatrist. If we are to make sense of it, we must ask ourselves how it can exercise the appeal which it undoubtedly does exercise. Why do people get a certain satisfaction from following their consciences and a dissatisfaction from not doing so, people who, as secularists, do not suppose that any religious sanctions attach to not following one's conscience? The secular humanist may be willing to say that he 'feels called upon' to adopt his course of action. My suggestion is that this is precisely the case. He is responding to the call of God. What he is aware of is God calling him. But his rejection of religion (probably based on unfortunate experiences with pseudo-religious people) makes it impossible for him to interpret this in terms of religion (of religion as he supposes it to be).

His acceptance of the call, however, is in fact an acceptance of God. There has been a real contact with God, and it is strengthened, indeed transformed, by his response to it. This is what he would be referring to if he spoke of the satisfaction which he gets from following his conscience. But probably he will not refer to it at all, for there is a natural reserve about such matters. He is more likely perhaps to refer to the dissatisfaction which he would feel if he went against his conscience. Would his situation make sense if he were not destined to a clear knowledge of God beyond the grave? A Christian will say that it will not make complete sense except on that condition. But it can make sufficient sense to get on with for the secular humanist. So far as he is concerned, following one's conscience is worth while for its own sake; it is something that he values, something that he *wants*. What he does not know is that the human project makes better sense than just this.

The general view which he takes of the world does not dispose him to recognize the human project for what in fact it is. Let us consider what his view of it presumably is. It is that the world is not the product of an intelligence, but that it has itself somehow produced intelligence. Here we meet another position which cannot be refuted by mere logic. To say that it is just the nature of the world to produce intelligent minds and that no explanation of it is called for may seem to be unreasonable (as indeed I think it is), but it is not in any way to contradict oneself. To go on to say that a world which began with no purpose subsequently acquired one (which is what the secularists' gospel implies) is surely even odder. But this, too, is irrefutable in just the same way. To say that some splendid future lies ahead for the spirit of man, which is the sort of thing which the secular humanist must say, seems very hard to believe if the spirit of man is itself some sort of cosmic accident. It is very near to saying in the same breath both that the world has not an overall purpose and that it has one. It may sound plausible at first to say that we ourselves can give the world and ourselves a purpose. But although we can give ourselves purposes in the sense of choosing this or that particular project, to bestow a project for life as a whole upon a world entirely devoid of projects should seem a hopeless task. How could we invent our own framework?

It will be useful to keep such considerations in mind, but of themselves, of course, they do not settle the problem of God. That can be settled, I shall say, only by the awareness of God. The case which I am beginning to develop is that this awareness is to be found in the most fundamental form (but not by any means exclusively) in our moral experience. One needs to talk about the awareness of God to people who are without it or, more probably, suppose themselves to be without it because they do not understand what it is. An egoistic hedonist seems to be without it; he has perhaps rejected it. A secular humanist, if he is not an egoistic hedonist in disguise, is really a theist in disguise. So I began by considering these two types of person because they are the people to whom talk about this awareness is naturally addressed. Those who have it already do not need to be considered for present purposes. But there are also those who are quite uncertain whether they have it or not. They have just a suspicion of God. They need to know how such an awareness grows up out of a suspicion. So far I have only suggested the area, so to speak, of our experience in which, I think, it most obviously does so, the area of our moral experience.

Before analysing our moral experience more closely, I want to make clear that I am not proposing an argument from conscience according to which an inference is made from the existence of a law to the existence of a lawgiver. What I am proposing is an interpretation of our moral experience. I argue that other interpretations of it are implausible, but the inferences which can be drawn from that conclusion will not prove of themselves that my interpretation is the right one. Again, it is something which has to be *seen*. To interpret something for anyone is only to put him in a position from which he can, if he will, see the answer for himself. Whether he sees it or not is up to him, not to the interpreter.

There is an obstacle ahead of us which, I must confess, I find rather baffling. It is the fact that a good many theists have little use for the claim that our moral evidence is evidence for God or, as I should prefer to put it, evidence *of* God. If a theist believes that God enters into our experience, it seems very strange that he should not enter *basically* into our awareness of ourselves as moral beings. (And if someone who calls himself a theist denies that God enters into our experience in any way, I do not know what he means by calling himself a theist.) One more point must be emphasized before I move on. I am not suggesting that the moral evidence declares its full meaning to us in a flash. As with all metaphysical conclusions, in which the central conclusion about God is always implicit, there may be for some time, perhaps for a very long time, a stage in which there is only a suspicion that we are in fact faced with evidence of God. For one thing, it may seem to lead to conclusions which are unacceptable, perhaps contradictory of truths which we cannot deny. The only way to turn such a suspicion into a certainty is to take a long cool look at what is offered to us as evidence. By a 'cool' look I do not mean a detached one, a mere spectator's look; it is *our* situation which we are examining.

When we start to look at ourselves engaged in a human project, we come to realize that there must be some project which is proper to us as human beings, a project which is *the* human project. We do mean something by talking about a human being. We must mean that we have certain powers which we are capable of developing, mental ones as well as bodily ones. A determinist will say that what this means is simply that we shall in fact develop in those particular ways which circumstances will dictate. If we accept that view, then the present discussion stops. Let us consider again what it would imply. It would imply that it would be an illusion to believe that we can at least sometimes, of our own free choice, direct our minds to some particular topic, excluding from it some other topic which presents itself to our attention. At the present moment I am thinking about the question of moral responsibility. A question about my holiday arrangements might be competing for my attention. I propose to say that I am simply *aware* of my ability to exclude it—at least to the extent that I can go on thinking about moral responsibility. If I allowed that question to disappear from the field of my attention, I should be morally responsible for abandoning my present project. I am free to choose in the sense that at this moment my decision is not the inevitable outcome of my history up to date, as the determinist would have it. I claim to be aware that it is my choice here and now which will decide the outcome and that this choice is not itself determined. No ingenious sophistry can overthrow this fact of experience.

If I recognize my moral freedom in regard to particular projects, I shall recognize it also in regard to *the* human project. And by *the* human project, I must mean the development of my own powers. The human project is a project of self-development. I am not compelled to develop my powers. I could decide to take no interest in them. I could pack up on the whole business by taking an overdose of something. What I am proposing is that, if we take a long cool look at our human powers, we can come to the conclusion that they *ought* to be developed. This is, I believe, the way to trace the notion of moral obligation to its deepest root in experience. We discover *value* in our human powers because we do not feel entitled to throw them away. Our own experience shows itself to us as possessing a value without which nothing else would seem valuable to us. It has value already, but this value needs to be developed. And this value is not something which we have produced by ourselves. For the value of an experience derives from *what* is experienced. We may say that we have a capacity for experience and that this is itself a value in a sense, a potential value. But even so it would remain that what is *actually* value is something which we receive. Such, in brief, are the considerations which lead me to say that the acknowledgement of value is the awareness of God's summons. It is a summons to accept value and to go on accepting it as it reveals itself to us more fully. We *have* value because we receive it from a source of value. That is what I mean, for a start, by God. We know him as giving us value. That is why the demand upon us to develop ourselves is an absolute, unconditional, demand. It is a summons to the absolute, the unconditioned. We are free to resist it (it is in our awareness of moral freedom that we become aware of it), but the demand is still there all the same. God's attitude to us never changes, although we can ignore it.

If this way of looking at things can be at least entertained, it will be seen to fit in with a good deal which might be otherwise very puzzling and in particular with what was said earlier about the value which people and things have in themselves. We found that a secular humanist recognizes people as having value in themselves; he recognizes an absolute obligation to aim at their welfare. Would such an *absolute* obligation make sense if we regarded other people simply as objects of our thought, our interest and our love, just these particular objects (in a world full of other objects) who happen to be connected with us in various particular ways? There is nothing absolute about people regarded simply in that fashion. An adequate explanation of this state of affairs will have to be a metaphysical one; it will have to lie behind people regarded simply as finite beings with no relationship to the infinite. Why should I be obliged to devote myself to the interests of other people if we are all on the same level and have no link with any other level? If, however, created persons and created things stand in a relationship to God of such a kind that we may call them 'reflections' of him, and if they are part of a divine plan, then, it would seem, we have an explanation or at any rate a clue to one.

These rather breathless metaphysical excursions seemed unavoidable because, as soon as the name of God is mentioned, a whole crop of misapprehensions commonly arises and until something is done about them further discussion may be useless. To simplify matters in the course of this exposition I have passed over a number of objections which, though important, did not seem to demand immediate attention. I shall conclude by saying something about them. As regards the question of moral obligation, it might be objected that I have spoken of it as a general obligation to develop our human powers, but that it presents itself to us in fact as the obligation to help our neighbour in this particular difficulty or in some other specific way. I am not denying that this is the sort of context in which the notion or rather the fact of it presents itself. It is, no doubt, the claim which our neighbours make on us which makes us first suspect what it really is to be a moral being. What I am saying is that it is the awareness of ourselves as summoned to self-fulfilment which leads us, in the last analysis, to accept the fact of obligation as a real fact. It may also be objected that I have hardly touched on the arguments so often advanced by positivists to show that the fact of moral obligation is a socio-logical phenomenon needing no religious explanation. My answer is that, if we once satisfied ourselves that it was the result of historical accidents, we should then be able to free ourselves from its bondage, and we should have to take up with egoistic hedonism. And I have said as much as it deserves about that. In any case, as has often been pointed out, to push back the problems of moral obligation into a distant past is not to abolish it. In the end, however, it is, as usual, our own awareness of it which is decisive. When I accept an absolute obligation, I am aware that so far from lapsing into the determinisms of history I am emerging from them, exercising my personal freedom in the completest way.

It may also be objected that, although the recognition of other people as 'reflec-tions' of God would certainly explain their value, it would not follow from this that we should have to devote ourselves to them if this meant neglecting our own interests. The answer to this, I take it, is that what we prove really to want (to put it with all simplicity) is just God himself, but that this means that we also want his plan for the world. His will is our peace. And thus it does not prove to make sense to talk about our own interests and the interests of other people as though there could be in the last analysis a conflict between them. That we are all in it together is something which the present generation sees more clearly than its predecessors, although what that really means is not often appreciated. That is why a further objection is likely to break out now. You are telling us, someone may say, that we ought to love people for God's sake. That is just what we do not want to do. We want to love them for their own sakes. And to that I reply that to love people because they are creatures of God, 'reflections' of God, is the only way to love them as they really are. To say that they are God's creatures is not just to mention an interesting fact about them. It is the essential truth about them. They have value indeed in themselves, but only because God gave it to them. Unless we saw God in them as the source of value, we should not *really* see that they had it. But I have also put forward the view that we do not in fact really see value until we see it in ourselves, that is, until we are aware of God's action on ourselves.

But the most strident of the objections, I suspect, will be made against my bland assertion that the value of an experience comes from *what* is experienced. *We* give meaning to things, it will be said; *we* are valuable ourselves. I am not denying this if it means what it ought to mean. What ought to be meant by our giving meaning to things is that they are meant for us to know. By acting on us they are doing a job, and they need us in order to do it. But we do not alter them by knowing them. When it is said that we are valuable in ourselves this should mean that the value which we receive is our living substance. The fact that we receive it does not mean that we are passive to it in the sense of being just kicked around by it. It means that it is given to us, making us what we are. When you listen to music, if you do it properly, you simply attend to it. It makes you what you are for the time being and very nice too. It *makes* us active in a very big way, but only on condition of our submitting to it. If you start interfering with it, you can't properly enjoy it. To say that our value comes to us from God is obviously only another way of saying that he creates us and not just when we start to exist but all the time. A theist, if he is to be consistent, must say this. Yet people who call themselves theists are constantly harping upon the way in which religion concentrates on God and abolishes man in the process. If you regard religion as obedience to arbitrary commands, that would indeed be the case. But that is completely to misunderstand the relationship in which we stand to God. We are made for him in the sense that he is for us. He fulfils us. That means that we become fully active. But for this to happen we must first listen to him, attend to him and receive from him. To say that we are in our whole being gifts of God is not to depress our status but to show its true dignity.

Chapter 61

Morality does not imply the existence of God

Kai Nielsen

I

IT is the claim of many influential Jewish and Christian Theologians (Brunner, Buber, Barth, Niebuhr and Bultmann—to take outstanding examples) that the only genuine basis for morality is in religion. And any old religion is not good enough. The only truly adequate foundation for moral belief is a religion that acknowledges the absolute sovereignty of the Lord found in the prophetic religions.

These theologians will readily grant what is plainly true, namely, that as a matter of fact many non-religious people behave morally, but they contend that without a belief in God and his law there is no ground or reason for being moral. The sense of moral relativism, scepticism and nihilism rampant in our age is due in large measure to the general weakening of religious belief in an age of science. Without God there can be no objective foundation for our moral beliefs. As Brunner puts it,[1] 'The believer alone clearly perceives that the Good, as it is recognized in faith, is the sole Good, and all that is otherwise called good cannot lay claim to this title, at least in the ultimate sense of the word . . . The Good consists in always doing what God wills at any particular moment.' Moreover, this moral Good can only be attained by our 'unconditional obedience' to God, the ground of our being. Without God life would have no point and morality would have no basis. Without religious belief, without the Living God, there could be no adequate answer to the persistently gnawing questions: What ought we to do? How ought I to live?

Is this frequently repeated claim justified? Are our moral beliefs and conceptions based on or grounded in a belief in the God of Judaism, Christianity and Islam? In trying to come to grips with this question, we need to ask ourselves three fundamental questions.

1. Is being willed by God the, or even a, *fundamental* criterion for that which is so willed being morally good or for its being something that ought to be done?

Kai Nielsen edited extract from *Ethics Without God* (Prometheus Books, 1973), copyright 1973, reprinted by permission of the publisher and the author.

1. Brunner, Emil (1947), *The Divine Imperative*, translated by Olive Wyon, London: Lutterworth Press, chapter IX.

2.   Is being willed by God the *only* criterion for that which is so willed being morally good or for its being something that ought to be done?

3.   Is being willed by God the only *adequate* criterion for that which is so willed being morally good or being something that ought to be done?

I shall argue that the fact that God wills something—if indeed that is a fact—cannot be a fundamental criterion for its being morally good or obligatory and thus it cannot be the only criterion or the only adequate criterion for moral goodness or obligation.

By way of preliminaries we should first get clear what is meant by a fundamental criterion. When we speak of the criterion for the goodness of an action or attitude we speak of some measure or test by virtue of which we may decide which actions or attitudes are good or desirable, or, at least, are the least undesirable of the alternate actions or attitudes open to us. A moral criterion is the measure we use for determining the value or worth of an action, principle, rule or attitude. We have such a measure or test when we have some generally relevant considerations by which we may decide whether something is whatever it is said to be. A fundamental moral criterion is (*a*) a test or measure used to judge the legitimacy of moral rules and/or acts or attitudes, and (*b*) a measure that one would give up last if one were reasoning morally. (In reality, there probably is no single fundamental criterion, although there are fundamental criteria.)

There is a further preliminary matter we need to consider. In asking about the basis or authority for our moral beliefs we are not asking about how we came to have them. If you ask someone where he got his moral beliefs, he, to be realistic, should answer that he got them from his parents, parent surrogates, teachers.[2] They are beliefs which he has been conditioned to accept. But the validity or soundness of a belief is independent of its origin. When one person naïvely asks another where he got his moral beliefs, most likely he is not asking how he came by them, but rather, (*a*) on what authority he holds these beliefs, or (*b*) what good reasons or justification he has for these moral beliefs. He should answer that he does not and cannot hold these beliefs on any authority. It is indeed true that many of us turn to people for moral advice and guidance in moral matters, but if we do what we do simply because it has been authorized, we cannot be reasoning and acting as moral agents; for to respond as a moral agent, one's moral principle must be something which is subscribed to by one's own deliberate commitment, and it must be something for which one is prepared to give reasons.

Keeping these preliminary clarifications in mind, we can return to my claim that the fact (if indeed it is a fact) that God has commanded, willed or ordained something cannot, in the very nature of the case, be a fundamental criterion for claiming that whatever is commanded, willed or ordained *ought* to be done.

---

2. Nowell-Smith, P. H. (1966); 'Morality: Religious and Secular' in Ramsey, Ian (ed.), *Christian Ethics and Contemporary Philosophy*, London: SCM Press.

II

Some perceptive remarks made by A. C. Ewing will carry us part of the way.[3] Theologians like Barth and Brunner claim that ethical principles gain their justification because they are God's decrees. But as Ewing points out, if 'being obligatory' means just 'willed by God', it becomes unintelligible to ask why God wills one thing rather than another. In fact, there can be no reason for his willing one thing rather than another, for his willing it *eo ipso* makes whatever it is he wills good, right or obligatory. 'God wills it because it ought to be done' becomes 'God wills it because God wills it'; but the first sentence, even as used by the most ardent believer, is not a tautology. 'If it were said in reply that God's commands determine what we ought to do but that these commands were only issued because it was good that they should be or because obedience to them did good, this would still make judgments about the good, at least, independent of the will of God, and we should not have given a definition of all fundamental ethical concepts in terms of God or made ethics dependent on God.'[4] Furthermore, it becomes senseless to say what the believer very much wants to say, namely, 'I ought always to do what God wills' if 'what I ought to do' and 'what God wills' have the same meaning. And to say I ought to do what God wills because I love God makes the independent assumption that I ought to love God and that I ought to do what God wills if I love him.

Suppose we say instead that we ought to do what God wills because God will punish us if we do not obey him. This may indeed be a cogent self-interested or prudential reason for doing what God commands, but it is hardly a morally good reason for doing what he commands since such considerations of self-interest cannot be an adequate basis for morality. A powerful being—an omnipotent and omniscient being—speaking out of the whirlwind cannot by his mere commands create an obligation. Ewing goes on to assert: 'Without a prior conception of God as good or his commands as right, God would have no more claim on our obedience than Hitler or Stalin except that he would have more power than even they had to make things uncomfortable for those who disobey him.'[5] Unless we assume that God is morally perfect, unless we assume the perfect goodness of God, there can be no necessary 'relation between being commanded or willed by God and being obligatory or good'.[6]

To this it is perfectly correct to reply that as believers we must believe that God is wholly and completely good, the most perfect of all conceivable beings.[7] It is not open for a Jew or a Christian to question the goodness of God. He must start with

---

3. Ewing, A. C. (1961), 'The Autonomy of Ethics' in Ramsey, Ian (ed.), *Prospect for Metaphysics*, London: Allen and Unwin.
4. Ibid., p. 39.
5. Ibid., p. 40.
6. Ibid., p. 41.
7. See Rees, D. A. (1961), 'Metaphysical Schemes and Moral Principles' in *Prospect for Metaphysics*, op. cit., p. 23.

that assumption. Any man who seriously questions God's goodness or asks why he should obey God's commands shows by this very response that he is not a Jew or a Christian. Believers must claim that God is wholly and utterly good and that what he wills or commands is of necessity good, though this does not entail that the believer is claiming that the necessity here is a logical necessity. For a believer, God is all good; he is the perfect good. This being so, it would seem that the believer is justified in saying that he and we—if his claim concerning God is correct—ought to do what God wills and that our morality is after all grounded in a belief in God. But this claim of his is clearly dependent on his assumption that God is good. Yet I shall argue that even if God is good, indeed, even if God is the perfect good, it does not follow that morality can be based on religion and that we can know what we ought to do simply by knowing what God wishes us to do.

III

To come to understand the grounds for this last rather elliptical claim, we must consider the logical status of 'God is good.' Is it a non-analytic and in some way substantive claim, or is it analytic? (Can we say that it is neither?) No matter what we say, we get into difficulties.

Let us first try to claim that it is non-analytic, that it is in some way a substantive statement. So understood, God cannot then be by definition good. If the statement is synthetic and substantive, its denial cannot be self-contradictory; that is, it cannot be self-contradictory to assert that X is God but X is not good. It would always in fact be wrong to assert this, for God is the perfect good, but the denial of this claim is not self-contradictory, it is just false or in some way mistaken. The 'is' in 'God is the perfect good' is not the 'is' of identity, perfect goodness is being predicated of God in some logically contingent way. It is the religious experience of the believer and the events recorded in the Bible that lead the believer to the steadfast conviction that God has a purpose or vocation for him which he can fulfil only by completely submitting to God's will. God shall lead him and guide him in every thought, word and deed. Otherwise he will be like a man shipwrecked, lost in a vast and indifferent universe. Through careful attention to the Bible, he comes to understand that God is a wholly good being who has dealt faithfully with his chosen people. God is not by definition perfectly good or even good, but in reality, though not of logical necessity, he never falls short of perfection.

Assuming that 'God is good' is not a truth of language, how, then, do we know that God is good? Do we know or have good grounds for believing that the remarks made at the end of the above paragraph are so? The believer can indeed make such a claim, but how do we or how does he know that this is so? What grounds have we for believing that God is good? Naïve people, recalling how God spoke to Job out of the whirlwind may say that God is good because he is omnipotent and omniscient. But this clearly will not do, for, as Hepburn points out, there is nothing logically improper about saying 'X is omnipotent and omniscient and morally wicked.'[8] Surely in the world as we know it there is no logical connection between being powerful and knowledgeable and being good. As far as I can see, all that God proved to Job when he spoke to him out of the whirlwind was that God was an immeasurably powerful being; but he did not prove his moral superiority to Job and he did nothing at all even to exhibit his moral goodness. (One might even argue that he exhibited moral wickedness.) We need not assume that omnipotence and omniscience bring with them goodness or even wisdom.

What other reason could we have for claiming that God is good? We might say that he is good because he tells us to do good in thought, word and deed and to love one another. In short, in his life and in his precepts God exhibits for us his goodness and love. Now one might argue that children's hospitals and concentration camps clearly show that such a claim is false. But let us assume that in some way God does exhibit his goodness to man. Let us assume that if we examine God's works we cannot but affirm that God is good.[9] We come to understand that he is not cruel, callous or indifferent. But in order to make such judgments or to gain such an understanding, we must use our own logically independent moral criteria. In taking God's goodness as not being true by definition or as being some kind of conceptual truth, we have, in asserting 'God is good', of necessity made a moral judgment, a moral appraisal, using a criterion that cannot be based on a knowledge that God exists or that he issues commands. We call God good because we have experienced the goodness of his acts, but in order to do this, in order to know that he is good or to have any grounds for believing that he is good, we must have an independent moral criterion which we use in making this predication of God. So if 'God is good' is taken to be synthetic and substantive, then morality cannot simply be based on a belief in God. We must of logical necessity have some criterion of goodness that is not derived from any statement asserting that there is a deity.

IV

Let us alternatively, and more plausibly, take 'God is good' to be a truth of language. Now some truths of language (some analytic statements) are statements of identity, such as 'puppies are young dogs' or 'a father is a male parent.' Such statements are definitions and the 'is' indicates identity. But 'God is good' is clearly not such a statement of identity, for that 'God' does not have the same meaning as 'good' can easily be seen from the following case: Jane says to Betsy, after Betsy helps an old lady across the street, 'That was good of you.' 'That was good of you' most certainly does not mean 'that was God of you.' And when we say 'conscientiousness is good' we do not mean to say 'conscientiousness is God.' To say, as a believer does, that God is good is not to say that God is God. This clearly indicates that the word God

---

8. Hepburn, Ronald (1958), *Christianity and Paradox*, London: C. A. Watts, p. 132.
9. This is surely to assume a lot.

does not have the same meaning as the word good. When we are talking about God we are not talking simply about morality.

'God is the perfect good' is somewhat closer to 'a father is a male parent', but even here 'God' and 'the perfect good' are not identical in meaning. 'God is the perfect good' in some important respects is like 'a triangle is a trilateral.' Though something is a triangle if and only if it is a trilateral, it does not follow that 'triangle' and 'trilateral' have the same meaning. Similarly, something is God if and only if that something is the perfect good, but it does not follow that 'God' and 'the perfect good' have the same meaning. When we speak of God we wish to say other things about him as well, though indeed what is true of God will also be true of the perfect good. Yet what is true of the evening star will also be true of the morning star since they both refer to the same object, namely Venus, but, as Frege has shown, it does not follow that the two terms have the same meaning if they have the same referent.

Even if it could be made out that 'God is the perfect good' is in some way a statement of identity, (*a*) it would not make 'God is good' a statement of identity, and (*b*) we could know that X is the perfect good only if we already knew how to decide that X is good.[10] So even on the assumption that 'God is the perfect good' is a statement of identity, we need an independent way of deciding whether something is good; we must have an independent criterion for goodness.

Surely the alternative presently under consideration is more plausible than the alternative considered in section III. 'God is good' most certainly appears to be analytic in the way 'puppies are young', 'a bachelor is unmarried' or 'unjustified killing is wrong' are analytic. These statements are not statements of identity; they are not definitions, though they all follow from definitions and to deny any of them is self-contradictory.

In short, it seems to me correct to maintain that 'God is good', 'puppies are young' and 'triangles are three-sided' are all truths of language; the predicates partially define their subjects. That is to say—to adopt for a moment a Platonic sounding idiom—goodness is partially definitive of Godhood, as youngness is partially definitive of puppyhood and as three-sidedness is partially definitive of triangularity.

To accept this is not at all to claim that we can have no understanding of good without an understanding of God; and the truth of the above claim that God is good will not show that God is the, or even a, fundamental criterion for goodness. Let us establish first that and then how the fact of such truths of language does not show that we could have no understanding of good without having an understanding of God. We could not understand the full religious sense of what is meant by God without knowing that whatever is denoted by this term is said to be good; but, as 'young' or 'three-sided' are understood without reference to puppies or triangles

10. Finally we must be quite clear that X's being good is but a necessary condition for X's being the perfect good. But what would be a sufficient condition? Do we really know? I think we do not. We do not know how to identify the referent of 'the Perfect Good'. Thus in one clear sense we do not understand what such a phrase means.

though the converse cannot be the case, so 'good' is also understood quite independently of any reference to God. We can intelligibly say, 'I have a three-sided figure here that is most certainly not a triangle' and 'colts are young but they are not puppies.' Similarly, we can well say 'conscientiousness, under most circumstances at least, is good even in a world without God.' Such an utterance is clearly intelligible, to believer and non-believer alike. It is a well-formed English sentence with a use in the language. Here we can use the word good without either asserting or assuming the reality of God. Such linguistic evidence clearly shows that good is a concept which can be understood quite independently of any reference to the deity, that morality without religion, without theism, is quite possible. In fact, just the reverse is the case. Christianity, Judaism and theistic religions of that sort could not exist if people did not have a moral understanding that was, logically speaking, quite independent of such religions. We could have no understanding of the truth of 'God is good' or of the concept God unless we had an independent understanding of goodness.

That this is so can be seen from the following considerations. If we had no understanding of the word young, and if we did not know the criteria for deciding whether a dog was young, we could not know how correctly to apply the word puppy. Without such a prior understanding of what it is to be young, we could not understand the sentence 'puppies are young.' Similarly, if we had no understanding of the use of the word good, and if we did not know the criteria for deciding whether a being (or if you will, a power or a force) was good, we could not know how correctly to apply the word God. Without such a prior understanding of goodness, we could not understand the sentence 'God is good.' This clearly shows that our understanding of morality and knowledge of goodness are independent of any knowledge that we may or may not have of the divine. Indeed, without a prior and logically independent understanding of good and without some non-religious criterion for judging something to be good, the religious person could have no knowledge of God, for he could not know whether that powerful being who spoke out of the whirlwind and laid the foundations of the earth was in fact worthy of worship and perfectly good.

From my argument we should conclude that we cannot decide whether something is good or whether it ought to be done simply from finding out (assuming that we can find out) that God commanded it, willed it, enjoined it. Furthermore, whether 'God is good' is synthetic (substantive) or analytic (a truth of language), the concept of good must be understood as something distinct from the concept of God; that is to say, a man could know how to use 'good' properly and still not know how to use 'God'. Conversely, a man could not know how to use 'God' correctly unless he already understood how to use 'good'. An understanding of goodness is logically prior to, and is independent of, any understanding or acknowledgment of God.

V

In attempting to counter my argument for the necessary independence of morality—including a central facet of religious morality—from any beliefs about the existence or powers of the deity, the religious moralist might begin by conceding that (*a*) there are secular moralities that are logically independent of religion, and (*b*) that we must understand the meanings of moral terms independently of understanding what it means to speak of God. He might even go so far as to grant that only a man who understood what good and bad were could come to believe in God. 'Good', he might grant, does not mean 'willed by God' or anything like that; and 'there is no God, but human happiness is nonetheless good' is indeed perfectly intelligible as a moral utterance. But granting that, it is still the case that Jew and Christian do and must—on pain of ceasing to be Jew or Christian—take God's will as their final court of appeal in the making of moral appraisals or judgments. Any rule, act or attitude that conflicts with what the believer sincerely believes to be the will of God must be rejected by him. It is indeed true that in making moral judgments the Jew or Christian does not always use God's will as a criterion for what is good or what ought to be done. When he says 'fluoridation is a good thing' or 'the resumption of nuclear testing is a crime', he need not be using God's will as a criterion for his moral judgment. But where any moral judgment or any other moral criterion conflicts with God's ordinances, or with what the person making the judgment honestly takes to be God's ordinances, he must accept those ordinances, or he is no longer a Jew or a Christian. This acceptance is a crucial test of his faith. In this way, God's will is his fundamental moral criterion.

That the orthodox Jew or Christian would reason in this way is perfectly true, but though he says that God's will is his fundamental criterion, it is still plain that he has a yet more fundamental criterion which he must use in order to employ God's will as a moral criterion. Such a religious moralist must believe and thus be prepared to make the moral claim that there exists a being whom he deems to be perfectly good or worthy of worship and whose will should always be obeyed. But to do this he must have a moral criterion (a standard for what is morally good) that is independent of God's will or what people believe to be God's will. In fact, the believer's moral criterion—'because it is willed by God'— is in logical dependence on some distinct criterion in virtue of which the believer judges that something is perfectly good, is worthy of worship. And in making this very crucial judgment he cannot appeal to God's will as a criterion, for, that there is a being worthy of the appellation 'God', depends in part on the above prior moral claim. Only if it is correct, can we justifiably say that there is a God.

It is crucial to keep in mind that 'a wholly good being exists who is worthy of worship' is not analytic, is not a truth of language, though 'God is wholly good' is. The former is rather a substantive moral statement (expressing a moral judgment) and a very fundamental one indeed, for the believer's whole faith rests on it. Drop this and everything goes.

It is tempting to reply to my above argument in this vein: 'but it is blasphemy to judge God; no account of the logical structure of the believer's argument can be correct if it says that the believer must judge that God is good.' Here we must beware of verbal magic and attend very carefully to precisely what it is we are saying. I did not—and could not on pain of contradiction—say that God must be judged worthy of worship, perfectly good; for God by definition is worthy of worship, perfectly good. I said something quite different, namely that the believer and non-believer alike must decide whether there exists or could conceivably exist a force, a being ('ground of being') that is worthy of worship or perfectly good; and I further said that in deciding this, one makes a moral judgment that can in no way be logically dependent on God's will. Rather, the moral standard, 'because it is willed by God', is dependent for its validity on the acceptance of the claim that there is a being worthy of worship. And as our little word 'worthy' indicates, this is unequivocally a moral judgment for believer and non-believer alike.

There is a rather more baroque objection[11] to my argument that (a) nothing could count as the Judaeo-Christian God unless that reality is worthy of worship and (b) it is our own moral insight that must tell us if anything at all is or ever possibly could be worthy of worship or whether there is a being who possesses perfect goodness. My conclusion from (a) and (b) was that rather than morality being based on religion, it can be seen that religion in a very fundamental sense must be based on morality. The counter-argument claims that such a conclusion is premature because the judgment that something is worthy of worship is not a moral judgment; it is an evaluative judgment, a religious evaluation, but not a moral judgment. The grounds for this counter-claim are that if the judgment is a moral judgment, as I assumed, then demonolatry—the worship of evil spirits— would be self-contradictory. But although demonolatry is morally and religiously perverse, it is not self-contradictory. Hence my argument must be mistaken.

However, if we say 'Z is worthy of worship' or that, given Judaeo-Christian attitudes, 'if Z is what ought to be worshipped then Z must be good', it does not follow that demonolatry is self-contradictory or incoherent. Not everyone uses language as Jews and Christians do and not everyone shares the conventions of those religious groups. To say that nothing can be God, the Judaeo-Christian God, unless it is worthy of worship, and to affirm that the judgment of something as worthy of worship is a moral judgment, is not to deny that some people on some grounds could judge that what they believe to be evil spirits are worthy of worship. By definition, they could not be Jews or Christians—they show by their linguistic behaviour that they do not believe in the Judaeo-Christian God who, by definition, is perfectly good. Jews and Christians recognize that believers in demonolatry do not believe in God but in evil spirits whom such Joycean characters judge to be

---

11. This objection has been made in an unpublished paper by Professor T. P. Brown.

worthy of worship. The Christian and the demonolater make different moral judgments of a very fundamental sort reflecting different views of the world.

VI

The dialectic of our general argument about morality and divine commands should not end here. There are some further considerations which need to be brought to the forefront. Consider the theological claim that there is an infinite self-existent being, upon whom all finite realities depend for their existence, but who in turn depends on nothing. Assuming the intelligibility of the key concepts in this claim and assuming also that we know this claim to be true, it still needs to be asked how we can know, except by the use of our own moral understanding, that this infinite, self-existent being is good or is a being whose commands we ought to obey. Since he—to talk about this being anthropomorphically by the use of personal pronouns—is powerful enough, we might decide that it would be 'the better part of valour' to obey him, but this decision would not at all entail that we ought to obey him. How do we know that this being is good, except by our own moral discernment? We could not discover that this being is good or just by discovering that he 'laid the foundation of the world' or 'created man in his image and likeness'. No information about the behaviour patterns of this being would of itself tell us that he was good, righteous or just. We ourselves would have to decide that, or, to use the misleading idiom of the ethical intuitionist, we would have to intuit or some-how come to perceive or understand that the unique ethical properties of goodness, righteousness and justness apply to this strange being or 'ground of all being' that we somehow discover to exist. Only if we independently knew what we would count as good, righteous, just, would we be in a position to know whether this being is good or whether his commands ought to be obeyed. That most Christians most of the time unquestionably assume that he is good only proves that this judgment is for them a fundamental moral judgment. But this should hardly be news.

At this point it is natural to reply: 'Still, we would not even call this being God unless he was thought to be good. God, whatever else he may or may not be, is a fitting or proper object of worship.' A person arguing thus might continue: 'This is really a material mode statement about the use of the word God; that is to say, we would not call Z God unless that Z were a fitting or proper object of worship or a being that ought to be worshipped. And if we say "Z is a fitting object of worship" or "Z ought to be worshipped" we must also be prepared to say "Z is good". Z could not be one without being the other; and if Z is a fitting object of worship, Z necessarily is a being we would call God. Thus, if Z is called God, then Z must also of necessity be called good since in Judaeo-Christian contexts what ought to be worshipped must also be good. (This is a logical remark about the use of the phrase "ought to be worshipped" in Judaeo-Christian contexts.) God, by definition, is good. Though the word God is not equivalent to the word good, we would not call a being or power "God" unless that being was thought to be good.'

The above point is well taken, but it still remains the case that the believer has not derived a moral claim from a non-moral religious one. Rather, he has only indicated that the word God, like the words Saint, Santa Claus, Hunky, Nigger, Mick or Kike, is not a purely descriptive term. 'God', like 'Saint', etc., has an evaluative force; it expresses a pro-attitude on the part of the believer and does not just designate or even describe a necessary being or transcendent power or immanent force. Such a believer—unlike Schopenhauer—means by 'God' something toward which he has an appropriate pro-attitude; employing this word with its usual evaluative force, he could not say, 'God commands it but it is really evil to do it.' If, on the other hand, we simply think of what is purportedly designated or described by the word God— the descriptive force of the word—we can say, for example, without paradox, 'an objective power commands it but it is evil to do it.' By simply considering the reality allegedly denoted by the word 'God', we cannot discover whether this 'reality' is good. If we simply let Z stand for this reality, we can always ask, 'Is it good?' This is never a self-answering question in the way it is if we ask, 'Is murder evil?' Take away the evaluative force of the word 'God' and you have no ground for claiming that it must be the case that God is good; to make this claim, with our admittedly fallible moral understanding, we must decide if this Z is good.

'But'—it will be countered—'you have missed the significance of the very point you have just made. As you say yourself, "God" is not just a descriptive word and God-sentences are not by any means used with a purely descriptive aim. "God" normally has an evaluative use and God-sentences have a directive force. You cannot begin to understand them if you do not take this into consideration. You cannot just consider what Z designates or purports to designate.'

My reply to this is that we can and must if we are going to attain clarity in these matters. Certain crucial and basic sentences like 'God created the Heavens and the earth' and 'God is in Christ', are by no means just moral or practical utterances and they would not have the evaluative force they do if it were not thought that in some strange way they described a mysterious objective power. The religious quest is a quest to find a Z such that Z is worthy of worship. This being the case, the evaluative force of the words and of the utterance is dependent on the descriptive force. How else but by our own moral judgment that Z is a being worthy to be worshipped are we enabled to call this Z 'my Lord and my God'? Christians say there is a Z such that Z should be worshipped. Non-believers deny this or remain sceptical. Findlay,[12] for example, points out that his atheism is in part moral because he does not believe that there can possibly be a Z such that Z is a worthy object of worship. Father Copleston,[13] on the other hand, says there is a Z such that Z ought to be

12. Findlay, J. N. (1955), 'Can God's Existence be Disproved?' in Antony Flew and Alasdair Macintyre (eds), *New Essays in Philosophical Theology*, New York: Macmillan Company, pp. 47–56.
13. Russell, Bertrand and Copleston, F. C. (1957), 'The Existence of God: A Debate' in Bertrand Russell, *Why I am not a Christian*, London: Allen and Unwin, pp. 145–7.

worshipped. This Z, Father Copleston claims, is a 'necessary being' whose non-existence is in some important sense inconceivable. But both Findlay and Copleston are using their own moral understanding in making their respective moral judgments. Neither is deriving or deducing his moral judgment from the statement 'there is a Z' or from noticing or adverting to the fact—if it is a fact—that Z is 'being-itself', 'a reality whose non-existence is unthinkable', 'the ground of being' or the like.

Morality cannot be based on religion. If anything, the opposite is partly true, for nothing can be God unless he or it is an object worthy of worship and it is our own moral insight that must tell us if anything at all could possibly be worthy of worship.

It is true that if some Z is God, then, by definition, Z is an object worthy of worship. But this does not entail there is such a Z; that there is such a Z would depend both on what is the case and on what we, as individuals, judge to be worthy of worship. 'God is worthy of worship' is—for most uses of 'God'—analytic. To understand this sentence requires no insight at all but only a knowledge of English; but that there is or can be a Z such that Z is worthy of worship depends, in part at least, on the moral insight—or lack thereof—of that fallible creature that begins and ends in dust.

In her puzzling article, 'Modern Moral Philosophy',[14] Miss Anscombe has made a different sort of objection to the type of approach taken here. Moral uses of obligation statements, she argues, have no reasonable sense outside a divine-law conception of ethics. Without God, such conceptions are without sense. There was once a context, a religious way of life, in which these conceptions had a genuine application. 'Ought' was once equated, in the relevant context, with 'being obliged', 'bound' or 'required'. This came about because of the influence of the Torah. Because of the 'dominance of Christianity for many centuries the concepts of being bound, permitted or excused became deeply embedded in our language and thought.'[15] But since this is no longer so unequivocally the case these conceptions have become rootless. Shorn of this theistic Divine Law, shorn of the Hebrew–Christian tradition, these conceptions can only retain a 'mere mesmeric force' and cannot be 'inferred from anything whatever'.[16] I think Miss Anscombe would say that I have shown nothing more than this in my above arguments. What I have said about the independence of morality from religion is quite correct for this 'corrupt' age, where the basic principles of a divine-law conception of ethics appear merely as practical major premises on a par with the principle of utility and the like. In such contexts a moral 'ought' can only have a psychological force. Without God, it can have no 'discernible content' for the conception of moral obligation 'only operates in the context of law.'[17] By such moves as I have made above, I have, in effect,

14. Anscombe, Elizabeth (January 1958), 'Modern Moral Philosophy' in *Philosophy*, vol. 33, no. 8.
15. Ibid., p. 5.
16. Ibid., p. 8.
17. Ibid., p. 18.

indicated how moral obligation *now* has only a delusive appearance of content. And in claiming that without God there still can be genuine moral obligations I have manifested 'a detestable desire to retain the atmosphere of the term "morally obligatory" where the term itself no longer has a genuine use.'[18] 'Only if we believe in God as a law-giver can we come to believe that there is anything a man is categorically bound to do on pain of being a bad man.'[19] The concept of obligation has, without God, become a Holmesless Watson. In our present context, Miss Anscombe argues, we should, if 'psychologically possible', jettison the concepts of moral obligation, moral duty and the like and approach ethics only after we have developed a philosophical psychology which will enable us to clarify what pleasure is, what a human action is and what constitutes human virtue and a distinctively 'human flourishing'.[20]

I shall not be concerned here with the larger issues raised by Miss Anscombe's paradoxical, excessively obscure, yet strangely challenging remarks. I agree, of course, that philosophical psychology is important, but I am not convinced that we have not 'done' ethics and cannot profitably 'do' ethics without such a philosophical psychology. I shall, however, be concerned here only to point out that Miss Anscombe has not shown us that the notion of moral obligation is unintelligible or vacuous without God and his laws.

We have already seen that if so-and-so is called a divine command or an ordinance of God, then it is obviously something that the person who believes it to be a divine command or ordinance of God will believe he ought to obey, for he would not call anything a *divine* command or an ordinance of *God* unless he thought he ought to obey it. But we ourselves, by our own moral insight, must judge that such commands or promulgations are worthy of such an appellation. Yet no moral conceptions follow from a command or law as such. And this would be true at any time whatsoever. It is a logical and not a historical consideration.

Now it is true that if you believe in God in such a way as to accept God as your Lord and Master, and if you believe that something is an ordinance of God, then you ought to try to follow this ordinance. But if you behave like this it is not because you base morals on religion or on a law concept of morality, but because he who can bring himself to say 'my God' uses 'God' and cognate words evaluatively. To use such an expression is already to make a moral evaluation; the man expresses a decision that he is morally bound to do whatever God commands. 'I ought to do whatever this Z commands' is an expression of moral obligation. To believe in God, as we have already seen, involves the making of a certain value judgment; that is to say, the believer believes that there is a Z such that Z is worthy of worship. But his value judgment cannot be derived from just examining Z, or from hearing Z's commands or laws. Without a pro-attitude on the part of the believer toward Z, without a decision by the individual concerned that Z is worthy of worship, nothing

18. Ibid., p. 18.
19. Ibid., p. 6.
20. Ibid., pp. 1, 15, 18.

of moral kind follows. But no decision of this sort is entailed by discoveries about Z or by finding out what Z commands or wishes. It is finally up to the individual to decide that this Z is worthy of worship, that this Z ought to be worshipped, that this Z ought to be called his Lord and Master. We have here a moral use of 'ought' that is logically prior to any law conception of ethics. The command gains obligatory force because it is judged worthy of obedience. If someone says, 'I do not pretend to appraise God's laws, I just simply accept them because God tells me to', similar considerations obtain. This person judges that there is a Z that is a proper object of obedience. This expresses his own moral judgment, his own sense of what he is obliged to do.

A religious belief depends for its viability on our sense of good and bad—our own sense of worth—and not vice versa. It is crucial to an understanding of morality that this truth about the uses of our language be understood. Morality cannot be based on religion and I (like Findlay) would even go so far as to deny in the name of morality that any Z whatsoever could be an object or being worthy of worship. But whether or not I am correct in this last judgment, it remains the case that each person with his own finite and fallible moral awareness must make decisions of this sort for himself This would be so whether he was in a Hebrew–Christian tradition or in a 'corrupt' and 'shallow' consequentialist tradition or in any tradition whatsoever. A moral understanding must be logically prior to any religious assent.

Questions for discussion

1. Can one be truly moral without having any religious beliefs?
2. To what extent might belief in God influence the way in which one thinks of one's day-to-day actions?
3. What problems arise from the suggestion that 'X is good because God wills X'?
4. What problems arise from the suggestion that 'God wills X because X is good'?
5. Might one hold both that X is good because God wills X and that God wills X because it is good?
6. 'God commands you to treat people fairly.' Supposing that the statement is true, does it give us definitive grounds for treating people fairly? If so, why? If not, what are the implications for discussions concerning morality and religion?
7. 'One cannot believe that moral truth is ultimately grounded in God's nature without also abandoning one's right and need to decide on moral questions for oneself.' Is that statement true?
8. Might one have moral reason for defying God?

Advice on further reading

One's whole approach to debates concerning morality and religion is bound to be deeply affected by one's view of morality in general. If you think, for example, that 'Hitler was a bad man' can only be understood as expressing someone's feelings, then you shall have no time for anything like the positions developed above in the extracts from Kant, Owen, and Trethowan. For these authors, and for most philosophers who think that moral matters are significant when it comes to philosophy of religion, moral discourse does more than indicate our attitudes to people and how they behave. They have what is often referred to as 'cognitive content'.

But do they? Your reflections on this question shall be greatly helped by some knowledge of the history of moral philosophy. For brief but reliable surveys, see Alasdair MacIntyre, *A Short History of Ethics* (2nd edn, Notre Dame, Indiana, 1998), Richard Norman, *The Moral Philosophers: An Introduction to Ethics* (2nd edn, Oxford, 1998), and D. D. Raphael, *Moral Philosophy* (Oxford, 1981). For a survey of the history of Christian thinking on morality, a good text to start with is Servais Pinckaers, *The Sources of Christian Ethics* (Washington, DC, 1995).

There are numerous books discussing key philosophical questions concerning morality (such as 'Can moral judgements be thought of as asserting truths?' and 'Is there any such thing as moral knowledge?'). Ones of particular philosophical interest (which sometimes touch on the relation between morality and religious belief), include:

R. B. Brandt, *A Theory of the Good and the Right* (Oxford, 1979).

John Finnis, *Natural Law and Natural Rights* (Oxford, 1980).

R. M. Hare, *The Language of Morals* (Oxford, 1952).

Alasdair MacIntyre, *After Virtue* (London, 1981).

J. L. Mackie, *Ethics: Inventing Right and Wrong* (Harmondsworth, 1977).

Philippa Foot, *Virtues and Vices* (Oxford, 1978).

Bernard Williams, *Ethics and the Limits of Philosophy* (Cambridge, Massachussetts, 1985).

For those approaching moral philosophy for the first time, there are some helpful anthologies currently available. These include:

David E. Cooper (ed.), *Ethics: The Classic Readings* (Oxford, 1998).

Louis P. Pojman (ed.), *Moral Philosophy: A Reader* (2nd edn, Indianapolis, Indiana, 1998).

Peter Singer (ed.), *Ethics* (Oxford and New York, 1994).

For some notable general studies on the topic of morality and religion, see:

Robert Merrihew Adams, *Finite and Infinite Goods: A Framework for Ethics* (New York and Oxford, 1999).

William Warren Bartley III, *Morality and Religion* (London, 1971).

Peter Byrne, *The Moral Interpretation of Religion* (Grand Rapids, Michigan, and Cambridge, UK, 1998).

Paul W. Diener, *Religion and Morality: An Introduction* (Louisville, Kentucky, 1997).

W. G. Maclagan, *The Theological Frontier of Ethics* (London, 1961).

P. L. Quinn, *Divine Commands and Moral Requirements* (Oxford, 1978).

For extremely useful volumes which include many important essays on the topic of morality and religious belief (volumes which also come with copious bibliographical recommendations), see:

Paul Helm (ed.), *Divine Commands and Morality* (Oxford, 1981).

G. Outka and J. P. Reeder (eds), *Religion and Morality* (Garden City, New York, 1973).

D. Z. Phillips (ed.), *Religion and Morality* (New York, 1996).

I. T. Ramsey (ed.), *Christian Ethics and Contemporary Philosophy* (London, 1966).

For discussions of Kant on God as a postulate of practical reason (with helpful advice on yet further reading), see:

Bernard M. G. Reardon, *Kant as Philosophical Theologian* (Basingstoke and London, 1988), ch. 3.

Keith Ward, *The Development of Kant's View of Ethics* (Oxford, 1972).

Ralph C. S. Walker, *Kant* (London, 1978), ch. X.

Allen W. Wood, *Kant's Moral Religion* (Ithaca, New York, 1970).

Allen W. Wood, 'Rational Theology, Moral Faith and Religion', in Paul Guyer (ed.), *The Cambridge Companion to Kant* (Cambridge, 1992).

For more on Aquinas on morality and religion, see John Finnis, *Aquinas: Moral, Political and Legal Theory* (Oxford, 1998), Anthony Lisska, *Aquinas's Theory of Natural Law: An Analytic Reconstruction* (Oxford, 1996), and Ralph McInerny, *Ethica Thomistica* (Washington, DC, 1982) and *Aquinas on Human Action* (Washington, DC, 1992). For a stimulating essay on Aquinas and moral goodness (one which is also relevant to reflection on the problem of evil), see Eleonore Stump and Norman Kretzmann, 'Being and Goodness', in Thomas V. Morris (ed.), *Divine and Human Action* (Ithaca and London, 1988).

It is interesting and thought-provoking to see how people coming from the traditions of different world religions respond to practical ethical problems. For examples of some of them doing so, see Regina Wentzer Wolfe and Christine E. Gudorf (eds), *Ethics and World Religions: Cross Cultural Case Studies* (Maryknoll, New York, 1999).

Part VII

People and life after death

Introduction

Is death the end?

ON 7 July 1776 James Boswell (1740–95) visited David Hume in Edinburgh.[1] Hume was dying. According to Boswell, he looked 'lean, ghastly, and quite of an earthy appearance'.[2] But he also seemed to be 'placid and even cheerful'.

Boswell asked him 'if it was not possible that there might be a future state'. Hume replied 'that it was a most unreasonable fancy that he should exist forever'. When Boswell asked him if 'the thought of annihilation never gave him any uneasiness', Hume said: 'Not the least.'

Boswell, who devoutly believed in a life to come, was amazed by this response. Yet, when reflecting on his meeting with Hume, he also felt bound to observe, 'I could not but be assailed by momentary doubts while I had actually before me a man of such strong abilities and extensive inquiry dying in the persuasion of being annihilated.'

For Hume, death is the end of human life. For Boswell, it is not. But which of them is right? Is it really the case that we perish at death? Or is there life for us after it? These are questions which everyone asks sooner or later. They are also questions which have provoked the attention of philosophers from ancient times to the present. And they are questions in which religious believers have an investment, since most religious traditions teach that people will survive death in some form or other.

People and life after death

But why should one suppose that this is so? And how might one conceive of life after death if one supposes that it is so?

In Chapter 62 (which has been specially written for this volume) Stephen T. Davis addresses both of these questions, while providing a solid and helpful account of ways in which philosophers have dealt with them through the ages. Philosophical discussions of life after death have been greatly influenced by differing views of what people are. Are they essentially physical entities? Are they essentially non-physical? Are they partly physical and partly non-physical? Davis explains how philosophers have answered these questions. He also explains why some have thought it reasonable to believe in life after death, why others have taken a different view, and what we might make of their verdicts today.

Since Davis provides a fine introduction to the topic of people and life after death, I

---

1. Boswell is, perhaps, most famous for his association with Samuel Johnson (1709–84), whose biography he wrote.
2. James Boswell, 'An Account of my Last Interview with David Hume, Esq.'. The text is conveniently reprinted in Norman Kemp Smith (ed.), *David Hume: Dialogues Concerning Natural Religion* (Indianapolis, Indiana, 1947).

will not waste space here repeating him. Instead, I will offer a short preface to Chapters 63–5, in which three celebrated thinkers (Plato, Bertrand Russell, and Peter Geach) offer their views on the question 'Is death the end?'.

Plato on life after death

The extract from Plato comes from the *Phaedo*, which purports to be an account of the final hours of Socrates. The setting is the death cell of Socrates in Athens. Socrates has been condemned to die by drinking poison. In this situation he is visited by friends, who want to share his last moments with him.

Early in the dialogue Socrates professes a strong belief to the effect that his execution means little, since he will survive it. The true philosopher, he says, should be happy to die. Why? Because death is a release from what most prevents us from acquiring true knowledge. Real philosophers, so Socrates suggests, are continually preparing for death. For it frees them from distractions that inhibit the quest for truth.[3]

Or does it? As the excerpt from the *Phaedo* begins, one of Socrates's friends (Cebes) begs to take issue with him on the matter.[4] Taking the word 'soul' to mean that which makes Socrates to be a living thing, Cebes wonders whether the soul of Socrates can really survive his death. In responding to Cebes, Socrates offers three arguments in favour of survival, arguments which presumably represent Plato's own thinking.

According to the first, we survive death, since opposites come from opposites and since life must therefore come from death.

According to the second, the notion of life after death seems to be supported by the fact that we cannot account for the fact that we know certain things except on the assumption that we have somehow existed before our present lives.

According to the third, people have to survive death, since their souls, being immaterial, lack parts and cannot therefore perish.

Are these arguments good ones? Philosophers since Plato have mostly found them unconvincing. Some have suggested that though things may have opposites, it does not follow that if something comes to be there is something from which it comes which is its opposite. Others have denied that our knowledge can only be accounted for on the supposition we have enjoyed a former life. Yet others have challenged the claim that something immaterial cannot cease to exist.

But Plato's arguments are sophisticated ones. And they did much to influence subsequent discussions of the subject. Why? Largely because they uncompromisingly assume what many take to be obvious: that the question of human survival is a question about the survival of something *incorporeal*.

---

3. Here Plato seems to be ascribing to Socrates the Platonic view that knowledge can only be achieved as we move beyond the impact on us of sense experience. According to Plato, sense experience cannot, by itself, tell us what things are.

4. 'When Socrates had said that' at the start of the extract refers back to what I have just reported as Socrates's view of death as reported by Plato.

Russell

Is it, however? As Davis explains, the assumption has been firmly rejected by a variety of thinkers. It relies on the belief that people are essentially different from their bodies and able to exist apart from them. But is this belief a tenable one? Some would say that we have no reason to embrace it and that we have positive reason for rejecting it. And their line of thinking is much in evidence in what Russell has to say. He draws attention to what he takes to be a dependence of the mental on the physical. And he finds the perishing of our bodies to be *prima facie* reason for thinking that death, for us, is indeed the end.

In that case, however, why do people believe in life after death? Russell takes belief in human survival to derive from fear of death. He also suggests that it springs from a misguided view of human beings as things of great value. But do people believe in life after death only for the reasons cited by Russell? As Davis indicates, some do not. As he also observes, some people see belief in life after death as inseparably connected with belief in human resurrection—a topic which Russell completely ignores.

Geach and resurrection

Yet the notion of resurrection is, however, much to the foreground in Chapter 66. For Geach is of the opinion that 'apart from the *possibility* of resurrection' there can be no life after death. Why so? In developing his answer to this question, Geach offers a sustained attack on the Platonic notion of people as essentially immaterial and therefore able to survive the destruction of their bodies.

Can one survive as a mind apart from the existence of one's body? Appealing to concepts such as *seeing* and *feeling*, Geach suggests not.

Might I survive as a disembodied spirit? According to Geach, a disembodied spirit would not be *me*, for I am a human person and am therefore something which essentially enjoys sensuous experiences.

Might I survive death by becoming reincarnated? According to Geach, it is hard to make sense of references to reincarnation.

On Geach's account, personal identity over time requires bodily continuity. So if I am to survive my death, then there has, after my death, to be a living person who is somehow materially continuous with the person I am now.

But is that right? Something like Geach's view of personal identity is probably the dominant one among contemporary philosophers. It is also defended by some philosophers of the past (e.g. Aristotle and Aquinas). But it has had some notable philosophical opponents. And there are still philosophers who argue that people can exist apart from what is material. Hence, for example, while Geach finds little sense in the suggestion that I can exist as a disembodied mind, Richard Swinburne finds the suggestion relatively unproblematic. Or, as he puts it:

A person has a body if there is one particular chunk of matter through which he has to operate on and learn about the world. But suppose he finds himself able to operate on and learn about the world within some small finite region, without having to use one particular chunk of matter for this purpose. He might find himself with knowledge of the position of objects in a room (perhaps by having visual sensations, perhaps not), and able to move such objects just like that, in the ways in which we know about the positions of our limbs and can move them. But the room would not be, as it were, the person's body; for we may suppose that simply by choosing to do so he can gradually shift the focus of his knowledge and control, e.g., to the next room. The person would be in no way limited to operating and learning through one particular chunk of matter. Hence we may term him disembodied. The supposition that a person might become disembodied . . . seems coherent.[5]

With this point made, Swinburne goes on to argue that if X can be without Y, then X and Y are distinct. And since he thinks that I can exist without my body, he concludes that I am not my body and can survive without it.

   When reading Geach, you should bear in mind arguments such as those of Swinburne. And you should try to adjudicate on them. For, in many ways, they take one to the core of most philosophical debates on the question of life after death.

   5. Sydney Shoemaker and Richard Swinburne, *Personal Identity* (Oxford, 1984), pp. 23 f.

Chapter 62

Philosophy and life after death: the questions and the options

Stephen T. Davis

I. Introduction

Do people live after death? This is surely one of the most important questions that is asked in the philosophy of religion. Naturally there are only two possible answers to it. Either human persons will live after death or else they will not. Let us call all theories that deny life after death, 'Death Ends All' views. There are three main sorts of theory that affirm life after death: reincarnation, immortality of the soul, and resurrection of the body.

Here, we will first consider the claim that life after death is not just false but incoherent. Next, we will consider two philosophical problems that bear significantly on our issue, viz., the relationship between the mind and the body, and the problem of personal identity. Then we will discuss one important 'death ends all' theory. Finally, we will discuss reincarnation, immortality, and resurrection, respectively.

II. Flew on 'surviving death'

In a famous essay written some forty-five years ago, 'Can a Man Witness His Own Funeral?',[1] Antony Flew argues that the notion of life after death is incoherent. He offers three related arguments for this conclusion. First, one statement typically made by those who affirm life after death—'We all of us survive death'—is self-contradictory. In an airplane crash, there are two mutually exclusive and exhaustive categories, the dead and the survivors. So the question, 'Did Jones (one of the passengers) survive the crash?' makes perfect sense, but the question 'Did Jones survive Jones's death?' does not. Accordingly, the sentence 'We all of us survive death' has no clear meaning.

Second, another statement typically made by those who accept life after death— 'We all of us live forever'—is simply empirically false. Notice, Flew says, that *the* paradigm true statement throughout the history of logic is the statement 'All men

1. Antony Flew, 'Can a Man Witness His Own Funeral?', *The Hibbert Journal*, vol. 54 (1956). Flew has widened and updated his critique of survival of death theories in more recent publications, e.g., *The Logic of Mortality* (Oxford: Basil Blackwell, 1987), but the basic line is similar.

are mortal.' This generalization is as massively confirmed as any generalization can possibly be, and it is, Flew says, the 'flat contrary' of 'We all of us live forever.'

Flew is aware of a possible objection to his first two arguments. One way to decide whether a given state of affairs is logically possible is to ask whether it is coherently imaginable. And a defender of life after death might claim that 'survival of death' is coherent after all because it is possible to imagine one's own funeral.

But here Flew offers some distinctions (1) *What it would it be like to witness my own funeral.* Of course this is imaginable, Flew says. It is quite possible for me to close my eyes and imagine people witnessing my funeral—I am in the casket, my mother is crying, a priest is offering prayers, etc. But imagining this picture does nothing to support the claim that life after death is imaginable. What *would* support the claim would be imagining (2) *what it would be like to witness me witnessing my own funeral.* But the problem is that this picture is not imaginable: if it is really me who is witnessing the funeral, then it is not my funeral; and if it is really my funeral, then I cannot witness it because I am dead in the coffin.

But, says Flew (speaking for his imagined critic), why can't I imagine (3) *what it would be like to witness myself as an invisible, incorporeal spirit witnessing my own funeral, i.e., the funeral of my body*? But, says Flew (now speaking in his own voice), this does not differ in any significant or empirically relevant way from (1), i.e., from imagining my own funeral without being there at all (except as a corpse in the coffin). All talk about an 'invisible, intangible spirit' and of its 'being there' is devoid of any empirical sense. So life after death theories either presuppose the absence of genuine death or else violate the normal use of such terms as 'I' or 'me.' Flew's conclusion is that his first two objections still stand.

Third, Flew introduces his dictum, 'People are what you meet.' Person words (by which Flew means words like 'I,' 'me,' 'you,' 'father,' 'mother,' 'butcher') refer not to mysterious elusive things like souls, but to real human persons, i.e., bodies plus behaviour. We know this because children who have no idea what a soul or immaterial essence might be can use person words perfectly well. Persons are publicly locatable and observable things. You don't ever take a walk or have a conversation with an immaterial essence. You engage in such activities with other human beings—not just with their bodies, of course (the term 'father's body' would normally mean 'father's corpse'), but with their bodies plus behaviours. Since the bodies and behaviours of human beings do not survive death, Flew's overall conclusion is that human beings do not and cannot live after death.

Flew no longer develops his critique of life after death in precisely this way, but his argument has had a lasting impact on the discussion, and is still occasionally cited. In one sense, this is surprising, since the argument is hardly convincing.

For one thing, Flew's *ex cathedra* claims about the incoherence of 'surviving death' will only be convincing to those whom we might call lexical fundamentalists. These are people who stubbornly insist that the meaning of a word is indelibly established by its original usage; thus Flew's dogged insistence that you might 'survive a plane crash' but never 'survive your own death.' But it is obvious that as new human situations arise, words sometimes get stretched in meaning in order to make valid, and quite communicable, points. If talk of 'surviving death' communicates with people, as opposed to systematically misleading them, that way of talking is fine.

Similarly, it would be surprising indeed if anyone who says 'We all of us live forever' means that sentence to deny that 'All men are mortal.' I would have thought that the reverse is true—those who speak in this way would want to be interpreted as *insisting* on the mortality of all human beings. This, in fact, is precisely their point—*we all die*, and after we die we go on living forever in another form or world. I have never heard of a believer in life after death who wanted to deny that everyone must die.

Finally, Flew's dictum, 'People are what you meet,' has clearly overlooked something, viz., a first person perspective. If the range of the term 'people' is 'other people,' that is, people besides me, then Flew's dictum is beyond reproach. But it is obvious that by introspection, human beings know themselves as something different from and other than 'body plus behaviour.' It is perfectly possible for me to know many things about myself (e.g., my present mood, my first impression of Kant, my sense that a certain person whom I know is pompous) that may never have been evident in my body or behaviour.

Whatever this missing something is, and it has been called by many names in philosophy (the mind, the soul, the realm of the mental, consciousness), those who believe in the life after death theory known as immortality (as well as those who believe in reincarnation) hold that it is the thing that survives death. Flew has not refuted that claim.

III. The mind–body problem

Two philosophical problems, the mind–body problem and the problem of personal identity, are importantly related to life after death theories. Let me briefly define each problem, sketch the strengths and weaknesses of some of the most important theories, and point out the relevance of those theories to the problem of life after death.

Human beings have or are bodies and engage in bodily activities such as walking, talking, sleeping, writing, etc. Bodies are physical objects that take up space, have physical location, and can be tested and measured scientifically. In addition, bodily events are accessible to other people. If I walk or talk or sleep, others are perfectly capable of observing those activities. But human beings also engage in various sorts of 'mental' activities—thinking, feeling, remembering, experiencing pain, formulating intentions, making decisions, etc. And those sorts of events do not take up space, are not located anywhere, cannot be measured scientifically, and are 'private' in the sense that they are directly accessible only to the person who thinks the thought, makes the decision, etc.

The mind–body problem, broadly stated, is: How are the physical and mental aspects of human beings related? How are the body and the mind (assuming there is such a thing as a mind) related in the human person?

Several major theories of the mind and body have been suggested in the history of philosophy. Monistic theories limit human nature to one and only one metaphysical class. Momentarily we will consider the monistic theory called materialism. Dualistic theories claim that human beings consist of both physical bodies and nonphysical (or incorporeal) minds, and that the mind (or soul), an ongoing existing thing, is the essence of the person. (There are other versions of mind–body dualism beside the 'substance dualism' that I have been describing, e.g., the so-called 'bundle theory,' usually associated with Hume and with some versions of Buddhism, but we will not be able to discuss them here.)

The dualistic theory known as interactionism is most commonly associated with Descartes.[2] One of the things that Descartes thought followed directly from his famous *Cogito, ergo sum*, is 'I am a thinking being.' That is, my essence or nature is to think (as well as, presumably, to engage in other 'mental' activities like feeling, intending, remembering, deciding, etc.). That aspect of human beings that does the thinking Descartes called the soul or mind; it is indivisible and unextended, and is the essence of the person. Human bodies are corporeal, divisible, and extended, and are really just very complicated machines whose behaviour can be explained mechanistically.

Descartes was convinced that minds and bodies are so metaphysically dissimilar that they cannot causally interact with each other—not directly, at any rate. The mind cannot directly cause bodily events, and the body cannot directly cause mental events. Yet we know intuitively that our minds and bodies are (as Descartes says) 'intimately conjoined'; mind–body causal interaction seems to happen all the time. I perform the mental event of deciding to raise my hand, and the physical event of my hand going up occurs; I perform the physical event of placing my hand in the fire, and the mental event of my feeling pain occurs.

How then do we explain apparent mind–body causal interaction when that interaction appears to be metaphysically impossible? Descartes's solution was to posit a location in the body—the pineal gland (which is an actual gland at the base of the medulla oblongata)–where mind and body (indirectly) causally interact. The medical science of Descartes's day did not know the function of the pineal gland, and Descartes simply posited the idea that mind and body exercise their influence on each other there.

Descartes also suggested the existence of what he called 'animal spirits'—these are pure, subtle gasses that pass through tubes in the body and are the means by which the mind and body communicate with each other through the pineal gland. Descartes's picture was apparently something like this: When I raise my hand, my

---

2. See especially the Second Meditation and *The Passions of the Soul* in Elizabeth S. Haldane and G. R. T. Ross (eds), *The Philosophical Works of Descartes*, vol. I (Cambridge: Cambridge University Press, 1970).

mind makes the decision, communicates this decision via the animal spirits to the pineal gland, which communicates via the animal spirits to my hand. Medical science of today, of course, knows nothing of animal spirits.

The majority of contemporary philosophers who discuss the mind–body problem oppose interactionism as well as the other dualistic theories, and part of the reason for this fact may be the legacy of Descartes and his ignorant guesswork about the pineal gland and animal spirits. It may be that interactionism can be defended, but certainly not in this way.[3]

The other mind–body theory that we will discuss is materialism. Materialists need not worry about causal interaction between metaphysically different sorts of entities, because they claim that there are no mental entities. Everything is physical; the only things that exist consist of atoms in motion. Most philosophers who discuss the mind–body problem today defend one or another version of materialism. Let me briefly explain one such theory; it is called 'Identity Theory.'[4]

Identity Theory is based on the claim that all mental events and processes are brain events. This is not meant as an a priori or linguistic claim, but rather as an empirical one—as a matter of fact, it turns out that all mental events are physical events. And the word 'are' here is meant in the sense of strict numerical identity. So the identity theorist's claim is that 'Making a decision to raise your hand' or 'Feeling a slight pain in one's arm' turn out to be *nothing more than* events that occur in the brain. We used to think of them as mental events, but we now see that they are simply brain processes.

Identity theorists defend their view in part on the basis of considerations of simplicity. And it must be admitted that theirs is a simpler ontology than is posited by dualists. The only realities they countenance are physical realities. Of course, considerations of simplicity are only probative in cases where two competing theories are equal or roughly equal in explanatory power, and it has yet to be determined that materialism and dualism are equal in explanatory power.

Identity Theory has been subject to rigorous criticism, and the objections have spawned ever more subtle variations in the theory as well as neighbouring theories.[5] Let me briefly mention what seems to be the overall point, as well as three aspects of it. The general theme of the criticisms is that physical or brain events simply cannot possess all the attributes that we are quite sure mental events possess, and that therefore mental events cannot be brain events.

For one thing, some mental states seem to be characterized by what philosophers call 'intentionality.' That is, they have a sort of 'aboutness'; they point towards things outside themselves as objects or targets. My decision to open the door is

3. For a much better way of defending dualism, see William D. Hart's essay, 'Dualism,' in Samuel Guttenplan (ed.), *A Companion to the Philosophy of Mind* (Oxford: Blackwell, 1994), pp. 265–9.
4. See especially the essays by U. T. Place, J. J. C. Smart, and D. M. Armstrong in C. V. Borst (ed.), *The Mind/Brain Identity Theory* (London: Macmillan, 1970).
5. See, for example, the essays collected especially in Parts III and IV of David M. Rosenthal (ed.), *The Nature of Mind* (New York: Oxford University Press, 1991).

about the door; my aversion to lima beans is about lima beans. Now critics of Identity Theory point out that physical states, e.g., the firing of certain nerve endings in the brain, have no intentionality. Brain events are simply electrical-chemical events in a human body—they don't refer to or represent or aim at anything.

For another, it seems absurd to many philosophers to say, as identity theorists must, that mental events (like the brain events they are supposedly identical to) have physical location, size, shape, or velocity. Mental events have no location (despite Descartes' claim that the soul's 'seat' in the body is the pineal gland). If they did, and if as claimed they are entirely physical, then surgeons would in theory be able to locate somewhere in my brain the decision to shut the door or my dislike of lima beans. Indeed, it has been charged against identity theory that if I were to close my eyes and formulate in my mind an imagined picture of an elephant, a surgeon would in theory be able to find an elephant-shaped something located somewhere in my grey matter.

Finally, mental states are characterized by what philosophers call 'privacy,' i.e., they are directly available only to the person who has them. I can be directly aware of my decision to shut the door, but you can only observe that I have apparently made a decision to shut the door by observing my door-shutting behaviour. But if identity theory is true, then my decision to shut the door is nothing more than a certain combination of physical events in my brain. Thus, in principle, if we knew enough about the brain and knew where to look, other people could observe my decision. And this has seemed to many philosophers absurd.

Of the life after death theories that we will discuss later, 'Death Ends All' theorists need not commit themselves to any particular mind–body theory. Believers in reincarnation and immortality, however, must be dualists. That is, if some version of mind–body materialism turns out to be true, those two theories are false. Believers in resurrection can be either dualists or materialists.

IV. The problem of personal identity

The second philosophical problem that is importantly related to life after death theories is the problem of personal identity. It is sometimes understood as an epistemological problem, viz., *how we could know* that, say, a given person before us is the same person as someone we once knew. But I believe the problem should rather be understood as a metaphysical one, viz., *establishing the criteria* that can be used for identifying and re-identifying persons. On what basis can someone, say, who exists in the afterlife be identified with someone who once lived on earth?

The problem of personal identity can be thorny and frustrating. Much of the discussion of the problem revolves around 'test cases'—imagined stories that often read like science fiction. John Locke began the trend with his story about the soul of a prince entering the body of a cobbler.[6] Contemporary test cases

6. John Locke, *An Essay Concerning Human Understanding*, ed. Alexander C. Fraser, vol. I (New York: Dover Publications, 1959), II, 27, 15.

typically involve body exchange, brain fusion, brain fusion, teletransportation, and the like.

There are three main approaches to this problem. Those who accept what is called the 'memory criterion' (which includes not just memory but other mental characteristics such as personality and dispositions) argue that a given person X is identical to a given person Y if and only if X and Y have the same mind (and thus memories, personality traits, etc.). And we do sometimes identify people on the basis of the memory criterion alone. For example, when we receive an email message we assume that the message was indeed written by the person it was purportedly written by if the message shows that its author has the memories and personality characteristics that we associate with the person by whom the letter claims to have been written.

Those who accept what is called the 'bodily criterion' argue that X is identical to Y if and only if X and Y have the same body (at two different times). And we do frequently identify people on this basis too—I recognize someone walking down the hall as the dean of the college by his physiognomy, attire, voice, etc. The deepest issues here concern questions such as: Is either criterion a necessary or sufficient condition (or both) of personal identity? Does one criterion take precedence over the other?

A third position has surfaced in recent years. Some who discuss the problem have given up on the task of trying to establish necessary and sufficient conditions of personal identity. There appear to be two main reasons for this. First, some philosophers hold that there are certain objections to all theories of personal identity that cannot be met, e.g., the so-called 'duplication objection.'[7] Second, some philosophers hold that in certain imagined but logically possible test cases personal identity seems either indeterminate or indecidable apart from arbitrary stipulation. The philosophers who take this third position no longer talk about personal identity in cases of survival of death. Instead of asking whether some X in the afterlife will be identical to some Y who lives now, they instead ask whether Y will be X's 'closest continuer' or has 'psychological continuity' with X.[8]

Advocates of 'Death Ends All' theories of survival of death need not commit themselves to any particular approach to the problem of personal identity. Defenders of reincarnation and immortality must reject the second and third theories in favour of the first. That is, they must argue (1) that the problem of personal identity can be solved, and (2) that the memory criterion can be sufficient by itself to establish personal identity. This is for the obvious reason that neither reincarnation nor immortality posits any bodily continuity between our premortem and postmortem selves. Defenders of resurrection must similarly argue that the problem of

---

7. See chapter 7 of Stephen T. Davis, *Risen Indeed: Making Sense of the Resurrection* (Grand Rapids, Michigan: Eerdmans, 1993) for a discussion of this objection.
8. Probably the foremost philosopher who fits in this third category is Derek Parfit. See Part III of his *Reasons and Persons* (Oxford: Oxford University Press, 1986).

personal identity can be solved, but can appeal to either the memory or the bodily criterion (or both) in establishing personal identity.

V. 'Death ends all' theories

For obvious reasons, defenders of 'Death Ends All' theories spend little time talking about the nature of the next life. Their efforts are usually directed towards showing why the prospects for life after death are dim, and drawing implications from that point for our lives here and now.

There are, of course, weaker senses in which even a 'death ends all' theorist can claim that we live on after death. I say 'weaker' because such notions do not involve persons as conscious, individual entities continuing after death. I may live on in the sense that my atoms merge, or my personality merges, into some greater whole. I may live on in the sense that others will remember me, or in the sense that I will remain eternally precious to God, or in the sense that my descendants will carry my genes into the future. But since here we are concerned with life after death in the full-blooded sense, I will discuss these options no longer.

Many philosophers take such a 'death ends all' approach, including many of the ancient Stoics, most of the modern Existentialists, and such well-known twentieth-century philosophers as Bertrand Russell, A. J. Ayer,[9] and Kai Nielsen. Let me focus in this section on the arguments of the great and now largely ignored ancient philosopher Epicurus (341–270 BCE).

Epicurus was the founder of the school of philosophy known as Epicureanism. He wrote works on many different philosophical topics, but fortunately he neatly summed up his thoughts about death in one, frequently quoted, sentence. It says: 'Death, the most dreaded of evils, is . . . of no concern to us, for while we exist death is not present, and when death is present we no longer exist.'[10]

Epicurus believed that fear of death was one of the chief reasons for human unhappiness, and he held that this fear has two sources, fear that dying will be painful, and fear of a terrible afterlife to be afflicted by the gods. Both are mistaken, he said. Dying may be painful, but it is soon over. And there is no life after death and thus no hell. Since I will not be there to experience anything, I should no more fear death than I should fear falling asleep. Rational Epicureans, he insisted, keep death in proper perspective.

Is Epicurus's argument (from the sentence quoted above) successful? Perhaps it can be stated in logical form as follows:

1.   At all times, either I exist or I am dead.

9. Although Ayer's disbelief in life after death was at least temporarily softened by a now famous near-death experience, as recounted in his 'What I Saw When I Was Dead,' reprinted in Paul Edwards (ed.), *Immortality* (New York: Macmillan, 1992).

10. See his 'Letter to Menoecius,' IIb, in Epicurus, *Letters, Principal Doctrines and Vatican Sayings*, ed. Russell M. Geer (Indianapolis, Indiana: Bobbs-Merrill, 1964), p. 54.

2.   When I exist, I am not dead.
3.   When I am not dead, my death is of no concern to me.
4.   Therefore, when I exist, my death is of no concern to me.
5.   When I am dead, I do not exist.
6.   When I do not exist, my death is of no concern to me.
7.   Therefore, when I am dead, my death is of no concern to me.
8.   Therefore, at no time is my death of concern to me.

But, premise (3) can be disputed. Indeed, those who find Epicurus's argument unconvincing will argue that it is precisely when I am not dead that my future death *is* of concern to me. Epicurus was apparently committed to the claim that something can be bad for me only if I experience it. Since I do not experience the state of *being dead* (although I probably will experience dying), the state of being dead is not bad for me.

But this seems false. Things that I do not experience *can* be bad for me. If event E1 causes event E2, and if I do not experience E1, and if E2 is bad for me, then surely it makes sense to say that E1 is bad for me. Suppose I am fired from my job because of a decision that was made at a meeting that was held last without my knowledge. Then surely the meeting was bad for me even though I did not experience it.[11]

But what about Epicurus's claim that people fear death because they fear the pain of dying and the threat of a painful afterlife? If this were true, that is, if these were the only or even the most important reasons that people fear death, Epicurus might be on firm ground. But these are definitely not the only reasons people fear death. (a) Some fear death because it is unknown; (b) some fear death because they will have to face it alone; (c) some fear death because it means separation from their friends and loved ones; (d) some fear death because their hopes and goals for the future will remain unattained; (e) some fear death because they suspect their loved ones might fare badly after they are gone; (f) some fear death because they believe it means annihilation of themselves.

If Epicurus's general claims about 'death ends all' are true, his theory does seem to assuage some of the reasons that people fear death, e.g., the fear of hell. But its weakness is that it does not assuage others, particularly reasons (d), (e), and (f) above. Indeed, so far as the fear of annihilation is concerned, Epicurus's argument seems rather to underscore it.

Epicurus may be correct that there is no life after death. He may be correct that we should face death with equanimity. But he was surely wrong in his thinking that his argument could overcome the human fear of death. For many people, the fear of non-being, of no longer existing, is the chief reason to fear death. Let me quote the

11.   There are other complications and difficulties involved in evaluating Epicurus's argument that I am not able to explore here. See 'How To Be Dead and Not Care: A Defense of Epicurus,' by Stephen E. Rosenbaum, and 'Some Puzzles About the Evil of Death,' by Fred Feldman, both reprinted in John Donnelly (ed.), *Language, Metaphysics and Death*, 2nd edn (New York: Fordham University Press, 1994).

Spanish philosopher Miguel de Unamuno, from his 1912 work, *Tragic Sense of Life*: 'I must confess, painful though the confession be, that in the days of the simple faith of my childhood, descriptions of the tortures of hell, however terrible, never made me tremble, for I always felt that nothingness was much more terrifying.'[12]

VI. Reincarnation

Reincarnation can be defined as the theory that one and the same human mind (or soul or essence or jiva) successively animates two or more different bodies. That is, after death, my body permanently disintegrates, but my immaterial essence will be reborn in another body. And after that incarnation it will be reborn again many times or perhaps even an infinite number of times. Now reincarnation comes in many packages, but (as already noted) reincarnationalists must hold to some variety of mind–body dualism and must hold that satisfaction of the bodily criterion is not essential to personal identity.

It will be helpful to sketch the outlines of an actual reincarnation theory. Perhaps the most philosophically sophisticated reincarnational theory (along with certain Buddhist views) is the Vedantic school of Hinduism.[13] Ultimate reality in Advaita Vedanta is *Brahman*. Brahman is pure being and pure consciousness, the only truly real thing. The phenomenal world, which is called *maya*, is illusory and dreamlike. It is the product of the creative power of Brahman, not through conscious acts of creation but through Brahman being so full of reality that it constantly emits emanations or radiations of reality. Maya is not ultimately real just in this sense: unlike Brahman, it is contingent and temporary. One aspect of maya is the existence of *jivas*, which might be called life monads; they are similar to the immaterial minds or souls of western dualism. Limitless numbers of jivas exist, and are from time to time incarnate in bodies (human and nonhuman) as empirical selves. When one body dies, the jiva that was incarnate in it is reborn in another.

The Vedantic theory also contains a *karma* doctrine. A jiva's station in life is a karmic function of its deeds in previous lives. The karmic imprint of previous lives is carried from one incarnation to the next by what is called the subtle body. The gross body is the physical organism, and the subtle body would be called mental by western philosophers. It is a body in the sense that it is part of the realm of maya. Its function is to register and transmit the moral and spiritual influences of previous lives.

Karma is an impersonal law that says, in effect, that jivas reap in one life what they have sown in prior lives. Through a long series of incarnations, it is possible for jivas to be purged of ignorance (*avidya*) and evil, and to attain true self-consciousness. Since reality for Vedantists is monistic or nondual this would primarily entail consciousness of the illusoriness of all differentiation and consciousness of each

12. Miguel de Unamuno, *Tragic Sense of Life* (New York: Dover Publications, 1954), p. 43.
13. See the sections from Sankara in S. Radhakrishnan and C. Moore (eds), *A Source Book in Indian Philosophy* (Princeton: Princeton University Press, 1957).

jiva's own essential oneness with Brahman. The eternal and immutable spiritual reality of each jiva, its nonempirical self, is called *atman*. Liberation (*moksha*) and escape from rebirth are achived when one realizes that *atman is Brahman*.

Let us consider three of the most serious objections that are raised against reincarnation. The first has to do with the equivocal nature of the evidence for the doctrine. Such phenomena as instincts, child prodigies, love at first sight, and déjà vu are sometimes said to be evidence for reincarnation, but they obviously have little probative value, since it is quite possible to give convincing explanations of these phenomena that do not involve reincarnation. The more serious evidence for reincarnation is the phenomenon of yoga memory—the experience of certain people, usually children, who claim to be someone else reborn and to 'remember' the previous life. Consideration of such cases was almost entirely unsystematic and anecdotal until the work of the contemporary medical doctor Ian Stevenson, who in several books discusses intelligently various cases of yoga memory.[14]

There are two issues here. The first is whether the cases Stevenson discusses can be relied upon. To my knowledge, no one accuses Stevenson of dishonesty, but criticisms of his methods and conclusions have been raised. For one thing, in the vast majority of the cases Stevenson discusses, there was contact between the two families—the family into which the child was born and the family the child claimed via yoga memory previously to belong to—before Stevenson was ever on the scene. For another, Stevenson seems to dismiss far too easily the possibility of fraud on the part of the child. For a third, Stevenson has never even attempted to answer the objections of his several critics, and proceeds as if these critics did not exist.[15]

The second issue is this: assuming Stevenson's cases (and other cases of yoga memory) are genuine in the sense that there was no deliberate fraud, egregious error, etc., what is the most sensible explanation of those phenomena? One explanation, of course, is reincarnation. But are there other, more plausible, explanations?

Suppose that telepathic communication between human minds occurs (and I myself have neither knowledge nor even any particularly firm opinion on the matter). If so, there is the possibility that those who have experienced yoga memory have learned what they know about the past person whom they claim to be identical to by telepathic communication with living humans who know those same facts about the deceased person. This may be completely unknown to the yoga rememberer. Indeed, here is a crucial conundrum for reincarnation: claims based on purported yoga memory will be believable if they can be verified; verification will normally be achieved via the testimony of people who are in a position to know the

14. A good place to begin reading Stevenson's work is Ian Stevenson, *Twenty Cases Suggestive of Reincarnation* (New York: American Society for Physical Research, 1966).
15. See the discussion by Paul Edwards, as well as the articles he cites, on pp. 10–14 of the Introduction of his previously cited book, *Immortality*. See also his more recent *Reincarnation: A Critical Examination* (Amhurst, New York: Prometheus Books, 1996).

relevant facts; but that always opens the possibility that the yoga rememberer was somehow in telepathic communication with those same people. So the point is this: one great difficulty for reincarnation is the fact that the strongest evidence for it admits a variety of explanations.

The second serious objection to reincarnation concerns the relationship between me and my karmic heir, the future person whom believers in reincarnation will claim is the reincarnation of me. Suppose that I will die in twenty years and that I will have a karmic heir (call him 'Tom') who will be born soon thereafter. Notice that karma seems just only if Tom *is* me. Otherwise it will hardly be fair for him to experience the karmic consequences of my deeds. But the problem is that it does not seem that Tom is me.

Notice that Tom will share nothing of my body. Reincarnation theories insist on this much; Tom's body will be totally different from mine. Furthermore, apart from the possibility of a few yoga memories (which only a tiny minority of human beings claim to experience), he will share precisely none of my memories. What is there then that holds Tom and me together? What is it that identifies the two of us as two different temporal episodes in the life of one and the same person?

In some reincarnational theories the only connecting thread is the fact that we possess the same jiva (or other sort of immaterial essence) together with its karmic imprints and latent memories. But is that enough for identity? It appears doubtful. This is perhaps enough to consider that there are causal connections and maybe even similarities between me and Tom, but hardly enough to support a claim of numerical identity. So the second serious criticism of reincarnation, even if we will all have karmic heirs, is that reincarnationalists cannot convincingly argue that my karmic heir will be me.

The third serious difficulty in reincarnation concerns karma. This is said to be an impersonal law, like gravity, which ensures that whatever occurs to a person, whether it be good or bad, is a just consequence of past actions. In fact, if you ask a typical Hindu for an argument in favour of reincarnation, that argument is likely to be that reincarnation *cum* karma explains the problem of suffering and apparent injustice. If karma is true, there is no such thing as undeserved suffering.

Some philosophers argue that karma as an impersonal law cannot possibly work. Recall that the theory posits no personal judge or administrator of karma who decides that a given jiva's past lives merit, say, a present life as a poor beggar. The idea is that karma works impersonally just like gravity or thermodynamics. Now it seems that some karmic consequences probably can be explained by impersonal karma, e.g., the moral harm that I do to myself in a given life because I have been, say, bitter and selfish for years. But in a case where, say, I suffer for years from a painful disease or am unjustly robbed of my inheritance and the karmic explanation is that this is a just consequence of my misdeeds in past lives, it is not easy to see how the system is supposed to work. What exactly is the impersonal causal connection between the misdeeds in past lives and the painful events in this life? If the pain is not due to misdeeds in the present life, it is hard to see how karmic 'decisions' as to what are the just and proper consequences are to be made.[16]

VII. Immortality of the soul

The life after death theory known as the immortality of the soul is the doctrine that after death my body permanently disintegrates, but my immaterial essence or soul lives on forever in an immaterial world. Immortality is accordingly a near neighbour of reincarnation—both are based on mind–body dualism; both hold that the immaterial essence survives death; and defenders of both doctrines must argue that the satisfaction of bodily criterion is not essential for personal identity. The important difference is that immortality posits after death not a successive series of bodily incarnations here on earth, but rather one eternal and uninterrupted life in a spiritual world.

Plato was a great defender of immortality, and in several of his dialogues[17] he suggested various ingenious arguments in favour of the doctrine. So was Immanuel Kant, who offered a famous 'moral argument' in favour of God and immortality.[18] Unfortunately, none of these arguments strikes us as cogent; it is difficult to find any contemporary philosophers who defend any of the classic arguments for immortality. Immortality is still accepted in some circles today, but doubtless the heyday of the doctrine was the Victorian era, especially in Britain. The great interest then was to look to spiritualist phenomena—seances, trance mediumship, automatic writing, etc.—as possible evidence for immortality. Unfortunately, it has never been convincingly shown that spiritualistic phenomena amount to genuine communication with those who have died and are, as it is said, on 'the other side.'

But in one sense, the prospects for immortality look brighter than they did thirty or forty years ago. As already noted, philosophers such as Flew were then arguing that the very idea of nonbodily existence is not just false but incoherent. But very many philosophers now hold that immaterial existence is at least logically possible (whether it is or will be actual is another matter).

They have been helped by an important article, written in 1953 but not widely noticed until later, by the philosopher H. H. Price. In his 'Survival and the Idea of "Another World",'[19] Price paints an apparently quite coherent picture of a dream-like or image-like world of immaterial objects. Price's notion was that souls inhabit

16. This and other points are well argued in Bruce R. Reichenbach, *The Law of Karma: A Philosophical Study* (Honolulu: The University of Hawaii Press, 1990). On this point, see pp. 96–100, 121–2 , 159, 189–90.
17. See especially the *Phaedo* and Book X of the *Republic*. Both are found in *The Collected Dialogues of Plato*, ed. Edith Hamilton, Hunting Cairns, (New York: Pantheon Books, 1961).
18. Immanuel Kant, *Critique of Practical Reason*, trans. L. W. Beck (Indianapolis, Indiana: Bobbs-Merrill, 1956), pp. 126–36.
19. Price's article has been widely reprinted, but originally appeared in *Proceedings of the Society for Psychical Research*, vol. 50 (1953), pp. 1–25.

a coherent immaterial world, one in which imaging replaces perceiving. Through these images—which might be visual, auditory, or telepathic—souls can be aware of each other and even of an environment as complex and vivid as ours. Objects and persons can be 'seen' as telepathic apparitions. Such a world, Price suggests, may have different causal laws than our world does (e.g., wish-fulfilment might be operative), but it will seem to its denizens just as real a world as ours does to us. A product of telepathically interacting minds, Price's world is envisioned as being located in a space all its own, and need not be an agreeable place.

Price was not predicting that we will all one day inhabit the sort of world he describes—indeed, Price himself was agnostic on the question of life after death. He was simply trying to paint a picture of a possible or intelligible immaterial world. Nor has his theory escaped criticism;[20] still, I believe most philosophers who write about this topic hold that the world Price describes is at least coherent.

Let me now discuss what many take to be the most serious objection to immortality, viz., the so-called 'mind–body unity' argument. It runs as follows: in ordinary human life we observe a rule, viz., that cessation of or change in certain physical or especially brain processes is always correlated with a cessation of or change in consciousness. Radical changes in or even the termination of consciousness can be produced by such physical events as a blow to the head, the ingesting of certain drugs, extreme fatigue, sleep, Alzheimer's disease, anesthesia, certain sorts of brain surgery, cutting off the flow of blood to the brain, etc. It seems sensible to conclude, then, that consciousness depends on a functioning nervous system. And it seems sensible to conclude from this—so the argument goes—that consciousness cannot survive bodily death. When my body dies, I die: when my body no longer lives, I no longer exist.[21]

The usual reply of the defender of immortality is this: the mind–body unity argument does not rule out the claim that while consciousness depends on a functioning brain during bodily life, it does not any longer depend on a functioning brain after bodily death. During life, the body is, so to speak, the instrument of the mind, but after bodily death the mind no longer uses that instrument—just as a violinist can pick up and play another violin if the first one is ruined. It is true that the bodily signs of consciousness are absent after bodily death, but it does not follow that consciousness has permanently ceased. What needs to be proved by mind–body unity arguers, but instead is only assumed, is not just that the mind uses and depends on a body during earthly life but that this relationship of use and dependence is essential to the mind. There is, then, no way to decide, just on the

20. See, for example, John Hick, *Death and Eternal Life* (New York: Harper and Row, 1976), pp. 265–77. Hick sees an inevitable tension between (1) Price's wish-fulfilment theme, and (2) his insistence on the public, non-solipsistic nature of the world he describes. If it is a publicly created and inhabited world, how can wish-fulfilment be an important force in shaping it? What happens if the wishes of certain individuals conflict?

21. Paul Edwards explains clearly the mind–body unity argument in his essay, 'The Dependence of Consciousness on the Brain,' in his *Immortality*, cited above, pp. 292–307.

basis of the evidence cited by mind–body unity arguers, whether the argument refutes immortality of the soul.

But by far the most debated contemporary topic in the area of immortality concerns out of body experiences (OBE's) and especially near-death experiences (NDE's). There is no doubt that some people, typically in the context of life-threatening medical emergencies, have such experiences. And there seem to be some striking commonalities in many of them—an initial sense of distress and fear followed by calm and joy; a sense of being outside one's body and of observing the resuscitation efforts; a feeling of moving down a long tunnel or road towards a bright light; an experience of being met by previously deceased friends or relatives; and a sense of approaching some sort of border or boundary and of being sent back, almost against one's wishes, into bodily recovery and everyday life.[22]

Is the fact that some people have such experiences evidence of life after death? It is true that most people (not quite all) who have them subsequently believe in life after death, whether they previously did so or not. It is also true that if the self or mind can indeed leave the body, and can act and perceive apart from the body, that would seem to refute the mind–body unity argument, constitute powerful evidence for some version of mind–body dualism, and at least indirectly support the possibility of survival. But the problem is that it is exceedingly difficult to prove that the self really does leave the body in such experiences. This despite reports in a few cases of patients 'returning' from NDE's with knowledge of distant events that occurred subsequent to their hospitalization, and which nobody at the hospital or in the family knew until checking later. Some have argued that OBE's are quite natural events, explainable responses of the brain to certain sorts of bodily events, and that the sense of being outside one's body is entirely subjective. Furthermore, it needs to be pointed out that a *near-death experience* is not an *experience of death*. Those who have a NDE and live to tell about it manifestly do not die, though they do experience some of the symptoms (e.g., no heartbeat) associated with death.

VII. Resurrection of the body

Resurrection can be defined as follows: it is the doctrine that after death my body disintegrates, but at some point in the future God will miraculously raise it from the ground and reconstitute me as a person. Bodily resurrection is an aspect of the traditions of Judaism, Christianity, and Islam, as well as many other religions. But it is in Christianity that the doctrine finds its most philosophically sophisticated statements.

In Christian thought resurrection and immortality have a complicated relationship. The majority report, so to speak, of Christian theologians from the second century onward combines the two in a view that might be called temporary

---

22. Many such cases are discussed in Robert Almeder, *Death and Personal Survival: The Evidence for Life After Death* (Lanham, Maryland: Rowman and Littlefield, 1992), pp. 163–201.

disembodiment. The idea is this: when I die, my body disintegrates, but I continue to exist; for an interim time I exist in the presence of God as a disembodied soul only; then one future day God will raise my body, reunite it with my soul, and constitute me a whole and complete person again. Temporary disembodiment was seen by many theologians as a neat way of reconciling Jesus' statement to the good thief on the cross, '*Today* you will be with me in paradise,' with the Pauline notion that resurrection only occurs in the last days.[23]

Despite this point, it must be insisted that resurrection is a very different theory from immortality. For one thing, it does not have to be based on mind–body dualism (although, as we have seen, it usually is). Resurrection based on an entirely materialist notion of human beings is quite possible.[24] For another, immortality of the soul posits survival of death as a natural property of souls, while resurrection (at least in Christian versions) insists that death would mean permanent annihilation for the human person were it not for a miraculous intervention of God that allows for life after bodily death.

The specific resurrection of Jesus Christ on Easter morning is taken by Christians to be the earnest or 'first fruits' of the resurrection of all other people, which is called the 'general resurrection' (see Rom. 8: 11; I Cor. 15: 20, 23; Phil. 3: 20–1; I Thess. 4: 14; I John 3: 2). So the ability of Christians to defend the possibility and indeed the plausibility of the general resurrection depends in part on their ability to defend the possibility and plausibility of the resurrection of Jesus.[25] This means, of course, dealing with two important issues that we will not be able to discuss here, viz., (1) Hume-like arguments against the rational believability of miracles, and (2) the concerns of scripture scholars about the New Testament evidence for the resurrection of Jesus.

One venerable objection to resurrection, which was raised in the time of the church fathers and is still raised today, is this: What if a Christian dies at sea and his body is eaten by various sea creatures who then scatter to the seven seas? How can God possibly resurrect that Christian? What the fathers typically did in response to this objection was to appeal to the divine nature. No human being would be able to locate and reconstitute the relevant atoms of the Christian's body, but an all-knowing and all-powerful God could. And as long as (1) the basic building blocks of matter endure through time (as of course they normally do) and (2) God's only problem is to locate, collect, and reassemble them, the church fathers were surely right. Such a being could do that.

The objection we have been discussing makes an important assumption, but it is one the church fathers (unlike most contemporary defenders of resurrection) were

23. A classic statement of temporary disembodiment is found in Thomas Aquinas, *Summa Contra Gentiles* (Notre Dame, Indiana: Notre Dame University Press, 1975), 4.79.11.
24. As is argued in Stephen T. Davis, *Risen Indeed*, pp. 110–31.
25. For a theologically and philosophically sophisticated attempt to do just this, see William Lane Craig, *Assessing the New Testament Evidence for the Historicity of the Resurrection of Jesus* (Lewiston, Main: The Edwin Mellen Press, 1989).

all willing to make. It is that resurrection entails that God must use the very same matter, the same atoms or 'stuff' of which the premortem body consisted. That is, if God wants to resurrect a given person who lived and then died, God must find and reassemble the same material of which this person's premortem body consisted. Otherwise it will not be the same person. As noted, contemporary defenders of resurrection rarely make this assumption. Most of them hold that it could be entirely new matter, but as long as it is structured or configured in the old way, personal identity is retained. And so far as personal identity is concerned, they appear to be correct—it could well be not just a replica but the same person. But this does not rule out the possibility of God resurrecting people in the patristic way too, if that is what God chooses to do.

But there is an equally venerable and much more serious objection to resurrection based on the patristic model. It is usually presented like this: what if another Christian is eaten by cannibals, so that the material of her body becomes material in their bodies? And suppose God later wants to resurrect all of them, both the Christian and the cannibals? Who gets which bodily particles? On what basis does God decide?

Here it seems that God must have some sort of criterion or policy for deciding which constituents of matter go where. Augustine made the suggestion that atoms will be raised in that human body in which they *first* appeared.[26] Others have suggested that some constituent parts of human bodies are essential to those bodies and others are not. So in raising Jones, for example, God need only locate those atoms that are or were essential to Jones, having already made sure that they have never appeared (or have never appeared as essential atoms) in somebody else's body. Perhaps God will use them as building blocks around which to reconstruct the rest of Jones's body out of new atoms.

The prevailing world-view of our scientific age is materialism. Very many people today hold that the only things that exist are material things. So it is not surprising that a majority of contemporary philosophers who talk about human nature and the mind–body problem tend toward various versions of physicalism. No believer in resurrection can embrace metaphysical materialism, because all religious traditions that affirm resurrection also affirm the existence of God, a non-physical being, who does the resurrecting. Still, those who believe in resurrection can at least agree with the majority to this extent—they affirm that life after death as a pure mind or disembodied spirit is a radically attenuated and crippled mode of life. Genuine and true human life, to the extent that it is possible after bodily death, is only possible via resurrection of the body.

26. See Aurelius Augustine, *The Enchiridion on Faith, Hope, and Love* (Chicago: Henry Regnery, 1961), LXXXVIII.

Chapter 63

Life after death: an ancient Greek view

Plato

WHEN Socrates had said that, Cebes rejoined: 'The other things you say, Socrates, I find excellent; but what you say about the soul is the subject of much disbelief: people fear that when it's been separated from the body, it may no longer exist anywhere, but that on the very day a person dies, it may be destroyed and perish, as soon as it's separated from the body; and that as it goes out, it may be dispersed like breath or smoke, go flying off, and exist no longer anywhere at all. True, if it did exist somewhere, gathered together alone by itself, and separated from those evils you were recounting just now, there'd be plenty of hope, Socrates, and a fine hope it would be, that what you say is true; but on just this point, perhaps, one needs no little reassuring and convincing, that when the person has died, his soul exists, and that it possesses some power and wisdom.'

'That's true, Cebes,' said Socrates; 'but then what are we to do? Would you like us to speculate on those very questions, and see whether that is likely to be the case or not?'

'For my part anyway,' said Cebes, 'I'd gladly hear whatever opinion you have about them.'

'Well,' said Socrates, 'Let's consider it, perhaps, in this way: do the souls of human beings exist in Hades when they have died, or do they not? Now there's an ancient doctrine, which we've recalled, that they do exist in that world, entering it from this one, and that they re-enter this world and are born again from the dead; yet if that is so, if living people are born again from those who have died, surely our souls would have to exist in that world? Because they could hardly be born again, if they didn't exist; so it would be sufficient evidence for the truth of those claims, if it really became plain that living people are born from the dead and from nowhere else; but if that isn't so, some other argument would be needed.'

'Certainly,' said Cebes.

'Well now, consider the matter, if you want to understand more readily, in connection not only with mankind, but with all animals and plants; and, in general, for all things subject to coming-to-be, let's see whether everything comes to be in this way: opposites come to be only from their opposites—in the case of all things that actually have an opposite—as, for example, the beautiful is opposite, of course, to the ugly, just to unjust, and so on in countless other cases. So let's consider this: is it necessary that whatever has an opposite comes to be only from its opposite? For example, when a thing comes to be larger, it must, surely, come to be larger from being smaller before?'

'Yes.'

'And again, if it comes to be smaller, it will come to be smaller later from being larger before?'

'That's so.'

'And that which is weaker comes to be, presumably, from a stronger, and that which is faster from a slower?'

'Certainly.'

'And again, if a thing comes to be worse, it's from a better, and if more just, from a more unjust?'

'Of course.'

'Are we satisfied, then, that all things come to be in this way, opposite things from opposites?'

'Certainly.'

'Now again, do those things have a further feature of this sort: between the members of every pair of opposites, since they are two, aren't there two processes of coming-to-be, from one to the other, and back again from the latter to the former? Thus, between a larger thing and a smaller, isn't there increase and decrease, so that in the one case we speak of "increasing" and in the other of "decreasing"?'

'Yes.'

'And similarly with separating and combining, cooling and heating, and all such; even if in some cases we don't use the names, still in actual fact mustn't the same principle everywhere hold good: they come to be from each other, and there's a process of coming-to-be of each into the other?'

'Certainly.'

'Well then, is there an opposite to living, as sleeping is opposite to being awake?'

'Certainly.'

'What is it?'

'Being dead.'

'Then those come to be from each other, if they are opposites; and between the pair of them, since they are two, the processes of coming-to-be are two?'

'Of course.'

'Now then,' said Socrates, 'I'll tell you one of the couples I was just mentioning, the couple itself and its processes; and you tell me the other. My couple is sleeping and being awake: being awake comes to be from sleeping, and sleeping from being awake, and their processes are going to sleep and waking up. Is that sufficient for you or not?'

'Certainly.'

'Now it's for you to tell me in the same way about life and death. You say, don't you, that being dead is opposite to living?'

'I do.'

'And that they come to be from each other?'

'Yes.'

'Then what is it that comes to be from that which is living?'

'That which is dead.'

'And what comes to be from that which is dead?'

'I must admit that it's that which is living.'

'Then it's from those that are dead, Cebes, that living things and living people are born?'

'Apparently.'

'Then our souls do exist in Hades.'

'So it seems.'

'Now *one* of the relevant processes here is obvious, isn't it? For dying is obvious enough, surely?'

'It certainly is.'

'What shall we do then? Shan't we assign the opposite process to balance it? Will nature be lame in this respect? Or must we supply some process opposite to dying?'

'We surely must.'

'What will this be?'

'Coming to life again.'

'Then if there *is* such a thing as coming to life again, wouldn't this, coming to life again, be a process from dead to living people?'

'Certainly.'

'In that way too, then, we're agreed that living people are born from the dead no less than dead people from the living; and we thought that, if that were the case, it would be sufficient evidence that the souls of the dead must exist somewhere, whence they are born again.'

'Yes, and besides, Socrates,' Cebes replied, 'there's also that theory you're always putting forward, that our learning is actually nothing but recollection; according to that too, if it's true, what we are now reminded of we must have learned at some former time. But that would be impossible, unless our souls existed somewhere before being born in this human form; so in this way too, it appears that the soul is something immortal.'

'Yes, what are the proofs of those points, Cebes?' put in Simmias. 'Remind me, as I don't recall them very well at the moment.'

'One excellent argument,' said Cebes, 'is that when people are questioned, and if the questions are well put, they state the truth about everything for themselves— and yet unless knowledge and a correct account were present within them, they'd be unable to do that; thus, if one takes them to diagrams or anything else of that sort, one has there the plainest evidence that that is so.'

'But if that doesn't convince you, Simmias,' said Socrates, 'then see whether maybe you agree if you look at it this way. Apparently you doubt whether what is called "learning" is recollection?'

'I don't doubt it,' said Simmias; 'but I do need to undergo just what the argument is about, to be "reminded". Actually, from the way Cebes set about stating it, I do almost recall it and am nearly convinced; but I'd like, none the less, to hear now how you set about stating it yourself.'

'I'll put it this way. We agree, I take it, that if anyone is to be reminded of a thing, he must have known that thing at some time previously.'

'Certainly.'

'Then do we also agree on this point: that whenever knowledge comes to be present in this sort of way, it is recollection? I mean in some such way as this: if someone, on seeing a thing, or hearing it, or getting any other sense-perception of it, not only recognizes that thing, but also thinks of something else, which is the object not of the same knowledge but of another, don't we then rightly say that he's been "reminded" of the object of which he has got the thought?'

'What do you mean?'

'Take the following examples: knowledge of a person, surely, is other than that of a lyre?'

'Of course.'

'Well now, you know what happens to lovers, whenever they see a lyre or cloak or anything else their loves are accustomed to use: they recognize the lyre, and they get in their mind, don't they, the form of the boy whose lyre it is? And that is recollection. Likewise, someone seeing Simmias is often reminded of Cebes, and there'd surely be countless other such cases.'

'Countless indeed!' said Simmias.

'Then is something of that sort a kind of recollection? More especially, though, whenever it happens to someone in connection with things he's since forgotten, through lapse of time or inattention?'

'Certainly.'

'Again now, is it possible, on seeing a horse depicted or a lyre depicted, to be reminded of a person; and on seeing Simmias depicted, to be reminded of Cebes?'

'Certainly.'

'And also, on seeing Simmias depicted, to be reminded of Simmias himself?'

'Yes, that's possible.'

'In all those cases, then, doesn't it turn out that there is recollection from similar things, but also from dissimilar things?'

'It does.'

'But whenever one is reminded of something from similar things, mustn't one experience something further: mustn't one think whether or not the thing is lacking at all, in its similarity, in relation to what one is reminded of?'

'One must.'

'Then consider whether this is the case. We say, don't we, that there is something that is equal—I don't mean a log to a log, or a stone to a stone, or anything else of that sort, but some further thing beyond all those, the equal itself: are we to say that it is a reality or not?'

'We most certainly are to say that it is,' said Simmias; 'unquestionably!'

'And do we know it, know what it is?'

'Certainly.'

'Where did we get the knowledge of it? Wasn't it from the things we were just mentioning: on seeing logs or stones or other equal things, wasn't it from those that we thought of that object, it being different from them? Or doesn't it seem different to you? Look at it this way: aren't equal stones and logs, the very same ones, sometimes evidently equal to one, but not to another?'

'Yes, certainly.'

'But now, were the equals themselves ever, in your view, evidently unequal, or equality inequality?'

'Never yet, Socrates.'

'Then those equals, and the equal itself, are not the same.'

'By no means, Socrates, in my view.'

'But still, it is from those equals, different as they are from that equal, that you have thought of and got the knowledge of it?'

'That's perfectly true.'

'It being either similar to them or dissimilar?'

'Certainly.'

'Anyway, it makes no difference; so long as on seeing one thing, one does, from that sight, think of another, whether it be similar or dissimilar, that must be recollection.'

'Certainly.'

'Well now, with regard to the instances in the logs, and, in general, the equals we mentioned just now, are we affected in some way as this: do they seem to us to be equal in the same way as is the thing itself, that which it is? Do they fall short of it at all in being like the equal, or not?'

'Very far short of it.'

'Then whenever anyone, on seeing a thing, thinks to himself, "this thing that I now see seeks to be like another reality, but falls short, and cannot be like that object: it is inferior", do we agree that the man who thinks that must previously have known the object he says it resembles but falls short of?'

'He must.'

'Now then, have we ourselves been affected in just that way, or not, with regard to the equals and the equal itself?'

'Indeed we have.'

'Then we must previously have known the equal, before that time when we first, on seeing the equals, thought that all of them were striving to be like the equal but fell short of it.'

'That is so.'

'Yet we also agree on this: we haven't derived the thought of it, nor could we do so, from anywhere but seeing or touching or some other of the senses—I'm counting all those as the same.'

'Yes, they are the same, Socrates, for what the argument seeks to show.'

'But of course it is from one's sense-perceptions that one must think that all sensible items are striving for that thing which equal is, yet are inferior to it; or how shall we put it?'

'Like that.'

'Then it must, surely, have been before we began to see and hear and use the other senses that we got knowledge of the equal itself, of what it is, if we were going to refer the equals from our sense-perceptions to it, supposing that all things are doing their best to be like it, but are inferior to it.'

'That must follow from what's been said before, Socrates.'

'Now we were seeing and hearing, and were possessed of our other senses, weren't we, just as soon as we were born?'

'Certainly.'

'But we must, we're saying, have got our knowledge of the equal before those?'

'Yes.'

'Then it seems that we must have got it before we were born.'

'It seems so.'

'Now if, having got it before birth, we were born in possession of it, did we know, both before birth and as soon as we were born, not only the equal, the larger and the smaller, but everything of that sort? Because our present argument concerns the beautiful itself, and the good itself, and just and holy, no less than the equal; in fact, as I say, it concerns everything on which we set this seal, "that which it is", in the questions we ask and in the answers we give. And so we must have got pieces of knowledge of all those things before birth.'

'That is so.'

'Moreover, if having got them, we did not on each occasion forget them, we must always be born knowing, and must continue to know throughout life: because this is knowing—to possess knowledge one has got of something, and not to have lost it; or isn't loss of knowledge what we mean by "forgetting", Simmias?'

'Certainly it is, Socrates.'

'But on the other hand, I suppose that if, having got them before birth, we lost them on being born, and later on, using the senses about the things in question, we regain those pieces of knowledge that we possessed at some former time, in that case wouldn't what we call "learning" be the regaining of knowledge belonging to us? And in saying that that was being reminded, shouldn't we be speaking correctly?'

'Certainly.'

'Yes, because it did seem possible, on sensing an object, whether by seeing or hearing or getting some other sense-perception of it, to think from that of some other thing one had forgotten—either a thing to which the object, though dissimilar to it, was related, or else something to which it was similar; so, as I say, one of two things is true: either all of us were born knowing those objects, and we know them throughout life; or those we speak of as "learning" are simply being reminded later on, and learning would be recollection.'

'That's quite true, Socrates.'

'Then which do you choose, Simmias? That we are born knowing, or that we are later reminded of the things we'd gained knowledge of before?'

'At the moment, Socrates, I can't make a choice.'

'Well, can you make one on the following point, and what do you think about it? If a man knows things, can he give an account of what he knows or not?'

'Of course he can, Socrates.'

'And do you think everyone can give an account of those objects we were discussing just now?'

'I only wish they could,' said Simmias; 'but I'm afraid that, on the contrary, this time tomorrow there may no longer be any human being who can do so properly.'

'You don't then, Simmias, think that everyone knows those objects?'

'By no means.'

'Are they, then, reminded of what they once learned?'

'They must be.'

'When did our souls get the knowledge of those objects? Not, at any rate, since we were born as human beings.'

'Indeed not.'

'Earlier, then.'

'Yes.'

'Then our souls did exist earlier, Simmias, before entering human form, apart from bodies; and they possessed wisdom.'

'Unless maybe, Socrates, we get those pieces of knowledge at the very moment of birth; that time still remains.'

'Very well, my friend; but then at what other time, may I ask, do we lose them? We aren't born with them, as we agreed just now. Do we then lose them at the very time at which we get them? Or have you any other time to suggest?'

'None at all, Socrates. I didn't realize I was talking nonsense.'

'Then is our position as follows, Simmias? If the objects we're always harping on exist, a beautiful, and a good, and all such reality, and if we refer all the things from our sense-perceptions to that reality, finding again what was formerly ours, and if we compare these things with that, then just as surely as those objects exist, so also must our souls exist before we are born. On the other hand, if they don't exist, this argument will have gone for nothing. Is this the position? Is it equally necessary that those objects exist, and that our souls existed before birth, and if the former don't exist, then neither did the latter?'

'It's abundantly clear to me, Socrates,' said Simmias, 'that there's the same necessity in either case, and the argument takes opportune refuge in the view that our souls exist before birth, just as surely as the reality of which you're now speaking. Because I myself find nothing so plain to me as that all such objects, beautiful and good and all the others you were speaking of just now, have the fullest possible reality; so in my view it's been adequately proved.'

'And what about Cebes?' said Socrates. 'We must convince Cebes too.'

'It's adequate for him, I think,' said Simmias; 'though he's the most obstinate of people when it comes to doubting arguments. But I think he's been sufficiently convinced that our souls existed before we were born. Whether they will still exist, however, after we've died, doesn't seem, even to me, to have been shown, Socrates; but the point Cebes made just now still stands—the popular fear that when a human being dies, his soul may be dispersed at that time, and that that may be the end of its existence. Because what's to prevent it from coming to be and being put together from some other source, and from existing before it enters a human body, yet when it has entered one, and again been separated from it, from then meeting its end, and being itself destroyed?'

'You're right, Simmias,' said Cebes. 'It seems that half, as it were, of what is needed has been shown—that out souls existed before we were born; it must also be shown that they will exist after we've died, no less than before we were born, if the proof is going to be complete.'

'That's been proved already, Simmias and Cebes,' said Socrates, 'if you will combine this argument with the one we agreed on earlier, to the effect that all that is living comes from that which is dead. Because if the soul does have previous existence, and if when it enters upon living and being born, it must come from no other source than death and being dead, surely it must also exist after it has died, given that it has to be born again? So your point has been proved already. But even so, I think you and Simmias would like to thrash out this argument still further; you seem afraid, like children, that as the soul goes out from the body, the wind may literally blow it apart and disperse it, especially when someone happens not to die in calm weather but in a high wind.'

Cebes laughed at this, and said. 'Try to reassure us, Socrates, as if we were afraid; or rather, not as if we were afraid ourselves—but maybe there's a child inside us, who has fears of that sort. Try to persuade him, then, to stop being afraid of death, as if it were a bogeyman.'

'Well, you must sing spells to him every day,' said Socrates, 'till you've charmed it out of him.'

'And where', he said, 'shall we find a charmer for such fears, Socrates, now that you're leaving us?'

'Greece is a large country, Cebes, which has good men in it, I suppose; and there are many foreign races too. You must ransack all of them in search of such a charmer, sparing neither money nor trouble, because there's no object on which you could more opportunely spend your money. And you yourselves must search too, along with one another; you may not easily find anyone more capable of doing that than yourselves.'

'That shall certainly be done,' said Cebes; 'but let's go back to the point where we left off, if you've no objection.'

'Of course not; why should I?'

'Good.'

*

'Well then,' said Socrates, 'mustn't we ask ourselves something like this: What kind of thing is liable to undergo this fate—namely, dispersal—and for what kind of thing should we fear lest it undergo it? And what kind of thing is not liable to it? And next, mustn't we further ask to which of those two kinds soul belongs, and then feel either confidence or fear for our own soul accordingly?'

'That's true.'

'Then is it true that what has been put together and is naturally composite is liable to undergo this, to break up at the point at which it was put together; whereas if there be anything non-composite, it alone is liable, if anything is, to escape this?'

'That's what I think,' said Cebes.

'Well now, aren't the things that are constant and unvarying most likely to be the non-composite, whereas things that vary and are never constant are likely to be composite?'

'I think so.'

'Then let's go back to those entities to which we turned in our earlier argument. Is the reality itself, whose being we give an account of in asking and answering questions, unvarying and constant, or does it vary? Does the equal itself, the beautiful itself, that which each thing itself is, the real, ever admit of any change whatever? Or does that which each of them is, being uniform alone by itself, remain unvarying and constant, and never admit of any kind of alteration in any way or respect whatever?'

'It must be unvarying and constant, Socrates,' said Cebes.

'But what about the many beautiful things, such as human beings or horses or cloaks or anything else at all of that kind? Or equals, or all things that bear the same name as those objects? Are they constant, or are they just the opposite of those others, and practically never constant at all, either in relation to themselves or to one another?'

'That is their condition,' said Cebes; 'they are never unvarying.'

'Now these things you could actually touch and see and sense with the other senses, couldn't you, whereas those that are constant you could lay hold of only by reasoning of the intellect; aren't such things, rather, invisible and not seen?'

'What you say is perfectly true.'

'Then would you like us to posit two kinds of beings, the one kind seen, the other invisible?'

'Let's posit them.'

'And the invisible is always constant, whereas the seen is never constant?'

'Let's posit that too.'

'Well, but we ourselves are part body and part soul, aren't we?'

'We are.'

'Then to which kind do we say that the body will be more similar and more akin?'

'That's clear to anyone: obviously to the seen.'

'And what about the soul? Is it seen or invisible?'

'It's not seen by human beings, at any rate, Socrates.'

'But we meant, surely, things seen and not seen with reference to human nature; or do you think we meant any other?'

'We meant human nature.'

'What do we say about soul, then? Is it seen or unseen?'

'It's not seen.'

'Then it's invisible?'

'Yes.'

'Then soul is more similar than body to the invisible, whereas body is more similar to that which is seen.'

'That must be so, Socrates.'

'Now weren't we saying a while ago that whenever the soul uses the body as a means to study anything, either by seeing or hearing or any other sense—because to use the body as a means is to study a thing through sense-perception—then it is dragged by the body towards objects that are never constant; and it wanders about itself, and is confused and dizzy, as if drunk, by virtue of contact with things of a similar kind?'

'Certainly.'

'Whereas whenever it studies alone by itself, it departs yonder towards that which is pure and always existent and immortal and unvarying, and by virtue of its kinship with it, enters always into its company, whenever it has come to be alone by itself, and whenever it may do so; then it has ceased from its wandering and, when it is about those objects, it is always constant and unvarying, because of its contact with things of a similar kind; and this condition of it is called "wisdom", is it not?'

'That's very well said and perfectly true, Socrates.'

'Once again, then, in the light of our earlier and present arguments, to which kind do you think that soul is more similar and more akin?'

'Everyone, I think, Socrates, even the slowest learner, following this line of inquiry, would agree that soul is totally and altogether more similar to what is unvarying than to what is not.'

'And what about the body?'

'That is more like the latter.'

'Now look at it this way too: when soul and body are present in the same thing, nature ordains that the one shall serve and be ruled, whereas the other shall rule and be master; here again, which do you think is similar to the divine and which to the mortal? Don't you think the divine is naturally adapted for ruling and domination, whereas the mortal is adapted for being ruled and for service?'

'I do.'

'Which kind, then, does the soul resemble?'

'Obviously, Socrates, the soul resembles the divine, and the body the mortal.'

'Consider, then, Cebes, if these are our conclusions from all that's been said: soul is most similar to what is divine, immortal, intelligible, uniform, indissoluble, unvarying, and constant in relation to itself; whereas body, in its turn, is most similar to what is human, mortal, multiform, non-intelligible, dissoluble, and never

constant in relation to itself. Have we anything to say against those statements, my
dear Cebes, to show that they're false?'

'We haven't.'

'Well then, that being so, isn't body liable to be quickly dissolved, whereas soul
must be completely indissoluble, or something close to it?'

'Of course.'

'Now you're aware that when a human being has died, the part of him that's
seen, his body, which is situated in the seen world, the corpse as we call it, although
liable to be dissolved and fall apart and to disintegrate, undergoes none of those
things at once, but remains as it is for a fairly long time—in fact for a very considerable time, even if someone dies with his body in beautiful condition, and in the
flower of youth; why, the body that is shrunken and embalmed, like those who've
been embalmed in Egypt, remains almost entire for an immensely long time; and
even should the body decay, some parts of it, bones and sinews and all such things,
are still practically immortal; isn't that so?'

'Yes.'

'Can it be, then, that the soul, the invisible part, which goes to another place of
that kind, noble, pure, and invisible, to "Hades" in the true sense of the word, into
the presence of the good and wise God—where, God willing, my own soul too must
shortly enter—can it be that this, which we've found to be a thing of such a kind
and nature, should on separation from the body at once be blown apart and perish,
as most people say? Far from it, my dear Cebes and Simmias; rather, the truth is far
more like this: suppose it is separated in purity, while trailing nothing of the body
with it, since it had no avoidable commerce with it during life, but shunned it;
suppose too that it has been gathered together alone into itself, since it always
cultivated this—nothing else but the right practice of philosophy, in fact, the cultivation of dying without complaint—wouldn't that be the cultivation of death?'

'It certainly would.'

'If it is in that state, then, does it not depart to the invisible which is similar to it,
the divine and immortal and wise; and on arrival there, isn't its lot to be happy,
released from its wandering and folly, its fears and wild lusts, and other ills of the
human condition, and as is said of the initiated, does it not pass the rest of time in
very truth with gods? Are we to say, that Cebes, or something else?'

'That, most certainly!' said Cebes.

'Whereas, I imagine, if it is separated from the body when it has been polluted
and made impure, because it has always been with the body, has served and loved it,
and been so bewitched by it, by its passions and pleasures, that it thinks nothing else
real save what is corporeal—what can be touched and seen, drunk and eaten, or
used for sexual enjoyment—yet it has been accustomed to hate and shun and
tremble before what is obscure to the eyes and invisible, but intelligible and grasped
by philosophy; do you think a soul in that condition will separate unsullied, and
alone by itself?'

'By no means.'

'Rather, I imagine, it will have been interspersed with a corporeal element, ingrained in it by the body's company and intercourse, through constant association and much training?'

'Certainly.'

'And one must suppose, my friend, that this element is ponderous, that it is heavy and earthy and is seen; and thus encumbered, such a soul is weighed down, and dragged back into the region of the seen, through fear of the invisible and of Hades; and it roams among tombs and graves, so it is said, around which some shadowy phantoms of souls have actually been seen, such wraiths as souls of that kind afford, souls that have been released in no pure condition, but while partaking in the seen; and that is just why they are seen.'

'That's likely, Socrates.'

'It is indeed, Cebes; and they're likely to be the souls not of the good but of the wicked, that are compelled to wander about such places, paying the penalty for their former nurture, evil as it was. And they wander about until, owing to the desire of the corporeal element attendant upon them, they are once more imprisoned in a body; and they're likely to be imprisoned in whatever types of character they may have cultivated in their lifetime.'

'What types can you mean, Socrates?'

'Those who have cultivated gluttony, for example, and lechery, and drunkenness, and have taken no pains to avoid them, are likely to enter the forms of donkeys and animals of that sort. Don't you think so?'

'What you say is very likely.'

'Yes, and those who've preferred injustice, tyranny, and robbery will enter the forms of wolves and hawks and kites. Where else can we say that such souls will go?'

'Into such creatures, certainly,' said Cebes.

'And isn't the direction taken by the others as well obvious in each case, according to the affinities of their training?'

'Quite obvious, of course.'

'And aren't the happiest among those and the ones who enter the best place, those who have practised popular and social goodness, "temperance" and "justice" so-called, developed from habit and training, but devoid of philosophy and intelligence?'

'In what way are those happiest?'

'Because they're likely to go back into a race of tame and social creatures similar to their kind, bees perhaps, or wasps or ants; and to return to the human race again, and be born from those kinds as decent men.'

'That's likely.'

'But the company of gods may not rightly be joined by one who has not practised philosophy and departed in absolute purity, by any but the lover of knowledge. It's for those reasons, Simmias and Cebes, my friends, that true philosophers abstain from all bodily desires, and stand firm without surrendering to them; it's not for any fear of poverty or loss of estate, as with most people who are lovers of riches;

nor again do they abstain through dread of dishonour or ill-repute attaching to wickedness, like lovers of power and prestige.'

'No, that would ill become them, Socrates,' said Cebes.

'Most certainly it would! And that, Cebes, is just why those who have any care for their own souls, and don't live fashioning the body, disregard all those people; they do not walk on the same paths as those who, in their view, don't know where they are going; but they themselves believe that their actions must not oppose philosophy, or the release and purifying rite it affords, and they are turned to follow it, in the direction in which it guides them.'

Chapter 64

Belief in life after death comes from emotion, not reason

Bertrand Russell

BEFORE we can profitably discuss whether we shall continue to exist after death, it is well to be clear as to the sense in which a man is the same person as he was yesterday. Philosophers used to think that there were definite substances, the soul and the body, that each lasted on from day to day, that a soul, once created, continued to exist throughout all future time, whereas a body ceased temporarily from death till the resurrection of the body.

The part of this doctrine which concerns the present life is pretty certainly false. The matter of the body is continually changing by processes of nutriment and wastage. Even if it were not, atoms in physics are no longer supposed to have continuous existence; there is no sense in saying: this is the same atom as the one that existed a few minutes ago. The continuity of a human body is a matter of appearance and behavior, not of substance.

The same thing applies to the mind. We think and feel and act, but there is not, in addition to thoughts and feelings and actions, a bare entity, the mind or the soul, which does or suffers these occurrences. The mental continuity of a person is a continuity of habit and memory: there was yesterday one person whose feelings I can remember, and that person I regard as myself of yesterday; but, in fact, myself of yesterday was only certain mental occurrences which are now remembered and are regarded as part of the person who now recollects them. All that constitutes a person is a series of experiences connected by memory and by certain similarities of the sort we call habit.

If, therefore, we are to believe that a person survives death, we must believe that the memories and habits which constitute the person will continue to be exhibited in a new set of occurrences.

No one can prove that this will not happen. But it is easy to see that it is very unlikely. Our memories and habits are bound up with the structure of the brain, in much the same way in which a river is connected with the riverbed. The water in the river is always changing, but it keeps to the same course because previous rains have worn a channel. In like manner, previous events have worn a channel in the brain, and our thoughts flow along this channel. This is the cause of memory and

Bertrand Russell 'Do We Survive Death?' from *Why I am not a Christian and Other Essays on Religion and Related Subjects* (George Allen & Unwin and Simon & Schuster, Inc, 1957), reprinted by permission of Routledge, an imprint of Taylor & Francis Books Ltd, on behalf of The Bertrand Russell Peace Foundation.

mental habits. But the brain, as a structure, is dissolved at death, and memory therefore may be expected to be also dissolved. There is no more reason to think otherwise than to expect a river to persist in its old course after an earthquake has raised a mountain where a valley used to be.

All memory, and therefore (one may say) all minds, depend upon a property which is very noticeable in certain kinds of material structures but exists little if at all in other kinds. This is the property of forming habits as a result of frequent similar occurrences. For example: a bright light makes the pupils of the eyes contract; and if you repeatedly flash a light in a man's eyes and beat a gong at the same time, the gong alone will, in the end, cause his pupils to contract. This is a fact about the brain and nervous system—that is to say, about a certain material structure. It will be found that exactly similar facts explain our response to language and our use of it, our memories and the emotions they arouse, our moral or immoral habits of behavior, and indeed everything that constitutes our mental personality, except the part determined by heredity. The part determined by heredity is handed on to our posterity but cannot, in the individual, survive the disintegration of the body. Thus both the hereditary and the acquired parts of a personality are, so far as our experience goes, bound up with the characteristics of certain bodily structures. We all know that memory may be obliterated by an injury to the brain, that a virtuous person may be rendered vicious by encephalitis lethargica, and that a clever child can be turned into an idiot by lack of iodine. In view of such familiar facts, it seems scarcely probable that the mind survives the total destruction of brain structure which occurs at death.

It is not rational arguments but emotions that cause belief in a future life.

The most important of these emotions is fear of death, which is instinctive and biologically useful. If we genuinely and wholeheartedly believed in the future life, we should cease completely to fear death. The effects would be curious, and probably such as most of us would deplore. But our human and subhuman ancestors have fought and exterminated their enemies throughout many geological ages and have profited by courage; it is therefore an advantage to the victors in the struggle for life to be able, on occasion, to overcome the natural fear of death. Among animals and savages, instinctive pugnacity suffices for this purpose; but at a certain stage of development, as the Mohammedans first proved, belief in Paradise has considerable military value as reinforcing natural pugnacity. We should therefore admit that militarists are wise in encouraging the belief in immortality, always supposing that this belief does not become so profound as to produce indifference to the affairs of the world.

Another emotion which encourages the belief in survival is admiration of the excellence of man. As the Bishop of Birmingham says, 'His mind is a far finer instrument than anything that had appeared earlier—he knows right and wrong. He can build Westminster Abbey. He can make an airplane. He can calculate the distance of the sun. ... Shall, then, man at death perish utterly? Does that incomparable instrument, his mind, vanish when life ceases?'

The Bishop proceeds to argue that 'the universe has been shaped and is governed by an intelligent purpose,' and that it would have been unintelligent, having made man, to let him perish.

To this argument there are many answers. In the first place, it has been found, in the scientific investigation of nature, that the intrusion of moral or aesthetic values has always been an obstacle to discovery. It used to be thought that the heavenly bodies must move in circles because the circle is the most perfect curve, that species must be immutable because God would only create what was perfect and what therefore stood in no need of improvement, that it was useless to combat epidemics except by repentance because they were sent as a punishment for sin, and so on. It has been found, however, that, so far as we can discover, nature is indifferent to our values and can only be understood by ignoring our notions of good and bad. The Universe may have a purpose, but nothing that we know suggests that, if so, this purpose has any similarity to ours.

Nor is there in this anything surprising. Dr. Barnes tells us that man 'knows right and wrong.' But, in fact, as anthropology shows, men's views of right and wrong have varied to such an extent that no single item has been permanent. We cannot say, therefore, that man knows right and wrong, but only that some men do. Which men? Nietzsche argued in favor of an ethic profoundly different from Christ's, and some powerful governments have accepted his teaching. If knowledge of right and wrong is to be an argument for immortality, we must first settle whether to believe Christ or Nietzsche, and then argue that Christians are immortal, but Hitler and Mussolini are not, or vice versa. The decision will obviously be made on the battle-field, not in the study. Those who have the best poison gas will have the ethic of the future and will therefore be the immortal ones.

Moreover, it is only when we think abstractly that we have such a high opinion of man. Of men in the concrete, most of us think the vast majority very bad. Civilized states spend more than half their revenue on killing each other's citizens. Consider the long history of the activities inspired by moral fervor: human sacrifices, persecutions of heretics, witch-hunts, pogroms leading up to wholesale extermination by poison gases, which one at least of Dr. Barnes's episcopal colleagues must be supposed to favor, since he holds pacifism to be un-Christian. Are these abominations, and the ethical doctrines by which they are prompted, really evidence of an intelligent Creator? And can we really wish that the men who practiced them should live forever? The world in which we live can be understood as a result of muddle and accident; but if it is the outcome of deliberate purpose, the purpose must have been that of a fiend. For my part, I find accident a less painful and more plausible hypothesis.

Chapter 65

What must be true of me if I survive my death?

Peter Geach

EVERYBODY knows that men die, and though most of us have read the advertisement 'Millions now living will never die', it is commonly believed that every man born will some day die; yet historically many men have believed that there is a life after death, and indeed that this after-life will never end. That is: there has been a common belief both in *survival* of bodily death and in *immortality*. Now a philosopher might interest himself specially in immortality, as opposed to survival; conceding survival for the sake of argument, he might raise and examine conceptual difficulties about *endless* survival. But the question of immortality cannot even arise unless men do survive bodily death; and, as we shall see, there are formidable difficulties even about survival. It is these difficulties I shall be discussing, not the special ones about endless survival.

There are various views as to the character of the afterlife. One view is that man has a subtle, ordinarily invisible, body which survives the death of the ordinary gross body. This view has a long history, and seems to be quite popular in England at the moment. So far as I can see, the view is open to no philosophical objection, but likewise wholly devoid of philosophical interest; the mind–body problem must after all be just the same for an ethereal body as for a gross one. There could clearly be no philosophical reasons for belief in such subtle bodies, but only empirical ones; such reasons are in fact alleged, and we are urged to study the evidence.

Philosophy can at this point say something: about what sort of evidence would be required. The existence of subtle bodies is a matter within the purview of physical science; evidence for it should satisfy such criteria of existence as physicists use, and should refer not only to what people say they have seen, heard, and felt, but also to effects produced by subtle bodies on physicists' apparatus. The believer in 'subtle bodies' must, I think, accept the physicist's criteria of existence; there would surely be a conceptual muddle in speaking of 'bodies' but saying they might be incapable of affecting any physical apparatus. For what distinguishes real physical objects from hallucinations, even collective hallucinations, is that physical objects act on one another, and do so in just the same way whether they are being observed or not; this is the point, I think, at which a phenomenalist account of physical

Peter Geach 'Immortality' from *God and the Soul* (Routledge and Kegan Paul, 1969), reprinted by permission of Taylor & Francis Books Ltd and the author.

objects breaks down. If, therefore, 'subtle bodies' produce no physical effects, they are not bodies at all.

How is it, then, that 'subtle bodies' have never forced themselves upon the attention of physicists, as X-rays did, by spontaneous interference with physical apparatus? There are supposed to be a lot of 'subtle bodies' around, and physicists have a lot of delicate apparatus; yet physicists not engaged in psychical research are never bothered by the interference of 'subtle bodies'. In the circumstances I think it wholly irrational to believe in 'subtle bodies'. Moreover, when I who am no physicist am invited to study the evidence for 'subtle bodies', I find that very fact suspicious. The discoverers of X-rays and electrons did not appeal to the lay public, but to physicists, to study the evidence; and so long as physicists (at least in general) refuse to take 'subtle bodies' seriously, a study of evidence for them by a layman like myself would be a waste of time.

When *philosophers* talk of life after death, what they mostly have in mind is a doctrine that may be called Platonic—it is found in its essentials in the *Phaedo*. It may be briefly stated thus: 'Each man's make-up includes a wholly immaterial thing, his mind and soul. It is the mind that sees and hears and feels and thinks and chooses—in a word, is conscious. The mind is the person; the body is extrinsic to the person, like a suit of clothes. Though body and mind affect one another, the mind's existence is quite independent of the body's; and there is thus no reason why the mind should not go on being conscious indefinitely after the death of the body, and even if it never again has with any body that sort of connexion which it now has.

This Platonic doctrine has a strong appeal, and there are plausible arguments in its favour. It appears a clearly intelligible supposition that I should go on after death having the same sorts of experience as I now have, even if I then have no body at all. For although these experiences are connected with processes in the body—sight, for example, with processes in the eyes, optic nerves, and brain—nevertheless there is no necessity of thought about the connexion—it is easy to conceive of someone who has no eyes having the experience called sight. He would be having the same experience as I who have eyes do, and I know what sort of experience that is because I have the experience.

Let us now examine these arguments. When a word can be used to stand for a private experience, like the words 'seeing' or 'pain', it is certainly tempting to suppose that the giving these words a meaning is itself a private experience— indeed that they get their meaning just from the experiences they stand for. But this is really nonsense: if a sentence I hear or utter contains the word 'pain', do I help myself to grasp its sense by giving myself a pain? Might not this be, on the contrary, rather distracting? As Wittgenstein said, to think you get the concept of pain by having a pain is like thinking you get the concept of a minus quantity by running up an overdraft. Our concepts of seeing, hearing, pain, anger, etc., apply in the first instance to human beings; we willingly extend them (say) to cats, dogs, and horses, but we rightly feel uncomfortable about extending them to very alien creatures and speaking of a slug's hearing or an angry ant. Do we know at all what it would be to apply such concepts to an immaterial being? I think not.

One may indeed be tempted to evade difficulties by saying: 'An immaterial spirit is angry or in pain if it feels *the same way* as I do when I am angry or in pain'. But, as Wittgenstein remarked, this is just like saying: 'Of course I know what it is for the time on the Sun to be five o'clock: it's five o'clock on the Sun at the very moment when it's five o'clock here!'—which plainly gets us no forrader. If there is a difficulty in passing from 'I am in pain' or 'Smith is in pain' to 'an immaterial spirit is in pain', there is equally a difficulty in passing from 'Smith feels the same way as I do' to 'an immaterial spirit feels the same way as I do'.

In fact, the question is, whether a private experience does suffice, as is here supposed, to a give a meaning to a psychological verb like 'to see'. I am not trying to throw doubt on there being private experiences; of course men have thoughts they do not utter and pains they do not show; of course I may see something without any behaviour to show I see it; nor do I mean to emasculate these propositions with neo-behaviourist dialectics. But it is not a question of whether seeing is (sometimes) a private experience, but whether one can attach meaning to the verb 'to see' by a private uncheckable performance; and this is what I maintain one cannot do to any word at all.

One way to show that a word's being given a meaning cannot be a private uncheckable performance is the following: We can take a man's word for it that a linguistic expression has given him some private experience—e.g. has revived a painful memory, evoked a visual image, or given him a thrill in the pit of the stomach. But we cannot take his word for it that he attached a sense to the expression, even if we accept his *bona fides*; for later events may convince us that in fact he attached no sense to the expression. Attaching sense to an expression is thus not to be identified with any private experience that accompanies the expression; and I have argued this, not by attacking the idea of private experiences, but by contrasting the attaching of sense to an expression with some typical private experiences that may be connected with the expression.

We give words a sense—whether they are psychological words like 'seeing' and 'pain', or other words—by getting into a way of using them; and though a man can invent for himself a way of using a word, it must be a way that other people *could* follow—otherwise we are back to the idea of conferring meaning by a private uncheckable performance. Well, how do we eventually use such words as 'see', 'hear', 'feel', when we have got into the way of using them? We do not exercise these concepts only so as to pick out cases of seeing and the rest in our separate worlds of sense-experience; on the contrary, these concepts are used in association with a host of other concepts relating, e.g., to the physical characteristics of what is seen and the behaviour of those who do see. In saying this I am not putting forward a theory, but just reminding you of very familiar features in the everyday use of the verb 'to see' and related expressions; our ordinary talk about seeing would cease to be intelligible if there were cut out of it such expressions as 'I can't see, it's too far off', 'I caught his eye', 'Don't look round', etc. Do not let the bogy of behaviourism scare you off observing these features; I am not asking you to believe that 'to see' is itself a word for a kind of behaviour. But the concept of seeing can be maintained only because it has threads of connexion with these other non-psychological concepts; break enough threads, and the concept of seeing collapses.

We can now see the sort of difficulties that arise if we try to apply concepts like *seeing* and *feeling* to disembodied spirits. Let me give an actual case of a psychological concept's collapsing when its connexions were broken. Certain hysterics claimed to have a magnetic sense; it was discovered, however, that their claim to be having magnetic sensations did not go with the actual presence of a magnet in their environment, but only with their belief that a magnet was present. Psychologists did not now take the line: We may take the patients' word for it that they have peculiar sensations—only the term 'magnetic sensations' has proved inappropriate, as having been based on a wrong causal hypothesis. On the contrary, patients' reports of magnetic sensations were thenceforward written off as being among the odd things that hysterical patients sometimes say. Now far fewer of the ordinary connexions of a sensation-concept were broken here than would be broken if we tried to apply a sensation-concept like seeing to a disembodied spirit.

If we conclude that the ascription of sensations and feelings to a disembodied spirit does not make sense, it does not obviously follow, as you might think, that we must deny the possibility of disembodied spirits altogether. Aquinas for example was convinced that there are disembodied spirits but ones that cannot see or hear or feel pain or fear or anger; he allowed them no mental operations except those of thought and will. Damned spirits would suffer from frustration of their evil will, but not from aches and pains or foul odours or the like. It would take me too far to discuss whether his reasons for thinking this were good; I want to show what follows from this view. In our human life thinking and choosing are intricately bound up with a play of sensations and mental images and emotions; if after a lifetime of thinking and choosing in this human way there is left only a disembodied mind whose thought is wholly non-sensuous and whose rational choices are unaccompanied by any human feelings—can we still say there remains the same person? Surely not: such a soul is not the person who died but a mere remnant of him. And this is just what Aquinas says (in his commentary on I Corinthians 15): *anima mea non est ego*, my soul is not I; and if only souls are saved, *I* am not saved, nor is any man. If some time after Peter Geach's death there is again a man identifiable as Peter Geach, then Peter Geach again, or still, lives: otherwise not.

Though a surviving mental remnant of a person, preserving some sort of physical continuity with the man you knew, would not be Peter Geach, this does not show that such a measure of survival is not possible; but its possibility does raise serious difficulties, even if such dehumanized thinking and willing is really conceivable at all. For *whose* thinking would this be? Could we tell whether *one* or *many* disembodied spirits thought the thoughts in question? We touch here on the old problem: what constitutes there being two disembodied minds (at the same time, that is)? Well, what constitutes there being two pennies? It may happen that one penny is bent and corroded while another is in mint condition; but such differences cannot be what make the two pennies to be two—the two pennies could not have these varied fortunes if they were not already distinct. In the same way, differences of memories or of aims could not constitute the difference between two dis-embodied minds, but could only supervene upon a difference already existing. What does constitute the difference between two disembodied human minds? If we could find no ground of differentiation, then not only would that which survived be a mere remnant of a person—there would not even be a surviving individuality.

Could we say that souls are different because in the first instance they were souls of different bodies, and then remain different on that account when they are no longer embodied? I do not think this solution would do at all if differentiation by reference to different bodies were merely retrospective. It might be otherwise if we held, with Aquinas, that the relation to a body was not merely retrospective—that each disembodied human soul permanently retained a capacity for reunion to such a body as would reconstitute a man identifiable with the man who died. This might satisfactorily account for the individuation of disembodied human souls; they would differ by being fitted for reunion to different bodies; but it would entail that the possibility of disembodied human souls stood or fell with the *possibility* of a dead man's living again *as a man*.

Some Scholastics held that just as two pennies or two cats differ by being differ-ent bits of matter, so human souls differ by containing different 'spiritual matter'. Aquinas regarded this idea as self-contradictory; it is at any rate much too obscure to count as establishing a possibility of distinct disembodied souls. Now this recourse to 'spiritual matter' might well strike us merely as the filling of a con-ceptual lacuna with a nonsensical piece of jargon. But it is not only Scholastic philosophers who assimilate mental processes to physical ones, only thinking of mental processes as taking place in an *immaterial* medium; and many people think it easy to conceive of distinct disembodied souls because they are illegitimately ascribing to souls a sort of differentiation—say, by existing *side by side*—that can be significantly ascribed only to bodies. The same goes for people who talk about souls as being 'fused' or 'merged' in a Great Soul; they are imagining some such change in the world of souls as occurs to a drop of water falling into a pool or to a small lump of wax that is rubbed into a big one. Now if only people *talked* about 'spiritual matter', instead of just thinking in terms of it unawares, their muddle could be more easily detected and treated.

To sum up what I have said so far: The possibility of life after death for Peter Geach appears to stand or fall with the possibility of there being once again a man identifiable as Peter Geach. The existence of a disembodied soul would not be a survival of the person Peter Geach; and even in such a truncated form, individual existence seems to require at least a persistent possibility of the soul's again entering into the make-up of a man who is identifiably Peter Geach.

This suggests a form of belief in survival that seems to have become quite popular of late in the West—at any rate as a half-belief—namely, the belief in reincarnation. Could it in fact have a clear sense to say that a baby born in Oxford this year is Hitler living again?

How could it be shown that the Oxford baby was Hitler? Presumably by memories and similarities of character. I maintain that no amount of such evidence would make it reasonable to identify the baby as Hitler. Similarities of character are of themselves obviously insufficient. As regards memories: If on growing up the Oxford baby reveals knowledge of what we should ordinarily say only Hitler can have known, does this establish a presumption that the child is Hitler? Not at all. In normal circumstances we know when to say 'only he can have known that'; when queer things start happening, we have no right to stick to our ordinary assumptions as to what can be known. And suppose that for some time the child 'is' Hitler by our criteria, and later on 'is' Goering? or might not several children simultaneously satisfy the criteria for 'being' Hitler?

These are not merely captious theoretical objections. Spirit-mediums, we are told, will in trance convincingly enact the part of various people: sometimes of fictitious characters, like Martians, or Red Indians ignorant of Red Indian languages, or the departed 'spirits' of Johnny Walker and John Jamieson; there are even stories of mediums' giving convincing 'messages' from people who were alive and normally conscious at the time of the 'message'. Now a medium giving messages from the dead is not said to be the dead man, but rather to be controlled by his spirit. What then can show whether the Oxford child 'is' Hitler or is merely 'controlled' by Hitler's spirit? For all these reasons the appearance that there might be good evidence for reincarnation dissolves on a closer view.

Nor do I see, for that matter, how the mental phenomena of mediumship could ever make it reasonable to believe that a human soul survived and communicated. For someone to carry on in a dramatic way quite out of his normal character is a common hysterical symptom; so if a medium does this in a trance, it is no evidence of anything except an abnormal condition of the medium's own mind. As for the medium's telling us things that 'only the dead can have known', I repeat that in these queer cases we have no right to stick to our ordinary assumptions about what can be known. Moreover, as I said, there are cases, as well-authenticated as any, in which the medium convincingly enacted the part of X and told things that 'only X could have known' when X was in fact alive and normally conscious, so that his soul was certainly not trying to communicate by way of the medium! Even if we accept all the queer stories of spirit messages, the result is only to open up a vast field of queer possibilities—not in the least to force us to say that mediums were possessed by such-and-such souls. This was argued by Bradley long ago in his essay 'The Evidences of Spiritualism', and he has never been answered.

How could a living man be rightly identifiable with a man who previously died? Let us first consider our normal criteria of personal identity. When we say an old man is the same person as the baby born seventy years before, we believe that the old man has material continuity with the baby. Of course this is not a criterion in the sense of being what we judge identity by; for the old man will not have been watched for seventy years continuously, even by rota! But something we regarded as disproving the material continuity (e.g. absence of a birthmark, different finger-prints) would disprove personal identity. Further, we believe that material continuity establishes a one–one relation: one baby grows up into one old man, and one old man has grown out of one baby. (Otherwise there would have to be at some stage a drastic change, a fusion or fission, which we should regard as destroying personal identity.) Moreover, the baby-body never coexists with the aged body, but develops into it.

Now it seems to me that we cannot rightly identify a man living 'again' with a man who died unless *material* conditions of identity are fulfilled. There must be some one—one relation of material continuity between the old body and the new. I am not saying that the new body need be even in part materially *identical* with the old; this, unlike material continuity, is not required for personal identity, for the old man need not have kept even a grain of matter from the baby of seventy years ago.

We must here notice an important fallacy. I was indicating just now that I favour Aquinas's doctrine that two coexisting souls differ by being related to two different bodies and that two coexisting human bodies, like two pennies or two cats, differ by being different bits of matter. Well, if it is difference of matter that makes two bodies different, it may seem to follow that a body can maintain its identity only if at least some identifiable matter remains in it all the time; otherwise it is no more the same body than the wine in a cask that is continuously emptied and refilled is the same wine. But just this is the fallacy: it does not follow, if difference in a certain respect at a certain time suffices to show non-identity, that sameness in that respect over a period of time is necessary to identity. Thus, Sir John Cutler's famous pair of stockings were the same pair all the time, although they started as silk and by much mending ended as worsted; people have found it hard to see this, because if at a given time there is a silk pair and also a worsted pair then there are two pairs. Again, it is clear that the same man may be in Birmingham at noon and in Oxford at 7 p.m., even though a man in Birmingham and a man in Oxford at a given time must be two different men. Once formulated, the fallacy is obvious, but it might be deceptive if not formulated.

'Why worry even about material continuity? Would not mental continuity be both necessary and sufficient?' Necessary, but not sufficient. Imagine a new 'Tichborne' trial. The claimant knows all the things he ought to know, and talks convincingly to the long-lost heir's friends. But medical evidence about scars and old fractures and so on indicates that he cannot be the man; moreover, the long-lost heir's corpse is decisively identified at an exhumation. Such a case would bewilder us, particularly if the claimant's *bona fides* were manifest. (He might, for example, voluntarily take a lie-detecting test.) But we should certainly not allow the evidence of mental connexions with the long-lost heir to settle the matter in the claimant's favour: the claimant cannot be the long-lost heir, whose body we know lies buried in Australia, and if he honestly thinks he is then we must try to cure him of a delusion.

'But if I went on being conscious, why should I worry which body I have?' To use the repeated 'I' prejudges the issue; a fairer way of putting the point would be: If there is going to be a consciousness that includes ostensible memories of my life, why should I worry about which body this consciousness goes with? When we put it that way, it is quite easy to imagine circumstances in which one would worry— particularly if the ostensible memories of my life were to be produced by processes that can produce entirely spurious memories.

If, however, memory is not enough for personal identity; if a man's living again does involve some bodily as well as mental continuity with the man who lived formerly; then we might fairly call his new bodily life a resurrection. So the upshot of our whole argument is that unless a man comes to life again by resurrection, he does not live again after death. At best some mental remnant of him would survive death; and I should hold that the possibility even of such survival involves at least a permanent *capacity* for renewed human life; if reincarnation is excluded, this means: a capacity for resurrection. It may be hard to believe in the resurrection of the body: but Aquinas argued in his commentary on I Corinthians 15, which I have already cited, that it is much harder to believe in an immortal but permanently disembodied human soul; for that would mean believing that a soul, whose very identity depends on the capacity for reunion with one human body rather than another, will continue to exist for ever with this capacity unrealized.

Speaking of the resurrection, St Paul used the simile of a seed that is planted and grows into an ear of corn, to show the relation between the corpse and the body that rises again from the dead. This simile fits in well enough with our discussion. In this life, the bodily aspect of personal identity requires a one–one relationship and material continuity; one baby body grows into one old man's body by a continuous process. Now similarly there is a one–one relationship between the buried seed and the ear that grows out of it; one seed grows into one ear, one ear comes from one seed; and the ear of corn is materially continuous with the seed but need not have any material identity with it.

There is of course no philosophical reason to expect that from a human corpse there will arise at some future date a new human body, continuous in some way with the corpse; and in some particular cases there appear strong empirical objections. But apart from the *possibility* of resurrection, it seems to me a mere illusion to have any hope for life after death. I am of the mind of Judas Maccabeus: if there is no resurrection, it is superfluous and vain to pray for the dead.

The traditional faith of Christianity, inherited from Judaism, is that at the end of this age Messiah will come and men rise from their graves to die no more. That faith is not going to be shaken by inquiries about bodies burned to ashes or eaten by beasts; those who might well suffer just such death in martyrdom were those who were most confident of a glorious reward in the resurrection. One who shares that hope will hardly wish to take out an occultistic or philosophical insurance policy, to guarantee some sort of survival as an annuity, in case God's promise of resurrection should fail.

Questions for discussion

1. Are there reasons for thinking that any historical individual has survived death?
2. 'Death is not an event in life. Death is not lived through' (Wittgenstein, *Tractatus Logico-Philosophicus* 6.4311). Are there good reasons for saying that?
3. Is death something to be feared?
4. According to Descartes: 'My essence consists solely in the fact that I am a thinking thing. It is true that I may have (or, to anticipate, that I certainly have) a body that is very closely joined to me. But nevertheless, on the one hand I have a clear and distinct idea of myself, in so far as I am simply a thinking, non-extended thing; and on the other hand I have a distinct idea of body, in so far as this is simply an extended, non-thinking thing. And accordingly, it is certain that I am really distinct from my body and can exist without it.' (*Meditations on First Philosophy* VI, trans. John Cottingham, Cambridge, 1986, p. 54). Is Descartes right?
5. What might be meant by the suggestion that we shall live again as resurrected?
6. According to John Hick (*Philosophy of Religion*, 4th edn, Englewood Cliffs, New Jersey, 1990, p. 128): 'Even if we discount the entire range of psychical phenomena, it remains true that the best cases of trance utterance are impressive and puzzling, and taken at face value are indicative of survival and communication after death.' Is Hick correct?
7. 'The seriousness of our endeavour to shape our lives according to ideals of truth, wisdom, love and compassion, and all that they entail in terms of the development of virtue, together with the sense of inadequacy in our actual achievement, warrant the presumption that a single life cannot be all that we are destined to have. To grant that would make a mockery of our moral experience' (Joseph Prabhu, 'The Idea of Reincarnation', in Steven T. Davis (ed.), *Death and Afterlife*, London, 1989, p. 66). Is that view true? If not, why not? If so, what does it imply when it comes to the topic of life after death?
8. Is the notion of life after death an appealing one? If so, why? If not, why not?
9. Can people be thought to be immortal even if they cease to exist at death?
10. It has often been said that with death comes the vision of God (the 'beatific vision'). But what might be meant by this claim? And does it make sense?

Advice on further reading

Discussions of life after death invariably adopt or presume views concerning the nature of human beings, especially views on the relationship between mind and body and views on the question of personal identity. In approaching the topic, therefore, you would be well advised to consult some general introductions to the philosophy of mind and/or the notion of personal identity. There are many available, but ones to be especially commended for clarity and/or comprehensiveness include (note that they represent a wide range of approaches to their subject-matter):

D. M. Armstrong, *The Mind–Body Problem: An Opinionated Introduction* (Boulder, Colorado, and Oxford, 1999).

David Braine, *The Human Person* (London, 1993).

Keith Campbell, *Body and Mind* (2nd edn, Notre Dame, Indiana, 1984).

Paul Churchland, *Matter and Consciousness* (Cambridge, Massachussetts, 1988).

Anthony Kenny, *The Metaphysics of Mind* (Oxford, 1989).

Jaegwon Kim, *Philosophy of Mind* (Boulder, Colorado, 1996).

H. D. Lewis, *The Elusive Mind* (London and New York, 1969).

H. D. Lewis, *The Elusive Self* (London and Basingstoke, 1982).

Colin McGuinn, *The Character of Mind* (2nd edn, Oxford, 1997).

Gilbert Ryle, *The Concept of Mind* (Harmondsworth, 1963).

Sydney Shoemaker and Richard Swinburne, *Personal Identity* (Oxford, 1984).

Richard Swinburne, *The Evolution of the Soul* (Oxford, 1986).

Jenny Teichman, *The Mind and the Soul: An Introduction to the Philosophy of Mind* (London and New York, 1974).

Godfrey Vesey, *Personal Identity: A Philosophical Analysis* (Ithaca, New York, 1974).

For good collections of essays (historical and contemporary) on the philosophy of mind and personal identity see:

John Perry (ed.), *Personal Identity* (Berkeley, Los Angeles, and London, 1975).

David Rosenthal (ed.), *The Nature of Mind* (New York and Oxford, 1991).

Richard Warner and Tadeusz Szubka (eds), *The Mind–Body Problem* (Oxford, and Cambridge, Massuchessetts, 1994).

For collections dealing specifically with life after death, see:

Paul Edwards (ed.), *Immortality* (New York, 1992).

Steven T. Davis (ed.), *Death and Afterlife* (London, 1989).

Antony Flew (ed.), *Body, Mind, and Death* (New York, 1964).

Some notable book-length treatments of life after death (adopting a variety of positions on the question) are:

Paul Badham and Linda Badham, *Immortality or Extinction?* (London, 1982).

C. J. Ducasse, *Belief in Life After Death* (Springfield, Ilinois, 1961).

John Hick, *Death and Eternal Life* (London, 1979).

Hans Küng, *Eternal Life* (New York, 1984).

H. D. Lewis, *The Self and Immortality* (London and Basingstoke, 1973).

H. D. Lewis, *Persons and Life After Death* (London and Basingstoke, 1978).

Terence Penelhum, *Immortality* (Belmont, California, 1973).

Terence Penelhum, *Survival and Disembodied Existence* (London, 1970).

John Perry, *Personal Identity and Immortality* (Indianapolis, Indiana, 1979).

D. Z. Phillips, *Death and Immortality* (London and Basingstoke, 1970).

Bruce Reichenbach, *Is Man the Phoenix? A Study of Immortality* (Grand Rapids, Michigan, 1978).

Simon Tugwell, *Human Immortality and the Redemption of Death* (London, 1990).

Discussions of life after death have often involved reference to reincarnation and to the testimony of psychical researchers. For sophisticated discussions of reincarnation, see Paul Edwards, *Reincarnation: A Critical Examination* (London, 1996) and Bruce Reichenbach, *The Law of Karma* (London, 1990). For relevant texts on psychical research, see C. D. Broad, *Lectures on Psychical Research* (London and New York, 1962), P. Kurtz (ed.), *A Skeptic's Guide to Parapsychology* (Buffalo, New York, 1985), and H. D. Lewis, 'Religion and the Paranormal', in H. D. Lewis, *Persons and Life After Death*.

The intelligibility and credibility of the claim that life after death either does or must involve resurrection is considered in many of the works cited above. But Christian belief in the resurrection of Jesus has also sparked off much discussion of the notion of resurrection and can hardly be ignored by philosophers who turn to it. For an introduction to issues and questions raised by belief in Jesus's resurrection, the text to start with is Stephen T. Davis, Daniel Kendall, and Gerald O'Collins (eds), *The Resurrection: An Interdisciplinary Symposium on the Resurrection of Jesus* (Oxford, 1997). For a philosophical debate on the resurrection of Jesus, see Garry R. Habermas and Antony Flew, *Did Jesus Rise from the Dead?* (San Francisco, California, 1987). For a general study on the resurrection of Jesus written with an eye on philosophy, see Peter Carnley, *The Structure of Resurrection Belief* (Oxford, 1987). See also Brian Davies, 'The Resurrection and Christian Belief', in Paul Burns and John Cumming (eds), *The Bible Now* (Dublin, 1981).

As you think about the arguments in Plato's *Phaedo*, you would do well to consult some commentaries on them. Especially valuable are:

David Bostock, Plato's *Phaedo* (Oxford, 1986).

David Gallop, Plato's *Phaedo* (Oxford, 1975).

R. Hackforth, Plato's *Phaedo* (Cambridge, 1972).

Geach's approach to life after death owes much to philosophical ideas to be associated with Thomas Aquinas and Ludwig Wittgenstein. For introductions to Aquinas on human beings and life after death, see Brian Davies, *The Thought of Thomas Aquinas* (Oxford, 1992), ch. 11, Anthony Kenny, *Aquinas on Mind* (London and New York, 1993), and Herbert McCabe, 'The Immortality of the Soul', in Anthony Kenny (ed.), *Aquinas: A Collection of Critical Essays* (London, 1969). For an excellent introduction to Wittgenstein on the human person (written with a special eye on theological matters), see Fergus Kerr, *Theology After Wittgenstein* (2nd edn, London, 1997). Note also that Geach develops his views on reincarnation in chapter 1 of his book *God and the Soul* (London, 1969).

Index

In this index, publications discussed in the text are given under authors only. None of the works listed in the Further Reading sections are indexed.

personal relationships 650–3,
    662; *see also* the individual
personalistic thinkers 376–81
phenomenology 70, 88, 657–8,
    726–7; *see also* religious
    experience
Phillips, D. Z. 10
    on belief 22, 23–4, 134
    on morality and God 639
    Religion Without Explanation
    24
Phillips, R. P. 204–5, 206, 207
philosophers
    academic 122
    definition 1
    Dominican 5
    in early church 488
    Franciscan 5–6
    influence
    Islamic 179–81
    Jewish 5, 158, 181
    medieval 4–6, 10, 17–19, 181–3
    modern 6, 9–10, 72, 122,
        183–4, 488
    as religious believers 381
    see also individual
        philosophers *and*
        philosophies
philosophical psychology 682
philosophy
    defintion 1–2
    derivation 1
    faith and 17
philosophy of religion
    belief and 6, 8, 9–10, 17–126
    as a concept 1
    definition 2
    history of 2, 3–10
    role 24
physical evil, *see* pain
Pieper, Josef 557
Pike, Nelson
    on Boethius 467, 468
    on future contingents
        468–74
    on omniscience of God 444,
        467–74
place, time and 234–5, 493
Plantinga, Alvin 7, 10, 20
    on divine simplicity 552–3,
        554, 556, 557, 561
    on evil and free will 576–7,
        603–4, 605, 609
    on existence of God 20–1, 23,
        42–94, 136, 310

Kretzmann's criticism of
    95–107
    on natural laws 401–2
    on natural theology 20–1, 42
    ontological arguments 20–1,
        23, 310, 342–51
    proper basicality concept
        21–2, 42–94
Plato 189, 190, 464
    on being 517
    Christian tradition, influence
        on 3
    on divinity 3, 179
    Euthyphro 637
    on God 3, 488, 509
    on immortality of the soul
        705
    on the individual 3
    influence 130, 488
    on life after death 3, 690, 705,
        710–22
        Geach's criticism of 691–2,
            727–33
    on material world 246
    neoplatonism 4
    Phaedo 3, 216–17, 690
pleasure 611, 612; *see also*
    emotions/feelings
Plotinus 4, 509, 517
political power 406–7
Pollock, John 90
positivists/positivism 46, 108–9
possibility/impossibility
    absolute 418, 419
    Duns Scotus on 6
    of existence of God 338–9,
        340–1
    logical possibility 404–6, 409
    of miracles 399–400, 400–2,
        425, 431–6
    of omnipotence 404–6, 409,
        418–19
    relative 418
possible worlds concept 6, 7,
    310, 342–52
power 406–10, 413–14
    active 398, 416–17, 418–19
    Aquinas on 416–17
    causal 406, 407, 413–14
    creative 406
    God as sole source of 413
    infinite 417–18
    legal 406–7
    moral character and 407–8
    passive 398, 416–17

political 406–7
    to sin 412–14, 418, 419
    see also omnipotence of God
prayer 8; *see also* religious
    practices
precedence 489, 491
predetermination, *see* future
    contingents
predicates 166, 338, 339–40
    determining 339
    real 339–40
    see also grammar
present, *see* past/present/future
    continuum
presumption
    of atheism 20, 36–41
    of guilt 40
    of innocence 37, 38, 39, 40
Price, H. H. 605–6
pride 80–1
principles
    in principle, definition of
        149
    Verification Principle 132–4,
        147–52
privacy concept 698; *see also*
    mind/body relationships
probability 267
    of miracles 431–2, 435
    see also possibility
probabilistic arguments *see*
    inductive arguments
proof, *see* evidence/
    evidentialism
proper basicality concept 21–2,
    42–94, 102–7
    applications of 83–6
    Aquinas and 43
    classical foundationalism
        and 68–71, 81
    criteria for 84–5, 105–6
    evidentialism and 43–59
property simplicity 537, 538,
    539, 548–50, 551–3, 554,
    556–62; *see also* divine
    simplicity
propositional evidence 104
propositional logic 59–60, 104
propositions
    analytic 339
    synthetic 339
providence 464–6
Pseudo-Dionysius, *see*
    Dionysius the Areopagite
psychoanalysis 359–60

2